Becoming a teacher

FIFTH EDITION

Becoming a teacher

ISSUES IN SECONDARY EDUCATION

FIFTH EDITION

*Edited by Meg Maguire, Simon Gibbons,
Melissa Glackin, David Pepper
and Karen Skilling*

 Open University Press

Open University Press
McGraw-Hill Education
8th Floor, 338 Euston Road
London
England
NW1 3BH

email: enquiries@openup.co.uk
world wide web: www.openup.co.uk

and Two Penn Plaza, New York, NY 10121-2289, USA

First published In this fifth edition 2018

A catalogue record of this book is available from the British Library

ISBN-13: 978-0-335-24325-9
ISBN-10: 0-33-524325-8
eISBN: 978-0-335-24326-6

Library of Congress Cataloging-in-Publication Data
CIP data applied for

Typeset by Transforma Pvt. Ltd., Chennai, India
Printed and bound by CPI Group (UK) Ltd, Croydon, CR0 4YY

Praise page

Contents

Contributors

Louise Archer is Karl Mannheim Professor of Sociology of Education at University College London, Institute of Education. Until 2017, Louise was the Professor of Sociology of Education at King's College London. Her research addresses educational identities and inequalities in relation to ethnicity, social class and gender. She currently directs several large inter/national projects looking at identities, aspirations and inequalities in science participation, including the 10-year ESRC-funded Aspires/Aspires2 projects, the Enterprising Science project and the UK Youth Equity Pathways study.

Paul Black is Professor Emeritus of Science Education at King's College London. He was Chair of the government's Task Group on Assessment and Testing in 1987–91 and Deputy Chair of the National Curriculum Council from 1989–91. His published reports, notably *Working Inside the Black Box* and *Assessment for Learning: Putting it into Practice*, have been widely read and have influenced practice in many schools. He is an Honorary Life Member of the Association for Science Education, and in 2014 received the John Nisbet Fellowship Award of the British Educational Research Association for his 'Outstanding contribution to educational research over his career'.

Jeremy Burke was a mathematics teacher in four inner-city London schools, including being a head of department in two schools and then a senior leader. He moved to work in a university where he directed mathematics education courses. At King's College London, as a senior lecturer, he was Director of the PGCE and Director of the MA. His research has focused on the sociology of education and Dowling's Social Activity Method, on which he has published in the UK and internationally.

Bob Burstow taught for more than 30 years in secondary schools in and around London, including 10 as a deputy head. Following his time as a senior lecturer at King's College London, where he was a co-developer of the Masters in Teaching and Learning (MTL) for Greater London, he is currently a Visiting Research Fellow, working with colleagues in universities and schools, researching the ethical issues surrounding school-based research. His book, *Effective Teacher Development*, was published by Bloomsbury in December 2017.

Simon Coffey is Senior Lecturer in Education (Modern Languages) at King's College London. His research interests focus on ways to promote creativity in the classroom and on sociological aspects of learning, including the social history of language learning and the analysis of autobiographical narratives. As well as publishing in academic books and journals, he is co-author of the popular *Modern Foreign Languages 5–11: A Guide for Teachers* (3rd edn, David Fulton 2017). He is joint editor of the *Language Learning Journal*.

Catarina F. Correia worked for nearly a decade as a researcher and teaching fellow in chemistry. In 2012, she changed her research focus to science education. Two years later, she joined King's College London as a research associate on the EU FP7 *Assess Inquiry in Science, Technology and Mathematics Education* (ASSISTME) project. Catarina is a member of the research specialist group in the Association for Science Education (ASE). Her research interests are in classroom assessment, inquiry-based pedagogy, curriculum development and teacher education.

Tania de St Croix is a Lecturer in the Sociology of Youth and Childhood at King's College London, where she is the Programme Director for the MA Education, Policy and Society. Her research and teaching concern how practitioners and young people are affected by, and respond to, education policy, and how these processes interact with equality, youth participation, and democratic workplaces. Her book *Grassroots Youth Work: Policy, Passion and Resistance in Practice* was published in 2016 by Policy Press.

Justin Dillon is Professor of Science and Environmental Education at the University of Exeter. He was Head of the Graduate School of Education at Bristol University from 2014–17. He has research interests in professional development and learning inside and outside the classroom. He has co-authored a range of edited collections including *Learning to Teach Science* (Falmer 1995), *Becoming a Teacher* (OUP 1995, 2001, 2007 and 2011) and *The Re-emergence of Values in the Science Curriculum* (Sense 2007).

Jenny Driscoll practised as a Family Law barrister for more than a decade, specializing in child protection, before moving to King's College London, where she is Programme Director for the MA Child Studies and MA International Child Studies. Her academic interests cover children's rights and child protection, including support for children in state care and care leavers. Current research projects include an ESRC-funded project on the role of schools in safeguarding. Jenny is a member of the Board of Trustees of the British Association for the Study and Prevention of Child Abuse and Neglect (BASPCAN).

Carla Finesilver taught secondary mathematics in mainstream, PRU and special schools in London for 10 years, including setting up and heading the mathematics department at a specialist school for pupils with Specific Learning Difficulties.

She is a Lecturer in Mathematics Education at King's College London, teaching on the PGCE, and is Programme Director for the MA Mathematics Education. Her current research interests include visuospatial representation, individual differences in mathematical thinking, and inclusive pedagogies and practices for learners with Special Educational Needs and disabilities.

Sharon Gewirtz is Professor of Education in the School of Education, Communication and Society at King's College London, where she also co-directs the Centre for Public Policy Research. She has been involved in research in the sociology of education and education policy for more than 25 years, during which time she has published widely on issues of equality and social justice in education, teachers' work, and the changing culture and values of schooling and higher education in the context of managerial reform.

Simon Gibbons began his career as a teacher of English, media and drama in an East London comprehensive school. After 10 years working in London schools, ultimately as the Head of English in a large comprehensive, he moved, via a role as a Local Authority Consultant, into the university sector and is the Director of Teacher Education at King's College London and a Senior Lecturer in English and Education. His research primarily focuses on English as a school subject, both its historical development and its contemporary state. His first book, *The London Association for the Teaching of English 1947–1967: A History*, was published in 2014, followed in 2017 by *English and its Teachers: A History of Policy, Pedagogy and Practice.*

Melissa Glackin is a Lecturer in Science Education at King's College London, where she is in charge of the biology PGCE. Melissa has worked as a secondary school science teacher and in a range of roles on out-of-classroom programmes. Her research interests include teaching and learning science outside the classroom, teachers' beliefs and self-efficacy, teacher professional development and environmental education curriculum development. She is an invited fellow of the National Association of Environmental Education (NAEE).

Chris Harrison is a Reader in Science Education at King's College London, where she teaches on the PGCE and MA. She has research interests in assessment, science education and professional learning. Chris is internationally recognized as a leader and innovator in the field of formative assessment, completing a 10-year research project relating to classroom assessment, as well as publishing and creating training programmes for teachers. Chris is currently leading the UK component of an international programme to investigate how new teachers are educated to assess students in the classroom.

Jill Hohenstein is Senior Lecturer in Psychology in Education at King's College London and is the School's Director of Post graduate Research. Trained as a developmental psychologist, her research examines the ways that children and adults learn in informal settings, including museums, with a particular focus on language and cognitive development. She is co-author of *Museum Learning: Theory and Research as Tools for Enhancing Practice* (Routledge 2017).

Eva Jablonka is a Professor at Freie Universität Berlin, in the Department of Education and Psychology. She previously worked as Professor of Mathematics Education at King's College London. Her research interests include mathematical modelling, mathematical literacy, comparative classroom studies and sociological theories in mathematics education. Her recent work has focused on the emergence of disparity in achievement in classrooms and on students in transition from school to university.

Jane Jones is Senior Lecturer and Head of MFL Teacher Education. She taught languages for many years in schools and is interested in all dimensions of language learning. Her research interests are formative assessment (for which she is internationally recognized), primary to secondary transition and teachers as critical researchers of their practice. She has worked on 20 EU projects exploring these dimensions and published in many international journals. She believes that effective pastoral care and the promotion of students' well-being are critical to supporting their learning.

Heather King is a Lecturer in Science Education at King's College London. Her work focuses on the pedagogical practices of educators both in and outside the classroom. In particular, recent studies have explored ways of supporting secondary science teachers to enhance the engagement and participation of students from marginalized communities. Other research interests include the role of natural history education for social and environmental justice, and the potential of museum experiences for supporting lifelong learning.

Constant Leung is Professor of Educational Linguistics, King's College London. Previously he taught in schools and worked as advisory teacher and manager in local education authorities for 15 years. His research interests include curriculum development and language policy. He joined King's College London in 1999 and is active in promoting continuous professional development for teachers working with linguistically diverse students. He has published extensively on language education issues both nationally and internationally.

Gerard Lum is Senior Lecturer in Philosophy and Education Management at King's College London. His research is in the philosophy and theory of education, and he has a particular interest in epistemological issues relating to education. In his recent work he has been concerned with questions about occupational knowledge, professional education, professional ethics and the nature of assessment. His book *Vocational and Professional Capability: An Epistemological and Ontological Study of Occupational Expertise* is published by Continuum.

Meg Maguire taught for many years in London schools and is Professor of the Sociology of Education at King's College London. She has a long-standing interest in education policy and practice, social justice issues, the life and work of school teachers, teacher education and the challenges of inner-city schooling. Her publications include *How Schools Do Policy* (with Stephen Ball and Annette Braun, Routledge 2012) and *Ethics and Education Research* (with Rachel Brooks and Kitte te Riele, Sage 2014). She is lead editor of the *Journal of Education Policy*.

Alex Manning worked in London schools as a secondary science teacher and Head of Year before joining King's College London. Her teaching responsibilities at King's are primarily concerned with the recruitment of teachers and initial education, while her research focuses on the bigger picture of teacher retention. She is interested in teachers' motivations for joining the profession and how these relate to notions of resilience, and how teachers can be supported to remain in the classroom.

Bethan Marshall is a Senior Lecturer in Education and is involved in teacher education. She specializes in issues relating to the teaching of English and assessment on which she has written extensively, including her books *English Teachers: An Unofficial Guide* (Routledge 2000) and *Testing English: Formative and Summative Practice in English* (Continuum 2011). Until last year she was Chair of the National Association for the Teaching of English. At present she is researching the differences in the teaching of English in Canada, England and Scotland.

Brian Matthews taught in London schools before leading the PGCE at Goldsmith's College. At King's College London he contributes to the science PGCE programme and was involved in research funded by the EU into Strategies for Assessment of Inquiry Learning in Science (SAILS). Previously he led a research project on emotional engagement in science education. Brian's research interests include science inquiry, gender and young people's emotions (www.engagingeducation. co.uk). His publications include *Engaging Education: Developing Emotional Literacy, Equity and Co-Education* (McGraw-Hill/OUP 2016).

David Pepper is a Lecturer in International Education at King's College London, where he previously completed his PhD on the validation of the OECD's Programme for International Student Assessment (PISA). This is also where he completed his MRes on student dips in attainment during lower secondary education, while working in education policy in the UK. David has worked with researchers and policy-makers in many other countries via international research and development projects, and is the Programme Director of the MA International Education.

Karen Skilling is a Lecturer in Mathematics Education. She is the PGCE Course Director and convenes the MA module 'Recent Developments in Mathematics Education' at King's College London. Karen was awarded a scholarship by the Australian Research Council attached to a three-year longitudinal, mixed methods project investigating the Middle Years Transition, Engagement and Achievement in Mathematics (MYTEAM). This project was followed by a Post-Doctoral Fellowship at Oxford University (Department of Education). Karen's research interests include engagement and motivation, self-regulation and metacognition, mathematics transition from primary to secondary school, and STEM projects.

Emma Towers taught for 10 years in a London primary school before coming to King's College London in 2012 to complete her PhD. Her doctoral study explored the reasons why teachers and headteachers stay working in inner London primary schools. At King's she teaches on undergraduate and postgraduate courses. Her main research interests include teachers' lives and career trajectories, urban education and teacher identity.

Mary Webb taught for many years in primary and secondary schools and is Senior Lecturer in Information Technology in Education at King's College London. Mary's research has examined pedagogy and formative assessment across both computer science as a subject in the curriculum and the uses of new technologies for learning and teaching throughout the whole curriculum. Mary is on the International Federation of Information Processing (IFIP) Education Executive and is lead editor for the World Conference on Computers in Education, 2017.

Chris Winch taught in primary schools in Yorkshire for 11 years. He is currently Professor of Educational Philosophy and Policy at King's College London and Honorary Vice President of the Philosophy of Education Society of Great Britain. His main research is in the areas of philosophy of education and vocational education. One of his current interests is in the nature of teaching as a profession. He is the author of, among other books, *Teachers' Know-How: A Philosophical Investigation* (Wiley 2017).

Foreword

Some people change the world. And some people change the people who change the world. That is you.

(Kij Johnson 2016)

It is perhaps a cliché but nevertheless true that teaching is one of the most demanding yet rewarding of occupations. It is demanding because of the complexity, breadth and weight of the responsibilities associated with the role and because of the distinctive mix of expertise and dispositions – or habits of mind – that are required to do it well. Teachers are not only responsible for teaching their subjects, developing students' cognitive capabilities, and helping them to do well in the exams that will give them access to the next stage of education or to training for their chosen occupations; t[hey] are also responsible for helping their students to be emotionally secure and socially adept individuals – to be empathic, well organized, creative, collaborative and critically reflective people. For many teachers, it will also be important to teach their students to be able to recognize injustices within schools and the wider society and to be motivated and equipped to challenge and address these. There is nothing more rewarding as a teacher than seeing your students learn and grow as a consequence of your teaching and the opportunities you have given them, and nothing more important than educating the next generation to be knowledgeable, curious, critical citizens, able to fulfil their potential and make a positive difference in the world.

As a newly qualified teacher – or if you are at the start of your training – this is likely to feel like a daunting set of responsibilities and what you will need first and foremost is the confidence to feel that teaching is something you will be able to do and do well. This collection is an indispensable resource for those of you wishing to build that confidence. Written in a highly accessible style by leading experts in their respective fields, it will help you to think about fundamental questions such as these:

- What is a good teacher and what kind of teacher do you want to be?
- What aims should underpin the curriculum and who should determine them?

- How do students learn and what are the implications of this for how we should teach?

- What does good school leadership look like and is running a school a science or an art?

- How can schools and teachers contribute to social justice?

The collection will also help you prepare for the nitty gritty of good teaching practice, for example, by helping you to arrive at your own answers to the following questions:

- How can you create a classroom climate that encourages students to become engaged and active learners?

- How can you ensure that your teaching is attentive to the diverse mix of student identities, capabilities, experiences and interests you are likely to encounter in the classroom?

- How can you frame questions in ways that will facilitate productive classroom dialogue, thinking and learning?

- How can you make best use of digital technologies to enhance your students' learning?

- How can you create a nurturing environment in which your students feel secure and able to talk openly about any anxieties and problems they may be experiencing?

- What role can and should teachers play in safeguarding children from exploitation, abuse or neglect?

- How can student performance data be used responsibly within schools to inform productive conversations about how school processes and practices can be improved?

The book concludes with a chapter by the editorial team that will help you to consider how best to navigate the 'maze of professional development' on offer as you continue in your career. As the political theorist, Antonio Gramsci (1971: 350) reminds us: 'Every pupil is always a teacher; and every teacher is always a pupil.' As teachers, we need to practise – and model – a readiness to continually learn and grow. Some of this will happen naturally in the course of your day-to-day teaching as you learn from your students and the colleagues you will be working with, but it is also helpful from time to time to stand back and think strategically about how best to make the most of the professional development opportunities that are available to you or how to proactively create these for yourselves and your colleagues.

Clearly it is impossible for one volume to incorporate everything you will ever need to know about teaching, but what this book does is provide an engaging introduction to some of the fundamental questions you will be asking as a teacher and the key challenges you are likely to encounter. Each chapter is underpinned by rich insights from research and scholarship, in many cases undertaken by the authors themselves, and some chapters also include helpful suggestions for further reading. As the editors say in their Introduction, it is a book that you are likely to want to dip in and out of as questions occur to you. However, if you are minded to read the book from cover to cover, that would also be a hugely enriching thing to do. I have just done that myself and enjoyed it immensely. I cannot recommend it highly enough!

Sharon Gewirtz
Professor of Education
King's College London

References

Gramsci, A. (1971) *Selections from the Prison Notebooks*, eds Q. Hoare and G. Nowell Smith. New York: International Publishers.

Johnson, K. (2016) *The Dream-Quest of Vellitt Boe*. New York: Tor.

Introduction

MEG MAGUIRE, SIMON GIBBONS, MELISSA GLACKIN, DAVID PEPPER AND KAREN SKILLING

If you are becoming a teacher, this book has been written for you. It has been written by a group of people who have two things in common. The first is that they have devoted most of their lives to education – teaching, researching or both. The second is that they have all worked in the School of Education, Communication and Society at King's College London. This unique and powerful combination has resulted in what you hold in your hands – thoughts, ideas, words, questions, answers, wit and wisdom.

You will notice that this is the fifth edition. Meg Maguire and Justin Dillon, the original editors, explained that the original motivation behind *Becoming a Teacher* followed a visit from Her Majesty's Inspectorate, which encouraged staff to look critically at the level of reading that King's students did during their PGCE year. Despite searching, Meg and Justin could not find a textbook that addressed the issues that they knew concerned their students and subsequently they wrote one themselves. Although this first text was for internal consumption, it proved to be very useful and, with the help of Open University Press, they produced, in 1997, a more polished version. This first edition proved to be popular too, and had to be reprinted. However, education changes rapidly and books date – even if many ideas remain valid over decades. Twenty years and four editions later, four new members have joined the editorial team to produce this fifth edition of *Becoming a Teacher*.

This edition contains 26 chapters. There are new contributions on education policy changes, international influences, learning and emotions, student engagement, teachers' lives and careers, and safeguarding in schools. There are seven new contributors and many new ideas and issues. However, the overall philosophy of the book remains unchanged. This is not a 'tips for teachers' book, although some chapters do focus on technical issues. Each chapter is designed to give you some background in terms of the historical context, and to illuminate the key issues that you will be faced with every day. Some of the chapters should enable you to make sense of what goes on in school and should help you to gain an overview of a particular topic. Our intention is that this book will give you some evidence from the literature to back up, or maybe to challenge, your own opinions and experience.

Teaching relies on confidence. You need to be confident in your knowledge of your subject. Your students need to be confident in you as a teacher. Confidence can develop through experience and through feedback from other people. This book is designed to help you to become more confident in your understanding of what learning to teach involves. There will be much in this book that you have not thought of before, things that you disagree with or things that you feel are obvious. It is designed to be dipped into rather than read from beginning to end and, we hope, will point you in the direction of further reading.

How to use the book

Each chapter is designed to be read on its own, although you will find recurrent themes across the book. If you are doing an assignment on a topic such as behaviour or social justice, or you feel that there are areas of education about which you know very little, then you can use the chapters here as starting points. Some of the chapters are linked in terms of content, so if you are interested in learning, you will find that the chapters on learning, differentiation and grouping and assessment for learning are interrelated. Indeed, the complexity and interwoven nature of education are what makes it such a fascinating area to work in.

The book is divided into four major parts. We have called Part 1 Becoming a teacher, because it sets the scene – addressing some fundamental areas of concern for a new teacher, such as what it means to be a teacher, how government reforms and your life and experiences outside teaching impact this work. Part 2, Policy, society and schooling, provides a grounding in the broader context in which education sits. As well as looking at education from an international perspective, this part raises questions about values in education, current policy shifts and social justice. In the classroom, some of your concerns will be more immediate than those outlined above, and Part 3, Teaching and learning, is a collection of interrelated articles addressing issues such as classroom management, English as an additional language and assessment for learning. In each chapter you will find practical advice based on sound theoretical understandings as well as some key issues to consider. Part 4, Across the curriculum, appears daunting. The responsibilities of teachers beyond that of being a subject specialist have grown steadily over the years. The authors of the chapters in this part provide information about roles and responsibilities in areas including environmental and sustainable education, digital technologies, literacy and numeracy. As well as looking at how the form tutor's role is changing in school, the part contains Chapter 26, which examines continuing professional development.

And, finally, in putting this book together, we have tried to emphasize the three Rs: reading, reflection and research. Effective teachers are able to learn from their experiences, reflecting on both positive and negative feedback. The best teachers are often those who not only learn from their experience but also learn from the experiences of others. Reading offers access to the wisdom of others as well as providing tools to interpret your own experiences. We have encouraged the authors contributing to this book to provide evidence from research to justify the points that they make. We encourage you to reflect on that evidence and on the related issues discussed in this book during the process of becoming a teacher. Over to you.

PART 1

Becoming a teacher

1

Becoming a teacher

KAREN SKILLING, SIMON GIBBONS, MELISSA GLACKIN, MEG MAGUIRE AND DAVID PEPPER

Introduction

This book is based on a central premise, which is that every child, every school and every education system depends for its success on the quality of its teachers. Teachers matter! Teachers who are passionate about their work and their subject, who have engaging relationships with their students and convey their enthusiasms to their classes are the teachers that we all remember making a difference in our own lives and to our learning. Some of us still have life-long interests and involvements with certain subjects or activities or creative forms because we were introduced to these by teachers; our interests were aroused by teachers rather than within our families. Teachers matter because they influence the academic progress of our young people and they matter because of their impact on students' social and emotional development (Hattie 2003). They also matter for society more widely because teachers are educating citizens for a yet as unknown future.

In this first chapter, we want to introduce some of the discussions and debates that will be returned to in more detail in the subsequent chapters in this collection. We start by briefly exploring some of the research that explores why people choose teaching as a career. We also lay out some of the main qualities, values and dispositions that characterize the 'good' teacher – although we realize that this is a contentious concept. We also consider some of the key pedagogical and personal aspects of teaching. Fundamentally, we want to start thinking about the role, the occupation and the identity of teachers, and the part they play in sustaining the common good and in enriching lives and communities where they work. All teachers are educating for a future that will contain many environmental, social and economic changes bringing many unknown challenges. As Melissa Glackin and Justin Dillon argue in Chapter 22, education must give future generations the skills to cope and embrace these changes. For all these reasons, teaching is the most exciting, daunting, demanding and important occupation in any society.

Who teaches and what motivates them?

Trainee teachers come to teaching from a range of backgrounds and various experiences. Some come straight from having completed their first degree while other trainee teachers will already have some experience of working in different occupational settings. They may already have experience of working to tight deadlines, working in teams and engaging in problem-solving activities. In addition, many of them will have spent some time working in schools – perhaps as Teaching Assistants – or they may have direct experience of their own children's schooling. All of them will have been to school themselves and some will come from families where siblings and/or parents are teachers. So, it seems fair to state that many, but certainly not all, trainee teachers will have some idea of what is involved in working as a teacher, as well as a realistic view of the complexities of classroom life when they choose to become teachers.

Research findings into why people decide to become teachers are fairly consistent across the world (Heinz 2015). The main reasons that are consistently given include the intrinsic value of teaching as a career, the fact that people choosing teaching believe they have some capability to do this work well – that is, 'perceived teaching ability' (Watt *et al.* 2012: 804) – wanting to work with children and young people, and the desire to make a difference in some way (as Alex Manning and Emma Towers discuss in Chapter 4). However, even though many trainees will have an appreciation of teaching as an occupation, sometimes the pressures of classroom life, particularly in high-poverty schools, can be stressful and sometimes disheartening. Teaching is a highly political and politicized activity and in a time of high-stakes accountability, there have been many calls for reforms to teacher education and sometimes teachers feel that they are being overly criticized. Sometimes it may seem that everyone is an educational expert! But to put all this into some perspective, as Vocke and Foran (2017: 86) have said, 'Teaching remains an extraordinarily noble profession with intrinsic rewards that few other professions enjoy. And, to be clear, no other profession would be possible were it not for outstanding teachers.'

What sorts of qualities do teachers need?

So far, we have been referring to the teacher, the 'good' teacher, and the 'outstanding' teacher, as if this were an uncontentious and straightforward matter. In thinking about the qualities that we would want to see in our teachers, and in ourselves as teachers, one way into this vexed question might be to start with what sort of learners we want to encourage. Do we want to produce compliant students who can apply what they have learned? Do we want problem-solvers and flexible learners? Do we want specialists or generalists? Depending on the sort of learner we have in mind may influence how the 'good' teacher is constructed. Are there any common strands that are recognizable as key components of a good teacher? What might we, as a society, want to prioritize in teaching at particular moments in time? In what follows we consider four main themes through which we hope to raise questions about the central qualities involved in being and becoming a teacher: (1) the role of knowledge; (2) classroom management skills; (3) personal qualities and the pastoral role; and (4) pedagogical qualities.

Knowledge and teaching

One of the most long-standing and divisive questions to do with schools and schooling relates to what is being taught. Even where there is some general consensus – for example, most people would subscribe to children being helped to learn to read – there will still be questions about how best to support this learning, what books and materials are most useful, how to pace and assess this learning experience. In most secondary schools there is a consensus about areas of knowledge and subjects that should be encountered. In England, this consensus is framed by the production of the National Curriculum. Indeed, if you are becoming a secondary school teacher, your first degree will generally lie within one of the specified subjects of the National Curriculum. But there will still be questions about what aspects of your subject should be taught at which time and stage, as well as how this teaching is to be conducted.

In many countries of the northern hemisphere, the work of E.D. Hirsch has been extremely influential in discussions about knowledge and schooling. In England and Wales, some influential educationalists as well as senior education ministers, like Nick Gibb, have been convinced of the power of his arguments. Basically, Hirsch believes that a knowledge-based curriculum will help disadvantaged children close the gap in attainment between themselves and their more privileged peers. He also claims that more progressive pedagogy – a skills-based approach, for instance – can lead to the opposite outcome in schools (Simons and Porter 2015). In contrast, other commentators argue that Hirsch's views displace other aspects of knowledge (Simons and Porter 2015). Knowing about something (knowing *that*) needs to be complemented with knowing *how*. Unwin and Yandell (2016: 78) argue that it is content that engages the interest of the learner and, they add, 'might not some content be more interesting – more valuable even – than other content?' Rather than what they see as a culturally conservative view of knowledge, they prefer a resolution through what they call an entitlement curriculum where all students experience the knowledge and the skills that all learners are entitled to meet. Classrooms are places where what is known is brought back to life by every new learner; teaching is not about exposing learners to an inert version of high-status knowledge. The point of this discussion about knowledge is that obviously teaching is intimately connected to learning about some things (and not others) and, therefore, what counts as a good teaching will to some extent depend on how these questions about knowledge are understood and responded to in practice (see Chris Winch's Chapter 2 in this volume for further discussion).

Classroom management skills

As Jeremy Burke discusses in Chapter 12, there are some core skills that contribute towards good teaching and effective classroom management. Good planning and organization, the capability to teach effectively in a mixed attainment classroom, command of subject knowledge and how to apply that knowledge, assessment, data management and record-keeping are all important skills in teaching. However, in thinking about classroom management skills, perhaps there is 'one ring to bind them all'. All of these variables depend on the degree to which a teacher can maintain a positive and open climate in the classroom. Classrooms are busy places and teachers and school students are in constant negotiation over boundaries, relationships, curriculum content, sequencing and pacing. So, while there are no simple 'tips' that will ensure a calm and co-operative classroom environment all the time, it does not mean that new teachers cannot be helped with these issues either. There are some basic requirements that can help and these strategies become honed over time and become embedded into a teachers' repertoire. Tom Bennett, an experienced teacher, has been appointed as the UK government's 'Behaviour Tsar' and it is useful to have a look at his advice in this area of the work of the teacher (Bennett 2010; 2015). It is also important to remember that this is just one perspective (see Rogers 2017). However, trainee teachers worry about classroom 'control' and seek out good ideas to help them manage well in their school experience settings. Experienced teachers know only too well that controlling – or creating a climate to allow learning to happen – is intimately bound up with a knowledge of the students.

Good classroom management depends centrally on the capacity of teachers and students to establish respectful relationships. Teachers need to be able to listen to and 'read' their students. This all takes time and practice to refine, and even for the most experienced of teachers, it can sometimes go wrong. Teachers need to be empathetic and they need to be aware of the complexities that may be part of the social worlds of their students (see Jenny Driscoll's Chapter 21 on keeping students safe and Brian Matthews' Chapter 17 on emotional learning). Dealing with adolescents is not always straightforward or predictable. At all times there is the need for respect for persons that is sometimes ignored when adults deal with young people.

Personal qualities of good teachers

Teaching involves a complex set of interpersonal skills. These skills are not innate; these are dimensions and dispositions that grow in supportive contexts. If your school is a caring and sensitive place to work, this will spill over to influence staff–student relationships and will be apparent to parents and the local community. But what sorts of interpersonal skills do we think teachers need? Here it is probably most appropriate to see what students themselves have to say. In 2015, an anonymous student blogged about their perfect teacher and we are going to draw on their comments because they so aptly make the point about working effectively with adolescents in school (https://www.theguardian.com/teacher-network/2015/oct/11/show-care-students-view-what-makes-perfect-teacher). This is how they started out:

> The perfect teacher. In Ofsted's eyes, that probably means exemplary lesson plans and 30 immaculately marked books with targets for improvement. But, as a 16-year-old, I'm not sure I agree. What students love about the best teachers – the ones whose lessons are discussed at the dinner table, whose names are always remembered and whose impact is never forgotten – is quite different.

They go on to say that the perfect teacher has deep subject knowledge but that 'a deep knowledge and understanding of their children is just as important'. 'Shouting students into submission just engenders dislike; a perfect teacher works to gain the respect of their students.' 'We genuinely like the teachers who smile . . . We know you're not here to be our friend, but some sort of relationship is important.' 'As children and teenagers, we are constantly changing and you – who see us through that time, pick us up from the wrong paths, failed tests and mistakes – are the truly great ones.' This student added that students like to be praised and not shamed in public. They finished off by writing that perhaps the perfect teacher doesn't really exist but that the best teachers are those 'who never give up on me and have taught me that I should never give up on myself'. We think this says a great deal about what is involved in being a good teacher!

Pedagogical skills

But there are also certain pedagogical skills that contribute towards being a good teacher. We have already highlighted the need for teachers to be able to plan and organize for learning, to assess learning and to be able to use data and research evidence in a thoughtful way in order to refine their practice. Teachers need to be able to create and maintain a positive learning environment in their classrooms if they are to be effective. Many of these skills become the underpinning mechanisms that are all part of teacher education programmes in schools or wherever else training is taking place. However, there are important and perhaps less tangible pedagogical skills that go towards making a difference in the classroom.

If we simply take pedagogy to mean all the different ways that teachers can work with their students to promote learning, then perhaps we might want to highlight emotional dispositions such as bringing enthusiasm and imaginative approaches to what is being explored or taught or tested out. Pedagogy may be refined through taking an active classroom research-focused approach; teachers may try out different ways of working with similar materials in different classrooms to see what approach seems to be more effective. Teachers may try working in partnerships – team teaching – to add different perspectives to what is being taught/learned. By taking a risk, and making their own teaching more open to scrutiny, teachers' pedagogical practices may be developed or extended. Risk-taking and dealing with why things go wrong can sometimes provoke greater insights and personal learning about teaching, but they may also be painful at times! How teachers might be supported in their professional progression is returned to in the final chapter of this book.

In some ways there is a contradiction in what we are saying. We would advocate that teachers, when thinking about their teaching and learning objectives, try to devise engaging ways in which to motivate and encourage their students to explore and learn see Karen Skilling's Chapter 11 in this volume). Sometimes it may be useful to draw on social media and technology to flip the lesson, for example, see Chapter 24 by Mary Webb. On other occasions, it may be that well-selected activities and games will promote the questioning that is desired. It might be that a drama-based activity, or a visit to a theatre or museum may consolidate learning in a far more effective manner than studying a textbook or completing a worksheet. However, and somewhat contradictorily, we would also want to advocate a form of consistency in pedagogy; the students should feel supported and safe in trying new approaches and techniques and while we are suggesting risk-taking and creativity in pedagogy, students need the reassurance of consistency, perhaps through careful questioning and giving them an opportunity to take ownership of their learning, however it is being approached. Indeed, this is part of a socially just approach to classroom practice (see Louise Archer's Chapter 9).

Pastoral role

One last aspect, which is discussed more fully by Jane Jones in Chapter 25, relates to the pastoral role of the teacher. Students know if their teachers are interested in their progress and are approachable, particularly if students are looking for advice or support about complex social and/or emotional challenges. As Jenny Driscoll discusses in Chapter 21, society expects schools and teachers to address, support and educate young people in relation to matters like substance use and abuse, sexuality and relationships, what to do to keep safe and what to do if things are going wrong. Teachers need to know what they can do, as well as what they cannot, in this context. Teachers need to be ready and prepared to 'make a difference' in these sometimes complex areas of young people's lives.

The pastoral role of the teacher and the statutory duties that schools have to uphold mean that this aspect of the occupational role of the teacher and the school extends outwards into the local communities as well as in the work that schools do with parents and carers. Being able to communicate well with the wider community and with parents and carers is a fundamental part of being a good teacher. Sometimes, this capacity to relate and work well beyond the classroom and the school boundaries is easier to manage, for example, regular contact takes place on a day-to-day basis in the primary school where children are collected by their carers. However, secondary schools put a great deal of effort into sustaining good school–home links, through their outward-looking websites, regular social events, sporting events and performances. It is well recognized that good school–home links support learning and achievement; these links can support and promote diversity by celebrating the experiences and valuable community learning in which students are vested.

Concluding thoughts

We started this chapter by asserting our claim that what really matters in education and really does make a difference is the *good* teacher. Whatever technological changes are introduced into teaching, however much the curriculum is reformed or assessment systems rejigged, the teacher is the ultimate key to educational change and school improvement. It is what teachers think, what teachers believe and what teachers do at the level of the classroom that shapes the kind of learning that young people experience. So it is no surprise that governments and policy-makers frequently try to reform and reshape what it is to be a teacher (see Chapter 3 by Simon Gibbons in this volume). However, as Unwin and Yandell (2016: 135) argue, classrooms 'remain extraordinarily complex places' and teaching involves a network of dispositions, biography, experiences, values and commitments as well as skills and knowledge.

What we have been arguing in this chapter, then, is that teachers do need a set of knowledge skills (*that* as well as *how*) and they also need a range of pedagogical skills including the capacity to organize and successfully plan for, assess and extend the learning of their students. They also need higher-order pedagogical skills. Teachers need to be creative and imaginative in their work; they need to be able to use 'intuitive, rational and reflective thinking' as well as having the 'confidence to take risks in learning and a sense of cognitive self-efficacy in a range of learning contexts' (Eraut 2000: 267). They need to keep learning and become actively involved in their own continuing professional development (see Chapter 26).

Many of you who are reading this chapter are becoming teachers yourselves, or perhaps you are involved in supporting a trainee teacher. Our case is that becoming a teacher is more than just a matter of training in basic skills and classroom procedures, essential as these all are as a starting place. It is also about choices and personal and professional decisions, judgement and even intuitions. It is also a matter of values, morals and ethics. Palmer (2007: 11) believes that 'Good teachers possess a capacity for connectedness. They are able to weave a complex web of connectedness among themselves, their subjects, and their students so that students can learn to weave a world for themselves.'

- What do you think a good teacher looks like?
- What sort of teacher do you want to be?

References

Bennett, T. (2010) *The Behaviour Guru: Behaviour Management Solutions for Teachers.* London: Continuum Books.

Bennett, T. (2015) New behaviour tsar: Tom Bennett's top ten tips for maintaining classroom discipline, *Times Educational Supplement*, 17 June, https://www.tes.com/news/school-news/breaking-views/new-behaviour-tsar-tom-bennetts-top-ten-tips-maintaining-classroom, accessed 2 May 2017.

Hargreaves, A. (1999) Series Editor's Foreword, in S. Acker, *The Realities of Teachers' Work: Never a Dull Moment.* London: Cassell.

Hattie, J. (2003) Teachers make a difference: what is the research evidence?, http://research.acer.edu.au/cgi/viewcontent.cgi?article=1003andcontext=research_conference_2003, accessed 23 April 2017.

Heinz, M. (2015) Why choose teaching? An international review of empirical studies exploring student teachers' career motivations and levels of commitment to teaching, *Educational Research and Evaluation*, 21(3): 258–97.

Murray, J. and Mutton, T. (2016) Teacher education in England; change in abundance, continuities in question, in The Teacher Education Group, *Teacher Education in Times of Change*. Bristol: Policy Press, pp. 57–74.

Palmer, P.J. (2007) *The Courage to Teach. Exploring the Inner Landscape of a Teacher's Life*. San Francisco, CA: Jossey-Bass.

Rogers, B. (2017) Bill Rogers on behaviour management, https://www.tes.com/news/school-news/breaking-views/watch-bill-rogers-behaviour-management, accessed 11 May 2017.

Simons, J. and Porter, N. (2015) *Knowledge and the Curriculum: A Collection of Essays to Accompany E.D. Hirsch's Lecture at Policy Exchange*. London: Policy Exchange, https://policyexchange.org.uk/wp-content/uploads/2016/09/knowledge-and-the-curriculum.pdf, accessed 27 April 2017.

Unwin, A. and Yandell, J. (2016) *Rethinking Education. Whose Knowledge Is It Anyway?* Oxford: New Internationalist Publications.

Vocke, D.E. and Foran, J.V. (2017) Why choose teaching? *Kappa Delta Pi Record*, 53(2): 80–6.

Watt, H.M.G. and Richardson, P.W. (2012) An introduction to teaching motivations in different countries: comparisons using the FIT-Choice scale, *Asia-Pacific Journal of Teacher Education*, 40(3): 185–97, http://users.monash.edu.au/~hwatt/articles/WattandRichoIntroAPJTE2012.pdf, accessed 20 March 2017.

2

On being a teacher
CHRIS WINCH

Introduction

This chapter will try to answer the question 'When you become a teacher, what exactly is it that you become?' The issue of occupational identity has always worried teachers, as it is bound up with their standing with the public, with other professions and with the state and politicians. It is a question endlessly chewed over by academics, who have come up with various accounts of what it is to be a teacher. All of these have problems. This chapter will review the various possibilities and then take a look at what recent governments have thought of the issue, sketching out some possibilities for the future development of teachers' occupational identity.

A brief historical survey

In the period from the 1960s until 1988, teachers enjoyed an historically unprecedented degree of autonomy within the educational system. This was particularly true of primary teachers, as we shall shortly see. This was not always the case; in particular the Revised Code of Inspection that existed from 1862 until 1898 provided for the regular inspection of teachers with a view to determining their pay scales according to the results of a test conducted by one of Her Majesty's Inspectors. The work of teachers was, therefore, under scrutiny from headteachers and government officials and there was little room for professional independence or initiative. The Revised Code 'payment by results' system testifies to the lowly status and low trust accorded to teachers at this period and echoes Adam Smith's views in his *Wealth of Nations* of 1776, where he argues that there should be a discretionary element in the pay of state-funded teachers otherwise the schoolmaster 'would soon learn to neglect his business' (Smith [1776] 1981, Book V: 785).

By the 1960s, great changes had occurred. The 1944 Education Act had provided for curricular control by Local Education Authorities (LEAs) which, in practice few, if any, exercised with any degree of vigour. The 11+ selection exam for the grammar schools imposed a *de facto* curriculum on those classes which were prepared in order to pass this exam. However, given the unwillingness or inability of headteachers to exercise control of the curriculum within their schools, inevitably much of the power to do this passed to the classroom teacher within the constraints imposed by the 11+. The demise of the 11+ led to a further weakening in curricular control and the period after the passing of the Plowden Report of 1967, which explicitly sanctioned experimentation within the classroom and even questioned the pre-eminence of the traditional aim of primary education in terms of grounding in the basics (see Alexander 1984: Chapter 1), allowed teachers to experiment, not only with curricula and pedagogy, but also with what they considered to be the aims of primary education (see Mortimore *et al.* 1988 for evidence of this process). The picture was somewhat different in secondary schools. Those 80 per cent of children who were not in grammar schools attended secondary schools, in which, by and large, they did not prepare for any public examinations (Taylor 1963). Furthermore, the schools were given considerable latitude within their non-academic brief to innovate, which many did. The rise of the comprehensive school, and the advent of the CSE examination altered the situation somewhat, but still gave schools considerable freedom to innovate if they so wished.

This 'golden age' of teacher autonomy came to an abrupt end in 1988. A unitary exam for nearly all 16-year-olds, the GCSE, came into being. But much more important, the Education Reform Act of 1988 set a universal statutory curriculum and scheme of summative assessment to which all schools and teachers in England and Wales had to conform. At a stroke, teachers' *de facto* ability to set their aims, their curricula and their assessment procedures, came to a halt. Primary and secondary teachers had, henceforth to work to guidelines as to what they should teach and they also had to teach in such a way that children were adequately prepared to take the Key Stage Assessments at ages 7, 11, 14 and 16, on which schools were, to a large extent, to be judged by the government and the public. However, teachers and their representatives were able to affect the construction of the National Curriculum (see Cox 1991 for an account of what happened to the English curriculum, Graham 1993 for a more general account), there was a degree of scope for interpretation of the requirements of the curriculum in terms of construction of schemes of work and lesson plans, and teachers were free to teach in a way that conformed to their professional judgement.

By 1992, however, further legislation ushered in mandatory regular formal inspection of schools according to a comprehensive set of criteria published in an inspection handbook. Individual teachers were to be judged on their performance in the classroom and the results of inspections for schools were to be published. In practice, therefore, the formative assessment and pedagogical methods of teachers were to be subject to scrutiny and potential sanction. Finally, in 1997, the advent of the National Literacy and National Numeracy Strategies brought state control of pedagogical methods onto the agenda, through detailed prescription of the methods to be employed in English and Mathematics for one hour each day, in the primary school. In nine years, therefore, teachers had apparently moved from a position of unparalleled autonomy to one of unparalleled control by the state. Did this signify, as many have argued, the demise of teachers as *professionals* and their emergence as low-level *technicians*, putting into effect recipes written by state agencies and policed by agents of the state? The position is actually much more complicated and interesting than this stark judgement suggests, but, in order to see this, it is first necessary to understand what could be meant by such a claim that teachers were *deprofessionalized*, or even *proletarianized*, that is, reduced to the status of unskilled workers.

What is a professional?

For many years it was common for teachers to be described as 'professionals' and for them to describe themselves as such. At first sight, such a description suggests that they are of the same kind of professional as doctors, lawyers and clergymen. However, the standard account of a professional found in the textbooks of sociologists of work casts some doubt on that claim. Professionals are supposed to have access to specialized, abstract and difficult-to-acquire knowledge, which they put into practice in the course of their work. Their ability to put this esoteric knowledge into practice constitutes, arguably, the core of their expertise and hence of their professional status (Eraut 1994). It justifies the public trust reposed in them, their ability to regulate their own affairs and their ability to control entry into the profession through the possession of a licence to practise guaranteed by the state, usually through a legislative instrument. It is sometimes also argued that the professions, unlike other occupations, are uniquely concerned with human well-being through their attention to fundamental human needs of health, justice, spiritual salvation and learning and moral development (this has been powerfully argued, for instance, by David Carr, see Carr 1999 and 2000).

However, these accounts of what it is to be a professional pose difficulties for anyone who wishes to call teachers a professional group in any straightforward sense. In the first place, it is not clear what teachers' esoteric professional knowledge actually is. One answer would be that it is *subject knowledge*, the material that they teach. However, this attribute would not normally serve to distinguish teachers from other individuals, who are not teachers, who have also acquired such knowledge through pursuing a university degree. Perhaps it lies in their ability to put this knowledge into practice, in the way in which a surgeon puts knowledge of anatomy, physiology and biochemistry into practice in diagnosis and in the operating theatre, or a lawyer who puts knowledge of the law into practical effect in the courtroom. The surgeon requires, in addition to the ability to make on-the-spot medical judgements, manipulative and managerial abilities. The lawyer has to deploy forensic and rhetorical powers to win cases. Such knowledge involves the practical interpretation of their theoretical knowledge in context in such a way as to achieve the desired result. In this sense, these professionals conform to the Aristotelian notion of a technician, by employing reason to achieve a given end. In their case, the reason involves interpreting a body of theoretical knowledge so that it is relevant to the needs of this particular patient or client in this particular operating theatre or courtroom. On this analogy, teachers have to deploy their subject knowledge in the same way, interpreting the subject matter in such a way that children learn it effectively.

If this story is true, then teachers are a kind of *high-level* technician, like a surgeon or a lawyer. Just as lawyers and doctors do not individually determine the aims of health care or justice (although they may have a say in determining them), so teachers do not determine the aims of education, nor what should be taught, but possess expertise in the pedagogic methods of transforming subject knowledge into a form suitable for pupils to acquire. It might be added that surgeons and doctors do not determine their own 'curriculum' either, in the sense that the knowledge that they deploy is framed by scientists and legislators rather than by doctors and lawyers themselves (although, again, they may contribute). In some cases, even the 'pedagogy' of doctors is prescribed (certain surgical techniques and drugs rather than others are recommended, and the effectiveness of the doctor or surgeon is to some extent judged on whether or not they employ such techniques). The puzzle about teachers is this: if teachers insist on calling themselves professionals, then why do they often complain when their work is brought into greater likeness with other occupations whose professional status is unquestioned, by endowing them with a body of theory to inform their practice?

Part of the answer undoubtedly lies in the fact that teachers do not control their own affairs in the way that these other professions do. They do not control a licence to practise and their power to influence the curriculum, pedagogic methods, assessment procedures, as well as their power to discipline their own membership is very limited. Furthermore, there is a high level of turnover in teaching; many teachers leave after a few years' practice and teaching enjoys one of the highest levels of casualization of any occupation (see Gallie *et al.* 1998). Recent and proposed changes to the necessity for a teacher to obtain Qualified Teacher Status (QTS) and the partial removal of teacher qualifications from universities has increased the gap between teaching and other professions (HMSO 2016). In terms of social status, therefore, it is in a weak position compared to other professions.

But many would also maintain that the description of teachers' professional knowledge given above is seriously incomplete. Some maintain that the ethical role of teachers as guardians of human well-being puts them in a pre-eminent position regarding determination of the aims of education, as well as curriculum and pedagogy, even though it is arguable that other interests in society have some role in determining these things (see Carr 1999 for a discussion that tends along these lines). But even if we were to allow that to be unrealistic, a very powerful school of thought maintains that teachers have, or should have, the knowledge of *how children learn* and it is this knowledge, above all, that is the mark of their professional expertise (see Donaldson 1992; Wood 2007, for the problematic nature of this claim). At its most extreme this view is encapsulated in the old *cri de guerre* of the 'progressive' teacher: 'we teach children not subjects'. This view is extreme as it discounts the significance of subject knowledge as something to be imparted to children and, by implication, discounts the need for teachers to have it as well. However, there is a broad consensus among teachers that they do have expertise on how children learn and that this constitutes a significant part, if not the core, of their occupational knowledge.

Before dealing with this issue, however, I want to question the claim that the professions have a unique stake in determining human welfare. It is undoubtedly true, as Carr maintains, that they deal in fundamental human goods (although some varieties of cosmetic surgery and legal claim-chasing may cast some doubt on certain cases), but it is also true that other occupations such as farming, plumbing, train driving and business activity are not only concerned with enhancing life, but also with ensuring it. Some occupations, such as nursing, are particularly concerned with *caring*, where the occupational expertise seems to be precisely single-minded concern with the physical welfare of a patient or client. But, significantly, such occupations are not classified as professions, at the most, as semi-professions (Etzioni 1969).

Professionals, craft workers and technicians

If teachers were professionals in the traditional sense, they would have at their disposal a body of applicable theoretical knowledge concerning how students learn, which they could employ in appropriate conditions. Alternatively, and possibly in addition, they would possess a body of normative theory (theory that recommends or directs) concerning what should be taught, rather as lawyers and doctors have rules concerning how they should proceed. Commentators on the nature of professionalism, such as Freidson (1986), argue that the key quality of professionals is that they are technicians, that is, those whose work involves applying theoretical knowledge to practice. However, there has traditionally been considerable resistance to the view that applicable theory constitutes the professional knowledge of teachers. This is particularly evident with the case of the National Curriculum. When it was introduced in 1988, many teachers complained that they were reduced to technicians from their previous professional status. However, according to the analysis in some of the literature on professionalism, they were just gaining attributes of professionalism that they previously lacked (Freidson 1986).

How can this reaction be explained? The post-11+ period had brought unparalleled autonomy to teachers. They were, in effect, responsible for their own curricula and even their own *aims* of education (Mortimore *et al.* 1988). These responsibilities were removed in 1988, so it is understandable that teachers thought that their professional autonomy had been radically diminished. That does not, however, explain their rejection of the 'technician' label which, post-1988 seemed more applicable to them as professionals than before. Indeed, by being given a body of normative theory within which to work and exercise their professional judgement, it could be said that they were losing an indeterminate status, exercising powers on behalf of society that they could not possibly exercise, and gaining the position of other professionals, as trusted interpreters of the aims and general direction of an important public service. Indeed, just as doctors and lawyers are thought to have an important, though not decisive, say in the nature and workings of the medical and legal systems, so teachers would now have an important, although not decisive, say in the nature and general direction of education. Their anomalous position would be removed and their professional status confirmed.

Why was this not the reaction of the majority of spokespeople for teachers? To understand this, we need to look at another influential account of the nature of teachers' knowledge. This account suggests that teachers are not technicians (the archetype of the technician, in the public mind, is the skilled industrial worker, who applies theory to practice, such as an engineer or electrician), but more akin to the pre-industrial craft worker, such as the potter, the wheelwright or the agricultural labourer. Craft knowledge is implicit, informal and non-codifiable, and is manifested in practice rather than in any book of rules and principles. Craft workers learn their trade through *apprenticeship*, in which they acquire expertise through observation and gradually increasing participation in the craft activity. As they do this, they learn the aims, ethos and ethics of the craft and to pass them on to future generations. Craft work does not involve the application of theory to practice but the application of manual skills and situated judgement to the materials at hand, oriented to the particular purposes of clients (Sturt 1976). The craft worker's knowledge is, above all, of local needs and conditions, not about applying general principles to particular situations, nor about applying theory to practice. Thus, teachers learn their trade through practising it and they become masters of their craft through understanding the needs of the children that they teach and the communities that they serve. By understanding these needs, they will devise aims and construct curricula that serve those needs. The craft conception of the teacher then includes the ability to devise aims and curricula, as well as pedagogies.

Seen in this light, it would not be surprising that a significant body of teachers would resist the removal of their control over aims and curricula and would see the role of the technician, albeit the 'professional' technician, as a demeaning one (but see Silcock 2002 for a more complex view). However, the craft conception of the work of teachers leads to a serious difficulty. A craft worker does not, on the whole, set the aims and general principles of the craft, these are handed down traditionally and only gradually modified over generations. Therefore, the analogy between the teacher and the craft worker is a misleading one. And there is a further difficulty, for the craft knowledge of the craft worker is essentially non-academic and practical. If teachers are craft workers, their knowledge of what curriculum to follow and the principles of pedagogy to adopt are intuitive, rather than rational. But if this is the case, then in what sense can teachers claim a similar status to doctors, lawyers and clergy? Much of their professional knowledge is, as we have seen, applied theory and there seems to be no room for theory in the knowledge of teachers. How could they even be entitled to a professional training, let alone professional status, if their knowledge is craft knowledge?

And there is worse to follow. Suppose a craft teacher's 'knowledge' is not really knowledge at all, but prejudice picked up in the staffroom? Teachers might claim to 'know' that some kinds of children are less able than others, that you can't teach reading using phonics, etc. Others again might deny these very propositions. What is the basis for such knowledge claims? It won't do to say 'intuition' or 'experience' because these are not justifications for action, but rather a claim to authority which is itself questionable. If the much-prized professional knowledge of teachers turns out to be, on inspection, prejudice, then it is a poor substitute for the 'technical' knowledge of other professions. But if, on the other hand, there is no knowledge for teachers that is analogous to the surgeon's knowledge of biochemistry or the lawyer's of civil or criminal law, then how can they avoid being an occupation whose much-vaunted professional expertise is a kind of folk wisdom of dubious provenance? There is some evidence, unfortunately, that teachers have, at least until the recent past, seen themselves as belonging to such an occupation (see Alexander 1984: Chapter 2, for some of the evidence). Hoyle (1974) suggested that the majority of teachers saw themselves as what he called 'restricted professionals' or workers who have no interest in theoretical knowledge and whose practice is based on experience and intuition, rather like that of a traditional craft worker. But unlike a craft worker, the supposed knowledge is not of the behaviour of wood, stone or clay, but of the actions, beliefs and attitudes of people.

However, the knowledge of the traditional craft worker is, in a sense, self-validating. A potter who does not intuitively understand the properties of clay will not be able to successfully make pots and this will become rapidly apparent. It is not so clear that one could easily detect the lack of knowledge of the teacher. Children who do not learn what an observer thinks that they should learn do not necessarily count against this. A teacher might plausibly say that her aims for education were the development of an integrated personality, not someone able to read and write, as, for example, Rousseau appears to have thought. A teacher might also say that one should not aim too high in teaching some children as high expectations are not appropriate for some kinds of children (see comments in Alexander 1984; Thrupp 1999). It is not a simple matter to distinguish the good from the bad teacher merely on the basis of one's own view of what education should be, if others do not share that view.

Some of these problems are solved by the existence of a national curriculum, which works to a set of aims and indicates, in broad terms, what should be taught. A teacher can then be judged against the extent to which he or she meets those aims and successfully reaches the aims of the relevant sections of the National Curriculum. However, this does not solve the difficulty concerning the *empirical* part of a teacher's knowledge, or the knowledge of how children learn and the best way to teach them that is supposed to constitute part of the core of a teacher's knowledge. We cannot depend on staffroom prejudices, but what if we have no reliable empirical theory to go on either?

Do we have research-based knowledge of teaching and learning?

At first sight, this seems a strange question to ask. After all, tens, if not hundreds of millions, of pounds must be spent every year on educational research across the developed world. Surely that expenditure cannot be in vain? The problem is, though, that we do not really know. Much work that was, at one time, thought to be highly significant is now thought to be compromised and maybe of little or no value. In their day, theories such as various forms of developmental, intelligence, verbal deficit and psycholinguistic theory have all enjoyed periods of prestige and influence and have then declined in the face of damaging counter-evidence. This is not the only educational research of course, much work consists of smaller-scale studies of specific aspects of teaching and learning or how particular schools function. But this more context-specific research poses its own problems, for how does one draw more general lessons from it? Research in education is always under attack, on the one hand, from those who denounce the general and overarching theories inferred from the small empirical base on which large theoretical claims are made, on the other hand, from those who claim that small-scale, context-dependent studies, whatever their virtues, cannot be generalized to larger contexts. This seems to be such a problem that there is an influential body of thought that doubts that empirical educational research does have, or even could have, any practical value (see Barrow 2005, for example).

The problem seems to be that, despite the huge amount of money and effort spent on it, we do not really have a clear enough picture of what is and is not reliable in educational research. Furthermore, very often interpretations differ as to what the available evidence tells us, and it is all too tempting for academics to discount research whose results they do not like and to praise research whose results they do. We are still a long way from getting a clear view of what we do know and what we don't and hence are still a long way from having a reliable knowledge of the theory underpinning successful pedagogies that could form the basis for teacher education.

However, it also seems that we have little choice but to successfully develop such a knowledge base, for the alternatives are not very appetising. If teacher knowledge is a kind of craft knowledge, like that of a potter or a wheelwright, then it should best be imparted within schools rather than in academic settings, just as one should learn to be a potter in a potter's workshop and a wheelwright in a wheelwright's shop. But if this 'knowledge' is, in reality, nothing more than prejudice or unjustified belief which may well be false, then it cannot be a good idea to rely on schools alone to educate future generations of teachers. Since it is not possible to rely on knowledge claims that may often be little more than prejudice, one cannot dispense with research, both conceptual and empirical. However, the amount and quality of research currently available may not be sufficient to sustain the professional education of teachers and, even if it does exist, may not be universally accepted by all those involved in the education of teachers.

It does seem, therefore, that in the absence of credible empirical knowledge about teaching and learning, the professional knowledge of teachers might largely rest with their subject knowledge and their ability to put that subject knowledge into practice in designing syllabuses, schemes of work and lessons. This ability is sometimes known as pedagogic content knowledge and is, arguably, the core competence of teachers. In-depth knowledge of the subject allows a teacher to make necessary and appropriate decisions concerning *what* to teach and *how* to teach it. Clearly, a necessary condition of having this ability is good subject knowledge. However, it is also important to know how that knowledge is selected and presented to students and, above all, what are the most effective ways of teaching it. Pedagogic content knowledge therefore seems to span both the subject and the professional knowledge of teachers and to constitute the core of their expertise, particularly in secondary education.[1]

At the secondary level, most teachers are involved in teaching subjects and are expected to develop syllabuses and lessons that effectively enable students to learn in those subjects. Teachers' expertise in knowing how students learn is, therefore, to a large extent bound up with their pedagogic content knowledge. There are good reasons, however, for thinking that such knowledge is simply a *knack* of applying subject knowledge, which can be gained with some experience in the classroom. There is, for example, a large amount of research within particular subjects which claims to provide teachers with vital know-how concerning the best methods for teaching particular subjects and even claiming authority on the sequencing of subject matter. If this research is reliable, then the problem for secondary teachers in particular is that of understanding and applying that relevant research in their daily practice. But if it is not, then pedagogic content knowledge has to be acquired through experience and through working with experienced teachers. One of the pressing problems for teachers concerning pedagogic content knowledge is that, especially in some subject areas, it is highly contested. This is not merely because different researchers disagree about findings, but also because they often start from different and contested philosophical assumptions about the nature of the subject knowledge and its acquisition in their subject areas. See, for example, the debate between Wally Suchting and Ernst von Glasersfeld about science education (von Glasersfeld 1990; Suchting 1992). Nor is this problem confined to secondary education; consider the debates about, for example, the teaching of writing and reading in primary education that have raged over the years.

If this is true, then it leaves teaching in a position unlike that of other professions, in that knowledge of how to carry out relevant professional tasks is, on the one hand, based on research and, in a lot of cases, hotly contested, or on the other, not dependent on research or theory, but on having mastered the informal rules of successful practice. One should distinguish between two claims here. One is that there *could* be no research-based empirical theory concerning how one should teach, a position that seems to be adopted by some influential commentators such as Carr and Barrow. On this account, we should not wait upon good educational research to guide the practice of teachers, because in its nature educational knowledge is not of the kind that could be yielded in this way, any more than the practice of a nineteenth-century wheelwright was dependent on theoretical knowledge of botany, economics and psychology.

Another, more optimistic, view is that educational research has not *sufficiently developed* to a point at which it can form the basis for teachers' practice. Even in those cases where knowledge obtained is reasonably reliable, it has not always been incorporated into practice. A greater effort needs to be made to evaluate extant research and to disseminate that which has been validated according to rigorous procedures and been replicated in a wide variety of practically relevant situations. It is, after all, most unlikely that there could be *no* knowledge of how children best learn and of how to teach them. One argument, found in Barrow (1984), is that teachers should never act on generalizations since all findings are only valid in the situations in which they have been obtained. Unfortunately, this claim is self-refuting as it is the kind of generalization it is meant to deny. If Barrow is right, then the generalization that one should not act on generalizations means that there is at least one generalization that one should act on, namely, his own. And if that is so, why not on others?

Educational research sceptics hardly ever deny that there are educational facts, just that there are general educational facts (e.g. Barrow 2005). For example, they believe that some schools are more effective than other schools and that some methods of teaching reading are better than others, but claim that research cannot reveal these facts. However, they and others like them act as if they do know some educational facts: they send their children to some schools rather than others in the belief that such schools are more effective, they make judgements about the quality of teachers, of certain kinds of lessons, about the efficacy of methods of teaching reading and so on. How do they do it? According to Barrow:

> More often than not educational truths, however, will be revealed rather by a combination of reasoning, reflection and informal experience. So this is not a counsel of despair. It is an argument to the effect that we need to emphasise other things in educational research than empirical inquiry on the model of the natural sciences.
>
> (2005: 29)

But we have seen that this really will not do. Common sense may be nothing more than prejudice and different people may lay claim to different versions of common sense. It may, for example, be the case that the choice is based on the social class composition of the children in the school (Ball 2003). As Phillips (2005) points out, what seems obvious may only become so after research has confirmed it.

> Consider the classic question of whether it promotes learning better to distribute practice examples on a new mathematics skill over time, or mass the practice following the teaching of the skill. *After the research has been done*, it might seem intuitively obvious that massing the practice until mastery is achieved is the more effective, but would we have made this choice beforehand? (And be alert here, for I might be playing a prank! Maybe the research shows that massed practice is *less* effective!) My point is that intuitions are unreliable here, and certainly do not substitute for careful research
>
> (Phillips 2005: 591)[2]

It does rather look as if carrying out good, reliable educational research is unavoidable if we wish to improve the work of teachers. In the past we have, maybe, been too hasty in expecting quick results and broad conclusions from small amounts of evidence. In the meantime, however, we have to make do with what we have.

The government's views of teacher knowledge

Past and present governments appear to tackle this tricky subject non-specifically. Generally speaking, standards for classroom teachers suggest that there is knowledge about learning and that even Newly Qualified Teachers (NQTs) should possess it.

Thus, teachers should 'understand how young people develop and that the progress and well-being of learners are affected by a range of developmental, social, religious, ethnic, cultural and linguistic influences' (Training and Development Agency for Schools 2010a: 12).

However, by 2012, this requirement had been diluted to the following:

Teachers should:

- have a secure understanding of how a range of factors can inhibit pupils' ability to learn, and how best to overcome these;
- demonstrate an awareness of the physical, social and intellectual development of children, and know how to adapt teaching to support pupils' education at different stages of development.

(DfE 2011)

It is thus implied, although not stated, that teachers are expected to draw on a body of knowledge in order to inform their teaching strategies. But it is not clear upon whom teachers are supposed to rely when obtaining this knowledge. Despite the fondness of governments over the last two decades for basing a lot of initial teacher education in schools, they seem to realize that one could not reliably expect that teachers possess that knowledge (see DfE 2015; HMSO 2016). The very fact that the 1997–2001 government thought it necessary to introduce National Literacy and Numeracy Strategies suggests that it did not believe that the knowledge of practising teachers was sufficient for two central parts of the National Curriculum. Detailed prescription of the English and Mathematics curriculum at Key Stages 1 and 2 is present in the latest iteration of the National Curriculum. The government at the time of writing (like its last seven predecessors) also regards university departments of education with some suspicion, suspecting that they are not really committed to evidence-informed practice. To some extent the problem can be alleviated by the kind of evaluation of research undertaken by organizations such as the EPPI (Evidence for Policy and Practice Information and Co-ordinating) Centre, the Educational Endowment Foundation (EEF) and the IEE (Institute for Effective Education) at York University for the evaluation of educational research, which attempts to draw together and draw general lessons from a review of all the relevant, good-quality research on a particular topic (see the comments of Hegarty 2000 on the knowledge base). It is also worth noting the influence of meta-reviews and meta-evaluations of large bodies of educational research such as are to be found in, for example, Hattie (2009).

However, both the conduct and the interpretation of meta-reviews, which would form the basis for evidence-informed research, require specialist skills and must therefore be done by qualified specialists.

Carrying out, understanding and interpreting research are the key expertise of the professional, qualified researcher and are not something that teachers can be expected to do as part of their normal professional duties. If such skills were taught either as part of their initial academic education or their professional education, then arguably at least some of the profession would be in a position to take on such a role. But such expertise is not available through initial teacher education, nor is it available to serving teachers except through such high-level and specialized qualifications as the EdD, MPhil and PhD.

If that is the case, then how will teachers obtain such knowledge in a form useful to them in their professional practice? Research findings could indeed be taught to them as part of their initial teacher education, if there were a consensus on what research should underlie practice. But, as we have seen, there is not. So should the government decide, in conjunction with centres like EEF, EPI and the IEE, what research is useable by teachers, rather in the way that the National Institute for Clinical Excellence evaluates and rules on which drugs should be prescribed to patients in the NHS? So, for example, primary teachers could consult *What Works for Struggling Readers?* (Slavin *et al.* 2009) in order to devise an effective programme for pupils who are having difficulty in learning how to read. In such a case the situation would be that those methods deemed to work will be put onto the syllabus of BA Education and PGCE courses and then taught as prescriptions for practice to intending teachers.

The current government proposes to address this by suggesting that there will be a British education research journal that will publish research findings relevant to teaching in an accessible way:

> We will also support the establishment of a new, peer-reviewed British educa-tion journal by the new College of Teaching, helping to spread cutting edge national and international research in an accessible and relevant format so that teachers can use it to improve their teaching. We hope that, in time, this will play a similar role in teaching as the *British Medical Journal* has in the medical profession – helping to raise standards and spread evidence-based practice.
>
> (HMSO 2016: 42)

However, the vague way in which such knowledge is described in the Teaching Standards (see above) makes it unclear whether it is believed that there is such knowledge. Standards are defined *behaviourally*. Teachers' understandings of factors influencing learning are manifested in the way that they use that knowl-edge. There are no academic components to teachers' qualification structure. Even though a teacher may have a qualification at level 7 (Masters level) as a newly qualified teacher, neither academic subject knowledge nor research-based cur-ricular or pedagogic knowledge is required in the qualification, provided compe-tence specifications are met. The same goes for the proposed level 6 apprenticeship in teaching, where no academic or theoretical content is specified. Contrast the qualification framework for secondary teachers in France, which is based largely on subject knowledge and which has a higher-tier qualification (the Aggrégation) for those who have excellent subject knowledge. The qualification for headship in England, NPQH, a qualification for the most senior kind of teacher, is not accredited at level 7 and needs further academic work by the student before it can be upgraded to a level 7 qualification by a university. The provenance of the knowledge that teachers at all levels are supposed to have is far from clear: is it staffroom 'common sense' or rigorously filtered research findings, critically interrogated academic research or an amalgam of all these things? It does not look as if the last feature is what the writers of the standards have in mind, since a specifically academic component is missing. There is, for example, no evidence from the standards document that Masters qualifications are needed to move up the promotional scales, even though they are now the level at which many NQTs are qualified. Professional standards for NQTs do not require the ability to put theoretical knowledge into practice, as we have seen.[3] Indeed, this would be difficult given the importance that the government attaches to school-based routes to QTS. At the time of writing there are *four* distinct routes to Qualified Teacher Status that are work-based rather than college-based. There are considerable year-to-year changes in these programmes. The discontinued Registered Teacher Programme took candidates with qualifications at NQF level 4 or above and worked as follows:

> Once on the programme your training will be tailored to your own individual needs and lead to qualified teacher status (QTS). Your school will also work with a local higher education institution to ensure that you receive suitable training to extend your subject knowledge to degree level.
>
> (TDA 2010b)

It appears that, in this programme, the professional knowledge and professional curricular knowledge will be developed entirely within the school, while the higher education institution has the job of bringing academic subject qualifications up to level 5 or 6 (honours degree level is not specified – this would be NQF level 6). The likelihood is that it will shortly be replaced with the level 6 apprenticeship in teaching. With this programme, the link with a higher education institution will no longer be mandatory.[4] All these considerations incline one to think that the current government standards would not make teachers professionals in the sense described above. They would tend, rather, to make them a kind of technician, but not the kind who uses their knowledge base to inform professional judgement, but one who uses recipes given by someone else to carry out practice, in other words, a low-level technician rather than one in the professional sense. With some routes, such as the Registered Teacher Programme, and the proposed level 6 apprenticeship in teaching, the preferred model seems to be craft knowledge developed in the workplace under the tutelage of experienced practitioners. Of course, it might still be the case that applying one's subject knowledge to the creation of syllabuses, schemes of work and lesson plans within the framework of the National Curriculum would require professional judgement based on subject knowledge. Here, perhaps, the claim that teachers have been reduced to 'mere' technicians, i.e. recipe followers in all areas of the curriculum, would be least convincing, despite the frequent claims that this is what the National Curriculum has done (see Silcock 2002 for teachers' reactions). However, the overall picture is one of a series of governments over the last 30 years that are not particularly interested in teachers building up a rigorous knowledge base in partnership with academic and research institutions with which to inform their professional practice, but is rather interested in craft knowledge and/or technical recipes as the preferred model of professional knowledge. For further information about routes into teaching, see Chapter 3.

One can conclude, therefore, that the enhancement of teachers' professional status does, to a considerable extent, rest on the development of such a knowledge base. This is most likely to happen if two conditions are fulfilled. First, all teachers undertake a programme that qualifies them to Masters level as an initial qualification and which includes a critical training in understanding and evaluating educational research and theory; second, that teachers themselves are stakeholders in the development of such theory, testing, commenting on and participating in the generation of findings relevant to classroom practice (Winch 2017).

Concluding thoughts

- Will a coherent picture of what a teacher should be emerge in England?
- To what extent will teachers have more say in what research, if any, will affect the work of teachers?
- Will universities continue to play a role in influencing the teaching profession?

Notes

1 In some respects, the issues for primary educators are different. For example, the knowledge of applied linguistics necessary to be an accomplished curriculum leader in English in the primary school is imparted to pupils as skill and understanding in reading and writing rather than as factual information. Which is not to say, of course, that subject knowledge is nothing more than facts – it also concerns methods of enquiry and verification (see Hirst 1974).
2 By 'massing the practice', Phillips means to give the pupils a lot of practical examples to do, immediately or shortly after explanation of, for example, a new mathematical operation.
3 The proposed apprenticeship for teachers was originally to be a level 7 qualification, but it is highly doubtful whether it meets the QAA academic standards for a professional Masters qualification.
4 Troops to Teachers is another work-based programme which, at the time of writing, does require one day a week in a university environment.

References

Alexander, R. (1984) *Primary Teaching*. London: Holt.
Ball, S.J. (2003) *Class Strategies and the Education Market: The Middle Classes and Social Advantage*. London: Routledge.
Barrow, R. (1984) *Giving Teaching Back to Teachers*. Brighton: Harvester Wheatsheaf.

Barrow, R. (2005) The case against empirical research in education, in R. Barrow and L. Foreman-Peck, *Is Educational Research Any Use?* London: Philosophy of Education Society, pp. 13–29.

Carr, D. (1999) Professional education and professional ethics, *Journal of Applied Philosophy*, 16(1): 33–46.

Carr, D.(2000) *Professionalism and Ethics in Teaching*. London: Routledge.

Cox, B. (1991) *Cox on Cox*. London: Hodder & Stoughton.

DfE (Department for Education) (2011) *Teachers' Standards*, https://www.gov.uk/government/publications/teachers-standards, accessed 30 October 2016.

DfE (Department for Education) (2015) *The Carter Review*. London, HMSO.

Donaldson, M. (1992) *Human Minds*. London: Allen Lane.

Eraut, M. (1994) *Developing Professional Knowledge and Competence*. Brighton: Falmer.

Etzioni, A. (ed.) (1969) *The Semi-Professions and their Organization: Teachers, Nurses and Social Workers*. London: Collier-Macmillan.

Freidson, E. (1986) *Professional Powers: A Study of the Institutionalization of Formal Knowledge*. Chicago: University of Chicago Press.

Gallie, D., White, M., Cheng, Y. and Tomlinson, M. (1998) *Restructuring the Employment Relationship*. Oxford: Clarendon Press.

Graham, D. (1993) *A Lesson for Us All: The Making of the National Curriculum*. London: Routledge.

Hattie, J. (2009) *Visible Learning*. London: Routledge.

Hegarty, S. (2000) *Characterising the Knowledge Base in Education*, www.oecd.org/dataoecd/18/22/1855192.pdf. Accessed 1st February 2017

Hirst, P.H. (1974) *Knowledge and the Curriculum*. London: Routledge.

HMSO (2016) *Educational Excellence Everywhere*, https://www.gov.uk/government/publications/educational-excellence-everywhere, accessed 30 October 2016.

Hoyle, E. (1974) Professionality, professionalism and control in teaching, *London Education Review*, 3(2): 15–17.

Mortimore, P., Sammons, P., Stoll, L., Lewis, D. and Ecob, R. (1988) *School Matters: The Junior Years*. Wells: Open Books.

Phillips, D. (2005) The contested nature of empirical educational research, and why philosophy of education offers so little help, *Journal of Philosophy of Education*, 39(4): 577–97.

Silcock, P. (2002) Under construction or facing demolition? Contrasting views on English teacher professionalism across a professional association, *Teacher Education*, 6(2): 137–55.

Slavin, R., Lake, C. and Madden, N. (2009) *What Works for Struggling Readers?* York: Institute for Effective Education.

Smith, A. ([1776] 1981) *The Wealth of Nations*. Indianapolis: Liberty Press.

Sturt, G. (1976) *The Wheelwright's Shop*. Cambridge: Cambridge University Press.

Suchting, W. (1992) Constructivism deconstructed, *Science and Education*, 1(3): 223–54.

Taylor, W. (1963) *The Secondary Modern School*. London: Faber & Faber.

TDA (Training and Development Agency for Schools) (2010a) *Professional Standards for Teachers*, http://www.tda.gov.uk/upload/resources/pdf/s/standards_a4.pdf, accessed 16 September 2010.

TDA (Training and Development Agency for Schools) (2010b) *Registered Teacher Programme*, http://www.tda.gov.uk/Recruit/thetrainingprocess/typesofcourse/employmentbase, accessed 16 September 2010.

Thrupp, M. (1999) *Schools Making a Difference – Let's Be Realistic!* Buckingham: Open University Press.

Von Glasersfeld, D. (1990) An exposition of constructivism: why some like it radical, *Journal for Research in Mathematics Education. Monograph*, Vol. 4, Constructivist Views on the Teaching and Learning of Mathematics, pp. 19–29, 195–210.

Winch, C. (2017) *Teachers' Know-how*. Oxford: Wiley-Blackwell.

Wood, D. (2007) *How Children Think and Learn: The Social Contexts of Cognitive Development* (2nd edn). Oxford: Blackwell.

3

New teachers: reforming or transforming ITE
SIMON GIBBONS

Introduction

Reports like that written by Barber and Mourshed (2007) point to the – perhaps commonsensical – fact that the most important element in the overall quality of a jurisdiction's school system is the quality of the teachers within it. In part, this relies on creating a context in which the teaching profession is seen to have high status, so that it is an attractive career to all those who might be suited to it, and in part this clearly relies on recruitment processes that ensure that the best candidates enter the profession. No less important, however, is the nature and quality of the initial teacher education that new entrants to the profession experience. Not only will the quality of training impact on the quality of teaching, it will influence the length of time a given individual will remain in the profession – this is at least the view of the government in England, which uses retention in the profession over time as one measure of the quality of teacher training institutions. Systems for recruiting teacher trainees and organizing initial teacher education vary across the globe; in terms of recruitment, for example, some countries – like England – favour restricting the numbers of trainees admitted to teacher training in order to ensure high-quality entrants, while other jurisdictions have a more open door to training with the selection of the best-quality new teachers made at the point of employment by schools. Getting initial teacher education right is clearly a huge contributory factor to the overall social and economic health of a nation. It is also true to say that the way that teacher training is organized is, to a large extent, a reflection of the view that is held by politicians and policy-makers about the nature of teaching itself – is it a profession, a craft, or simply a technical skill?

Given the critical importance of teacher education, it is unsurprising that in England the field has been one that has seen sustained policy intervention, increasingly so in the past two decades, apparently as part of the overall drive to raise standards in the system. While some reforms in the area may honestly be viewed as attempts to implement evidence-based initiatives, it is also true to say that it is not too hard to see ideological motives behind some policy shifts. The result has been to produce a more diverse, arguably fragmented, landscape of teacher education. The impact of these reforms on the success of the school system is difficult, as yet, to judge.

This chapter will consider how teacher education in England, in particular, is currently constructed. Some brief historical context will be offered, but the focus will predominantly be on recent developments and the current situation, where an array of training routes now exist but which are linked, ostensibly at least, by the existence of a single set of Teachers' Standards that determine the competencies new entrants to the profession must demonstrate. There will, too, be a consideration of possible future directions for initial teacher education. A reading of this chapter should enable you to reflect more clearly on your own experiences in your training year, allow you to consider the context in which you are working and encourage you to refine your thinking about the nature of teaching.

Some brief historical context

As Wendy Robinson's clear and helpful account, 'Teacher training in England and Wales: past, present and future perspectives' (2006), shows, shifts in the nature of initial teacher education have been common for more than two hundred years. The metaphor of the swinging pendulum has often been used to illustrate how the focus of training has shifted back and forth between trainees spending more, or less, time in academic learning within higher education and practical training in school settings. For convenience sake, it might be said that the current era of teacher training dates from the James Report of 1972 (DES 1972), a report which came at a time when it is probably fair to say that the balance of training was weighted towards higher education. The James Report made recommendations that sought to bring some overall coherence to the field and in a sense paved the way for the more direct government regulation of teacher training that intensified in the 1980s with the establishment of central agencies increasingly controlling numbers of trainees and structures of programmes. From the 1990s there was an increased emphasis on a partnership model for the training of teachers, with schools playing an increasingly substantial role in initial teacher training (ITT) and regulations set down which ensured that by far the majority of time on a given programme was spent in school settings gaining practical experience.

Thus, by the end of the twenty-first century's first decade, the pendulum had certainly swung in the direction of school-based training, a fact reflected in the variety of routes by then available to a prospective new entrant to the profession. These consisted of well-established higher education-based routes such as the Bachelor of Education (BEd) (mainly taken by intending primary school teachers), BA/BSc with QTS (an honours degree that also incorporated teacher training) and postgraduate courses (PGCEs) (based in schools for 24 out of the 36 weeks for primary and secondary teachers). Training based entirely in schools was in place through the establishment of SCITTs (School Centred Initial Teacher Training), though such organizations often worked in partnership with HEIs in order to offer academic accreditation along with the professional qualification. Employment-based routes, like the Graduate Teacher Programme (GTP) and the Registered Teacher Programme (RTP), were essentially introduced to allow individuals to stay in their jobs while undertaking initial teacher training. The Overseas Trained Teacher programme (OTTP) enabled experienced teachers who had gained their qualifications overseas to obtain Qualified Teacher Status (QTS) in England and Wales. Assessment Only (AO) training enabled people with substantial school experience to qualify with little or no additional training. Teach First was also introduced with the aim of attracting the most academically successful students into teaching; this independently run programme was set up to be substantially work-based, with participants (as those on Teach First were named) placed as employees in challenging schools after a relatively short period of training in a summer school.

Recent shifts in policy and practice in initial teacher education

Since the election of the Coalition government in 2010, and with the subsequent election of a Conservative administration in 2015, changes to initial teacher education have gathered pace, particularly in the area of the shift from university to school-based training. The move was signalled in the earliest days of the Coalition, with the Secretary of State for education telling the National College:

> We will reform teacher training to shift trainee teachers out of college and into the classroom ... Teaching is a craft and it is best learnt as an apprentice observing a master craftsman or woman. Watching others, and being rigorously observed yourself as you develop, is the best route to acquiring mastery in the classroom.
>
> (Gove 2010)

We shall return later to the notion of teaching as craft, and to what extent different ideas about effective teacher training inevitably enshrine differing notions of what it is to be a teacher, and this area is explored further in Chris Winch's Chapter 2 in this volume. For the moment, we will concentrate on the direct consequences of this stated aim to shift teacher training into the classroom in terms of policy and its implementation.

Gove's speech was followed by the Conservative coalition's first Education White Paper, *The Importance of Teaching*, in which the pledge was made to 'increase the proportion of time trainees spend in school, focussing on core teaching skills' (DfE 2011a: 9). Subsequently, the implementation plan, *Training our Next Generation of Outstanding Teachers* (DfE 2011b) outlined how the moves to a school-led system would work; by increasing the number of SCITTs, allowing successful schools to become teaching schools, expanding Teach First, and – perhaps most influentially – replacing the GTP and introducing the new School Direct routes into teaching. There were also plans to develop Teach Next – an extension of Teach First aimed at attracting career changers – and Troops to Teachers, a means to fast-track ex-service personnel into the classroom. There was also the suggestion that universities be encouraged to open so-called University Training Schools, institutions that might be analogous to teaching hospitals, and the first of these linked to Birmingham and Cambridge universities eventually opened in 2015. Additionally, the Researchers in Schools initiative was launched to attract PhD graduates into the profession.

From very modest beginnings the School Direct routes into teaching have grown exponentially. The initial plan had been for around 500 places to be School Direct provision; by the time of the publication of the 2016–17 initial teacher training census more than 15,000 trainees were on school-led routes, making up 56 per cent of the total number in training (DfE 2016a). School Direct has taken two forms – a salaried route that is essentially a like-for-like replacement of the GTP, and a non-salaried route in which trainees are recruited to a particular school but are still technically students of the ITT provider that the school has partnered with. Across both versions of School Direct, schools have greater say in the recruitment of trainees and there was originally an expectation that, on successful completion of the training year, employment within the training school would be offered – this, however, has not always been the case.

The arguments for a school-led system are in many ways rooted in a common-sensical notion that classroom experience, 'on the job' training, is the most effective way to learn the skills of a teacher. Comparing the effectiveness of school-based and university-based training is fraught with difficulties, and analysing different measures reveals different results. There was a time when Ofsted, in its annual report, would specifically comment on the difference in quality of different training routes; in essence, the inspections of ITT would generally point to trainees being more confident on aspects like behaviour management if they were following predominantly school-based routes, but would point to stronger subject knowledge training on more traditional PGCE and BEd/BA routes into teaching. Some statistics point to higher completion and employment rates on some of the school-led routes, but this may inevitably occur as these routes tend to feature smaller cohorts, and the trainees may already be working in the schools in which they train. Such factors may also account for the high rankings of SCITTs in league tables like those published in *The Good Teacher Training Guide* (Smithers and Coughlan 2015), a report which comes down unequivocally on the side of school-based training in its rankings. NASBTT (the National Association for School-Based Teacher Training) strongly advocates the benefits of school-led routes (see, for example, NASBTT 2015). Clearly there are some forms of evidence to support a move from university to school-based training; however, it is difficult to escape the thinking that, in part at least, Michael Gove's rejection of university teacher training was as much part of an ideological stance as an evidence-informed one – the Secretary of State famously included those in university education departments as part of 'the blob' that was threatening to destroy education (see, for example, Gove 2013 for a clear expression of this view).

On the face of it, the rise of the School Direct routes would indeed seem to mean more initial teacher education is happening in schools and that the involvement of university education departments in the training of teachers has been concurrently diminished. These were the stated aims of the policy-makers. However, the picture is far from that simple and when considering the detail of school-based training, we cannot avoid William Blake's assertion that to generalize is to be an idiot. School Direct functions in many different ways and its operation varies across providers. Many of the non-salaried, tuition fee-paying, School Direct programmes in fact operate very similarly – almost identically – to existing so-called traditional PGCE programmes, with trainees on the school-based route following the same programme as their colleagues on the PGCE, leading to the same academic qualification to accompany their Qualified Teacher Status. In essence, many university providers have simply retained or even expanded their existing PGCE cohorts through the addition of non-salaried School Direct trainees. Although many of the salaried School Direct programmes do not carry a PGCE qualification and are, essentially, fully school-based, even this is not universally the case. The reality is that it is very difficult to generalize purely on the basis of which route a given trainee is on, as to what the provision entails – the balance of academic and practical work, the engagement with research, and so on will be dependent on the specific nature of the provision and partnership arrangements. Similarly although SCITTs are nominally school-based, many of these providers will have relationships with universities that allow for the award of a PGCE with the programme, often at a Masters level – this could mean any number of types of relationships from university staff teaching on SCITT programmes, to SCITT trainees attending university, to SCITTs becoming franchised to deliver university-approved programmes and modules.

So while, at a big picture level, the data would indeed point to an increasingly school-led system, and policy-makers can – with some legitimacy – claim that more school-led training is happening, it is difficult to say with any certainty that the aims set out by Michael Gove have been achieved. Even when, physically, teacher training has been shifted out of a university provider, this may only be a geographical arrangement and Gove's aims were clearly not just to move the physical location of training, but to change the very nature of it. The reality is that only by examining the provision at an individual level can a judgement be made as to what the balance between theory and practice is on any given programme. This has the potential, of course, to lead to a very confusing system for those seeking entry to the profession – a fact that is unlikely to have helped recruitment in the short term. Recruitment figures for training courses in 2016–17, while buoyant in a few subjects, like history and geography, showed numbers falling well short of the teacher supply model targets in many subjects, with computing, for example, only recruiting 68 per cent of the target (DfE 2016(a)).

The choices for someone entering the profession are now wider than ever, with routes available within traditional PGCE and BEd programmes, BA/BSc degrees with QTS attached, Teach First, School Direct salaried and non-salaried, with each route varying depending on the particular provider or school taking the lead. Careful research is needed by an incoming trainee to make sure they are getting the kind of course and training for which they feel they are best suited. There is also the potential for the development of misconceptions in those in positions of employing newly qualified teachers; unless, as a headteacher, you are employing a new teacher graduating from a programme you know well, it is very difficult to be clear exactly what type of education and training a new entrant has had in their ITT year.

The Carter Review of ITT

In part, at least, the increasing diversity of pathways led to the review of teacher training led by Sir Andrew Carter that published its findings in 2015 (DfE 2015). Acknowledging in its report a system that had become 'complex and sometimes confusing' (DfE 2015: 14), the aim of the review was ostensibly to 'identify which core elements of high quality ITT across phases and subject disciplines are key to equipping trainees with the required skills and knowledge to become out-standing teachers' and to 'improve transparency of training offers and access to courses' (2015: 3). Somewhere at the heart of the decision to conduct this review there seems to have been a desire to bring some sort of consistency – perhaps conformity – across the system. By appointing a man who himself led a SCITT and having a review group relatively under-represented by those working within university provision, it might have perhaps been the hope that the final report would come out strongly in favour of school-led provision. In fact, the recommen-dations of the review were far less straightforward than this and indeed there were strong messages in the review about the value of research and evidence-based teaching which did not seemingly point to the classroom-based craft notion of the profession that central policy had been pushing. Although there was a call in the report to make clear the distinction between Qualified Teacher Status and an academic qualification like the PGCE – a point viewed by some as an intended threat to the existence of the PGCE – this was not one of the recommendations acted upon by the Conservative coalition government (2010–15).

Many of the Carter Review recommendations suggested that core content frameworks should exist so that there would be some sort of comparability across provision – Carter was apparently confused by a system where an ITT course could lead to no academic credit, or academic credit ranging from a level 6 award to a postgraduate award with up to 120 Masters credits. Following the publication, three working groups were set up to make recommendations for guidance on the core content for ITT courses, behaviour management training and standards for school-based mentors. When the reports of these working groups appeared in 2016 (DfE 2016b; 2016c; 2016d), the government stopped short of making mandatory its recommendations, although there was the indication that future allocations (that is the number of training places awarded to a given provider by the DfE) and Ofsted judgements of the different institutional provisions (all the courses and providers are regularly inspected) might be informed by the extent to which ITT providers embraced the three reports' findings so they may well have some impact on provision across the sector.

The Teachers' Standards

The one area of consistency across the various routes that can be taken into the profession is the requirement to demonstrate that one has met the statements of competence laid out in the Teachers' Standards. The current version of these Standards was first published following a review led by Sally Coates, then principal of Burlington Danes Academy, which published its findings in 2011 (DfE 2011c).

The Standards themselves are in fact the fifth incarnation of such competencies, following versions in the 1990s and 2000s, and are unique in that they apply to all teachers, not just those in their initial training year. The Standards (DfE 2013) are divided into two sections – 'Teaching' and 'Personal and professional conduct'. In reducing the apparent number of Standards in the 'Teaching' section, there seems to have been an attempt to encourage a more holistic view of competence, rather than reducing the ability to teach to an extensive set of boxes to be ticked, as was the criticism of some previous iterations of QTS Standards. In reality, the number of sub-bullets within each of the eight Standards in Part 1 means, if taken individually, the total number of competency statements is not significantly lower than before. However, the reorganization does at least encourage more of a sense that different elements of a teacher's work are interrelated. As with any system of assessment, though, the interpretation and use of the Standards by particular providers will have an effect; many trainees on courses are expected to produce evidence to demonstrate how they have 'met' the Standards – where a course insists that evidence is provided for each sub-bullet and where each Standard is graded discretely, then the more holistic view of competence is at risk of being compromised.

The second section of the Teachers' Standards is interesting, detailing as it does what are seen to be the personal and professional codes of conduct that ought to govern the behaviour of teachers throughout their careers. It is laid down that teachers should not undermine fundamental British values (as they are defined within the government's Prevent Strategy – something Jenny Driscoll picks up in Chapter 21); statements such as these can generate discussions about the moral and ethical dimensions of the teacher's work.

Views of teaching

At the heart of a discussion about initial teacher education and training is the conception one has of teaching – is it a craft, a technical skill or a professional endeavour? One could argue that, in the years of the New Labour government (1997–2010), the view of teacher as technician was forefronted, particularly in the advancement of National Strategy programmes where teachers were, in essence, asked to deliver certain curriculum content using prescribed classroom strategies. Although such strategies were presented as being evidence-based, and some of this evidence was presented to teachers (for example, in the document *Roots and Research* (Harrison 2002), which presented the research base for the Key Stage 3 English Strategy), there was no real invitation for teachers to engage with the theory that underpinned the empirical work. As we have seen, Michael Gove's view was that of teaching as a craft – whether or not he took this view from an informed or ideological position is debatable. I presume, along with the majority of my colleagues involved in ITT – both in higher education establishments and schools – and prefer to argue that teaching is in fact a profession, and that teachers themselves – from their initial training year – should be engaged in active reflection as they develop their expertise.

Orchard and Winch's highly readable pamphlet *What Training Do Teachers Need? Why Theory Is Necessary to Good Teaching* (2015) deals clearly with the question of the nature of teaching by illustrating how both the technical and craft views are not, in and of themselves, effective concepts of what teaching is, as Winch further explores in his chapter 'On being a teacher'. It is hard to argue with the view expressed that the idea of teacher as technician is flawed – for this idea to hold water would require the rejection of the knowledge all teachers have that classrooms are complex places; no two classes are the same, and the success of a lesson can depend on so many contextual factors that it is inconceivable that there could be simple implementation of a teaching method that is deemed to work. Orchard and Winch's central problem with teaching as craft is that it becomes too reliant on the dubious concept of 'common sense' when it comes to taking decisions in the classroom, and that it runs the risk of unquestioned acceptance of popular – if unproven – educational ideas (the example they give is the highly debatable field of 'learning styles', about which it became very fashionable for teachers to speak). While not denying that teaching involves both elements of technical skill and craft knowledge, ultimately Orchard and Winch argue that there needs to be a more robust definition of what it is to be a good teacher. A professional teacher like this takes decisions grounded not in common sense or intuition, but in a knowledge of theory and research.

> A teacher who is able to make good situational judgements does not rely on hearsay or unreflective practice. She draws on a well-thought-through and coherent conceptual framework, on knowledge of well-substantiated empirical research, and on considered ethical principles, to arrive at decisions in the classroom context.
>
> (Orchard and Winch 2015: 14)

The idea of the teacher as a professional has a long history and takes various forms, but central to this concept of professionalism is teachers taking some responsibility for the development of their own practice, and within this there is the core notion of the value of an engagement with educational theory and research. It is this engagement that is potentially at most risk from a shift to a dominantly school-led ITT system; even if school-based teacher trainers and mentors champion the value of educational theory and research, the reality is that the nature of the profession, and the fact that most mentors will themselves be full-time teachers, means that there will be little time for such activity. It is the university-based element of teacher training that affords the expertise, the capacity and the scope for genuine engagement with research.

Even as the shift of training to schools has been gathering pace, however, the call for teachers to engage with research has emerged strongly from various quarters. It is there in the Carter Review, it comes through forcefully in the Sutton Trust/CEM report on *What Makes Great Teaching* (Coe, Aloisi, Higgins and Major 2014) and is central to the development of what began as the College of Teachers and is now the Chartered College of Teaching, an organization in part designed to enable teachers to access 'robust research and evidence of effective practice' (Claim Your College 2015: 13). There are those who would take the argument further, however, to say that the teacher professional is not simply a teacher with the skills and knowledge to evaluate emerging research and theory, not simply a teacher who identifies best practice and puts this to work, but that to be a genuine professional, a teacher has to, herself, be involved in research, testing out what works by entering what has been called a dialogue with research:

> When productive, this process of dialogue – which might be either metaphorical or literal – should culminate in classroom teachers themselves investigating the merits of research-based proposals by testing them through action research in their own teaching. This approach is based therefore on the premise that research can be helpful in improving the quality of classroom teaching, but equally on a second premise that research cannot be helpful except through quite complex processes culminating in classroom teachers engaging in dialogue with research-based proposals.
>
> (McIntyre 2005, quoted in Wilson 2013: 3)

Seeing teaching as a profession and the teacher as a professional who should be actively engaged in interrogating research and putting it to the test in their own practice certainly projects an image of the profession as high status. For some, a teacher's own sense of themselves as a professional is critical for education reform more generally to have any lasting effect (see, for example, Friedman, Galligan, Albano and O'Connor 2009) and treating teachers as technicians to implement others' ideas has a damaging effect (Day and Smethem 2009). Clearly, however, there are all manner of implications if the view of a teacher as a professional is to be properly endorsed and supported by policy-makers. In some parts of the world – one might look at Finland with the five-year training to be a teacher in a wholly Masters level workforce – this has been done and the effect on the status of the profession has been marked. The fact that initiatives in England like the Chartered College of Teaching are expected, ultimately, to be self-funded by the profession suggests that even if there is official rhetoric about the value of engagement with theory and research through vehicles like the Carter Review, there is not the will to follow this up with hard policy moves that would raise the status of teaching as a profession. It is hard to see how further moves to school-based training can satisfy the tension that arises from rhetoric, on the one hand, of teaching as craft, and evidence, on the other, that forefronts the need for teachers to actively engage with research.

New thinking

It might be argued that the rapid shift to school-based training in the most recent decade has forced academics within some universities – assuming that they wish to continue to be involved in ITT – to begin to rethink their role and the contribution HEIs can and perhaps should make to training. The arguments about the effects the move to school-led training are having on university education departments clearly emerge from the research into School Direct undertaken at Manchester Metropolitan University (Brown, Rowley and Smith 2015). One group that has recently emerged to begin to articulate a new vision for teacher education has come together under the title of the Teacher Education Exchange and has published *Teacher Development 3.0: How We Can Transform the Professional Education of Teachers* (Teacher Education Exchange 2017). This pamphlet, starting from the position that teacher quality 1.0 is essentially the traditional university-based teacher education model and that 2.0 was the reformist agenda that led to programmes like Teach First and the school-led system, argues that a new model for initial training needs to be promoted. The central arguments in Teacher Education 3.0 are that there needs to be innovation in the field of initial and continuing professional development and training so that universities and schools can work together in new ways to provide a long-life teaching force suitably equipped for the challenges of education today. Though embryonic, the work of this group is significant in that it is trying to shift the debate from one that sees the pendulum swing back and forth in order to seek a new kind of equilibrium in the work of schools and HEIs in the training of teachers. For this group, innovation is the key word in seeking to explore new models of teacher training and education and to find new solutions to the enduring problems of the supply and retention of high-quality teachers.

Moving forward

Predicting the future direction of policy and practice in any area of education is difficult. With respect to ITT, given the history and current context, it is a tricky, if not to say foolish, enterprise. Debates about the nature of teaching will influence ideas for training, and the beliefs of policy-holders will have an impact on the direction of travel. In the immediate future, *Education Excellence Everywhere* (DfE 2016e) pointed to some potentially significant further changes in the sector. At the time of writing, it is difficult to know how much of this White Paper will see a life in legislation, and exactly when this might happen, given the fact that governmental priorities necessarily lie elsewhere. The proposal to make Qualified Teacher Status more rigorous by delaying the award of the professional accreditation until an undefined point in a newly qualified teacher's first post is still very much on the table. If enacted, such a policy may not have a significant effect on the initial training year beyond the name of the award received on graduation, but it would raise many quality assurance questions. There is also potential to make entry to the profession even more confusing for applicants who may not be clear about at which point they might be deemed to be qualified (and thereby, one assumes, entitled to be paid the appropriate salary). The role of universities and other accredited providers in a system that delays the award of QTS beyond the training year is unclear at this stage. One assumes there would need to be some form of regulation since a system which transfers the award of QTS to individual employing schools could be open to abuse.

In terms of initial teacher training itself, doubtless the pendulum will continue to swing one way and then the other. New players are poised to enter the game, too. The Institute for Teaching (see https://ift.education/#institute-for-teaching) is in the process of being established by the Ark Academy chain and would ultimately be, in effect, a private ITT provider, potentially able to undercut established universities in terms of tuition fees and thereby heralding greater marketization of the sector. There are, too, developments that would provide an apprenticeship route into teaching (see http://schoolsweek.co.uk/schools-plan-for-no-degree-teaching-apprenticeship-route-sent-to-government/). This kind of model of teacher training may seem to work against the raising of the status of the profession as a whole, and it may appear to jar with the efforts that have been made to raise the entry qualifications for postgraduate teacher training, where incremental bursaries have targeted applicants with first-class degrees on the basis that such applicants will be higher-quality teachers. However, there are clearly pragmatic considerations afoot.

In part, moves like the suggestion of teaching apprenticeships are another element in the drive to address the perennial problem of recruitment to the profession. The immediate practical problem for any government is to ensure that sufficient numbers of well-qualified, well-trained teachers are available to satisfy school staffing needs. What might be considered 'quick-fix' solutions to this – for example, increasing the number of possible training routes, offering substantial financial incentives to train – do not seem to have provided the answers in England. In the short term, this may lead to a return to a stronger role for universities in training, since the capacities of such institutions make it more likely that the economies of scale one talks about when defining numbers of new teachers needed will be met. That there is currently a shortage of teachers – particularly in certain subjects and particular geographic regions – is in no doubt, and there is more to it than the success or failure of particular policy initiatives.

This fact is reinforced by the ongoing problem of teacher retention, something addressed by Alex Manning and Emma Tower in Chapter 4. It is fair to say that the problem of teachers leaving the profession may at times be overstated in press reports – understandably so since it makes for a good story (see, for example, *Guardian*, 22 March 2016, where it was claimed nearly half of all teachers planned to leave in the next five years). It is also fair to say that the stock government response to questions about retention is unsatisfactory – to say that there are more teachers in schools now than at any time before may be true, but even if it is, it is avoiding the issue. The official statistics, as recorded in parliamentary briefing papers, reveal some stark numbers: an overall 'wastage' rate of over 10 per cent; a striking 19 per cent of newly qualified teachers no longer working in state education after two years, with the five-year drop-out figure rising to 28 per cent (House of Commons Library 2016). Whether this is in line with comparable public-sector professions, as the briefing paper suggests, it is still clearly a worry. Retention is important to ensure there are teachers ready to assume middle and senior management positions, to secure professional knowledge and to support the in-school training of teachers. This is to say nothing of the waste of public money when trainees may be in receipt of substantial tax-free bursaries and then leave the profession shortly after training.

Concluding thoughts

This chapter has laid out some of the fundamental dilemmas that bedevil teacher training and its reform. Issues of recruitment and retention cannot be separated from the persistent problems perceived with teaching as a career in England – the relative lack of status of the profession when compared with medicine or the law, the demands of the job in the context of a high-stakes, accountability-heavy, performance-driven, standards-based reform school landscape. Making teaching a more attractive career proposition clearly needs more than attractive and coherent initial training, but a view of training that enshrines a concept of teachers as active professionals, pursuing an enterprise that is intellectually stimulating and underpinned by theories of learning and development could be a strong part of raising the status, and the evidence seems to suggest that teachers engaged in research make the strongest classroom practitioners. It may be interesting to reflect during your own training year as to what extent a view of teaching as craft, technical skill or profession is promoted through your various experiences.

Longer-term policy-making is required if the evidence around professionalism is going to transform teacher training and replace the unhelpful arguments about the school vs university training divide that has hitherto existed with new and innovative ideas about how best to create the kinds of teachers that schools now need. History does not necessarily give cause for optimism, however, in a country that has often seen education policy as something that changes rapidly as successive secretaries of state and governments seek to make their mark. Some would argue that taking decision-making for education away from policy-makers might pave the way for longer-term thinking and planning – do you think this is a desirable or conceivable possibility?

References

Barber, M. and Mourshed, M. (2007) How the world's best-performing school systems come out on top, http://mckinseyonsociety.com/downloads/reports/Education/Worlds_School_Systems_Final.pdf, accessed 18 January 2017.

Brown, T., Rowley, H. and Smith, K. (2015) *The Beginnings of School Led Teacher Training: New Challenges for University Teacher Education*, http://www.esri.mmu.ac.uk/resgroups/schooldirect.pdf, accessed 1 February 2017.

Claim Your College (2015) *The Profession's New College of Teaching: A Proposal for Start Up Support*, http://www.princes-ti.org.uk/documents/College-of-teaching-expression-of-interest2.pdf, accessed 1 February 2017.

Coe, R., Aloisi, C., Higgins, S. and Major, L. (2014) *What Makes Great Teaching: Review of the Underpinning Research*. Durham: Durham/CEM/The Sutton Trust.

Day, C. and Smethem, L. (2009) The effects of reform: have teachers really lost their sense of professionalism? *Journal of Educational Change*, 10: 141–7.

DES (Department of Education and Science) (1972) *Teacher Education and Training*. London: Her Majesty's Stationery Office.

DfE (Department for Education) (2011a) *The Importance of Teaching*, https://www.gov.uk/government/uploads/system/uploads/attachment_data/file/175429/CM-7980.pdf, accessed 12 January 2017.

DfE (Department for Education) (2011b) *Training Our Next Generation of Outstanding Teachers: Implementation Plan*, http://www.educationengland.org.uk/documents/pdfs/2011-teacher-training-plan.pdf, accessed 12 January 2017.

DfE (Department for Education) (2011c) *First Report of the Independent Review of Teachers' Standard*, https://www.gov.uk/government/uploads/system/uploads/attachment_data/file/175433/first_report_of_the_review_of_teachers_standards.pdf, accessed 12 January 2017.

DfE (Department for Education) (2013) *Teachers' Standards: Guidance for School Leaders, School Staff and Governing Bodies*, https://www.gov.uk/government/uploads/system/uploads/attachment_data/file/301107/Teachers__Standards.pdf, accessed 12 January 2017.

DfE (Department for Education) (2015) *Carter Review of Initial Teacher Training (ITT)*, https://www.gov.uk/government/uploads/system/uploads/attachment_data/file/399957/Carter_Review.pdf, accessed 12 January 2017.

DfE (Department for Education) (2016a) *Initial Teacher Training Census for the Academic Year 2016–17, England*, https://www.gov.uk/government/uploads/system/uploads/attachment_data/file/572290/ITT_Census_1617_SFR_Final.pdf, accessed 20 January 2017.

DfE (Department for Education) (2016b) *A Framework of Core Content for Initial Teacher Training (ITT)*, https://www.gov.uk/government/uploads/system/uploads/attachment_data/file/536890/Framework_Report_11_July_2016_Final.pdf, accessed 12 January 2017.

DfE (Department for Education) (2016c) *Developing Behaviour Management Content for Initial Teacher Training (ITT)*, https://www.gov.uk/government/uploads/system/uploads/attachment_data/file/536889/Behaviour_Management_report_final__11_July_2016.pdf, accessed 12 January 2017.

DfE (Department for Education) (2016d) *National Standards for School-Based Initial Teacher Training (ITT) Mentors*, https://www.gov.uk/government/uploads/system/uploads/attachment_data/file/536891/Mentor_standards_report_Final.pdf, accessed 12 January 2017.

DfE (Department for Education) (2016e) *Education Excellence Everywhere* (cm9230). London: HM Government.

Friedman, A., Galligan, H., Albano, C. and O'Connor, K. (2009) Teacher subcultures of democratic practice amidst the oppression of educational reform, *Journal of Educational Reform*, 10: 249–76.

Gove, M. (2010) Speech by Secretary of State for Education to the National College Annual Conference, 16 June, https://www.gov.uk/government/speeches/michael-gove-to-the-national-college-annual-conference-birmingham, accessed 12 January 2017.

Gove, M. (2013) I refuse to surrender to the Marxist teachers hell-bent on destroying our schools: Education secretary berates 'the new enemies of promise' for opposing his plans, *Daily Mail*, 23 March, http://www.dailymail.co.uk/debate/article-2298146/I-refuse-surrender-Marxist-teachers-hell-bent-destroying-schools-Education-Secretary-berates-new-enemies-promise-opposing-plans.html, accessed 1 February 2017.

Guardian (2016) Nearly half of England's teachers plan to leave in next five years, https://www.theguardian.com/education/2016/mar/22/teachers-plan-leave-five-years-survey-workload-england, accessed 1 February 2017.

Harrison, C. (2002) *Key Stage 3 English: Roots and Research*. London: Department for Education and Skills.

House of Commons Library (2016) *Teachers' Supply, Retention and Workload*, http://researchbriefings.files.parliament.uk/documents/CBP-7222/CBP-7222.pdf, accessed 1 February 2017.

McIntyre, D. (2005) Bridging the gap between research and practice, *Cambridge Journal of Education*, 35(3): 357–82.

NASBTT (2015) Press release: The truth about school based teacher training, http://www.nasbtt.org.uk/wp-content/uploads/The-Truth-About-School-Based-Teacher-Training-30.11.2015-1.pdf, accessed 1 February 2017.

Orchard, J. and Winch, C. (2015) *What Training Do Teachers Need? Why Theory is Necessary to Good Teaching*. Salisbury: Philosophy of Education Society of Great Britain.

Robinson, W. (2006) Teacher training in England and Wales: past, present and future perspectives, *Education Research and Perspectives*, 33(2): 19–36.

Smithers, A. and Coughlan, M. (2015) *The Good Teacher Training Guide*. Buckingham: University of Buckingham Centre for Education and Employment Research, http://www.buckingham.ac.uk/wp-content/uploads/2016/03/GTTG15.pdf, accessed 1 February 2017.

Teacher Education Exchange (2017) *Teacher Development 3.0: How We Can Transform the Professional Education of Teachers*. London: Teacher Education Exchange.

Wilson, E. (2013) *School Based Research: A Guide for Education Students*. London: Sage.

4

Teachers' lives and careers: becoming and staying a teacher
ALEX MANNING AND EMMA TOWERS

Setting the scene

It might seem somewhat odd to see this chapter in a book entitled *Becoming a Teacher*, however we want to broaden the scope from 'becoming' to 'remaining' a teacher. There seems little point in concentrating on becoming without also focusing on how to sustain the teacher role. In this chapter we start by presenting some of the issues involved in teacher recruitment and retention in the English context. We also explore some of the reasons why people choose to teach and what may motivate them to remain in teaching. We then offer some ways for you to consider how you might navigate your own teaching career, so you are making informed decisions about how you achieve job satisfaction within the profession.

First, it is useful to provide an overview of the teaching workforce landscape in England. Rising numbers of school students together with a growing shortage of teaching recruits as well as concerns over the numbers of teachers who report that they are considering leaving the profession have combined to create a crisis in teacher recruitment and retention (Wilshaw 2015; Lynch *et al.* 2016). A common figure, often cited within discussions of teacher recruitment and retention, is that 50 per cent of teachers leave the profession within the first five years. Teacher attrition is an international problem. Indeed, Rinke (2014) entitled her US-based book *Why Half of Teachers Leave the Classroom*. Figures on the school workforce in England (DfE 2016) show that teacher retention rates reduce after each year of qualifying. These figures do not take into account the variation between the retention rates in primary and secondary schools; teachers of different subjects in the secondary phase; different locations such as rural and urban areas; and different types of schools.

While research undertaken over a decade ago, such as the Smithers and Robinson's (2005) study on teacher turnover and wastage in England reported that more primary school teachers than secondary teachers left the profession, more recent research has suggested that the numbers of teachers leaving schools in the state-funded sector are largely similar across the primary and secondary phases (DfE 2016). Although there is not currently robust evidence showing the leaving rates of specific subject teachers in secondary schools, the demand for teachers in certain EBacc (English Baccalaureate) subjects such as the sciences, especially physical sciences, languages and geography has continued to grow (Lynch *et al.* 2016). However, reports by the NFER (Lynch *et al.* 2016) suggest that higher numbers of teachers of EBacc subjects are considering leaving the profession in comparison to those who teach non-EBacc subjects. Further evidence shows there are regional differences in teacher retention. Inner and Outer London and the South East have seen the highest rates of teachers leaving their schools (DfE 2016). Overall, schools serving 'deprived' inland communities have higher rates of leavers than those in deprived coastal schools (DfE 2016).

It is difficult to gain an accurate picture of the teacher recruitment and retention issue, in part because there is a wide array of (often contradictory) data sources which make it challenging to understand exactly what is happening at any point in time (Worth, Bamford and Durbin 2015). In his annual report (Ofsted 2016), Sir Michael Wilshaw, then the Chief Inspector of Schools for England, noted that a lack of accurate government statistics meant that, 'It is difficult to understand accurately the extent to which shortages exist at a local level, or the number of teachers moving abroad or between the independent and state sectors' (Ofsted 2016: 125).

Recruitment and retention are two distinct issues in teacher supply. Recruitment is about attracting individuals into the profession, while retention focuses on keeping those same individuals in their posts. Recruitment has a long history of featuring in government policy agendas, however retention is a relative newcomer to the political landscape. While recruitment numbers may experience shortfalls, there are thousands of 'qualified teachers, not currently employed as teachers by the government' (Frijters *et al.* 2004: 4). Retention, therefore, is of paramount importance.

While individuals are entering the profession, their career trajectories are by no means a simple linear progression. Teachers do not all start as newly qualified teachers (NQTs) and work steadily in a specific number of schools, achieving promotion in the process. While some follow the pathway described here, many do not, and alternative career trajectories have been described by Troman and Woods (2000). While working in the challenging occupation of teaching and experiencing different career stresses, some individuals adopted adaptive strategies including 'retreatism', 'downshifting' and 'self-actualization'. Retreatism involves 'leaving the job' (Troman and Woods 2000: 260). Downshifting includes 'reducing workload, responsibility and status' (Troman and Woods 2000: 262); and self-actualizing can mean 'rerouting' (Troman and Woods 2000: 265) within education or 'relocating' (Troman and Woods 2000: 267) to another school. These three trajectories also produce turnover in the teaching workforce but may be far less susceptible to statistical monitoring and, while this research is quite old, these adaptive strategies are still in play in teachers' career decisions.

'Push' and 'pull' factors for entering, staying and learning teaching

Teachers enter the profession for a variety of reasons such as the enjoyment from having 'contact with young people' (Huberman 1993: 114), the 'desire to help society improve' (Kyriacou and Coulthard 2000: 117), 'making a difference' to children's lives and learning (Maguire, Wooldridge and Pratt-Adams 2006), having 'a love of children' (Moran *et al.* 2001: 21) and the desire to promote a particular subject (Watt *et al.* 2012).

Similarly, there are a number of reasons why teachers move schools or leave the profession. Ingersoll divided the reasons for leaving into the following broad categories: retirement, staff reorganization, personal reasons (e.g. pregnancy) and, finally, job dissatisfaction or the desire to pursue different opportunities (Ingersoll 2003: 149–50). Broadly speaking, job satisfaction is the feeling of contentment in a role. However, this contentment can be difficult to define, and factors that are involved can be contradictory. For example, one factor might 'push' an individual to leave the profession while also acting as a positive 'pull' into teaching as a career, as we detail in what follows.

- *Pupils* are traditionally thought of as a pull factor, as a motivation to enter the profession and are cited as a reason to stay (Hunter-Quartz *et al.* 2010). Our own research on primary and secondary teachers' lives and career decision-making found many teachers cited the pupils as a key pull factor. For example, statements from secondary teachers such as 'I love teaching the children' (cited in Manning 2016: 125); 'I really enjoy the kids. I like the kids we've got, you get attached to them'; and 'the kids are enough to keep me motivated' (2016: 139) were repeated in interviews with teachers describing why they stayed in their posts. Similar sentiments were expressed by primary teachers: 'Oh, I love the kids, I really love the kids, no matter what kind of class it is' (Towers 2017: 265). The flipside of this argument is that challenging pupil behaviour is regularly cited as a decision to leave; Smithers and Robinson (2001: 25) reported that 45 per cent of teachers in England and Wales included behaviour as a factor in their reasons for leaving. However, teachers may be more concerned about the way that behaviour is managed in their schools rather than the behaviour itself. 'It just feels like it's inconsistent . . . that's frustrating, like the children's behaviour is inconsistent as a result . . . it just needs to be consistent and they don't talk to each other, senior management as a team' (cited in Manning 2016: 145).

- *Leadership* can also be a push/pull factor in relation to staying or leaving. At the school and department level, leadership is perceived as important; inadequate leadership affects teachers' decisions to leave their posts (Smithers and Robinson 2005: 52). Conversely strong leadership can be a reason to remain: 'I really appreciate [the Head], I think he's a good guy, he looks out for me and he cares about me' (cited in Towers 2017: 256). Good leadership provides support for teachers, which again contributes to a context of satisfaction, this is particularly relevant for recent entrants to the profession in the induction period (Burkhauser 2016).

- *Forming good relationships with colleagues* in schools is crucial for staying in post (Dinham and Sawyer 2004). Collaborative and cohesive school cultures play a central role in enhancing teachers' commitment to their jobs (Gu and Day 2007). Primary school teachers and headteachers in Towers' (2017) study reported that having friendly colleagues was an important pull factor: 'I've got strong relationships with members of staff here' (cited in Towers 2017: 221) and 'the people have kept me here, the staff . . . I really like everybody here' (2017: 165). One of the teachers in Manning's (2016) study claimed that good staff relationships was one of the main reasons they remained in post. Conversely, if teachers do not feel they can work and collaborate with supportive colleagues, this may result in them leaving their school. One teacher in Manning's study described their previous department 'as the most dysfunctional' one they had ever worked in (2016: 118).

- *Salary* is another reason why some teachers leave their posts. Ingersoll (2003) found that 54.3 per cent of school teachers in the US claimed that their job dissatisfaction was linked to poor salary. The role of salary is a complex and often contradictory one as it can act as both a push and a pull factor in the decision to remain in teaching (Purcell *et al.* 2005). When referring to reasons why teachers stayed, Smithers and Robinson (2003: 52) found that salary was not so much a 'push' factor for teachers in England and Wales, but it did remain a 'pull' factor. They suggested that an acceptable salary would influence teachers' decisions to stay and 'put up with the other hassles' of teaching (2003: 65). In contrast, Frijters *et al.* (2004) found that those who had left teaching in England and Wales were often earning lower salaries, suggesting that they did not leave for pay issues alone.

However, there are factors which are less dualistic and do not contribute to the teacher's stay/leave dilemma. These factors are more straightforwardly push factors.

- The media sometimes create 'bad press' for teachers and, as a consequence, the profession can experience *status loss* (Smithers and Robinson 2001; Buchanan *et al.* 2013). Teachers can feel demoralized by inaccurate portrayals of the teaching role. According to Fuller *et al.* (2013: 465), 'Teachers still feel there is a significant gap between the status of teaching and other high-status professions, particularly in relation to teaching being a respected and valued authority.'

- Various UK governments have been and continue to be active in terms of education-based *initiatives and policy*. This initiative overload has undoubtedly led to an increase in teacher *workload* and related pressures of the *time* allowed to complete a given task or undertake a specific role. Workload pressures induced by increased demands for accountability and performance have contributed to a rise in teacher attrition in England (NAO 2016). Despite the introduction of 'The Workload Agreement' (DfES 2003) and the 'Workload Challenge' (DfE 2015), teachers continue to report experiencing high workloads (NUT 2015). For example, a 2016 study on the effect of recent reforms on secondary schools found that many teachers were struggling to 'cope with the pressures emanating from the greater focus on data and accountability measures, workload intensification and a sense of reduced classroom autonomy' (Neumann *et al.* 2016: 8).

- *Pupil achievement* can be a factor in teachers' decisions to move between schools. Boyd *et al.* (2005) claim that some teachers wish to work in schools where pupil results are higher, resulting in a flow of teachers from low- to high-achieving schools. Allen *et al.* (2016) found that teachers generally wanted to move to schools with higher attainment and lower disadvantage. However, it may be more complex than this. In all schools the demands of increased bureaucracy and accountability can distract teachers from what they regard as essential pastoral work with pupils. This can be particularly frustrating for teachers in disadvantaged schools who generally prioritize the health and well-being of their students over and above the demands for increasing accountability. The pressure to focus on attainment rather than well-being is arguably felt more acutely by teachers working in schools of lower attainment and higher disadvantage; another factor which may go some way to explaining the pattern of 'movers' from low- to high-attaining schools.

- *Parents* who are integrated into the life of the school are key to the success of their children (Desforges and Abouchaar 2003; Towers 2017). Unsupportive and challenging parents can have a detrimental effect on teachers and schools and can contribute to teacher attrition (Maguire *et al.* 2006). Headteachers and school leaders know this and work to ensure parents work in partnership with the teachers and schools. For example, a headteacher in Towers' (2017: 208) study reported: 'If a parent has got problems we have to help them resolve those problems in order for their children to flourish.'

- *Lack of quality resources* – for example, textbooks, ICT equipment and other teaching resources – can make teaching more difficult (Knapp and Plecki 2001). Buckley *et al.* (2005) have explored the part played by wider school facilities in teacher satisfaction. They detail: *air quality* and impact on health, and therefore absenteeism; *thermal comfort,* in relation to being able to control the temperature of the environment; *lighting,* with respect to intensity level and amount of daylight; and *noise levels.* Buckley *et al.* speculatively suggest that work environments have a greater impact than might sometimes be expected, not just on morale, but possibly on attrition rates too.

Factors in recruitment and retention can be interconnected; they can overlap and impact on one another. For example, school leadership may impact on the level of support available for staff (Donnelly 2003), or the level of parental support could impact on pupil behaviour (Desforges and Abouchaar 2003; Moscovici 2008). Similarly, factors can contribute to a snowball effect, compounding a difficult situation. Poor resources/facilities are unlikely to result in an individual deciding to leave a school, however this could be an additional push for someone already experiencing job dissatisfaction. In other words, the reasons individuals enter and leave the profession are complex and may be due to one or several of the factors we have mentioned. We would also argue that certain factors might be exacerbated in specific contexts. For example, in disadvantaged urban schools, teachers often have to contend with complex demands and challenges (which are less likely to be present in more privileged schools) while under pressure to meet strict attainment targets. Such factors have impacted acutely on teacher turnover. As Ingersoll (2003) states, turnover in itself need not be a negative entity; we recognize new members joining a school/department can bring novel ideas and fresh eyes to revaluate current practices. 'Too little turnover in any organisation may indicate stagnancy. Effective organisations usually benefit from a limited degree of turnover' (Ingersoll and Smith 2003: 2). However, very high teacher turnover rates are cause for concern, particularly in occupational settings that depend on good interactions as well as consistent high-quality teaching over time.

The 'paradox' of teaching

Teaching can be intensely rewarding and uplifting and those who choose to teach are generally fuelled by a passion for the job and a commitment to their students. However, teaching is also a relentless profession, fraught with tensions, difficulties and fatigue. Teaching can be exhausting, not least as a result of increased responsibilities, conflicts and problems with staff and children. Furthermore, teaching can at times mean boredom and repetition where teachers are required to work within the confines of internal and external policy directives. The 'paradox' in teaching is that a teacher can be 'in love with one's work, but daily talk of leaving it' (Nias 1989: 191). It is this 'paradox' which beginning teachers need to take heed of when making decisions about their futures in teaching. In his research on teachers' lives, Huberman (1993) refers to a 'crossroads' in a teacher's career; a time when teachers need to decide whether to continue or to leave teaching. He identified several key factors which contributed to a potential decision to exit teaching: 'fatigue, routine, frustration [and] nervous tension' (1993: 145). Certainly, as detailed at the beginning of this chapter, fewer teachers remain in the profession as each year passes, but there are a number of teachers who do maintain their commitment and dedication to their profession for longer periods. These teachers are motivated by a number of different and perhaps somewhat contradictory factors to remain in their jobs. Some of these may pertain to you as you progress in your teaching career.

If, or when, you arrive at a 'crossroads' in your career, it is useful to reflect on those reasons which prompted you to become a teacher and consider factors that may influence your decision to continue in the profession. Teachers' motivations for remaining in their posts can be complex, multifaceted, and dependent on their individual situation and circumstances (Day et al. 2007; Tricarico et al. 2015). However, there are some common motivations which teachers cite as reasons to stay: having a strong sense of self-belief and the feeling that they are making a difference to students' lives and learning; having a good and supportive leadership team and headteacher; opportunities for continuing professional development (CPD); and good and collaborative relationships with colleagues. Given that many teachers cite 'making a difference' as a reason to enter the teaching profession, they need to feel they are indeed making a difference if they are to sustain their commitment. Teachers who stay and report that they feel confident in their work and feel they are doing a good job invariably increase their motivation and commitment (Canrinus and Fokkens-Bruinsma 2011). This sense of self-belief is inextricably linked to the other factors which have been discussed. Schools that nurture teachers' career trajectories by providing opportunities for professional development and collaboration are more likely to retain happy and healthy teachers (Burkhauser 2016). Happy and healthy teachers are therefore more likely to cope when faced with challenges and difficulties in their teaching lives.

In addition to considering the reasons which prompted you to decide to teach and hopefully to remain in teaching, it is also useful to take time to reflect on your *identity* as a teacher, which may help in understanding why you do the job you do. Day *et al.* (2006: 601) suggest that identity is the 'key influencing factor on teachers' sense of purpose, self-efficacy, motivation, commitment, job satisfaction and effectiveness'.

Understanding your teacher identity and its influence in staying and leaving

Turning directly to those of you who are reading this chapter and who are in the process of becoming teachers, being aware of your *teacher identity* from the very beginning of your career, while you are training to teach, is valuable when reflecting on the reasons for doing what you do, so you can perhaps reflect more meaningfully on your practice. Teacher identity is a complex and multifaceted phenomenon; and here we are going to draw on the way that Day *et al.* (2006) understand this concept. They say that teachers have a professional and personal identity. They also claim that teachers have what they call a situated identity.

Situated identities involve a number of school-located influences which include a teacher's unique relationships with their students and colleagues; the teacher's role as a subject expert (particularly in the case of the secondary teacher); and the teacher's professional role or responsibility within the school (Alsup 2006). The professional strand of the teacher's identity involves longer-term policy and social trends surrounding the role of the teacher, which can exist at a national or local level. These external influencers necessarily impact on your teacher identity and can be in harmony with, or in conflict with, your own values.

Teacher identity involves a combination of a teacher's professional and personal identities (Pearce and Morrison 2011). A teacher's 'significant personal investment' (Day *et al.* 2006: 603) in their work suggests that the personal identity of a teacher is intimately connected to their professional self. Again there are various influences on 'personal identity'; these include relationships with friends and family, values, beliefs and interests. Indeed, teaching is a deeply personal endeavour, the individual can be fully imbued in the role. As a result, 'teacher identity' incorporates an individual's multiple identities that are continually constructed and reconstructed in response to a variety of ever-changing influences.

Teachers are being encouraged, more and more, to consider their performance and outputs by national policies and school leadership, rather than focus on their inner selves, their values and their reasons for what they do. Much less time is dedicated to how they interpret their identity as teachers. Olsen (2010) warns that it is imperative for teachers to examine their own 'interpretive frame' if they are to become better and more reflective teachers. He claims that our values and beliefs shape our practices so, positively, they guide what we do. He warns, however, that,

'If we do not unearth, examine, and adjust our interpretive frame as we become teachers, then it controls the kind of teachers we become' (Olsen 2010: 45). These interpretive frames impact on the teacher's ability to sustain the teacher role.

Teachers' identities are central to their lives, their careers and the decisions they make about their futures. Your sense of identity as a teacher is intimately connected to your motivations and the career decisions you make. Therefore, being mindful of *who* you are as a teacher will help you better understand *why* you do the work you do and can help you shape the teacher you want to be for the future. It may, therefore, be useful to consider your developing teacher identity, and to reflect on how your personal self and your teacher self work together in a variety of ways, both profound and subtle, influenced by a number of factors in your personal and professional life, to produce your teacher self.

Concluding thoughts

In this chapter we have discussed which factors motivate people to become teachers and which elements influence the decision to stay in teaching. We have encouraged you to consider the various aspects of your identity which may influence the kind of teacher you are, and the kind of teacher you wish to become in the future. It is important to note that in being a teacher you will never occupy a static position; being a teacher is a dynamic and fluid process which interacts with a range of external and internal influences throughout the course of your career. Being aware that teachers have many, often overlapping and sometimes complex, motivations for both becoming a teacher and staying in the profession can be helpful when considering your own career decisions. Teachers can have paradoxical feelings about the nature of their work where 'push' factors may appear to outweigh 'pull' factors and influence their decisions to leave the profession. We argue that if teachers can be afforded the time and space to reflect on their identities and consider their reasons for being a teacher, then they are better equipped to make informed career decisions.

We contend that, as teachers, it is crucial that you take time to reflect on your own teacher identity and consider your own motivations for choosing to be, and hopefully remaining, in the teaching profession. In Figure 4.1, we have provided a tool which lists the kinds of questions, arising from this chapter, that you may wish to consider as you progress in your career. By reflecting on your responses to these questions, this tool may help you come to considered decisions about the next steps in your teaching career. If you feel you are not currently satisfied with being a teacher, it is worth noting which factors may possibly change your feelings of dissatisfaction. For example, how would you feel if you could change your role in your school? Or if you could change schools? Or even change sector, such as moving from the primary phase to the secondary phase? Additionally, even if you are satisfied in your profession, a 'Yes' answer may be a shifting 'Yes' or a 'Yes, but/Yes, and . . . '. In this case, it is worth considering what elements of your job *keep* you in your role, what elements of your job you would be happy to *lose*, and what you

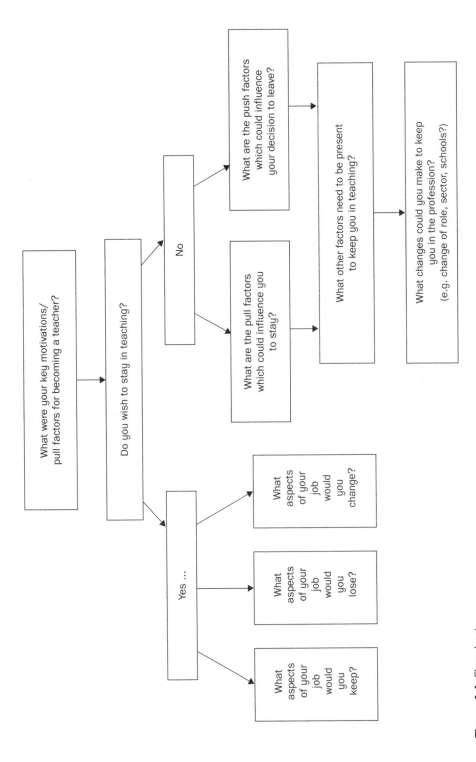

Figure 4.1 Flowchart

might *change*. In order to help you with your reflections on these various questions, we would encourage you to annotate the tool using the space provided in the boxes. At a time when teacher recruitment and retention is one of the most pressing issues in our education system, it is essential that individuals, like you, are making well-informed career decisions and that we are not losing teachers unnecessarily from the profession.

References

Allen, R., Belfield, C., Greaves, E., Sharp, C. and Walker, M. (2016) *The Longer-Term Costs and Benefits of Different Initial Teacher Training Routes.* London: Institute for Fiscal Studies.

Alsup, J. (2006) *Teacher Identity Discourses: Negotiating Personal and Professional Spaces.* Mahwah, NJ: Lawrence Erlbaum Associates.

Boyd, D., Lankford, H., Loeb, S. and Wyckoff, J. (2005) Improving science achievement: the role of teacher workforce policies. Unpublished paper.

Buchanan, J., Prescott, A., Schuck, S., Aubusson, P. and Burke, P. (2013) Teacher retention and attrition: views of early career teachers, *Australian Journal of Teacher Education*, 38(3): 110–29.

Buckley, J., Schneider, M. and Shang, Y. (2005) Fix it and they might stay: school facility quality and teacher retention in Washington, DC, *The Teachers College Record*, 107(5): 1107–23.

Burkhauser, S. (2016) How much do school principals matter when it comes to teacher working conditions? *Educational Evaluation and Policy Analysis*, 0162373716668028.

Canrinus, E. and Fokkens-Bruinsma, M. (2011) Motivation to become a teacher and its relationships with teaching self-efficacy, professional commitment, and perceptions of the learning environment. Paper presented at 24th International Congress for School Effectiveness and Improvement, January.

Day, C., Sammons, P. and Stobart, G. (2007) *Teachers Matter: Connecting Work, Lives and Effectiveness.* Maidenhead: McGraw-Hill.

Day, C., Stobart, G., Sammons, P., Kington, A., Gu, Q., Smees, R. and Mujtaba, T. (2006) *Variations in Teachers' Work, Lives and Effectiveness.* Final report for the VITAE Project. London: DfES.

Desforges, C. and Abouchaar, A. (2003) *The Impact of Parental Involvement, Parental Support and Family Education on Pupil Achievement and Adjustment: A Literature Review* (Vol. 433). Nottingham: DfES Publications.

DfE (Department for Education) (2015) *Workload Challenge: Analysis of Teacher Consultation Responses.* Research Report, February. London: DfE.

DfE (Department for Education) (2016) *School Workforce in England: November 2015* (SFR 21/2016, 30 June). London: DfE.

DfES (Department for Education and Skills) (2003) *Raising Standards and Tackling Workload: A National Agreement.* London: DfES.

Dinham, S. and Sawyer, W. (2004) Mobility and highly effective teachers: re-visiting beliefs about 'over-stayers', *Critical Studies in Education*, 45(2): 83–97.

Donnelly, J. (2003) *Managing Urban Schools: Leading from the Front.* London: Kogan Page.

Frijters, P., Shields, M.A. and Price, S.W. (2004) *To Teach Or Not to Teach? Panel Data Evidence on the Quitting Decision.* Bonn: IZA.

Fuller, C., Goodwyn, A. and Francis-Brophy, E. (2013) Advanced skills teachers: professional identity and status, *Teachers and Teaching*, 19(4): 463–74.

Gu, Q. and Day, C. (2007) Teachers' resilience: a necessary condition for effectiveness. *Teaching and Teacher Education*, 23(8): 1302–1.

Huberman, A.M. (1993) *The Lives of Teachers*. London: Cassell.

Hunter-Quartz, K., Olsen, B., Anderson, L. and Barraza-Lyons, K. (2010) *Making a Difference: Developing Meaningful Careers in Education*. New York: Paradigm.

Ingersoll, R.M. (2003) The teacher shortage: myth or reality? *Educational Horizons*, 81(3): 146–52.

Ingersoll, R.M. and Smith, T. (2003) The wrong solution to the teacher shortage, *Educational Leadership*, 60(8): 30–3.

Knapp, M.S. and Plecki, M.L. (2001) Investing in the renewal of urban science teaching, *Journal of Research in Science Teaching*, 38(10): 1089–100.

Kyriacou, C. and Coulthard, M. (2000) Undergraduates' views of teaching as a career choice, *Journal of Education for Teaching: International Research and Pedagogy*, 26(2): 117–26.

Lynch, S., Worth, J., Bamford, S. and Wespieser, K. (2016) *Engaging Teachers: NFER Analysis of Teacher Retention*. Slough: NFER.

Maguire, M., Wooldridge, T. and Pratt-Adams, S. (2006) *The Urban Primary School*. Maidenhead: Open University Press.

Manning, A. (2016) Urban science teachers: exploring how their views and experiences can influence decisions to remain in post or not. Unpublished doctoral thesis. King's College London.

Moran, A., Kilpatrick, R., Abbott, L., Dallat, J. and McClune, B. (2001) Training to teach: motivating factors and implications for recruitment, *Evaluation and Research in Education*, 15(1): 17–32.

Moscovici, H. (2008) Science teacher retention in today's urban schools: a study of success and failure. *Urban Education*, 44(1): 88–105.

NAO (National Audit Office) (2016) *Training New Teachers*. (Report No: HC 798 SESSION 2015–16), https://www.nao.org.uk/wpcontent/uploads/2016/02/Training-new-teachers.pdf, accessed 25 April 2017.

Neumann, E., Towers, E., Gewirtz, S. and Maguire, M. (2016) *A Curriculum for All? The Effects of Recent Curriculum, Assessment and Accountability Reforms on Secondary Education*, https://www.teachers.org.uk/sites/default/files2014/curriculum-for-all-64pp-10845.pdf, accessed 5 February 2017.

Nias, J. (1989) *Primary Teachers Talking: A Study of Teaching as Work*. London: Routledge.

NUT (2015) NUT commissioned YouGov poll of 1020 teachers carried out in June/July 2015 and published in October 2015, https://www.teachers.org.uk/news-events/press-releases-england/nutyougovteacher-survey-government-education-policy, accessed 15 October 2017.

Ofsted (Office for Standards in Education) (2016) *The Annual Report of Her Majesty's Chief Inspector of Education, Children's Services and Skills 2015/16*. London: TSO, https://www.gov.uk/government/uploads/system/uploads/attachment_data/file/57418Ofsted_annual_report_education_and_skills_201516_web-ready.pdf, accessed 15 May 2017.

Olsen, B.S. (2010) *Teaching for Success: Developing Your Teacher Identity in Today's Classroom*. Boulder, CO: Paradigm Publishers.

Pearce, J. and Morrison, C. (2011) Teacher identity and early career resilience: exploring the links, *Australian Journal of Teacher Education*, 36(1): 48–59.

Purcell, K., Wilton, N., Davies, R. and Elias, P. (2005) *Education as a Career: Entry and Exit from Teaching as a Profession* (DfES research report no. 690). London: DfES.

Rinke, C.R. (2014) *Why Half of Teachers Leave the Classroom: Understanding Recruitment and Retention in Today's Schools*. London: R&L Education.

Ross, A. and Hutchings, M. (2003) *Attracting, Developing and Retaining Effective Teachers in the United Kingdom of Great Britain and Northern Ireland.* OECD Country Background Report, http://www.oecd.org/edu/school/2635748.pdf, accessed 13 April 2007.

Smithers, A. and Robinson, P. (2001) *Teachers Leaving.* London: National Union of Teachers.

Smithers, A. and Robinson, P. (2003) *Factors Affecting Teachers' Decisions to Leave the Profession.* London: DfES Publications.

Smithers, A. and Robinson, P. (2005) *Teacher Turnover, Wastage and Movements Between Schools.* London: DfES Publications.

Towers, E. (2017) 'Stayers': a qualitative study exploring why teachers and headteachers stay in challenging London primary schools. Unpublished doctoral thesis, King's College London.

Tricarico, K.M., Jacobs, J. and Yendol-Hoppey, D. (2015) Reflection on their first five years of teaching: understanding staying and impact power, *Teachers and Teaching,* 21(3): 237–59.

Troman, G. and Woods, P. (2000) Careers under stress: teacher adaptations at a time of intensive reform, *Journal of Educational Change,* 1(3): 253–75.

Watt, H.M., Richardson, P.W., Klusmann, U., Kunter, M., Beyer, B., Trautwein, U. and Baumert, J. (2012) Motivations for choosing teaching as a career: an international comparison using the FIT-Choice scale, *Teaching and Teacher Education,* 28(6): 791–805.

Weiss, E.M. (1999) Perceived workplace conditions and first-year teachers' morale, career choice commitment, and planned retention: a secondary analysis, *Teaching and Teacher Education,* 15(8): 861–79.

Wilshaw, M (2015) Keynote speech at North East Summit, Newcastle, https://www.gov.uk/government/speeches/schools-northeast-summit-2015, accessed 15 January 2016.

Worth, J., Bamford, S. and Durbin, B. (2015) *Should I Stay or Should I Go? NFER Analysis of Teachers Joining and Leaving the Profession.* Slough: NFER.

PART 2
Policy, society and schooling

5

International assessments
DAVID PEPPER

Introduction

One history of international comparisons of education policy and practice begins with travellers returning home with tales of their observations overseas – including the peculiarities of education there – since time immemorial. This history proceeds with a period of education 'policy borrowing' between countries in the eighteenth and nineteenth centuries before the significance of cultural contexts for education policies and practices in each nation state received more attention from the turn of the twentieth century. This history ends optimistically with the formation of a social science of comparative education, safeguarded by academics in universities, in the 1960s (Noah and Eckstein 1969). In a parallel development in the same decade, however, the first international assessment of school students' educational attainment was conducted, sowing the seeds of a new wave of policy borrowing between education systems. Since the turn of the millennium, three major international assessments have been regularly repeated, seeking and receiving a great deal of media and policy attention (Pereyra, Kotthoff and Cowen 2011; Pons 2017). This chapter focuses on these international assessments and makes the following key points about their results:

- Reports of international rankings conceal small differences between countries' results.
- Reports of *changes* in international rankings mask countries' joining or leaving assessments.
- The results provide a snapshot of a limited range of learning outcomes at one point in time.
- The education policies and practices responsible for changes in the results remain opaque.
- A much wider range of policies and practices influence the results but are not attended to.

- We need additional methods to help us understand education in different cultural contexts.
- We also need additional methods to inform education policies and practices in our context.

The next two sections will help you to reflect critically (as opposed to uncritically) on the designs and uses of international assessments, with a particular focus on England. The final section then concludes the chapter with some reflections for the relevance of international assessments to becoming a teacher.

The designs of international assessments

This section begins with a little historical background on international assessments of educational attainment in schools, and then focuses on the three which predominate today:

1. PISA (Programme for International Student Assessment)
2. TIMSS (Trends in International Mathematics and Science Study)
3. PIRLS (Progress in International Reading Literacy Study).[1]

The first international assessments

The earliest of the international assessments was the First International Mathematics Study (FIMS) in 1964, in which 12 countries participated, including the UK (but only England and Scotland). Mathematics was selected because it was thought the subject would be universal and culturally neutral but this did not prove to be the case and major technical and practical difficulties were encountered (Brown 1996). The Second International Mathematics Study (SIMS) was not attempted until 1982, when 20 countries participated, including England, Wales and Scotland from the UK, and with more success (Brown 1996). While the International Association for the Evaluation of Educational Achievement, which bears only limited resemblance to its acronym (IEA), was created by national governments to conduct FIMS and SIMS, the funding for the International Assessment of Educational Progress (IAEP) in 1988 and 1991 came from the US government. The IAEP assessed not only mathematics but also science and initially involved six countries, including England, Scotland and Wales from the UK, and subsequently grew to involve 20 countries. The IEA, stressing its independence as an international collaborative enterprise, then took over where IAEP left off, with its next study including mathematics and science.

The advent of TIMSS, PIRLS and PISA

The Third International Mathematics and Science Study, conducted in 1995, lends its acronym to the contemporary incarnation of this IEA assessment, namely TIMSS, which has been conducted every four years since 1999. The IEA has also conducted

Table 5.1 Key features of PISA, TIMSS and PIRLS

	PISA	TIMSS	PIRLS
Organization	OECD	IEA	IEA
Ages/grades	Aged 15	Grade 4 (Age ~10) Grade 8 (Age ~14)	Grade 4 (Age ~10)
Subjects	Reading Mathematics Science Financial literacy Collaborative problem-solving	Mathematics Science	Reading
Organizing concept	Literacy	Curriculum	Curriculum
Methods	Tests Questionnaires	Tests Questionnaires	Tests Questionnaires
Frequency	Every 3 years	Every 4 years	Every 5 years
Since	2000	1999	2001

its international assessment of reading (PIRLS) every five years since 2001. When the Organisation for Economic Cooperation and Development (OECD) first conducted PISA in 2000, it was therefore a latecomer to international comparisons of student attainment in mathematics and science but ahead of PIRLS in assessing reading. The OECD's extension of its competences from economic to education matters reflected a wider trend in governance which left education as one area of public policy which governments could still use as a lever for economic growth. Table 5.1 summarizes the similarities and differences between the key features of PISA, TIMSS and PIRLS, which are explored in the remainder of this section.

Participants

PISA has been administered every three years since 2000, growing in scale from 32 to 72 OECD members and associates by 2015. In addition, the OECD launched PISA for Development with eight low- and middle-income countries in 2013. Over a similar period, TIMSS grew from 38 to 57 countries by 2015 and PIRLS grew from 35 to 54 countries by 2016. Differences between the PISA and IEA assessments prevent any straightforward comparison of the numbers of countries.[2] Regardless, these assessments sample a large number of students across participants: 540,000 in PISA 2015; 580,000 in TIMSS 2015; and 325,000 in PIRLS 2011. These samples represent very large populations; for example, the PISA 2015 sample represented 29 million students. Nonetheless the fact that the assessments are surveys rather than censuses means that small differences between countries in the results should not be interpreted as 'true' differences. Finally, the samples do not represent individual schools, which would require 'oversampling' with a much larger number of students than the 30 currently surveyed in each participating school.

Ages or grades

Both TIMSS and PIRLS assess students in Grade 4 but TIMSS also assessed students in Grade 8. In recent cycles, the UK government has entered England for participation in PIRLS and in TIMSS but, for reasons that are unclear, only in Grade 8. In practice, there is also some variation between countries in which grades are actually assessed as students start school at different ages. As children are relatively young when they start school in England, this means students in Year 5 (aged 10) and Year 9 (aged 14) are assessed. The variation in the number of years of schooling that students have experienced could have a bearing on performance, particularly at Grade 4. However, students who begin school when they are younger may be less ready for formal schooling, so additional years of schooling may not result in increased educational attainment. On the contrary, the average score of children whose parents or carers often engaged them in pre-primary numeracy activities was relatively high in TIMSS 2011 at Grade 4. Another implication of the grade design in TIMSS and PIRLS is that, since some countries require students to repeat a grade, older students could participate in these assessments. Since this grade retention seems to hinder rather than help students, any impact on results is likely to be negative.[3]

Organizing concepts

This brings the discussion to a notable difference between the IEA and OECD assessments, which you can explore in more detail by comparing released test items.[4] In TIMSS and PIRLS, the organizing concept is the curriculum. The aim of the assessment is then to understand the relationship between the attained curriculum (what the assessments indicate students have learnt), the implemented curriculum (what teachers report they have taught) and the intended curriculum (what policies state students were expected to learn). The concept of the curriculum therefore explains why students are sampled for the IEA studies on the basis of their grade, not their age.

By contrast, the organizing concept in PISA is literacy. This usage is not limited to reading literacy but extends to mathematics literacy and science literacy for real-world situations, enabling full participation in society. To this end, in PISA 2015, financial literacy and collaborative problem-solving were assessed for the first time.[5] PISA therefore aims to assess the preparedness of students aged 15 for real-world situations as they complete their compulsory education. The starting age and grade retention issues noted with respect to TIMSS and PIRLS are therefore not the same as for PISA but another issue arises.

Both TIMSS and PISA assess students in secondary education but in some countries only primary education is compulsory, or lower secondary education is compulsory but not enforced. As students in these countries get older, they are more likely to leave school and begin full-time work, which makes the issue more pronounced for PISA. For example, one explanation of the success of Vietnam in PISA is that a substantial minority of children leave school before the end of lower secondary education.[6] Under the reasonable assumption that these are students from disadvantaged backgrounds with lower levels of attainment, this leaves students from more advantaged backgrounds with higher levels of attainment in schools and sampled for PISA.

Test and questionnaire items

In PISA, TIMSS and PIRLS standardized tests are used to assess students' performance in reading, mathematics and science. In addition, questionnaires are administered to students, teachers and even parents in TIMSS 2015 to help identify factors that might explain students' performance.[7] These tests and questionnaires are increasingly computer-based, which has implications for what can be assessed and what is actually assessed. While TIMSS focuses on maths and science every fourth year and PIRLS focuses on reading every fifth year, PISA focuses on one subject every three years. This means more PISA test items were administered to students for reading in 2000 and 2009, mathematics in 2003 and 2012 and science in 2006 and 2015. It also means that the PISA questionnaires about these subjects were only administered in those years. Consequently, the PISA results for the main subject should give a better overview of the subject as a whole, its individual parts and correlated variables than results for the minor subjects in each round of the assessment. In PISA 2015, the focus on science led to some discussion of a puzzling international correlation between more scientific inquiry in schools, a more scientific epistemology and more interest in a career in science but less scientific literacy.

Samples of students and items

The international assessments are dependent on the co-operation of schools and their students, so the OECD and IEA try to balance the subject overview and assessment burden with a matrix sample for the administration of items. This means students are randomly allocated different bundles of test items so that their scores on the bundles they do not receive can be imputed from the bundles they do receive. This can result in a substantial amount of error for some students, so results for individual students are not reliable. However, this error evens out at aggregate level, meaning that results are more reliable for countries, boys/girls, and so on. A matrix sample was also attempted for the PISA 2015 student questionnaire but, as many constructs are assessed through this questionnaire, students responded to even fewer items for each construct than before, and there was reportedly a lack of data to support analyses of correlations with performance.

Test and questionnaire languages

The IEA and PISA assessments are administered in the language of instruction of students' schools, which means there is a challenging task of translating test and questionnaire instruments between languages. While IEA instruments are translated into the 'target' language and back-translated to check for accuracy, PISA instruments are generally independently translated from English and French versions and then consolidated. However, there have been some anomalies within and between the PISA and IEA assessments, and Hong Kong provides some examples. In IEA assessments, students in Hong Kong have been administered IEA instruments incorporating Chinese and English versions of instructions and items to reflect the fact that the language of instruction varies within and between their schools. By contrast, in PISA, students have been administered a Chinese-only version of PISA instruments to reflect Hong Kong's argument that this is a better reflection of whether students are prepared for real-world situations in China as a whole. Also in PISA, only one of the source languages is used to translate the items for Hong Kong and some other participants. However, the OECD (2004) has reported that reliability is higher for items developed using both source languages. On the other hand, none of these anomalies impacts on the headline finding in Hong Kong, which is that its mean score in PISA, TIMSS and PIRLS is consistently high.

Linguistic differences

More fundamentally, the idiosyncrasies of languages may impact on the difficulty of items. Some languages require more words, longer words or less frequently used words to express the same meaning, which impacts on the reading demands of items but in ways that currently cannot be accounted for (El Masri, Baird and Graesser 2016). Compared with English, the PISA 2006 instruments were longer by 20 per cent in French, 17 per cent in German, 11 per cent in Spanish and 8 per cent in Finnish (Eivers 2010). Chinese, Japanese and Korean number names have a more transparent logic than English (11, 12, 13 are ten-one, ten-two, ten-three, and 20, 21, 22 are two-ten, two-ten-one, two-ten-two). This may help children to make quick progress to more sophisticated calculation methods but whether this would have an enduring impact that can help to explain much of the difference observed in international assessments is open to question (Askew *et al.* 2010). Beyond language alone, the idiosyncrasies of each education system and the wider cultural context impact how students interpret information in the assessment instruments, particularly the student questionnaires, in ways that militate against any straightforward comparison of variables that could explain differences in performance between education systems (Pepper *et al.* 2016).

The use of international assessments

Alexander (2010) identified a number of prosperous countries competing for the accolade of a 'world-class' education system and noted that in England it was the then Labour government's 'ambition for this country to have the best school system in the world' (DCSF 2009: 2). The language of 'world-class schools' continued under the subsequent government but the emphasis shifted. While the Labour government's statement of policy had made passing reference to evidence from world-class education systems, the Coalition government set out on 'a direction of travel on the curriculum and qualifications which allows us to learn from, and outpace, the world's best' (DfE 2010: 7). More recently, the Conservative government asserted that 'every child and young person in this country deserves a world class education' (DfE 2016: 5). This meant supporting the development of world-leading teachers, curricula, assessments and qualifications. This might imply that international comparisons would only be required to establish whether the 'world class' accolade had been attained in international assessments. After all, it is difficult to lead while following examples. In fact, as this section will show, the policy pronouncements of this and previous governments demonstrate that international surveys assessments have been used not only to justify the need for education reforms in England but also to follow selected examples from 'high-performing jurisdictions' (DfE 2011).

First of all, it is important to consider the IEA's and OECD's intended uses for their surveys, and the 'stakes' associated with these uses. On the one hand, PISA, TIMSS and PIRLS have low stakes for students who participate in these surveys because their responses to the tests and questionnaires do not inform any decisions about them, either in or beyond school. On the other hand, TIMSS and PIRLS should 'enable participating countries to make evidence-based decisions for improving educational policy' (IEA 2016). Similarly, PISA should 'allow policy makers around the world to ... set policy targets against measurable goals achieved by other education systems, and learn from policies and practices applied elsewhere' (OECD 2016: 3). The IEA's and OECD's intended uses of the assessments are therefore high stakes in that they are to inform discussions and decisions which have implications for students (and teachers!) across education systems. This section will explore some recent uses of the results of the major international assessments in England with some comparisons from other education systems, starting with Germany.

PISA shock and dismay

The 'PISA shock' in Germany has become a seminal and particular example of the influence of international assessments on education policy and practice. When the first PISA results were published, Germany was below the OECD average in all three subjects and the difference between the most and least disadvantaged students was the greatest of all participating countries. This challenged the nation's understanding of its education system, and even its social and cultural achievements, leading to the introduction of national education standards and assessments (Ertl 2006). Initially, however, the effect of early and largely social selection of students into different types of secondary schools was a taboo subject and there was a lack of political will for a fundamental reform of the school system (Gruber 2006). However, according to an OECD (2010) report on 'strong performers and successful reformers in education', a long-term process of reducing the social segregation of students between school types is now under way in Germany. In PISA 2015, Germany was above the OECD average in the three subjects and in terms of its share of high- and low-performing students. However, as explored below, using international surveys to draw conclusions about the impact of changes in education policies and practices is problematic.

There was no such PISA shock in the UK as the country performed above the OECD average in all three subjects in PISA 2000 and, although this performance seemed to decline over the course of subsequent PISA cycles, the Labour government focused on improvements in performance in TIMSS in England. By contrast, the Conservatives have focused on PISA, with the Secretary of State for Education, Michael Gove, going so far as to call the OECD official responsible for the assessment, Andreas Schleicher, 'the most important man in British education'. Under Mr Gove's tenure, the Coalition government expressed dismay that: 'In the most recent OECD PISA survey in 2006 we fell from 4th in the world in the 2000 survey to 14th in science, 7th to 17th in literacy, and 8th to 24th in mathematics' (DfE 2010: 2). This analysis of rankings neglected the growth in the number of OECD members and associates participating in PISA in 2003 and 2006. Some of these new participants were relatively high-performing but this does not fully explain the change in rankings, nor the fact that TIMSS portrayed a rather different picture.

An independent analysis compared the mathematics scores for England, which suggest an improvement in TIMSS between 1999 and 2007 but a decline in PISA between 2000 and 2009 (Jerrim 2013). Although there are differences in what is assessed in the two assessments with, for example, more emphasis on algebra in TIMSS and more emphasis on data in PISA (Wu 2009), the divergence in results for England is not observed in the results for other education systems. However, the assessments struggled with non-responses from schools in England in the early part of the period and England received a special dispensation to bring the administration of PISA 2006 and subsequent cycles forward in the school year from April to September to avoid a clash with GCSE examinations. Consequently, we cannot conclude England's performance in mathematics either improved or declined over this period. Furthermore, the PISA 2015 and TIMSS 2015 results suggest that England's performance has been stable since samples stabilized in PISA 2006 and TIMSS 2007. Nonetheless, the PISA results provided a general justification for 'whole-system reform' in England, for, it was argued, 'It is only through such whole-system reform that education can be transformed to make a nation one of the world's top performers' (DfE 2010: 7). The following sections will show how this 'whole-system reform' in England borrowed freely from other education systems, including for National Curriculum reforms, and reflect on the most recent results from PISA 2015.

'Whole-system reform' in England

The purpose of this section is not to evaluate whether recent reforms in England constitute the whole system reform championed by government but to show how some major reforms borrowed policies found overseas, including recent National Curriculum reforms. International comparisons have informed successive reviews of the National Curriculum. Indeed, a website with UK government funding to provide up-to-date information on curriculum and assessment in several countries was first established in the 1990s.[8] It included a comparison of the philosophical underpinning of the National Curriculum in several countries (Le Metais 1997) and led to the development of distinctive values, aims and purposes for the National Curriculum in England and Wales for the first time in 2000. These values, aims and purposes were included in the National Curriculum handbook for schools but not the subject booklets for teachers, which meant that teachers were often not aware of them. More recent incarnations of the National Curriculum have drawn not only on the original international comparison but also on this national experience, integrating philosophical underpinnings, using terminology such as *importance*, *aims*, *values* and *purposes*, into the programmes of study for each subject. As for the website that provided the original international comparison: the government withdrew its funding as part of the cutbacks that followed the global financial crisis in 2008, indicating that policy-makers favoured PISA, TIMSS and PIRLS over the other types of international comparison emphasized in Alexander (2010).

In the most recent review, which led to the implementation of a revised National Curriculum for schools in September 2014, references to examples from selected high-performing jurisdictions were prominent (DfE 2011). These jurisdictions included Alberta in Canada, Finland, Flemish Belgium, Hong Kong, Massachusetts in the USA, New Zealand, Victoria and New South Wales in Australia, and Singapore. The review involved mapping curriculum content for English, maths and science in these jurisdictions, a process first initiated ahead of the primary curriculum review completed towards the end of the Labour government and aborted by the incoming Coalition government. This review described the mapping of curriculum content as an important resource for the development of the new National Curriculum. In particular, the mapping led this review to reject year-by-year prescription and retain Key Stage-by-Key Stage prescription to curriculum content. The review also argued for this content to cover fewer things in more depth in primary education to ensure that all children could progress. This is not to say that all high-performing jurisdictions took these approaches; rather the review was satisfied that most favoured depth and several favoured Key Stage-by-Key Stage prescription. The curriculum mapping for this review therefore implies either that the remaining jurisdictions were high-performing despite their year-by-year prescription and preference for breadth or, more plausibly, that unobserved practices are just as important in explaining their performance. These practices may include some that are less easily borrowed, such as a consensual approach to the development of education policies.

The things outside the schools

International assessments necessarily examine a limited range of practices and, as comparative and international educationalists are wont to note: 'In studying foreign systems of Education we should not forget that the things outside the schools matter even more than the things inside the schools, and govern and interpret the things inside' (Sadler 1900, as quoted in Bereday 1964). Furthermore, PISA, TIMSS and PIRLS are cross-sectional surveys, providing a snapshot of one cohort in each cycle, rather than longitudinal surveys tracking the progress of cohorts of students. Nor are they, for that matter, randomized controlled trials comparing intervention and control groups. The OECD (2016: 3) does caution that PISA therefore 'cannot identify cause-and-effect relationships between policies/practices and student out-comes', and IEA (2016) seems to choose its words carefully when it says that TIMSS and PIRLS provide information which 'can be examined in relation to achievement to explore factors that contribute to academic success'. But how these factors should be explored is left for national policy-makers and others to consider.

The PISA 2015 national report for England is consistent with the cautious words of the OECD when it notes that 'due to the host of factors influencing pupils' test scores, some of which cannot be observed within the data, PISA can typically only identify correlations between variables, rather than establishing causation' (Jerrim and Shure 2016: 19). However, the OECD goes on to note that PISA 'can show educators, policy makers and the interested public how education systems are similar and different – and what that means for students', which emphasizes the importance of variables observed in PISA. In the same spirit, the national report for England goes on to suggest that

> One could choose to compare England to other countries where achievement levels have risen or declined substantially over a sustained period of time. This may provide a better way of identifying countries that have initiated change in educational outcomes, and therefore in identifying policies . . .

Crucially, however, it adds that these policies 'could then be tested in England' as 'identifying exactly what has led to change in a country's performance is a notoriously difficult task' (OECD 2016: 20). Thus, if international assessments provide food for thought, the proof of the pudding is – if anywhere – in other methods. The interaction of unobserved and observed variables, including some that are not easily reproduced, means that:

> We cannot wander at pleasure among the educational systems of the world, like a child strolling through a garden, and pick off a flower from one bush and some leaves from another, and then expect that if we stick what we have gathered into the soil at home, we shall have a living plant.
> (Sadler 1900, as quoted in Bereday 1964)

Continued policy borrowing

In recent years, Conservative-led governments have introduced free schools to England, taking inspiration from US charter schools and Swedish free schools, although neither of these countries falls into the high-performing category, and despite evidence that this policy could increase educational inequalities and social segregation (Wiborg 2010). Inspiration has otherwise tended to come from high-performing education systems in the Far East, ranging from 'textbook borrowing' from Singapore to 'teacher borrowing' from China. It is important to note here that the education systems which are the subject of such borrowing are not static. Current performance may therefore come at a price that is no longer tolerated, such as long hours of study outside of school with implications for children's wider development in countries such as Japan and Korea. When the UK government (2015) announced its ambition for England to be the best in Europe for reading by 2020, this perhaps not only reflected a recognition that there is a gulf in PIRLS between Europe and parts of Asia but also a realization that it could undermine children's wider well-being.

A further point to note is that current performance may also reflect the enduring influence of previous policies. In contrast to the focus on the Far East in England, the PISA shock in Germany had triggered a 'mass pilgrimage' of politicians and officials to the 'promised land' of Finland, which was the top-ranked country for reading and the top-ranked country in Europe for mathematics and science in PISA 2000 (Gruber 2006). However, Oates (2015) has argued that PISA has provided snapshots of a successful education system that is now in decline following decentralization. A highly qualified teaching profession with high social status but under more central control than outsiders realized (because it took unexpected forms such as evaluation rather than inspection) has given way to less central control – notably a gradual end to the use of state-approved textbooks. Although Finland remains one of the highest-ranked countries in PISA (despite the increased number of participants), its mean scores in the three subjects are substantially lower now than in the early 2000s. Indeed, with Estonia the highest-ranking European country in the PISA 2015 results focusing on science and published in December 2016, an international conference hosted by Estonia's Ministry of Education and Research (2017) initiated a new wave of education pilgrimages, but to a different shore of the Baltic Sea.

Closing the gap in England

Policy-makers under successive governments in England have referred to the need to 'close the gap'. Rather than the difference between England and high-performing education systems, however, this has referred to the relatively large difference between students in England with the highest and lowest performance in PISA. Furthermore, the PISA 2015 results confirmed the persistence of this gap. The overall picture was that, compared with the average score of students across OECD members, the average score of students in England was higher for science, slightly higher for reading but the same for maths.[9] However, while the difference between the highest- and lowest-performing students was similar to the OECD average difference for reading, it was greater for mathematics and greater still for science.[10] In science this reflected the fact that there were not only very high-performing students but also very low-performing students in England. Across the three subjects, the attainment gap was reported as equivalent to eight or more years of schooling. The question for policy-makers in England will be whether they can learn from somewhere like Canada, which has a high score and a small gap in reading, mathematics and science and is arguably, in cultural terms, a near neighbour. Yet identifying the 'factors' will be as difficult as ever and it will be important to understand the importance of student experiences of practices in England. These would include the 'ability grouping' discussed in Francis *et al.* (2017) and differentiation more generally (see Coffey's Chapter 13 in this volume) in England. However, while the government has acknowledged the link between socio-economic background and educational attainment through remedial policies such as Pupil Premium, the fact remains that the attainment gap in PISA has remained quite stable between cycles, raising the possibility that wider social policy addressing socio-economic inequality itself is crucial.

Concluding thoughts

International assessments are one way of comparing education policies and practices in different countries. The assessments focus on student attainment in reading, mathematics and science at the level of education systems rather than individual schools or students. They were once intermittent and isolated but they are now regular and influential. The publication of PISA, TIMSS and PIRLS results every few years is reported in international media and influences the education policy agenda in and far beyond the UK. The impact on teaching practices therefore tends to be indirect, through education policies. However, an optimist might argue that the teaching profession can influence education policies. Furthermore, teachers themselves exercise some discretion in how policies are implemented. For these reasons, it is important we develop our understandings of the results of the international assessments, differences in their designs, and their limitations, as highlighted in this chapter and summarized as follows.

In England, there is a recent history of the government highlighting analyses of international assessment results that are consistent with its policy agenda, yet omitting those which are not. In particular, analyses suggesting the education system had declined in PISA but improved in TIMSS have proven superficial. As participation in the international assessments at system, school and student level is variable, our use of results needs to go deeper than rankings and even deeper than scores. The degree of change in scores over time and the degree of difference between the scores for education systems is crucial to making sense of international assessments results and using them responsibly.

Although the international assessments share many characteristics, notable differences in their designs impact on their results and their relevance to teachers in secondary schools. While PIRLS has assessed students against a reading curriculum in England at age 10, TIMSS has assessed students in England at age 14 against a mathematics curriculum and a science curriculum. By contrast, PISA assesses students aged 15 on their literacy in English, mathematics and science. PIRLS results will therefore be of more interest to English teachers with reference to students entering secondary education. PISA and TIMSS results will therefore be of more interest to English, mathematics and science teachers with reference to students approaching their GCSEs. Whether mathematics and science teachers give more weighting to curricula in TIMSS or literacies in PISA is a matter of judgement. On the one hand, PISA emphasizes students' preparedness for real-world situations and, on the other, released test items suggest that GCSE is more similar to TIMSS than PISA.

The design limitations of international assessments mean that any attempt at using them to explain student attainment should be tentative and provisional until corroborated with information based on other methods. Indeed, the national report on the PISA 2015 results in England acknowledged that using international assessments to draw conclusions about the impact of changes in education policies and practices is problematic. The limitations are two-fold. First, the international assessments focus on education systems and struggle to account for wider cultural contexts. Second, the international assessments are a snapshot of a cohort's performance rather than a longitudinal or controlled study of students' progress. Any successful attempt at transferring an education policy between education systems therefore presupposes research not only encompassing the wider range of practices which constitute cultural contexts but also the re-formulation and trialling of the policy in the recipient education system.

Finally, this chapter raises three questions for your consideration:

1. Do PISA, TIMSS or PIRLS assess the types of learning outcomes you consider important for your students to develop?
2. If you go beyond the rankings, what perspectives on education in your context do these international assessments give you?
3. If an education reform is proposed on the basis of these international assessments, is that reason enough for changing policy and practice?

Notes

1 This section draws on relevant information available from: www.oecd.org/pisa/, http://timssandpirls.bc.edu/ and https://www.nap.edu/read/9174/chapter/9.
2 Some regions, states and provinces participate in PISA and in the IEA studies in their own right. In PISA, these 'economies' participate without the remainder of the country. In the AEA studies, these are 'benchmarking entities' for the remainder of the participating country (seven in TIMSS 2015 and nine in PIRLS 2016).
3 See the Education Endowment Foundation toolkit on repeating a year: https://educationendowment foundation.org.uk/resources/teaching-learning-toolkit/repeating-a-year/.
4 See the PISA, TIMSS and PIRLS websites to 'take the test'.
5 Karen Skilling and Eva Jablonka explore financial literacy in the school curriculum of selected countries in Chapter 19.
6 Lower secondary school enrolment data collected by the Ministry of Education and Training in Vietnam were published by UNESCO: http://unesdoc.unesco.org/images/0023/002327/232770e.pdf.
7 TIMSS and PIRLS use a 'curriculum questionnaire' to gather background information from the organizations responsible for the surveys in participating countries.
8 See: www.inca.org.uk for details.
9 While the science and reading scores were statistically significantly different, the reading scores were not.
10 This is the difference between the 10th percentile and the 90th percentile of students in England and across OECD members.

References

Alexander, R.J. (2010) 'World class schools' – noble aspiration or globalised hokum? *Compare: A Journal of Comparative and International Education*, 40(6): 801–17.
Askew, M., Hodgen, J., Hossain, S. and Bretscher, N. (2010) *Values and Variables: Mathematics Education High-Performing Countries*. London: King's College London.

Bereday, G.Z.F. (1964) Sir Michael Sadler's 'Study of Foreign Systems of Education', *Comparative Education Review*, 7(3): 307–14.

Brown, M. (1996) FIMS and SIMS: the first two IEA International Mathematics Surveys, *Assessment in Education: Principles, Policy and Practice*, 3(2): 193–212.

DCSF (Department for Children, Schools and Families) (2009) *Your Child, Your Schools, Our Future: Building A 21st Century Schools System*, https://www.gov.uk/government/uploads/system/uploads/attachment_data/file/344452/21st_century_schools.pdf. Accessed 30 January 20.

DfE (Department for Education) (2010) *The Importance of Teaching: The Schools White Paper 2010*, https://www.gov.uk/government/uploads/system/uploads/attachment_data/file/175429/CM-7980.pdf. Accessed 30 January 20.

DfE (Department for Education) (2011) *The Framework for the National Curriculum: A Report by the Expert Panel for the National Curriculum Review*, https://www.gov.uk/government/uploads/system/uploads/attachment_data/file/175439/NCR-Expert_Panel_Report.pdf. Accessed 30 January 20.

DfE (Department for Education) (2016) *Educational Excellence Everywhere*, https://www.gov.uk/government/uploads/system/uploads/attachment_data/file/508447/Educational_Excellence_Everywhere.pdf. Accessed 30 January 20.

Eivers, E. (2010) PISA: Issues in implementation and interpretation, *Irish Journal of Education*, 38: 94–118.

El Masri, Y.H., Baird, J.-A. and Graesser, A. (2016) Language effects in international testing: the case of PISA 2006 science items, *Assessment in Education: Principles, Policy and Practice*, 23(4): 427–55.

Ertl, H. (2006) Educational standards and the changing discourse on education: the reception and consequences of the PISA study in Germany. *Oxford Review of Education*, 32(5): 619–34.

Estonia Ministry of Education and Research (2017) PISA and its meaning for policy and practice around the Baltic Sea, https://www.hm.ee/en/pisaconference, accessed 3 May 2017.

Francis, B., Archer, L., Hodgen, J., Pepper, D., Taylor, B. and Travers, M.-C. (2017) Exploring the relative lack of impact of research on 'ability grouping' in England: a discourse analytic account, *Cambridge Journal of Education*, 47(1): 1–17.

Gruber, K.H. (2006) The German 'PISA-shock': some aspects of the extraordinary impact of the OECD's PISA study on the German education system. In H. Ertl (ed.) *Cross-National Attraction in Education: Accounts from England and Germany*. Didcot: Symposium Books.

IEA (2016) About TIMSS and PIRLS International Study Center, https://timssandpirls.bc.edu/about.html, accessed 3 May 2017.

Jerrim, J. (2013) The reliability of trends over time in international education test scores: is the performance of England's secondary school pupils really in relative decline? *Journal of Social Policy*, 42(2): 259–79.

Jerrim, J. and Shure, N. (2016) *Achievement of 15-Year-Olds in England: PISA 2015 National Report*. Paris: OECD.

Le Metais, J. (1997) *Values and Aims in Curriculum and Assessment Frameworks*. London: SCAA.

Noah, H.J. and Eckstein, M.A. (1969) *Towards a Science of Comparative Education*. London: Macmillan.

Oates, T. (2015) *Finnish Fairy Stories*. Cambridge: Cambridge Assessment.

OECD (2004) *Learning for Tomorrow's World: First Results from PISA 2003*. Paris: OECD.

OECD (2010) *Strong Performers and Successful Reformers in Education: Lessons from PISA for the United States*. Paris: OECD.

OECD (2016) *PISA 2015: PISA Results in Focus*. Paris: OECD.

Pepper, D., Hodgen, J., Lamesoo, K., Kõiv, P. and Tolboom, J. (2016) Think aloud: using cognitive interviewing to validate the PISA assessment of student self-efficacy in mathematics, *International Journal of Research and Method in Education*, 1–14.

Pereyra, M.A., Kotthoff, H.G. and Cowen, R. (2011) *PISA Under Examination: Changing Knowledge, Changing Tests, and Changing Schools*. Rotterdam: Sense Publishers.

Pons, X. (2017) Fifteen years of research on PISA effects on education governance: a critical review, *European Journal of Education*, 52(2): 131–44.

Wiborg, S. (2010) Learning lessons from the Swedish model, *Forum*, 52(3): 279–84.

Wu, M. (2009) A comparison of PISA and TIMSS 2003 achievement results in mathematics, *Prospects*, 39(1): 33–46.

6

Ideology, evidence and the raising of standards
PAUL BLACK

Introduction

A teacher's classroom work is constrained by a framework of rules and beliefs about curriculum and assessment. In England and Wales that framework underwent a revolution when the National Curriculum and assessment system was put in place, for the first time, by the Education Reform Act of 1988. This chapter is about that revolution, about its consequences, and about the broader lessons that can be learnt from it. Its account is set out in four main sections as follows.

The first section discusses the background – the ideas and beliefs that helped drive the development of the new policies. The second gives a brief description of the development of our first National Curriculum while the third section describes the related developments of the national system of assessment (Chapter 14 deals with the principles and methods of assessment that are directly relevant to classroom work and technical aspects of assessment). Finally, the fourth section addresses fundamental purposes by returning to the themes of the first section, looking at beliefs and assumptions that stand in the way of a more coherent and effective approach to education policy.

While some of what is described is now history, this is offered both to inform understanding of present systems in the light of their origins, and to aid reflection both on the ways in which they provide support for principles of teaching and learning, and on the ways in which they present obstacles to the best classroom practices. Many of the obstacles have arisen from the myriad pressures that bear on policy-makers – pressures which will not go away, so it is important to understand these, but also to look beyond them. Overall, therefore, the first three sections of this chapter use a historical lens to show how politicians have been unable to frame policies which match the aims and achievements of education with the needs of a rapidly changing society because of:

- Their narrow beliefs about the aims of education
- Their mistrust of researchers and of their findings
- Their simplistic view of the effects of assessment on the learning of pupils
- Their lack of respect for the professional expertise of teachers.

They, therefore, have been unable to frame policies which match the aims and achievements of education with the needs of a rapidly changing society.

Then the fourth section outlines ways in which a coherent policy for the improvement of education might help to redeem the situation which we now inherit.

Nostalgia, fear and myth

The world of politics is driven by a mixture of rationality, myth and expediency. In education, three powerful myths have driven political thinking and public opinion. This section examines those myths in turn.

The first myth is that standards have fallen. This myth, which has been a feature of public debate in England for well over a century, is not confirmed by any thorough review of evidence: policy is often driven by selective evidence and hearsay.

Between 1970 and 1971 and 1991 and 1992, the percentage of pupils obtaining no graded examination results as school leavers fell from 44 per cent to 6.2 per cent (due in part to the raising of the school leaving age from 15 to 16 so that all pupils were in school to take the age 16 examinations). The percentage of those leaving school before the age of 17 who gained five or more higher grades at GCSE (or the earlier equivalents) was about 7 per cent (DfE 1994) in 1970, whereas in the last few years it had risen to 59 per cent in 2013, but then fell to 53 per cent as schools began entering some pupils one school year earlier (DfE 2016). Despite year on year fluctuations, the trend for over 30 years has been of steady increase, which points to the enormous success of teachers in our comprehensive schools.

A second myth is that this 'fall in standards' has been due to the adoption of 'progressive' methods of teaching. This flies in the face of the evidence of Eric Bolton, former head of the national inspectorate, based on his experience of thousands of hours of observation by his staff:

> The evidence of inspection is that poor standards of learning are more commonly associated with over-direction by teachers, rather than with teachers opting out and allowing pupils to set the pace and style of learning.

> Far from having an education service full of trendy teachers led, willy-nilly, this way and that by experts and gurus (the 'Educational Mafia'), we have a teaching profession that is essentially cautious and conservative: a profession that is highly suspicious of claims from within or without its ranks that there is a particularly fool-proof way of doing things. Teachers are too close to the actual, day-to-day complexity of classrooms, and to the variability of people and pupils, to be anything else but pragmatic and commonsensical in their thinking and actions.

> (Bolton 1992: 16–19)

The third myth is that learning would be improved by a return to traditional methods. Here again, the evidence contradicts the myth. Numerous research studies have shown the debilitating consequences of rule-bound traditional learning. The study by Nuthall and Alton-Lee (1995) of the methods pupils use to answer tests showed that long-term retention depends on the capacity to understand and so reconstruct procedures, and the work of Boaler (1997) showed that more open methods produce better attitudes and performance in mathematics than traditional methods (see also Chapter 19 in this volume). There is also evidence which suggests that children learn more effectively if they are listened to and helped to understand by themselves (Weare 2005). An extensive survey of teaching methods in Chicago public schools showed that teachers who teach for understanding achieved higher results on the state's standardized tests than those who just 'teach to the tests' (Newmann *et al.* 2001). The results of such studies are entirely consistent with contemporary research on the ways that children learn (Pellegrino *et al.* 1999). Consider the following from a review of such work:

> Even comprehension of simple texts requires a process of inferring and thinking about what the text means. Children who are drilled in number facts, algorithms, decoding skills or vocabulary lists without developing a basic conceptual model or seeing the meaning of what they are doing have a very difficult time retaining information (because all the bits are disconnected) and are unable to apply what they have memorized (because it makes no sense).
>
> (Shepard 1992: 303)

This dominance of mythology is linked to neglect of research, or to selective use of research results, and a distrust of change. The following quotations help to explain this neglect (the first is about a former Conservative Minister – Sir Keith Joseph):

> Here Joseph shared a view common to all Conservative educationists: that education had seen an unholy alliance of socialists, bureaucrats, planners and Directors of Education acting against the true interests and wishes of the nation's children and parents by their imposition on the schools of an ideology (equality of condition) based on utopian dreams of universal co-operation and brotherhood.
>
> (Knight 1990: 155)

> Tories really did seem to believe in the existence of left-wing, 'education establishment' conspiracies.
>
> (Lawton 1994: 145)

Such suspicion is shared by many in the other parties. Thus one can understand why research evidence is untrustworthy – those responsible for this evidence are part of the conspiracy.

However, any plea that policy should pay more attention to research findings should imply an assumption that research has established all that needs to be known about ways to enhance learning. An authoritative review by the US National Research Council (NRC) recommended that: 'Accumulated knowledge and ongoing advances of the cognitive and measurement sciences should be synthesized and made available in usable form to multiple educational constituencies. These constituencies include educational researchers, test developers, curriculum specialists, teachers and policy-makers' (2001: 299). The clear implication is that there ought to be a national body charged to formulate such synthesis in 'usable form'. Many organizations have attempted fragments of this task, but there is little evidence of any national groups being willing to take on this task and being supported for doing so.

After 1997, the Labour government was only a little less suspicious of educational research, and its record of taking research findings seriously is a very uneven one. Indeed, there has hardly been any change since 1997 in another relevant policy, namely the application of the ideology of the marketplace to education. The application of a market model to education has been criticized by many, notably in the reports of the NCE (1995), in the analysis offered by Stephen Ball (Ball 1994: Chapter 7), and in a review of the effect of over a decade of parental choice of schools in Scotland: 'Parental choice has led to an inefficient use of resources, widening disparities between schools, increased social segregation and threats to equality of educational opportunity' (Adler 1993: 183).

A market implies consumer choice between expensive products of high quality and cheaper products of poorer quality, while demand is linked to willingness and ability to pay, not to need. The right-wing Hillgate Group has commented that 'Consumer sovereignty does not necessarily guarantee that values will be preserved' (McKenzie 1993). Keith Joseph believed in the 'blind, unplanned, uncoordinated wisdom of the market' (1976: 57), but it is clear that markets favour those who have the knowledge and the power to choose effectively – the children of the less well informed will suffer (Ball 2003).

A notable extension of the market model has been implemented in England by the government support for schools, both academies and free schools, which can be set up without regard for the need for extra school places in their district. One consequence of this policy is that the majority of state-funded schools in England are now under the direct control of the Department for Education. Another is that the regional co-ordination work of the local education authorities has been undermined, thus reducing their effective in-service programmes for teachers and their capacity to offset the effects of social inequalities on the children of disadvantaged parents.

There are other myths which are prevalent among politicians, some teachers and many of the general public. One is that selective education systems produce better pupil learning overall than comprehensive systems. The House of Commons Select Committee on Education and Skills conducted an investigation into this issue in 2003–2004. Their conclusion was: 'We have found no evidence that selection by ability or aptitude contributes to the overall improvement of educational standards' (Select Committee 2004: report (8), para. 258). Nevertheless, in 2016, the UK Prime Minister set out a policy to extend selective secondary education, although in this case the research evidence that this policy will not achieve its declared aim of helping the disadvantaged, is now so well known that it is doubtful whether it can command parliamentary support.

Another myth is that it is better, notably in mathematics, to use setting or streaming of classes rather than mixed ability classes. Reviews of research investigations in which the results of the two approaches are compared do not support this belief (Harlen and Malcolm 1999; Francis *et al.* 2016; and, for mathematics, Burris *et al.* 2006).

Thus, it seems that many changes, or refusals to change, in our education policy have been and still are based on a combination of nostalgia, folk wisdom, and fear of change, driven in some areas by an inappropriate market model for education. Such views are protected by a neglect of evidence, so that we do not learn from experience (Whitty 2002). Taken together, they constitute an eclectic ideology, one which seems to have remained powerful despite changes in the ruling party.

The curriculum: pragmatic, traditional, unprincipled

The Education Reform Act 1988 devoted about three lines to the principles on which the curriculum should be based – it was to promote the spiritual, moral, cultural, mental and physical development of pupils. It then moved to list the 10 subjects, which were thereby established as if they were self-evident 'goods'. Then, as the separate formulations for these subjects were developed, and have since been revised, there have been few attempts to check that they serve these principles either separately or in a mutually coherent way. Furthermore, these subjects, with the notable exception of design and technology, were the subjects which constituted my own grammar school education in the 1940s and 1950s. It is easy to expose the intellectual poverty of this way of specifying a national curriculum and its consequences (White 1990), but the specification survived the 1997 change in government and is enshrined without debate, as did much of the rest of the Conservative policy (see Whitty 2002: Chapter 8; Tomlinson 2005: Chapter 5).

Some other countries have policies in education that contrast sharply with England's (Scotland has always been different, and Wales and Northern Ireland have changed significantly since devolution gave them control over education) and do not share these weaknesses. The policy in Scotland has been (until recently) to develop and trust teachers' own assessments, aligning these with the overall curriculum development, and to avoid the use of national testing (Hayward *et al.* 2008), while similar changes were developed in Wales (Daugherty 2009). In Finland, a policy document on the framework for the curriculum (National Board of Education 1994) discussed changes in social needs and values, and went on to emphasize that our new understanding of learning showed the need to emphasize 'the active role of the student as the organiser of his [*sic*] own structure of knowledge' and the need for 'organizing teaching into inter-curricular issues and subjects'.

The Norwegian Ministry document on the Core Curriculum (Royal Ministry of Church, Education and Research 1994) was in chapters with titles as follows:

- The spiritual human being
- The creative human being
- The working human being
- The liberally educated human being

- The social human being
- The environmentally aware human being
- The integrated human being.

Here we have governments who, in sharp contrast to our own approach since 1988, present to their country a deeply argued rationale for the aims of their curriculum.

Education policy has to confront concerns about the changing world of the child and the adolescent. Changes in family stability and in the stability of employment, and the increasing power of the media, have meant that young people face an environment that is rich in information and vicarious experience, poor in first-hand experience, weaker than it ever was in emotional security and support, and overshadowed by the threat of unemployment (Beck 1992). Where the world of the child has been impoverished, the task of the school is both more complex and more vital. Yet it has to be carried out in a society where the authority of teachers, as with other professionals, is not taken for granted.

A nostalgia-driven return to traditional policies ignores such problems, and cannot provide for the contemporary needs of young people and of society. In 1995, a group of European industrialists stressed the importance of literacy, numeracy and of science and technology, but added to these critical thinking, decision-making, the need to be able to learn new skills, the ability to work in groups, a willingness to take risks and exercise initiative, curiosity, and a sense of service to the community (ERT 1995). British employers see the same needs (Ball 1990: 103).

A similar argument has been expressed in working papers of the inter-country meetings of the European Commission (2010). More recent debates in the UK that have expressed similar concerns, some to do with basic literacy and numeracy skills, some with broader issues such as citizenship, and spiritual and moral education, are all evidence of the inadequacy of the 1988 formulations, which subsequent revisions have failed to redress. Moreover, a curriculum which has a focus on basic skills as separate targets ignores the fact that problems in the real world require interactions and choices between them, and insofar as this limitation is ignored in the related assessments, these are bound to be of limited validity. This point, and its implications for the role of teachers, was emphasized by Stanley *et al.* as follows:

> . . . the teacher is increasingly being seen as the primary assessor in the most important aspects of assessment. The broadening of assessment is based on a view that there are aspects of learning that are important but cannot be adequately assessed by formal external tests. These aspects require human judgement to integrate the many elements of performance behaviours that are required in dealing with authentic assessment tasks.
>
> (2009: 31)

The need for changes in the role of teachers in assessment policies will be discussed below.

National assessment: the rise and fall of the TGAT

In 1987, the Cabinet Minister then responsible for education, Kenneth Baker, invited me to chair the Task Group on Assessment and Testing (TGAT) to advise on assessment policy for the new National Curriculum. I accepted because my experience made me optimistic that valid, and therefore helpful, external national tests could be set up. I was also optimistic because government statements seemed to recognize the importance of teachers' own assessments in any national scheme (DES 1987: para. 29; 1988a: Appendix B). The task group members represented a wide range of interests and relevant experience. Five had been members of public examination boards – one as chairman, two had directed different subject areas of the government's Assessment of Performance Unit, one was director of the National Foundation for Educational Research, another the director of one of the leading agencies for post-16 vocational examinations, while two others were distinguished researchers in examining. The group also included the Chief Education Officer of one of the largest local authorities, a senior Her Majesty's Inspector (HMI) from Ofsted (the national inspectorate) and two headteachers, one secondary, one primary.

The TGAT proposals (DES 1988a; 1988b) emphasized the centrality of teachers' own assessments in promoting the day-to-day learning of pupils. They went on to recommend that national assessments should be based upon a combination of teachers' own assessments and the results of external tests, on the grounds that external tests helped establish common standards and criteria, but were of limited reliability and limited in the range of learning aims that they could validly test.

These proposals were at first accepted as government policy, and then abandoned one by one in the next few years (Black 1993; 1997). It was clear at an early stage that Baker's acceptance of the TGAT report might not have wholehearted support from his Prime Minister:

> The fact that it was then welcomed by the Labour Party, the National Union of Teachers and the *Times Educational Supplement* was enough to confirm for me that its approach was suspect. It proposed an elaborate and complex system of assessment – teacher dominated and uncosted. It adopted the 'diagnostic' view of tests, placed the emphasis on teachers doing their own assessment and was written in an impenetrable educationalist jargon.
>
> (Thatcher 1993: 594–5)

A more explicit rejection was delivered later by Thatcher's new Education Minister, Kenneth Clarke:

> The British pedagogue's hostility to written examinations of any kind can be taken to ludicrous extremes . . . This remarkable national obsession lies behind the more vehement opposition to the recent introduction of 7-year-old testing. They were made a little too complicated and we have said we will simplify them . . . The complications themselves were largely designed in the first place in an attempt to pacify opponents who feared above all else 'paper and pencil' tests.
>
> (Clarke 1991)

The TGAT argument, that priority should be given to supporting assessment by teachers, was accepted by Baker. However, the agencies responsible for developing the national assessment policy devoted hardly any of their time or resources to teachers' assessments – they concentrated on external testing (Daugherty 1995; Black 1997). This should not have been a surprise in view of earlier reversals. Consider, for example, Baker's statement in 1989: 'The balance – characteristic of most GCSE courses – between coursework and an externally set and marked terminal examination has worked well. I accept the Council's judgement that assessment by means of coursework is one of the examination's strengths' (quoted in Daugherty 1995: 131).

In 1991, the Prime Minister, John Major, reversed this conclusion: 'It is clear that there is now far too much coursework, project work and teacher assessment in GCSE. The remedy surely lies in getting GCSE back to being an externally assessed exam which is predominantly written' (quoted in Daugherty 1995: 137). Government directives then, without either consultation or consideration of evidence, reduced the coursework component of GCSE.

In 2013, the government initiated a new programme for revision of the school curriculum and of the assessment system. In the development of this work, the role of coursework assessment was further considered. The outcome was that it was further reduced, so that it was only specified for such 'performance' subjects as art and music. For example, in science, the use of 'controlled assessment' as a restricted form of school-based assessment was abandoned. One consequence was evident discord between the specified aims of the new curricula and the pressures of assessments. For example, the DfE's GCSE subject content for Combined Science said that the GCSE's specifications should enable students '[to] . . . develop and learn to apply observational, practical, modelling, enquiry and problem-solving skills, both in the laboratory, in the field and in other learning environments'. However, this aim is only to be assessed indirectly through test items in the written papers. In addition, schools now have to attest that the students they entered had carried out a set of routine laboratory exercises – a condition of entry that will have no effect on the GCSE marks.

Underlying this flux of debate is a basic question – how can policy and practice in testing and assessment raise the standards of pupil work in schools? Many politicians have a simple answer to this question – set tests and make schools accountable for them and improvements will follow automatically. There is hardly any evidence to support this belief. Indeed, such policies lead to a system where short, written, external tests dominate the curriculum, tests which cannot reflect some of the important aims of education.

One outstanding example of such weakness was exposed by a study of the national Key Stage 3 science tests set in the four successive years 2003–2006 (Fairbrother 2008). At that time, these were used to judge the work of secondary school teachers. Analyses of the questions and of the marking schemes showed that these called mainly for knowledge recall and simple comprehension with almost no attention to skills of analysis, synthesis and evaluation. Moreover, the question demands were broken up into small steps, and for over 90 per cent of the marks the mainly atomized mark scheme allocated 1 or 0 for each of these steps. Similar findings were reported in Black *et al.* (2004).

Yet the pressure on schools to do well in such tests means that they distort and damage learning (Fairbrother *et al*. 1995; Gipps *et al*. 1995); there is also evidence that while above-average pupils have improved on tests, the absolute standards of those well below the average have fallen (Bell 1995), and that testing pressures have adverse effects on the anxiety and motivation of many pupils (ARG 2002). Furthermore, as schools concentrate on drilling pupils to do well in sets of short test items, they can improve their scores on these particular tests, but do so by giving less attention to developing in pupils the skills needed to apply their learning to complex and realistic tasks. Further distortion arises in two ways. One is that some schools bend admission, or exclusion, practices to 'cherry-pick' pupils whose results may do them credit in the future (Gillborn and Youdell 2000). The other is that some schools were tempted to 'play the system' by focusing attention on pupils close to the critical C/D borderline, to enhance the – reported – number who have attained above this, to the neglect of any who are well below it. It is hard to predict how the recent change, from the A, B, C, D, E scale to the finer-grained 9-point scale, will affect this situation and how this change might interact with the new Progress 8 performance measure.

To make matters worse, it is also clear that the results of short external tests are bound to be of limited reliability. The evidence available (Gardner and Cowan 2005; Black and Wiliam 2006, and more recent reports by Ofqual) indicates that GCSE, or A levels, involve rather large margins of error, notably for students whose marks are close to grade boundaries. Other countries have accepted the limitations of external testing. In Sweden, national tests serve as a benchmark to calibrate schools but the results for individual pupils are left to teachers to determine (Eckstein and Noah 1993). In the Australian state of Queensland, while all are now required by the National Government to take tests in basic literacy and numeracy, external testing for pupils' certification was abandoned in 1982 and to date there is no sign that they will ever be reintroduced (Cumming and Maxwell 2004), and a carefully developed set of procedures and criteria to ensure the quality of teachers' own assessments, involving inter-school moderation procedures, underpins the judgements of teachers and their schools (QCAA 2016).

Research evidence clearly indicates a quite different answer to the basic question. Dramatic improvement in pupils' achievement can be made by changes in the way that teachers use assessment to give feedback to guide pupils' learning. The key to raising standards lies in supporting the work of teachers in the classroom, not in attempting to control and harass them from the outside (Black and Wiliam 1998a; 1998b; Black *et al*. 2002; 2003).

Other countries have realized this. In France, national testing has been deployed, not to blame teachers at the end of a teaching year, but to help them by providing diagnostic information about their new classes of pupils at the start of a school year (Black and Atkin 1996: 101–11). The National Board of Education in Finland has written (1994: 29) that:

The task of evaluation is to encourage all students – in a positive way – to set their own aims, to plan their work and to make independent choices.

For this to take place, all students gradually need to learn to analyse their own studies and those of others through the use of self-evaluation and group evaluation. The ability to do that in the future means the ability to survive in a situation where there is more and more uncertainty and where the individual is subjected to all kinds of choices and sudden changes. Practical ideas about how to achieve such reform have been developed with teachers.

Can we find new directions?

My aim here is to discuss six issues that need to be confronted in any attempt to formulate a coherent policy for the improvement of education. The *first issue* is concerned with the process of change. An OECD review of 23 case studies, spread over 13 countries, which examined the progress of different educational innovations, revealed striking differences between the models of change that were adopted (Black and Atkin 1996: 1–11). At one extreme, there were top-down models in which central authority tells everyone what to do. Where this was done, either very little happened at classroom level, or teachers, being disoriented, delivered an impoverished interpretation of the intentions.

The opposite approach, which was to leave as much as possible in the hands of schools and of teachers, also had difficulties, for the process was slow and such delegation implied that only a very general framework could be prescribed. However, there are powerful arguments, of principle and from empirical evidence, that this is the most effective and acceptable strategy (Posch 1994; Fullan 2015). Where matters are interlinked in complex ways and where one has to be sensitive to the local context in which this complexity is situated, then only those who have freedom of manoeuvre can turn a good idea into a really effective innovation. This approach has been adopted in business and industry (Peters and Waterman 1982), where the response has been to move from long hierarchical chains to so-called 'flat' management structures. If new aims for education are to be achieved, we have to give teachers freedom to work out the best ways for their school:

> While the existence of central national and regional (local government) institutions is necessary to guarantee social equity in education and to supply guidelines and expertise, it is essential that educational institutions at every level should have autonomy to implement the changes they see as necessary.
>
> (ERT 1995: 18)

The OECD study also concluded that worthwhile educational reform cannot happen quickly – it takes several years for the majority of teachers to turn innovation plans into practice through changes in their classroom work. This timescale is long compared with the interval between elections. More alarmingly, it may be too long in relation to the pace at which our society, and – therefore – at which its demands on education, are changing.

This issue was further explored in a collection of brief articles by members of the US National Academy of Education (2015). In one of these, Jennings emphasizes:

> ... more must be done to connect what is learned through education research to the policy-making process. To state it differently, the politicians should use what is learned through education research to enact sound legislation and to make other policies that affect the schools. A related necessity is that those who hold public office should use this information correctly; they should understand it well enough not to misuse its findings.
>
> (2015: 313)

This author goes on to describe several cases where even well-intentioned reforms have produced undesirable effects because unforeseen and secondary conse-quences have led to effects opposite to those intended.

Teachers are the focus of my *second issue*. Where teachers have low status, they become targets for blame, and are treated with remarkable insensitivity in England:

> We are struck by the extent to which German and French education systems place responsibility on the shoulders of professional teachers. It contrasts sharply with the mood of distrust of professionals which has grown in this country [England] in recent years, not without government encouragement. This mood has been carried too far and must be reversed.
>
> (NCE 1993: 340)

Such treatment is not only unjust, it is also counter-productive, for in any but the most narrow mechanical view of teaching, it must be recognized that teachers are the sole and essential means to educational improvement. If they do not share the aims of an innovation, it cannot happen effectively.

Furthermore, to define teachers as mere providers of the market goods that the parent customers require is to misconstrue their fundamental role. A former Chair of the Headmasters' Conference, Father Dominic Milroy, wrote:

> They [parents] know that, for the child, the encounter with the teacher is the first major step into outside society, the beginning of a long journey towards adulthood, in which the role of the teacher is going to be decisive ... all edu-cation is an exercise in collaborative parenting, in which the profession of teaching is seen as a complement to the vocation of parenthood ... Teachers are, therefore, not in the first instance agents either of the National Curricu-lum Council (or whatever follows it) or of the state. They are bridges between individual children and the culture to which they belong ... This culture consists partly of a heritage, which links them to the past, and partly of a range of skills and opportunities, which links them to the future. The role of the teachers is, in this respect, irreplaceable.
>
> (Milroy 1992: 57–9)

This perspective replaces the notion of teachers as paid agents with a concept of partnership in which the role of teachers is to take authority for developing young adults. Indeed, parents give this authority to the school and the teachers because they want their children to learn the many ideas and skills that they cannot themselves give them, and society reinforces this when it sets up a curriculum within which parents are not free to pick and choose if their children go to schools funded by their taxes. The teacher is a pivotal agent of change, sharing authority with parents for the development of children, and representing society as the agent to achieve nationally agreed aims for education.

This issue was raised above in the quotation from the 2009 article by Stanley *et al.* However, the argument there was that broader aims of education cannot be assessed by external agencies. The same article goes on to make a further point, as follows:

> Evidence from education systems, where teacher assessment has been implemented with major professional support, is that everyone benefits. Teachers become more confident, students obtain more focused and immediate feedback, and learning gains can be measured. An important aspect of teacher assessment is that it allows for the better integration of professional judgement into the design of more authentic and substantial learning contexts.
>
> (2009: 82)

The Queensland QCAA is one such system. A limited development project in England to explore and improve teachers' own summative assessment work (Black *et al.* 2011) has shown both that such work, and particularly the component of inter-school moderation, can be professionally rewarding, but that it requires long-term investment to develop the teacher skills and procedures that are needed. In the present system in England, in which three different awarding organizations compete for schools as customers, it is difficult for any one of them to invest in such long-term development

A *third issue* is the need to clarify what society wants teachers to achieve, which is to say that we need a fresh consensus about the educational aims that society wants schools to pursue. This is lacking because of rapid social change, because our society is divided about its fundamental beliefs and values and because society has weakened in many ways the support given to the developing child outside school.

A national curriculum that stresses details of subjects, flimsily related to a few very broad aims, leaves schools in a very difficult position. It might make sense to give schools no direction at all. It might be better to set out for them the broad framework of aims that society wants them to achieve and leave them to find the detailed ways to achieve such aims. It surely makes no sense at all to specify the detailed ways but to leave them to decide the overall aims.

My *fourth issue* has already been discussed above. We need a new policy for assessment, one which will support the assessment aspect of teachers' work, which will have helpful rather than damaging effects on good teaching by assessing those aspects of learning that young people need to be effective in a changing society, and which will give information, to individuals and to the public, that is both relevant and trustworthy. This issue was explored in a thorough review by the Assessment Reform Group (ARG 2006).

The *fifth issue* is that we need to have a proper respect for evidence, which means that we have to be willing to review existing evidence, to monitor the progress of our educational changes and to research in depth some of the most important problems that this raises. This implies that the level of investment in research in education should be very sharply increased.

If we are to be able to work effectively at these five issues, I believe we shall need to take up a *sixth*, which is that we need to build up a much better public understanding of the complexities of teaching and learning. The public ought to be far better informed about educational issues than they are at present. Myths about our schools are too powerful and policy thinking about our education is too weak. There ought to be a sustained effort to help the public, and especially politicians and their policy advisers, to achieve a more realistic, and therefore more complex, understanding of the realities of schools, of classrooms, of testing and of educational change.

However, the above list of six issues does not do justice to the complexity of the relationship between educational policy and effective change. It is easy to point out the mistakes and errors of others, more difficult to focus on the ways to work for a better future. Such problems as striking the right balance between over-prescription and policy stagnation, and the need to achieve sustainable changes that are relevant to the inevitable, increasingly rapid pace of social change, all call for more subtle and comprehensive analyses, such as that attempted by Fullan (2003). We all need to formulate and work for networks of optimum relationships between the different responsible agents, i.e. between governments, parents, teacher and employers, relationships based on mutual respect and agreed general principles.

Concluding thoughts

- Is it fair to expect teachers to take partial, or even sole, responsibility for the high-stakes summative assessment of their pupils?
- How can teachers reassure parents that their summative assessments of their children are comparable in quality and in standards of judgement with those of other teachers and from other schools?
- Should teachers be expected to invest the extra time that will be needed for them to develop and implement new methods to ensure that their assessment practices help their pupils to become more confident and effective learners?

References

Adler, M. (1993) An alternative approach to parental choice, in *National Commission on Education, Briefings*. London: Heinemann.

ARG (Assessment Reform Group) (2002) *Testing, Motivation and Learning: A Report from the Assessment Reform Group*. Cambridge: University Faculty of Education.

ARG (Assessment Reform Group) (2006) *The Role of Teachers in the Assessment of Learning: A Report from the Assessment Reform Group*. London: Institute of Education.

Ball, S.J. (1990) *Politics and Policy Making in Education*. London: Routledge.

Ball, S.J. (1994) *Education Reform: A Critical and Post-structural Approach*. Buckingham: Open University Press.

Ball, S.J. (2003) *Class Strategies and the Education Market: The Middle Classes and Social Advantage*. London: Routledge.

Beck, U. (1992) *Risk Society: Towards a New Modernity*. Newbury Park, CA: Sage.

Bell, C. (1995) In a different league? *British Journal of Curriculum and Assessment*, 5(3): 32–3.

Black, P. (1993) The shifting scenery of the National Curriculum, in P. O'Hear and J. White (eds) *Assessing the National Curriculum*. London: Paul Chapman.

Black, P. (1997) Whatever happened to TGAT?, in C. Cullingford (ed.) *Assessment vs. Evaluation*. London: Cassell.

Black, P. and Atkin, J.M. (eds) (1996) *Changing the Subject*. London: Routledge.

Black, P. and Wiliam, D. (1998a) Assessment and classroom learning, *Assessment in Education*, 5(1): 7–71.

Black, P. and Wiliam, D. (1998b) *Inside the Black Box: Raising Standards Through Classroom Assessment*. London: NFER Nelson.

Black, P. and Wiliam, D. (2006) The reliability of assessments, in J. Gardner (ed.) *Assessment and Learning*. London: Sage, pp. 214–39.

Black, P., Harrison, C., Hodgen, J., Marshall, M. and Serret, N. (2011) Can teachers' summative assessments produce dependable results and also enhance classroom learning? *Assessment in Education*, 18(4): 451–69.

Black, P., Harrison, C., Lee, C., Marshall, B. and Wiliam, D. (2002) *Working Inside the Black Box: Assessment for Learning in the Classroom*. London: NFER Nelson.

Black, P., Harrison, C., Lee, C., Marshall, B. and Wiliam, D. (2003) *Assessment for Learning: Putting it into Practice*. Buckingham: Open University Press.

Black, P., Harrison, C., Osborne, J. and Duschl, R. (2004) *Assessment of Science Learning 14–19*. London: Royal Society, https://royalsociety.org/~/media/Royal_Society_Content/policy/publications/2004/4294969761.pdf. Accessed 30 January 2017.

Boaler, J. (1997) *Experiencing School Mathematics: Teaching Styles, Sex and Setting*. Buckingham: Open University Press.

Bolton, E. (1992) The quality of teaching, in *Education – Putting the Record Straight*. Stafford: Network Press, pp. 13–19.

Burris, C.C., Heubert, J.P. and Levin, H.M. (2006) Accelerating mathematics achievement using heterogeneous grouping, *American Educational Research Journal*, 43(1): 105–36.

Clarke, K. (1991) Education in a classless society, 'The Westminster Lecture', given to the Tory Reform Group, June.

Cumming, J.J. and Maxwell, G.S. (2004) Assessment in Australian schools: current practice and trends, *Assessment in Education*, 11(1): 94–108.

Daugherty, R. (1995) *National Curriculum Assessment. A Review of Policy 1987–1994*. London: Falmer.

Daugherty, R. (2009) Trusting the judgment of teachers: changing assessment policies in Wales. *Education Review* 22(1): 61–8.

DES (Department of Education and Science) (1987) *The National Curriculum 5–16: A Consultation Document*. London: Department of Education and Science and the Welsh Office.

DES (Department of Education and Science) (1988a) *Task Group on Assessment and Testing. A Report*. London: Department of Education and Science and the Welsh Office.

DES (Department of Education and Science) (1988b) *Task Group on Assessment and Testing: Three Supplementary Reports.* London: Department of Education and Science and the Welsh Office.

DfE (Department for Education) (1994) *Educational Statistics for the United Kingdom,* Statistical Bulletin 1/94. London: DfE, https://www.education.gov.uk/researchandstatistics/statistics/allstatistics/a00193166/1994-secondary-school-performance-tables. Accessed 30 January 2017.

DfE (Department for Education) (2016) *Revised GCSE and Equivalent Results in England 2014 to 2015,* https://www.gov.uk/government/uploads/system/uploads/attachment_data. Accessed 30 January 2017.

Eckstein, M.A. and Noah, H.J. (1993) *Secondary School Examinations: International Perspectives on Policy and Practice.* New Haven, CT: Yale University Press.

ERT (European Round Table of Industrialists) (1995) *Education for Europeans: Towards the Learning Society.* Brussels: ERT.

European Commission (2010) *Assessment of Key Competences: Draft Background Paper for the Belgian Presidency Meeting for Directors-General for School Education.* Brussels: European Council of Ministers.

Fairbrother, R. (2008) The validity of the Key Stage 3 science tests, *School Science Review,* 89(329): 107–13.

Fairbrother, R.W., Dillon, J. and Gill, P. (1995) Assessment at Key Stage 3: teachers' attitudes and practices, *British Journal of Curriculum and Assessment,* 5(3): 25–31, 46.

Francis, B., Archer, L., Hodgen, J., Pepper, D., Taylor, B. and Travers, M.-C. (2016) Exploring the relative lack of impact of research on 'ability grouping' in England: a discourse analytic account, *Cambridge Journal of Education* pp 1–17. Published online: 4 January 2016.

Fullan, M. (2003) *Change Forces with a Vengeance.* London: RoutledgeFalmer.

Fullan, M. (2015) *The New Meaning of Educational Change* (5th edn). London: Cassell.

Gardner, J. and Cowan, P. (2005) The fallibility of high stakes '11-plus' testing in Northern Ireland, *Assessment in Education,* 12(2): 145–65.

Gillborn, D. and Youdell, D. (2000) *Rationing Education.* London: Routledge.

Gipps, C., Brown, M., McCallum, B. and McAlister, S. (1995) *Intuition or Evidence? Teachers and National Assessment of 7-Year-Olds.* Buckingham: Open University Press.

Harlen, W. and Malcolm, H. (1999) *Setting and Streaming: A Research Review. SCRE Research Series No. 18.* Edinburgh: Scottish Council for Research in Education, http://www.scre.ac.uk/pdf/setting.pdf. Accessed 30 January 2017.

Hayward, L., Dow, W. and Boyd, B. (2008) *Assessment is for Learning: Report to the Scottish Government.* Glasgow: Universities of Strathclyde and Glasgow HEI Research and Development Sub-group.

Jennings, J. (2015) Research and policy: the need to tie the knot, in M.J. Feuer, A.I. Berman and R.C. Atkinson (eds) *Past as Prologue: The National Academy of Education at 50 – Members Reflect.* Washington, DC: National Academy of Education, pp. 313–15.

Joseph, K. (1976) *Stranded in the Middle Ground.* London: Centre for Policy Studies.

Knight, C. (1990) *The Making of Tory Education Policy in Post-War Britain 1950–1986.* London: Falmer.

Lawton, D. (1994) *The Tory Mind on Education 1979–94.* London: Falmer.

McKenzie, J. (1993) *Education as a Political Issue.* Aldershot: Avebury.

Milroy, D. (1992) Teaching and learning: what a child expects from a good teacher, in various authors, *Education – Putting the Record Straight.* Stafford: Network Press.

National Board of Education (1994) *Framework for the Comprehensive School 1994.* Helsinki: Painatuskeskus (in English).

National Research Council (2001) *Knowing what Students Know: The Science and Design of Educational Assessment. Report of the Board on Testing and Assessment.* Washington, DC: National Academy Press.

NCE (National Commission on Education) (1993) *Learning to Succeed: Report of the National Commission on Education.* London: Heinemann.

NCE (National Commission on Education) (1995) *Learning to Succeed: The Way Forward.* London: NCE.

Newmann, F.M., Bryk, A.S. and Nagaoka, J.K. (2001) *Authentic Intellectual Work and Standardized Tests: Conflict or Coexistence?* Chicago: Consortium on Chicago School Research, http://www.consortium-chicago.org. Accessed 30 January 2017.

Nuthall, G. and Alton-Lee, A. (1995) Assessing classroom learning: how students use their knowledge and experience to answer classroom achievement test questions in science and social studies, *American Educational Research Journal*, 32(1): 185–223.

Pellegrino, J.W., Baxter, G.P. and Glaser, R. (1999) Addressing the 'two disciplines' problem linking theories of cognition with assessment and instructional practice, *Review of Research in Education*, 24: 307–53.

Peters, T. and Waterman, R. (1982) *In Search of Excellence.* New York: Harper and Row.

Posch, P. (1994) Strategies for the implementation of technology education, in D. Layton (ed.) *Innovations in Science and Technology Education*, Vol. V. Paris: UNESCO.

QCAA (2016) Queensland Curriculum and Assessment Authority: On-line statement of P-12 assessment policy, https://www.qcaa.qld.edu.au/downloads/approach2/qcaa_assessment_policy.pdf. Accessed 30 January 2017.

Royal Ministry of Church, Education and Research (1994) *Core Curriculum for Primary, Secondary and Adult Education in Norway.* Oslo: Akademika a/s (in English).

Select Committee (2004) *House of Commons Education and Skills Committee. Secondary Education: Schools Admissions, 4th Report, Session 2003–2004*, July 22nd 2004, http://www.publications.parliament.uk/pa/cm/cmeduski.htm. Accessed 30 January 2017

Shepard, L.A. (1992) Commentary: what policy makers who mandate tests should know about the new psychology of intellectual ability and learning, in B.R. Gifford and M.C. O'Connor (eds) *Changing Assessments: Alternative Views of Aptitude, Achievement and Instruction.* Boston: Kluwer.

Stanley, G., MacCann, R., Gardner, J., Reynolds, L. and Wild, I. (2009) *Review of Teacher Assessment: What Works Best and Issues for Development. Report Commissioned by the Qualifications and Curriculum Authority.* Oxford: Oxford University Centre for Development.

Thatcher, M. (1993) *The Downing Street Years.* London: HarperCollins.

Tomlinson, S. (2005) *Education in a Post-Welfare Society* (2nd edn). Maidenhead: Open University Press.

Weare, K. (2005) *Improving Learning Through Emotional Literacy.* London: Paul Chapman.

White, J. (1990) *Education and the Good Life: Beyond the National Curriculum.* London: Kogan Page.

Whitty, G. (2002) *Making Sense of Education Policy.* London: Sage Publications.

7

Policy imperatives

MEG MAGUIRE AND TANIA DE ST CROIX

Introduction

When we are immersed in the day-to-day pressures and joys of working in a class-room, the frequent reforms and heated debates of education policy might feel somewhat remote. However, we cannot ignore them, because all aspects of teaching and learning to teach are influenced (explicitly and implicitly) by govern-ment policy. Until the late 1980s, 'you would have been hard-pressed to find many educationalists who thought that their world extended much beyond that of the classroom or their institutions' (Bottery 2000: 1). Since the late 1980s, the educa-tional policy climate and its impact on schooling have reversed this situation. The state has become determined to control, manage and transform society, including through the governance and reform of education provision. This new arrangement involves contracting out services previously supplied by the state so that while the financial support may still come from the centre, in many cases, the responsibility for delivery is placed elsewhere – what Ball (2012: 102) describes as 'deconcentra-tion rather than devolution'. In this process, the previously crucial role of the local authority has largely been subordinated to national policy imperatives. In the UK, as elsewhere, the role and work of schools and teachers are still heavily prescribed by central government.

What is being demanded of schools and their role in national prosperity and social cohesion is encoded in a vast and complex litany of policy statements, docu-ments and legislation. This means that schools and teachers need to be familiar with policies that are planned for them, must know how to put these policies into practice, and will be held accountable for doing so. It is also important for teachers and school leaders to develop the skills of *thinking critically* about policy and its consequences for their schools, their students, their colleagues and themselves. Thinking critically is not the same as simply criticizing something; it includes being fully informed, reflecting on the claims made about education by different people and groups, evaluating the quality of evidence and reasoning that informs these claims, and questioning 'common-sense' understandings.

For the purposes of this chapter, we are taking 'policy' to refer to the plans for education developed by politicians and their advisers. However, with Jones

(2016: 1), we recognize that any policy agenda is informed by the wider social context – 'social and cultural, economic and political' – and this includes global trends and pressures. Thus, macro factors influence national and local policy debates and policy responses, as we shall see. It is impossible in one short chapter to provide a detailed account of specific pieces of policy reform or pedagogical policies such as assessment for learning or behaviour for learning, important though these undoubtedly are. Nor would a summary of specific policies currently affecting education be desirable – not least, because the rate of change in education policy means that any overly specific account given here may well be out of date by the time the book is printed!

What we want to do in this chapter, then, is provide an overview of reform through a consideration of four key policy imperatives that have been influential for some time, and are likely to remain prominent in the foreseeable future. These are:

1. The insertion of market forces as a lever for reform and change
2. The rise of accountability in the form of managerialism
3. Cultures of performativity
4. The social mobility agenda.

This approach represents an attempt to group and classify a wide range of policies that are, in practice, interrelated and interwoven. There is a large literature in each individual policy arena, and so all we are able to do here is provide an overview of the sorts of debates, ideas and policies that continue to shape education provision.

Before we attempt this, there are three key points that need to be considered. First, at the heart of all social policy is a tension between what should be taken to be a *public* or a *private* responsibility and this conflict is reflected in education provision as in other aspects of social welfare policy. This tension continues to generate 'a process which is never settled and always evolving' (Drakeford 2000: 183). Thus, debates continue about what the state can and should be providing in a time of global financial crisis and the onward sweep of the 'privatisation of public assets' (Gamble 2009: 15). There are conflicts between freeing up individuals to make their own decisions and make their own choices, set alongside calls for the state to take responsibility for the 'weakest' members of society. There are highly contested struggles over who is best placed to provide welfare services such as education and health. In recent years, successive governments have suggested that what counts is *what* is provided (for example, good GCSE results) – and that how it is provided, who provides it or for what reason are all secondary factors. As you read the chapter, you might want to reflect on what you think about this.

Second, in this chapter we are tracing what we see as the dominant policy agenda that circumscribes the work of schools and teachers. Thus, we do not intend to explore specific legislative and policy intentions in any great depth. Our intention in this chapter is to provide some indication of the fundamentals of policy intentions. But, in saying this, it is important to appreciate that there are other overlapping and sometimes conflicting policy agendas. In policy terms, different policies co-exist and sometimes contradict one another. Schools may have to make careful, and sometimes painful, decisions about where their policy priorities lie. In the need to survive, they may sometimes feel pressed into particular ways that do some violence to their integrity, culture, ethos and social circumstances (Maguire *et al.* 2011).

Third, in this chapter we are going to speak in the main about English policy-making. The UK is made up of four educational 'departments' that share some common features as well as many points of difference. In terms of educational policy-making, however, England has been the most 'radical' in terms of its policy agenda (Jones 2016) and thus is worthy of particular analysis. There are similarities in the four settings such as class inequality and limited social mobility, but there are differences too. Relations between teachers, parents and local governments vary and 'on such key themes of current policy as selection and social inclusion there are strong differences of inflection, in which much is at stake' (Jones 2016: 3). One example of this high stakes policy conflict was reflected in the 2017 campaign led by Prime Minister May to restore selective secondary grammar schools in England. The 'differences of inflection' referred to by Jones can also be seen in our four policy drivers, to which we now turn – market forces in education, accountability, performance and social mobility.

Market forces

In this section we consider what has been, and still is, the most influential and wide-ranging policy reform in education in the twentieth and twenty-first centuries: the insertion of market forces into education provision at all levels and stages, from nursery schools through to universities, and in virtually all parts of the world (Verger *et al.* 2016). In the UK, since the 1980s, various governments of all political complexions have sought to make schools more like businesses. Parents have been positioned as consumers and choosers of their children's schools. Their choice has been facilitated by the provision of examination data that purports to signal which schools are 'better' in each local area. Schools are largely funded on the basis of the numbers of their students; hence there is a drive to ensure parental satisfaction in order to maintain recruitment and funding; less popular and less well-funded schools will close and in this way, market forces will drive a more efficient and effective provision. Or so it is claimed.

In October 1976, the then Labour Prime Minister Jim Callaghan launched what he called a 'great debate' at Ruskin College, Oxford, about what he saw as major problems in the education system. He argued that school leavers were ill-prepared for the economy in a changing world and lacked basic skills of literacy and numeracy. He raised concerns about those young people who were underachieving and argued that there was a need to reform school examinations and the governance of schools. While no one today would be surprised to hear a politician talking in this way about education provision (note the continuity in education concerns), in 1976 this was a revolutionary moment. Until then, education, schools and teaching had not been the provenance of politicians and being Secretary of State for Education was seen as a political cul-de-sac in career terms. Politicians left education to teachers and their unions. As a pamphlet published by the Association of School and College Leaders (ASCS 2013: n.p.) puts it, 'Callaghan resisted the pressure to "keep off the (educational) grass" owned and tended by teachers. Even before he had stood up to speak, critics were rounding on him and arguing that the state was fettering educational freedom.' However, the dominant argument was that schools were failing to deliver what was needed for economic and individual prosperity. Uneconomic and inefficient education provision was not able to respond effectively to individual or societal needs. This critique was circulated in the media and was taken up by politicians of all parties. It was claimed that a market-led approach would solve this problem (Marginson 1997). Following the Great Debate, the Conservatives were elected into power from 1979–97 and during this extended period they inserted market forces into public-sector provision, including education. This was a major shift that continues to influence policy-making in the public sector to this day.

From the 1980s onwards, educational provision in the UK was restructured to incorporate a neo-liberal approach towards policy and practice. In education, a quasi-market form was inserted; education provision was to be supplied by competitive providers and the purchasers of the service were funded by the state (Le Grand 2011). In 1988, the government introduced a national curriculum and national testing. The publication of national league tables reflecting each secondary school's success at national examinations became a lever for consumer choice. Different types of schools were set up to promote diversity of choice in the education marketplace – and this diversity has extended over time to include free schools and multi-academy chains. Since the introduction of quasi-market forces into education, the public provision of education has once more become an individualized good, and a private responsibility, albeit still largely funded by the taxpayer. While many researchers have demonstrated the way in which market choice tends to privilege middle-class choosers (Reay 2013) and, rather than reducing inequality, market forces drive up the gap between the poor and the rich, nevertheless, all governments still seem to have been convinced of the power of market forces in driving their policy agenda.

However, in the educational arena, the ideology of neo-liberalism and marketization has some complicated outcomes. As Connell (2013) argues, if you have a market, then there will be winners and losers. This is the nature of competition. As she says, 'There need to be known losers, if people are to be required to pay to become winners' (2013: 105). In this marketplace, educational institutions are coerced into strategies of performativity and 'the education system as a whole comes to stand, not for the common interest and self-knowledge of the society, but for ways to extract private advantage at the expense of others' (2013: 106).

There are many examples of market forces driving education provision, including curriculum packages; assessment techniques; the provision of supply teachers, and so on, as well as the education and training of teachers. Some concern centres around the question of whether market forces encourage moves towards education privatization and whether this is desirable or not. For example, Hatcher and Hirtt (1999) described what they called endogenous and exogenous forms of privatization in education. Endogenous forms are typified by bringing in market-like mechanisms such as managerialism (see below). Exogenous forms of privatization involve the generation of profit from contracting out some aspects of schooling such as the provision of school meals. In reality, many policy developments may seem to blur this distinction because the notion of 'profit' in education is opaque, and education is still free at the point of use.

One example of this blurring can be seen in the introduction of free schools, which were introduced in England by the Academy Act, 2010. Free schools are all-ability state-funded schools, proposed and set up by groups of parents, community groups, businesses, religious groups and charities (DfE 2013). Like other academy schools, free schools are outside local education authority control, they do not have to follow the National Curriculum, can set up their own admissions policies and are not bound by national union agreements. They do not have to employ qualified teachers. 'They are often seen as a dramatically new way of establishing new schools and encouraging the supply side of the quasi-market in schooling' (Walford 2014: 315).

Free schools were justified on the basis of posing a solution to two policy problems: the need to raise attainment in areas of social deprivation and increasing democratic involvement in schooling (Hatcher 2011). However, they have been contentious right from the start. Proponents argue that these schools bring imagination and creativity to education as well as enhancing parental and community involvement. These schools are free to experiment and test out alternatives – which some certainly do (see the websites for School 21 and Michaela Community School, for example). Those who are more sceptical are concerned about free schools undermining local authority capacity to plan for places; their extremely generous start-up funding; and ultimately, that they signal more moves towards the semi-privatization of schooling, albeit still funded by the state (Miller *et al.* 2014). While we have only briefly outlined one policy move, the free school, it does seem that, in policy terms, quasi-market competition in a range of different forms is here to stay – for the time being!

Accountability and managerialism

While markets have been the dominant influence on English education policy for some time, they work alongside and in relation to other imperatives. One of these is accountability. The centrality of this concept can be seen by how often it is mentioned in government texts and political speeches; for example, one education policy document included 73 mentions of the words 'accountability' and 'accountable' (DfE 2016). Few would disagree that teachers and schools should be accountable to a variety of constituencies (students, parents and local communities, for example) across a range of dimensions that might include effectiveness, safeguarding, ethical practice and the efficient use of resources. Accountability could be seen as particularly vital now that schools are run by a wide range of independent organizations. Yet it is crucial to note that there are different ways of putting accountability measures into practice, and that these mechanisms will have particular effects in the school and in the classroom.

Everybody working or learning in an English school today will be only too aware of the importance of Ofsted inspections, league tables and student attainment. These approaches are not the only way to assure accountability – the Finnish education system, for example, has been consistently successful in international student assessments and yet is based on trust, collective responsibility and mutual learning between schools (Sahlberg 2010). In contrast, the approach taken in England (and in many other places) tends to rely on a top-down system of tests, comparisons and ranking that can be described as 'managerial accountability' or managerialism.

At the heart of managerialism lies the desire to extract the methods of the business environment and insert them into public services such as health and education, ostensibly to make these services more efficient, effective and accountable. The focus in managerial accountability is in using 'what works' to achieve ends that are frequently related to the international success of the economy. In education, this often means a preoccupation with whether our education system makes us competitive on a global stage, and international assessments, such as PISA (see Chapter 5), become a key justification for reform. This is often done in a somewhat alarmist way; we are told that 'our education standards have remained static, at best, while other countries have moved ahead' (DfE 2016: 3).

In a market-oriented policy context, the nation state plays a central role in ensuring that the education system produces the flexible, up-skilled workers that are seen as being necessary for today's technologically advanced economy. Managerial accountability is a form of control that is both organizational and individualized, in which those on the ground are charged with 'delivering' what those in government have decided is best. Schools must deliver on national targets, they have to deliver on national strategies for raising standards, and they are regularly assessed and inspected in order to ensure that they are sticking to the script. Technical 'problems' such as teachers who are seen as ineffective, or schools labelled as 'failing' or 'coasting', are subject to further scrutiny and regulation, and those seen as successful are rewarded with greater autonomy. Operating alongside a system in which schools are funded largely according to the number of students they are able to attract in a system of parental choice, good Ofsted judgements and league table placings become vital for the reputation, resourcing and viability of a school.

One danger is that schools, needing to be accountable by fulfilling these centrally determined targets, will strive to organize and present themselves in a way that is compliant, but which involves a great deal of 'fabrication' – manipulating their performance to tell a positive story (Maguire *et al.* 2011). Often, these fabrications or attempts to 'game the system' are used to justify further reforms, which then have their own consequences. This can be seen in relation to the measures used in the school league tables. Between 1992 (when league tables were first introduced) and 2010, secondary schools were ranked according to the proportion of students who attained grade C or above in at least five GCSEs 'or equivalent'. Enterprising schools began to introduce a raft of 'equivalent' qualifications, often in vocational subjects that were disproportionately targeted at lower attaining students who were seen as unlikely to achieve five grade Cs at GCSE. While some of these courses were valued by students, the Wolf Review of vocational education argued that many were 'dead end' (Wolf 2011: 8) qualifications with 'little to no market value' (Wolf 2011: 7) that were disproportionately aimed at working-class students. Such problems – alongside calls for a more 'traditional' curriculum – led to the Conservative-led Coalition government, elected in 2010, introducing the English Baccalaureate (EBacc) attainment measure. The EBacc consists of a grade C or above in English, mathematics, two sciences, history or geography, and a language. While the introduction of EBacc as a league table measure reduced the popularity of low-status qualifications in schools, it also led to reduced choice for students who wanted to study arts, vocational and other non-eligible subjects (Parameshwaran and Thomson 2015).

Another major consequence of the old league table ranking mechanisms was the incentive for schools to focus on students at the C/D borderline, potentially neglecting those perceived to be less academic — students from low-income families and certain minority ethnic groups were particularly affected by this 'rationing' (Gillborn and Youdell 2000; Parameshwaran and Thomson 2015). To combat this, the Conservative government introduced Progress 8 as the headline accountability measure to be used in league tables from 2016. Progress 8 captures the progress in attainment of all students between primary school and year 11. This reform has been welcomed by many teachers for its inclusiveness, yet is criticized for relying on sometimes inaccurate data from primary schools, which are themselves incentivized to show that their students are progressing (Neumann *et al.* 2016). Over time, it will be interesting to see whether certain groups of students are, once again, disadvantaged by this system – for example, students with challenging home lives and behaviour issues who may be perceived as less likely to progress. It will also be interesting to see whether and in what ways schools change the curriculum they offer.

High-stakes managerial accountability can produce unintended consequences, which often disadvantage groups of students who are already facing the greatest challenges. When new policies are brought in to address the problems, the accountability goalposts are moved and schools, teachers and students can face a challenging period of adjustment. Some would argue that 'gaming' practices are inherently incentivized in high-stakes managerial forms of accountability. Targets, testing, performance management techniques, inspection and reporting become 'a system for delivering government policy, not for discussion of what the aims of education might be; and when governmental policies are so clearly predicated upon economistic ends, managerialism is doubly controlling' (Bottery 2000: 79).

None of this is to suggest that teachers and schools should not be accountable. Where accountability takes the form of managerialism, however, there is a real danger of erosion in democratic participation, co-operation, and inter-school learning. Alongside this, we need to take into account the high levels of stress and bureaucracy that tend to accompany managerial accountability, and the particular effects that this has on students and learning, and on educators and teaching.

Performativity

As we have argued, the contemporary educational context is characterized by growing industries of testing, measuring and assessment, which have become so normalized that it is difficult to imagine schooling without them. If something cannot be tested or measured, it is not valued – and in the fashion for quantifying more aspects of life, we have seen the introduction of mechanisms for the indexing of more nebulous qualities such as well-being, resilience and 'grit'. It is clear that some measurements 'count' more than others, and in this context, test and exam results, league tables, and Ofsted gradings have high stakes because they are used to categorize, compare and rank schools, teachers and students.

The overwhelming emphasis on performance, measurement, comparison and competition in market-based education systems is referred to by education policy scholars as 'performativity' (Ball 2008; Perryman 2009). In performative cultures, we are encouraged to take responsibility for continuous improvement against externally defined measures, to compare ourselves to others and to think about how we could do better. We begin to exist through calculation (Ball 2003) so that tests, league tables and 'value added' scores come to represent our 'true' achievements. Performativity changes what teachers and students do, their identities as educators and learners, and how they feel about themselves:

> Performativity works best when it is inside our heads and our souls. That is, when we do it to ourselves, when we take responsibility for working harder, faster and better as part of our sense of personal worth and the worth of others . . . it also offers us the possibility of being better than we were or even being the best – better than others.
>
> (Ball 2008: 52)

These systems are persuasive and seductive because of the satisfactions involved in meeting our targets or improving our scores, yet success is never enough and is sometimes not even possible. This can be seen every summer when exam results are announced – if results have gone up, the exams are derided as having been 'too easy' or 'dumbed down', whereas if results have gone down, we are told that standards are falling, that teachers have failed and the students have not worked hard enough. We are not suggesting that holding high aspirations for school students is unimportant; rather, that there is a risk of constant fault-finding and a lack of sensitivity to the incremental gains that have occurred in children's and young people's learning. Children (and teachers) do not thrive in a setting where they are constantly berated or tested and found wanting (Stobart 2008). The constant pressure to achieve more and work harder sends a message to students that they should measure themselves against narrow and competitive visions of success, over and above collaboration and creativity (Keddie 2016).

In 2017, Prime Minister May announced that teachers would be trained in understanding and identifying mental health issues in children and young people (May 2017); however, this announcement did not address the problem of the endemic performative cultures that seem to belie expressions of care and compassion. Recent research has highlighted that children – girls in particular – are experiencing an intensification in stress, anxiety and depression, some of which appears to be school-related (Children's Society 2016). Of course, these issues are complex and the rise in mental ill health among children and young people is not caused by testing and examinations alone. Yet teachers have reported increased levels of stress placed on students by recent policy changes, including the renewed focus on exams and a reduction in time for creative, vocational and active subjects (Neumann *et al.* 2016). This stress is not confined to students who are struggling with their school work; high-attaining students can be particularly aware of and affected by performative pressures (Keddie 2016).

Teachers, too, suffer ill-health, stress and demoralization in the performative environment. Teachers' performance is constantly measured through target attainments, students' examination results, their capacity to meet centrally imposed standards and a whole range of performance indicators and measurable outcomes. The introduction of performance-related pay has intensified these pressures for teachers on the ground:

> A lot of staff failed performance management last year based on their data targets and it has been made very clear that the same will happen again this academic year even if all other targets are achieved, thus blocking pay progression.
>
> (head of department, quoted in Neumann *et al.* 2016)

Through devices such as appraisal for individuals, performance assessments as part of promotion and pay increments, target setting for the whole school and other tactics of managerialism, teachers are cajoled to conform to a battery of measures and performance indicators (Mahony and Hextall 2000). These processes are stressful in themselves, as well as taking time away from teaching. All of this is exacerbated by systems of surveillance that ensure that teachers are continuously assessed, and schools exist in a state of perpetual anxiety, particularly now that Ofsted gives almost no notice of inspections (Page 2017).

Performance issues are never straightforward. There are benefits for students and for teachers in working hard, reflecting on what they have achieved, and trying to improve what they do. Yet there are dangers of high-stakes accountability mechanisms, enforced through cultures of managerialism and performativity: students might become anxious, teachers feel stressed and may leave the profession, and educational inequalities might be exacerbated. It is difficult to know what teachers can do about these issues, but it is important to understand the policies that are behind the systems causing stress, to think critically about them, and to encourage our students to do the same.

Social mobility

Turning now to our final policy imperative, a wide range of research reports have been published by various think tanks, individual research teams, third-sector providers as well as different governments that detail different aspects of continuing educational disadvantage in the UK (Strand 2015; Cullinane and Kirby 2016). The consensus is that educational disadvantage still exists across the UK and that there is a need to challenge this outcome. Some policy-makers and politicians justify their concerns from the perspective of human capital theory.

According to this perspective, we need to harness the talents of everyone if we are to be economically successful. In a global economy, we need citizens who have acquired good literacy, numeracy and IT skills in order to increase their productivity in the marketplace. Schools need to encourage the uptake of these skills as well as the 'right' dispositions towards the labour market to ensure wealth creation. Education is about investing in people to assure this outcome. Others argue that we need to dismantle educational disadvantage more from a social justice perspective; reduced educational attainment places individuals in more insecure positions, impacts their mental and physical health and excludes them from participating in society (Joseph Rowntree Foundation 2016). One significant finding from all this policy work is that while there are dimensions in patterns of attainment that correlate with aspects of identity – girls are less likely to achieve in STEM subjects; minority students are disadvantaged when applying for prestigious universities regardless of their prior attainment; students living in 'care' have very poor educational outcomes – overriding all these issues is one clear and consistent conclusion which is that social class, more than anything else, is the 'strongest predictor of educational achievement in the UK' (Perry and Francis 2010: 2).

In 2016, the Sutton Trust published a report that summed up the situation as follows: White, working-class males in receipt of free school meals are the lowest achievers at GCSE as only 24 per cent get five A*–C grades at GCSE, including English and mathematics. In the report, Cullinane and Kirby (2016) illustrated that this group had been the lowest or second lowest attaining group for more than a decade and that while working-class girls did slightly better on the same measure (36 per cent), they were also in the lowest performing ethnic group. The Social Mobility and Child Poverty Commission (2014: 5) put this in stark terms: 'just 42 per cent of disadvantaged students (are) getting five good GCSEs including English and maths, compared to 67 per cent of other children'. (For a full and detailed account of class and ethnic outcomes over time, see Strand's 2015 DfE study.)

The government response to this long-standing pattern of educational disadvantage has been to focus on social mobility in its education policy work. The argument was and is still made that education offers a chance at social mobility, for if you work hard and are successful in school, then you will access better life chances than your parents. Social mobility has become a promise and an aspiration in the rhetoric of educational conversations (Reay 2013). The evidence shows that while there was some degree of social mobility in the 1970s (the golden age of social mobility), this was due more to changes in the occupational structure and the decline of blue-collar labour. Goldthorpe (2013) argues that social mobility can be seen in two distinct ways – first, as either declining or, second, as levelling out. He argues that there are problems with the economic analysis and the 'in decline' case does not stand up. In contrast, if a social class analysis were taken into account, he claims that the 'levelling off' account would be shown to be more accurate: 'Relative mobility rates remained much the same as for decades previously, although if any directional change were in evidence it was an actual increase in fluidity among women' (Goldthorpe 2013, n.p.).

Why this argument matters is because for some time now, policy-makers have concentrated on attempts to raise social mobility through narrowing the attainment gap in schools. However, if Goldthorpe is correct, and social mobility is not the policy problem as it is currently constituted, then education policy activity to support disadvantaged children to become more mobile might not have much effect. Those who are already better placed to access opportunities and advantage will still be able to do this. Goldthorpe adds that attempting to increase social mobility through education is 'uncertain'. What he believes is needed is a broader set of policies of equality that allows everyone to achieve their potential. Education policy may not be the answer – what might be needed are policies that 'reduce inequalities of condition, of which those associated with social class would appear the most fundamental' (Goldthorpe 2013, n.p.). As Reay (2013: 661) put it, 'Social justice requires much more than the movement of a few individuals up and down an increasingly inequitable social system.'

Thinking policy: 'doing' policy

In this chapter we have broadly taken policy as the plans for education that are developed by politicians and their advisers in response to problems that need resolutions. Here we have explored four policy imperatives that look set to continue to play a dominant part in what happens in our schools: market forces, accountability and managerialism, performativity and social mobility. All schools have to be compliant with policy demands that are mandated, particularly in relation to national forms of accountability. Schools also have to have due regard for other policy imperatives but may have more autonomy in working out their responses in the light of their situated contexts; for example, in respect of Religious Education or Sex and Relationship Education. Some types of schools will have more space to make decisions of their own in terms of their approaches to pedagogy, teacher employment and financial matters, as we have outlined in this chapter. Indeed, at any one time, schools will be involved with enacting many different and sometimes conflicting policies (Ball *et al.* 2012). It can be insightful to see the range of policies that schools currently upload to their outward-facing websites. How policies are reconstructed and how they are enacted in different schools can provide insights into alternative pedagogical approaches as well as into different sets of beliefs and values.

One key matter that we have not addressed in this chapter is what exactly does happen to policies when they are put into practice – for policies can sometimes have unintended consequences. Estelle Morris (2008), briefly Labour Secretary for Education and Skills (2001–02), has written about aspects of neo-liberal interventions into education: 'Those who would have us import the extremes of market principles into the education service should reflect on what can happen when competition is allowed to run unchecked.' It may be worth considering her question in more detail particularly in the light of our need for an education system that allows all of our young people to flourish (Sentamu 2017).

Concluding thoughts

- What sorts of policy problems do you think we face in our education system?
- What role should government have in education?
- Is it possible to ensure accountability in an inclusive manner?
- Where would you place the policy priority for the next five years if it were up to you?

References

ASCS (2013) The Great Education Debate: setting the scene, https://www.google.co.uk/search?q=ASCS+Great+education+debate+setting+the+sceneandie=utf-8andoe=utf-8andclient=firefox-bandgfe_rd=crandei=DuuqWLLeJK2stgefgImAC, accessed 12 January 2017.

Ball, S.J. (2003) The teacher's soul and the terrors of performativity, *Journal of Education Policy*, 18(2): 215–28.

Ball, S.J. (2008) Performativity, privatisation, professionals and the state, in B. Cunningham (ed.) *Exploring Professionalism*. London: Institute of Education.

Ball, S.J. (2012) The reluctant state and the beginning of the end of state education, *Journal of Educational Administration and History*, 44(2): 89–103.

Ball, S.J., Maguire, M. and Braun, A. (2012) *How Schools Do Policy: Policy Enactments in Secondary Schools*. London: Routledge.

Bottery, M. (2000) *Education, Policy and Ethics*. London: Continuum.

Children's Society (2016) *The Good Childhood Report 2016*. London: The Children's Society.

Connell, R. (2013) The neoliberal cascade and education: an essay on the market agenda and its consequences, *Critical Studies in Education*, 54(2): 99–112.

Cullinane, C. and Kirby, P. (2016) Class differences: ethnicity and disadvantage: The Sutton Trust, http://www.suttontrust.com/researcharchive/class-differences-ethnicity-and-disadvantage/, accessed 5 January 2017.

DfE (Department for Education) (2013) *Free Schools*, http://www.education.gov.uk/schools/leadership/typesofschools/freeschools. Accessed 11 October 2017

DfE (Department for Education) (2016) *Education Excellence Everywhere* (cm9230). London: HM Government.

Drakeford, M. (2000) *Privatisation and Social Policy*. Harlow: Pearson Education Limited.

Gamble, A. (2009) *The Spectre at the Feast: Capitalist Crisis and the Politics of Recession*. London: Palgrave.

Gillborn, D. and Youdell, D. (2000) *Rationing Education*. London: Routledge.

Goldthorpe, J.H. (2013) Understanding – and misunderstanding – social mobility in Britain: the entry of the economists, the confusion of politicians and the limits of educational policy, *Journal of Social Policy*, 42(3): 431–50.

Hatcher, R. (2011) The Conservative–Liberal Democrat Coalition government's 'free schools' in England, *Educational Review*, 63(4): 485–503.

Hatcher, R. and Hirtt, N. (1999) The business agenda behind Labour's policy, in M. Allen (ed.) *Business, Business, Business: New Labour's Education Policy*. London: Tufnell Press.

Jones, K. (2016) *Education in Britain: 1944 to the Present* (2nd edn). Cambridge: Polity.

Joseph Rowntree Foundation (2016) We can solve poverty in the UK, https://www.jrf.org.uk/report/we-can-solve-poverty-uk, accessed 7 January 2017.

Keddie, A. (2016) Children of the market: performativity, neoliberal responsibilisation and the construction of student identities, *Oxford Review of Education*, 42(1): 108–22.

Le Grand, J. (2011) Quasi-market versus state provision of public services: some ethical considerations, *Public Reason*, 3(2): 80–9.

Maguire, M., Perryman, J., Ball, S.J. and Braun, A. (2011) The ordinary school – what is it? *British Journal of Sociology of Education*, 32(1): 3–18.

Mahony, P. and Hextall, I. (2000) *Reconstructing Teaching: Standards, Performance and Accountability*. London: RoutledgeFalmer.

Marginson, S. (1997) *Markets in Education*. Sydney: Allen and Unwin.

May, T. (2017) The shared society, speech at the Charity Commission annual meeting, https://www.gov.uk/government/speeches/the-shared-society-prime-ministers-speech-at-the-charity-commission-annual-meeting, accessed 5 February 2017.

Miller, P., Craven, B. and Tooley, J. (2014) Setting up a free school: successful proposers' experiences, *Research Papers in Education*, 29(3): 351–71.

Morris, E. (2008) Be wary of market forces in education, *Guardian*, 28 October.

Neumann, E., Towers, E., Gewirtz, S. and Maguire, M. (2016) *A Curriculum for All? The Effects of Recent Key Stage 4 Curriculum, Assessment and Accountability Reforms on English Secondary Education*. London: National Union of Teachers.

Page, D. (2017) The surveillance of teachers and the simulation of teaching, *Journal of Education Policy*, 32(1): 1–13.

Parameshwaran, M. and Thomson, D. (2015) The impact of accountability reforms on the Key Stage 4 curriculum: how have changes to school and college performance tables affected pupil access to qualifications and subjects in secondary schools in England? *London Review of Education*, 13(2): 157–73.

Perry, E. and Francis, B. (2010) *The Social Class Gap for Educational Achievement: A Review of the Literature*. London: RSA Projects.

Perryman, J. (2009) Inspection and the fabrication of professional and performative processes, *Journal of Education Policy*, 24(5): 611–31.

Reay, D. (2013) Social mobility, a panacea for austere times: tales of emperors, frogs, and tadpoles, *British Journal of Sociology of Education*, 34(5–6): 660–77.

Sahlberg, P. (2010) Rethinking accountability in a knowledge society, *Journal of Educational Change*, 11(1): 45–61.

Sentamu, J. (Archbishop of York) (2017) We need an education system that works for the whole of society, *School Week*, 2 February 2017, http://schoolsweek.co.uk/we-need-an-education-system-that-works-for-the-whole-of-society/, accessed 12 March 2017.

Social Mobility and Child Poverty Commission (2014) *Cracking the Code: How Schools Can Improve Social Mobility*. London: SMCP.

Stobart, G. (2008) *Testing Times: The Uses and Abuses of Assessment*. London: Routledge.

Strand, S. (2015) Ethnicity, deprivation and educational achievement at age 16 in England: trends over time: Annex to compendium of evidence on ethnic minority resilience to the effects of deprivation on attainment. London: Department for Education, https://www.gov.uk/government/uploads/system/uploads/attachment_data/file/439867/RR439B-Ethnic_minorities_and_attainment_the_effects_of_poverty_annex.pdf.pdf, accessed 4 January 2017.

Verger, A., Fontdevila, C. and Zancajo, A. (2016) *The Privatization of Education: A Political Economy of Global Education Reform*. New York: Teachers College, Columbia University.

Walford, G. (2014) From city technology colleges to free schools: sponsoring new schools in England, *Research Papers in Education*, 29(3): 315–29.

Wolf, A. (2011) *Review of Vocational Education: The Wolf Report*, https://www.gov.uk/government/uploads/system/uploads/attachment_data/file/180504/DFE-00031-2011.pdf, accessed 5 February 2017.

8

School management and leadership
GERARD LUM

Introduction

There was a time when it was sufficient to think of schools simply as having head-teachers. Today the talk is all of 'managers' and 'leaders'. Indeed, over the last two decades there has been an explosion of interest around the globe in ideas relating to school management and leadership. There are those who will understandably be suspicious of the use of this terminology: factories have managers, and leaders might seem more appropriate in the military or political sphere. Why would one wish to have managers or leaders in schools if not to make schools more like production lines or army training camps? We thus get an inkling of the kind of dispute likely to arise in connection with the issue of school management and leadership.

Certainly, the change in nomenclature reflects marked changes in thinking about the way schools could or should be run. In England, it was the Education Reform Act of 1988 which first brought to the fore the idea that headteachers might be thought of as managers. Headteachers were called upon to manage the quite radical educational changes that followed in the wake of the Act, such as the implementation of the newly devised National Curriculum. And because the Act reduced quite radically the role of local authorities in the running of schools, head-teachers and school governors had to take on a range of functions previously managed by the local authorities; in particular, with the introduction of 'Local Management of Schools' in 1991, headteachers became responsible for the financial control of their schools.

The suggestion that the role of headteacher should also include 'leadership' began to take hold in the mid-1990s with the idea that it is the responsibility of the head to 'lead' the school on a journey of improvement, an idea taken up with enthusiasm by the incoming New Labour government of 1997. Of course the quest for school effectiveness and improvement is itself far from unproblematic, for there are any number of questions to be asked about what it is for a school to be 'effective' or 'improved'. At the same time, there is a sense in which no one would want schools to be anything other than effective or improved where possible. And it is just this recognition of the potential need for *change* that has turned attention to the role not just of headteachers but of *all* teachers who are in a position to take responsibility and help bring about that change. Accordingly, the ethos of school leadership is by no means restricted to the head or principal of a school. Indeed anyone joining the teaching profession today needs to understand what is meant by school management and leadership, not just so that they can make sense of the organizational landscape in which they find themselves, but because they will themselves, as teachers, be called upon to engage in forms of school management and leadership.

What is the difference between management and leadership? Well, while it is true that some may use these terms interchangeably or perhaps choose to regard leadership as just one aspect of management, many do see fit to distinguish between them (see, for example, Bennis 1989). Indeed, some would distinguish between management and administration, while in some countries the word 'administration' is used in preference to 'management' (Bush 2003). Insofar as there is a difference in the use of such terms, one broad consensus is that while management is about maintaining or improving the functioning of an organiza-tion, leadership is about influencing or shaping the 'goals, motivations, and actions of others' (Cuban 1988: xx) with a view to changing or transforming the organiza-tion (Kotter 1990). It would be a mistake, of course, to read too much into the supposed meaning of one word as against another, for whatever term is used, the substantive issue remains that of how schools are run. Yet the political appeal of 'leadership' with its connotations of change and improvement has brought this term to particular prominence, not least in England where a National College for School Leadership was set up in 2000 with the express purpose of offering a range of 'school leadership' programmes. And another reason why it is leadership rather than management that has become the buzz word in education of late is that the very word 'management' has in some quarters come to be seen as 'deeply unfash-ionable' (Crawford 2004: 63) due to its association with 'managerialism' – a notion to which we shall shortly return.

This growing interest in educational leadership has given rise to a burgeoning literature on the subject. Anyone approaching this literature for the first time will discover a bewildering array of variations on the leadership theme: such things as 'distributed leadership' (Gronn 2000; Harris 2013), 'shared leadership' (Lambert 2002), 'collaborative leadership' (Kochan and Reed 2005), 'invitational leadership' (Novak 2005), 'effective leadership' (Harris *et al.* 2013), 'decentralised leadership' (Bryant 2004), 'transformational leadership' (Burns 1978) as against 'transactional leadership' (Goldring 1992), 'deep leadership' (Hargreaves 2006; Harris *et al.* 2009), 'teacher leadership' (Leithwood *et al.* 1999), 'student leadership' (Harris *et al.* 2009),'contingent leadership' (Bush 2003), 'instructional leadership' (Leithwood *et al.* 1992), 'cultural leadership' (Foskett and Lumby 2003), 'moral leadership' (Sergiovanni 1992), 'wise leadership' (Crawford 2004), 'passionate leadership' (Davies and Brighouse 2008) and even 'bastard leadership' (Wright 2001). We need not concern ourselves for the moment with this hotchpotch of different concep-tions, what has been aptly dubbed the 'alphabet soup of leadership' (MacBeath 2003), except to say that what they all have in common is that they all attempt variously to articulate something of how it is thought schools should be organized and run, by whom, and what is thought to be required of those involved in this task. Again, it would be a mistake to place too much store by the use of one word rather than another, for while some of these expressions have overlapping meanings and might even be used synonymously, others are interpreted differently by different commentators, with the very same term sometimes being recruited to promote widely disparate ideas of how a school should be run.

Two kinds of complexity contribute to this complicated picture. One kind of complexity arises from the fact that the concept of leadership, like the concept of education, is a *contested* concept in the sense that a person's view of how a school should be run and the kind of relationships that should exist between the head-teacher and the wider school community will vary according to the values they hold, the moral and political priorities they happen to have. In short, different people will have different views about these issues. Another kind of complexity arises from the fact that how we respond to the question of how schools should be run may well depend on how we go about answering still more fundamental questions: questions about how staff might best be motivated, the kind of knowledge or skills leadership requires, the nature of the school as an organization, and so on. In other words, questions about school leadership will often come down to questions about such things as human psychology and interaction, human knowledge and capability, and the nature of organizations. Answering these questions by no means removes values from the picture but may serve to clarify what is involved in achieving that which is valued and in so doing identify any inconsistencies between methods and aims or, indeed, between different aims.

The purpose of this chapter is to try to unravel some of these complexities and to provide an insight into some of the disputes that lie at the heart of this hugely contentious issue. It is certainly not the intention here to provide the reader with a list of dos and don'ts in respect of school management and leadership, or to add to the already vast literature speculating on what strategies may or may not contribute to the proper and effective running of a school. Rather, the task here is to enable those new to teaching to see through the fog of rhetoric generated by the current official preoccupation with leadership, to make sense of the culture which currently predominates in schools, and to understand what might be at stake in adopting one conception of school management and leadership rather than another.

The dichotomies of educational leadership

It is of no small significance that the editor of one voluminous collection of work on educational leadership (English 2005) saw fit to use its introductory chapter to map out four 'binaries' or dichotomies that seem to permeate contemporary debates about educational leadership. One of these dichotomies arises from the distinction we have already encountered between management and leadership. For inasmuch as we understand the first as concerned with bureaucratic or administrative tasks, and the latter with unifying the organization around the leader's 'vision' or sense of 'mission', a difficulty arises in that while managing apparently lacks the wherewithal to provide organizational cohesion or momentum, the very idea of leadership, in emphasizing adherence to an orthodoxy, seems to put the organization at risk of being insufficiently sensitive to truth and falsity. On this view, it would seem that we have to *choose* between management and leadership, between truth and unity. This is, of course, assuming that these conceptions of management and leadership are valid in the first place and that they accurately represent the kind of capabilities substantively at issue.

More significant here, I want to suggest, are the other three dichotomies to which Fenwick English draws attention, in part because they serve to illustrate the quite radical polarization of views that has come to characterize educational debate in the UK, the USA and elsewhere of late, and also because it would seem that in order to have a coherent and plausible conception of school management and leadership it will be necessary to somehow go beyond these dichotomies, to engage, as English says, in their 'deconstruction' (2005: x).

One of these dichotomies revolves around the famously controversial issue of whether education should be run along business lines. On one side of this divide are those who believe that schools, like businesses, should be accountable to the market and that they should compete with one another for 'consumers' in an education 'marketplace'. According to this model, education is to be regarded as a product, defined in terms of measurable outcomes and delivered by teachers whose performance can be monitored and induced by performance-related pay. Among those in opposition to this model are those who would regard it as being fundamentally at odds with principles of social justice and who would see the school as having an important part to play in the advancement of society rather than merely being such as to perpetuate its existing inequalities and injustices. Similarly, it might be objected that an education run on business lines and motivated essentially by self-interest lacks the kind of moral compass essential to the education of children.

Another well-known polarity arises from the question of whether running a school should be thought of as a science or as an art, and also from the closely related question of the extent to which it is appropriate to think of educational problems as being amenable to scientific modes of investigation and explanation. While some will be happy to employ statistical and quasi-scientific methods to gain the measure of the achievements of schools, others will contest the assumed pre-eminence of the scientific paradigm, perhaps seeing science as offering just one methodology, one form of knowledge among many. They may thus be of the view that the most important educational problems require a different approach, a different kind of explanation.

Lastly, there is the opposition that is made between theory and practice. The dissension here concerns the kind of skills or knowledge thought necessary for educational leadership. On one side are those who would see practical knowledge and experience as paramount and regard theory as being in large part irrelevant or superfluous to practice, the perceived shortfall perhaps being referred to as a 'theory–practice gap' (cf. English 2002). On the other side are those who see all meaningful, purposeful practice as necessarily theory-laden and who would regard theoretical understanding as a prerequisite of expert performance.

Such, then, are the oppositions which have come to beleaguer and divide opinion on the question of school management and leadership. And of course it is not difficult to see how current arrangements in England sit within this scheme of things. With the introduction of the Education Reform Act of 1988, the pendulum swung quite decidedly towards the business/scientific/practice end of these dichotomies (cf. Lum 2003; Barker 2010). State schools have ever since been required to operate very much on business lines in order to compete with one another in an education market, with statistical measures used to gauge the operational effectiveness of each and every school. With the ends of education taken as a given and specified in terms of set criteria and attainment levels, the only thing left open for consideration is how those ends are to be achieved, with this admitting only of technical or quasi-scientific solutions. The resulting emphasis on performance and measurable outcomes, on monitoring and appraisal, is a characteristic feature of the New Public Management of public services (Clarke and Newman 1997) and, in education, the stark, top-down, technicist managerialism that has attracted so much criticism over the last two decades (see Gewirtz 2002). Meanwhile, the newly re-titled National College for Teaching and Leadership is unabashed in its emphasis on practice as opposed to theory. Certainly the College's programmes pay scant attention to theory from a critical perspective (Thrupp 2005). With its essentially competence-based methodology and use of 'skills assessment', the approach of the National College is to equate good leadership with the facility to exhibit certain behaviours, 'skills' or 'styles'. Those seeking to gain the 'National Professional Qualification for Headship', initially a mandatory qualification for new headteachers in England, must demonstrate or provide evidence of the requisite, officially designated behaviours. There seems little doubt, then, that the current official conception of school leadership is firmly entrenched at the business/scientific/practice end of these all-pervasive dichotomies.

One might have expected the welter of different conceptions of leadership mentioned earlier to have done something to counter these extremes, yet many have been conspicuously ineffectual in this regard. Take, for example, the notion of 'distributed leadership', said to be of some 'popularity' (Harris 2005: 10) currently, according to which leadership practice should be 'distributed over leaders, followers, and the school's situation or context' (Spillane *et al.* 2004: 11). Or the idea of 'shared leadership', which has it that 'leadership must be a shared, community undertaking ... the professional work of everyone in the school' (Lambert 2002: 37). Or again, 'invitational leadership' which 'appreciates individuals' uniqueness and calls forth their potential' (Novak 2005: 44); or yet again, the idea of 'teacher leadership' which 'suggests that teachers rightly and importantly hold a central position in the ways schools operate and in the core functions of teaching and learning' (York-Barr and Duke 2004: 255). What all of these different variations on school leadership have in common is a claim to the effect that sufficient importance should be attached to the contribution of teachers in processes of decision-making and in determining the ethos and general direction of school. In other words, they all 'emphasise *inclusivity* and *teacher participation*' (Gold *et al.* 2003: 128; original emphasis). Certainly such approaches would be a useful antidote to authoritarian forms of leadership in which the school is led from the top by a single dominant leader wielding techniques of command and control. However, they are distinctly less useful in countering the kind of command and control that accompanies technicist managerialism and which demands not so much obedience to a leader *per se* but compliance to officially sanctioned standards, systems and processes, with the head's role being one of communicating and enforcing those standards, systems and processes. In fact, the National College has even been able to appropriate the idea of 'distributed leadership' and parade it as one of its officially sanctioned strategies. In official hands, distributed leadership becomes less about teacher participation in genuine decision-making than about legitimizing the top-down allocation of responsibilities. Indeed, one of the ways in which the National College has until now been able to 'uncritically relay managerialist education policy into schools' (Thrupp 2005: 14) is precisely by appropriating the language of inclusivity and distorting the original meaning of notions such as distributed leadership (cf. Gronn 2003). Under the circumstances, it is hardly surprising that one commentator has judged the whole issue of school leadership to be 'full of word magic of the worst kind' (Hodgkinson 1993: 21).

But perhaps another reason why many of these writings have failed to have any substantial impact on current arrangements is that they tend to be articulated primarily in terms of *values*. Such writings are littered with insistent claims about what 'rightly', 'must' or 'should' be done in schools. The intention is to appeal to our social and moral sensibilities, our sense of justice and fairness. The problem is that while there will certainly be those who will readily be persuaded that this or that approach is in the interests of everyone, that is, schools, teachers, children and society, others will be of the view that the interests of children and society are best served when schools and teachers are held to account by precisely the kind of arrangements we already have in schools. In other words, whether or to what extent a person finds such claims compelling will often depend less on any reasoning or reasons than on whether those claims happen to coincide with their ethical and political predilections.

Of course, in the absence of *any* reasons or reasoning such claims may be little better than truisms or platitudes – what one commentator has referred to as 'bumper sticker homilies' (English 2008: 165). Certainly there is a long tradition of this sort of writing in the popular management press – the kind of books found in airport bookshops with such titles as '10 Strategies for Successful Leadership'. Eugenie Samier (2005) has referred to this kind of literature as a form of kitsch. For, as Samier says, this kind of writing 'requires no knowledge, understanding, critique, or analysis' (2005: 38) and significantly, it is a form of writing that is susceptible to being recruited to any cause: 'because of its unreflective, uncritical nature, and dominance by emotional appeal, kitsch lends itself easily to the injection of propaganda' (2005: 38). When this happens, clichés are taken up and promulgated as official watchwords, elevated to the status of mission statements, or passed down through the school as fashionable slogans. They are as 'platitudes plucked out of the air' (Hussey 1998: 150) and likely to be just as counter-productive when discovered to be lacking in both substance and sincerity.

None of this is to deny that there are rich and meaningful accounts of educational leadership in the literature that stand in contradistinction to current policy and practice. Thomas Sergiovanni's account of leadership is a case in point. His conception of the school as a 'moral community' (Sergiovanni 2005: 33) stands in marked contrast to the business/market-oriented approach. Far from being something amenable to quasi-scientific rules and measurable outcomes, running a school, according to Sergiovanni's view, is akin to 'trying to get a giant amoeba to move from one side of the street to another' (2005: 7). And good leadership for Sergiovanni is more about 'leading with ideas' (2005: 20) than adopting pre-specified behaviours, 'skills' or 'styles'. Perceived in terms of the binaries, an account such as this seems simply to make a case for the opposite viewpoint from that which informs official arrangements. And therein lies the difficulty. For if required to choose between them, we would no doubt choose according to our predilections, according to whether we are inclined by belief or temperament to give overriding priority to, say, community as against accountability, comprehensiveness as against exactitude, mind as against behaviour, and so on. But to construe the issue in these dichotomous terms is to invite not an answer but partisanship; it is to invoke a schism which divides people according to their contingent preferences, political leanings or emotional instincts. In short, to frame the issue in these terms is to allow substantive educational concerns to be displaced by expressions of partiality. It would seem that if we are to progress any further with the issue of school management and leadership we must find a way of going beyond these dichotomies.

Towards a more coherent conception of educational leadership

There are few, if any, who would dispute that there are well-run schools and less well-run schools, effective headteachers and less effective headteachers. Although there may be occasions when people differ in their judgements about such things, we think it reasonable to presume that, on the whole, these are not merely matters of subjective opinion but matters of *fact*. The question here is what *kind* of fact. We tend to assume that all objective facts about the world are amenable to being described by science. But, as the American philosopher John Searle has been at pains to point out, not all facts, not even all 'objective' facts, can be reduced to the facts of natural science. To illustrate the point Searle asks us to imagine a group of observers trying to describe a game of American football using only the 'brute' facts of science:

> What could they say by way of description? Well, within certain areas a good deal could be said, and using statistical techniques certain 'laws' could even be formulated. For example, we can imagine that after a time our observer would discover the law of periodic clustering: at statistically regular intervals organisms in like colored shirts cluster together in a roughly circular fashion (the huddle). Furthermore, at equally regular intervals, circular clustering is followed by linear clustering (the teams line up for play), and linear clustering is followed by the phenomenon of linear interpenetration. Such laws would be statistical in character, and none the worse for that. But no matter how much data of this sort we imagine our observers to collect and no matter how many inductive generalizations we imagine them to make from the data, they still have not described American football.

(Searle 1969: 52)

It is not merely facts about football, such as the fact one team 'won', that elude description in terms of the natural sciences, but facts extending into every area of human involvement and activity. The fact that a particular piece of paper counts as 'currency', that someone is 'married', is a 'graduate' or is 'employed', the fact that someone was 'jogging', 'dancing' or 'playing' – facts such as these are simply not amenable to scientific explication. Certainly, we can use science to describe the raw physics or chemistry of things; science can describe the piece of paper in my wallet, down to the last molecule if need be, but science cannot capture the fact that it is a five pound note. Facts of this kind are objective in the sense that they are certainly not just a matter of subjective opinion, yet unlike the facts of science these facts are *utterly dependent upon human agreement*. It would seem that much of our ordinary, everyday experience consists of this kind of *constructed* social reality, a reality of quite astonishing metaphysical complexity (see Searle 1995).

The point here is that when we refer to the facts of such things as well-run schools or effective headteachers, it is usually to this kind of fact that we refer – and we can see the kind of mistake that might arise if we were to restrict our conception of these facts to the things that science can describe. This has a number of important implications, not least for how we conceive of the school as an organization. When we speak, for example, of improving 'the school', what we are referring to is not something that exists independently of the people who make up the school community, rather, what we are referring to is something that exists in the *minds* of those people. All this is of a piece with Thomas Barr Greenfield's account of organizations as 'social inventions': 'organizations are ideas held in the human mind, sets of beliefs – not always compatible – that people hold about the ways they should relate to one another. Within these relationships, people act to realize values, to attain goals important to them' (1973: 560).

We can see why Sergiovanni likens running a school to 'trying to get a giant amoeba to move from one side of the street to another', for a school is not a 'thing' in any conventional sense. We can see also how acknowledging facts of this kind allows us to break away from the traditional dichotomy of science versus art, according to which we must choose between school leadership understood as something amenable to scientific description and precise measurement, or as something essentially subjective and open to personal interpretation. For it would seem that to most intents and purposes, neither is the case. That a school is well run or a headteacher effective are not simply matters of personal opinion, yet neither are they such as can be described using scientific methods.

A related issue concerns the kind of knowledge thought necessary for leadership and here we come up against another of the traditional dichotomies: the distinction between theory and practice. I have argued elsewhere (Lum 2007) that the persistence of this dichotomy in thinking about knowledge derives from a tendency to confuse knowledge with the antecedent and consequent conditions of knowledge. Certainly we can often meaningfully distinguish theory and practice understood as the antecedent conditions of knowledge, that is, as different kinds of educational provision. It is entirely reasonable to want to distinguish between, say, learning from a text and learning from a practical exercise. Similarly, it is often feasible to make a distinction in the consequent conditions of knowing, that is, in the outcomes of learning. Colloquially, we might say that someone 'knows how' or 'knows that', or we might say that they know 'the theory' or 'the practice' of something. The mistake comes about by confusing these more evident conditions of knowledge for knowledge itself, with what a person actually knows. We can get a sense of why this is mistaken by thinking about cases where the distinction clearly does not hold up. For example, it does not account for how someone could gain the wherewithal to construct a flat-pack wardrobe (knowing how) from reading the instructions (knowing that). A far better way of thinking about knowledge, I have suggested, is to think of it as the facility to make sense of a particular 'world' of meanings, purposes and involvements. That 'world' might be the world of mathematics or music, art or architecture, the world of flat-pack furniture, or indeed the 'world' of an occupation, such as teaching or running a school. On this view, professional capability is not so much about knowing particular facts or having certain physical dexterities, rather:

> It is first and foremost about learning to perceive, experience, cope with, in short, to *be* in a particular 'world' . . . As we go about our lives acting in a particular occupational capacity a certain coherence is disclosed to us, a world of profoundly interconnected meanings and involvements inextricably related to our purposes, goals and values – purposes, goals and values which must be approximate in some sense to those of our fellow practitioners . . . Our becoming vocationally capable is primarily about our gaining certain fundamental understandings and abilities relating to how that particular world works, how to cope in it and find our way around it – rather than necessarily being able to exhibit the secondary and derivative behavioural or propositional manifestations of those understandings. In becoming capable we learn to adopt a particular stance, a certain interested and purposeful viewpoint which in turn structures our consciousness and our experience. We thus come to be equipped with a certain kind of 'readiness'; we are able to see things *as* certain things, we are able to interpret what we experience and extrapolate from it in a way which is appropriate to the world in which we wish to operate.
> (Lum 2009: 113)

Our understanding of this world can be informed by either theoretical or practical provision. The more concrete that world, the more important is practical experience, the more abstract, the more important is the theoretical approach. And it would be difficult to think of a world more abstract than the world of the school, a world that exists entirely in the minds of the community involved in and served by that enterprise. At the same time, running a school necessitates having appropriate and effective dealings with that community, and it is only to be expected that the quality and effectiveness of those engagements will be enhanced by practical experience. Just as this shows the dichotomy of theoretical and practical knowledge to be false, so too, the supposed dichotomy of management and leadership. There is no incompatibility between management and leadership on the view offered here because it is possible to develop understandings pertinent to a 'world' which incorporates the functions of both management and leadership and which allows a synthesis of judgement such as will provide for both truth *and* organizational unity.

We are perhaps now in a position to understand the full significance of Sergiovanni's phrase 'leading with ideas', for there is an important sense in which the school only exists in the realm of ideas. This is not to give precedence to theory as opposed to practice. Rather, it is to acknowledge the centrality of people's understandings in creating and sustaining the world of the school and the role of the headteacher in contributing to and guiding that sphere of understandings. By the same token, we can also understand the intuition that lies behind demands for leadership to be 'distributed' or 'shared' among the staff of the school. It is not merely that the world of the school will be enriched by the contribution of teachers; it is rather that their exclusion from this process would undermine the existence of the school as an organization. To say that teachers would lack motivation if excluded is to understate the matter; it is rather that the school can only properly exist in and through the collective understandings of its teachers.

Needless to say, all this is at some remove from the official line which urges school leaders to communicate their 'vision', which in practice may amount to little more than a mix of trite clichés and measurable outcomes. And we can also see the inadequacy of conceiving of the role of the headteacher as simply one of adopting certain behaviours or 'styles'. To conceive of leadership this way is to neglect not only the understandings that constitute the school, but also leadership's important moral dimension. The National College approach has been to conceive of leadership as the ability to use different 'styles' so as to influence different people in different situations. The upshot, as Michael Smith (2002) has rightly noted, is a view of the school leader as someone prepared to treat members of the school community as a means to an end, who deliberately manipulates people and believes that such manipulation is justified if it allows them to achieve their ends – hardly appropriate behaviour for the leader of a 'moral community'. In contrast, on the view presented here, to be a leader is to adopt a certain interested and purposeful stance, that is, certain things must come to *matter*. And there is a fundamental difference between a person for whom things matter, and a person who merely *acts* as though they do.

Further moral implications arise out of questions about the role of leadership in relation to the so-called 'market' in education. Characterized in terms of an opposition between the public and the private, the instincts of many will be to take sides according to their ideological inclinations. But again, to frame the matter in these dichotomous terms offers no resolution of the issue but only the opportunity for opposing sides to mark out their political allegiances. Here is not the place to enter into the question of how demands for parental choice might be reconciled with the wider needs of children, schools and society. What we can say, however, is that current arrangements clearly skew the ends of education towards the quantifiable and measurable. Overriding priority is attached to demonstrable attainment, to 'thin skills' rather than 'rich knowledge' (Davis 1998, *passim*). To judge school leaders in these terms is to place them under intolerable pressure as they try to accommodate demands for tangible 'improvement' and a favourable position in the 'league tables', while simultaneously striving to achieve something more substantial for their pupils.

Concluding thoughts

These, then, are the kind of dissensions that confront those entering the teaching profession in England and a good many other countries today. The intention here has been to lay bare some of the debates at the heart of this hugely contentious issue. If there has been one overarching theme here, it is this: the words we use to describe the task of running our schools matter less than how we conceive of that enterprise, for the kind of education children receive ultimately hangs on this. Simply describing arrangements as 'distributed', 'shared' or 'democratic' does not make them so. Certainly, leadership is about far more than the top-down implementation of officially decreed diktats. Indeed, good leadership should be first and foremost about *supporting* colleagues in the work that they do. And when leadership roles are devolved to others, this should mean a good deal more than devolved accountabilities. For ultimately, leadership is about helping to shape the very idea of the school and to nurture that idea in the minds of everyone involved in the life of the school.

References

Barker, B. (2010) *The Pendulum Swings: Transforming School Reform.* Stoke-on-Trent: Trentham Books.

Bennis, W. (1989) *On Becoming a Leader.* Cambridge, MA: Perseus Books.

Bryant, M. (2004) Cross-cultural perspectives on school leadership: themes from Native American interviews, in N. Bennett *et al.* (eds) *Effective Educational Leadership.* London: Open University/Paul Chapman.

Burns, J.M. (1978) *Leadership.* New York: Harper and Row.

Bush, T. (2003) *Theories of Leadership and Management.* London: Sage.

Clarke, J. and Newman, J. (1997) *The Managerial State: Power, Politics and Ideology in the Remaking of Social Welfare.* London: Sage.

Crawford, M. (2004) Inventive management and wise leadership, in N. Bennet *et al.* (eds) *Effective Educational Leadership.* London: Open University/Paul Chapman.

Cuban, L. (1988) *The Managerial Imperative and the Practice of Leadership in Schools.* Albany, NY: State University of New York Press.

Davies, B. and Brighouse, T. (eds) (2008) *Passionate Leadership in Education.* London: Sage.

Davis, A. (1998) *The Limits of Educational Assessment.* Oxford: Blackwell.

English, F.W. (2002) Cutting the Gordian knot of educational administration: the theory–practice gap, *UCEA Review*, 44(1): 1–3.

English, F.W. (ed.) (2005) *The Sage Handbook of Educational Leadership: Advances in Theory, Research, and Practice.* London: Sage Publications.

English, F.W. (2008) *The Art of Educational Leadership: Balancing Performance and Accountability.* London: Sage Publications.

Foskett, N. and Lumby, J. (2003) *Leading and Managing Education: International Dimensions*. London: Paul Chapman Publishing.

Gewirtz, S. (2002) *The Managerial School*. London: Routledge.

Gold, A., Evans, J., Earley, P., Halpin, D. and Collarbone, P. (2003) Principled principles? *Education Management and Administration*, 31(2): 127–38.

Goldring, E.B. (1992) System-wide diversity in Israel, *Journal of Educational Administration*, 30(3): 49–62.

Greenfield, T.B. (1973) Organisations as social inventions: rethinking assumptions about change. *Journal of Applied Behavioural Science*, 9(5): 551–74.

Gronn, P. (2000) Distributed properties: a new architecture for leadership, *Educational Management and Administration*, 28(3): 317–38.

Gronn, P. (2003) *The New Work of Educational Leaders*. London: Paul Chapman.

Hargreaves, D.H. (2006) *Deep Leadership – 1: A New Shape for Schooling?* London: Specialist Schools and Academies Trust.

Harris, A. (2005) Reflections on distributed leadership, *Management in Education*, 19(2): 10–12.

Harris, A. (2013) *Distributed School Leadership: Developing Tomorrow's Leaders*. London: Routledge.

Harris, A., Day, C., Hopkins, D., Hadfield, M., Hargreaves, A. and Chapman, C. (2013) *Effective Leadership for School Improvement*. London: Routledge.

Harris, A., Ireson, G., McKenley-Simpson, J., Sims, E., Smith, P. and Worral, N. (2009) *Deep Leadership: Emerging Learning from the Development and Research Network*. London: Specialist Schools and Academies Trust.

Hodgkinson, C. (1993) *The Philosophy of Leadership*. Oxford: Blackwell.

Hussey, D. (1998) *Strategic Management: From Theory to Implementation*. Oxford: Butterworth-Heinemann.

Kochan, F.K. and Reed, C.J. (2005) Collaborative leadership, community building and democracy in education, in F. English (ed.) *The Sage Handbook of Educational Leadership: Advances in Theory, Research, and Practice*. London: Sage.

Kotter, J. (1990) *A Force for Change: How Leadership Differs from Management*. New York: Free Press.

Lambert, L. (2002) A framework for shared leadership, *Educational Leadership*, May: 37–40.

Leithwood, K., Jantzi, D. and Steinbach, R. (1999) *Changing Leadership for Changing Times*. Buckingham: Open University Press.

Leithwood, K., Steinbach, R. and Begley, P. (1992) Socialization experiences: becoming a principal in Canada, in F. Parkray and G. Hall (eds) *Becoming a Principal: The Challenges of Beginning Leadership*. Boston, MA: Allyn and Bacon.

Lum, G. (2003) Towards a richer conception of vocational preparation, *Journal of Philosophy of Education*, 37(1): 1–15.

Lum, G. (2007) The myth of the golden mean, in J. Drummond and P. Standish (eds) *The Philosophy of Nurse Education*. London: Palgrave Macmillan.

Lum, G. (2009) *Vocational and Professional Capability: An Epistemological and Ontological Study of Occupational Expertise*. London: Continuum.

MacBeath, J. (2003) The alphabet soup of leadership, *Inform*, 2. Cambridge: University of Cambridge.

Novak, J.M. (2005) Invitational leadership, in B. Davies (ed.) *The Essentials of School Leadership*. London: Sage.

Samier, E. (2005) Toward public administration as a humanities discipline: a humanistic manifesto, *Administrative Culture (Halduskultuur Journal)*, 6: 6–59.

Searle, J.R. (1969) *Speech Acts*. London: Cambridge University Press.

Searle, J.R. (1995) *The Construction of Social Reality.* London: Penguin Press.

Sergiovanni, T. (1992) *Moral Leadership.* San Francisco: Jossey-Bass.

Sergiovanni, T. (2005) *Leadership: What's in it for Schools?* London: RoutledgeFalmer.

Smith, M. (2002) The school leadership initiative: an ethically flawed project? *Journal of Philosophy of Education,* 36(1): 21–39.

Spillane, J.P., Halverson, R. and Diamond, J.B. (2004) Towards a theory of leadership practice: a distributed perspective. *Journal of Curriculum Studies,* 36(1): 3–34.

Thrupp, M. (2005) The National College for School Leadership, *Management in Education,* 19(2): 13–19.

Wright, N. (2001) Leadership, 'bastard leadership' and managerialism: confronting twin paradoxes in the Blair education project, *Educational Management and Administration,* 29(3): 275–90.

York-Barr, J. and Duke, K. (2004) What do we know about teacher leadership? Findings from two decades of scholarship, *Review of Educational Research,* 74(3): 255–316.

9

Social justice in schools: engaging with equality
LOUISE ARCHER

Introduction

In this chapter I suggest that an understanding of social justice can be a useful tool for teachers who want to work in equitable ways and who wish to foster a classroom environment that is experienced as 'fair' and respectful by pupils from diverse communities. I illustrate how the concept of social justice can help us to analyse and address unequal power relations within schools and classrooms and can help professionals to become more attuned to 'hidden' inequalities.

What do we mean by 'social justice'?

The term 'social justice' is often used by academics as a means for engaging with issues of inequality – although it has perhaps been less commonly employed within policy and practitioner circles. In one sense, the notion of social justice is just another way of talking about and engaging with issues of equality and 'fairness'. Indeed, we could ask why it is even necessary – especially given the proliferation of terminology within this area in recent years, such as: social exclusion/inclusion; social equity; equal opportunities; equality and diversity; equality of outcomes. However, as I argue below, the strength of 'social justice' is that it provides a robust and comprehensive toolkit for engaging with inequalities – due primarily to the ways in which it has been meticulously theorized.

So how might we conceptualize 'social justice'? In her book, *Action for Social Justice in Education*, Morwenna Griffiths postulates that 'social justice is a verb' (Griffiths 2003: 55). In other words, it is a dynamic project – never complete, finished or achieved 'once and for all', it is always subject to revision. Drawing on the work of Young (1990) and Fraser (1997), we might usefully identify three key forms of social justice (see also Power and Gewirtz (2001; 2002) for an example of this framework in practice):

- *Relational justice*: this is about ensuring cultural recognition and respect. It refers to fair and just relationships within society.

- *Distributive justice*: this concerns the allocation and distribution of material and discursive goods and resources within society. It is about making sure that economic, cultural and other resources are shared out equitably.

- *Associational justice*: this refers to people's ability to have a say and participate in decisions that affect their own lives. It is about ensuring that people are enabled to be active and equitable participants in society.

This tripartite conceptualization of social justice offers a complex and holistic approach to identifying and understanding different forms of inequality. Yet as Gewirtz (2006) argues, the three aspects of social justice are not simple, discrete categories. Rather, they overlap, inter-relate and can contradict one another. This alerts us to how the task of promoting social justice within schools will never be simple or straightforward – there is no single, 'one-size-fits-all' approach. However, the three components do provide a useful model for helping to identify the different sorts of equity issues that might be at stake within any given context.

So how might this concept of social justice help us to engage with issues of equality and diversity within schools? The following sections outline and discuss some key features of contemporary debates pertaining to three core axes of social difference within UK society and schools, namely, gender, race/ethnicity and social class. Due to constraints of space, I have chosen to concentrate on gender, 'race'/ethnicity and social class – there are other important axes, such as sexuality, dis/ability, and so on (DePalma and Atkinson 2008). Gender, 'race'/ethnicity and social class have been organized here as separate sections purely for ease of presentation and comprehension. This approach should not be interpreted as indicating that I treat them as separate, free-standing social categories. Rather, I would argue that they are all inextricably interlinked (see Archer 2005 regarding my re/theorization of 'difference').

Each section starts by outlining the theoretical and policy context and then moves on to illustrate social justice issues for teachers and schools through a discussion of related research evidence. It should be noted, however, that the chapter provides merely a brief snapshot and introduction to issues and research in each area – it cannot fully represent the depth and complexity of issues and work within the field.

Gender

Theoretical and policy context

Since the mid-1990s, one of the most enduring educational issues has been the 'boys' underachievement debate'. Newspapers regularly contain headlines expressing concerns about a 'crisis' in relation to boys' underachievement – often, in the UK, around the time when national examination results are published. But this is not just a UK issue; governments around the world have instigated a plethora of initiatives designed to increase boys' attainment at school. Many of these interventions have been substantially funded, for example the $4 million 'lighthouse' schools programme in Australia and the $1.2 million study in the USA into whether single-sex teaching can raise boys' achievement (see Francis and Skelton 2005 for a full discussion and overview). In the UK too, there has been a proliferation of research and initiatives, such as the 'Playing for Success' national programme (a football-themed initiative to encourage after-school homework).

Despite the overwhelming media and policy concern with boys' underachievement, the evidence pertaining to the existence, or the size, of any gender gap in achievement is rather less clear-cut. Indeed, while the popular headlines scream out each summer that girls are outperforming boys at GCSE and A level, these overall aggregate figures hide important underlying trends. For instance, girls do not outperform boys in *all* subjects: 'female outperformance of boys is strongly connected to their overwhelmingly higher achievement at language and literacy subjects, which somewhat skews the achievement figures overall' (Francis and Skelton 2005: 3).

An international study of 15-year-olds across OECD countries (OECD 2015) has found that, on the whole, boys do better than girls in mathematics in all countries (although this is largely explained by differences in self-confidence/anxiety, such that when comparing boys and girls with a similar level of confidence in mathematics, the gender attainment gap disappears). Girls' levels of post-16 participation in subjects like physics and engineering also remain persistently and significantly below those of boys (for example, see Archer and DeWitt 2017). However, on the whole, the OECD research suggests that girls continue to outperform boys in reading but that a greater proportion of boys than girls fail to attain baseline proficiency in the three core areas (reading, mathematics and science).

In light of these findings, it has been argued that the scale of concern with boys' 'underachievement' fails to take account of the complexity of the picture and is disproportionate to the issue: 'although there are grave concerns among British policy-makers and journalists about "boys' underachievement", Britain is actually one of the five countries where the OECD PISA study (2003) identifies the gender gap as narrowest' (Francis and Skelton 2005: 3).

Serious questions have also been raised about the use of broad-brush statistics within the boys' underachievement debate. For instance, the foundational book by Epstein *et al.* (1998) argues that it is not true to say that all boys are underachieving and all girls are achieving. Rather, they point to complex racialized, classed and gendered patterns of achievement – posing the question as to which boys and which girls are under/achieving. Attention has also been drawn to statistics that demonstrate how boys' achievement is actually rising year on year. Furthermore, data on post-16 employment and earnings indicates that boys tend to be more advantaged than girls in the labour market. Hence feminist academics have argued that the boys' underachievement debate is not only misleading, but is also potentially harmful because it hides the issues and problems experienced by many girls, directs resources towards boys at the expense of girls and deflects attention from more significant achievement gaps in relation to 'race' and social class.

Research evidence: social justice issues for teachers

There is a considerable and wide-ranging body of feminist (and pro-feminist) research pertaining to gender equality in schooling. The journal *Gender and*

Education is also an excellent source for current research and thinking. Below, however, are a couple of selected themes together with some illustrations from research, which raise some pertinent issues for teachers wanting to address gender equity within schools.

The popular focus on addressing 'boys' underachievement' within schools has entailed a range of negative implications for girls, whose needs have slipped off the policy agenda. As a study by Osler and Vincent (2003) details, this situation is playing a key role in generating *girls' hidden exclusion*. For instance, the types of social exclusion often experienced by girls (such as verbal/psychological bullying, truancy, self-exclusion and leaving school due to pregnancy) are often overlooked and inadequately resourced because policy-makers and practitioners are working with a notion of exclusion that is based on the most common features of boys' exclusion. Hence, Osler and Vincent argue, girls' exclusion has become more difficult for professionals to recognize and address.

Particular attention has also been given to the crucial role played by *teachers' gendered expectations and stereotypes* in reproducing gender inequalities within schools. Teachers' (unwitting) gendered expectations of their students can impact on their interactions in class and can play a role in shaping students' aspirations and expectations (for instance, steering them towards particular gender-stereotypical aspirations and career expectations – see, for example, Osgood *et al.* 2006). Indeed, there is a wealth of research evidence documenting how teachers are more likely to describe boys as being 'naturally intelligent' and girls as 'plodding achievers', irrespective of the child's actual attainment (see, for example, Walkerdine 1990). This has been found to be exacerbated particularly within subjects like physics, which are often stereotypically aligned with masculinity (see Carlone 2003). Indeed, it has been argued that many professionals work with an implicit (unwitting) model of the 'ideal pupil' that is constructed in masculine terms. Against this, girls may be relegated to a 'helpful', 'sensible' servicing role (Skelton and Francis 2009), for example, being expected to help facilitate boys' learning and deferring to boys' dominance in the classroom. Numerous studies have also documented how boys continue to take up proportionally more space in schools and playgrounds, dominating these spaces both physically and discursively (see, for example, Skelton 2001; Connolly 2003).

Another important area of concern relates to *students' constructions of gender identity* – particularly the ways in which the 'coolest' and most popular forms of masculinity and femininity are configured. Research has been particularly instructive in developing our understandings of how gender identities are constructed within matrices of power, and how the dominance of particular hegemonic forms of masculinity and femininity can impact negatively on the lives and experiences of 'other' students. Studies, such as those conducted in Australia by Martino and Palotta-Chiarolli (2005), highlight the pain and misery endured by those students with marginalized masculinities and femininities, who experience ridicule and relentless pressure to conform to a very narrow dominant form of popular masculinity/femininity. For instance, Martino and Palotta-Chiarolli (2005) detail boys' and girls' accounts of sexualized bullying that is tolerated in schools because the perpetrators are interpreted as 'just being cool' or 'normal'.

The value of schools working to help students to deconstruct gender stereo-types and to develop broader, more inclusive gender identity constructions is not 'merely' a social justice issue. Large-scale national research undertaken by Warrington and Younger (2002) demonstrates that boys tend to record higher levels of achievement in schools where gender constructions are less extreme and polarized. It has thus been argued that: 'teachers need to develop ways of getting their pupils to reflect and critique "taken-for-granted" but gendered assumptions of classroom/media texts, ways of being organised, managed and assessed, engaging with learning, and so forth' (Francis and Skelton 2005: 149).

To this end, practical assistance and ideas for professional development activities can be found in the following: Mills (2001) – for tackling dominant forms of masculinity and cultures of violence in schools; Martino and Palotta-Chiarolli (2005) – for challenging gender stereotypes among students and staff and reformulating student-welfare policies; Rowan *et al.* (2002) – for addressing gender and literacy; and Keddie *et al.* (2008) – in relation to deconstructing gender stereotyping within secondary schools.

'Race' and ethnicity

Theoretical and policy context

While issues of 'race' and ethnicity tend to occupy the centre-stage of American education policy discourse, they have not achieved such a high-profile status in the UK. This is not to say that questions of 'race'/ethnicity do not feature within UK education debates, but rather that racialized inequalities within schooling have not been positioned as a social justice imperative to quite the same extent. Indeed, it has been argued that there has been a distinct dearth of mainstream discussion and interventions focusing on 'race', ethnicity and achievement in the UK (Gillborn 2008).

For many years, education policy has focused on the differential achievement of students from different ethnic backgrounds. Traditionally, concerns have primarily been expressed about the underachievement (and low rates of progression into post-16 education) of African Caribbean students (especially African Caribbean boys) and, to a slightly lesser extent, Pakistani and Bangladeshi students (see Archer and Francis 2007). However, since the early 2000s, most minority ethnic groups have recorded greater increases in attainment at age 16 than has been noted among White British students (Stokes *et al.* 2015).

Calls have been made, however, to use such statistics with caution – not least because the broad-brush categories employed often lump together groups with very different levels of achievement and there can be considerable variation within 'ethnic groups', not least by gender and social class.

Criticisms have also been made of the ways in which much contemporary education policy engages with issues of 'race'/ethnicity. For instance, attention has been drawn to the subtle yet sustained erasure of the language of 'race' and ethnicity from policy work (Lewis 2000). Reviewing statistical evidence and policy initiatives in this area, Archer and Francis (2007) argue that issues of 'race'/ethnicity have been subject to a pernicious turn in recent policy discourse. In particular, we have argued that education policy explanations of (and proposed strategies for engaging with) underachievement among minority ethnic students tend to deny or ignore racism as a factor. Instead, emphasis tends to be placed on 'cultural', personal and family factors (for example, the notion of a 'poverty of aspirations' within some communities). This approach can pathologize these students and their families and shift the locus of blame/attention away from social structures and institutions and on to minority ethnic families – who are positioned as the primary site of both 'the problem' and any solutions. Furthermore, we have argued that such policy approaches tend to naturalize differences in achievement between ethnic groups and effectively remove the means for engaging with inequalities.

Of course, the pathologization of minority ethnic students and families within education policy is not a recent or new phenomenon. In the 1960s, minority ethnic pupils were treated as explicit educational problems, who were 'bussed' out to different schools in order to 'spread the burden' of educating them. As Mullard (1985) discusses, a 'compensatory' approach dominated, in which minority ethnic students were perceived in terms of 'lack' – hence the primary issue was seen to be how to address and compensate for these pupils' deficits of skills, intelligence, language and so forth. Minority ethnic students were framed as 'problems' that need 'solving' – with interventions being designed to speed up students' assimilation into the mainstream (for example, encouraging them to 'give up' their 'alien' ways).

There have been various discursive shifts over the years in terms of how education policy has approached the schooling of minority ethnic students – although, as critics point out, these have often been built upon problematic conceptualizations of 'race' and ethnicity. For instance, the advent of multiculturalism sought to 'celebrate diversity' yet it attracted criticism for reproducing simplistic, stereotypical views of minority ethnic groups. In particular, the focus upon celebrating aspects of 'culture' has been critiqued for reifying and homogenizing ethnic differences and propagating stereotypical representations of ethnic groups (the 'saris, samosas, steel bands' syndrome). At the same time, this approach also ignored structural inequalities such as racism and could not account for more complex patterns of (under-)achievement (for an extended discussion, see Gillborn 2008).

Anti-racism developed as an alternative to multiculturalism, emphasizing (as the name suggests) the role of racism within minority ethnic students' experiences of schooling. Yet this movement also attracted criticism for its homogenization of all minority ethnic groups under a single banner and for its rather simplistic understanding of racism. Indeed, the MacDonald Report (MacDonald et al. 1989) – set up in response to the murder of a student, Ahmed Iqbal Ullah, by a White peer in the playground of his school – delivered a condemning analysis of the ineffectiveness of the anti-racist policies of the school in question at the time.

The MacPherson Report (MacPherson 1999) – released after the murder of Black London teenager Stephen Lawrence – instigated a new policy awareness regarding the role of institutional racism. The report heralded in new legislation, in the form of the Race Relations Amendment Act (2000), which places a duty on public institutions to tackle racism and promote good race relations. And yet, it has been argued that, in general, different administrations have tended to maintain a 'colour-blind' stance (Gillborn 2001; Majors 2001). Furthermore, it has been argued that most governments seem not to attach the same importance (and do not devote the same resources) to addressing racial and ethnic differences in achievement as compared, for example, to gender. This, Gillborn (2008) argues, indicates an implicit acceptance of racial inequity within British education policy and reflects 'tacit intentionality' on the part of the government – that is, an intention to maintain power structures that privilege Whites (see Strand 2010). In recent years, policy attention has focused primarily on White, working-class under-achievement (for example, House of Commons 2014), although Black Caribbean students and mixed White and Black Caribbean students continue to be two of the lowest-attaining ethnic groups (Strand 2015).

Research evidence: social justice issues for teachers

A considerable amount of research has been conducted to illuminate the social justice issues within schools. The journal *Race, Ethnicity and Education* also provides a useful reference point for reading further about current research and theory in this area. Detailed below are some core themes that may be of particular interest to teachers wishing to grapple with the issues.

A key issue facing minority ethnic students is that of *racist stereotyping*. This not only relates to the tendency for some teachers and schools to hold lower expectations of Black and minority ethnic students, but also to more subtle, complex, specifically racialized stereotypical discourses (Gillborn 2008). In other words, popular discursive constructions of particular groups of students can result in an array of differential implications for the students concerned. For instance, a number of studies have drawn attention to the disjuncture between teachers' expectations for Black girls, and the views and aspirations of the girls and their parents. As I argue elsewhere, there is dominant popular perception that average achievement is 'good enough' for Black girls and boys – whereas Black students and their families often talk about 'wanting more' (Archer 2006). Consequently, aspirational Black students may be forced to negotiate circuitous, strategic, 'backdoor' routes to achieve educational success (Mirza 1992). For example, Loretta, an 18-year-old Black African student from one study, described her experience of being dissuaded from applying to university:

> I was told not to apply because, you know, I just wouldn't get the grade and whatever . . . and the teacher turned round and said to me, 'Well, I think 14.50 [the application fee] is a lot of money.' And I said, 'Do you know what? When I go to university, whatever I make, I'm sure it will cover that 14.50, so I'll just spend it ahead.' I'm really cheeky when I want to be.
>
> (Archer *et al.* 2003: 103)

Loretta did in fact receive three offers of a university place and had achieved the requisite grades at the time of her mock examinations. Loretta's story is, unfortunately, borne out time and again within other research studies. For instance, Marilyn, a young Black woman from another study (Archer *et al.* 2004), recounted:

> I said to Mr W before, like, because – you know when we had to go down to the library and do all the Connexions? He goes, 'Oh, Marilyn, so what do you want to do when you grow up?' And I said I wanted to be a lawyer and he just laughed and he goes, 'You!' and I went, 'Yes' and he goes, 'I don't think so.'

Attention has also been drawn to how dominant stereotypes about Black masculinity operate as pernicious racist discourses. For instance, Sewell (1997) discusses how the identities and behaviours of Black boys in school are often interpreted as being aggressive, problematic and challenging (see also Byfield 2008). These images are also underpinned by popular associations of Black masculinity as hyper-heterosexual and 'macho' – a construction that has its roots in historical racist representations of blackness (hooks 1992; Mama 1995).

'Asian' and Chinese pupils have also long been subject to particular forms of stereotyping – although these have often taken more 'positive' guises, representing such pupils as 'clever', 'quiet', 'behavers and achievers' (Archer and Francis 2005a). However, even these seemingly 'positive' stereotypes have been shown to be experienced as negative and homogenizing by the young people concerned. More recently, there has been a discursive split within representations of 'Asian' pupils – whereby 'achievers' (Indian, predominantly Sikh and Hindu pupils) have been representationally differentiated from 'believers' – namely, Muslim pupils from Pakistani and Bangladeshi backgrounds. The impact of Islamophobia on representations of Muslims (but particularly boys) as 'problematic' pupils is documented elsewhere (Archer 2003). A sustained critique has also been mounted regarding racist popular constructions of Asian/Muslim girls as passive and oppressed 'hapless dependants' whose families are more concerned with getting them married off than pursuing an education (for example, Ahmad 2001; Shain 2003; Bhopal 2010).

In addition to the issue of stereotyping, minority ethnic pupils continue to experience *verbal and physical violence* within schools. For instance, Muslim young people in a town in the north-west of England recounted their near-daily experiences of being spat at, insulted and attacked (Archer 2003). They also, however, described more subtle manifestations of racism from their peers – for instance, explaining their confusion about how their White peers would be friendly in school but would 'ignore us' in public at the weekends. A study by Becky Francis and myself also records how British-Chinese pupils regularly experience name-calling and how British-Chinese boys complain that they are regularly taunted (as 'Bruce Lee') and are forced to fight by their male peers (Archer and Francis 2005b; 2007). As pupils from across minority ethnic backgrounds point out, there is still a challenge for schools in how to resolve incidents of violence. The issue seems particularly acute in the case of those boys who choose to use violence back in retaliation – with many complaining that an even-handed punishment of both sides is 'unfair' – not least when the original abuse may remain unaddressed (and hence is perceived to be sanctioned by the school). This illustrates the complexity of enacting social justice in schools – although it does also indicate how addressing racism may also entail a complementary focus on challenging hegemonic forms of masculinity.

Attention has also been drawn to the importance of ensuring an equitable *school ethos and organization*, in which parents' and students' various needs and values are valued and respected. Within educational policy, this is often discussed in terms of the provision of special resources (for example, halal food, prayer rooms) and the adoption of practices and rules that can accommodate cultural and religious differences (for example, flexible rules around uniform, permitting the wearing of hijab, etc.). However, critics have argued that such measures can only go so far, and that additional efforts may be required with respect to ensuring, for instance, that the curriculum represents the histories, interests and identities of diverse ethnic, cultural and religious groups. Debates also continue around the imbalances that exist in terms of state funding of faith schools – with proportion-ally far more 'White' faith/denominational schools being supported as compared, for instance, to Muslim faith schools (see, for example, Parker-Jenkins *et al.* 2004). Important concerns have also been raised that the voices of Black and minority ethnic parents remain absent from many schools at both formal and informal levels (see Crozier and Reay 2005).

Social class

Theoretical and policy context

Within current education policy, issues pertaining to social class tend to be framed in terms of working-class pupils' (under-)achievement and low rates of progression into post-16 education. Statistics indicate that young people from poorer socio-economic backgrounds (and those on free school meals) achieve lower academic results than their more affluent peers (DfE 2016). Students from working-class backgrounds also remain severely and persistently under-represented at university level (Archer *et al.* 2003) – with recent analysis suggesting that the proportion of working-class students attending Russell Group universities has stalled over the last decade and remains well below the proportion of those from more affluent backgrounds (TES 2016). Various initiatives and outreach schemes have been introduced over the years in an effort to support achievement and to encourage more working-class young people to stay on in further and higher education – although arguably these have had little whole-scale effect.

While it is widely agreed that the achievement and progression of working-class young people are an issue that requires policy attention, there are also quite stark differences of opinion regarding the potential causes of, and solutions to, the issue. For instance, many policies have been criticized for adopting a deficit approach to working-class young people and their families because they assume that lower rates of achievement and post-16 progression are the result of students' 'faulty cognitions' and/or lack of information/knowledge (see, for example, Thomas 2001). These assumptions are evidenced within policy references to students' 'low aspirations' and family cultures that do not value education. In contrast, critics have argued that the generation of patterns of working-class achievement and post-16 progression is far more complex, being produced through an interplay of structural and institutional inequalities together with social, cultural, emotional and identity factors (as illustrated further below).

Alongside these policy debates, social class also remains a hotly contested concept within sociological and academic circles. Opinion is divided as to how best to define, understand and theorize social class, and debates rage as to whether the concept of social class is even still relevant and useful. Within these debates it is noticeable that a 'culturalist' approach to theorizing social class is proving attractive (see, for example, Savage 2000; Skeggs 2004), particularly among educationalists concerned with promoting social justice (see, for example, Reay 2002). This approach treats class as a complex concept that is as much to do with people's tastes, consumption, values and feelings about their identities and lived experiences as it is to do with their 'objective' position in occupational and economic terms.

Research evidence: social justice issues for teachers

So what can research tell us about the social justice issues facing schools with respect to working-class students? The work of Diane Reay (2002; 2006) provides a particularly useful starting point for reading further about social class inequalities and schooling. The following provides a thumbnail sketch/brief overview of some key themes emerging from recent studies conducted with young people in UK secondary schools.

Attention has been drawn to the social justice implications of the *school as a classed institution*. For instance, various studies record how working-class young people report feeling excluded by the 'middle class', 'posh' language, ethos and curriculum of schools. For instance, interviews conducted with working-class girls in two separate London studies (Archer *et al.* 2004; 2005) revealed how the girls felt alienated by their schools' middle-class institutional habitus. They described feeling estranged from the 'high brow' speech of some of their teachers and complained that there was a gulf of understanding between their 'common' selves and 'posh' teachers – who, they felt, were not 'on their level'. This finding has also been noted in relation to working-class students in higher education (see, for example, Read *et al.* 2003). A number of working-class students also experienced aspects of the curriculum as irrelevant to their own lives. For instance, a student in one study (Archer 2006) was adamant that learning Spanish is irrelevant because 'it's unlikely for me to go out to Spain'. She continued, 'I can't speak enough language anyway, even English, I'm common and that's that' – revealing the psychic damage inflicted on those who are already judged to be 'lacking' and of lesser 'value' within dominant systems.

Various studies have also flagged up how *classed relations between teachers, students and parents* are implicated within the reproduction of inequalities. For instance, many working-class young people report experiencing a gulf of understanding and (an albeit sometimes unintentional) lack of respect from teachers/schools due to the disjuncture between the classed backgrounds, identities and assumptions of home and school (Archer *et al.* 2010). For instance, some students' report feeling 'misunderstood' by teachers and studies have highlighted how young people's attempts to generate a sense of value and worth in their lives (for example, through particular 'styles' of ways of being) may be interpreted as inappropriate or 'anti-education' by middle-class professionals (see Archer *et al.* 2007). Furthermore, students have complained that interactions with their families at parents' evenings can be disrespectful. As one girl put it: 'Some of the things they say . . . it's making them look at my mum stupidly, and I'm like "Don't talk to my mum like that, she's right there, she understands what you're saying, she's not dumb"' (quoted in Archer *et al.* 2004).

Working-class parents also describe feeling 'looked down on' by schools and are subsequently wary about further contact. This may, in turn, be interpreted by schools as evidence that these parents do not care sufficiently about their children's education – so feeding into a cycle of bad feeling and/or miscommunication. For similar reasons (and exacerbated by tighter constraints on time and resources), working-class parents also tend to be less fully or less frequently involved in consultations regarding how their children's schools are organized and run (Crozier and Reay 2005). Class differences between home and school can entail a lack of understanding from both sides regarding the identities, motivations and contexts of the other. There is also, of course, evidence of instances of more overt class prejudice – for instance, in one study a teacher's description of working-class families as a 'bolshie and obnoxious', 'underclass' of 'just bloody useless parents' (Archer 2006). All of these examples illustrate the symbolic violence that may be experienced as the result of living in positions of inequality and subordination and how knowing that you are 'looked down on' within society constitutes what Sennett and Cobb (1993) have termed the 'hidden injuries' of class.

A further important consideration concerns the ways in which *material inequalities* can impact on the lives and education of working-class students. Less affluent families obviously have fewer economic (financial) resources with which to support their children's learning – whereas middle-class families benefit from having the money to pay for more (or more exotic) school trips, electronic mobile devices/Internet, reference materials, extra tutoring and a whole host of extra-curricula 'enrichment' activities (see Vincent and Ball 2006). Financial resources are not the only type of resource, however, and working-class families may experience tighter constraints on resources such as time and physical space. For instance, some working-class young people may find it more difficult to do their homework due to a lack of space at home and/or because they provide important caring responsibilities for parents or siblings. Where families experience different levels of material and cultural wealth, this can also generate symbolic violences; for example, where young people feel looked down on because they cannot afford to purchase particular uniforms or go on school trips. Disparities in wealth also strongly shape the types of school that students attend – an issue exacerbated by 'school choice' policies. Indeed, working-class students are disproportionately represented in 'sink' and 'demonized' schools with poorer physical environments and resources (Reay and Lucey 2003). They are also less likely to see higher education (particularly the more prestigious institutions) as either open or affordable (Archer *et al.* 2010).

Concluding thoughts

This chapter has discussed how the concept of social justice can be a useful tool for education professionals. However, this is not to imply that teachers are responsible for either causing or indeed solving all societal problems and injustices! As Gewirtz (2006) discusses, there are no 'purely' egalitarian policies or practices, and the extent to which particular actions are equitable will be mediated by the context and according to the different parties involved. Indeed, it would be unrealistic to expect teachers to be able to change national government policies – and of course we must be mindful that teachers must work within particular sets of requirements, responsibilities and constraints, all of which demand attention, time and resources. However, it is suggested that by developing an understanding of the complexity of enacting social justice in practice and by fostering an awareness of the various types of issues that might be encountered, teachers may be able to create small (but significant) changes in their classrooms and schools. To this end, I have outlined a model for understanding social justice and have tried to draw attention to a few equity issues (in relation to gender, 'race'/ethnicity and social class) which may not otherwise be necessarily apparent – as they often arise as (unintended) implications from wider policies or 'common-sense' ways of thinking. This mode of reflection might be particularly valuable for teachers who come from 'dominant' (for example, White or middle-class) backgrounds, because we are rarely obliged to reflect on our privilege and the taken-for-granted assumptions that it can bring. At times this can be a difficult, even painful, process with no easy answers (Francis *et al.* 2017) – but it also carries the potential to be incredibly important and fruitful. In sum, the chapter has tried to open up ways of thinking about 'equality' – in all its complexity – as part of a collective project of creating an education system that can be experienced as fair and socially just by all students, teachers and parents.

References

Ahmad, F. (2001) Modern traditions? British Muslim women and academic achievement, *Gender and Education*, 13(2): 137–52.

Archer, L. (2003) *'Race', Masculinity and Schooling: Muslim Boys and Education*. Buckingham: Open University Press.

Archer, L. (2005) Re/theorising 'difference' in feminist research, *Women's Studies International Forum*, 27: 459–73.

Archer, L. (2005) The impossibility of girls' educational 'success': entanglements of gender, 'race', class and sexuality in the production and problematisation of educational femininities. Paper for ESRC Seminar Series 'Girls in Education 3–16', Cardiff, 24 November 2005.

Archer, L. and DeWitt, J. (2017) *Understanding Young People's Science Aspirations*. London: Routledge.

Archer, L. and Francis, B. (2005a) 'They never go off the rails like other ethnic groups': teachers' constructions of British Chinese pupils' gender identities and approaches to learning, *British Journal of Sociology of Education*, 26(2): 165–82.

Archer, L. and Francis, B. (2005b) British Chinese pupils' and parents' constructions of racism, *Race, Ethnicity and Education*, 8(4): 387–407.

Archer, L. and Francis, B. (2007) *Understanding Minority Ethnic Achievement: Race, Class, Gender and 'Success'*. London: Routledge.

Archer, L., Halsall, A. and Hollingworth, S. (2007) Class, gender, (hetero)sexuality and schooling: working class girls' engagement with schooling and post-16 aspirations, *British Journal of Sociology of Education*, 28(2): 165–80.

Archer, L., Halsall, A., Hollingworth, S. and Mendick, H. (2005) *'Dropping Out and Drifting Away: An Investigation of Factors Affecting Inner-City Pupils' Identities, Aspirations and Post-16 Routes*, Final Report to the Esmee Fairbairn Foundation. London: IPSE.

Archer, L., Hollingworth, S. and Halsall, A. (2007) 'University's not for me – I'm a Nike person': inner-city young people's negotiations of 'new' class identities and educational engagement, *Sociology*, 41(2): 210–37.

Archer, L., Hollingworth, S. and Mendick, H. (2010) *Urban Youth and Schooling*. Maidenhead: Open University/McGraw-Hill.

Archer, L., Hutchings, M. and Ross, A. (2003) *Higher Education and Social Class: Issues of Exclusion and Inclusion*. London: RoutledgeFalmer.

Archer, L., Maylor, U., Read, B. and Osgood, J. (2004) *An Exploration of the Attitudinal, Social and Cultural Factors Impacting on Year 10 Student Progression: Final Report to London West Learning and Skills Council*. London: IPSE.

Bhopal, K. (2010) *Asian Women in Higher Education: Shared Communities*. Stoke-on-Trent: Trentham Books.

Byfield, C. (2008) *Black Boys Can Make It: How They Overcome the Obstacles to University in the UK and USA*. Stoke-on-Trent: Trentham Books.

Carlone, H.B. (2003) (Re)producing good science students: girls' participation in high school physics, *Journal of Women and Minorities in Science and Engineering*, 9(1): 17–34.

Connolly, P. (2003) Gendered and gendering spaces: playgrounds in the early years, in C. Skelton and B. Francis (eds) *Boys and Girls in the Primary Classroom*. Buckingham: Open University Press.

Connolly, P. (2008) A critical review of some recent developments in quantitative research on gender and attainment in the UK, *British Journal of Sociology of Education*, 29(3): 249–60.

Crozier, G. and Reay, D. (eds) (2005) *Activating Participation*. Stoke-on-Trent: Trentham Books.

DePalma, R. and Atkinson, E. (eds) (2008) *Invisible Boundaries: Addressing Sexualities Equality in Children's Worlds*. Stoke-on-Trent: Trentham Books.

DfE (Department for Education) (2016) *Revised GCSE and Equivalent Results in England: 2014 to 2015*, https://www.gov.uk/government/statistics/revised-gcse-and-equivalent-results-in-england-2014-to-2015, accessed 20 February 2017.

DfES (Department for Education and Skills) (2003) *Using the National Healthy School Stand to Raise Boys' Achievement*. Wetherby: Health Development Agency.

DfES (Department for Education and Skills) (2005) *Standards*, http://www.standards.dfes. gov.uk/ethnicminorities/raising_achievement. Accessed 30 May 2006.

DfES (Department for Education and Skills) (2006a) *Ethnic Minority Achievement*, at http://www.standards.dfes.gov.uk/ethnicminorities/, accessed 30 May 2006.

DfES (Department for Education and Skills) (2006b) *Black Pupils' Achievement Programme*, http://www.standards.dfes.gov.uk/ethnicminorities/raising_achievement/bpa programme/, accessed 30 May 2006.

Donald, J. and Rattansi, A. (1992) *Race, Culture and Difference*. London: Sage.

Epstein, D., Elwood, J., Hey, V. and Maw, J. (1998) Schoolboy frictions: feminism and 'failing boys', in D. Epstein, J. Elwood, V. Hey and J. Maw (eds) *Failing Boys?* Buckingham: Open University Press.

Francis, B. (2006) Heroes or zeroes? The discursive positioning of 'underachieving boys' in English neo-liberal education policy, *Journal of Education Policy*, 21(2): 187–200.

Francis, B., Mills, M. and Lupton, R. (2017) Towards social justice in education: contradictions and dilemmas, *Journal of Education Policy*, 32 (4): 414–431.

Francis, B. and Skelton, C. (2005) *Reassessing Gender and Achievement*. London: Routledge.

Fraser, N. (1997) *Justice Interruptus*. New York: Routledge.

Gewirtz, S. (2002) *The Managerial School*. London: Routledge.

Gewirtz, S. (2006) Towards a contextualised analysis of social justice, *Educational Philosophy and Theory*, 38(1): 69–81.

Gillborn, D. (1990) *Race, Ethnicity and Education: Teaching and Learning in Multi-ethnic Schools*. London: Unwin Hyman.

Gillborn, D. (2001) Racism, policy and the (mis)education of Black children, in R. Majors (ed.) *Educating Our Black Children*. London: RoutledgeFalmer.

Gillborn, D. (2005) Education policy as an act of white supremacy: whiteness, critical race theory and education reform, *Journal of Education Policy*, 20(4): 485–505.

Gillborn, D. (2008) *Racism and Education: Coincidence or Conspiracy?* London and New York: Routledge.

Griffiths, M. (2003) *Action for Social Justice in Education: Fairly Different*. Maidenhead: Open University Press.

hooks, b. (1992) *Black Looks*. London: Turnaround Press.

House of Commons (2014) *Underachievement in Education by White Working Class Children*, http://www.parliament.uk/business/committees/committees-a-z/commons-select/education-committee/inquiries/parliament-2010/white-working-class-underachievement/, accessed 20 February 2017.

Keddie, A., Mills, C. and Mills, M. (2008) Struggles to subvert the gendered field: issues of masculinity, rurality and class, *Pedagogy, Culture and Society*, 16(3): 193–205.

Lewis, G. (2000) Discursive histories, the pursuit of multiculturalism and social policy, in G. Lewis, S. Gewirtz and J. Clarke (eds) *Rethinking Social Policy*. London: Open University and Sage.

Macdonald, I., Bhavnani, R., Khan, L. and John, G. (1989) *Murder in the Playground*. London: Longsight Press.

MacPherson, W. (1999) *The Stephen Lawrence Enquiry: Report of an Enquiry by Sir William MacPherson*. London: Stationery Office.

Majors, R. (2001) Introduction, in R. Majors (ed.) *Educating Our Black Children*. London: RoutledgeFalmer.

Mama, A. (1995) *Beyond the Masks: Race, Gender and Subjectivity*. London: Routledge.

Martino, W. and Palotta-Chiarolli, M. (2005) *Being Normal is the Only Way to Be: Adolescent Perspectives on Gender and School*. Sydney: University of New South Wales Press.

Mills, M. (2001) *Challenging Violence in Schools*. Buckingham: Open University Press.

Mirza, H. (1992) *Young, Female and Black*. London: Routledge.

Mullard, C. (1985) Multiracial education in Britain, in M. Arnot (ed.) *Race and Gender: Equal Opportunities Policies in Education*. Milton Keynes: Open University Press.

NCIHE (1997) *Higher Education and the Learning Society: The Dearing Report*. London: Stationery Office.

OECD (2015) *The ABC of Gender Equality in Education: Aptitude, Behaviour, Confidence, PISA*. Paris: OECD Publishing, http://dx.doi.org/10.1787/9789264229945-en. Accessed 10 Aug 2016

Osgood, J., Francis, B. and Archer, L. (2006) Gendered identities and work placement: why don't boys' care? *Journal of Education Policy*, 21(3): 305–42.

Osler, A. and Vincent, V. (2003) *Girls and Exclusion: Rethinking the Agenda*. London: RoutledgeFalmer.

Parker-Jenkins, M., Hartas, D. and Irving, B.A. (2004) *In Good Faith: Schools, Religion and Public Funding*. Ashgate: Aldershot.

Power, S. and Gewirtz, S. (2001) Reading education action zones, *Journal of Education Policy*, 16(1): 39–51.

Read, B., Archer, L. and Leathwood, C. (2003) Challenging cultures? Student conceptions of 'belonging' and 'isolation' at a post-1992 university, *Studies in Higher Education*, 28(3): 261–77.

Reay, D. (2002) Shaun's story: Troubling discourses of white working-class masculinities, *Gender and Education*, 14: 221–33.

Reay, D. (2006) The zombie stalking English schools: social class and educational inequality, *Sociology*, 42(4): 691–708.

Reay, D. and Lucey, H. (2003) The limits of choice: children and inner-city schooling, *Sociology*, 37: 121–43.

Rowan, L., Knobel, M., Bigum, C. and Lankshear, C. (2002) *Boys, Literacies and Schooling*. Buckingham: Open University Press.

Savage, M. (2000) *Class Analysis and Social Transformation*. Buckingham: Open University Press.

Sennett, R. and Cobb, J. (1993) *Hidden Injuries of Class*. Cambridge: Polity Press.

Sewell, T. (1997) *Black Masculinities and Schooling*. Stoke-on-Trent: Trentham Books.

Shain, F. (2003) *The Schooling and Identity of Asian Girls*. Stoke-on-Trent: Trentham Books.

Skeggs, B. (2004) *Class, Self, Culture*. London: Sage.

Skelton, C. (2001) *Schooling the Boys*. Buckingham: Open University Press.

Skelton, C. and Francis, B. (2009) *Feminism and the Schooling Scandal*. London: Routledge.

Stokes, L., Rolfe, H., Hudson-Sharp, N. and Stevens, S. (2015) *A Compendium of Evidence on Ethnic Minority Resilience to the Effects of Deprivation on Attainment. DfE Research Report*. London: HMSO.

Strand, S. (2010) Do some schools narrow the gap? Differential school effectiveness by ethnicity, gender, poverty and prior attainment, *School Effectiveness and School Improvement*, 21(3): 289–314.

Strand, S. (2015) *Ethnicity, Deprivation and Educational Achievement at Age 16 in England: Trends over Time. Annex to Compendium of Evidence on Ethnic Minority Resilience to the Effects of Deprivation on Attainment*. London: HMSO.

TES (2016) Proportion of working-class students at some top universities lower than a decade ago, 18 February, https://www.tes.com/news/school-news/breaking-news/proportion-working-class-students-some-top-universities-lower-a, accessed 20 February 2017.

Thomas, L. (2001) *Widening Participation in Post-Compulsory Education*. London: Continuum.

Vincent, C. and Ball, S. (2006) *Choice and Class Practices*. London: Routledge.

Vincent, C. and Martin, J. (2005) Parents as citizens: making the case, in G. Crozier and D. Reay (eds) *Activating Participation*. Stoke-on-Trent: Trentham Books.

Walkerdine, V. (1990) *Schoolgirl Fictions*. London: Verso.

Warrington, M. and Younger, M. (2002) Speech at the 'Raising boys' achievement' conference, Homerton College, Cambridge, 11 July.

Young, I.M. (1990) *Justice and the Politics of Difference*. Princeton, NJ: Princeton University Press.

PART 3
Teaching and learning

10

An introduction to key learning theories and their application in educational practice
HEATHER KING AND JILL HOHNSTEIN

Introduction

Learning is commonplace and ubiquitous – it is something we all do every day, whether consciously or unconsciously. We learn, we practise, we become proficient. But how can we best understand and explain learning? And, perhaps most significantly for us as educators, how can we best support learning? In this chapter we seek to answer these questions by introducing some of the key theories that address learning, and by implication, also offer guidance and insights for teaching.

As Illeris (2007) has argued, learning can refer to an outcome, a process or to an interaction. As an outcome, learning can be defined as a relatively permanent change in thought, ability or behaviour that results from experience. As a process, learning describes the mental and physical processes leading to changes in knowledge and ability. As an interaction, learning emphasizes the significance of the interplay between an individual and his or her environment (including other people) which shapes the nature of the learning. Theories of learning variously emphasize the aspects of outcomes, processes or interaction, with some focusing on changes within a single individual, while others see learning as a social affair. Others acknowledge the individual and the social elements of learning but focus on its outward expression. In short, learning theories and their implications for practice overlap and build upon one another.

As a body of knowledge, theories of learning offer rich insights for teaching. However, the cumulative nature of such theories can make it difficult to organize a chapter discussing their various contributions! Our chosen approach here is first of all to introduce the key theories of learning, beginning with those that primarily focus on the individual before moving on to theories that focus on learning as a social affair. In the second half of the chapter, we turn our attention to the way in which these theories, in conjunction with perspectives on student motivation and students' mental models, among others, may be applied to our understanding of teaching. Our aim, therefore, is to help you understand what may be happening to your students as and when they learn, and moreover to support you to reflect on your own professional practice.

An introduction to key theories of learning

We begin our discussion of learning theories by considering those which seek to explain how changes in knowledge or abilities occur within the individual learner. For the most part, it is possible to align the theories with one of two categories: behaviourist or cognitivist. Some, however, span both. Behaviourism acknowledges the role of the environment and the effects of externally observable inputs, which, in turn, prompt externally observable outputs. Cognitivist theories, meanwhile, focus primarily on the internal workings of the mind.

Behaviourism is generally related to the philosophy of Hobbes ([1651] 1968), who suggested that humans are simply material systems, operating by way of inputs and outputs, and thus constructs such as 'mind' and 'free will' do not affect the way people function. Extreme behaviourism claims that infants enter the world as 'blank slates' and learn about the world through various forms of association, including conditioning, both classical (Pavlov 1927) and operant (Thorndike 1898; Skinner 1974). Classical conditioning can be thought of as the training of behaviour on the basis of stimulus and response. For example, a dog has innate responses (salivation) to a stimulus (food), which gradually become associated (through repeated pairing) with a new stimulus (a bell). The learned behaviour here is the salivation in response to the sound of a bell. Operant conditioning may be defined as shaping behaviour through incentives and punishments. A monkey may learn to press a lever to dispense food by at first giving it food when it approaches the part of the cage where the lever is positioned. Then, as time progresses, food is given only when the monkey touches the lever. Finally, the monkey must actually press the lever to receive food. While these examples are from the animal world, the same principles are thought to also apply in human learning. For example, it used to be common in foreign language classrooms for students to respond with the word in the foreign language that matched the teacher's utterance of the English word. Thus, the teacher's utterance of 'thank you' would be paired by French-learning students with the word 'merci'. The teacher's use of praise, or positive evaluation, to reinforce the accurately paired responses can be seen as an example of the application of operant conditioning. That is, the praise will be seen by the students as a reward and will serve to inform them of their correct response, which will in turn allow them to more firmly establish the use of the word 'merci' in their vocabulary. While the behaviourist perspective has lost the respect of researchers over the years due to its emphasis on the observable at the expense of internal thought processes, its elements can be found in much of human behaviour, including the aforementioned pairing of response and evaluation.

Building on the behaviourist tradition which sees learning as a series of inputs and outputs is the theory of learning as information processing (Newell and Simon 1972). In this theory, a key metaphor is that of the computer program: there is a series of specialist features in human cognition that develop over time, including working memory, long-term memory and executive function: these can be seen as the mind's 'hardware'. The 'software' is the sets of experiences and environmental 'input' that learners receive over time. With this model of learning, then, children take in information which is then processed by the mechanisms in the mind, and some output is produced (e.g., being able to come up with the multiplication tables). The way information is processed is clearly cognitive but the learner is entirely dependent upon the 'input' he or she gets from those around them. Over time, inputs and outputs form a connected network that serves to link concepts which are then accessed as 'knowledge'. In addition to its behaviourist roots, Newell and Simon's theory also suggests that the brain's internal processes are key in shaping the nature of knowledge. In this way, the theory also resonates with ideas that have their basis in cognitivist perspectives.

Cognitive theories consider what is going on in the mind, and in this way propose mechanisms to explain changes in learners' abilities to solve problems, understand complex situations, and work with relatively abstract notions. One set of cognitivist theories stipulates that a learner progresses with age through a series of stages, each affording a greater degree of intellectual ability. Jean Piaget (1952; Piaget and Inhelder 1958) is perhaps the best known of the stage theorists. His ideas suggest that when babies are born, and for the first two years of life in the sensorimotor period, their primary objective is to explore the world around them using their developing skills to move about, sense and manipulate objects, and understand their own agency. From age 2 until age 7, children are said to pass through a period known as the pre-operational stage, in which they tend to be egocentric in their thoughts and not be able to complete 'operations' that older children can do. Once children have entered the concrete operations stage (age 7–12) of Piaget's theory, they are able to operate on the things around them. For example, they can begin to conceive volume, number and mass, and, significantly, identify changes (or not) in these measurements. A classic Piagetian task involves pouring equal amounts of liquid into two glasses of the same shape and size. After the child has agreed that the glasses contain the same amount of liquid, the liquid from one glass is then poured into a different-sized glass (either taller and thinner or shorter and squatter). Children who are able to mentally reverse the operation of pouring the liquid will understand that the total volume is conserved. Children who have not passed into the concrete operations stage will say that the amount of liquid has changed, tending to focus on only one of the dimensions of the glasses (e.g., height). After the age of 12, children pass into the formal operations (or adult) stage of cognitive development. This stage is characterized by the ability to think abstractly about many different concepts and to use logical reasoning. Over the years, many people have challenged the idea that children pass through a discrete set of stages, particularly at the ages Piaget proposed. For example, several researchers, including Metz (1995) and Adey et al. (2002), have argued that children are capable of dealing with abstract notions at the relatively young age of 7 if, that is, they have appropriate guidance and practice. Despite the questioning of the precise ages at which children move from one stage to another, there has been relatively little challenge to Piaget's idea that there are discrete stages or the order in which they occur.

Piaget (1952; Piaget and Inhelder 1958) proposed that children (and other learners) have a need to feel that the information they receive from the world matches with their understanding of the world, a concept he referred to as 'equilibrium'. When meeting ideas that the learner already understands well, or does not experience as new, there is no conflict and equilibrium is maintained. However, when the child encounters a new piece of information, there are two different processes the mind can engage in to make sense of the new material: assimilation and accommodation. When the information does not challenge previous understandings, the learner can just assimilate the information into the existing structure. For example, children may know that fish have a general oblong shape, with fins, and that they live in water. They may also know that there are different varieties of fish, including goldfish, cod, sharks and tuna. When the child encounters something with similar properties and is told it is also a fish but is called a trout, he or she has little problem assimilating this new type of fish into his or her extant set of fish. However, to explain the progression from one stage to another, Piaget and his followers proposed that an encounter with a new construct or experience which refutes an existing belief will prompt the reorganization of one's mental framework. This 'accommodation' of a new concept results in a new way of thinking, and ultimately the progression into the next stage of conceptualization. To follow from the example of fish above, when this same child learns about whales, which have a similar shape to fish, complete with fins, and also live in the water, but are not fish because they breathe by surfacing and have warm blood (unlike fish), in order to successfully understand, the child must accommodate her fish concept to exclude whales and other fish-shaped mammals. This process of accommodation can at times prove rather tricky for children.

The process through which learners build or construct new mental models based on previous knowledge shaped by their stage of development that Piagetian theory above describes is known as constructivism. There are many 'forms' of constructivism that variously preface the role of social groups (Berger and Luckmann 1966; Vygotsky 1978; Rogoff 1990; see Palincsar 1998 for a full account), highlight the role of context (discussed further below) or focus solely on the learner (von Glasersfeld 1995; see Hardy and Taylor 1997 for a full discussion). However, broadly speaking, constructivism proposes that learners actively create their own understandings, to make sense of the world around them. In other words, constructing new understanding is an active process on the part of the learner. Learning is not achieved by 'pouring' content into a learner's brain – the learners must engage in effort to make sense of such content and build the appropriate mental schema for themselves.

In emphasizing the learner's role in constructing information, constructivism can be to seen to underscore the notion of discovery learning. Often attributed to Bruner (1961), discovery learning involves the learners using prior experience combined with experimental trial and error to 'discover' the answer to a problem and to make sense of the information by themselves. As such, both discovery learning and constructivism emphasize the learner's agency in learning situations; however, discovery learning is sometimes interpreted as occurring in a vacuum, in the absence of other people. Critiques of discovery learning, therefore, do not doubt the importance of the individual constructing mental models; rather they question the extent to which individuals are able to apply problem-solving rules or strategies without appropriate help (Kirschner, Sweller and Clark 2006). Without due guidance, the individual may construct mental models that do not conform to canonical understanding, or more basically, become frustrated if they are unable to 'discover' an answer. Inquiry-based learning (Schwab 1966) similarly challenges learners to explore ideas and to discover the nature of phenomena and relationships between variables. It is particularly associated with science learning: indeed, both discovery learning and inquiry-based learning are purported to be the foundational principles of many hands-on exhibits in science centres.

The support and guidance by others, such as parents, teachers or one's peers, form the central pillar of social constructivist theories (Vygotsky 1978). The support is usually afforded in the form of language or demonstration, although the 'other' person need not be physically present. For example, a learner may interact with the ideas of another by engaging with the products of their work, such as reading a book, or viewing an art work (Bakhtin 1981).

Other interpretations of constructivism emphasize the role of the context in enabling learning. For example, Lave and Wenger (1991) argue that learning is more likely if the learning is part of one's daily life. The concepts to be learnt are thus not abstract, but instead involve making meaning out of the real activities of one's environment. Moreover, they suggest that the learning is co-constructed with others in the social context. Thus, the theory of situated learning foregrounds the role of the social process but also embeds learning in particular physical and social contexts. The theory also holds that knowledge is acquired situationally and thus only transfers to similar situations. Indeed, a classic study of shoppers by Lave (1988) illustrates this point. In the study, adult shoppers were found to be able to add complex figures to calculate a shopping bill when in the context of a supermarket, yet unable to add up a similar set of numbers when presented as a formal 'test'. The participants' skills of totting up a shopping bill had been acquired situationally as a result of regular experience and the individual's need to be able to accurately determine how much their shopping would cost. In lieu of any context, the addition task became abstract, unfamiliar and lacking in meaning, resulting in participants failing the task. Since studies of this type, other scholars have suggested that situational learning can transfer to other contexts if participants are afforded enough practice. Bransford and Schwartz (1999), for example, report studies which found greater evidence of an individual's application of a skill to a new context when asked to do it again on a second day.

Alongside practice and repetition, learning can be supported by the active role of the educator. Sometimes the 'coaching' is implicit or tacit, such as in the case of a parent almost subconsciously steering their child's choice of words or actions. In more formal education settings such as the classroom, the coaching tends to be more explicit – the teacher assumes a particular position in the room and may define their role as one of instruction. To be most effective in their instruction, the teacher needs to have a sense of the learner's initial ability and an ideal destination. In describing the distance between the starting point and the end, Vygotsky (1978) coined the term 'zone of proximal development' (ZPD). Specifically, the ZPD is defined as the area between what an individual can accomplish on their own and that which they could achieve with the help of someone more experienced. It therefore identifies an individual's potential level of understanding or skill in a more dynamic way than do many forms of knowledge assessment. Take, for example, a child working on problems of multiplication. This child may be able to work through problems that involve single-digit numbers by him- or herself. However, this same child can potentially solve problems involving the multiplication of two-digit numbers with the aid of a teacher or parent. The child's ZPD with respect to multiplication lies between multiplying single-digit numbers and two-digit numbers. The role of the educator, meanwhile, is most significant when helping the child to make sense of concepts at the upper end of their ZPD rather than either above or below. With practice at the upper end of the ZPD, the child will eventually be able to multiply two-digit numbers on his or her own.

In the paragraphs above we have discussed the implications arising from individually focused theories, and those that consider the role of the social environment. A final perspective, which to a certain extent builds on both ends of the learning spectrum, concerns theories of identity development. The notion of identity development has gained considerable interest in recent years (for example, see Nasir and Hand 2008; Barton and Tan 2010; Seth *et al.* 2011). As Wenger (1998: 125) has noted, learning is 'not just an accumulation of skills and information, but a process of becoming, to become a certain person or, conversely, to avoid becoming a certain person'. In this way, identity can be thought of as the pivot between the individual and the social world in which the individual operates. Over time, experiences and interests build up and combine to create a degree of coherence which is expressed as an identity: individuals see themselves, and importantly others similarly recognize them, as being 'science-y', or a 'languages person', or someone who is 'arty', and so on. Without time and regularity of experience, however, new knowledge, skills and opinions can remain fragmented, unconnected to other experiences, and a coherent identity fails to form (Gee 2000).

In considering learning as identity, itself shaped in turn by various experiences over time, the sheer multiplicity of players and events that determine learning becomes clear. The theory of learning as identity formation also underscores the complexity of learning, especially if considered in conjunction with theories from behaviourist or cognitivist and social constructivist traditions. We turn now to consider how an understanding of such theories can help us as educators to support and facilitate the complex process of learning.

Applying learning theories to educational practice

In the middle decades of the last century, behaviourism was the favoured theory to explain and guide educational approaches. In some respects, it still holds sway in the ways that school systems are designed today. For instance, many schools now opt in to a rewards/points system that allows students to accumulate points for good behaviour and high marks, and then trade them in for attractive 'prizes', such as book vouchers or leisure centre passes. Behaviourism also offers us insights into the ways in which either positive or negative reinforcements affect and incentivize future learning behaviours. For example, upon receiving praise for attempting to answer a question, students may be more willing to try to answer others. If, however, a student receives admonishment, or ridicule, or some other negative response for answering a question incorrectly, they are unlikely to try again. Their peers observing this interaction may also be wary of trying at all.

In understanding the ways in which praise and admonishment affect behaviour we point to the work of Dweck and Leggett (1998). These authors propose that the manner by which an individual completes a task will depend on the extent to which he or she is driven by a performance orientation or a mastery orientation. A performance orientation is related to extrinsic motivation and is exemplified by the desire to achieve a particular score or grade, or response from a teacher. Mastery orientation, on the other hand, describes the situation when an individual pays attention and expends effort because they want to understand the material at hand. Hidi and Renninger's (2006) framework, meanwhile, connects motivation with developing interest. They suggest that one's interest and commitment to a task can exist at four sequential phases progressing from situational interest when a learner's attention is initially piqued through to well-developed personal interest which is self-sustaining.

Clearly, the aim for an educator is to create a learning environment which promotes intrinsic motivation and mastery orientation by providing experiences which foster deep self-sustaining interest. This is no small order, particularly for educators responsible for a whole class of very different children! To encourage mastery orientation, research suggests that learners be supported in developing learning strategies that allow them to cope in difficult situations and experience success (Pintrich 2003). Strategies here include in-depth questioning and debate with peers (King 1990; 1994), use of assessment as a tool for learning, rather than selection (Smeding *et al*. 2013), creating meaningful (possibly hands-on) activities for students to work through rather than repeated worksheets (Ames 1992), and allowing students to choose among tasks, which may also reduce comparison between students in terms of performance (Ames 1992).

Of course, learners considered to be mastery-orientated also want to perform well, and this can complicate the notion of a learner being either mastery- or performance-orientated. However, the key point here for educators is that being solely performance-orientated can be damaging for learning. For example, in a classic study by Deci and Ryan (1985), pre-schoolers who were offered a prize for their drawing – an activity they enjoyed – thus prompting performance orientation, subsequently stopped wanting to draw when there was no longer a prize offered, a phenomenon sometimes referred to as the undermining effect. Second, as research by Midgley *et al*. (2001) indicates, learners who have adopted a mastery orientation approach tend to continue to want to learn and see the experience as a valuable step in their learning journey. Those with a performance orientation are more likely to feel frustration and avoid situations where they could potentially fail again in the future.

With respect to content acquisition, cognitive theories, including stage theory and its various corollaries, have been key in providing the foundation to many cumulative approaches such as the spiral curriculum proposed by Bruner (1960). Based on the principles of constructivism, the spiral curriculum is premised on the notion of students revisiting a topic several times throughout their school careers, but with each visit they engage with more and more complex ideas. In this way, the new information presented each time relates to the prior learning and can readily be accommodated into the students' mental models with the final result being a body of knowledge that is reinforced and solidified.

Constructivist theories of learning are also particularly significant in reminding us that learners do not arrive at new situations as a blank slates. Rather, they come to new ideas with prior conceptions which are built upon in a process of accommodation, resulting in new information being added to an existing mental schema. This process requires effort: a learner must collect, assess, sort and systematize the new ideas to create a larger whole (diSessa 1988). Educators similarly need to exert effort to provide empathetic understanding and patience necessary to guide learners' thinking in ways that align with canonical explanations. To do this, educators need to help learners see that new ideas are more plausible and potentially useful than prior notions (Posner Strike, Hewson and Gertzog 1982).

Information processing theories of learning similarly highlight the role of mental models and tend to stress elements of memory in learning (e.g., Clark and Paivio 1991). In using mental models in this way, the focus for scholars in this area is to develop techniques to help learners acquire more information and, more significantly, acquire new insights. For example, studies in this area have long focused on the manner by which knowledge may be constructed by encouraging the learner to analogize from a familiar concept to one that is less familiar (Bassok and Holyoak 1989; Vosniadou 1989). For instance, young children might be taught that the way in which bacteria infect the body can be compared to the situation in which an army attacks: germs attack the body's cells, making them weak, in the same way that armies attack countries or factions. Older pupils learning about physics could be given a demonstration of the way that a wheeled vehicle will slow down as it crosses from a smooth to a more friction-filled surface, with an explanation that the process of refraction of light is similar as light is slowed as it passes through glass, causing it to bend.

Theories that emphasize the role of social interaction (as in social constructivism) are useful in structuring the design of education efforts. For example, in considering a learner's ZPD, and assisting in a learner's sense-making and connection-building, an educator must carefully structure the form and extent of any support they offer. Wood *et al.* (1976) refer to such support as scaffolding. The term is particularly apt as such support should necessarily diminish and fade over time as the edifice of one's knowledge becomes secure and self-standing.

In considering activities for learners, meanwhile, the emphasis on social interaction highlights the importance of providing opportunities for learners to express, rehearse and develop their ideas in discussion with others. The role for the educator here is to help learners externalize their thoughts and reflect on their validity. Externalization in an educational setting often takes the form of verbal conversation or writing, but can equally include drawing and symbolic physical movements such as gestures. In expressing ideas 'out loud' in this way, learners are provided with the opportunity to overtly monitor their ideas for incongruities, and thereafter self-correct (Gelman and Lucarriello 2002). The notion of dialogic teaching wherein learners are encouraged to examine meanings in peer-to-peer dialogue is an example of externalization in practice. Educators may also prompt learner externalization by asking key questions that challenge learners to operate at the higher end of their ZPD. To ensure that learners are developing in the ways intended, educators have many language-related tools at their disposal. They can repeat a learner's statement to emphasize its contribution to the discussion and its role in connecting ideas (Edwards and Mercer 1987; O'Connor and Michaels 1996). They can also rephrase or reformulate a learner's contribution so that the idea is more explicitly aligned to a particular position (Mortimer and Scott 2003). In the context of reading, learners can be encouraged to predict what will follow based on their understanding of what has gone before (as proposed in the Directed Activities Related to Text (DART) approach to reading). In this way, the learner's response enables the educator to keep track of what sense is being made, and if necessary shape and guide further communication as appropriate.

As noted above, situated theories of learning similarly emphasize the importance of social interaction, but more specifically prompt consideration of the location and context of the learning experience. Research studies have found that learning is best enabled if it occurs in an everyday, familiar, social context (Greeno 2006; Kolodner 2006) wherein the learning task reflects an authentic aspect of everyday life (Blumenfeld, Kempler and Krajcik 2006). Although not always practically possible, a situated approach to learning is useful in reminding educators of the importance of not just contextualizing their lessons, but moreover making the lessons personally and locally relevant to the learners before attempting to move on and apply new conceptual understandings to more abstract ideas and content.

Finally, viewing learning as a process of identity formation can help us to challenge the notion of teaching as a form of delivery. Rather than learning being the 'passing' of knowledge from one to the next, theories of identity development emphasize the ways in which learning is a result of changes in one's identity, and that identity development takes time and involves a multiplicity of experiences. Furthermore, and as with the principles of conceptual change, only those experiences and ideas which seem personally fruitful and relevant will adhere and resonate with learners.

In thinking about learning as identity formation, three perspectives can help. The first is to recognize that learning comprises an ecology wherein contributing experiences from a variety of settings operate within an ecosystem – the more links that are generated between multiple experiences, the richer the overall learning (Barron 2006; see also Bronfenbrenner 1979). Indeed, the US National Research Council (2009) has noted that education should not be considered the preserve of schools, and should instead be shared explicitly with resources in the community including family interactions, the media and Internet, and also cultural settings. The second is to acknowledge that learners possess unique resources in the form of culturally based funds of knowledge (Moll *et al.* 1992). As noted earlier in this chapter, learners do not arrive at new experiences as empty slates. Rather they come with a host of prior experiences that may or may not overtly align with the canonical knowledge selected for coverage in the curriculum. For example, a child may have a detailed knowledge of car engines from assisting her father in his car repair business. However, this same child may be unaware of scientific principles which define the processes she observes. By exploring a student's funds of knowledge and seeking to link these prior experiences to the topic of the lesson, a teacher values the learner's experiences and in so doing the learner affirms her beliefs in her abilities. From self-belief grows identity which, with further support, can foster interest and motivation in turn strengthening identity in a positive feedback loop. The third perspective notes the role played by 'significant' individuals in shaping a learner's emergent identity. As Sjaastad (2012) has argued, significant persons can influence a young person's decisions and self-perceptions of identity. For example, parents contribute to the formation of a student's feeling of what they ought to be like, while teachers affirm students' beliefs in their actual attributes. Acknowledging the role played by significant persons again emphasizes the importance of social interaction in the learning process.

Concluding thoughts

In this chapter we have introduced some of the key theories of learning guiding educational practice both in the past, and currently. In discussing the theories we have indicated whether their conceptual foundations sought to emphasize processes occurring within the individual or, alternatively, viewed learning as a social affair.

In attempting to summarize a number of theoretical contributions, we have but scratched the surface of research conducted across the fields of psychology, sociology and education. Nonetheless, we hope that we have provided a starting point for further study. More importantly, in summarizing key theories and highlighting their particular perspectives, we hope we have drawn attention to the ways that different learning theories are utilized for different issues, but that all have value in explaining and supporting education. We also hope that this chapter will serve as a springboard for further deliberation about the application of learning theory in the rapidly changing context of contemporary education. How, for example, might theories of learning inform our understanding of educational practice beyond the conventional classroom setting? How will teachers manage learning opportunities and respond to student motivations in an increasingly marketized climate with its emphasis on performance scores and results over the individual's experience of learning? And how should we apply our understanding of learning theories to inform, guide, and if necessary, push back on, new policy directions around curriculum development and assessment? Similarly phrased questions concerning issues of performativity and the design of educational opportunities run throughout this book. Building from an understanding of learning theory, we argue, will be an important first step in attempting to answer them.

References

Adey, P., Robertson, A. and Venville, G. (2002) Effects of a cognitive stimulation programme on Year 1 pupils, *British Journal of Educational Psychology*, 72(1): 1–25.

Ames, C. (1992) Classrooms: goals, structures and student motivation, *Journal of Educational Psychology*, 84: 261–71.

Bakhtin, M. (1981) *The Dialogic Imagination: Four Essays* (ed. M. Holquist). Austin, TX: University of Texas Press.

Barron, B. (2006) Interest and self-sustained learning as catalysts of development: a learning ecology perspective, *Human Development*, 49: 193–224.

Barton, A.C. and Tan, E. (2010) 'We be burnin'!' Agency, identity, and science learning, *Journal of the Learning Sciences*, 19(2): 187–229.

Bassok, M. and Holyoak, K.J. (1989) Interdomain transfer between isomorphic topics in algebra and physics, *Journal of Experimental Psychology: Learning, Memory, and Cognition*, 15(1): 153–66.

Berger, P.L. and Luckman, T. (1966) *The Social Construction of Reality: A Treatise in the Sociology of Knowledge*. Garden City, NY: Anchor Books.

Blumenfeld, P.C., Kempler, T.M. and Krajcik, J. (2006) Motivation and cognitive engagement in learning environments, in R.K. Sawyer (ed.) *The Cambridge Handbook of the Learning Sciences*. New York: Cambridge University Press, pp. 475–88.

Bransford, J.D. and Schwartz, D.L. (1999) Rethinking transfer: a simple proposal with multiple implications, *Review of Research in Education*, 24(3): 61–100.

Bronfenbrenner, U. (1979) *The Ecology of Human Development: Experiments by Nature and Design*. Cambridge, MA: Harvard University Press.

Bruner, J.S. (1960) *The Process of Education*. Cambridge, MA: The President and Fellows of Harvard College.

Bruner, J.S. (1961) The act of discovery, *Harvard Educational Review*, 31(1): 21–32.

Clark, J. and Paivio, A. (1991) Dual coding theory and education, *Educational Psychology Review*, 3: 149–210.

Deci, E. and Ryan, R. (1985) *Intrinsic Motivation and Self-determination in Human Behavior*. New York: Plenum Press.

diSessa, A.A. (1988) Knowledge in pieces, in G. Forman and P.B. Pufall (eds) *Constructivism in the Computer Age*. Hillsdale, NJ: Erlbaum, pp. 49–70.

Dweck, C. and Leggett, E. (1988) A social-cognitive approach to motivation and personality, *Psychological Review*, 95: 256–73.

Edwards, D. and Mercer, N. (1987) *Common Knowledge: The Development of Understanding in the Classroom*. London: Methuen/Routledge.

Gee, J.P. (2000) Identity as an analytic lens for research in education, *Review of Research in Education*, 25: 99–125.

Gelman, R. and Lucarriello, J. (2002) Role of learning in cognitive development, in R. Gallistel (ed.) *Stevens' Handbook of Experimental Psychology: Learning, Motivation, and Emotion* (3rd edn, Vol. 3). New York: Wiley, pp. 395–443.

Greeno, J.G. (2006) Learning in activity, in R.K. Sawyer (ed.) *The Cambridge Handbook of the Learning Sciences*. New York: Cambridge University Press, pp. 79–96.

Hardy, M. and Taylor, P. (1997) Von Glasersfeld's radical constructivism: a critical review, *Science and Education*, 6: 135–50.

Hidi, S. and Renninger, K.A. (2006) The four-phase model of interest development, *Educational Psychologist*, 41(2): 111–27.

Hobbes, T. ([1651] 1968) *Leviathan*. Harmondsworth: Penguin.

Illeris, K. (2007) *How We Learn: Learning and Non-Learning in School and Beyond*. London: Routledge.

King, A. (1990) Enhancing peer interaction and learning in the classroom through reciprocal questioning, *American Educational Research Journal*, 27(4): 664–87.

King, A. (1994) Guiding knowledge construction in the classroom: effects of teaching children how to question and how to explain, *American Educational Research Journal*, 31: 338–68.

Kirschner, P.A., Sweller, J. and Clark, R.E. (2006) Why minimal guidance during instruction does not work: an analysis of the failure of constructivist, discovery, problem-based, experiential, and inquiry-based teaching, *Educational Psychologist*, 41(2): 75–86.

Kolodner, J.L. (2006) Case-based reasoning, in R.K. Sawyer (ed.) *The Cambridge Handbook of the Learning Sciences*. New York: Cambridge University Press, pp. 225–42.

Lave, J. (1988) *Cognition in Practice: Mind, Mathematics and Culture in Everyday Life*. New York: Cambridge University Press.

Lave, J. and Wenger, E. (1991) *Situated Learning: Legitimate Peripheral Participation*. Cambridge: Cambridge University Press.

Metz, K. (1995) Reassessment of developmental constraints on children's science instruction, *Review of Educational Research*, 65: 93–127.

Midgley, C., Kaplan, A. and Middleton, M. (2001) Performance-approach goals: good for what, for whom, under what circumstances, and at what cost? *Journal of Educational Psychology*, 93: 77–86.

Moll, L., Amanti, C., Neff, D. and Gonzalez, N. (1992) Funds of knowledge for teaching: using a qualitative approach to connect homes and classrooms, *Theory into Practice*, 31(2): 132–41.

Mortimer, E. and Scott, P. (2003) *Meaning Making in Secondary Science Classrooms*. Buckingham: Open University Press.

Nasir, N.S. and Hand, V. (2008) From the court to the classroom: opportunities for engagement, learning, and identity in basketball and classroom mathematics, *Journal of the Learning Sciences*, 17(2): 143–79.

Newell, A. and Simon, H. (1972) *Human Problem Solving*. Oxford: Prentice-Hall.

NRC (National Research Council) (ed.) (2009) *Learning Science in Informal Environments: People, Places, and Pursuits*. Washington, DC: National Academies Press.

O'Connor, M.C. and Michaels, S. (1996) Shifting participant frameworks: orchestrating thinking practices in group discussion, in D. Hicks (ed.) *Discourse, Learning, and Schooling*. New York: Cambridge University Press, pp. 63–103.

Oppezzo, M.A. and Chin, D.B. (2011) Practicing versus inventing with contrasting cases: the effects of telling first on learning and transfer, *Journal of Educational Psychology*, 103(4): 759–775.

Palincsar, A.S. (1998) Social constructivist perspectives on teaching and learning, *Annual Review of Psychology*, 49: 345–75.

Pavlov, I. (1927) *Conditioned Reflexes*. New York: Dover.

Piaget, J. (1952) *Origins of Intelligence in Children*. New York: International Universities Press.

Piaget, J. and Inhelder, B. (1958) *The Growth of Logical Thinking from Childhood to Adolescence*. New York: Basic Books.

Pintrich, P. (2003) A motivational science perspective on the role of student motivation in learning and teaching contexts, *Journal of Educational Psychology*, 95: 667–86.

Posner, G.J., Strike, K.A., Hewson, P.W. and Gertzog, W.A. (1982) Accommodation of a scientific conception: toward a theory of conceptual change, *Science Education*, 66(2): 211–27.

Rogoff, B. (1990) *Apprenticeship in Thinking: Cognitive Development in Social Context*. Oxford: Oxford University Press.

Schwab, J. (1966) *The Teaching of Science*. Cambridge, MA: Harvard University Press.

Seth, J., Schwartz, S.J., Luyckx, K. and Vivian, L. (eds) (2011) *Handbook of Identity Theory and Research*. New York: Springer.

Sjaastad, J. (2012) Sources of inspiration: the role of significant persons in young people's choice of science in higher education, *International Journal of Science Education*, 34(10): 1615–36.

Skinner, B.F. (1974) *About Behaviourism*. New York: Alfred A. Knopf.

Smeding, A., Darnon, C., Souchal, C., Toczek-Capelle, M.C. and Butera, F. (2013) Reducing the socio-economic status achievement gap at university by promoting mastery-oriented assessment. *PLOS One*, https://doi.org/10.1371/journal.pone.0071678. Accessed August 2016

Thorndike, E.L. (1898) Animal intelligence: an experimental study of the associative processes in animals, *Psychological Monographs: General and Applied*, 2(4): i–109.

Venville, G.J. and Dawson, V.M. (2010) The impact of a classroom intervention on grade 10 students' argumentation skills, informal reasoning, and conceptual understanding of science, *Journal of Research in Science Teaching*, 47(8): 952–77.

Von Glasersfeld, E. (1995) *Radical Constructivism: A Way of Knowing and Learning. Studies in Mathematics Education Series: Book 6*. Bristol: Falmer Press.

Vosniadou, S. (1989) Analogical reasoning as a mechanism in knowledge acquisition: a developmental perspective, in S. Vosniadou and A. Ortony (eds) *Similarity and Analogical Reasoning*. New York: Cambridge University Press, pp. 413–37.

Vygotsky, L.S. (1978) *Mind in Society: The Development of Higher Psychological Processes*. Cambridge, MA: Harvard University Press.

Wenger, E. (1998) *Communities of Practice: Learning, Meaning, and Identity*. Cambridge: Cambridge University Press.

Wood, D.J., Bruner, J.S. and Ross, G. (1976) The role of tutoring in problem solving, *Journal of Child Psychology and Psychiatry*, 17: 89–100.

11

Engaging in learning: learning to engage
KAREN SKILLING

Introduction

Promoting student engagement, participation and interest in learning is considered important by educational researchers because of its contribution to improved achievement outcomes and by teachers who shape student behaviour, emotions and thinking at school. Student engagement has received much attention from the field of educational psychology (including motivation and cognition theories) over the last three decades and there is a growing interest in the construct of engagement from research and teaching perspectives. In the first part of this chapter, engagement literature is discussed with the aim of defining and conceptualizing student engagement. The second part of the chapter reports on teachers' beliefs about and practices that promote student engagement.

Specifically, this chapter aims to do the following:

- Define and conceptualize the engagement construct including different types and how they operate in an interrelated way
- Consider the relationship between types of engagement and underlying motivational factors that are likely to influence the way in which students engage in learning
- Alert beginning teachers to the signs of engagement they might expect to see students exhibiting and provide a framework that assists in categorizing these into types of engagement
- Offer insights into the instructional approaches that teachers use to promote student engagement and to dissuade student disengagement in learning.

What do we mean by student engagement?

When asked to describe a student who is 'engaged' in school, many responses are likely to include a range of compliant actions such as: paying attention in class; sitting near the front; answering and asking questions; getting on with set work; completing homework; and studying for tests. When asked to describe 'disengaged' students, responses often include: not listening to the teacher; sitting near the back of the room; not making eye contact with the teacher; being easily distracted and often distracting others; refusing to do class work or procrastinating over work; rarely completing homework or studying for tests.

Nearly all of the signs of engagement mentioned above reflect how students behave and participate (or not) in classrooms. While behaving in ways that are conducive to learning is important, this alone does not necessarily require students to be immersed in the learning processes that lead to deep understanding of material or make connections between essential concepts. Those interested in engagement are centrally concerned with student learning and have noted that it is not just how students behave in school but how they feel towards learning and the approaches they take towards mastering skills and comprehending complex material and processes. It is students who are highly engaged in the ways they *act*, *feel* and *think* who achieve higher levels of educational outcomes (Martin *et al.* 2012), whereas those students who are disengaged from school are likely to experience low achievement, feel alienated from school, and are more likely to disengage from learning and drop out from school altogether (Wang and Eccles 2012). The next section sets out to define the different types of engagement that reflect student actions, feelings and thinking, and how they operate in an interrelated way.

Types of engagement

Following an extensive review of 44 studies of student engagement, Fredricks *et al.* (2004) established a framework that distinguishes three types of engagement including behavioural engagement, emotional engagement, and cognitive engagement. Although three types of engagement are categorized by Fredricks and her colleagues (2004), it is understood that types of engagement overlap and the engagement construct is uniquely viewed as multidimensional. Therefore, it is likely that two or three types of engagement operate together in an interrelated way, reflecting the way individuals *act*, *feel* and *think*. Although some researchers have suggested additional dimensions of engagement reflecting the social aspects of learning on behaviour (Linnenbrink-Garcia *et al.* 2011) and the degree of students active involvement in learning (agentic engagement) (Reeve and Tseng 2011) for now, the current tripartite conceptualization of engagement is widely agreed upon.

Definitions of engagement

Behavioural engagement is concerned with levels of participation and involvement in academic, social or extra-curricular activities associated with school, including 'effort, persistence, concentration, attention, asking questions and contributing to class discussion' (Fredricks *et al.* 2004: 62). *Emotional engagement* is concerned with students' positive and negative affective reactions to teachers, schoolwork, peers and school. There is increasing interest in the long-term effect of emotions and other non-cognitive aspects such as interest, values and attitudes that influence motivation and achievement (Pekrun and Linnenbrink-Garcia 2014).

Cognitive engagement, which appears to be more strongly linked to improving student learning (Harris 2011), has been more difficult to clearly define because it draws upon two different perspectives. One perspective focuses on the psychological investment in learning and stresses the learning efforts students make to understand and master knowledge and skills (Fredricks *et al.* 2004; 2016), reflecting motivational constructs. The other draws on academic achievement literature that focuses on practices that aim to enhance learning and instruction such as self-regulation strategies and metacognitive processes. It has been suggested that scholars integrate both perspectives, however some researchers highlight key differences between cognitive engagement and self-regulation (Wolters and Taylor 2012) and others argue that cognitive engagement and self-regulation should be considered in separate but interconnecting ways (Boekaerts 2016).

Characteristics of engagement

Characteristics of engagement include consideration of its duration, intensity and changeability. Although engagement is seen as dynamic and ongoing, it is unlikely that students will exhibit high levels of dynamic and continuous engagement throughout their school day or throughout an entire lesson and therefore variations in its duration are expected. When talking about student engagement, it is important to consider whether reference is being made to particular tasks or reflective of a pattern of involvement in a range of tasks over time, as this is likely to vary.

Furthermore, the intensity of cognitive investment or commitment a student makes might be reflected generally or involve a heightened intensity in one particular type of engagement. For example, in relation to behavioural engagement, a student may complete work as asked (low investment) or be more proactive such as asking clarifying questions (high investment). Considering cognitive engagement, a student may read through their notebook as test preparation (low investment) or use sophisticated learning strategies such as preparing summaries and completing practice questions (high investment).

Additionally, patterns of engagement for individual students are likely to be changeable and fluctuate (Skilling *et al.* 2016). For instance, when students are introduced to a new concept they might display high levels of interest (emotional engagement) and ask a range of clarifying questions (behavioural and cognitive engagement) but then subsequently display reduced interest and participation when a similar concept is presented – possibly reflecting a gain in understanding rather than indicating reduced interest, value and effort. Therefore, engagement is 'idiosyncratic' (Williams and Ivey 2001) and unstable in nature, and we may expect to see individual students exhibiting different types of engagement at varying levels of intensity depending on the activities to hand and other contextual and motivational factors.

Given the fluctuations, intensities and complexity of engagement, it seems erroneous to refer to students as either *engaged* or *disengaged*. It also raises the broader issue about how the dis/engagement construct is perceived. Some researchers are of the view that engagement and disengagement are separate constructs underpinned by separate but similar motivational factors while others perceive an engagement continuum extending from high levels of engagement through to eventual disengagement. There have been fewer studies specific to disengagement and, of these, teachers' conceptions mainly focus on behavioural and emotional indicators (Fredricks *et al.* 2016). For example, student disengagement is often characterized by students' lack of persistence and effort, off-task behaviours, overt negative emotions and lack of interest. However other research has identified that disengaged students also convey disengaging cognitive indicators such as a low task value, as well as ineffective and unsophisticated strategy use (Skilling 2013). Whether or not engagement and disengagement are separate constructs is of ongoing interest to researchers and Martin *et al.* (2012) suggest that while both constructs are significantly correlated, they uniquely explain variance in academic functioning, concluding that they are complementary but distinct.

While it is important to note the theoretical issues and conceptions about engagement, for many teachers, concerns about student engagement derive from direct experiences in their classrooms. For teachers, knowing that engagement is a strong predictor of learning outcomes and that it is malleable is significant. This is because teachers can alter their approach to instruction within their classroom environments, potentially influencing some of the factors that shape student engagement. This may raise the following questions for teachers: Are there a group of factors that underlie significant shifts in dis/engagement? How are students who are neither highly engaged nor disengaged identified and what should be done to promote engagement and arrest declines towards disengagement? Can disengaged students be re-engaged and are there specific influential factors for this?

Later in this chapter, the range of engagement and disengagement that teachers perceive in their classrooms is discussed, exploring the underlying signs that teachers perceive an indicating student engagement. However, before this, the following section considers the relationship between motivation and engagement.

Motivation and engagement

The reasons for fluctuations in student engagement are often difficult to determine. A way to understand why and how student engagement fluctuates is to explore motivational and contextual factors that influence how students feel, think and behave. The terms motivation and engagement are frequently used interchangeably, however, although they are linked, they are distinct. Motivation explains why individuals behave in particular ways in different situations. It is concerned with the psychological processes that underlie visible engagement characteristics (Skinner and Pitzer 2012), so that motivation is viewed as encompassing the internal, private and unobservable factors of the outer, public and observable engagement (Skilling 2014). In terms of operational processes, there is a broad agreement that motivation occurs before (and often during) activities that lead to engagement and in turn engagement mediates learning outcomes, including achievement. A recent study that considered the operational ordering of motivation and engagement found support for motivation as the impetus for engagement yet also found that 'prior engagement also explains significant variance in subsequent motivation' (Martin *et al.* 2017: 157), suggesting that there is a cyclical process to consider between these two constructs.

While in the past, motivation theories of learning were viewed in mechanistic ways, over time research from the field of psychology and those interested in academic achievement have influenced thinking about student engagement and hence the expansion of research interest in this field. Where previously the drive and needs of individual students were seen as being the source of energy for student behaviours in classrooms, with the teachers playing a less active facilitator role, more recent perspectives identify sources of motivation arising from multiple factors. In addition to student needs and individual goals, factors relating to cognitions, emotions, values as well as environmental aspects are viewed as extremely influential in learning settings.

Different motivational theories tend to focus on one source of motivation when aiming to understand and describe the psychological characteristics that influence achievement. For example, achievement goal theorists are interested in explaining academic motivation by considering two fundamental goal orientations of individuals, mastery and performance, and are concerned with investigating the avoidance and approach components that influence these (Anderman and Patrick 2012). This can be contrasted to self-regulation theorists who are concerned with how individuals use strategic thinking and complex processes to store information, choosing which cognitive strategies to employ and making judgements about their own thinking (Zimmerman 2002). Researchers who favour particular motivational theories tend to view student engagement through different lenses, according to the underlying tenets of each theory.

This inevitably leads to variations in the conceptualizations of engagement as different motivational factors are emphasized, depending on the construct at the heart of each theoretical perspective. Drawing on the examples from the previous paragraph, goal theorists use goal orientation theory to explain motivation and engagement (Anderman and Patrick 2012). They do this by adopting the model of engagement proposed by Fredricks *et al.* (2004) and focus on the goals that students display towards tasks *before* and *during* the participation in tasks. Self-regulation theorists see the advantages of integrating perspectives from the field of motivation, engagement and self-regulation. Looking through their lens, self-regulation theorists pay great attention to the processes students use to *initiate* and *sustain* high levels of focus and effort on learning activities and pay particular attention to cognitive engagement (Cleary and Zimmerman 2012).

There are also researchers who have blended more than one theoretical perspective when researching engagement. A framework known as the 'Motivation and Engagement Wheel' reflects a host of important motivation theories and specifically integrates motivational and engagement constructs (Martin 2003; 2007). This framework captures 11 motivational factors drawn from seven theories of motivation. Martin identifies congruencies between certain motivational factors and organized them by four higher-order clusters. There are two adaptive (positive) clusters. The first, adaptive motivation, includes factors relating to positive orientations and thinking about learning, including self-efficacy, mastery orientation and valuing. Adaptive engagement, which is reflective of positive behaviour for learning, includes persistence, planning and task management. The two maladaptive (negative) clusters include: maladaptive motivation such as anxiety, failure avoidance and uncertain control, all of which impede academic learning; and maladaptive behaviour such as self-handicapping and disengagement reflecting problematic behaviours (Martin 2003; 2007; Martin et al. 2012). This comprehensive and multidimensional framework aims to integrate thinking between motivation and engagement and is proposed as being particularly useful in educational settings, helping to inform those involved in learning about various cognitive and behavioural factors that are likely to influence student learning.

For teachers, however, student interactions in the classroom are more obviously linked to learning environments and the demands of different tasks and subjects (Fredricks et al. 2004; Fredricks and McColskey 2012) and it can be difficult to determine the underlying motivational processes influencing the ways students engage (Skilling et al. 2016). Difficulties may also arise because there are some features that are shared between engagement and motivation. For example, positive motivation such as persistence might be recognized as time spent on tasks and asking questions, but these are also characteristics that might be described as positive behavioural engagement. Understandably, teachers are generally not experts in motivation literature but they do spend many hours with students in school settings and can draw on their expertise and knowledge about how they perceive students are engaged in their classrooms. It is therefore important to know what teachers 'notice' about student engagement and what they perceive as 'signs' of engagement, involving not only behaviours and overt emotions but also the ways they gauge students are thinking about their learning. Determining what teachers believe about student engagement is important because these influence what they do and drive the instructional choices and efforts they make to promote student engagement (Hadré 2011; Skilling et al. 2016).

There have been calls for more research to investigate student engagement from teachers' perspectives, including what teachers understand by the concept of engagement and what they expect to see (Harris 2011). To address this, a growing body of research is addressing teacher beliefs about engagement, such as what teachers report as signs of engagement and the practices they use that promote student engagement both generally and for specific subjects (Skilling et al. 2015; Skilling et al. 2016; Durksen et al. 2017). Gaining insights into teacher beliefs about engagement is important for: (1) moving discussions of engagement beyond the more obvious behavioural indicators towards more comprehensive conceptions of the engagement construct: and (2) because teacher beliefs shape the instructional approaches they use in their classrooms and therefore it is important to identify teaching practices that are more likely to promote student engagement than hinder it.

What teachers say about student engagement: the engagement spectrum

This section draws on research reporting the signs or cues that teachers describe as engagement and disengagement in mathematics classrooms. It begins by reporting the responses of 31 teachers who took part in a qualitative study in

Table 11.1

Levels of engagement	Types of engagement		
	Behavioural (Participation and involvement)	Emotional (Interest and value learning)	Cognitive (Investment in learning)
Disengaged	Refuses to talk and work Off-task/distracts others Does not bring equipment/ books to class	Not interested Expresses dislike Expects failure Lacks drive	Poor organization Lack of bookwork Resists homework Does not study for tests
Variably engaged	Procrastinates/fiddles Clowns around Reluctant contributor Rushes work/not thorough	Disenchanted Easily disappointed Anxious if unsure Bored by repetition	Variable concentration Happy to be average Focuses on marks rather than understanding
Substantially engaged	On task/pays attention Frequent participation Asks/answers questions Interacts with peers/class Begins work/perseveres	Interested/positive Enjoys/likes learning Excited to improve Self-motivated Positive self-belief	Listens to others' explanations/questions Discusses applications Clarifies concepts Likes to help/explain Works ahead and studies

Source: Adapted from Skilling *et al.* (2016).

Australia (NSW),[1] which led to the development of a framework known as 'The Engagement Spectrum' (adapted in Table 11.1) (Skilling 2014; Skilling *et al.* 2016).

When asked to describe 'engaged' and 'disengaged' students in their classrooms, nearly all the teachers responded with multifaceted statements reflecting behavioural, emotional and cognitive aspects of engagement. For example, one teacher described engaged students by: 'Their level of interest, their level of concentration. Through observation; watching them too, talking to their friend about the work . . . whether they're on task. The questions that they fire, the conversation that comes out of things' (Skilling 2013: 116).

Applying this to the engagement framework (Fredricks *et al.* 2004) outlined at the beginning of this chapter, signs of behavioural engagement include 'concentration', 'on-task', 'questions'. Emotional engagement is indicated by 'interest'. Signs of cognitive engagement include 'talking . . . about the work' and 'conversation' (clarified as being class conversation about the lesson content and tasks).

While it is acknowledged that signs such as 'level of concentration' could indicate all three types of engagement (and indeed reflects the interrelated ways in which engagement operates), for the purpose of understanding the engagement construct more deeply, categorizing engagement by types is helpful for gaining greater insight into how it is perceived by a range of teachers.

Similarly, when teachers described a 'disengaged' student, their responses were also multifaceted, for example, another teacher reported that students' body language and preparedness to learn are significant signs:

> . . . their body language, how they walk into class. The fact that they are not prepared, they don't have their textbook, they don't have their diary . . .

Sometime they don't have a pen or pencil, so a lack of organisation, their general demeanor. They might come into class . . . and not interrupt but they will just sit and they won't talk . . .

(Skilling 2013: 120)

It can be seen from these types of responses that signs of engagement are indicated not only by what students say but also by the non-verbal cues that they display. Once all the teachers' responses were collated and categorized as either behaviourally, emotionally or cognitively engaged and disengaged, it became clear that some of the reported signs were more or less intense than others. For example, 'always asking and answering questions about the work' was deemed more intense and engaging than 'answering questions when asked' and 'hating maths' was seen as more extreme than 'losing interest in it'. Taking note of these variations in the way teachers expressed the signs they perceived for the different types of engagement called for a second level of analysis with the responses also being categorized by their level of intensity.

This two-way analysis led to the Engagement Spectrum framework (Skilling 2014; Skilling *et al.* 2016) classifying student engagement both by types and levels of intensity. An adapted version of the Engagement Spectrum is represented in Table 11.1 on p 152. In this table, the three types of engagement are listed – behavioural, emotional and cognitive. Next, three levels of engagement can be seen and profiles for students who are *disengaged, variably engaged* and *substantially engaged* are shown. It is from looking across at each 'profile' that some light is shed on the types of engagement characteristics teacher might identify with. Importantly, the *variably engaged* category, where students are neither disengaged nor highly engaged, highlights incongruities in individual student engagement, where clear signs of engagement are not always obvious or consistent.

While the Engagement Spectrum has been used to organize and summarize teachers' responses in the study (mathematics teachers in secondary schools), it also acknowledges the 'fuzziness' about particular teacher responses, although clarification at the time of interview helped in this process. The main aim of establishing this framework is to assist teachers to think more specifically about how they perceive student engagement, to consider engagement that is not immediately obvious and the underlying factors and opportunities they provide that influence engagement. The following section provides some further details about each engagement profile.

Disengaged

When asked about student disengagement, teachers generally referred to off-task behavioural indicators before mentioning emotional and cognitive ones. The indicators reported by teachers included specific acts of disengagement and also non-verbal signs. For example, teachers referred to disengaged students as being actively disruptive by 'distracting others . . . talking and whispering' and not bringing or not completing homework that was expected in class, they did not keep tidy notes, they regularly did not bring pens or notebooks, and made little effort to participate in class work. Non-verbal signs included 'avoiding eye contact', lack of greeting the teacher when entering the classroom, sitting towards the back of the room, and lack of participation in class tasks and discussion.

Disengaged students were reported as displaying negative emotions, and a lack of interest with reports of students 'hate', 'anger' and 'frustration' towards particular subjects. Other teachers reported their awareness of students' attitudes of not being interested or caring about their work. Some teachers commented on students who portrayed negative responses to new work, stating that the work was too difficult even before it was attempted. In terms of cognitive engagement, disengaged students were perceived by teachers to lack organizational skills in and outside of the classroom, such as not maintaining notes they could use for revision, not attempting homework and rarely preparing for tests.

Variably engaged

The variably engaged category in Table 11.1 reflects the descriptions given by teachers of students who were perceived to be neither totally disengaged nor substantially engaged. Such students were often regarded as being compliant and doing what was asked in class but avoided active and sustained involvement in class activities. The term 'variable' for this category of engagement is used because the reasons for the fluctuating engagement varied between individual students as outlined below.

Descriptions of variably engaged students included those who were 'quiet, and seated', appearing to listen but were 'switched off'. On the other hand, this also included students who delayed getting on with meaningful work or 'who avoided work by wasting time or procrastinating by spending too long on menial tasks'.

The level of students' concentration was also mentioned as influencing engagement levels. When students' concentration fell, they needed explicit encouragement from the teacher to maintain their participation on tasks. Teachers reported students as still willing to contribute, albeit for only parts of the lesson, and made occasional contributions to class discussions.

Although some teachers interpreted students' lack of participation as a lack of interest, others felt that there could be other reasons. For example, some teachers believed students' lower participation was due to other characteristics, such as being shy. Other teachers believed that although students were able to contribute to questions asked in class, they were 'scared to explore in front of the peer group' or 'panicked' if asked a question in the class. Several teachers noted that some students were anxious about 'getting things wrong in front of the other students' and this was likely to reduce their participation rather than reflect a lack of engagement.

On the other hand, teachers also noted that some students did not want 'to be seen as smart, to be seen as capable of doing it' but were happy not to be pushed into participating more obviously. Teachers perceived these types of students as capable but did not 'want to be seen as nerds', although one teacher noted that higher achieving students could become less engaged if they became bored when relearning procedures and doing more examples. It is therefore important to consider why student engagement may be variable, as a wide range of factors such as anxiety, uncertainty, shyness, fear of failure, and so on may be influencing students' levels of participation, enjoyment and cognitive involvement in class work rather than their engagement.

Substantially engaged

Substantially engaged students were reported as students indicating high levels of behavioural, emotional and cognitive engagement. In terms of participation, these students paid attention in class, were on task, often answered and asked questions and 'want to come up to the board to show the answer' with teachers commenting that you 'see smiles and "I get it, I get it"'. Another characteristic of substantially engaged was their high level of interest in understanding class material rather than just completing tasks, for example, one mathematics teacher stated that 'engaged' means:

> [Being] on task, interested in not only finishing the task but finishing it to the best of their ability, to a high standard, and wanting to know what they don't know, wanting to go that step further, rather than ticking and crossing, actually finding out why.
>
> (Skilling *et al.* 2016: 556)

Teachers also reported that substantially engaged students were often keen to help their peers and to share knowledge with others. Teachers identified high levels of cognitive engagement indicated by sustained concentration on work, self-motivated and strategic, staying behind to clarify questions and completing homework. It was also reported that such students interest in learning lead to more satisfaction and absorption in their class work and are interested in the future application of their knowledge and 'how it will be used'.

Substantially engaged students were not restricted to those who achieved highly as a number of teachers mentioned the efforts that lower-attaining students made to understand class work and appreciated the efforts they made despite finding work difficult. Teachers also perceived that they played a significant role in supporting students' efforts and could identify those students who were focused and wanting to learn.

In summary, by teasing apart and identifying signs for different types of engagement and categorizing these as *disengaged, variably engaged* and/or *substantially engaged* on a single framework, we can gain an overview for how teachers perceive students are engaged in their classrooms. In particular, considering why students display variable engagement provokes thinking about the underlying specific factors for individual students and promoting teacher sensitivity towards student differences. Further, although behavioural and overt emotions are readily visible in classrooms, this research aims to highlight the importance of not relying solely on these as indicators of engagement. This is because, in many circumstances, student emotions and the way students are thinking about their class work are not always obvious. However, as discussed in this section, many teachers do identify multiple types of engagement and the importance of student cognitive engagement and it is these teachers who are most likely to use multiple practices to promote overall student engagement. The following section now considers some of these practices.

What teachers do about student engagement: teacher practices for engagement

Researchers have identified effective practices associated with maintaining student engagement, and note four main strategies as effective for building student understanding and learning (Stipek *et al.* 1998). These include: encouraging students to take on challenges; a focus on conceptual understanding of concepts; promoting active student autonomy and feelings of control; and developing competency. Other practices such as providing feedback, pressing for understanding, nurturing students' needs, interest and value in learning as well as fostering collaboration, have also been associated with increased student engagement (Schweinle *et al.* 2006; Turner *et al.* 2011).

However, while teachers may be well informed about effective practices for promoting engagement, it is also essential that they believe that they can effectively use such practices to promote engagement. Consequently, teacher knowledge of practices that can promote student engagement is just as essential as their self-efficacy for promoting student engagement (Hadré *et al.* 2008). Bandura (1977) defines self-efficacy as 'beliefs in one's capacities to organize and execute the courses of action required to produce given attainments' (1977: 3). It is suggested that self-efficacy varies in strength; therefore, some teachers may be more efficacious than others. Variations in teachers' self-efficacy result in different teachers' choices and this is likely to shape their approach to instruction. For example, teachers with high self-efficacy beliefs tend to spend increased efforts planning lessons, they persist longer when faced with challenges, they are willing to try new strategies, they are more enthusiastic, they have more confidence in managing classroom behaviours, they also have high expectations of their students' capabilities and promote self-regulatory approaches in their students (Draper 2013; Chatzistamatiou *et al.* 2014). In the next section, there is some discussion about teachers who believed that the various practices they used could make a difference to student engagement, and other teachers whose beliefs about engaging students were limited so they used only a few practices or were uncertain about how to engage students at all. It begins with describing practices that promote engagement and is followed by several that hinder it.

Practices promoting student engagement[2]

Relevance and value

In one reported study (Skilling *et al.* 2016), more than half the teachers discussed the relevance and practical applications of learning mathematics and how it was connected to the 'real world', as a means of engaging their students. For example, mathematics was seen as having 'a place in life, in the simple things that you do' and many teachers addressed student questions about the future value of mathematics as being 'helpful to know when they get out in the real world . . . and relevance is really important'. It was often mentioned that students asked questions about why they were learning particular topics and many teachers aimed to address these positively by making links to how the content might apply beyond the classroom, citing the development of logic and reasoning skills that are useful across learning and work.

However, this was not always the case, with some teachers unwilling to address students' needs for understanding. For example, when asked about the relevance of the mathematics work students were being asked to do, one teacher responded, 'At 13 and 14 years of age . . . we are doing it because we are doing it. I don't think you are going to come up with a satisfactory story for a 13 year old so sometimes I just think, "What is the point?"' (Skilling *et al.* 2016).

Enhancing student autonomy and empowerment

The importance of student autonomy has been advocated by Reeve (2009), as a key factor in promoting student motivation and engagement in learning settings. For example, in the study, many teachers explained how they encouraged student autonomy in their classrooms and altered their teaching approach for the range of student achievement levels evident in their classrooms. These teachers welcomed students' questions, acknowledged their frustrations and encouraged independent student investigations. One teacher explained his beliefs about student autonomy as needing to be centred on the students and 'It should be about the kids themselves taking control of what they're doing . . . so it's not just me giving the answers, they're actually finding the answers themselves' (Skilling *et al.* 2016). The contrary situation where teachers favour a controlling approach in classrooms results in negative influences on student engagement (Reeve 2009).

Emphasizing student interest

Many teachers believed it was important to be sensitive to student interest and to show their own passion for learning. This sensitivity to student interest in learning was perceived quite differently to doing something 'interesting' simply to maintain students' on-task behaviour. For example, one teacher said, 'I am trying to make it a bit more fun and energetic in class, I think they get that vibe off me that it can be fun even though the work is not easy all the time' (Skilling *et al.* 2016). The same teacher also reported that she tended to give quite a bit of homework but this was not as a sanction but because she wanted to maintain her students' interest and knowledge of mathematics learning between lessons. Other teachers nurtured students' capabilities and interests by allowing them to create the warm-up for the class and other teachers captured students' interest by starting lessons 'with puzzles and things to get their brains ticking'.

Emphasizing interpersonal relationships

Teachers also saw making personal connections with students as being important for encouraging continued learning. For example, one teacher said: 'If you have a rapport, then I think you are going to get a lot more out of any student.' It was also seen as important to become sensitive to students' feelings, that establishing relationships mattered for building trust and 'that you are not going to make fun of them or make them embarrassed'. This was seen as particularly important for promoting help-seeking, with one teacher commenting: 'I figure if the kid is too scared to ask you a question, then what is the point of being a teacher? They are supposed to want to ask you so you can help them . . . I try and relate to them as much as possible' (Skilling *et al.* 2016).

Apart from noting particular practices that are more effective for promoting engagement, it also has also been found that the number and frequency of times when teachers use such practices make a difference to engagement. Raphael *et al.* (2008) found that teachers who used a wide range of practices to encourage engagement resulted in high levels of positive affect and engagement in their classrooms (up to 90 per cent). They were also able to uncover practices that undermined engagement and these included negative classroom atmosphere and discipline styles, low expectancy to complete tasks, low value of the task itself, and limited monitoring and support for task completion (Raphael *et al.* 2008).

Practices hindering student engagement

Low expectations and controlling teacher styles

Unfortunately some teachers expressed low expectations of student engagement and the practices they used for promoting engagement were limited. For example, one teacher reported that the students' revision strategies for an upcoming test were unlikely to 'make a difference to them' as she expected that the students were unlikely to undertake revision at home or would simply be looking through their notebooks. Other teachers believed that starting the Year 7 teaching programme at the beginning for all students was effective despite knowing that many students already had a good understanding of the material, with one teacher justifying this by reporting, 'revision can't hurt'. This teacher did not seem to consider the engagement and learning needs of the students who would be repeating material and would be unlikely to be challenged.

Although it has been identified that controlling teacher styles reduce student value, interest, self-initiative, perseverance and creativity in classrooms (Reeve 2009), some teachers used this teaching style in their classrooms. Although controlling teacher styles might influence students' on-task behaviours and effort in the short term, they are not supportive of long-term emotional and cognitive engagement (Reeve 2009). Teachers often believed that they were not controlling, for example, wanting to have 'a low-stress classroom' and to give students a 'bit of responsibility' but then emphasizing sanctions for off-task behaviours and imposing penalties such as demerits for those who did not complete work in class. Often these teachers believed they were supporting increased student participation but were unaware of how these controlling practices might impede students' desires to engage with mathematics learning independently.

Occasional and uncertain engagement: the absence of effective practices

For some teachers, engaging students in learning was seen as something that only required attention occasionally. Quite often teachers perceived engagement as separate from teaching content and cited the priority of completing the lesson content and complying with the set scheme of work. Teachers considered adhering to the curriculum outcomes to be their key purpose, even when they were aware that students' understanding and engagement would be compromised, reporting 'Even if you have some great ideas that could engage [students], there is just not the time for it' (Skilling *et al.* 2016). Additionally, some teachers viewed practical lessons as wasting time and alleviating boredom rather than potentially engaging students. In other cases, teachers considered engaging lessons for students involved doing 'different' activities such as conducting the lesson outside or visiting the computer room.

Unfortunately, some teachers reported an uncertainty about how to engage students and at times felt powerless because of factors outside of their control. Teachers who felt a sense of helplessness about their ability to successfully engage students also reported reduced attempts to try to engage students. For example, one teacher commented that: 'You walk out of some classes and think, I may as well have just shown a movie because what did we achieve?' and another reported that despite trying quite a few different things, 'I just don't know how I can get them to want to do it' (Skilling *et al.* 2016). Teachers who are unsure about which approaches to use to engage students often seemed to be limited to thinking of engagement only in terms of student behaviour. This is in contrast to those teachers who used a wide range of practices to promote engagement. For these teachers, their focus went beyond encouraging student participation, and included enhancing positive emotions and evoking deep thinking about tasks and activities.

Concluding thoughts

This chapter began with four key aims: (1) to define and conceptualize engagement; (2) to consider the relationship between types of engagement and the underlying motivations that influence student engagement in learning; (3) to alert beginning teachers to the signs of engagement they might expect to see and provide a framework that assists in categorizing these into types of engagement; and (4) to offer insights into the instructional approaches that teachers use to promote student engagement and to dissuade student disengagement.

By using a clearly defined framework for student engagement, the types of engagement and how it is conceived provide insights into this important construct in school settings. This framework might encourage you to consider how you think about student engagement and if you believe that it goes beyond how students *act*, to include how they *feel* and *think* about their learning.

The Engagement Spectrum incorporated a wide range of teachers' responses and was able to categorize engagement by types of levels and intensity. In particular, the nuance of variably engaged students is explored, concerning those students who are neither disengaged nor substantially engaged students, as these are the students who are most at risk of moving towards disengagement. In particular, this might provoke you as a beginning teacher to consider more carefully the range of engagement that exists in classrooms, how it fluctuates, and the underlying factors that might influence this.

Finally, the section on teaching practices considers practices that promote and hinder student engagement. It is noted that teachers whose confidence is high often use a wide range of practices to support students. On the other hand, teachers who perceived obstacles to engaging their students and believed it to be too difficult reported using few effective practices for engaging students. Teachers who feel powerless to engage students often limit their efforts to placating students' immediate and short-term interests, however, this reduced their attempts at influencing student cognition.

As you navigate the beginning years as a teacher you may want to consider the following questions. How will your beliefs about student engagement influence your approach to instruction? Further, who do you think is responsible for student engagement or is this a shared responsibility between students and teachers?

Notes

1 This study is nested within a larger research project. Further details of the findings of this study have been reported elsewhere: Skilling (2013; 2014) and Skilling *et al.* (2016).
2 Please see Skilling *et al.* (2016) for a fuller discussion on teacher practices for engagement.

References

Anderman, E.M. and Patrick, H. (2012) Achievement goal theory, conceptualization of ability/intelligence, and classroom climate, in S.L. Christenson, A.L. Reschly and C. Wylie (eds) *Handbook of Research on Student Engagement*. New York: Springer, pp. 173–92.

Bandura, A. (1977) Self-efficacy: toward a unifying theory of behaviour change, *Psychological Review*, 84: 191–215.

Bobis, J., Way, J., Anderson, J. and Martin, A.J. (2015) Challenging teacher beliefs about student engagement in mathematics, *Journal of Mathematics Teacher Education*, 19(1): 33–55.

Boekaerts, M. (2016) Engagement as an inherent aspect of the learning process, *Learning and Instruction*, 43: 76–83.

Chatzistamatiou, M., Dermitzaki, I. and Bagiatis, V. (2014) Self-regulatory teaching in mathematics: relations to teachers' motivation, affect and professional commitment, *European Journal of Psychology of Education*, 29(2): 295–310.

Cleary, T.J. and Zimmerman, B.J. (2012) A cyclical self-regulatory account of student engagement: theoretical foundations and applications, in S.L. Christenson, A.L. Reschly and C. Wylie (eds) *Handbook of Research on Student Engagement*. New York: Springer, pp. 237–58.

Draper, J. (2013) Teacher self-efficacy: internalized understandings of competence, in S. Phillipson, K.Y.L. Ku and S.N. Philipson (eds) *Constructing Educational Achievement: A Sociocultural Perspective*. New York: Routledge, pp. 70–83.

Durksen, T.L., Way, J., Bobis, J., Anderson, J., Skilling, K. and Martin, A.J. (2017) Motivation and engagement in mathematics: a qualitative framework for teacher–student interactions, *Mathematics Education Research Journal (Special Issue)*.

Fredricks, J.A. and McColskey, W. (2012) The measurement of student engagement: a comparative analysis of various methods and student self-report instruments, in S.L. Christenson, A.L. Reschly and C. Wylie (eds) *Handbook of Research on Student Engagement*. New York: Springer.

Fredricks, J.A., Blumenfeld, P.C. and Paris, A.H. (2004) School engagement: potential of the concept, state of the evidence, *Review of Educational Research*, 74: 59–109.

Fredricks, J.A., Wang, M-T., Linn, J.S., Hofkens, T.L., Sung, H., Parr, A. and Allerton, J. (2016) Using qualitative methods to develop a survey measure of math and science engagement, *Learning and Instruction*, 43: 5–15.

Hadré, P.L. (2011) Motivation for math in rural schools: student and teacher perspectives, *Mathematics Education Research Journal*, 23: 213–33.

Hadré, P.L., Davis, K.A. and Sullivan, D.W. (2008) Measuring teacher perceptions of the 'how' and 'why' of student motivation, *Educational Research and Evaluation*, 14(2): 155–79.

Harris, L. (2011) Secondary teachers' conceptions of student engagement: engagement in learning or in schooling? *Teaching and Teacher Education*, 27: 376–86.

Linnenbrink-Garcia, L., Rogat, T. and Koskey, K. (2011) Affect and engagement during small group instruction, *Contemporary Educational Psychology*, 36: 13–24.

Martin, A. (2003) The student motivation scale: further testing of an instrument that measures students' motivation. *Australian Journal of Education*, 47(1): 88–106.

Martin, A.J. (2007) Examining a multidimensional model of student motivation and engagement using a construct validation approach, *British Journal of Educational Psychology*, 77: 413–40.

Martin, A.J., Anderson, J., Bobis, J., Way, J. and Vellar, R. (2012) Switching on and switching off in mathematics: an ecological study of future intent and disengagement among middle school students, *Journal of Educational Psychology*, 104(1): 1–18.

Martin, A.J., Ginns, P. and Papworth, B. (2017) Motivation and engagement: same or different? Does it matter? *Learning and Individual Differences*, 55: 150–62.

Martin, A.J., Papworth, B., Ginns, P., Malmberg, L., Collie, R. and Calvo, R. (2015) Real-time motivation and engagement during a month at school: every moment of every day for every student matters, *Learning and Individual Differences*, 38: 26–35.

Pekrun, R. and Linnenbrink-Garcia, L. (2014) Introduction to emotions in education, in R. Pekrun and L. Linnenbrink-Garcia (eds) *International Handbook of Emotions in Education*. New York: Routledge, pp. 1–10.

Raphael, L., Pressley, M. and Mohen, L. (2008) Engaging instruction in middle school classrooms: an observational study of nine teachers, *Elementary School Journal*, 109(1): 61–81.

Reeve, J. (2009) Why teachers adopt a controlling motivating style toward students and how they can become more autonomy supportive, *Educational Psychologist*, 44(3): 159–75.

Reeve, J. and Tseng, C.M. (2011) Agency as a fourth aspect of students' engagement during learning activities, *Contemporary Educational Psychologist*, 50: 1–13.

Schweinle, A., Meyer, D.K. and Turner, J.C. (2006) Striking the right balance: students' motivation and affect in elementary mathematics, *Journal of Educational Research*, 99(5): 271–94.

Skilling, K. (2013) Factors that influence Year 7 students' engagement and achievement in mathematics. Unpublished doctoral dissertation, University of Sydney, Sydney, Australia.

Skilling, K. (2014) Teacher practices: how they promote or hinder student engagement, in J. Anderson, M. Cavanagh and A. Prescott (eds) *Curriculum in Focus: Research Guided Practice*. Proceedings of the 37th annual conference of the Mathematics Education Research Group of Australasia, Sydney, NSW: MERGA, pp. 589–98.

Skilling, K., Bobis, J. and Martin, A. (2015) The engagement of students with high and low achievement levels in mathematics, in K. Beswick, T. Muir and J. Wells (eds) *Proceedings of the 39th Psychology of Mathematics Education* conference, Vol. 4. Hobart, Australia: PME, pp. 185–92.

Skilling, K., Bobis, J., Martin, A.J., Anderson, J. and Way, J. (2016) What secondary teachers think and do about student engagement in mathematics, *Mathematics Education Research Journal*, 28(4): 545–66.

Skinner, E.A. and Pitzer, J.R. (2012) Developmental dynamics of student engagement, coping and everyday resilience, in S.L. Christenson, A.L. Reschly and C. Wylie (eds) *Handbook of Research on Student Engagement*. New York: Springer, pp. 21–44.

Stipek, D., Salmon, J.M., Givven, K.B., Kazemi, E., Saxe, G. and MacGyvers, V.L. (1998) The value (and convergence) of practices suggested by motivation research and promoted by mathematics education reformers, *Journal of Research in Mathematics Education*, 29(4): 465–88.

Turner, J.C., Warzon, K. and Christenson, A. (2011) Motivating mathematics learning: changes in teachers' practices and beliefs during a nine-month collaboration, *American Educational Research Journal*, 48(3): 718–62.

Wang, M.-T. and Eccles, J. (2012) The measurement of student engagement: a comparative analysis of various methods and student self-report instruments, in S.L. Christenson, A.L. Reschly and C. Wylie (eds) *Handbook of Research on Student Engagement*. New York: Springer.

Williams, S.R. and Ivey, K.M.C. (2001) Affective assessment and mathematics classroom engagement: a case study, *Educational Studies in Mathematics*, 47: 75–100.

Wolters, C.A. and Taylor, D.J. (2012) A self-regulated learning perspective on student engagement, in S.L. Christenson, A.L. Reschly and C. Wylie (eds) *Handbook of Research on Student Engagement*. New York: Springer.

Zazkis, R. and Hazzan, O. (1999) Interviewing in mathematics education: choosing the questions, *Journal of Mathematical Behaviour*, 17(4): 429–39.

Zimmerman, B. (2002) Becoming a self-regulated learner: an overview, *Theory into Practice*, 41: 64–70.

12

Making sense of classroom 'behaviour': relating the two discourses of regulation and instruction

JEREMY BURKE

Introduction

The argument is made here that strategies for classroom management are acquired in practice. It is not possible to provide a set of tactics that will deal with all classes and all students at all times. The relationship with a class is contingent on various factors. However, there are strong claims made, in policy texts that deal with behaviour management about the importance of teachers' charisma and school behaviour policies in sustaining learning environments. Neither of these portrayals of teaching deals with attracting and maintaining the interest of an audience per se, which is the bedrock of effective management. Rather, a generalized school behaviour policy and individual subjects present different practices, where the teaching of each requires a process of attraction and maintenance of attention, but with different ends in sight. This chapter looks at the issues involved in behaviour management and presents a description which might help analyse the strategies adopted.

Boys don't sing

A teacher is standing before a class of Year 9 boys. He is working hard on his presentation to get them to engage, suggesting that the lesson contains nothing to be scared about, rather that it should be fun. He then interjects, 'Excuse me, boys, can we cut the chat? I don't want to have to move anyone. That would be a shame. Both of you. Thank you. Don't answer back.' After little success, he says, 'Oh dear. We aren't very awake in this class, are we?' Things do not get easier. The teacher persists, 'Sit down. All of you. Right now. Sit down right now, Tyrone.' Then turning to another boy, he starts to become more insistent, 'Stop talking, please. Excuse me. You. Young man. Can you join in, please? Are you going to join in?' The boy shook his head and replied, 'I can tell you now. I ain't singing.'

The class was being taken by Gareth Malone, who was attempting to rise to the challenge of developing a choir in a boys' school, where, according to the title of the TV series, *Boys Don't Sing* (Channel 4, 2008). Here, despite the presence of cameras and the class teacher, Gareth Malone was having a great deal of difficulty in attracting the boys' attention and getting them to take part in the activity of singing. Given that this was a TV programme and that Gareth was not the usual teacher of the group, then some of these difficulties might not be surprising. Unsurprising too, was that he became quite cross with the class; he could scream! 'I just feel, like, what is the point of them being here?' From the other perspective, the pupils in the class might be asking the same question: what's the point of Gareth Malone being here? And this is precisely the issue. A teacher meeting a class that is new to them always has to try to find a way to get the students to attend to, and make some sense of, the message that is being presented. But this cuts both ways. The pupils have to be generally willing to see some point in the topic to which they are being required to attend.

What is classroom behaviour?

There is a substantial literature on the issue of class control and management but definitions are less than forthcoming. First, there is no agreed term. The Steer Report (2005) uses the terms 'behaviour management' and 'classroom management' which are fairly common. There are also various other expressions, such as 'classroom disciplinary climate' (Jenkins and Ueno 2017) and, more simply, 'classroom climate' (Haydn 2014). Doherty *et al.* (2016) use the term 'classroom trouble' and Dicke *et al.* (2014) 'classroom disturbances'. Each of these has some credibility, but the variation suggests that the issue is not quite tied down. If naming is not quite clear, then the recognition rules are also not well defined. A question arises as to how we might observe good classroom practice in respect of, say, 'classroom management'. Indeed, what do we mean here by 'good'? The ways of getting a description or measure of 'classroom management' are tricky. Jenkins and Ueno (2017: 128) approach this by saying, 'Broadly speaking, a favourable classroom climate is one in which there is a well ordered and calm environment in which learning can take place.' Evertson and Weinstein (2006: 4) define classroom management as 'the actions teachers take to create an environment that supports and facilitates both academic and social-emotional learning'. Doyle (2005: 96) says classroom management is defined as 'how order is established and maintained in classroom environments', but also observes that conceptions of orderliness will vary according to circumstances, e.g. between different lessons, or during lesson breaks, or across different subjects, so orderliness in Mathematics might look very different from, say, PE, or Art or Technology. Maguire *et al.* (2010: 159) echo this, observing, 'what is commended in one subject area (say Drama or English) may not be seen as appropriate behaviour elsewhere. What is regarded as acceptable at one stage/age might be less appropriate in a different phase of schooling.' There can also be differences in subjective views of what counts as good classroom management. Dicke *et al.* (2014) used a Likert-type scale for student teachers to report how effective they thought they had been in classroom management. This gives an individual's self-perception of what they were doing, or how effective they thought their practice with that class in that lesson had been, but it does not offer a *general* description of classroom management.

The difficulty in defining and describing 'classroom management' was acknowledged by Elliot, who observed with reference to 'teacher authority': 'this knowledge is often tacit, the skills and behaviours involved may not necessarily be fully recognized by the practitioners themselves or easily communicated to others who are eager to learn from those with high-level expertise' (2009: 200). This makes the acquisition of the skill of 'classroom management' difficult because saying quite what it is eludes the commentator. Dowling (1998) describes this as text which is weakly discursively saturated (DS-). That is, the principles of the practice cannot be easily or adequately expressed in text. There are many activities like this, such as swimming or cycling. One might imagine giving a lesson to a class of pupils on how to swim:

> Push off from the side of the pool so you are parallel with the surface of the water, head face down in the water.
> Push your right hand backwards under your body.
> Turn your head to the right to breathe as you bring your right arm out of the water in a roughly circular fashion ready to push your hand, with your palm facing down, smoothly into the water shortly in front of your head.
> Straighten your arm ready to push backwards under your body.
> Repeat on the left side.
> Meanwhile kick your legs alternately with a strong up and down movement.

And then tell them to jump in the pool.

This is a DS- practice which needs to be experienced in other ways than being told or reading it. Books on swimming include photographs and diagrams, and perhaps the best information is given in YouTube videos. It seems that classroom management also has DS- elements which makes general statements opaque to newcomers to the practice. Cowley (2006) sets out to describe in some detail about 'getting the buggers to behave'. She gives a weakly defined classification of 'teaching styles', including one which is listed as 'The firm but fair teacher' (2006: 75). This is her view of the 'ideal teacher/behaviour manager' of which she gives some 'characteristics' but not exactly a definition. She begins with these two:

> The teacher tells the class what is expected in terms of behaviour right from the start, and sticks to these rules consistently.
> There is some flexibility applied to rules on occasions where it seems appropriate.
> (2006: 75)

Two things strike me about this. First, which rules are expected? Who makes these up? To what do they refer? Given Maguire *et al.*'s (2010) observation about different subjects, different phases of education, and so on, then there might be some variability in these 'rules'. Second, if these rules are stuck to 'consistently', how does this square with a need for 'flexibility' to suit the occasion?

The state view/policy approach

If we recognize classroom management as having significant DS- aspects to its practice, then to some extent the field is open for competing views about the practice and, second, non-discursive descriptions may play a more significant part, e.g. cartoons, drawings, photographs, films. For example, a few years ago, Michael Gove, then Secretary of State for Education, spoke to camera describing the 'perfect teacher':

> [A] good teacher is someone who has a natural air of authority buttressed by being well trained in classroom management. If you've got someone who's been your mentor, or someone who's trained you, who teaches you the tricks of the trade, in order to make sure that children can behave and can have their full attention on task, and on your teaching, then all of those ingredients together go up to make the perfect teacher.
>
> (DfE 2010)

Here Gove introduces the concept of a 'natural air of authority', which presumably one either has, or not, whatever it is. However, even the natural air is insufficient as it has to be buttressed. This is an odd term as it denotes a firm support offered to a building, and here connotes a rigidity or some kind of toughness which can be associated with 'tricks of the trade'. This is perhaps not quite the 'flexibility' that Cowley had in mind for her ideal teacher/behaviour manager. While the description of a 'perfect teacher' is unclear in terms of developing some skill in managing a classroom, it does perhaps explain, for example, the promoting of the programme Troops to Teachers. This was a scheme to provide a second career in teaching for people who had been in the armed services. David Laws, then Education Minister, opined, 'the Troops to Teachers scheme would bring military values of leadership, discipline, motivation and teamwork into the classroom' (*Daily Telegraph*, 7 June 2013). He appears to have presumed that these attributes could be recontextualized in school settings, making an analogy between the army and schools to give a particular view of behaviour management in school.

Visual images of teaching and classroom management are frequently presented in film and Dahlgren (2017) observes that many Hollywood films present an image of teaching containing a similar political message: 'What public education needs, these scenes beg their audience to deduce, is a short sharp dose of "real world" discipline' (Dahlgren 2017: 75). Perhaps this was the buttressing that Gove was seeking. It does serve to indicate that one aspect of the state view of schools is as institutions of control and discipline.

A further element of buttressing was introduced by Nicky Morgan, then Secretary of State for Education, through the appointment of the 'Behaviour Tsar', Tom Bennett. In his recent report there is a definition of 'behaviour' as:

> any actions performed by any members of the student and staff communities. It includes conduct in classrooms and all public areas: how members work, communicate, relax and interact; how they study; how they greet staff; how they arrive at school, transition from one activity to another; how they use social media, and many other areas of their conduct.
>
> (Bennett 2017: 12)

Clearly if the definition incudes 'any actions', then all of the subsequent list, and more, would be contained in such a catch-all phrase. He goes on to say that, 'Schools in all circumstances can achieve high standards of behaviour' (Bennett 2017: 12), but does not actually state what constitutes 'high standards'. He later looks for evidence of 'behaviour' being a problem and relies on self-reported survey results of teachers which, like Dicke *et al.*'s (2014) study, do not readily generalize. Surveys might identify whether individual teachers feel there is a problem. They do not define what the problem is. The DfE website, on the other hand, does present two views of teaching to address the issue of classroom management.

The classroom teacher

The Get into Teaching (GiT) website is set out to encourage people to consider becoming a teacher. Clearly there is an element of marketing about the representations of teaching here. At the outset there is a banner photograph showing a teacher engaging with pupils. The banner rotates over time displaying four different images showing one mathematics and three science classes. In one picture there is a teacher, presented as a 'hero', in a chemistry lesson. He is standing, surrounded by girls, holding out his hands, palms down. He is smiling broadly, wearing red glasses. His pupils are smiling too, wearing blue safety glasses. He is at the centre of the action and the pupils are looking towards him for the next step. The depiction is one of a teacher absolutely having the attention of his class. He has the pupils copying his hand movements, and there is an expectation that something is going to happen. The teacher looks ecstatic at his performance. The picture also shows the girls are dressed in spotless school uniforms, all wearing ties and looking very tidy. The classroom wall behind them has a colourful display, neatly arranged. The girls' blue safety glasses match their blue uniform and the teacher's red glasses match stripes in his tie (GiT, n.d. a). The image is both of a charismatic teacher and a well-ordered environment. A similar image in another section of the web page is provided of a modern languages teacher, also wearing red glasses (perhaps it was part of the teachers' uniform?) and smiling ecstatically. She has her hands out, but this time with her palms facing up. She has girls beside her, wearing very new-looking school uniforms with blazers, shirts and ties, and they appear to be saying something in unison. Behind them is a dramatic and very colourful display showing numerals with their names, (for example, 8, ocho, huit) in Spanish or French (GiT, n.d. b). Again the image is of a teacher enthusiastically engaging her class. The pupils are controlled insofar that they appear to be following what the teacher is presenting.

This is not dissimilar to the images presented of teaching in many films showing how teachers, new to a school, manage to captivate otherwise uninterested students such as LouAnne Johnson in *Dangerous Minds* or Jaime Escalante in *Stand and Deliver*. Ellsmore (2005) notes that presentations of teachers in films, much as in the GiT images of teaching, posit them as adopting a charismatic authority. They become central to the action, attracting and holding the attention of their students though adjusting the curriculum offered and confronting the established practices in the institution. Dissolute and resistant teenagers become attentive and 'buy into' what the teacher has to say. We might consider that the teacher's message has been well conceived and marketed. Ellsmore interviews serving ('real') teachers about their views on the filmic ('reel') teachers and their response is generally sceptical. They observe that it takes time to develop a relationship with a class and that there are frequently support structures in place for new teachers. The state's presentation of dazzling performances (GiT) appear to be somewhat overstated, but there is a performance, a marketing aspect to teaching. Dahlgren (2017: 148) notes that a contrasting view of teaching is presented in other Hollywood films which show teachers as 'uniformly dull and pedantic, creating a stultifying and authoritarian classroom atmosphere for their students'. Presumably the GiT images are set in direct opposition to this kind of view of teaching. However, it is interesting to look at another area of the DfE website for policy views on classroom management.

The school behaviour policy

There is a section on the DfE website which gives 'departmental advice' to schools and here there is a document which provides advice for headteachers and school staff on 'Behaviour and discipline in schools' (DfE 2016). This looks at schools developing behaviour policies and the powers that school staff have to discipline students. At the outset it states:

1.   The headteacher must set out measures in the behaviour policy which aim to:

   • promote good behaviour, self-discipline and respect;
   • prevent bullying;
   • ensure that pupils complete assigned work;

   and which

   • regulate the conduct of pupils.

(DfE 2016: 4)

This looks like a lot of control is being proposed, although quite what constitutes good behaviour is not defined. Nor is any detail given about the nature or quality of 'assigned work' which stands here simply as a job to be done, rather than involving learning. Indeed, the set of bullet points might be replaced simply by the last one: 'regulate the conduct of pupils'. However, the concept of 'self-discipline' does sound like Foucault's (1977) analysis of the techniques for disciplining the populations in institutions such as prisons, hospitals and schools. Foucault uses the term *discourse* to include the sets of texts and exemplars of a practice which in turn become recognizable as that practice. Foucault examines disciplinary regimes where various practices are used to provide a subjectivity in that discourse:

> The workshop, the school, the army were subject to a whole micro-penalty of time (lateness, absences, interruptions of tasks), of behaviour (impoliteness,

disobedience), of speech (idle chatter, insolence), of the body ('incorrect' attitudes, irregular gestures, lack of cleanliness), of sexuality (impurity, indecency). At the same time, by way of punishment, a whole series of subtle procedures was used, from light physical punishment to minor deprivations and petty humiliations.

(Foucault 1977: 178)

The *Advice* to headteachers details the sanctions to be implemented when a pupil is identified as behaving poorly. These include: a verbal reprimand; extra work; writing lines; loss of privileges; missing break time; detention; school-based community service; regular reporting and being placed on report; uniform and other checks; and 'in more extreme cases schools may use temporary or permanent exclusion' (DfE 2016: 8).

Foucault draws on the idea of a prison designed by Jeremy Bentham in the early nineteenth century – the Panopticon. Here the prison is built around an open space in which stands a watch tower. The cells are lit from outside the building, but the central area remains relatively unlit. The prisoners cannot tell whether they are being watched, or not, and consequently tend to act as though they are. A modern-day example is the Gatso Speed Camera on roads. Drivers slow down by these camera boxes just in case there is a live camera there and they are fined for speeding. They do not take the chance. Foucault describes this as the effect of the 'gaze' from the watch tower and the associated punishment system. The DfE Advice to Headteachers is to set up a punishment system so that when the 'gaze' falls upon miscreant pupils, they might be corrected until they internalize the 'expected' behaviour. In schools the 'gaze' is provided by teachers and other staff. As each infringement of the behaviour policy is noticed and noted, it can lead to the type of 'authoritarian' classroom described earlier by Dahlgren (2017).

I wish to raise two further issues about the *Advice*. First is, as we have seen elsewhere, there is no definition of what constitutes 'good behaviour'. The document only says that:

3. The headteacher must decide the standard of behaviour expected of pupils at the school. He or she must also determine the school rules and any disciplinary penalties for breaking the rules.

(DfE 2016: 4)

This presents the headteacher as the sovereign power within the micro-state of the school. The head determines the law, that is the 'standard of expected behaviour' and the 'disciplinary penalties for breaking the rules'. However, Foucault argues that the effect of disciplinary power is to work its way through the operations, processes and language of the organization which ultimately holds not only pupils in its thrall, but also teachers. The fact that the state issues *Advice* to Headteachers, and then requires that the behaviour policy is published on a website for all to see, and then inspects schools through the gaze of Ofsted, suggests that heads too are caught in this disciplinary network. The policy appears to promote heads and teachers as martinets, which is echoed in comments by Tom Bennett, who said, 'Students must become "compliant" in order to be free' (*Daily Telegraph*, 24 March

2017). The state is seeking to regulate the moral discourse into which pupils are to be 'compelled' (Bennett 2017: 23).

A contrary finding is given by Jenkins and Ueno (2017) in their study of 'classroom climate' comparing English schools with other schools internationally. They found that 'There was only weak evidence that school climate was related to classroom climate.' This intimates that a teacher with a class of pupils might develop a 'climate' which was better, worse or different from that in the rest of the school. The suggestion, then, is that the required publicized behaviour policy does not necessarily impact too strongly in the classroom.

Earlier on I presented two images of teaching in schools as exemplified on the DfE (GiT) websites: the charismatic teacher in the classroom and the institution with a strong disciplinary structure. I now want to turn to look at two sociological analyses to address these.

Pedagogic relations

In talking about teaching, we can consider two voices, a transmitter (author) and an acquirer (audience). In the empirical classroom these positions would typically be the teacher as transmitter and the pupil as acquirer. Clearly there will be some situations with pupil-to-pupil interaction, where one assumes the transmitter voice, and indeed at times a student will tell a teacher something about which they do not know. So I will speak about author (transmitter) and audience (acquirer) as a general case. I shall draw on Dowling's (2009) definition of a *pedagogic relation* as one where the author retains the principles of the practice being pedagogized. That is, in an empirical classroom, the teacher can evaluate the performance of the pupils and assess how well they can reproduce what is being taught.

Dowling also looks at this from the other point of view. That is where the audience can evaluate the performance of the author (the transmitting voice). He describes this as an *exchange relation* and we can find examples of this in common performances. An analogy of this is a stand-up comedian facing a new audience. Recently I was at a comedy show where a well-known performer came on stage to perform his new schtick. After a few minutes someone, in the third row, commented loudly, 'That's not very funny.' This surprisingly disturbed the entertainer whom I should have thought would be used to such interruptions. This exemplifies an exchange relation where the audience (or at least one member of it) has passed judgement on the performance of the author.

This is sometimes what is referred to in a classroom as 'disturbance', where the audience, the pupils, do not recognize completely the authority of the author, the teacher. The move required is to interpellate the class as students of the teacher. That is, that the children in the class recognize themselves as 'students' and would respond to being spoken to as such. The term interpellation comes from Althusser (2001: 1971), who uses it to signify a self-recognition, by responding to a hailing. As Foucault was concerned about the way a person adopts or becomes a certain subject, Althusser describes the process of self-recognition within an ideological framework. In the classroom the attempted framework to be established is one of a pedagogic relation. To achieve this, the audience, the students, have to recognize themselves as the acquirers of the message being delivered. In the comedy show, the man in the audience was not accepting the authority of the entertainer. He judged his story was 'not funny'. The job of the entertainer, and to this extent is similar to that of a teacher, is to gain acceptance as the authoritative transmitter, the author in the relation with the audience.

Dowling also includes in his analysis of pedagogic and exchange relations the positioning of the person being evaluated. Focusing here on pedagogic relations, Dowling suggests that the audience may be attributed with a subjectivity as *apprentices* to the practice being taught or as *dependent* participants. A mode of apprenticeship offers entry into the practice with a progress to 'mastery' or some degree of competence. A mode of dependency requires that some procedures or limited actions are learned and performed.

Two discourses

Bernstein posited that pedagogic discourse, the practice being transmitted by a teacher, is composed of two separate discourses. The first he termed the *instructional* discourse (ID). This is associated with subject teaching such as English, Mathematics, Science etc. The second he termed the *regulative* discourse (RD). This is concerned with the deportment, dress, styles of address (Sir, Ma'am), time, place, and so on. It refers to a moral education and Bernstein asserts that moral discourse dominates the subject discourse. This does look similar to the DfE *Advice* on behaviour management which states, 'School staff, pupils and parents should all be clear of the high standards of behaviour expected of all pupils at all times.' This is certainly the message in the GiT images. Pupil deportment, dress and the orderliness of their surroundings make the exciting teaching possible. The RD 'buttresses' the ID. On the other hand, the starry charisma of the film characters, identified by Ellsmore (2005), allowed them to adjust what they were teaching in order to attract and maintain the attention of their classes. The film message, then, is one of ID trumping the RD – hence the slightly revolutionary, independent nature of *reel* teachers' actions.

Dowling takes the view that subject disciplines also have some regulative aspect since, *pace* Foucault, 'being a subject *of* always entails being subject *to*, which is to say it always entails a regulation on behaviour in some form or other' (Dowling 2009: 182). If this is the case, then the ID/RD relation is not the one given by Bernstein, but rather each aspect exists within any practice. However, recognizing that there are many regulatory practices in schools, Dowling differentiates disciplinary (specialized) practices and non-disciplinary (generalized) practices. Subjects such as English, mathematics, science, etc. refer to academic, specialized disciplines, but school behaviour policies are more general. The important thing is to mark out the two, as Jenkins and Ueno pointed out, because the school behaviour rules and the actions in classrooms are not necessarily closely related.

Interpellating the student

So far I have considered the issues of offering a pathway to subjectivity *of* a practice, where *apprenticeship* included some independent competence while *dependency* provided rather limited access to the principles of the practice of classroom management. I have also looked at the *willingness*, or not, of an audience to recognize the authority of the author, here the classroom teacher. I have also shown that 'behaviour management' is a DS- practice which is not well defined in the literature. Finally, I have differentiated specialized (school subjects) and generalized (whole school 'behaviour').

The way that I am reading 'behaviour management' or 'class control' or 'climate' is through a focus on the classroom interactions between a teacher and students. If there is a general (non-disciplinary) and local (disciplinary) discourse, then in both instances there is the possibility of positioning the audience as potential apprentices to, or dependents of, that discourse. In terms of the state's required school behaviour policy, the recommendation in the *Advice* mainly positions the audience as dependent – to 'regulate the conduct of pupils' in order to 'promote good behaviour' although without defining it. The document is almost entirely about the punishments and sanctions available if a pupil 'misbehaves' and breaks a school rule. School rules will include dress and deportment requirements, and so on, but if there is any resistance to the school rules, then the set of punishments are there in order to compel the pupil to conform. This takes a dependency view of the outcome. The pupil will never master the rules, to be subject of, but only dependent on the given, to be subject to.

Here an unwilling audience is *coerced* to attend to the required deportment, the moral code, of the institution through a process of individualization and punishment. However, if the audience is ready to accept the authority of the authorial voice, then all that is needed for attention is a *summons*. On the other hand, if the level of subjectivity being attributed to the audience is apprenticeship, then the heavy hand of 'discipline and punish' might not lead to the more independent action required to make some sense of the practice being pedagogized. Here the move is to *attract* an audience which is not immediately accepting of the authority of the authorial voice. This is the stuff of the filmic teachers: LouAnne, in *Dangerous Minds*, announces she is a marine and knows karate; Jaime Escalante in *Stand and Deliver* chops an apple in two with a meat cleaver. This is also presented in the GiT images, as the chemistry teacher is holding his hands out. These are actions to attract an audience, although perhaps overdramatic for 'real' teachers.

Table 12.1 Interpellating the student

Audience demeanour	Author attribution of subjectivity to audience	
	apprenticeship (high level of subjectivity)	dependency (minimal subjectivity)
Accepting	inviting	summoning
Not accepting	attracting	coercing

Nevertheless, some attraction is needed for pupils to see themselves as 'apprentices' in that lesson. If the audience is ready to accept being apprenticed to a practice, then the authorial move is to *invite* attention. These strategies can be illustrated in the schema in Table 12.1.

Returning to Gareth Malone and his boys in the singing class, he draws on a regulatory aspect of his pedagogy of pupils as being quiet and sitting still. He variously threatens moving boys, sending one outside the lesson and telling another to remain behind. These are all statements with punishments attached: if you do not do this, then a sanction will be incurred. This is the strategy of *coercing* attention to the authorial voice, but all that is being offered is the subjectivity of sitting quietly when told. The problem is that Gareth had not really set about *marketing* what he is offering. The boys are not in the class because they have chosen to be, so what is it that marks them out as any different from prisoners?

In the Channel 4 series *Educating East London*, an introductory short clip was of a teacher in a class of girls. Here the girls are making comments, perhaps causing a 'classroom disturbance' as Dicke *et al.* (2014) describe it. The teacher asks the girls to be quiet and one replies, 'It's only bantah.' The teacher, Mr Bispham, responds: 'I know it's only banter, but this is not the time for bantaah. This is the time for work-aah' (Channel 4, 2014). We might expect that there is some continuum from disruption to banter, and the move to close this down is the judgement of the teacher, at that time, with that particular group. The teacher here was calling students to account. The girls appear to be fully aware of the class rule about 'work' and the teacher can draw on that in seeking to end the off-task 'banter'. His strategy is to *summon* the girls to attend to the task in hand, interpellating them as students in his English lesson.

As a teacher myself, I was concerned to *attract* the attention of pupils in Mathematics lessons and a typical strategy I deployed was to provide a statement about something that appeared obvious, but to then find some surprise. For example, on one occasion I said to pupils, 'There are only eight different pentominoes. Can you find them all?' A pentomino is a shape made from five squares touching edge to edge. Constructing a pentomino is very simple. Pupils could draw them easily on squared paper. After a little while someone said, 'Oh, I've found nine pentominoes.' I then acted surprised, and said there were only eight. The pupil became more insistent and showed me nine. I continued to be surprised and said it must be a mathematical breakthrough. A discovery. The pupil with nine was then delighted until someone said, 'Um, I've found ten.'

At this point the class was hooked. How many pentominoes were there? How would we know if we had found them all, and the mathematics developed into two-dimensional isometries and proof (e.g. Wesslén and Fernandez 2005; Burke *et al.* 2007). The subjectivity attributed to the audience was one of apprenticeship. The offer was to engage in some serious (school) mathematics which, as Wesslén and Fernandez point out, could lead to teaching group theory to Year 8.

Turning back to consider the GiT images, they are indicative of an *invitation* strategy. The chemistry teacher has his pupils holding their hands out in expectation. The modern languages teacher has her pupils chanting something by the wall. Here the pupils, and teachers, are smiling, happy and ready to engage with what is about to be transmitted. So, I have argued that classroom management is a DS- practice. That it has to be learned in the situation and experienced. Each of these examples demonstrates an interaction between teachers and students as moves are made to gain the attention of the audience.

Classroom management

Dicke *et al.* (2015) refer to the 'shock' experienced by new teachers when they first take a class. This should be a shock only insofar that it is a new situation, a new experience – much like the 'shock' of getting into a swimming pool for the first time. However, this is not because of a group of pupils who are out to get the teacher, but rather that it takes some time to make sense of the signals being given by members of the class, for example, confusion, lack of interest, tiredness, excitement about something else, and so on. A better way of thinking about classroom management is learning to *read* the audience. Elliot noted that, 'The notion that skilled teachers prevent problems, rather than merely react to them, highlights the importance of sensitivity to classroom contexts' (2009: 200). Classroom management is the outcome of the relationship built between a teacher and their pupils. Initially a teacher has to establish authority. When new to a school, all teachers have to do this. Part of this is devising strategies to attract the attention of pupils in the first place: the move from exchange to pedagogic relations – if you like, from bantah to work-aah.

The state requires that all schools have, and publish, a 'behaviour policy' and sets out how this should include the rules and penalties for failing to adhere to the rules. This looks like Foucauldian technologies of gaze, discipline and punish. The behaviour policy in setting out a pattern of 'behaviour' is a practice to be learned, but not a practice over which students will often acquire the principles of evaluation. To that extent the audience for this is constructed as having a dependent subjectivity. The role offered to teachers is one of a martinet, and this is what Tom Bennett, the behaviour Tsar, promotes.

Disciplinary, or academic, subjects taught in schools will frequently offer an apprenticeship to that subject, to the top sets at least. To have pupils think about and make sense of what is being presented will often require a degree of flexibility, as suggested by Sue Cowley, so that the strategy for gaining attention is to invite an accepting audience or to attract in some way a non-accepting audience. The gaining of attention in all ways is, to an extent, an actorly performance. The filmic teachers clearly do this, and the GiT photographs suggest this too. However, as the teachers interviewed by Ellsmore, or the comments made by Dahlgren, point out, teaching is not the same as the very theatrical strategies adopted in film and the GiT site, and somewhat smaller and more subtle moves are made. My example was offering pupils the wrong answer and acting surprised when the students found out that it was wrong. This is a strategy for marketing the subject, but this requires some serious thought. Chocolates or merit marks might get a task done, but might not encourage the thinking needed by pupils to make sense of what is being taught.

The development of a relationship with a class is a DS- activity. One can pick up ideas and suggestions from mentors, or books that provide anecdotes of teaching, but ultimately the experience is to be lived and made one's own. The 'tricks of the trade', as Michael Gove expressed it, are relatively few, for example:

- Wait for silence before speaking.
- If you write something on the board, pupils will, somewhat mechanically, copy it down. This will gain quiet but little thought.
- Ask pupils to stand *behind* their chairs before releasing them at the end of the lesson. This gets all the chairs put away neatly.
- If your room is efficiently tidied up at the end of the lesson, then it looks like you have been in control to whoever walks in the room next – staff or pupils.

These 'tricks' are soon learned. The more important element of the practice is to recognize what difficulties pupils have with your subject and try to address these.

I started with Gareth Malone, and there are two further points to come from this episode with his class of boys. First, he says he is very clear about the goal he is trying to achieve. This is very important for teachers and is commonly referred to as 'planning'. There is no escape from this. You have to know what points you want the class to engage with, how you might offer an explanation and what you want the pupils to actually do to help them make sense of what they are being taught.

Second, he says he is determined not to give up. This is sometimes referred to as 'resilience' and is also a vital part of teaching. Learning a DS- activity is about trial and error. About reflecting on the ways things have gone, identifying what worked well and making adjustments for things that didn't. What does not work at all is to blame the class. I have heard so many times that 'some pupils are spoiling it for those who want to learn'. It is the responsibility of a teacher to identify those pupils who are not accepting the subjectivity of a student of their subject and working out what to do about it. There are all sorts of ways to do this, and one is to be methodical and at some point in the lesson talk to one or two pupils about their work. The next lesson talk to another two, and so on. Very soon all the pupils in the class have had some engagement with the teacher, who will be developing a sense of the class and its members. The school level and classroom level practices may be addressed differently, and there are moves between marketing and compelling to be considered, depending on the desired outcome.

Stickability, resilience, imagination, and a bit of an act are all part of 'classroom management', as is 'reading' the class and identifying who needs help and who will make ready progress. The strategies deployed will be contingent on the class, subject, topic, time of day, whether it's windy . . . and so on. Ultimately it is planning, clarity and determination that gets all of us to engage our audience.

Oh, and the boys, in the end, did sing.

Concluding thoughts

You might want to make use of the schema provided in this chapter when looking at classroom interactions between teachers and students and consider what is the outcome of the use of particular strategies.

References

Althusser, L. (2001) Ideology and ideological state apparatuses, in L. Althusser, *Lenin and Philosophy and Other Essays*. New York: Monthly Review, pp. 127–86.

Bennett, T. (2017) *Independent Review of Behaviour in Schools*. London: DfE, https://www.gov.uk/government/uploads/system/uploads/attachment_data/file/602487/Tom_Bennett_Independent_Review_of_Behaviour_in_Schools.pdf.

Bernstein, B. (2000) *Pedagogy, Symbolic Control and Identity: Theory, Research, Critique*. Oxford: Rowman and Littlefield.

Burke, J., Cowen, S., Fernandez, S. and Wesslén, M. (2007) Dynamic gliding, *Mathematics Teaching*, 195: 12–14.

Channel 4 (2008) *The Choir Series 2: Boys Don't Sing*. Presented by Gareth Malone for the BBC. Filmed and directed by Harry Beney and Rob McCabe. Twenty Twenty Productions Ltd.

Channel 4 (2014) *Educating the East End*, Thursday, 4 September, Channel 4, available on YouTube, https://www.youtube.com/watch?v=tBcX1W0sUZQ, accessed 24 January 2017.

Cowley, S. (2006) *Getting the Buggers to Behave*. London: Continuum.

Dahlgren, R.L. (2017) *From Martyrs to Murders: Images of Teaching in Hollywood Films*. Rotterdam: Sense Publishers.

DfE (Department for Education) (2010) We ask Michael Gove what he thinks makes a good teacher, http://www.youtube.com/watch?v=qUVMNh_vvPw, accessed 24 January 2017.

DfE (Department for Education) (2016) *Behaviour and Discipline in Schools: Advice for Headteachers and School Staff*, https://www.gov.uk/government/publications/behaviour-and-discipline-in-schools, accessed 24 January 2017.

Dicke, T., Elling, J., Schmeck, A. and Leutner, D. (2015) Reducing reality shock: the effects of classroom management skills training on beginning teachers, *Teaching and Teacher Education*, 48: 1–12.

Dicke, T., Parker, P.D., Marsh, H.W., Kunter, M., Schmeck, A. and Leutner, D. (2014) Self-efficacy in classroom management, classroom disturbances, and emotional exhaustion: a moderated mediation analysis of teacher candidates, *Journal of Educational Psychology*, 106(2): 569–84.

Doherty, C., McGregor, R. and Shield, P. (2016) Ordering within moral orders to manage classroom trouble, *Pedagogies: An International Journal*, 11(2): 127–45.

Dowling. P. (2009) *Sociology as Method: Departures from the Forensics of Culture, Text and Knowledge*. Rotterdam: Sense Publishers.

Dowling, P.C. (1998) *The Sociology of Mathematics Education: Mathematical Myths/Pedagogic Texts*. London: Falmer Press.

Doyle, W. (2005) Ecological approaches to classroom management, in C.M Evertson and C.S. Weinstein (eds) *Handbook of Classroom Management: Research, Practice, and Contemporary Issues*. Mahwah, NJ: Lawrence Erlbaum, pp. 97–125.

Elliot, J.G. (2009) The nature of teacher authority and teacher expertise, *Support for Learning*, 24(4): 197–203.

Ellsmore, S. (2005) *Carry on Teachers! Representations of the Teaching Profession in Screen Culture*. Stoke-on-Trent: Trentham Books.

Evertson, C.M. and Weinstein, C.S. (2006) *Handbook of Classroom Management. Research: Practice and Contemporary Issues*. Mahwah, NJ: Lawrence Erlbaum Associates, Inc.

Foucault, M. (1977) *Discipline and Punish: The Birth of the Prison*. London: Penguin Books.

GiT (n.d. a) https://getintoteaching.education.gov.uk/sites/default/files/hero_banner/x10471745_Chemistry_1204-09651_RGB.jpg.pagespeed.ic.8wAZATwaVb.jpg, accessed 24 January 2017.

GiT (n.d. b) https://getintoteaching.education.gov.uk/explore-my-options/training-to-teach-secondary-subjects/training-to-teach-languages, accessed 10 October 2017.

Haydn, T. (2014) To what extent is behaviour a problem in English schools? Exploring the scale and prevalence of deficits in classroom climate, *Review of Education*, 2(1): 31–64.

Jenkins, A. and Ueno, A. (2017) Classroom disciplinary climate in secondary schools in England: what is the real picture? *British Educational Research Journal*, 43(1): 124–50.

Maguire, M., Ball, S. and Braun, A. (2010) Behaviour, classroom management and student 'control': enacting policy in the English secondary school, *International Studies in Sociology of Education*, 20(2): 153–70.

Steer, A. (2005) *Learning Behaviour: The Report of The Practitioners' Group on School Behaviour and Discipline*, http://webarchive.nationalarchives.gov.uk/20130401151715/http://www.education.gov.uk/publications/eOrderingDownload/0281-2006PDF-EN-04.pdf, accessed 20 January 2017.

Wesslén, M. and Fernandez, S. (2005) Transformation geometry, *Mathematics Teaching*, 191: 27-29

Further reading

Dowling, P. and Brown, A. (2009) Pedagogy and community in three South African schools: an iterative description, in P. Dowling, *Sociology as Method: Departures from the Forensics of Culture, Text and Knowledge*. Rotterdam: Sense Publishers, pp. 149–91.

13

Differentiation in theory and practice
SIMON COFFEY

Introduction

Differentiation denotes both a philosophy of education which recognizes that pupils learn differently, and the range of measures and strategies that seeks to accommodate these differences. To differentiate means, according to my dictionary, 'to perceive, show or make a difference (in or between); to discriminate' (*Collins Concise English Dictionary* 1982: 311). However, the perception of difference is not always straightforward and depends to a large extent on cultural and institutional beliefs. This chapter considers differentiation at three connecting levels: systemic differentiation through school types, setting within schools, and pedagogic practices to differentiate between learners within a single classroom. The emphasis will be placed on the last of these and I present the what, why and how questions which face teachers across the curriculum as they seek to embed differentiated teaching into their practice, but awareness of the wider contextualizing layers of structural differentiation serves to remind us of the deeply ideological dimension of how learning is organized. The central message I wish to convey in this chapter is that, although the need to ensure that each pupil experiences meaningful and successful learning can often seem a daunting challenge given material and time constraints, differentiation *is* manageable when viewed as flexibility in planning, teaching and assessing.

Systemic differentiation

Schools are designed to meet the aims of a wider social structure and their organization cannot be understood without reference to the broader socio-historical conditions that create them and which they reproduce. In England, schools have always been particularly stratified to reflect a hierarchical view of society. Attendance at particular schools was at one time differentiated by wealth until free schooling became progressively more available, developing from charity schools to state-funded compulsory schooling first at elementary and then secondary level. Provision expanded during the eighteenth and, especially, nineteenth centuries in the wake of industrialization as the expanded middle class wanted to benefit from new opportunities for professional and social mobility. There was also an increasing recognition of the value of education for social cohesion and civic participation. Nonetheless, educational provision remained differentiated along lines of social class and elitist conceptions of the purposes of education according to whether schooling was viewed as preparation for future leadership, middling professions or manual work.

Education in schools has traditionally been differentiated along lines of gender, with the sexes believed to require different types of education for their different futures, and also to learn in different ways. The recommendation of the Hadow Report (1923: xv) that girls take their exams a year later than boys and have a shorter school day because 'the conditions of health are not the same . . . Girls are liable to seasons of lowered vitality, in which nervous fatigue is serious' can seem amusing today. The same report suggests that the aims of physical exercise should be differentiated by sex so that 'the aim in general should be to cultivate strength and precision among boys, and suppleness, grace, and lightness of movement among girls' (1923: 74). This quotation highlights the changing views on the criteria for differentiation. Systemic differentiation by gender has, nonetheless, continued across both the independent and maintained sectors.

Other common forms of systemic differentiation are by faith and by academic ability. In the first case, children from different faith communities are permitted to study together in an environment that supports the ethos of their family's religion. In some countries, state schooling is strictly secular and even in the UK many people believe that state funding should not be used to support sectarian differentiation. Recent research also confirms that faith schools are socially selective and take proportionately fewer disadvantaged pupils (Education Policy Institute 2016). In spite of this, recent governments have increasingly favoured the expansion of faith schools. Organizing schools around academic ability is especially tricky because of the more complex and contestable ways in which ability can be defined, in comparison to the biological or communitarian differences already mentioned, although, as we have seen, a historical perspective shows us clearly that even these seemingly obvious differences are not as tangible as they may first appear.

The view that schooling should be differentiated according to future work trajectories seemed logical in a relatively stable system of socially classed labour where children tended to follow the work and life patterns of their parents. The academic–vocational divide that had its precursor in the Victorian and Edwardian school legislation, was crystallized by the tripartite system established in the optimistic post-war period. In this system children were differentiated by a selective exam – effectively an intelligence test – at the age of 11 (called the 11+) and funnelled into the grammar school to follow a more academic curriculum, a secondary modern school to follow a general but less ambitious curriculum with more emphasis on technical subjects, and technical schools, which were the least 'academic', although actually few in number (around 7 per cent of children attended these). Most children attended the secondary modern. The ambition for the system was to provide free education for all (independent schools continued with their own traditional practices for those who could afford the fees) according to ability. In principle, the sought-after grammar school places, taking around 25 per cent of pupils, would be available for any child who could demonstrate aptitude for academic study through passing the 11+. In practice, of course, this tended to be children from the middle classes, not because the children were necessarily more innately able but because the parents used what sociologists now call social and cultural 'capital' – forms of social know-how learned from their own experience of privilege – to navigate the system by, for instance, having their children coached specifically to pass the 11+.

Setting within schools

The egalitarian ideology heralded by the social movements of the 1960s and 1970s, especially in Western Europe and North America, shook up the world of education and in the UK comprehensive schooling was introduced in most areas, though the 11+ still segregates children in a small number of counties and local boroughs. Comprehensive schools were believed to provide an egalitarian model of schooling whereby all children from a given catchment area would attend their local school, mixing between social class and levels of ability. Within the comprehensive school, children were often placed in either streams (i.e. ranked by ability into groups for all subjects) or, most commonly, 'sets' (ranked by ability for certain subjects) – both setting and streaming are referred to in the US as 'tracking'. The ideology of setting continues to be highly contentious and there is no consensus about its effectiveness. Some schools do not 'set' at all, while others set for some subjects and others set for just core subjects.

Research findings have repeatedly suggested that setting does not benefit most pupils in terms of academic progress and that the negative impact of ability group is greatest in lower sets. Having reviewed the literature on ability grouping, Francis *et al.* conclude that the 'evidence suggests that these [setting] practices are not of significant benefit to attainment, with a *negative impact for lower sets and streams* – those wherein pupils from lower socio-economic groups are over-represented' (2016: 3, original emphasis). Despite this finding, the belief in the value of setting is tenaciously adhered to by many teachers and parents, and supported by successive governments' recommendations (DfEE 1997; DCSF 2005), concerned that fully mixed ability classes will be disruptive and hinder the learning of the more able.

Differences in aptitude have long been recognized. In the past, such differences were understood as being immutable characteristics inherent within pupils and it was believed that pupils of different aptitudes would benefit from structural segregation by 11+ filtering or by streaming and/or setting by ability groups within a school. The move away from setting towards completely 'mixed ability', that is, *unset* groups, seemed a natural extension of the egalitarian ethos of comprehensivism and required teachers to rethink issues of organizing and planning for pupils' different learning needs. The ethos which underpins *explicit* differentiation as it is now interpreted in the UK[1] is therefore closely tied to a belief in mixed ability teaching, not least of all the importance of the social dimension. Of course, even where groups are set by ability, there is a range of varying aptitude within the group, as well as different motivations, so even the most rigorous selection process will never produce a truly homogeneous group of learners. It is for this reason that the term 'mixed ability' can be somewhat misleading as all groups are heterogeneous.

Differentiated learning

The different ways in which pupils learn result from complex cognitive, genetic and social differences, which we are still only beginning to understand. It is important to emphasize that differentiation in teaching is only as important as differentiation in learning. A traditional view of school learning was that, metaphorically speaking, pupils were receptacles and the job of the teacher was to fill them with knowledge. The process was conceived as linear, that is, incremental, so 'good' pupils retained more knowledge. In such a case, it was often seen that this type of pupil had a good memory, was motivated and paid attention, while 'bad' pupils did not retain knowledge, lacked motivation to learn and were easily distracted. Unsurprisingly, 'co-operation' and docility therefore became conflated with notions of intelligence.

We now recognize that learning is a much more complex process than the retention of information and that the traditional classroom privileged certain, culturally shaped ways of learning, interacting and seeing the world. There is still some dispute over terminology to describe difference; for example, less able, SEN, different needs, gifted and talented – see Cigman (2006) for a defence of the concept of the 'gifted child'. However, modern educationalists, faced with increasing diversity, unite in acknowledging that the 'one-size-fits-all' model of learning is no longer credible and so we are left with no alternative which can claim to be just and equitable other than to integrate into our teaching a flexibility that allows *all* pupils the opportunity to succeed.

What does differentiation look like in a school?

Most schools now include 'differentiation' explicitly or implicitly in their stated learning goals, acknowledging that teaching needs to reflect the highly individual needs of learners. Consider, for example, these two aims extracted from school mission statements:

1. We believe that every pupil can succeed and we challenge pupils to achieve their full potential by building differentiated targets into our teaching.
2. We will develop pupils' individual talents and encourage them to work positively on improving identified areas for development.

These statements reflect the remit of education in the twenty-first century: to prepare pupils for a lifetime of flexible 'learnability'. Skills and knowledge are no longer, if indeed they ever were, viewed as finite entities or attributes, things that some people can do or know and which will continue to serve them in their professional life. We cannot know which skills will be in demand in the future or which personal qualities will be privileged in the workplace and so the emphasis is now on developing flexible skills and approaches to learning. Differentiation – offering the appropriate level of challenge – allows pupils, to a greater extent, to plan their own learning and to negotiate their own targets. In other words, it encourages positive involvement and increased autonomy.

Why differentiate?

As the term 'differentiation' became established in educational discourse in the 1990s, it denoted an attitude to pupils and a repertoire of practices which many experienced teachers already recognized as 'good', child-centred teaching. As the focus on differentiated teaching and learning became more explicit, through in-service training and initial teacher education, many experienced teachers welcomed the acknowledgement of what had long been their experience in the classroom: 'Defining the word and operationalizing it was something new, although the actual practices were old, something which was part of experienced teachers' professional expertise and craft knowledge' (Kersher and Miles 1996: 19).

At last, the open discussion about difference and how to support different pupils meant that ideas could be cross-fertilized and new strategies developed to cater for different needs. Differentiation no longer needed to be dependent on anecdote and conventional wisdom but could take its place as a major cornerstone in the way lessons were planned and taught. Similarly, teachers new to the profession welcomed the range of differentiating strategies to support their management of the sometimes overwhelming diversity of any pupil cohort.

In summary, then, many teachers have always implicitly had different expectations from different students, especially as their personal knowledge of pupils grew, and these expectations often affected choices made about which pupils to ask what, which pupils to pair off together for an activity, and so forth. Now, however, differentiation enjoys full recognition as it forms both part of teachers' professional dialogue and an important dimension in pupils' developing autonomy as learners.

How to differentiate

Provide optimal challenge

As teachers differentiate between classes according to a broad set of variables (for example, age, set, previous learning, maybe gender ratio, even the time of day), so, within a class, teachers know that there are a range of pupil-preferred styles of learning, levels, competences, and so forth. Whether the class has been 'set' or not, *all* classes require sensitivity to differentiated needs, although, of course, where there is broad mix of ability, this breadth needs to be reflected in the scope of the teacher's differentiation strategies. Differentiation does *not* mean teaching individually tailored lessons to 30 individuals; no teacher is expected to provide private tuition on this scale! Even if this were feasible logistically, such exclusively individualized learning would undermine the richness of the group dynamic which characterizes in-school learning. The social aspect of learning in a group with pupils offering different types of help to one another is to be capitalized on by teachers in the interests of peer respect and school citizenship values. These different collaborations include coaching through modelling and explaining, and other types of scaffolding peer support.

Indeed, as exemplified at the end of this chapter, peer collaboration and modelling offer important mechanisms for providing differentiated support, and research has shown that such scaffolding does lead to improved competence (Tudge 1992). Clearly, social cohesion and a belief in pupil–teacher shared goals are important elements in ensuring a feeling of belonging and a positive attitude to the subject and, indeed, to school (Ireson and Hallam 2005). Differentiation strategies therefore always need to be underpinned by an environment of warmth and security in which pupils work together.

Differentiation means offering pupils *optimal* challenge, so that each child can experience success. The role of the teacher is to sustain appropriate levels of interest and engagement. During the thousands of lessons I have both taught and observed, I have concluded that the single most striking yardstick for measuring sustained pupil engagement (for which read 'successful learning') is sensitivity to the appropriate *level, pace* and *type* of learning to ensure optimal challenge. To unpack this statement let us consider each of the three components.

Level of learning

Clearly, pupils need to be set activities which are within their reach but which are not too easy. Both work that is too difficult and that which is too easy are likely to lead to distraction and, in the long term, to disaffection. If work is perceived to be too difficult, pupils will feel that they are not up to the task. This may be because the task does not build on the frame of knowledge and skills that has previously been developed, or it may be that the task has not been 'scaffolded' adequately with support material, further explanation or other sources of support, such as group work. Pupils often feel that the task is intrinsically too difficult for them rather than thinking that they need to enlist support. Indeed, they may not know what type of support is available or how to gain access to it. Provision of adequate support, or clear signposting towards it, is incumbent upon the teacher. Pupils in this case, faced with a task which they perceive as too hard, are likely to switch off. They may then display some form of bravado to parade an indifference to learning ('this is stupid – I don't care about this') or will simply remain quiet and internalize their confusion. In either case, the effects on personal self-esteem as well as on class morale are decidedly negative.

At the other extreme, if pupils are repeatedly set work which is too easy, they will soon realize that they are not being stretched and will also become bored. Here the danger is that teachers set work towards the middle of the ability band without allowing pupils with more aptitude in the subject the scope for challenge at the upper level. It is a common mistake for beginning teachers to set work that is too easy in the hope that it will 'please' pupils and keep them occupied. In fact, the opposite happens. I firmly believe that pupils enjoy the level of challenge that allows them, with effort, to succeed. This has a confidence-boosting effect on the individual and is good for class morale; differentiation is therefore tightly linked to the goal of pupil motivation (Miller 1998). Some teachers believe that they need to 'teach to the top and scaffold down', meaning that the main work targets more able or confident students but thought needs to be given to how this can be made accessible to the rest of the class through extra support.

So, how do we know where to pitch the level? Of course, this is never going to be an exact science, but in order to be able to provide the appropriate level of input, teachers need to know what pupils have done before, that is, new input needs to build on knowledge of pupils' previous learning. Personal knowledge of pupils' interests and abilities will also be a guide. Some assessment frames (like attainment target levels) suggest that pupils' knowledge/skill-base is developed in a linear, hierarchical fashion; however, the building process is not purely incremental. Rather, previous learning is constantly revisited, checked and integrated into new learning to provide a qualitatively expanded and highly individualized experience of the subject. Short-term and long-term plans (lesson plans, schemes of work, whole school curricula) need to take a broad perspective of learning aims to ensure that key overarching themes dovetail over time. Ollerton and Watson describe this type of planning as a 'three-dimensional activity that [takes] account of the student's passage through school' and advocate a 'spiral curriculum' which sees pupils revisiting 'ideas from different perspectives, different directions at different times' (2001: 55).

The ways in which new knowledge is integrated into existing cognitive schemata are personal yet shaped by cultural frames as well as neurobiological patterns. The Vygotskian ZPD (zone of proximal development) metaphor emphasizes individualized appropriation of new concepts through joint participation in an activity. Differentiation strategies support this view of learning as a process of social engagement, that pupils learn not through being *told* but through 'problem solving under adult guidance or in collaboration with capable peers' (Vygotsky 1978: 86, quoted in Daniels 2001: 57).

Pace of learning

Pace refers to the speed at which new items are presented sequentially and the time allowed for their assimilation. Different pupils need different time frames and different levels of support to digest new information but, again, this is not only about speed but also about the level of conceptual sophistication. If higher prior attainment pupils are expected to work too slowly, they will soon become bored, and if lower prior attainment pupils are not given adequate time to understand and assimilate a concept, they will become frustrated as they are less likely to grasp the follow-up. Teachers will use different levels of explanation and different levels of support to modify the input that pupils receive. *All* pupils, of course, require a clear exposition of concepts and clear modelling and guidelines for tasks that they are asked to complete. No matter how able pupils may be, it is important not to obscure 'content' by presenting the mechanics of the task in a confusing or ambiguous way. Many pupils need content to be contextualized through multiple text types, for instance, presenting concepts graphically or with pictures. Eye-catching, uncluttered material is helpful here. Key words should be reinforced at regular intervals and personalized in some way, by setting tasks that require pupils to process key concepts more deeply through personal research, re-phrasing, drawing out or explaining to others. Varying the pace of a lesson (what I call 'changing gear') helps maintain interest through the change of energy flows as some activities encourage quiet, independent work while others call for some exuberance through interaction or physical movement.

Type of learning

The type of learning that is taking place needs to be clear in the teacher's mind if varied modes of participation are to be included. Classifying different learning preferences and teaching inclusively to bring in pupils who may not excel in traditionally valued school learning patterns now constitute a far-reaching discourse affecting educational theory and practice. Stemming largely from Howard Gardner's (1993) theory of multiple intelligences, recognition of different learning styles has become widely entrenched in educational planning,[2] for example, Lazear (1997), Larsen-Freeman (2000). However, the learning styles concept is widely, and increasingly, contested and I do not advocate that teachers cater to a checklist of learner styles or 'intelligence types'. Rather, it is useful to think in terms of varying modes of participation across activities and assessments, setting up opportunities for individual, pair, group work and whole class work. It soon becomes clear to any new teacher that different pupils can develop their own effective strategies for learning when given adequate scope to do so, and this is why engendering autonomy and self-awareness through teaching learning skills is so important. Differentiation is all about equity of opportunity and so planning a range of different types of activity values personal preferred modes of participation. For example, combining speaking and writing activities (public and personal acts) into a lesson, or alternating text-based work with drawing, graphic schemata like mind maps or acting out. In the case of group work, pupils preparing for a presentation may find it helpful to be allocated roles which play to the personal strengths of each group member.

A convenient way to build these differentiated elements into our teaching is by the classic dyad: *differentiation by task/differentiation by outcome*. It is crucial, though, to remember that differentiation is not simply a top and tail reflection which concerns only the planning phase and the outcome of a task or lesson. Rather, it affects everything about the task *while* it is under way, that is, in terms of the support provided through ongoing help and variation in pace and level of explicitness. Essentially, 'differentiation by task' means that pupils in the same class are given different tasks to do, whereas 'differentiation by outcome' means that all pupils are given the same task but that this task has been designed to allow for a range of variable outcomes to offer different levels of challenge. Many other types of differentiation are often described, for instance, differentiation by support or by resource; however, teacher choices facilitating differentiated learning can be adequately discussed under the two types: by task and by outcome.

Furthermore, the suitability of differentiation strategies may vary across the curriculum. For example, some subjects may lend themselves more to open-ended tasks which can be interpreted differently where pupils are encouraged to interpret meaning subjectively, while other subjects may have a narrower range of expected outcomes, where learning outcomes require pupils to acquire more fixed types of propositional knowledge. I hesitate to say that these differences characterize different curriculum subjects *per se*, but possibly the way different disciplines tend to be taught.

Differentiation by task

Differentiating by the setting of different tasks can mean planning completely different activities for pupils so that they are almost following parallel curricula and, clearly, this is necessary where pupils have specific needs such as bilingual or near-bilingual children in a modern languages class (McLachlan 2002), or if isolated pupils within a class are being fast-tracked to take an exam early. However, this extreme version of individualized task setting is unusual because of practical limitations. Task differentiation usually means modifying resources in some way to provide more or less support (scaffolding) to groups within a class. In written work this could take the form of graded – or 'tiered' – exercises, moving from maximum guided support to freer pupil production. Some pupils may not need to do preliminary exercises, which are worked through by average or less able pupils, and so can move directly to a higher level of challenge to match their aptitude in the subject. In other cases, the teacher might set *core*, then *optional* activities, which serve as an extension for early finishers or more able pupils. It is important to give due thought to the nature of extension tasks: these should not simply be 'more of the same' but should be *qualitatively* stretching. Being given an increased quantity of unchallenging tasks just to stay occupied can demotivate even the most enthusiastic pupil. For this reason many teachers now prefer to use other terms such as 'stretch and challenge' instead of extensions. Bloom's classic taxonomy (see Bloom *et al.* 1956) can help remind us that some classroom activities are lower-order cognitive tasks (e.g. rote learning) while others promote higher-order thinking and greater emotional investment (e.g. working out patterns and formulating rules).

However, differentiation by task is not limited to graded worksheets and individual activities. One preparation-intensive but extremely enriching alternative to traditional teaching is the carousel approach (Cajkler and Addelman 2000), which enables individuals, pairs or groups to work around the room at different work stations structured to both challenge different skills sets and to facilitate different levels of challenge. In this case, the teacher and other staff present have very much a facilitating, supportive role, ensuring optimal challenge. Pupils of all levels generally respond well to this type of learning, enjoying the high degree of autonomy that is afforded.

The 'learning how to learn' agenda – see, for example, Black *et al.* (2006) and Pedder (2006) – plays a key role in developing pupil autonomy and can be furthered by open discussion of learning preferences ('what works for me is . . .'). It is a good idea to allow pupils the time and space to share their own approaches to work and study as well as to benefit from the teacher's guidance. When giving revision work, for instance, it is useful to discuss a range of strategies that pupils might employ, for example, mind maps, redrafting, testing one another aloud, pictorial prompts, and so forth. Unsurprisingly, research has shown that pupils feel best supported in doing 'self-regulated' or semi-autonomous tasks where there is an explicit focus on the learning *how* to learn (van Grinsven and Tillema 2006).

Differentiation by outcome

Tailoring learning outcomes

The most time-efficient and practical way of differentiating is to set pupils a common task which is open-ended and flexible so that the expected outcomes are staggered. This strategy also has the enormous benefit of keeping learning across the class on track. Differentiated outcomes are now often built into teachers' planning, as reflected in the format for lesson plans and schemes of work that is:

> All pupils will be able to . . .
> Most pupils will be able to . . .
> Some pupils will be able to . . .

The key here is to make expected outcomes explicit, often negotiated by pupils themselves with guidance from the teacher. It is very clear when, in an English lesson for example, two peers produce markedly different creative compositions from the same assigned title that pupils' interpretation of the task is extremely divergent. When faced with such an open-ended task, therefore, pupils need help in understanding what is expected, so minimal outcomes must be clearly stated and understood; in the English lesson this might be a writing frame or a prescribed set of elements which must be included in the text. This use of frames and models provides all pupils with a sense of security but does not restrain more able pupils from going beyond the minimum requirements. This last point is important as differentiating learning objectives can be perceived as limiting. Knowing pupils and encouraging them to work at their optimal level of challenge will increase their confidence.

Interacting with pupils

Given that much class time is spent speaking, the nature of this spoken interaction also represents a valuable opportunity for differentiation. The way new concepts are introduced, building on previous learning, and the way in which pupils are encouraged to revise previously covered items usually rely on teachers asking questions to the class. In a traditional setting, questions are asked, an answer is then given by a pupil and the teacher then provides feedback (usually saying if the answer is right or wrong). The restrictive nature of this traditional interaction routine (input-response-evaluation) has been recognized for some time – see Black *et al.* (2003) on formative assessment and Wragg and Brown (2001) on explanation strategies. Some creative forethought into the way questions might be asked in class to stimulate thinking at different levels ensures that all pupils can make a contribution corresponding to their current level and their preferred mode of participation. For example, questions can be directed to particular pupils or can be addressed to the whole class; questions can be open or closed to varying degrees – see Revell (1995) for a full discussion of effective questioning strategies for differentiated learning. Open questions clearly offer pupils more opportunities for creative expression, enabling them to structure their own responses. Open questions might also be particularly appropriate where there is a range of possible solutions. This type of questioning also provides the teacher with useful formative feedback. However, more closed answers can bring specific elements (key words and key themes) into focus and can reaffirm existing knowledge, allowing a larger number of pupils to experience success, especially where pupils chose from a range of given answers. Consider these question types in a history class. The class have recently been learning about the Industrial Revolution:

- Who were the Luddites (to class)?
- Who can tell me something about the Luddites (to class)?
- Lucy, can you tell us something about the Luddites (to one pupil)?
- (To one pupil) Maia, if you described somebody as a Luddite, would you mean that that person is conservative or that they embrace change? . . . Yes, I agree. Well done. Can you say where the word comes from?
- I would like each of you to think of at least one fact about the Luddites – more if you can – and note it down. You have one minute from now (to class).
- In pairs, write one sentence using the words Luddites and mechanization.
- (Teacher shows a picture of angry men destroying a mechanized loom) Describe what is happening here and why. You have two minutes to share ideas in groups of three.

Alternative questioning strategies include re-framing questions by giving an answer for pupils to think of an appropriate question or, for longer answers, asking pupils to present questions or use role play to present different points of view. This might work well, for example, in understanding the motivations of different historical characters such as the Luddites versus the factory owners or the mill hands.

There is also some research evidence (Myhill 2006) that reference-framing strategies in teacher–pupil interactions have a determining effect on pupil participation. For instance, pupils respond more positively when invited to draw on their own experience rather than with reference to an abstracted reality. This is true of all pupils but has been shown to be especially effective in increasing participation of disaffected, low-achieving boys. Myhill found that this group was three times more likely to refer to personal, out-of-school experiences.

Let us now turn to an example of differentiation in practice. The lesson described here posits models of good practice for differentiation with reference to a particular subject – French – although the principles which underlie the differentiation strategies described are general and can clearly be applied across the curriculum and not just in mixed ability classes.

Differentiation with a Year 9 mixed ability group: a French lesson

This lesson was taught by 'Lis' to a Year 9 mixed ability group. The topic is within the scheme of work unit on illnesses, parts of the body, remedies and the primary language objective is *j'ai mal au/à la . . .* , with the imperative tense being a secondary objective. Pupils had previously learnt parts of the body, although many make mistakes with the gendered article and some struggle with pronunciation. The whole lesson lasted one hour. Lis identified the following objectives for the lesson, staggered in way that differentiates by outcome:

- All pupils will revise parts of the body with gendered article and combine parts of the body with *j'ai mal au/à la . . .* to express some basic ailments: I've got a headache, I've got a sore throat, my leg hurts, etc.
- Some pupils will understand and say some basic remedies: stay in bed, take these tablets, drink plenty of water, get plenty of rest.
- Some pupils will be able to extend the minimal dialogues with conjunctions, present perfect phrases and extra turns using *si ça continue.*
- Some pupils will be able to say affected body parts but may not be able to use *au/à la* correctly and may only remember key vocabulary items from the chunk-learnt phrases.

After greeting the class, Lis discussed the objectives, written on the board, with pupils. She then presented the new language to the whole class by holding up pictures showing people suffering from affected body parts and repeating clearly key phrases: *j'ai mal à la jambe, j'ai mal au dos*, and so forth. Once the expressions had all been modelled by Lis, she used pupils with more confidence in French to model for others, *j'ai mal au __*, each pupil finishing the phrase according to the picture being held up. This led pupils to incorporate previously learnt vocabulary into new phrases. Lis chose different pupils to answer in quick-fire succession, moving from more to less confident pupils. This differentiated routine was then repeated but with a different prompt from Lis (*qu'est-ce que tu as?*) which required pupils to respond using a whole phrase beginning *j'ai mal au/à la*. It is a common strategy to instigate peer modelling by starting off routines with more confident pupils in this way (a discreet form of differentiation by task), however it is important not to overuse particular pupils when deploying this strategy as this can be perceived as favouritism. Such a risk can be avoided by using alternating strategies such as starting some activities with simpler, more closed questions and targeting less confident pupils to answer.

Next, pupils listened to a series of short, recorded dialogues of different people being asked and answering questions about what is wrong with them. Pupils were given one of three different worksheets to complete during the listening activity, each offering different levels of challenge. For example, one sheet required pupils to write a sequence number next to a picture while others required pupils to fill in a gap as well. This activity exemplifies how the same resource, in this case, audio-recorded dialogues, can be exploited to allow different tasks.

Lis then led a whole-class review. She went through the answers from the listening activity and as pupils answered some kept textbooks closed ('Look if you need to'), while others looked up the vocabulary item or its gender. There was a focus on pronunciation as pupils gave answers. Then all new expressions were reviewed through miming ailments, starting teacher to pupil (*qu'est-ce qu'il y a?*), then pupils to each other in pairs. Pupils were able to look at a simple, gapped dialogue on a PowerPoint slide if necessary, although most did not need this support. As she circulated in the room, Lis encouraged many pupils to go beyond the modelled dialogue. This teacher-focused part of the lesson allowed Lis both to assess pupils' progress and to reinforce the key objectives of the lesson.

The next activity aimed at developing reading skills. Each pupil was given a handout consisting of a series of patient–doctor dialogues, each more complex than the last.

Referring to the first three dialogues, pupils were invited to respond, at speed, to some true/false (*vrai/faux*) questions using mini-whiteboards; for example, Sandrine's leg hurts – *vrai ou faux?* The doctor advises M Viret to stay in bed – *vrai ou faux?* Mini-whiteboards allow all pupils to offer an answer without the risk to self-esteem of getting it wrong. This maximizes pupil participation and allows the teacher to check comprehension instantly. Next, some reading comprehension questions were given on PowerPoint for pupils to work through on their own, graded to become gradually harder ranging from *vrai/faux* to eliciting full responses. Lis asked the class to 'do as many as you can', so differentiated by outcome at this stage. A time limit was set for the whole class. Early finishers were given the following extension: write your own dialogue using the picture prompts at the bottom of the handout. The questions and the written texts were prepared to be progressively more challenging, some pupils would only do a few and others would finish. When Lis went over the answers with the class, she expected pupils who were more able in French to give fuller answers. She again did a quick assessment of how far pupils were progressing ('Hands up if you've answered 5/6/7 questions correctly'). All pupils were praised for their effort.

The match-up 'game' which followed was to give pupils the opportunity for speaking practice. Pupils worked in groups, some with light and dark blue cards and some with light and dark yellow sets. Blue cards showed a picture of an ailment to be matched to its written phrase. Yellow cards also showed a picture of an ailment to be matched up to a phrase but the picture card also had a 'suitable remedy' picture which pupils were asked to express in words to win the pair, for example *Reposez-vous! Prenez deux aspirines!* The children had played this type of match-up activity with Lis before and so were familiar with the routine and always enjoyed the game. Lis, a learning support assistant and a foreign language assistant all circulated among pupils during the card game activity to monitor and support. Some pupils were encouraged to go beyond the minimum turns from the cards, that is, to add an extra, unscripted turn such as *Qu'est-ce qui s'est passé? – J'ai eu un accident* or to add *Et si ça continue?* The activity was timed and lasted for 10 minutes.

The final activity was a writing task which was started off in class to be finished for homework. Pupils were asked to write a postcard to a French pen pal describing a holiday where a lot of things have gone wrong. Pupils were asked *to choose* between two writing frames, one with gapped out phrases and picture prompts or one that only had picture prompts. Pupils using only picture prompts were also asked to add their own unprompted sentences.

At the end of the lesson, after pupils had packed their bags and were waiting to be dismissed, Lis asked differentiated questions using a combination of flash-card pictures, mime and requests for remedies. She revisited the key objective of the lesson, asking different pupils to give examples using *j'ai mal au/à la* . . . This was the fundamental goal of the lesson (the *base* or *minimal* outcome) and so it was important for Lis to reinforce this expression with body parts vocabulary, so that *all* pupils would leave the room with this key phrase in mind, having a clear idea of the lesson's aims and feeling that they had achieved these. However, Lis also built into the plenary review opportunities to reinforce elements of the extended dialogues that some pupils had covered in the lesson.

Concluding thoughts

In this chapter we have seen how classroom differentiation in the UK emerged as a result of decreasing structural differentiation by ability – both of schools and within schools – which led to increasing mixed ability teaching. Faced with a broad range of pupil needs and personal differences, teachers needed to develop new strategies as well as to formalize existing 'craft knowledge' (Kersher and Miles 1996) in order to create optimal learning opportunities for different pupils within a single lesson. We have explored the conceptual principles underlying the notion of optimal learning within the learning level-pace-type trichotomy, which enables us to modify lesson content and to plan activities to suit a range of learning preferences. While differentiation may often require more detailed and lengthy planning, I have tried to emphasize in this chapter that differentiation is about building in flexibility and this does not always entail *extra* planning and materials but rather a broader and more creative vision of learning outcomes and how these can be achieved. Differentiation seen in this perspective is important in all contexts, including selective schools and schools where subject-setting practices are the norm. It is important for new teachers to consider what differentiation strategies best suit the specific pedagogy and learning goals of their curriculum subject. When planning lessons, it is useful to check whether the different activities planned include varying modes of participation to cater for different personalities and learning preferences. Finally, can we be sure that we are not dumbing down by differentiating, but are maintaining an 'optimal' level of challenge which is suitably stretching for the more able as well as supporting those with lower prior attainment? In schools committed to promoting differentiation, strategies are shared within and across departments not only informally but as an integral part of professional development. Similarly, differentiation in lesson planning will dovetail with differentiated goals built into schemes of work and these, in turn, reflect a whole school ethos which acknowledges diversity and opportunity for all.

Notes

1 It is worth remembering that the differentiation ethos and strategies described here are the product of specific cultural beliefs about the aims of education and these are not universal. For example, a review of research looking at differentiation reported: 'the literature revealed that differentiation is interpreted quite differently (both in the UK and the US)' (NFER 2003). In the UK, the focus is on differentiating the curriculum to cater for mixed ability classrooms whereas in the USA the emphasis is on streamed classes for gifted children. Furthermore, in France, where equality is seen as a cornerstone of republican democracy and is enshrined institutionally in national education, the idea of giving pupils different work to do seems inequitable to many teachers (Raveaud 2005).
2 Gardner's categories of 'intelligence' have been repeatedly adapted, including by Gardner himself, and remain contested conceptually (for example, see Richards and Rodgers 2001).

References

Black, P., Harrison, C., Lee, C., Marshall, B. and Wiliam, D. (2003) *Assessment for Learning: Putting it into Practice*. Buckingham: Open University Press.

Black, P., McCormick, R., James, M. and Pedder, D. (2006) Learning how to learn and assessment for learning: a theoretical enquiry, *Research Papers in Education*, 21(2): 119–32.

Bloom, B.S., Engelhart, M.D., Furst, E.J., Hill, W.H. and Krathwohl, D.R. (1956) *Taxonomy of Educational Objectives: The Classification of Educational Goals. Handbook I: Cognitive Domain*. New York: David McKay Company.

Cajkler, W. and Addelman, R. (2000) *The Practice of Foreign Language Teaching*. London: David Fulton.

Cigman, R. (2006) The gifted child: a conceptual enquiry, *Oxford Review of Education*, 32(2): 197–212.

Collins Concise Dictionary of the English Language (1982) Glasgow: William Collins.

Daniels, H. (2001) *Vygotsky and Pedagogy*. London: RoutledgeFalmer.

DCSF (Department for Children, Schools and Families) (2005) *Higher Standards, Better Schools for All: A Government White Paper*. London: Her Majesty's Stationery Office.

DfEE (Department for Education and Employment (DfEE) (1997) *Excellence in Schools: A Government White Paper*. London: Her Majesty's Stationery Office.

Education Policy Institute (2016) *Faith Schools, Pupil Performance and Social Selection. Report by Jon Andrews and Rebecca Jones*, http://epi.org.uk/wp-content/uploads/2016/11/Pupil_characteristics_and_performance_at_faith_schools.pdf, accessed December 2016.

Francis, B., Archer, L., Hodgen, J., Pepper, D., Taylor, B. and Travers, M.-C. (2016) Exploring the relative lack of impact on 'ability grouping' in England: a discourse analytic account, *Cambridge Journal of Education*, 1–17, http://dx.doi.org/10.1080/0305764X.2015.1093095, accessed December 2016.

Gardner, H. (1993) *Frames of Mind: The Theory of Multiple Intelligences* (2nd edn). London: Fontana.

Hadow Report (1923) http://www.educationengland.org.uk/documents/hadow1923/hadow1923.html, accessed January 2017.

Ireson, J. and Hallam, S. (2005) Pupils' liking for school: mobility grouping, self-concept and perceptions of teaching, *British Journal of Educational Psychology*, 75: 297–311.

Kersher, R. and Miles, S. (1996) Thinking and talking about differentiation, in E. Bearner (ed.) *Differentiation and Diversity in the Primary School*. London: Routledge.

Larsen-Freeman, D. (2000) *Techniques and Principles in Language Teaching* (2nd edn). Oxford: Oxford University Press.

Lazear, D. (1997) *Seven Ways of Teaching: The Artistry of Teaching with Multiple Intelligences*. Arlington Heights, IL: Skylight Publishing.

McLachlan, A. (2002) *New Pathfinder 1. Raising the Standard: Addressing the Needs of Gifted and Talented Pupils*. London: CILT.

Miller, D. (1998) *Enhancing Adolescent Competence*. London: Thomas Nelson.

Myhill, D. (2006) Talk, talk, talk: teaching and learning in whole class discourse, *Research Papers in Education*, 21(1): 19–41.

NFER (National Foundation for Educational Research) (2003) *What Works for Gifted and Talented Pupils: A Review of Recent Research*. Slough: NFER.

Ollerton, M. and Watson, A. (2001) *Inclusive Mathematics 11–18*. London: Continuum.

Pedder, D. (2006) Organizational conditions that foster successful classroom promotion of learning how to learn, *Research Papers in Education*, 21(2): 171–200.

Raveaud, M. (2005). Hares, tortoises and the social construction of the pupil: differentiated learning in French and English primary schools. *British Educational Research Journal*, 31(4): 459–479.

Revell, M. (1995) *The Differentiation Handbook: A Guide to Differentiation in Secondary Science Teaching*. Northants: Northamptonshire Inspection and Advisory Service.

Richards, J.C. and Rodgers, T.S. (2001) *Approaches and Methods in Language Teaching*. Cambridge: Cambridge University Press.

Tudge, J.R.H. (1992) Processes and consequences of peer collaboration: a Vygotskyan analysis, *Child Development*, 63: 1364–79.

van Grinsven, L. and Tillema, H. (2006) Learning opportunities to support student self-regulation: comparing different instructional formats, *Educational Research*, 48(1): 77–91.

Wragg, E.C. and Brown, G. (2001) *Explaining in the Secondary School*. London: RoutledgeFalmer.

14

Classroom assessment

CHRIS HARRISON AND CATARINA F. CORREIA

Introduction

Assessment for learning (AfL) raises attainment and motivates children to learn. Classrooms that function well rely on good use of questioning and focusing teaching on the evidence that is collected during learning. AfL classrooms are less teacher-directed, students are more proactive, and there is an emphasis on collaboration rather than competition. Rather than being a set of strategies that can be implemented in the classroom, AfL is above all a way of conceptualizing teaching and learning as a dynamic endeavour that relies on a constant dialogue between the teacher and students, among students themselves, and within each student.

While AfL has revolutionized classroom assessment over the last two decades, there is still considerable work to be done to raise the quality of classroom dialogue, of teachers' written feedback, and of peer and self-assessment to allow feedback to function well in many classrooms. Equally, the intertwining and play-off between formative and summative assessment purposes needs careful consideration to allow AfL to enhance learning.

This chapter offers a reflection on the opportunities and dilemmas that teachers may face while adapting their practice to create a truly effective AfL environment in the classroom. In the introduction, we start by looking into AfL as a continuous 'dialogue' between the teacher and students and among students, that supports learning. We proceed into reflection on how teacher 'noticing' of what is going on in the classroom shapes the 'dialogue' that takes place herein. We then focus on the essential aspects of classroom talk, written feedback, peer and self-assessment that need to be taken into account to facilitate an effective and rewarding AfL environment.

Teachers' beliefs about learning and assessment influence their classroom actions and decisions (Harrison 2015). One of the most influential drivers for the way assessment has been conceptualized over the last three decades has been the Black and Wiliam (1998) paper, which surveyed the evidence that linked assessment with improvement in learning. In this conceptualization, assessment is viewed as collecting evidence of students' current understanding with the purpose of deciding which steps are needed in order to improve. The goal of assessment, in the context of assessment for learning (AfL), requires a prospective view of learning in which the concern is not solely with the actual level of performance, but with anticipating future possibilities (Heritage 2007). Such assessment becomes formative if the teacher or learner takes some action in response to the assessment evidence.

Research on classroom assessment provides strong prescriptive messages about the characteristics of effective teacher assessment (Black and Wiliam 1998) and evidence-based claims about the effectiveness of these approaches for student learning (Black and Wiliam 1998; Black et al. 2003; Wiliam et al. 2004). In classrooms featuring formative assessment, teachers make frequent and interactive assessments of students' understanding. This enables them to adjust their teaching to meet individual student needs, and to better help all students reach high standards. Formative assessment today is now seen as more integrated into the teaching and learning process, rather than as a separate activity (Perrenoud 1998; Allal 2005; Black and Harrison 2010; Harrison 2011). Sometimes teachers use various strategies to help this process happen. So, a teacher might use mini-whiteboards for students to individually provide answers that he or she can quickly see and react to. The teacher can quickly spot whether students are giving the expected answer and can see alternative ways some students have of thinking about the answer. This feedback from the students to the teacher provides the teacher with information to influence the way he or she steers the lesson. The teacher might stop and instigate a discussion of the reasons for the range of answers that the students have given, and then direct the thinking using some of the ideas that arise in that discussion. Alternatively, the teacher might make a note of which students got the answer wrong and later come back to them and help them sort out their misunderstandings. The important point here is that the teacher is collecting and responding to assessment data as it arises in the classroom – he or she is using assessment to support the next stages of learning. It is the purpose that is important here as this is what shapes and drives the action. For this reason, many teachers refer to formative assessment as assessment for learning or AfL.

Since the 1998 Black and Wiliam review, a number of researchers have proposed and debated the definition and value of AfL (Black and Wiliam 2009; Klenowski 2009; Bennett 2011; Kingston and Nash 2011; Swaffield 2011). In essence, AfL is an approach to pedagogy that allows students to discuss and share their ideas with others (Black et al. 2002) and, in so doing, students reveal to themselves and others their current understanding. Teachers ask questions or introduce tasks that challenge current understanding and from the discussions that ensue it becomes clear what students know, partly know, and don't know. AfL pedagogy creates a dynamic assessment environment where both teachers and learners can take note of where strengths and weaknesses exist in the current learning, such that they can respond to any shortfall and so move learning forward. Over time there has been an increasing emphasis with AfL on students taking an active role in their own learning and assessment processes. It has also been recognized that it is not sufficient that students merely learn how to address their immediate learning challenges. AfL has a greater role in encouraging lifelong learning and so the approach that teachers take with AfL in their classrooms needs to enable and empower students to learn how to learn and to motivate them to keep on learning (Harrison and Howard 2009). Indeed, Boud argues that assessment is sustainable only if it 'meets the needs of the present without compromising the ability of students to meet their own future learning needs' (2000: 151). Teachers, when introduced to ideas to strengthen AfL, will tend to work on a range of strategies that develop classroom talk, both to improve how they probe and prompt learners in discussion and also in helping their students respond and interact with one another with increasing confidence. Teachers who elicit and use evidence from students' thinking as the basis for instructional decisions can positively affect student learning (Carpenter *et al.* 1989; Ruiz-Primo and Furtak 2007; Pierson 2008). For example, Pierson (2008) found a significant correlation between teachers' responsiveness to their students' ideas and students' learning and achievement in mathematics.

Common to all these practices is the active involvement of students, whose role changes from passive recipients of knowledge to active partners in the learning process (Swaffield 2011). The role of the teacher is to create activities which provide a forum in which the students can think about and develop their understanding of ideas through discussion with peers. Such practice enables teachers to use talk strategies that encourage students to explore ideas and compare their emerging understanding with other students. The teacher is then able to recognize areas of a topic that are problematic for some students and how students are connecting ideas and concepts. Finding out what makes sense makes prior knowledge more visible and subjects developing ideas to self- and peer critique through discussion (Penuel *et al.* 2017), which encourages next steps in learning.

Teacher noticing and AfL

Classrooms are complex environments where many things are taking place at the same time. As mentioned above, at the core of AfL practices is the idea of eliciting and collecting evidence of learning in order to make informed decisions that will support students in making progress in learning. The potential of AfL practices to inform student learning is shaped by three factors:

1. What teachers notice
2. How they interpret what they notice
3. What decisions they make based on these interpretations.

Noticing has been described as a complex skill that relies on expertise in choosing what to attend to and what to ignore (Jacobs *et al.* 2011). For the busy teacher choosing what to attend to and what to ignore is not straightforward, because it requires the teacher to make observations, interpretations, judgements and decisions in light of both short- and long-term learning aims. If the teacher notices that some students have alternative conceptions such as 'there is no gravity on the moon', when the focus of the lesson is on eclipses, do they stop and sort out misconceptions or focus on the positioning of the sun, moon and earth to explain the eclipse? Faced with such a dilemma, some teachers ignore the misconception, others correct it there, and some 'park' the incorrect idea and later work out when in the curriculum they can come back and deal with the misconception. All of the above are valid pedagogical decisions. In order to develop an expertise in consciously noticing, Mason (2011) highlights the importance of consciously focusing on noticing and reflecting on what to attend to while planning a lesson, and then on how that lesson went in light of what the teacher wanted to attend to.

Based on her work with teachers, Van Es (2011) has proposed a framework for supporting teachers in developing their noticing of student thinking. This framework describes what teachers frequently notice and how they notice it at different levels of expertise when observing other teachers' practice. Initially, teachers tend to focus their attention on general aspects of whole classroom behaviour and learning, and teacher pedagogy. Teacher reflections are evaluative and geared towards their own practice. As teachers develop their expertise in noticing, they start focusing more on particular aspects of student thinking and attempt to link these to specific teaching strategies observed. Teacher reflections are now geared towards making connections between observed events and principles of teaching and learning, and teachers tend to move away from evaluative judgements into proposing alternative pedagogical solutions that would address student needs.

Developing expertise in noticing requires time and professional development anchored on a reflection of what to attend to in a given context, and how this knowledge can be used to inform instruction (Jacobs *et al.* 2011). The message here for trainee teachers is to change the focus of their classroom observations at different stages of their training. So, while whole class observation might be useful in the early stages of teacher practice, moving to a focus of how specific tasks, prompts or questions promote or halt discussion with individual and groups of students, at a later stage, should prove more fruitful in developing the sense of noticing.

Classroom talk

Robin Alexander in his booklet *Towards Dialogic Teaching* argues that

> Children, we now know, need to talk, and to experience a rich diet of spoken language, in order to think and to learn. Reading, writing and number may be the acknowledged curriculum 'basics' but talk is arguably the true foundation of learning.
>
> (2004: 5)

Through his comparative research in the primary school classrooms of five countries, Alexander (2001) has shown that teachers organize the communicative process of teaching and learning in very different ways. In most of the classrooms he observed, teachers talked more than the students; but the balance and nature of contributions varied considerably, both between countries and between classrooms. One of the reasons for this variation was that in some classrooms a teacher's questions would elicit only brief responses from students, while in others they often generated much more extended and reflective talk. The concept of 'dialogic talk' emerged from these observations as a way of describing a particularly effective type of classroom interaction. This may be used when teachers are interacting with groups or with whole classes. 'Dialogic talk' sums up the interactions in which both teachers and students make substantial and significant contributions and through which students' thinking on a given idea or topic is helped to move forward (Alexander 2004). 'Dialogic talk' is reciprocal and cumulative, in that both teachers and learners learn from the process and the evidence produced can be utilized to inform the next steps towards improvement.

We know that by increasing 'wait time' (Rowe 1974) between teacher questions and accepting answers that more students volunteer answers and start to say more in their answers than previously. In some classrooms, the change in the classroom environment is enormous, moving from single-word answers from a handful of students to a purposeful discussion driven by several students. This multivariate change in the classroom environment creates more opportunities for feedback, both to the teacher and to the learners. Classroom talk becomes increasingly dynamic, reciprocal and continually evolving the more often it is used in the classroom, and provides a range of possibilities for the learner to engage in. However, such changes require more than increasing wait time; it requires the teacher to construct questions that encourage thinking and the skills to support and continue the discussion beyond the first answer that is given in class.

Many studies have mapped the type of talk that happens in classrooms (e.g. Scott, Mortimer and Aguiar 2006). If we look first at who does the most talking, it is clear from most UK classrooms that the teacher is responsible for most of what is said. In a study (King's-Medway-Oxfordshire-Formative-Assessment-Project, KMOFAP) that ran from 1999–2001 with Science, Mathematics and English secondary school teachers, we looked at how teachers generally started their lessons (Black *et al.* 2003). We found that teachers often began lessons with question and answer sessions intended to link the lesson with previous learning experiences. At the start of the KMOFAP project, we found that, on average, teachers dominated talk in most of these lesson starters by an average word count of 10:1. While teachers did try to engage learners by asking questions, the answers demanded tended to be limited to one-word or one-sentence answers. This approach, at the start of lessons, tipped the dominance of talk in favour of the teacher talk and therefore limited the learner in expressing their ideas and created difficulty for the teacher in collecting evidence of strengths and weaknesses in student understanding. With support from the King's team, the project teachers began to address this imbalance in the classroom talk. For example, one mathematics teacher partway through a topic on ratio, started a lesson with Year 8 by asking, 'What's similar and different about ratios and fractions?' This created a lively discussion around the idea of 'sideways fractions' and division and why the 'one' in a 3:1 ratio was not a third. What was evident in this classroom discussion was that the mathematical thinking went beyond procedural, and the conversation continued between some pairs of student when the class started an exercise on ratios that followed the starter. This was a good example of students testing and checking their own understanding rather than quietly trying to get correct answers in their mathematics class.

Teachers also introduced strategies to encourage more student engagement. Two of the KMOFAP mathematics teachers introduced the idea of 'no hands up' in whole class discussions. This meant that the teachers could select anyone in the class to answer and so all students were being required to think in these situations, as they might be called on to give an answer. By the end of the project, most of the KMOFAP teachers had introduced various techniques that reduced the dominance of teacher talk and this was achieved through helping students to find a voice by working on strategies to help students raise ideas. By doing this, the teacher encourages the use of talk in shaping and developing learning that reduces the teacher's role as orchestrator and controller of classroom talk, and instead repositions the teacher as an enabler of talk for thinking (Myhill 2006).

Despite several research projects highlighting the effectiveness of dialogic talk (Mercer and Littleton 2007; Kutnick and Colwell 2010; Scott *et al.* 2010), many classrooms still use questioning in a less productive way, with questions aimed at checking whether students remember factual information imparted to them in previous lessons. As such, most questions have low cognitive demand and do not encourage discussion and thinking. While we have attempted various approaches to support teachers in improving their classroom questioning, the most effective has been providing question stems that they then use to design questions for a specific topic (see Figure 14.1). Initially we developed these on the KMOFAP project to support mathematics teaching for the topic of ratios but quickly found that these stems were applicable both to other topics and other subject areas.

The AfL classroom requires teachers who are willing to set up situations where students feel comfortable expressing their views and ideas and where listening to student talk takes priority over correcting ideas, in the first instance. Deciding when to intervene and when to allow talk to continue is a key skill in the AfL classroom because the formative process requires a sufficient source of evidence for judgements to be made to inform planning. Stopping the talk too soon might mean that the teacher does not fully understand the problem that students are having with a particular concept, while allowing the talk to continue for too long may leave insufficient time in the lesson for ideas to be challenged and problems sorted out. The important point here is that learning does take time and a teacher simply

How can we be sure that . . . ?
Why is ____ an example of _____?
What is the same and what is different about . . . ?
Is it ever/always true/false that . . . ?
Why do ____, ____ and ____ all give the same answer?
How do you . . . .?
How would you explain . . . ?
What does that tell us about . . . ?
What is wrong with . . . ?
Why is _____ true?

Figure 14.1 Question stems

correcting a statement by a student is unlikely to shift that student's understanding and affect the understanding of the other students listening in. Clearly students are more likely to be willing to make improvements during the production of their work rather than returning to what they considered a finished piece completed several days earlier. This therefore requires a more dynamic approach where the teacher runs the assessment process alongside the learning process. In other words, it is the 'process used by teachers and students to recognize and respond to student learning in order to enhance the learning during the learning' (Bell and Cowie 1999: 32).

Written feedback

Students receive feedback when teachers collect in books and mark their work. Here again it is important that the feedback is used to improve either that piece of work or to understand what could be done to produce a similar piece of work of higher quality. So, the key focus is not a measure of how well someone has done but rather how they might improve by producing a stronger argument, a clearer explanation or by annotating their design. Feedback by comments provides the information for improvement in a more detailed and purposeful way than marks or grades could achieve. Comments also are more likely to encourage the learner to reflect and to think through the work again, particularly if the feedback asks questions or requires the learner to add something or change part of the assessed piece. Working with feedback helps learners develop a sense of what quality means in a particular area of work and this is what they need both to test and consolidate their current understanding but also to aspire to better achievement in the future. Research by Ruth Butler (1987; 1988) demonstrates that acquiring this approach to improving work can be inhibited if grades or marks are involved during the learning process because these take the focus away from improvement and centre on attainment. Research by Carole Dweck (2000; 2017) on 'growth mindset' complements this approach as it ensures that both teacher and learner are more aware of making learning a challenging but supportive endeavour that is not shaped by predetermined views of teaching and learning.

Self- and peer assessment

Group work is an important strategy in AfL because learners can use their peers as a resource (Heritage 2007) who both provide and check ideas as they arise in the classroom activities. Through discussing with others, a learner begins to get a view of how much and how well they understand the topic. This can then be strengthened through peer assessment exercises. In strongly developed AfL classrooms, learners are able to take charge of their learning and to use teacher and peer feedback to shape their own self-assessment of their current progress, which enables and equips them with the confidence and wherewithal to take their learning forward. Students come to realize through their experiences in the classroom and the way that teachers respond to their essays, reports and calculations that the role of school is to help them learn, rather than simply provide them with things to learn, and that the responsibility to move their learning forward requires them to be active and collaborative in the classroom.

More formalized peer and self-assessment exercises need to be modelled for students to understand their roles in these situations. Part of this arises from the ways in which the teacher interacts with students in class, noting strengths and weaknesses in answers and also in how the teacher provides written feedback to individuals. These practices set the style of language and the tone of the guidance for providing feedback and students tend to mimic these approaches when providing peer feedback. In all of our AfL projects, we have found that peer feedback provides a good developmental field for self-assessment. One of the history teachers that we worked with on our project in Scotland used to set up self-assessment scenarios by asking students to do a particular essay task for homework. In the following lesson, she would provide the students with three anonymized essays that the students looked at, in pairs, and decided the rank order for quality. The teacher asked different pairs to justify their ranking of the three essays and reach a consensus about the quality of each essay. Individual students were then asked to position their essay in the rank order of the essays – above the best, below the worst or somewhere in the middle. The teacher then provided each individual with the examination mark scheme for that essay and individuals self-assessed their essays. Finally, the pairs read one another's essays and discussed whether they thought their partner had correctly ranked and marked their essay and made suggestions how they might improve their essay next time. While this was quite a time-consuming exercise first time round, the teacher felt that the opportunity to work out what quality meant in that context was worth the time investment. She also acknowledged that the students reflected far more carefully on their own and others' essays through doing this exercise and the quality of their writing improved faster than her expectations had been for that class.

Self- and peer assessment practices not only support students' learning, but they also assist students in becoming better learners (Black *et al.* 2002). Showing examples of work that do and do not meet the success criteria can help students to understand more fully what is required and to reflect on the things they need to do in order to improve. Looking at the work of others can also help learners to understand the different approaches they could have taken and to appreciate that there are different ways of achieving success. Following any self- or peer assessment activity, students should be given sufficient time and opportunity to make improvements. Having assessed the work of others, students will find it easier to identify weaknesses in their own work and to see how they can make improvements. It can also lead to students reflecting on their own development and progress, comparing their current work with that produced previously and with their own personal targets.

However, through classroom assessment practices, student actions and interactions are always open to peer scrutiny and evaluation (Cowie 2005) and while, on the one hand, teachers want students to learn from their mistakes, they are also aware that some students will shy away from activities where their self-esteem may be negatively affected. The goal of AfL is not to eliminate failure, but rather to keep failure from becoming chronic and seen as inevitable in the mind of the learner (Stiggins 2005). It is therefore important to have agreed rules and practices when students assess one another's work so that guidance is clear and positive and comments do not affect self-esteem.

Concluding thoughts

The routines, behaviours and environment necessary for AfL to flourish take considerable time to develop and become effective. Taking a reflective stance while trialling different strategies and collaborating with other teachers can support you in developing an AfL mind-set that will drive your teaching and assessment practice.

- When teaching, what are the things that you typically pay attention to? What do you notice?
- How often do you have conversations with your students/stop the class to probe their understanding/ideas about what you are teaching?
- When is the best time to check with students which parts of a topic are insecure?
- What does self- and peer assessment look like in your classroom? How can you organize it so that your students strengthen their assessment skills?
- Which type of activities help students understand the importance of using peers as a resource?
- What is the balance between teacher-supported and student-supported learning in your classroom? How might you change this to help students become better learners?

References

Alexander, R. (2001) *Culture and Pedagogy: International Comparisons in Primary Education.* Oxford: Blackwell.

Alexander, R. (2004) *Towards Dialogic Teaching: Rethinking Classroom Talk.* Cambridge: Dialogos.

Allal, L. (2005) Assessment and the regulation of learning, *International Encyclopedia of Education,* 3: 348–52.

Bell, B. and Cowie, B. (1999) A model of formative assessment in science education, *Assessment in Education: Principles, Policy and Practice,* 6(1): 101–16.

Bennett, R.E. (2011) Formative assessment: a critical review, *Assessment in Education: Principles, Policy and Practice,* 18(1): 5–25.

Black, P. and Harrison, C. (2010) Formative assessment in science, in *Good Practice in Science Teaching: What Research Has to Say* (2nd edn). Buckingham: Open University Press, pp. 183–210.

Black, P. and Wiliam, D. (1998) *Inside the Black Box: Raising Standards Through Classroom Assessment.* London: School of Education, King's College London.

Black, P., Harrison, C., Lee, C. Marshall, B. and Wiliam, D. (2003), *Assessment for Learning: Putting it into Practice*, Open University Press, Buckingham, United Kingdom.

Black, P., Harrison, C., Lee, C. Marshall, B. and Wiliam, D. (2002), *Working inside the Black Box: Assessment for Learning in the Classroom*, Department of Education and Professional Studies, King's College, London.

Black, P. and Wiliam, D. (2009) Developing the theory of formative assessment, *Educational Assessment, Evaluation and Accountability*, 21(1): 5–31.

Boud, D. (2000) Sustainable assessment: rethinking assessment for the learning society, *Studies in Continuing Education*, 22: 151–67.

Butler, R. (1987) Task-involving and ego-involving properties of evaluation: effects of different feedback conditions on motivational perceptions, interest, and performance, *Journal of Educational Psychology*, 79(4): 474.

Butler, R. (1988) Enhancing and undermining intrinsic motivation: the effects of task-involving and ego-involving evaluation on interest and performance, *British Journal of Educational Psychology*, 58(1): 1–14.

Carpenter, T.P., Fennema, E., Peterson, P.L., Chiang, C.-P. and Loef, M. (1989) Using knowledge of children's mathematics thinking in classroom teaching: an experimental study, *American Educational Research Journal*, 26(4): 499–531.

Cowie, B. (2005) Student commentary on assessment for learning. *Curriculum Journal*, 16: 137–51.

Dweck, C. (2000) *Self-Theories: Their Role in Motivation, Personality, and Development (Essays in Social Psychology)*. London: Routledge.

Dweck, C. (2017) *Mindset Updated Edition: Changing the Way You Think to Fulfil Your Potential*. London: Hachette UK.

Harrison, C. (2011) Making assessment work in the classroom, in J. Dillon and M. Maguire (eds) *Becoming a Teacher: Issues in Secondary Teaching* (4th edn). Maidenhead: Open University Press, pp. 222–35.

Harrison, C. (2015) Assessment for learning in science classrooms, *Journal of Research in STEM*, 1(2): 78–6.

Harrison, C. and Howard, S. (2009) *Inside the Primary Black Box: Assessment for Learning in the Classroom*. London: Granada Learning.

Heritage, M. (2007) Formative assessment: what do teachers need to know and do? *Phi Delta Kappa*, 89(2): 140–5.

Jacobs, V.R., Lamb, L.L., Philipp, R.A. and Schappelle, B.P. (2011) Deciding how to respond on the basis of children's understandings, in M.G. Sherin, V.R. Jacob and R.A. Philipp (eds) *Mathematics Teacher Noticing: Seeing Through Teachers' Eyes*. New York: Routledge, pp. 97–116.

Kingston, N. and Nash, B. (2011) Formative assessment: a meta-analysis and a call for research, *Educational Measurement: Issues and Practice*, 30(4): 28–37.

Klenowski, V. (2009) Australian Indigenous students: addressing equity issues in assessment, *Teaching Education*, 20(1): 77–93.

Kutnick, P. and Colwell, J. (2010) Dialogue enhancement in classrooms: towards a relations approach for group working, in K. Littleton and C. Howe (eds) *Educational Dialogues: Understanding and Promoting Productive Interaction*. London: Routledge, pp. 192–215.

Mason, J. (2011) Noticing: roots and branches, in M.G. Sherin, V.R. Jacob and R.A. Philipp (eds) *Mathematics Teacher Noticing: Seeing Through Teachers' Eyes*. New York: Routledge, pp. 35–50.

Mercer, N. and Littleton, K. (2007) *Dialogue and the Development of Children's Thinking: A Sociocultural Approach*. London: Routledge.

Myhill, D. (2006) Talk, talk, talk: teaching and learning in whole class discourse, *Research Papers in Education*, 21(1): 19–41.

Penuel, W.R., DeBarger, A.H., Boscardin, C.K., Moorthy, S., Beauvineau, Y., Kennedy, C. and Allison, K. (2017) Investigating science curriculum adaptation as a strategy to improve teaching and learning, *Science Education*, 101(1): 66–98.

Perrenoud, P. (1998) From formative evaluation to a controlled regulation of learning processes: towards a conceptual field, *Assessment in Education: Principles, Policy and Practice*, 5(1): 85–102.

Pierson, J.L. (2008) The relationship between patterns of classroom discourse and mathematics learning. Doctoral thesis, University of Texas.

Rowe, M.B. (1974) Relation of wait-time and rewards to the development of language, logic, and fate control: Part II – Rewards, *Journal of Research in Science Teaching*, 11(4): 291–308.

Ruiz-Primo, M.A. and Furtak, E.M. (2007) Exploring teachers' informal formative assessment practices and students' understanding in the context of scientific inquiry, *Journal of Research in Science Teaching*, 44(1): 57–84.

Scott, P., Ametller, J., Mortimer, E. and Emberton, J. (2010) Teaching and learning disciplinary knowledge, in K. Littleton and C. Howe (eds) *Educational Dialogues: Understanding and Promoting Productive Interaction*. London: Routledge, pp. 289–303.

Scott, P.H., Mortimer, E.F. and Aguiar, O.G. (2006) The tension between authoritative and dialogic discourse: a fundamental characteristic of meaning making interactions in high school science lessons, *Science Education*, 90(4): 605–31.

Stiggins, R.J. (2005) *Student-Involved Assessment for Learning*. Upper Saddle River, NJ: Prentice Hall.

Swaffield, S. (2011) Getting to the heart of authentic assessment for learning, *Assessment in Education: Principles, Policy and Practice*, 18(4): 433–49.

van Es, E. (2011) A framework for learning to notice student thinking, in M.G. Sherin, V.R. Jacob and R.A. Philipp (eds) *Mathematics Teacher Noticing: Seeing Through Teachers' Eyes*, New York: Routledge, pp.134–51.

Wiliam, D., Lee, C., Harrison, C. and Black, P. (2004) Teachers developing assessment for learning: impact on student achievement, *Assessment in Education*, 11(1): 49–65.

15

Inclusion: individual differences, disabilities and Special Educational Needs

CARLA FINESILVER

The UK Government is committed to inclusive education of disabled children and young people and the progressive removal of barriers to learning and participation in mainstream education.

(DfE 2014: 25)

Introduction

The population of students in any school, like the general population, is one of diversity in many forms. There are wide-ranging differences between individuals in any given cohort, and these include many differences in specific and general strengths, weaknesses, capabilities and impairments that interact with both academic and non-academic aspects of school life. Some of these learner characteristics can manifest as additional or different learning needs that are considered significant compared to the majority of their peers; in English schools, these are commonly referred to as Special Educational Needs (SEN), although there are alternatives in use, such as Additional Learning Needs (ALN, as used more frequently in Further/Higher Education) or Additional Support Needs (ASN, as used in Scotland). The acronym SEND (or SEN/D) has recently become more frequently used, for example, in the current *Code of Practice* (DfE 2014), with the addition of the D to include disability status. Note that while adopting current official terminology for present purposes, it should be remembered that these are all contested terms due to the sensitive and complex nature of assigning such labels to certain people within a society, and the problematic assumptions and expectations that this can entail; this is addressed later in the chapter.

One of the Professional Standards for Qualified Teacher Status ('5: Adapt teaching to respond to the strengths and needs of all pupils') refers explicitly to SEND:

A teacher must: have a clear understanding of the needs of all pupils, including those with special educational needs; those of high ability; those with English as an additional language; those with disabilities; and be able to use and evaluate distinctive teaching approaches to engage and support them.

(DfE 2011b: 1)

Several of the other Standards also clearly indicate the need for teachers to ensure the educational environment they create is inclusive for students with diverse capabilities, both with and without formal SEND diagnoses. Recent governmental guidance elaborates further on Teaching Standard 5, indicating that teachers should have an understanding of cognitive, social, emotional, physical and mental health factors that can inhibit or enhance education, be able to analyse students' strengths and needs, recognize signs that might indicate SEND, and make adjustments to overcome barriers so all are able to access the curriculum (DfE 2016a).

This chapter provides a brief introduction to issues of inclusion in the classroom for those learners whose individual differences are considered to constitute Special Educational Needs and/or disabilities. While it refers to some of the more common SENDs teachers may expect to encounter in mainstream classrooms, it does not address specific diagnoses or go into the details of practical support in the classroom. There are many whole books on this topic (e.g. Peer and Reid 2011; Spooner 2013), and you will also find various publications tailored for the particular requirements of each of the different school subjects. After first addressing some of the key terminology, the remainder of the chapter provides some historical context on political and professional attitudes to inclusion in education, outlines current UK policies and systems for supporting students with SEND, and offers some general guidance on making your teaching and learning practices inclusive, for the benefit of those both with and without SEND.

Terminology

'Disabled' and 'Special Educational Needs' are currently legally defined terms in England, as used within educational policies that are statutory requirements. Disability is currently defined under the Equality Act 2010 as a physical or mental impairment that has a long-term and substantial adverse effect on the individual's ability to carry out normal day-to-day activities. Here, 'long-term' is defined as a year or more, and 'substantial' is defined as 'more than minor or trivial', and so this includes more people than many realize. Disability (along with race, sex, gender reassignment, pregnancy and maternity, religion or belief) is designated a legally 'protected characteristic'. This means that schools and other education providers must not directly or indirectly discriminate against disabled young people; further, they are expected to eliminate discrimination, promote equality of opportunity and foster good relations between disabled and non-disabled young people.

According to the current *SEND Code of Practice* (DfE 2014: 15), a learner is defined (somewhat recursively) as having Special Educational Needs if they have 'a learning difficulty or disability that calls for special educational provision to be made'. They are considered to have a learning difficulty or disability if they have 'a significantly greater difficulty in learning than the majority of others of the same age' (2014: 15), or 'a disability which prevents or hinders him or her from making use of facilities of a kind generally provided for others of the same age' (2014: 16). Special educational provision is thus 'educational or training provision that is additional to or different from that made generally for other children or young people of the same age by mainstream schools, maintained nursery schools, mainstream post-16 institutions or by relevant early years providers' (2014: 16).

Note that while, as mentioned above, the current acronym of choice is SEND, and there is significant overlap, SEN and disability are not interchangeable. This means that not all SENs result from disabilities, and not all disabilities cause SENs. Political and professional understandings of diversity, inclusion, Special Educational needs and disability have changed over time, and it should be noted that there is also significant national and cultural variation in the way these issues are understood and discussed.

Historical context: political and professional attitudes

Nineteenth to the early twentieth century

It is worth considering current principles within the historical context of the last century or so. Officially organized Special Education provision for those with learning difficulties might be said to have begun in 1847 with the Highgate Asylum for Idiots, prior to which those not cared for privately would most likely have been placed in workhouses or infirmaries (Warnock 1978); however, by 1897, London alone had 27 centres catering for some 1000 children judged 'capable of learning elementary subjects at some rate, however slow' (Hurt 1988: 127). Governmental involvement followed – for example, the Education Department Committee's Report on Defective and Epileptic Children in 1898. Legislative changes affecting education were not confined to those with disabilities; this was part of a much broader movement towards the principle of national state education for all. This social change was not without opposition from those with strong beliefs about keeping to one's 'place in society' – and receiving an education appropriate to that end; nevertheless, the school-educated population grew significantly, as did competing theories and practices for the stratification and segregation of this population. Expectations of children and schools tended to be conceptualized in terms of both social class and academic aptitude (as well as other factors, such as gender and ethnicity), and beliefs about differences in innate mental capacity of these subgroups were prevalent and relatively unchallenged. These all fed into and drew upon widespread presumptions about the limited learning potential of certain types of children, with little opportunity for them to prove different.

Legislating on how, where and whether different categories of child should be educated necessitated they be categorized – and an admission on the part of educationalists that many were borderline cases. The early twentieth century saw diagnostic change, in the rising popularity of 'Intelligence Quotient' (IQ) testing. Initially, the idea of actually measuring children's intelligence had considerable appeal, as an improvement on the cultural presumptions discussed above. Alfred Binet (developer of the first IQ test) intended it to be used to identify less able learners requiring special education, and the conception of academic ability as a spectrum was in some ways a helpful development. However, the idea of 'innate intelligence' as a fixed, unitary personal attribute persisted, even if less likely to be assumed *a priori*. Promotion of IQ resulted instead in the pinning of permanent labels on children after performance in a single test, and adjustment of their educational expectations accordingly. Labels were also assigned to scorers in the lower ranges that are generally considered derogatory (e.g. 'moron' for the IQ range 55–70).

The 1940s to the 1970s

Where previous legislation had treated the education of the 'handicapped' as an entirely separate issue to that of the rest of the population, the landmark Education Act 1944 included specialist provision within its list of requirements for all local education authorities. A key principle was also enshrined that any child considered educable had the legal right of access to schooling. The Act also brought in a new, and rather heterogeneous, category of 'educationally subnormal' (children of limited ability, developmentally retarded by more than 20 per cent for their age by disability or other conditions such as irregular attendance, ill-health, lack of continuity in their education or unsatisfactory school conditions), believed to amount to approximately 10 per cent of the school population, and made detailed suggestions regarding the nature of their school experience. This acceptance of multiple etiologies for underachievement appears strikingly contemporary, as does this proposal made in a 1946 Ministry of Education pamphlet on Special Education:

> They should be taught in small groups, in attractive accommodation and by sympathetic teachers. They should not, however, be isolated, but should be regarded as full members of the ordinary school and should share in general activities.
>
> (HMSO 1946, quoted in Warnock 1978: 21)

While intentions were good, there continued to be tensions over discrepancies in assessment, and some students were still deemed ineducable, and so ineligible for even special education. However, rising levels of parental dissatisfaction and appeals against LEA decisions led to further refinements of the law, and since the implementation of the Education (Handicapped Children) Act 1970, all children with disabilities, however severe, have been included in the framework of special education.

Late twentieth century to the present

A second landmark event of the twentieth century for children with educational difficulties was the publication of the *Warnock Report* (1978), from a committee appointed to review educational provision for children and young people 'handicapped by disabilities of body or mind'. Addressing the tangled nature of concepts of handicap, disability, incapacity and disadvantage, it stated bluntly the impossibility of establishing precise criteria for what constitutes educational handicap. This report also introduced the formal term Special Educational Needs (SEN), and the idea of using a multidisciplinary approach to look at the complex picture of abilities, disabilities, and all factors bearing on an individual's educational progress. It included statistical information which at the time was quite shocking: that at any time an estimated one in six children requires some form of special educational provision, and that one in five children are likely to qualify as having SEN at some time during their school career (Warnock 1978). This widely disseminated finding dealt a considerable blow to the historical tendency to dismiss those who do not succeed in traditional educational models as academically incapable. The idea that in an ordinary class of 30 students one might reasonably expect five to require special assistance of some sort is a powerful one, affecting how teachers, parents and peers perceived students experiencing difficulties. This period also saw greater realization of the wide spectrum of attainment to be found within the general population of school students – for example, the 'seven-year difference' in mathematics attainment at age 11 highlighted in Cockroft (1982). Overall, the effect was an increased awareness of the diversity that is likely to be present at any given time within each classroom; it is normal for students to progress at different and varying paces, and to need more support at different points in their education.

Further developments and refinements relating to SEND followed the *Warnock Report* (such as in the *Education Acts* of 1993 and 1996, and the *SEN Codes of Practice* from 1994 and 2001); these provided statutory guidance and practical advice for professionals to identify, assess and make provision for diverse learners. However, SEND policy was and is still seen by many as being applied in discriminatory and 'labelling' ways, which have continued to consider educational divergences from the norm as 'deficits' in a way which is ethically unacceptable (Warnock *et al.* 2010) and demanding of further re-conceptualization. An example of such re-conceptualization is the 'capability perspective' outlined by Terzi (2005), an educational adaptation of the *capability approach* philosophy developed by Amartya Sen and Martha Nussbaum. The capability approach considers disability as one aspect of normal human diversity, to be addressed within a distributive pattern of functionings and capabilities. For example, a student's specific learning difficulty is seen as a *limitation in particular functionings* resulting from the interaction of the personal characteristics of the child with the schooling environment. Where this environment is not appropriately designed and/or the individual is not receptive, the result is a limitation of capabilities, and thus of opportunities (Warnock *et al.* 2010).

Policy and official recommendations have continued to be refined (such as in the 2011 Green Paper on 'support and aspiration' in SEND), and statistics gathered. According to the Department for Education's most recent annual report (DfE 2016b), 1,228,785 students (14.4 per cent) in English schools were identified as having some kind of SEN for which they received support; this figure has seen a slight reduction from its highest point in 2010. A further 236,805 students (2.8 per cent) had a formal 'Statement of SEN' (pre-2014 system) or 'Education, Health and Care Plan' (EHC) (post-2014 system); this figure has remained constant since 2007. While it is certainly not the case that all stigma is banished to the past, for a student to be on an urban mainstream school's SEN Register is now comparatively unremarkable.

Current systems for supporting students with SEND

As discussed above, in previous generations, students characterized as having SEND were not generally educated with their peers, but changing attitudes, coupled with legislation, have resulted in significant moves towards inclusive education. While state-funded special(ist) schools do still exist in England (attended by 42.9 per cent of students with statements or EHC plans in 2016), for the majority of learners with an SEN and/or disability, inclusion in mainstream schools is considered the preferred path. It is a statutory requirement for every school to make 'reasonable adjustments' in order to ensure their academic and non-academic practices are suitable for students with additional or different needs, and provide individualized support if required.

Interactionist, bio-medical and social models of disability

The legislation and organizational frameworks relating to adjustments and support, as they currently stand, are compatible with what is sometimes described as an *interactionist* model. In an interactionist model of disability, individual, systemic or environmental barriers (e.g. physical aspects such as stairs or attitudinal aspects such as bias) interact with specific impairments (physical, cognitive, mental, sensory, emotional, developmental). An interactionist model of SEN assumes that environmental and individual child factors interact over time to result in the difficulties that give rise to Special Educational Needs (Wedell 2008). This may be contrasted with the *(bio-)medical model*, which views atypical characteristics, traits or impairments which cause disadvantage to that individual as deficits intrinsically rooted within the individual. Also in contrast is the *social model*, which suggests that the barriers faced are within the environment – that certain characteristics and impairments need not be disabling to a person, yet become disabling because of the ways in which society responds to them. Inclusive teaching practices tend towards the social model, accepting the need to differentiate and individualize learning so that each learner, whatever their characteristics and individual traits, can learn and develop according to their own needs and attributes. This is particularly the case in the early years of school, where learning is more 'child-centred' (Peer and Reid 2011). In contrast, in subject-centred formal assessment, that premise changes: there is a reversion to thinking of learning difficulties as if they are deficits intrinsic to the individual (i.e. the biomedical model), rather than focusing on the test environment within which they occur.

Support systems in schools

All schools are expected to have a clear approach to identifying and responding to SENs that is built into the overall approach to monitoring the progress and development of all students, so that those making less than expected progress given their age and individual circumstances may be identified. You, as teacher, will be involved in this process, and the following outlines the progression of a general case.

In cases where an initial concern has been raised, the first response should be targeting of the student's areas of weakness as part of normal teaching practice. Where progress continues to be less than expected, then the Special Educational Needs Co-ordinator (SENCO) should be alerted and, working with the student's teacher(s), should assess whether they have SEN. Concerns may also be initially expressed by parents (or those in the parental role), and the students themselves.

Once a student is identified as having SEN, schools are expected to put effective special educational provision in place, under the supervision of the SENCO. This follows an overall cycle of *Assess – Plan – Do – Review*. *Assessment* may involve multiple teachers and external professionals (such as an educational psychologist). *Planning* is likely to involve support staff (general teaching assistants (TAs) and/or specialist learning support assistants (LSAs)), and consultation with parents. Class or subject teachers take responsibility for *Doing*, although support staff may play a central role in interventions, such as small-group teaching or one-to-one support, in-class or temporarily withdrawn to an alternate learning environment. Again, external professionals may contribute. The *Review* process evaluates the effectiveness of support and any interventions; for students with an EHC plan, this is a formal requirement a minimum of once per year.

Education, Health and Care (EHC) needs assessments and plans

An EHC plan sets out detailed provisions to meet the Special Educational Needs of the student, to secure the best possible outcomes for them across education, health and social care and, as they get older, prepare them for adulthood. It is the responsibility of the local authority rather than the school, and includes a decision on the type of school or institution to be attended, as well as information such as the type, hours and frequency of support, and level of expertise required. The assessment process establishes the views, interests and aspirations of the parents and student, provides a full description of their Special Educational Needs and any health and social care needs, establishes desired outcomes across education, health and social care, and specifies the provision required. In particular, it co-ordinates the input of education, health and social care services, that work together to meet the child or young person's needs and support the achievement of the agreed outcomes.

Further details of the workings of EHC plans and in-school SEND support systems may be found in the *SEND Code of Practice* (DfE 2014). The main differences between this 2014 Code and its predecessors are that the most recent version strongly promotes a more joined-up approach with closer co-operation and continuity between education, health and social care systems, and that it covers the 0–25 age range, with a stronger focus on the transition from school to adulthood.

Classification and characterization of needs

The *SEND Code of Practice* identifies four 'broad areas of need', all of which may require particular modes of support. These are:

1. communication and interaction
2. cognition and learning
3. social, emotional and mental health difficulties
4. sensory and/or physical needs.

(DfE 2014: 97–8)

With some individuals, it may be possible to identify a clear and specific cause of the manifesting SEN; however, this is often not the case, as will be discussed below. Some of the classroom manifestations of these 'broad areas of need', and practices for addressing them, will be included in the following section. First, here is a sample of just a few of the conditions which might be interacting with the learning environment a teacher provides, resulting in additional or different learning needs for a given individual:

- Physical conditions – e.g. visual or auditory impairment, limited mobility, dysfunction of fine motor skills
- Medical conditions – e.g. epilepsy, diabetes, migraine, chronic fatigue/pain syndromes, asthma, eczema, clinical depression, anxiety disorder
- Developmental conditions – e.g. dyslexia, dyspraxia, attention deficit (hyperactivity) disorder, autistic spectrum, Tourette's syndrome
- Social conditions – e.g. poverty, abuse, trauma, bereavement, migration, English as an Additional Language (EAL).

One common public misconception is that knowing an individual's diagnosis means knowing in exactly what ways their educational experience will differ from that of a 'typical' student, and having a checklist of the necessary adjustments to be made. Labelling creates a spurious air of precision, implying certainty about causes of difficulties, although many quasi-medical labels are no more than 'a description dignified as a diagnosis' (Peer and Reid 2011). While the fact that we use different category labels for SEN at all indicates that there is some practical use in generalization, it is vital to remember that these are broad characterizations of diverse groups, and labels are only a rough guide into which the actual individuals we work with may not neatly comply. Many of these conditions do the following:

- Lie on a continuum (with formal diagnosis at an arbitrarily decided cut-off point)
- Fluctuate in severity (varying by the hour, day, month, ambient temperature, stress level, etc.)
- Can be comorbid (i.e. two or more inter-related conditions occurring together)

In considering issues of inclusion in education, it is necessary to consider the characteristics of the learning environment you create – both literally, as in the physical space in which it takes place, and in terms of the actual requirements of the activities in which you want students to participate. Here, the four 'broad areas of need' can be helpful, as well as overarching learning requirements such as information processing, executive functioning (memory, organization and planning), social interaction, focus/concentration and self-confidence. These will vary in importance between school subjects (e.g. in mathematics, sequencing, pattern recognition, and task-based strategizing are particularly important cognitive demands), so it is worth taking a moment to consider the particular characteristics of your own subject area.

The following examples are chosen to prompt reflection on inclusion (and exclusion) in the classroom of learners both with and without identified SENs.

Example: listening

The teacher communicating information or instructions to their class by speaking is something easily taken for granted ('But I *told* them . . . '), so consider some of the possible reasons listeners might not, despite their best intentions, catch everything the teacher says.

- They may have full or partial hearing loss, which might be permanent (such as damage to the auditory nerve) or temporary (such as an ear infection). This impairment of functioning could affect the whole range of hearing or just certain frequencies; for example, hearing loss in the high frequencies results in difficulty distinguishing between the sound of *f*, *s* and *th*, or *k* and *t*, and thus the confusing of similar words.

- They may have no hearing loss, but issues with processing the sounds of speech (either a diagnosed auditory processing disorder, or just having a longer than average delay between sounds entering the ear and words forming in the brain). Children with Speech, Language and Communication Needs (SLCN) may also have difficulties with the semantic aspect of language, i.e. understanding and recalling the meaning of words. In all of these cases there will be problems when the speaker moves on to a new phrase while the listener is still translating the meaning of the previous one.

- They may have a developmental condition that affects nuanced comprehension of the speaker's intended meaning, although all words are heard and processed effectively. For example, children on the autism spectrum are likely to take all speech very literally, and more experienced learners may be expending additional effort scrutinizing the speaker's tone of voice or accompanying gestures for indications that they might in fact be using irony or sarcasm, employing metaphor or making a joke.

- Co-existing with any of the above descriptions, a listener might have particularly high sensitivity to interference from background noise.

- Have overlapping characteristics (i.e. similar observable characteristics, diffi culties and/or support needs resulting from entirely different underlying causes

Furthermore, individuals classified as having SEN may:

- Not 'present' in the expected stereotypical ways for their condition(s)
- Have developed habits of concealing (or at least, not alerting the teacher attention to) their struggles – often in order to 'fit in' and avoid real or pe ceived stigma
- Have had their underlying difficulties exacerbated by missing significa chunks of school, not only directly caused by their condition(s), but by uns tled home circumstances (around 70 per cent of looked-after children ha some form of SEN) or exclusion (students with identified SEN accounting f more than half of all permanent and fixed term exclusions).

In most cases, by the time students reach secondary school, they will have alrea been identified as having SEN, and information on any relevant conditions th have, such as those listed above, will be available. In some of these cases they w also have a detailed EHC plan. However, there will be times when this is unava able (e.g. because the child has recently moved from another country). It may al be inaccurate (e.g. because a developmental condition is still undergoing diagr sis, a chronic medical condition has worsened, a recently occurring additior condition has not yet been identified). Additionally, as noted above, many releva conditions are not strictly categorical (i.e. you either 'have it' or you don't) but f on a continuum of severity or effective impairment. So, for example, a giv individual may exhibit some of the diagnostic characteristics of dyslexia autism, but have not met the necessary threshold during psychological testing 1 a formal diagnosis to be given.

Every individual, however they are categorized by our education system, w still have their own individual pattern of capabilities, strengths and weakness and these are not set in stone but change over time. Do not forget about the part ular strengths that students with SEND may have; for example, by seconda school many neuro-divergent learners will have developed ingenious coping str egies and workarounds for their cognitive difficulties and differences (or have t potential to do so, with support). For these reasons, considering and improving t inclusivity of your practice should not be thought of as something only for tho students with SEND, but for the entire cohort.

Inclusive practice for the benefit of all

A pupil has SEN where their learning difficulty or disability calls for speci educational provision, namely provision different from or additional to th normally available to pupils of the same age. Making higher quality teachii normally available to the whole class is likely to mean that fewer pupils w require such support.

(DfE 2014: 94–

Many other issues might be affecting an individual's capability to listen effectively to the teacher, such as being anxious, sleep-deprived, hungry, in discomfort or pain, on medication with unpleasant side-effects, concentrating on suppressing disruptive tics (Tourette's syndrome), or trying to filter out voices in the head (schizophrenia) – to name just a few.

Where a student is identified as having a hearing impairment, there are some standard inclusion practices: these include having them sit near the front of the class, remaining in a direct line of sight and facing them whenever speaking, and potentially using a microphone/transmitter. However, as it is clear that complications in listening to the teacher is an issue affecting a much wider group, it is possible to aim generally for inclusive practice without knowing every specific source of difficulty. First, do not assume that your own levels of sound detection, auditory processing speed, comprehension of language, and capability for focusing on speech are universal. Make sure you speak at an appropriate pace and volume without running words together; repeat key information and instructions verbally, and also present them in written form; and try to consider possible misinterpretations of your choice of words. It is also vital to maintain an environment where students experiencing any of the issues above are comfortable letting you know that they did not understand what you said; a child who is mocked or chastised for 'not listening' learns not to ask again, and to conceal their struggles.

Example: writing

When planning lessons and thinking about how the activities in your lessons may be experienced differently by the diverse student cohort, it is also wise to consider where the educational value lies in those activities. For example, another common classroom activity is students writing (for example, copying notes and examples of the lesson content from the board or a textbook, or producing written compositions); consider some of the potential difficulties this presents for individuals, that are not to do with the content of the text.

- They may have a permanent disability affecting their ability to grip or manipulate a pen (e.g. cerebral palsy), or a temporary impairment (e.g. tendinitis, broken finger). This might mean they cannot write at all, or that they can write, but it is slower and more effortful than for their peers, and the end product is harder to read.

- They may have unimpaired physical capacity to write, but issues with processing what they see and reproducing it (due to a diagnosed visual processing disorder, or a longer than average delay between eye and brain). As with spoken text, interpreting and producing written text cause particular difficulties for learners with certain developmental conditions, such as SLCN and Specific Learning Difficulties (SpLD).

- Some of these issues will be exacerbated by interference, such as poorly printed text, contrast issues, or a patterned background.

Unlike spoken text, reading may generally be done at the learner's individual pace; however, you can help by making sure any that you produce (such as on a projector screen or worksheet) is of a suitable size and clarity. There are various alternative strategies for writing (such as typing on a laptop rather than handwriting, or audio recording speech and using voice recognition software for notating it). In the case of copying notes, pre-printed notes could be provided for those who need them. However, it is also worth taking time to reconsider the importance of the information presented in text form: is all of it actually necessary to the lesson objectives, particularly in the case of copying information from one place to another?

Orienting to others' perspectives

If there is anything common to the diverse set of students with SEND, it is the greater probability of them being frustrated in lessons, and of under-performing in formal test situations – even with some additional support. On the basis of standardized assessment practices that are a poor fit for nonstandard patterns of strengths and weaknesses, they may be assumed to be of 'low ability', and given work that is not intellectually stimulating. This can include being placed in an inappropriate 'ability' grouping (see Chapter 13 for a discussion of the issues of setting and streaming). This experience of being prevented from performing to one's potential can be difficult to imagine for those who are able-bodied, neurotypical, and generally well in mind and body. Perhaps it may help somewhat to recall the details of a past illness, or the feeling after a night's severely disrupted sleep, or the emotional state following troubles at home, and to imagine how this might affect your performance in a test. Would you be happy to have your 'ability' and future potential for learning judged on this basis, day in and day out? Might it become a self-fulfilling prophecy? With students with SEN, there is a very particular danger of creating an inflexible learning environment where the 'bar' is simultaneously set too high and too low; too high in that the manner of presentation or types of activity demanded create barriers to learning, while too low in terms of the assumptions made about their (lack of) potential for rationality, creativity and higher-order thinking.

It is always worth asking students with SEN for their views and feedback on what inclusion and support strategies they find helpful, and some will have much to offer in terms of creativity and innovative approaches to learning, that may also benefit those without SENs. However, it should also be remembered that others will have little awareness of their additional or different needs compared to their more typical peers. Hendrickx expresses this strongly:

> When I have spoken to [neurodiverse] young people about their diagnosis and what it means, overwhelmingly, they do not know. They have been told the name of the condition and no more. They have had no information or explanation about how they are different, or more importantly, how everyone else is different.

> (2010: 156)

[They] may have assumed that everyone else felt the same way. It can be a real light-bulb moment when someone understands why they have been inadvertently offending people or getting low grades due to misunderstandings or differences in interpretation of language or intention.

(2010: 157)

The book from which these quotes are taken, *The Adolescent and Adult Neurodiversity Handbook*, not only contains many useful 'tips', but is unusual in that it includes substantial descriptions of the experience of living (and learning) with a variety of conditions, each written in the first-person voice by adults with diagnoses of autism, ADHD, dyslexia, dyspraxia, OCD and various other conditions. Texts such as these, or the increasing number of blogs and forums run for – and, importantly, *by* – people with disabilities and differences that affect participation in both learning and wider society, have great potential for raising awareness of the variety and scale of individual differences inherent in the population.

The support team

Teaching school subject(s) in a way which includes students with diverse needs requires an understanding of:

- The current SEND Code of Practice
- The inclusion and support systems within your school, including the roles and functioning of the SENCO, specialist and general support staff
- Ways of creating and maintaining effective working relationships between individual students, support staff and classroom teachers.

The SEND Code of Practice and the SENCO role have been discussed above. Regarding the other staff who may be involved, some features that have been identified as contributing to successful support teams are: clear specification of roles and responsibilities; well-organized resources; regular meetings to plan and evaluate; thorough record-keeping; and adaptability (Daniels and Anghileri 1995).

Working with support staff

Terms used to describe the 'learning support' or 'inclusion' staff vary between schools, e.g. teaching assistant (TA), learning support assistant (LSA), classroom assistant. There is also variation in the way they are organized within schools; this might include a particular TA working with a particular student within their classes across several subjects, LSAs with specialist training in assistive technologies for a particular category of SEND (such as visual or hearing impairment), or who are attached to a particular subject area in which they are familiar. These fellow professionals can be a superb resource of information and strategies; for example, they may have come to know a student with complex difficulties very well, and be able to tell you some of the teaching/learning strategies that have proved helpful (and less helpful) in other classes. Having them assisting in your lesson can be a great opportunity.

However, beginning teachers often find it quite challenging, if not daunting, to be managing the activities of other adults in their classroom, and there can be a tendency for some teachers to leave TAs to their own devices. This is not good practice: recent research and guidance such as the *Maximising the Impact of Teaching Assistants* project (Webster *et al.* 2015) has emphasized preparedness as the key issue for effective inclusion support practices, so it is best, when circumstances permit, to communicate in advance with support staff. In some schools there is time scheduled for this purpose, but unfortunately in others it can be difficult to find opportunities. As a general principle, the more information your support staff have about the lesson content, the ways you intend to teach it and the activities students will be engaging in, the better help they can provide. If there are any particular things you want them to do, this will work better with some prior discussion, or at least warning. With experienced support staff, a collaborative approach to planning can work very well indeed, in which they are given the chance to contribute and make suggestions. On the other hand, most of the learning support staff you work with will not be subject specialists, and some may lack confidence in supporting your subject. They may be unfamiliar with the content, or with your preferred teaching/learning approaches to it, and in such cases, communication in advance is also very important. If their explanations and methods differ from yours too greatly, this can increase the confusion for students, so it may be necessary for assistants to be guided to work in the way that you, the subject expert, think most appropriate.

Sometimes provisions made by the school may include withdrawing certain students from class for small-group or one-to-one support, occasionally or more frequently. This can be done by specialist support from staff secured by the school, such as literacy and numeracy specialist tutors running 'catch-up' intervention programmes; professionals from outside agencies may also be involved, such as educational psychologists, speech and language therapists, and mental health services. When there are interventions involving group or one-to-one teaching away from the main subject teacher, the students may benefit greatly from the focused specialist attention they receive while away from the main class, but there is also the potential for confusion on returning to class having missed material taught in your lesson. If you are in this position, it is particularly important to work closely with the other staff involved, to plan and assess the impact of support and interventions, and when and how they could be linked to your classroom teaching.

Concluding thoughts

Have you heard the phrase 'I've got x SEN(D) kids in my class'? It is not an uncommon phrase for beginning teachers (as well as some who are more experienced). While this is understood to be shorthand, and to come from a good intention to identify those students who may need additional or different support to achieve their potential, it is problematic. It gives the impression of learners with Special Educational Needs and/or disabilities as a quite separate category of person, set apart bilaterally from 'normal' humans.

It also implies homogeneity among those who carry that designation, when in fact there is huge diversity within it (and without). It should be clear by now that every individual has their own pattern of strengths and weaknesses, functionings and impairments, capabilities and needs, and this includes differing levels of self-awareness, reflexivity and metastrategic capability. These all interact in different ways with the classroom environment provided, and change over time and context. Consider how your own pattern of individual characteristics interacted with your school experience, and how it may have differed from that of other students. In particular, what were the cumulative effects over your school career, and beyond?

While inclusive educational practices are a legal and ethical right of individuals with SEND, there is more to this than diagnosis according to constructed categories, and then following of the guidelines set out in the Code of Practice. Identifying patterns of capability and need, and ensuring an appropriate learning environment that takes into account the diversity of the student cohort, are part of inclusive educational practice in a wider sense. Even two students with the same diagnosis will likely have much less in common than you would expect, so how can you make sure they are fully included in your lessons? While it should now be clear that there is no simple solution or single strategy guaranteed to 'work', there are principles to keep in mind. You can start by thinking in terms of capability rather than deficit. You can avoid falling into habits and continue to try out different teaching strategies, planning for diversity and designing your activities so that they may be presented and carried out in a range of different forms. You can learn what is helpful (or not) in different cases by watching and listening to student responses to your approaches, and by learning perceptively from what they communicate. You can keep a particular eye out for signs of progress that may be in smaller steps, at a slower pace, or qualitatively different from those you might have come to expect. You can make sure not to judge the content of a communication by its mode of presentation.

> It will never be easy to make an education system inclusive but it will always be indefensible to accept that it should be otherwise. Inclusion 'trips easily off the tongue but can be without meaning or substance' (Wade 1999: 81) but this must be avoided if education is to be a benefit which is truly available to all: a bridge and not a barrier.
>
> (Abbott 2011: 234)

Appreciate and enjoy the diversity within your classroom, and take pride in your role of building bridges and removing barriers to education!

References

Abbott, C. (2011) Aiming for inclusion: removing barriers and building bridges, in J. Dillon and M. Maguire (eds) *Becoming a Teacher: Issues in Secondary Education* (4th edn). Maidenhead: McGraw-Hill.

Cockroft, W.H. (1982) *Mathematics Counts: Report of the Committee of Inquiry into the Teaching of Mathematics in Schools*. London: HMSO, http://www.educationengland.org.uk/documents/cockcroft/index.html, accessed 4 May 2017.

Daniels, H. and Anghileri, J. (1995) *Secondary Mathematics and Special Educational Needs*. London: Cassell.

DfE (Department for Education) (2011) *Teachers' Standards*, https://www.gov.uk/government/publications/teachers-standards, accessed 4 May 2017.

DfE (Department for Education) (2014) *Special Educational Needs and Disability Code of Practice: 0 To 25 Years*, https://www.gov.uk/government/publications/send-code-of-practice-0-to-25, accessed 4 May 2017.

DfE (Department for Education) (2016a) *A Framework of Core Content for Initial Teacher Training*, https://www.gov.uk/government/uploads/system/uploads/attachment_data/file/536890/Framework_Report_11_July_2016_Final.pdf, accessed 4 May 2017.

DfE (Department for Education) (2016b) *Special Educational Needs: Analysis and Summary of Data Sources*, https://www.gov.uk/government/publications/sen-analysis-and-summary-of-data-sources, accessed 4 May 2017.

Equality Act 2010 (2010) http://www.legislation.gov.uk/ukpga/2010/15/contents, accessed 4 May 2017.

Hendrickx, S. (2010) *The Adolescent and Adult Neuro-Diversity Handbook: Asperger's Syndrome, ADHD, Dyslexia, Dyspraxia, and Related Conditions*. London: Jessica Kingsley Publishers.

Hurt, J.S. (1988) *Outside the Mainstream: A History of Special Education*. London: Batsford.

Peer, L. and Reid, G. (2011) *Special Educational Needs: A Guide for Inclusive Practice*. London: Sage Publications Ltd.

Spooner, W. (2013) *The SEN Handbook for Trainee Teachers, NQTs and Teaching Assistants*. London: David Fulton Publishers.

Terzi, L. (2005) A capability perspective on impairment, disability and special needs: towards social justice in education. *Theory and Research in Education*, 3(2): 197–223.

Warnock, H.M. (1978) *Special Educational Needs: Report of the Committee of Enquiry into the Education of Handicapped Children and Young People*. London: HMSO, http://www.educationengland.org.uk/documents/warnock/index.html, accessed 4 May 2017.

Warnock, M., Norwich, B. and Terzi, L. (2010) *Special Educational Needs: A New Look*. London: Continuum.

Webster, R., Russell, A. and Blatchford, P. (2015) *Maximising the Impact of Teaching Assistants: Guidance for School Leaders and Teachers*. London: Routledge.

Wedell, K. (2008) Evolving dilemmas about categorization, in L. Florian and M.J. McLaughlin (eds) *Disability Classification in Education: Issues and Perspectives*. Thousand Oaks, CA: Corwin Press.

16

English as an additional language: challenges of ethnicity, language and subject identity in the contemporary classroom

CONSTANT LEUNG

Becoming a fully professional teacher in contemporary Britain means developing effective practice with regard to pupils from diverse ethnic and linguistic minority families. This chapter, organized into five sections, offers a broad overview of this topic. The first section presents a picture of the ethnic and linguistic diversity in our schools. The second section traces the development of English as an Additional Language (EAL) as a curricular response to changing demographics. The third section is focused on the current policy and provision of EAL within the school curriculum. The discussion in the fourth section offers an account of the pedagogic principles underlying the official curriculum policy and their implications for classroom practice. The final section addresses wider professional issues related to EAL pupils and their language development.

This chapter takes account of the devolved nature of UK governance. The four constituent parts of the UK have different educational jurisdictions and administrations. The terms 'British' and 'UK' are used where the points being made are relevant to all parts of the country. Statistical data from the Department for Education (DfE) and the Office for National Statistics (ONS) tends to refer to England only; Northern Ireland, Scotland and Wales publish their national statistical data separately. For reasons of scope and space, I will only draw on DfE and ONS data in this discussion.

The term EAL itself is of relatively new coinage; previously it was referred to as ESL (English as a Second Language). Indeed, in other parts of the English-speaking world, the term ESL is still used alongside many others, for example, English Language Learning/Learners in the USA. For some, the notion of an 'additional' language is generally held to be ideologically more positive than 'second' language which might encourage a deficit view of pupils' linguistic repertoire. For this reason, sometimes pupils with EAL are also referred to as bilingual pupils.

A diverse school population

Ethnic and linguistic diversity in the UK school population has been increasing in recent years. According to data produced by the Department for Education/Office for National Statistics:

> The proportion of pupils from minority ethnic origins has been rising steadily since 2006. In primary schools, 31.4 per cent of pupils are of minority ethnic origins, an increase from 30.4 per cent in January 2015. Minority ethnic pupils made up 71 per cent of the increase in pupil numbers in primary schools between 2015 and 2016.
>
> In secondary schools, 27.9 per cent of pupils are of minority ethnic origins, an increase from 26.6 per cent in 2015.
>
> (DfE/ONS 2016: 8)

The ONS uses the following categories for data collection: 'White British', 'White non-British', 'Asian', 'Black', 'Mixed', 'Chinese', 'Any other' and 'Unclassified'. These categories are very broad and can be subject to different interpretations. It is also important to recognize that pupils with ethnic minority backgrounds are not necessarily from linguistic minority backgrounds. In other words, some ethnic minority pupils are English as first-language speakers, others are learners of EAL. For instance, many Asian and Black pupils are UK-born and have first-language fluency in English. Some of these pupils may also have knowledge of their home or local community language/s, e.g. Cantonese, English-based Creoles, Urdu or Yoruba. These pupils are sometimes referred to as bi/multilinguals.

For English as an Additional Language, the ONS (DfE/ONS 2016: 10) currently uses this working definition: 'A pupil is recorded to have English as an additional language if they are exposed to a language at home that is known or believed to be other than English.' Using this definition the ONS reports that:

> In primary schools, 20.1 per cent of pupils are exposed to a language known or believed to be other than English in their home. This is an increase of 0.7 percentage points since January 2015, and the figure has been steadily rising since 2006.
>
> In secondary schools, 15.7 per cent of pupils are exposed to a non-English language in their home. This rate has also steadily increased over the last ten years and by 0.7 percentage points since January 2015.
>
> (DfE/ONS 2016: 10)

It is clear that the ONS working definition of EAL is imprecise and vague; it certainly does not provide any accurate information on pupils' EAL proficiency. Indeed, the Department for Education (2016) has recently introduced an EAL proficiency screening and identification framework as part of the statutory data returns for all schools in England. Therefore, the official ethnic and EAL data need to be treated with some caution since they contain inadequacies (discussed further in a later section).

Furthermore, ethnic and linguistic diversity is not itself a static phenomenon. The pattern of international migration has changed quite significantly over recent years and it is likely to continue to change for the foreseeable future. Suffice it to say at this point that teachers have to assume that their knowledge of ethnic and linguistic diversity needs to be updated constantly and their classroom practices have to be adjusted and developed accordingly. Questions such as 'how to respond to the needs of EAL learners?' have to be re-visited and re-calibrated regularly. The sociologist Giddens (1991: 38–9) observes social and cultural changes in contemporary conditions and our actions are intertwined:

> To sanction a practice because it is traditional will not do . . . The reflexivity of modern social life consists in the fact that social practices are constantly examined and reformed in the light of incoming information about those very practices . . . We are abroad in a world which is thoroughly constituted through reflexively applied knowledge, but where at the same time we can never be sure that any given element of that knowledge will not be revised.

This observation applies directly to teaching in our time.

EAL: the historical context

To understand the current official EAL policy and practices, we need first to take a retrospective look at some relevant past events. EAL became an important issue in the British education system as a result of the inward migrations and settlement of peoples and languages since 1945, particularly in the 1950s, 1960s and 1970s. Martin-Jones (1989) described these migrations as principally of people entering Britain as either migrant workers or as refugees. At the same time she saw a significant divide between those entering from other parts of Europe, and those from former colonies and other economically less developed parts of the world. It was the languages of people from the latter which had the strong impact on EAL policy and practice in Britain during that period. I am speaking here of people who migrated to the UK in relatively large numbers in the 1950s, 1960s and 1970s from India, Pakistan, Bangladesh, the Caribbean, Hong Kong, East Africa (principally Kenya, Tanzania and Uganda), West Africa (mainly Nigeria and Ghana), Vietnam, Ethiopia and Eritrea, Somalia and Cyprus (see Peach 1996) and brought with them languages such as Punjabi, Urdu, Gujarati, Hindi, Bengali and Sylheti, Cantonese and Hakka Chinese, Caribbean Creoles, Yoruba, Twi, Cypriot Greek and Turkish, Kurdish, Tigrinya, Amharic and Somali (see ILEA 1989; Alladina and Edwards 1991). In recent years the profile of pupils with EAL has changed rapidly, for instance, as a result of the arrival of new migrant populations from Eastern Europe and elsewhere stimulated by major global economic and political developments.

Unfortunately, the entrance into the UK of migrants from former colonies and so-called developing countries was accompanied by a considerable amount of racial hostility and disdain for their languages. This led to, in the 1950s and 1960s, an official assimilationist approach (Department of Education and Science 1971), based on the idea that schools should set about erasing the languages and cultural practices of the children of new migrants as a precondition for their educational success. When the children from migrant families arrived at local schools with little English or speaking different varieties of English, the main educational concern was to help make them 'become "invisible", a truly integrated member of the school community . . . as soon as possible' (Derrick 1977: 16). In practice, where staff and material resources were available, the newly arrived migrant pupils were taught English in specially instituted full-time or part-time English language programmes that did not cover the subject content of the 'ordinary' curriculum available to all other pupils. The language teaching approach was informed by a combination of elements of language-as-grammar principles, common sense, and pragmatic every-day language use. For instance, the Ministry of Education (1963: 18) advised that:

> The teacher, through his [or her] own clear and natural speech should act as a constant example of the normal intonation, rhythm and pitch of ordinary conversation, using pictures, objects, actions and improvised dialogues to ensure comprehension and to enlarge vocabulary . . . Most teachers . . . would stress the importance of basing oral work on a carefully graded vocabulary and carefully introduced sentence patterns.

There was no systematic national guidance for this provision. The amount of time spent by pupils in these English language classes varied between a few months to eighteen months, depending on the local (county/city level) policy and resources. This separate provision was widely regarded as the most efficacious way of teaching English to migrant children; it also helped reduce the visibility of ethnically different pupils in the mainstream pupil population which had led to complaints of 'lowering standards' (see Leung and Franson 2001).

This separate teaching provision was later modified following the Bullock Report (DES 1975: 286), which stated that:

> No child should be expected to cast off the language and culture of the home as he (*sic*) crosses the school threshold [and] . . . the school should adopt positive attitudes to its pupils' bilingualism and wherever possible should help maintain and deepen their knowledge of their mother tongues.

Despite this declaration, the Bullock Report did not indicate how schools were to implement this aspiration.

A decade later another official report, the Swann Report (DES 1985), while reaffirming a generally positive attitude to the home and community languages of ethnic minority pupils, decisively ruled out any support for these languages by what it called 'mainstream' (i.e. publicly funded) schools:

> We find we cannot support the arguments put forward for the introduction of programmes of bilingual education in maintained schools in this country. Similarly we would regard mother tongue maintenance, although an important educational function, as best achieved within the ethnic minority communities themselves rather than within mainstream schools.
>
> (DES 1985: 406)

However, one principle upon which the Swann Report insisted, was that ethnic minority pupils for whom English was an additional language should at all times be educated in the mainstream classroom alongside their peers to avoid segregated provision and to guarantee equal access to the mainstream curriculum. The terms 'mainstream' and 'mainstreaming' were first used in official documents in the 1980s and 1990s to refer to the idea of inclusive educational practice that provided the same curriculum provision for all pupils, irrespective of their ethnic, language backgrounds and EAL proficiency. Official opinions and statements strongly recommended the mainstreaming of EAL provision. For instance, in a landmark investigation into the EAL provision and practice of the Calderdale education authority, the Commission for Racial Equality found the practice of providing separate non-mainstream schooling for pupils with EAL to be racially discriminating and contrary to 'the prevailing educational view' (1986: 6), and recommended that 'provision for second language speakers is made in conjunction with mainstream education . . .' (1986: 16). (Also see relevant parts of the Swann Report (DES 1985) and the Bullock Report (DES 1975). For a detailed discussion of the development of this approach to EAL, see Mohan, Leung and Davison 2001; Rampton, Harris and Leung 2001.)

As noted earlier, in recent years, the ethnic and linguistic profiles of pupils with EAL have changed substantially as a result of the arrival of new migrant populations from Eastern Europe and elsewhere, stimulated by major global economic and political developments. The patterns of inward migration are likely to continue to change as the political relationships between the UK, the European Union and the rest of the world develop in the next period. There is, however, little sign that the changing composition of the ethnic and linguistic profiles of the EAL learners will impact on the current 'mainstreaming' policy position. It is to the relationship between English as an Additional Language and the mainstream curriculum that we now turn.

EAL and the school curriculum: a glimpse of professional reality

At present, with the possible exception of some short-term English language induction courses, all pupils with EAL are expected to follow the school curriculum. This means that additional language learning opportunities, particularly for academic purposes, are to be provided in subject lessons. This has been the official policy disposition for the best part of 20 years. Hence, 'the teaching of English is the responsibility of all teachers' (National Curriculum Council 1991: 1). This official view has been reaffirmed in subsequent official curriculum guidance documents. For instance, the National Curriculum Framework document states that:

> 4.5 Teachers must also take account of the needs of pupils whose first language is not English. Monitoring of progress should take account of the pupil's age, length of time in this country, previous educational experience and ability in other languages.
>
> 4.6 The ability of pupils for whom English is an additional language to take part in the national curriculum may be in advance of their communication skills in English. Teachers should plan teaching opportunities to help pupils

develop their English and should aim to provide the support pupils need to take part in all subjects.

(DfE 2014a: 8)

The National Curriculum Framework does not regard EAL as a discipline in its own right; there is no dedicated curriculum specification for it. So, unlike English or Science, EAL is generally not given dedicated time slots in the subject-based teaching day. At the same time, to all intents and purposes, the curriculum specifications and assessment criteria for English (the National Curriculum subject) are used for both English as a first language speaking pupils and those who are still in the process of learning EAL; there is little specific guidance on EAL. For instance, the statutory guidance for teachers working with KS4 pupils (14–16 years) are advised:

Teachers should build on the knowledge and skills that pupils have been taught at key stage 3. Decisions about progression should be based on the security of pupils' linguistic knowledge, skills and understanding and their readiness to progress to the next stage. Pupils whose linguistic development is more advanced should be challenged through being offered opportunities for increased breadth and depth in reading and writing. *Those who are less fluent should consolidate their knowledge, understanding and skills, including through additional practice.*

(DfE 2014b, electronic publication, added italics)

In order to understand how EAL provision is organized in schools, it is important to know something about funding and staffing in schools. EAL provision is non-mandatory (unlike subjects such as English and Mathematics). Between the mid-1960s and late 1990s funding for EAL came from a special grant. This grant was commonly known as Section 11, earmarked 'to support the cost of employing additional staff to help minority ethnic groups overcome linguistic and other barriers which inhibit their access to, and take up of, mainstream services' (OFSTED 1994: 1). From 1998, the monies were administered under a DfEE grant scheme, known as Ethnic Minority Achievement Grant (EMAG). This grant was time-limited, often two or three years at a time. The actual amount of funding available to a school, via the local education authority, varied from one grant period to another depending on the total size of the grant and the competing demands from other schools. The vast majority of EAL teachers, often referred to as language support teachers, were employed through this funding.

Although since the 1960s this grant had been regularly renewed, the time-limited nature meant instability for schools in terms of curriculum planning, and for individual EAL staff in terms of their career and professional development. The amount of funding was in any case always well short of what was needed. This meant that generally EAL staff were very thin on the ground. This dedicated stream of school funding was abolished in 2011. Now there is a small allocation in the general school funding formula that is designed to provide time-limited support for EAL learners (currently the first three years in school), but schools are not required to report how the monies involved are used.

Given that EAL is not a curriculum discipline with its own programme of study and timetable slots, teachers working with EAL are expected to provide support in a variety of ways. Broadly speaking, specialist EAL teachers play a number of roles including:

- As a classroom teacher, working in partnership with subject teachers, with a special regard for EAL development within the context of the school curriculum

- As a curriculum adviser and developer to promote a more inclusive and whole-curriculum planning approach to responding to the needs of pupils with EAL

- As a day-to-day adviser and in-service professional development provider to other colleagues on EAL matters

- As a liaison person, particularly those EAL teachers who are speakers of a community language such as Turkish and Urdu, with minority parents and community organizations. (For a fuller account, see Bourne and McPake 1991.)

The extent to which any individual EAL teacher can contribute to the above roles depends on a number of individual and school circumstances. Professional experience has shown that, given the shortage of funds and qualified staff, EAL teachers can only meet some of the teaching and curriculum development demands in school. Many class or subject teachers working in classrooms with a high number of EAL pupils receive no assistance from EAL specialists. It is therefore important for all teachers to have some knowledge of some of the key concepts and principles which have been influential in shaping EAL teachers' classroom strategies. A knowledge of these principles may enable non-EAL teachers to begin to understand the teaching and learning issues involved.

Pedagogic principles and classroom strategies

As pointed out earlier, EAL is a cross-curricular teaching concern. Within this cross-curricular perspective two linked pedagogical principles have been promoted in the professional literature: (1) making learning activities and tasks personally meaningful and understandable; and (2) using learning activities to encourage active engagement.

Making learning activities and tasks personally meaningful and understandable

> [b]y ... encouraging children to apply their personal and already acquired knowledge to solving group problems, and from observing their efforts in a collaborative situation, to identify and provide any support that might be needed by individual children to acquire curriculum concepts and the language needed to express them.
>
> (Bourne 1989: 64; also see Mohan, Leung and Davison 2001: Chapter 10)

This approach is clearly built on the idea that subject-related classroom activities can be exploited to create supportive opportunities for EAL learners to develop their English language proficiency (see Leung 2016, for a further discussion).

Using learning activities to encourage active engagement

> Learning is best achieved through enquiry-based activities involving discussion . . .
>
> To learn a language it is necessary to participate in its meaningful use . . . The curriculum itself is therefore a useful vehicle for language learning . . . A main strategy . . . for both curriculum learning and language learning is the flexible use of small group work . . .
>
> (Bourne 1989: 63)

The National Curriculum Council (NCC 1991) advised teachers to use teaching techniques that would allow EAL learners to engage in class activities; these techniques include the use of familiar objects and activities that can assist first-hand understanding, obviating the need for sophisticated language (for a fuller discussion, see Leung and Creese 2010: Chapter 1). These principles are broadly consistent with a constructivist view of education which puts a great deal of premium on hands-on experiential learning, which would necessarily include the increasingly prominent use of digital technology. They also require the teacher to have a very clear understanding of at least two language development issues in the classroom context:

1. The link between curriculum knowledge and the language used to express that knowledge
2. The link between spoken and written English (and possibly other languages) used for interaction in the classroom, including teacher talk and teacher writing, and the learning and development of spoken and written English for assignments, assessments and tests in different subject areas.

Three helpful strategies

In the actual classroom teachers have to interpret these broad principles with reference to their EAL learners who may be at different stages of English language development. The three following ideas and strategies have been found to be helpful for teachers to put the principles into practice.

Contextual support using physical movements/actions, visual/audio material and realia

Unfamiliar concepts and complex ideas can often be made more comprehensive by using pictures, diagrams and visual and other sensory representations. For instance, the central ideas in the topic of paper-making may be visually supported by a series of pictures or drawings showing the process involving tree logging, making pulp, and so on. Even ephemeral and often domain-specific concepts such as cynicism and sarcasm in a particular narrative context may be exemplified by drama activities. In many ways the value of this kind of contextual support is quite well understood. An important issue here is not to assume that contextual support of this kind can be understood by all pupils. It is possible that sometimes even the most obvious picture, to the teacher, may not make any sense to some pupils. For some very young pupils, the picture of an inkwell or the image of a vinyl record may mean very little. The usefulness of any contextualization material and activity has to be constantly evaluated in relation to the pupils involved. A further issue is that while contextual support may help pupils understand the gist of what is going on, there is no guarantee that they will learn the language being used.

Opportunities for language development by teaching and modelling language in context

Cummins' (1992; 2008) distinction between basic interpersonal communication skills (BICS) and cognitive academic language proficiency (CALP) has been useful in helping teachers understand how to analyse language demands for their pupils. A teacher asking pupils to choose a colour on screen or on a cardboard colour chart is a classroom example of BICS. From EAL pupils' point of view, even if they do not understand the question or the names of the colours, the immediate meaning of the activity can be worked out by observing the actions of others. The physical context of the activity and the active engagement in the activity (e.g. by having to choose a colour) can provide an opportunity for highly focused language modelling by the teacher, and conscious and active language use by the pupil. The value of contextual information can be made more obvious if we picture a different scenario, this time the teacher asks the same question but without any visuals. This kind of use of highly contextualized language supported by visual and other materials can be helpful for pupils at all stages of developing listening, speaking, reading and writing in EAL, but its benefits are immediately obvious to those teachers who are working with pupils at an early stage of learning English.

Opportunities to develop language use for academic purposes

Meaning in speech in social situations can be interactionally built up. Imagine the following:

Pupil 1:	What are we doing?
Pupil 2:	Miss said we have to write down what we said.
Pupil 3:	Like what we did on Monday.
Pupil 1:	What, like we write down the things we made up?

Classroom conversations, even when they are curriculum-related, are full of examples of this kind of joint focus forming and meaning making. This is indeed one of the main characteristics of everyday spoken language. Furthermore, spoken language is often informal in that it is not necessarily made up of well-formed sentences; the phrase or the clause is more likely to be the unit of utterances (Kress

1994). Spoken language in social situations also tends to use lots of referring and pointing words such as '*it*', '*this*', '*here*' and '*there*', e.g. '*I think it's 20 degrees here and that's 40 degrees*' when a pupil tries to estimate the temperatures of different substances as part of a science activity. Some of these characteristics of everyday spoken language are not found in formal academic English. The ability to read and write effectively in an academic style cannot be assumed, even when a pupil appears to be able to handle here-and-now spoken English, and can read and produce some everyday texts such as simple stories and factual accounts.

The ability to read and understand academic texts, especially in the senior years of schooling, requires more than a knowledge of curriculum-related vocabulary and grammar (which is already quite a challenge for some pupils with EAL anyway). Pupils have to develop a knowledge of text types or genres. That is, they need to know something about the conventionally established ways of selecting and structuring information in specific formats for different purposes (for example, a narrative, instructions for games, a letter of complaint, a technical report), and the specific features of language expression involved (for example, the use of slang in a play dialogue or technical/scientific terms in a report). Furthermore, pupils need to be able to go beyond the literal meaning. Some texts, and not just literary texts, cannot be fully appreciated without an ability to understand and decipher humour, cynicism, sarcasm, irony and other culturally embedded meanings. (In face-to-face situations some of these implied meanings may also be more accessible because physical actions, contextual clues and facial expressions can assist interpretation.)

Furthermore, some of the knowledge and skills involved in the process of writing are sometimes 'hidden', so to speak; only the outcomes are visible. Many school writing tasks are concerned with representing ideas or describing events (for example, telling a story or reporting on the results of an experiment). The purpose of a great deal of writing in school is to show that one can communicate one's ideas and thoughts without the benefit of either contextual support or immediate contributions and feedback from others (as in a conversation). This involves pupils drawing on their existing knowledge and expertise to package ideas and produce a piece of text by themselves. This is a complex process. Beyond the level of knowing vocabulary, learning to write involves:

- Using different types of phrases and sentences to represent ideas
- Organizing sentences into sequences and sections (paragraphs)
- Selecting, organizing and presenting information and ideas in conventionally recognizable ways (genres).

Gibbons (1998: 101) provides a highly illuminating example of how language features change as pupils move from group talk to individual writing:

Text 1: (spoken by three 10-year-old students and accompanying action)
this . . . no it doesn't go . . . it doesn't move . . .
try that . . .
yes it does . . . a bit . . . that won't . . .

won't work it's not metal . . .
these are the best . . . going really fast.

Text 2: (spoken by one student about the action, after the event)
We tried a pin . . . a pencil sharpener . . . some iron filings . . . the magnet didn't
attract the pin . . .

Text 3: (written by the same student)
Our experiment was to find out what a magnet attracted. We discovered that a
magnet attracts some kinds of metal. It attracted the iron filings, but not the pin . . .

The above discussion shows that a great deal of the academic use of written
English in school is different from classroom spoken English in a number of ways;
some of the differences are related to vocabulary and grammatical choice; some
are concerned with information structuring; and others are related to the properties and constraints of the different modes of language. These differences often
reflect the different purposes served by spoken and written language in different
contexts. Thus, harnessing the knowledge and understanding achieved through
classroom activities mediated by the spoken language provides a mere starting
point. (For a fuller discussion on developing reading and writing in EAL, see Leung
2001; for a further discussion on EAL provision, see Leung 2005, 2016.)

Wider professional challenges

The development of the kind of EAL-sensitive pedagogic practice discussed in the
preceding section will no doubt require sustained professional development. There
are, however, wider questions concerning EAL that are inextricably connected to
questions of ethnicity and language which themselves are far from simple. Earlier
we mentioned that the official ethnic categories are 'White British', 'White non-
British', 'Asian', 'Black', 'Mixed', 'Chinese', 'Any other' and 'Unclassified'. For teachers,
there is a need to find ways of thinking about these categories which have some
practical utility for day-to-day interactions with pupils. There are a number of
potential problems which require attention. First of all, these categories may give
a potentially unhelpful impression that pupils belong to fixed, stable, homogeneous and comfortably knowable identities. In reality, pupils from ethnic minority
backgrounds are heterogeneous. For instance, the category 'Chinese' covers a
wide variety of backgrounds. Some of the pupils in this category are British-born,
others are from culturally diverse places such as China, Taiwan, Singapore and
other world locations; some are first language speakers of English (of different
varieties), others are EAL learners. Second, the putative 'fixed identities' can lead
to difficulty in envisioning these ethnic minority pupils as cultural and linguistic
insiders rather than permanent outsiders in the UK. Many ethnic minority pupils
are 'cultural insiders' in their local communities and English is their dominant
language. Third, the education system and the curriculum framework have yet to
take full advantage of the fact that many ethnic minority pupils might be at one and
the same time aligned to *both* UK/English/British ethnic identities and languages,

and those associated with other global locations. Gilroy ([1987] 1991) depicts the refusal to allow for change and variation in representations of broader British and minority ethnic identities as ethnic absolutism. Hall (1988) suggests that minority individuals, rather than seeking to preserve their ethnic identities unchanged, are actively and continuously engaged in a process of creating new ethnicities. Mercer (1994), among others, sees significant numbers of young members of UK-based 'visible' minority groups as being intimately connected *both* with the everyday mores of their UK locations *and* wider, African, Caribbean and Asian-derived diasporas. Hall provides a useful summary of the general position being proposed here when he identifies the concept of translation which:

> describes those identity formations which cut across and intersect natural frontiers, and which are composed of people who have been *dispersed* forever from their homelands. Such people retain strong links with their places of origin and their traditions, but they are without the illusion of a return to the past. They are obliged to come to terms with the new cultures they inhabit, without simply assimilating to them and losing their identities completely. They bear upon them the traces of the particular cultures, traditions, languages and histories by which they were shaped. The difference is that they are not and will never be *unified* in the old sense, because they are irrevocably the product of several interlocking histories and cultures, belong at one and the same time to several 'homes' (and to no one particular 'home'). People belonging to such *cultures of hybridity* have had to renounce the dream or ambition of rediscovering any kind of 'lost' cultural purity, or ethnic absolutism. They are irrevocably *translated* . . . They are the products of the new *diasporas* created by the post-colonial migrations. They must learn to inhabit at least two identities, to speak two cultural languages, to translate and negotiate between them. Cultures of hybridity are one of the distinctly novel types of identity produced in the era of late-modernity, and there are more and more examples of them to be discovered.
>
> (Hall 1992: 310)

Clearly, this 'translation' is a dynamic process (see Gilroy 2004 for a further discussion). To put it briefly, the essential point for teachers to grasp is that the majority of young ethnic minority pupils in England are daily engaged in the active construction of what Back (1996) terms new forms of 'Englishness'. Harris (2006) offers a detailed treatment of one example of this phenomenon. There are specific linguistic consequences of relevance to classroom teachers. More precisely, one of the factors with which any teacher needs to come to terms, is that there are two aspects of the actual patterns of language use of many pupils for whom English is an Additional Language:

1. Many such pupils with EAL are more linguistically comfortable with a local urban spoken English vernacular rather than with an ethnic minority 'community' language which they might encounter in family contexts (see Harris 1997, 1999; Leung, Harris and Rampton 1997 for examples of this phenomenon).

2. Even where these pupils begin their school careers in England with very limited English language proficiency, their entry to English tends to be connected

with a local, often urban, spoken vernacular English, learned informally, rather than with the spoken or written Standard English associated with the formal aspects of the school curriculum.

Hewitt made a number of observations on the significant ways in which urban youth, in their routine language use and participate in the 'destabilisation of ethnicity' (1991: 27). He suggested that an important but often overlooked part of their language use is what he describes as a 'local multi-ethnic vernacular' or a 'community English' that contains elements of minority languages such as Punjabi and Jamaican Creole. This language use is 'the primary medium of communication in the adolescent peer group in multi-ethnic areas' (1991: 32). The emergence of this 'multi-ethnic vernacular' is a consequence of the diaspora of the peoples from different parts of the world through migration and their coming together in parts of Britain (see the earlier discussion on this point). For Hewitt (1995: 97), the sources of this variety of English use are diasporic and global as well as local, contributing to:

> the obliteration of pure language forms deriving from a single cultural source, evident in some inner city areas (in the UK) and . . . the diasporic distribution of communicative forms which, while generated from and based in local communities, nevertheless reach out and extend lines of connection in a global way. The local penetration and mixing of language forms evident in some urban settings in the UK should, in fact, be seen perhaps as a reflex of the broader linguistic diasporic processes.

In addition, there is still a general acceptance of 'the widespread practice . . . based on little or no analysis or enquiry, of attributing to pupils drawn from . . . ethnic minority groups an expertise in and allegiance to any community languages with which they have some acquaintance' (Harris 1997: 14).

Harris calls this 'romantic bilingualism'. We now know that pupils from ethnic and linguistic minority communities are not necessarily fluent or knowledgeable in their putative 'home' language, and it would be useful for teachers to work with a more nuanced view of different types of EAL-labelled pupils. Following Harris (1999), there are three broad groups of pupils with EAL.

1. *The 'new' arrivals*: These pupils may be relatively recent arrivals in the country possessing a limited acquaintance with, and low levels of expertise in, the English language, together with little familiarity with contemporary British cultural and educational practices. In the past few years, many new arrivals have been from Eastern Europe.

2. *The low-key British bilinguals*: (1) Pupils born and brought up in a multilingual home in the UK. They have regular routine interaction with family and community languages other than English without claiming a high degree of expertise in these languages. They are entirely comfortable with the discourse of everyday English, particular local vernacular Englishes and with contemporary British cultural and educational practices. They have, however, along with fellow pupils of all ethnic backgrounds, including White British and non-British ones, difficulty in reproducing accurate and fluent written

Standard English in the preferred written genres favoured in specific school subject disciplines; (2) Pupils born and brought up in the UK who enter early years schooling with a dominant spoken language proficiency in a 'home'/'community' language originating from outside the UK, but not in English. As they progress through the school years these pupils are likely to progressively share some of the English language support needs as the pupils discussed in (1) above; (3) Pupils born outside the UK who enter the British schooling system some time between the ages of 5 and 16 and appear to gradually move from the 'new' arrival to the low-key British Bilingual category; and (4) Pupils of African-Caribbean descent who perhaps constitute a special case of (1) above in terms of their patterns of language use. That is, they may have substantial experience and expertise in a Creole language such as Jamaican Creole, which while having a lexical relationship with English is often not intelligible to English-speaking outsiders.

- *The high-achieving multilinguals*: These pupils have a good level of expertise or an untapped potential to rapidly acquire expertise in a 'home'/'community' language other than English. At the same time they also have a high degree of proficiency in the kinds of spoken and written Standard English required for school success. These may include newly arrived pupils who have previously attended English-medium international schools in other parts of the world.

It should be evident that each of these distinct groups of pupils will require distinct approaches to language and learning developed by sensitive teachers. The pedagogic principles discussed earlier should be translated into classroom strategies and teaching activities with reference to the actual pupils in the classroom.

Concluding thoughts

At a very high level of conceptual abstraction, EAL in England has been fully integrated into the mainstream curriculum. EAL, as a subject entity and a teaching-learning activity, is completely absorbed into the everyday processes of 'doing' the English-medium curricular activities. At the same time, little attention is paid to language pedagogy beyond requiring teachers to exploit opportunities to help pupils develop their English through meaningful use. There is also little discussion on language learning goals beyond participating in curricular activities. EAL in the English school system is thus a diffuse idea that has no curricular visibility. Currently, teachers of all subjects are expected to make use of at least some of the pedagogic principles and teaching know-how discussed earlier in this chapter without systematic professional development. For EAL provision to be provided with a subject and professional infrastructure on a par with other subjects such as English, Geography and Science, careful consideration will need to be given to accredited initial teacher education and continuous professional development. At the same time a differentiated EAL curriculum framework that meets the needs of the diverse groups of EAL learners at different ages and proficiency levels will need to be developed. Since EAL learners are in all curriculum areas, all subject teachers can help build a principled and practicable EAL pedagogy.

References

Alladina, S. and Edwards, V. (1991) *Multilingualism in the British Isles* (Vol. 2). London: Longman.

Back, L. (1996) *New Ethnicities and Urban Culture*. London: UCL Press.

Bourne, J. (1989) *Moving into the Mainstream: LEA Provision for Bilingual Pupils*. Windsor: NFER-Nelson.

Bourne, J. and McPake, J. (1991) *Partnership Teaching: Co-operative Teaching Strategies for English Language Support in Multilingual Classrooms*. London: HMSO.

Commission for Racial Equality (1986) *Teaching English as a Second Language*. London: CRE.

Cummins, J. (1992) Language proficiency, bilingualism, and academic achievement, in P.A. Richard-Amato and M.A. Snow (eds) *The Multicultural Classroom: Readings for Content-Area Teachers*. New York: Longman, pp. 16–26.

Cummins, J. (2008) BICS and CALP: empirical and theoretical status of the distinction, in B.V. Street and N.H. Hornberger (eds) *Encyclopedia of Language and Education* (2nd edn). New York: Springer, pp. 71–83.

Derrick, J. (1977) *Language Needs of Minority Group Children*. Slough: NFER.

DES (Department of Education and Science) (1971) *The Education of Immigrants: Education Survey 13*. London: HMSO.

DES (Department of Education and Science) (1975) *A Language for Life: Report of the Committee of Inquiry appointed by the Secretary of State for Education and Science under the Chairmanship of Sir Alan Bullock/[Committee of Inquiry into Reading and the Use of English]*. London: HMSO.

DES (Department of Education and Science) (1985) *Education for All: The Report of the Committee of Inquiry into the Education of Children from Ethnic Minority Groups* (The Swann Report). London: HMSO.

DfE (Department for Education) (2014a) *The National Curriculum in England: Key Stages 3 and 4 Framework Document*, https://www.gov.uk/government/collections/national-curriculum, accessed 10 Aug 2016.

DfE (Department for Education) (2014b) *Statutory Guidance: National Curriculum in England: English Programmes of Study*, https://www.gov.uk/government/publications/national-curriculum-in-england-english-programmes-of-study/national-curriculum-in-england-english-programmes-of-study, accessed 10 Aug 2016.

DfE (Department for Education) (2016) *School Census 2016 to 2017: Guide, Version 1.0*. London: DfE.

DfE/ONS (Department for Education/Office for National Statistics) (2016) *Schools, Pupils and their Characteristics: January 2016*. London: DfE/ONS.

Gibbons, P. (1998) Classroom talk and the learning of new registers in a second language, *Language and Education*, 12(2): 99–118.

Giddens, A. (1991) *Modernity and Self-Identity*. Cambridge: Polity Press.

Gilroy, P. ([1987] 1991) *There Ain't No Black in the Union Jack*. London: Routledge.

Gilroy, P. (2004) *After Empire: Melancholia or Convivial Culture? Multiculture or Post-colonial Melancholia*. London: Routledge.

Hall, S. (1988) New ethnicities. *ICA Documents*, 7: 27–31.

Hall, S. (1992) The question of cultural identity, in S. Hall and T. McGrew (eds) *Modernity and its Futures*. Cambridge: Polity Press/Open University, pp. 274–316.

Hampshire County Council (1996) *Bilingual Learners Support Service: Service Guidelines* (2nd edn). Hampshire: Hampshire County Council.

Harris, R. (1997) Romantic bilingualism: time for a change?, in C. Leung and C. Cable (eds) *English as an Additional Language: Changing Perspectives*. Watford: National Association for Language Development in the Curriculum (NALDIC), pp. 14–27.

Harris, R. (1999) Rethinking the bilingual learner, in A. Tosi and C. Leung (eds) *Rethinking Language Education: From a Monolingual to a Multilingual Perspective*. London: CiLT, pp. 70–83.

Harris, R. (2006) *New Ethnicities and Language Use*. Basingstoke: Palgrave Macmillan.

Hewitt, R. (1991) Language, youth and the destabilisation of ethnicity, in K. Lovren, G. Bolin and C. Palmgren (eds) *Ethnicity and Youth Culture*. Stockholm: Stockholm University, pp. 27–41.

Hewitt, R. (1995) The umbrella and the sewing machine: trans-culturalism and the definition of surrealism, in A. Alund and R. Granqvist (eds) *Negotiating Identities*. Amsterdam: Rodopi, pp. 91–104.

Inner London Education Authority (1989) *Catalogue of Languages: Spoken by Inner London School Pupils: RS 1262/89*. London: ILEA Research and Statistics.

Kress, G. (1994) *Learning to Write*. London: Routledge.

Leung, C. (2001) *English as an Additional Language: Language and Literacy Development*. Royston, Herts: United Kingdom Reading Association.

Leung, C. (2005) English as an additional language policy: issues of inclusive access and language learning in the mainstream, *Prospect*, 20(1): 95–113.

Leung, C. (2016) English as an Additional Language: a genealogy of language-in-education policies and reflections on research trajectories, *Language and Education*, 30(2): 158–74.

Leung, C. and Creese, A. (eds) (2010) *English as an Additional Language: Approaches to Teaching Linguistic Minority Students*. London: Sage, in association with National Association for Language Development in the Curriculum.

Leung, C. and Franson, C. (2001) Mainstreaming: ESL as a diffused curriculum concern, in B. Mohan, C. Leung and C. Davison (eds) *English as a Second Language in the Mainstream: Teaching, Learning and Identity*. Harlow: Longman-Pearson, pp. 165–76.

Leung, C., Harris, R. and Rampton, B. (1997) The idealised native speaker, reified ethnicities, and classroom realities, *TESOL Quarterly*, 31(3): 543–60.

Martin-Jones, M. (1989) Language education in the context of linguistic diversity: differing orientations in educational policy making in England, in J. Esling (ed.) *Multicultural Education Policy: ESL in the 1990s*. Toronto: OISE Press, pp. 36–58.

Mercer, K. (1994) *Welcome to the Jungle*. London: Routledge.

Ministry of Education (1963) *English for Immigrants*. London: HMSO.

Mohan, B., Leung, C. and Davison, C. (eds) (2001) *English as a Second Language in the Mainstream: Teaching, Learning, and Identity*. London: Longman.

National Curriculum Council (1991) *Circular Number 11: Linguistic Diversity and the National Curriculum*. York: NCC.

OFSTED (Office for Standards in Education) (1994) *Educational Support for Minority Ethnic Communities*. London: Ofsted.

Peach, C. (1996) Introduction, in C. Peach (ed.) *Ethnicity in the 1991 Census* (Vol. 2, pp. 1–24). London: HMSO.

Rampton, B., Harris, R. and Leung, C. (2001) Education and languages other than English in the British Isles. Working Papers in Urban Language and Literacies, no. 18. King's College London.

17

Why aren't we educating pupils?
Learning and the emotions
BRIAN MATTHEWS

Introduction

In this chapter, I argue that changes in the labour market, work and employment in capitalist societies, driven by the digital revolution, require an education system that will help pupils develop new skills for life and for work. Many of these new skills depend on emotional literacy, the ability to communicate and to empathize. Just as importantly, young people need to develop skills and tactics that help them cope with pressures and stresses as well as contributing towards making society more just and inclusive. This chapters explores these new soft skills and shows what teachers can do to integrate their subject learning with the development of these capabilities.

Changing society: changing skills

In this first section I highlight two aspects of the digital revolution that have impli-cations for education provision. First, the complexity that technology has brought to employment. Second, some of the social concerns that are raised by the use of social media.

Society is changing rapidly and much of this has to do with the development of digital technologies and platforms. For example, digital technologies have driven an increase in the gig economy (Brinkley 2016). A gig economy is one where people no longer have a job for life, but can have multiple jobs and are more likely to be self-employed. This can lead to greater freedom, with people being able to select the jobs they want. According to the Confederation of British Industry (CBI), it has led to greater employment and flexibility but requires changes in industry to give a sense of empowerment (CBI 2016; Standard Life 2016). However, on the other hand, there is a worry that people in the gig economy can feel insecure and experience a loss of power (TUC 2016). People may have no holiday pay or may not pay national insurance. People on zero-hours contracts can be uncertain about how much they will earn. Also, because of new technologies, some jobs are being routinized and then automated, so that in many occupations workers are being de-skilled and so become low paid. Andreas Schleicher, of the OECD Education Directorate, points out that: 'Today, because of rapid economic and social change, schools have to prepare students for jobs that have not yet been created, technologies that have not yet been invented and problems that we don't yet know will arise' (2010: 1). As society and work become more fractured, more people feel insecure (Tait 2016). These trends indicate that pupils will need strong emotional resilience and social connection with others who can help them to come to terms with such a society and they may also require new skills.

Second, the digital revolution can also impact on social relationships. There is a great deal of concern over the effects on young people as they come to rely on digital methods of communication (Havey and Puccio 2016; Alter 2017). The onset of social media means that face-to-face communication is decreasing, with people expressing views they would not voice if they were physically present with the other person and also they may miss important non-verbal communications (Rampages 2015; Havey and Puccio 2016). Turkle (2016) draws attention to the way digital technologies interrupt conversations, even down to families using phones at mealtimes, and argues that children's emotional development can be affected. Youngsters sometimes use phones even while talking to friends and family. Turkle points out that human interactions are essential for the development of empathy and engagement with others. The problem is that we are social people who like to be together, but technology can compartmentalize us. The lack of face-to-face interactions can feed social anxiety (Dent 2017). Social anxiety, or social phobia, 'is a fear of interaction with other people, that brings on self-consciousness, feelings of being negatively judged that can lead to feelings of inadequacy and embarrassment, and sometimes avoidance or depression' (Chelsea Psychology Clinic 2017). UK census data suggests there is an increase in anxiety and depression and an increase in mental health issues (Office of National Statistics 2016). Research in America has also indicated an increase in social anxiety (Primack *et al.* 2017) and found that young people who use social media more than 58 times a week are three times more likely to feel lonely than those who used it 11 times a week. Meanwhile, Fehm *et al.* (2008) found that Social Anxiety Disorder starts mainly in adolescence.

Is all of this just scaremongering? At times of social upheaval, change is often seen as to be feared and leading to social problems. However, there are many positive aspects to digital technologies, such as medical advances, data gathering on a huge scale for weather reporting, and detailing environmental concerns. There are both biological advances and mechanization of plant growth, so that a greater amount of food can be produced. Social media enables people to talk to one another across the globe, call for help and change arrangements at short notice. Important events and speeches can be watched in real time; disasters in different countries can be made public very quickly so aid can be sent. Transportation links have improved. Even your washing machine could not operate as it does without a computer.

Nobody knows which trends will continue, so it raises the question *What do pupils need?* in order to navigate a complex and changing environment. I argue that they will need to be flexible, able to respond to change, be resilient and able to collaborate with other people across diversity. Consequently, they need to develop their social and emotional skills so that they can understand and manage emotions, feel and show empathy for others, and establish and maintain positive relationships. There is a sense that to enter society, and live a fulfilled life, the most important thing is for pupils to be socially and emotionally secure. For example, a person who has to look at their phone regularly does so as an emotional response; this can be seen as a form of *emotional hijacking* and occurs when the emotions take over a person's actions. It is the same process that occurs when a pupil suddenly becomes very angry, and is a sign of emotional immaturity. In the midst of all of this, we need to think about what can we do as teachers to enable pupils to learn to connect with one another, communicate joys and fears, have relationships, and learn what it means to be human; to feel for others who are in trouble or less fortunate than themselves, and have sufficient empathy and resilience to want to do something about it.

Obviously, you want to teach your subject, but you also want pupils to like your subject and enjoy it. In other words, their emotional response is also important. Schools today are increasingly diverse and have a responsibility to ensure that pupils engage in learning, achieve academically, behave positively and get on with one another. Social and emotional learning (SEL) has been shown to provide a foundation for constructive academic forms of learning and in enhancing students' school life and careers (Ings 2017). This is done through pupils developing the skills and attitudes to enable them to manage emotions, develop empathy and establish positive relationships (Casel 2016; Place2be 2017). It is possible for secondary teachers to focus on teaching their subject so that pupils pass exams. They may hold the view that SEL is not central to their pedagogy. However, while pupils do need a set of understandings (knowledge) as well as skills and aptitudes, they also need the emotional capabilities to live well and work well. These capacities are often called life skills.

Which life skills do pupils need?

Life skills enable us to deal with the joys and difficulties that we experience as we grow and move through our life course. The skills we need vary as we go through life and depend on the culture we live in, but they enable us to develop our potential, make choices and enjoy ourselves. The World Health Organization (WHO 1997, 1 Part One) defines life skills for young people as a core set of skills that promote the health and well-being of adolescents. These are:

- Decision-making
- Problem-solving
- Creative thinking
- Critical thinking
- Effective communication
- Interpersonal relationship skills
- Self-awareness

- Empathy
- Coping with emotions
- Coping with stress.

The WHO argues that life skills development should start at an early age. Embedded in all of these capacities is the central ability to form positive relationships. Building relationships involves a willingness to learn, to seek new experiences, and to be open to new ideas and different people. Diversity should be positively embraced, not seen as a threat, and relationships need to extend across gender and sexualities, as well as age, dis/abilities, ethnic diversity, religion and social class. Crucially, well-being can be helped if one has an attitude of mind where one wants to develop, is willing to try something different and grow as a person. These are all key aspects of learning at all ages.

In one way or another, good life skills are dependent on the quality of relationships. Forming sound relationships is one of the main life skills needed for people to be able to have a fulfilled life. Clearly developing interpersonal abilities involves being able to build rapport, and be supportive while being able to be constructively critical. If a person is unable to develop effective communication skills, they can find it harder to express themselves successfully, can misunderstand people and so feel frustrated, which can lead to conflict. Being able to be self-reflective can also help develop rapport and support conflict resolution. While we all need a sound set of life skills, alongside the promotion and development of these capacities we need to be aware of factors that might mitigate against this. For example, many young people now report mental health issues that may get in the way of developing positive life skills and teachers need to be able to address these pressures.

Mental health, well-being and schools

Over the last 25 years there has been a 70 per cent increase in children experiencing problems with anxiety and mental health (Mind 2016). Since 2013, hospitalizations from self-harm have doubled, teenagers have started to poison themselves and do things that could lead to suicide (Bacino 2013). No one knows exactly why some people, rather than others, experience mental health problems, but around one in ten children experience difficulties, often associated with depression and worry, such as bullying (Department of Health 2013). Children in poverty are three times more likely to have a mental illness than children in wealthier homes; the *Mental Health Review* 'recognises the corrosive impact of stigma and discrimination on people experiencing mental health problems and those living in poverty' (Elliott 2016: 4). The report *Poor Mental Health* (Ayre 2016) found that almost a quarter of children living in poverty did not feel useful, compared to one in six (16 per cent) children from more affluent backgrounds. The *Good Childhood Report* (Rees, Goswami and Pople 2013; Pople et al. 2014) found that children in England came 30th out of 39 European and American countries for subjective well-being (which is self-reporting how one feels), and out of 11 countries around the world surveyed for well-being, England came ninth (Adamson 2013; UNICEF 2013).

More children and young people are reporting anxiety and stress. There is evidence that factors such as exam pressure often exacerbate stress and anxiety (NSPCC 2016). According to the NSPCC's Childline, exam stress has increased greatly: 58 per cent of counselling sessions it offered were about exam stress (7546). This represented a 200 per cent increase compared to 2012/13. As well as exams, pupils also have to cope with the pressures of SATs and routine assessments and end-of-term tests. On top of these stressors, pupils are regularly set targets to achieve. This increases competition and pressure, with many parents pushing their children to do well. Some schools stress academic success as being very important, often to the exclusion of everything else, including developing life skills. The situation is similar in America with the same pressures being exacerbated by pupils not having people to talk to, or not being able to express themselves (Dwyer 2014).

Teachers can play a part in helping their students to cope with some of these pressures. They have direct and regular contact with children and may be the first to spot the signs of mental health issues. They may also be the first people parents turn to when they are worried about their child. It is important therefore, that teachers are alert to the early signs that indicate when a pupil may need some support, and that they feel confident engaging in conversations about emotions, mental health and well-being. Schools which place a high value on positive relationships, and focus on promoting a nurturing environment where pupils can experience a sense of connectedness and belonging, can create the conditions where pupils and teachers are able to talk openly about mental health issues. Any support that teachers can offer pupils is likely to be most effective when it is part of a whole school approach to promoting positive mental health and well-being (life skills) incorporating the views of pupils, parents and staff. As part of a whole school approach, teachers, of all subjects, should consider what they do to teach all pupils about mental health and well-being, as well as supporting those in need. Teachers could ensure they find out how mental health and well-being are taught through dedicated PSHE lessons, so that they can make cross-curricular links and develop a unified approach.

When teachers have concerns about pupils, they also need to be able to draw on a range of interventions to support pupils' mental health, including access to counselling (see Chapter 21). It is recommended that counselling support is part of a whole school commitment to promoting mental health and well-being, and is linked to wider school systems, including pastoral support and external services. Charities can be approached to find out what support they can give. For example, Place2Be (2017) offers counselling to everyone in the school community – children, parents and staff – therefore ensuring that the support is fully accessible and non-stigmatizing. Similarly, a report by Public Health England offers a range of supports and examples of good practice (Public Health England 2015).

The aims of the education system could be extended to include being concerned with helping pupils develop life skills and well-being, and certainly doing more than it is currently doing to combat mental health problems. Then pupils will be more likely to grow as people. Additionally, pupils will learn more, be happier and less disruptive, and lead more fulfilled lives. It is worth noting that research has shown that people who are emotionally literate and kind to people are more likely to be happy and content with their lives (81 per cent), and to earn more (Ferrari and Freeman 2017), while of those people who described themselves as aggressive, only 10 per cent said they were happy (Edmonds 2017).

What life skills do pupils need to be prepared for the world of employment?

We all live in a fast-changing world. One aspect that will help pupils in this context is to achieve respectable academic qualifications to gain employment or become self-employed. However, the Confederation of British Industry (CBI) believes that there are other skills that are essential for employability (CBI Higher Education Task Force 2009; CBI 2010a). The CBI, in its report *Raising Expectations* (CBI 2008: 1), found that 52 per cent of employers were dissatisfied with school leavers' literacy skills. However, the next highest dissatisfaction rating was that 51 per cent of employers were unhappy with young people's employability skills. The CBI has been working with employers to define *employability skills* (CBI 2009) and has produced a list of seven elements, the first four of which are:

1. *Self-management* – readiness to accept responsibility, flexibility, time management, readiness to improve own performance.
2. *Team-working* – respecting others, co-operating, negotiating/persuading, contributing to discussions.
3. *Business and customer awareness* – basic understanding of the key drivers for business success and the need to provide customer satisfaction.
4. *Problem-solving* – analysing facts and circumstances and applying creative thinking to develop appropriate solutions.

The next three areas refer to communication, numeracy and information technology. Nearly all of the first four areas are directly related to social and emotional learning and include the ability of people to communicate well, be reflective, open-minded and self-organizing – what I have referred to as life skills (above). Elsewhere the CBI and other writers (Taylor 1998; Markes 2006; BCUCS 2010) have indicated the importance of these social and emotional skills in the workplace. For example:

> All employers are looking for young people with strong employability skills, including the ability to solve problems, work in teams, and manage their time effectively. But more needs to be done to address the weaknesses in the *soft* skills of school/college leavers and graduates.
>
> (CBI 2010b: 6)

This quotation illustrates the importance the CBI attaches to the social and emotional development of pupils so that they are able to cope with the contemporary work situation, either as employees or employers. There is evidence that people make decisions based on an intermix of rational and emotional factors, and the role of emotion is being seen as increasingly important as we understand more how the brain works (Damasio 1996; Curran 2008; Heath and Heath 2011). There are other reasons for achieving a good level of social and emotional development (soft skills) as well, as we shall see below.

Twenty-first-century skills

In parallel to the employability skills described in this chapter, there has been a global attempt to define what are frequently referred to as twenty-first-century skills (Blinkley *et al.* 2010; Jayaram 2012; Voogt and Roblin 2013). Because we live in a fast-changing world, the knowledge learned in school is being rapidly refined (OECD 1999; Hargreaves 2003). For people to work in this fluid and flexible environment, where (some) knowledge soon becomes out of date (Fisch 2007), what is needed are people who know *how* to learn, who are self-motivated, reflective, creative and effective self-managers, confident that they can get ideas from and work with others, no matter what their backgrounds are. The core twenty-first-century skills have been identified and are known as the 4Cs (P21 2016): collaboration; critical thinking; creativity; and communication.

- *Collaboration:* Working with others in groups and teams with respect for diversity. Ability to share and learn together with empathy and understanding. Accepting feedback and dealing constructively with criticism and praise. Ability to manage emotions in a range of situations.

- *Critical thinking:* Ability to think around a problem or situation, with others or individually. Ability to problem-solve and discover novel solutions or explanations. Critical thinkers realize that they could always be wrong, but strive to improve their thinking. They recognize the complexity of many issues and strive to make solutions that recognize the needs of others. They question social norms for prejudice and consider self- and vested interest.

- *Creativity:* Ability to analyse possibilities, extend thinking and question personal ideas as well as those of others. Able to adapt to new information and ideas. Creativity involves using imaginative ideas to produce appropriate solutions. Often it involves making connections between things in novel ways.

- *Communication:* Ability to express ideas, to individuals or groups, to explain underlying principles and realize the extent to which ideas are understood. Ability to convey ideas and emotions through multimedia and for a wide range of reasons.

This list of twenty-first-century skills also includes literacy, ICT skills and being culturally aware. In 2012, a global report called for the integration of twenty-first-century and employability skills (Jayaram 2012). The report was concerned about the rise in youth unemployment, particularly in the Organisation for Economic Co-operation and Development (OECD) area in Europe, and argued that if employment rates were to increase, a change in emphasis in education was

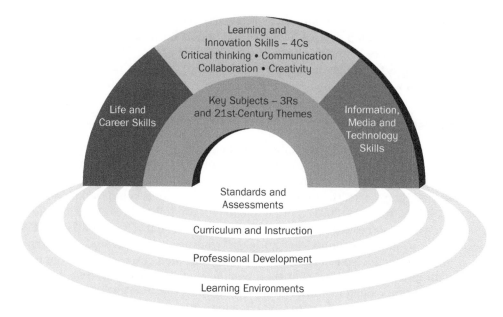

Figure 17.1 P21 framework for twenty-first-century learning

required. The report contained a figure from the Partnership for 21st Century Skills (P21 2016: 9) used to illustrate a holistic framework for the integration of the necessary skills (Figure 17.1).

This framework attempts to connect what students learn in school with the skills that employers are increasingly demanding in the workplace (P21 2016: 9). In industry, people have to work co-operatively with people with very different knowledge bases, and need enthusiasm and a desire to learn and develop. However, according to the CBI (2014: 48), the knowledge bases that pupils are exposed to in schools at present often sideline or omit social and emotional skills; that is, their emotional development. This is not to say that academic knowledge is not essential, but an overemphasis on this aspect can distract from the need to develop pupils' emotional learning. So far then, I have argued that to help pupils face and flourish in a fast-changing society it would be of benefit to them to develop SEL. However, we need to consider what is meant by emotional development.

Emotional literacy/intelligence

There are many definitions of emotional intelligence and literacy (Goleman 1996; Steiner 1997; Antidote 2010) and they include factors such as recognizing emotional states, having empathy, being able to relate to others and being motivated. The term *emotional intelligence* is commonly used as if the development of the emotions is an individual personal matter. However, Matthews (2006) has pointed out that communications and emotional connections always happen in a dynamic social context along with others and argues that emotional literacy is:

> both about self-development and the building of community so that one's own sense of emotional well-being grows along with that of others, and not at their expense ... It is a dynamic process through which the individual develops emotionally and involves culture and empowerment. For example, it includes understanding how the nature of social class, 'race' and gender (sexism and homophobia) impinges on people's emotional states to lead to an understanding of how society could change.
>
> (Matthews 2006: 178)

Hence the term *emotional literacy* is used to reflect its social nature (Matthews 2006: 35–47) and incorporates the ability to work with others and build for change to improve the lives of everyone. Teachers should help pupils develop socially and emotionally in ways that connect with others and their concerns.

This section has considered the knowledge, skills, aptitudes and life skills needed by young people as they move towards the world of employment. However, emotional well-being has other benefits as well.

Contributing to an emotionally literate society

It is generally agreed that pupils should be prepared to become active citizens in our society. There are many views on how this should be done. This can vary from teaching only a small amount of factual information to pupils, through to encouraging them to consider political issues with the aim of getting them to think about how our system could be improved. In order to enable pupils to contribute to these discussions, it would help if their emotional literacy were developed so that they could empathize with others, and have a commitment to doing something about social injustices. Yet, it is not that simple. For example, suppose different sexualities are not discussed at all; pupils who may be starting to identify as transgender may not be able to recognize their feelings, know that others feel the same way, and so become depressed and have their mental health affected (Mardell 2016). So, if there is silence on certain issues, they may not be discussed and pupils may be kept in ignorance. You have to know who is being discriminated against and suffering from injustice to be able to connect emotionally with that situation and have a commitment to do something about it. Paulo Freire, in *Pedagogy of the Oppressed* (1972), discusses the dehumanizing act of keeping people in ignorance. He says that one purpose of education is to work with oppressed and discriminated-against peoples to find out how they feel, to raise their consciousness about how they are being oppressed and silenced. It is then possible to be politically engaged with them and their agendas in order to improve society (see Chapter 9 in this volume).

However, the formal curriculum may hide the beliefs, norms and values that are unspoken, accepted as 'common sense' and so not considered as being open to change. To give an example, in the 1950s it was, to some extent, often accepted that boys should be educated for jobs and girls educated for the home – and hence do subjects such as cooking. Boys and girls were educated to accept these norms and values through the subjects they were taught. At that time gender concerns were rarely raised in schools and the pupils encountered a silence that hid gendered inequalities so that pupils did not discuss them and their consciousness was not raised. Leaving something unnamed makes it unspeakable.

Some educators argue that the role of education is to change society. Critical pedagogists (Kincheloe 2008) and transformative educationists (Mezirow 1991; O'Sullivan 1999; Biesta and Miedema 2002) take the view that one of education's roles is to make explicit the norms, values and beliefs of society and to hold these up for inspection. Pupils could debate such profound issues if the education system put value on these sorts of activities. However, for pupils to be able to do this, they would also have to be able to empathize with people in different circumstances from those they are in themselves. This means being able to deal emotionally with being confronted with views quite different from their own. For example, exploring issues around sexuality can be very challenging for pupils unless they are emotionally secure. In other words, the more young people have developed their emotional literacy, the greater the probability they will be able to participate in debates. Such engagements should help them become better able to be expressive and co-operative, and build their social competences (Holopainen *et al.* 2012). According to Bazalgette (2017), empathy is of fundamental importance in society, as it binds us together in communities and countries. Having empathy, which relies on face-to-face communication, enables us to understand others, to enter into their feelings and beliefs, and, to a large degree, makes it possible for societies to function more cohesively and inclusively.

So, the issue for you is what do you believe are your responsibilities to your pupils? To what extent do you think you should incorporate a critical or transformative pedagogy? Should you open up silences on sexualities and politics? In other words, how can you help pupils develop their social and emotional skills, along with critical thinking? Clearly, each subject area has different aspects to contribute: science teachers could debate the way modern technologies enable surveillance and control of the population, English teachers could look at the ways news is written and spoken and how some values, rather than others, are supported. In each of these cases the decisions that might be made intersect logical evidence with the social and emotional feelings of the pupils' outlook on life.

In the classroom: how to integrate the cognitive, social and emotional

So far this chapter has raised awareness about the changes in society, life skills, employability and twenty-first-century skills, and the need to be able to contribute to an emotionally literate society. These all have common threads underlying them: that pupils need to develop not only their cognitive skills, but also their social and emotional soft skills. Research in England has shown how developing social skills can enable pupils to learn to get on better with one another across gender and ethnic differences and lead to better behaviour in class (Matthews 2006; Banerjee 2010). My own research has focused on equity issues (Matthews 2005a) getting boys and girls to work together and help one another to learn (Matthews and Sweeney 1997), which can affect their emotional relationships and attitudes to equity (Feldman 2017). This links with agendas to improve well-being (DODS 2010). In order to realize this aim, cognitive learning has to be combined with social and emotional development. My research has been based on integrating SEL with academic learning and also tackling gender issues (Matthews 2006). In the classroom, pupils (single-sex but preferably in mixed gender and ethnicity groups) work together in collaborative groups during the course of normal subject lessons. While the pupil groups (generally two girls and two boys but can be single-sex) work on a collaborative task, a pupil-observer records how they interact with one another. For this an observation sheet is useful (Matthews 2005b). After the collaborative task – which can be filling in a worksheet or doing a practical task – is finished, the pupils fill in individually a 'Guesses' sheet where they record what they thought went on in the group and how they felt at the time. Then, the next vital stage, the observer runs a discussion on how the group functioned, as well as individual interactions. The key points discussed here could include:

- The pupils having to say what they thought went on and discussing their interactions
- Comparing their perceptions with what others say and being able to understand how different pupils can have different views; this is part of the pupils learning to empathize
- Discussing their feelings and emotions.

The observer is only used to support the pupils' awareness that it is legitimate to discuss feelings at the same time as learning (in the more 'traditional' sense). Then the observer is removed and the pupils run the procedures themselves in subsequent lessons (Matthews 2006; 2011).

In one group, documented in my research, two boys and two girls wrote that the group functioned well, but it was clear that one boy had dominated the conversations and told the others what to do. The next time the group worked together, about three weeks later, the girls and the other boy challenged his behaviour and had an argument with him. As a result, the group gradually worked better. The teacher had noted what had gone on and decided not to intervene but kept an eye on them.

In another group the conversation went as follows:

You hogged the apparatus (girl to two boys).
Well, you did the writing (boy to the two girls).
Only because you took the apparatus (girl's response).
Rubbish, when we started, you got out your books and pen straight away (boy's response).
So we won't show you the results (girl).
Oh, great, next time we won't tell you the results [as we do the experiment] (boy).

There was no verbal continuation of this argument, but the group did share its results. In the next experiment the apparatus was shared, although the boys still did more. The point is that the interactions were made explicit in both cases and, as a result, change occurred. Being explicit and legitimizing expressing emotions about the interactions enabled consciousness raising. Over a period of time, the pupils may start to develop emotional habits that mean they can express how they feel to one another on a more regular basis. One of the findings that came out of using this method is that the students reported that they discovered how to help one another learn academically in their lessons.

Once the teacher is familiar with these procedures, they may cease to use sheets and instead decide during the lesson to highlight aspects that they believe would benefit their students in discussing how they interact. Through the integration of the cognitive, social and emotional aspects of learning, it is possible to enable pupils to become more self-independent and co-independent, and critical thinkers. The use of sheets with pupils stating what they believed occurred, and then comparing these with the others' viewpoints in the group, contributes towards the growth of empathy, and should help reveal power relationships. It is possible that emotional habits will be developed where it will become routine for pupils to discuss emotional interactions. This helps build relationships based on understanding, and forges the integration of cognitive, social and emotional aspects. The laying of such a base could enable pupils, in all subject areas, to progress in those areas required to develop life skills and take part in society. However, what has been explained here is only one way of doing this. Teachers can explore other ways.

Thinking about your teaching

This chapter has briefly outlined some of the key social and emotional skills, over and above academic learning, that are required for students to flourish in a changing society. Engagement with emotions in subject lessons can help pupils develop socially, change their attitudes to schooling, and augment their life chances as well as improving their academic success. A key feature of interventions to ensure pupils discuss their communications is that they make explicit the classroom interactions that are taking place so that they can be inspected and open to change. Another benefit is that these interventions enable pupils to participate in sessions where feelings and emotions are routinely discussed. These strategies can enable pupils to work together and know they can work through difficulties for themselves. Therefore, as a teacher, you need to be aware of the decisions you have to make and what you can do in your classroom. I do not wish to pretend that such actions are easy and no list can be fully exhaustive, but this chapter has indicated that the following aspects could be helpful:

1. Understand life skills along with the employability and twenty-first-century skills; consider how to engage with these with your pupils within and across subjects

2. Realize that the individual does not exist except in the community and group in which they socialize, so that they need to understand others' diversity

3. Be aware of pupils as individuals and try to understand their needs, including mental health issues

4. Find ways of discussing injustice
5. Change your classroom pedagogy to enable pupils to mature, support and help one another
6. Make time for pupils to talk to one another about how they feel, and debate the power structures and social values that can help and hinder their development
7. Make explicit and break silences around values, including sexuality and diversity.

Concluding thoughts

You have many years ahead of you to be teaching and to contribute to changing education for the better. All I can do is to end with some questions for you to think about and discuss with others.

- Why am I teaching, and what do I hope to achieve?
- What are my responsibilities towards my students?
- How will pupils be different because of my teaching?
- Where is my balance between pupils learning my subject and developing socially and emotionally?

What do you think is not included in this chapter?

References

Adamson, P. (2013) *Child Well-Being in Rich Countries. A Comparative Overview*. Florence: UNICEF.

Alter, A. (2017) *Irresistible: Why We Can't Stop Checking, Scrolling, Clicking and Watching*. London: Bodley Head.

Antidote (2010) *Definition of Emotional Literacy*, http://www.antidote.org.uk/learning/about.php, accessed April 2010.

Ayre, D. (2016) *Poor Mental Health: The Links Between Child Poverty and Mental Health Problems*. London: The Children's Society.

Bacino, L. (2013) Shock figures show extent of self-harm in English teenagers. *Guardian*, 21 May 2014, http://www.theguardian.com/society/2014/may/21/shock-figures-self-harm-england-teenagers, accessed May 2017.

Banerjee, R. (2010) *Social and Emotional Aspects of Learning in Schools: Contributions to Improving Attainment, Behaviour, and Attendance*. Sussex: University of Sussex.

Bazalgette, P. (2017) *The Empathy Instinct: How to Create a More Civil Society*. London: John Murray.

BCUCS (2010) *Employability Skills: A Checklist*. Birmingham: Birmingham City University Careers Service.

Biesta, G. and Miedema, S. (2002) Instruction or pedagogy? The need for a transformative conception of education, *Teaching and Teacher Education*, 18: 173–81.

Blinkley, M., Erstad, O., Herman, J., Raizen, S., Ripley, M. and Rumble, M. (2010) *Assessment and Teaching of 21st Century Skills. Draft White Paper. Defining 21st Century Skills.* Melbourne: University of Melbourne/CISCO/INTEL/Microsoft.

Brinkley, I. (2016) *In Search of the Gig Economy.* London: The Work Foundation.

Casel (2016) Casel Website for Emotional Learning, http://www.casel.org/, accessed May 2017.

CBI (2008) *Raising Expectations: Enabling the System to Deliver.* London: Confederation of British Industry.

CBI (2009) *Future Fit: Preparing Graduates for the World of Work.* London: Confederation of British Industry.

CBI (2010a) *Fulfilling Potential: The Business Role in Education.* London: Confederation of British Industry.

CBI (2010b) *Ready to Grow: Business Priorities for Education and Skills. Education and Skills Survey 2010.* London: Confederation of British Industry.

CBI (2014) *Gateway to Growth.* London: CBI/Pearson.

CBI (2016) *People and Partnership.* Confederation of British Industry, www.cbi.org.uk/cbi-prod/assets/File/pdf/ETS_report_proof_X.pdf, accessed May 2017.

CBI Higher Education Task Force (2009) *Stronger Together: Businesses and Universities in Turbulent Times.* London: Confederation of British Industry.

Chelsea Psychology Clinic (2017) Is social anxiety on the rise?, http://www.thechelsea psychologyclinic.com/blog/social-anxiety-rise/, accessed May 2017.

Curran, I. (2008) *The Little Book of Big Stuff about the Brain: The True Story of Your Amazing Brain.* Carmarthen, Wales: Crown House Publishing.

Damasio, A. (1996) *Descartes' Error: Emotion, Reason and the Human Brain.* London: Papermac.

Dent, G. (2017) The disconnected age, *i News, Independent Newspaper*, 6 March, p. 15.

Department of Health (2013) *Annual Report of the Chief Medical Officer 2012: Our Children Deserve Better: Prevention Pays.* London: Department of Health, https://www.gov.uk/government/uploads/system/uploads/attachment_data/file/255237/2901304_CMO_complete_low_res_accessible.pdf, accessed 20 May 2017.

DODS (2010) Cameron launches 'Well-Being' Index, http://www.epolitix.com/latestnews/article-detail/newsarticle/cameron-to-launch-wellbeing-index-1/Politix, accessed May 2017.

Dwyer, L. (2014) When anxiety hits at school, *The Atlantic*, http://www.theatlantic.com/health/archive/2014/10/when-anxiety-hits-at-school/380622/, accessed May 2017.

Edmonds, L. (2017) Why it pays to be nice, *Evening Standard*, 9 March, p. 3.

Elliott, I. (2016) *Poverty and Mental Health. A Review to Inform the Joseph Rowntree Foundation's Anti-Poverty Strategy.* London: Mental Health Foundation, https://www.mentalhealth.org.uk/sites/default/files/Poverty%20and%20Mental%20Health.pdf, accessed May 2017.

Fehm, L., Beesdo, K., Jacobi, F. and Fiedler, A. (2008) Social anxiety disorder above and below the diagnostic threshold: prevalence, comorbidity and impairment in the general population, *Social Psychiatry*, 43: 257–65.

Feldman, L. (2017) *How Emotions Are Made: The Secret Life of the Brain.* London: Macmillan.

Ferrari, E. and Freeman, J. (2017) *The Power of Nice: A Study Exploring the Relationship Between Participant Ratings of How 'Nice' They Are, Their Behaviour, and Their Reported Levels of Health, Happiness and Success.* London: i2 media research.

Fisch, K. (2007) *Did You Know; Shift Happens – Globalization; Information Age*, http://www.youtube.com/watch?v=ljbI-363A2Q, accessed May 2017.

Freire, P. (1972) *Pedagogy of the Oppressed.* Harmondsworth: Penguin.

Goleman, D. (1996) *Emotional Intelligence: Why It Can Matter More Than IQ*. London: Bloomsbury.

Hargreaves, A. (2003) *Teaching in the Knowledge Society: Education in the Age of Insecurity*. Maidenhead: Open University Press.

Havey, A. and Puccio, D. (2016) *Sex, Likes and Social Media: Talking to Our Teens in the Digital Age*. London: Vermillion.

Heath, D. and Heath, C. (2011) Why emotion, not knowledge, is the catalyst for change, *Fast Company*, http://www.fastcompany.com/magazine/152/next-strategy-passion-provokes-action.html?page=0 per cent2C0, accessed May 2017.

Holopainen, L., Lappalainen, K., Junttila, N. and Savolainen, H. (2012) The role of social competence in the psychological well-being of adolescents in secondary education, *Scandinavian Journal of Educational Research*, 56(2): 199–212.

Ings, S. (2017) *Stalin and the Scientists: A History of Triumph and Tragedy, 1905–1953*. London: Faber.

Jayaram, S. (2012) *Skills for Employability: The Need for 21st Century Skills*. Washington, DC: Results for Development Institute.

Kincheloe, J. (2008) *Critical Pedagogy*. New York: Peter Lang Publishing.

Mardell, A. (2016) *The ABC's of LGBT+*. Miami, FL: Mango Media.

Markes, I. (2006) A review of literature on employability skill needs in engineering, *European Journal of Engineering Education*, 31(6): 637–50.

Matthews, B. (2005a) Emotional literacy as the engine of equity, *Emotional Literacy Update*, 3(21): 10–11.

Matthews, B. (2005b) *Engaging Education: Developing Emotional Literacy, Equity and Co-education*. Maidenhead: Open University Press.

Matthews, B. (2006) *Engaging Education: Developing Emotional Literacy, Equity and Co-education*. Buckingham: McGraw-Hill.

Matthews, B. (2011) Enjoying science: combining thinking skills and emotional literacy, in M. Hollins (ed.) *ASE Guide to Secondary Science Education*. Hatfield: Association for Science Education.

Matthews, B. and Sweeney, J. (1997) Collaboration in the science classroom to tackle racism and sexism, *Multi-Cultural Teaching*, 15(3): 33–6.

Mezirow, J. (1991) *Transformative Dimensions of Adult Education*. San Francisco, CA: Jossey-Bass.

Mind (2016) *Children and Young People: Mental Health Facts and Statistics*, http://www.mind.org.uk/information-support/guides-to-support-and-services/children-and-young-people/, accessed May 2017.

NSPCC (2016) *Exam Stress Rising Concern for Young People Contacting Us*. London: NSPCC.

OECD (1999) *Measuring Student Knowledge and Skills: A New Framework for Assessment*. Paris: Organisation for Co-operation and Development.

ONS (Office of National Statistics) (2016) *Anxiety and Depression Statistics*, https://www.ons.gov.uk/aboutus/transparencyandgovernance/freedomofinformationfoi/anxietyanddepressionstatistics, accessed May 2017.

O'Sullivan, E. (1999) *Transformative Learning: Educational Vision for the 21st Century*. London: Zed Books.

P21 (2016) *Framework for 21st Century Learning*, http://www.p21.org/our-work/p21-framework, Partnership for 21st Century Skills, accessed May 2017.

Place2be (2017) *Website: Place2Be*, https://www.place2be.org.uk/, accessed May 2017.

Pople, L., Raws, P., Mueller, D., Mahony, S., Rees, G., Bradshaw, J., Main, G. and Keung, A. (2014) *Good Childhood Report*. London: The Children's Society.

Primack, B.A., Shensa, A., Sidani, J.E., Whaite, E.O., Lin, L.Y., Rosen, D., Colditz, J.B., Radovic, A. and Miller, E. (2017) Social media use and perceived social isolation among young adults in the U.S., *American Journal of Preventive Medicine*, 41–8, http://www.colditzjb.com/2017/03/ajpm-2017/, accessed on 26 August 2017.

Public Health England (2015) *Promoting Children and Young People's Emotional Health and Wellbeing: A Whole School and College Approach.* London: Public Health England.

Rampages (2015) *Final Inquiry Project: The Negative Impacts of Social Media on Face-to-Face Interaction*, https://rampages.us/peasedn200/2015/12/01/final-inquiry-project/, accessed May 2017.

Rees, G., Goswami, H. and Pople, L. (2013) *Good Childhood Report*, http://www.childrenssociety.org.uk/good-childhood-report-2013-online/index.html, The Children's Society, accessed May 2017.

Schleicher, A. (2010) *The Case for 21st Century Learning*, http://www.oecd.org/document/2/0,3746,en_2649_201185_46846594_1_1_1_1,00.html, OECD, accessed May 2017.

Standard Life (2016) *Business: And Some.* London: Standard Life.

Steiner, C. (1997) *Achieving Emotional Literacy.* London: Bloomsbury.

Tait, C. (2016) *A Good Day's Work: What Workers Think About Work, and How Politics Should Respond.* London: Fabian Society.

Taylor, A. (1998) Employability skills: from corporate 'wish list' to government policy, *Journal of Curriculum Studies*, 30(2): 143–64.

TUC (2016) *Living on the Edge: The Rise of Job Insecurity in Modern Britain.* Trades Union Congress, https://www.tuc.org.uk/sites/default/files/Living%20on%20the%20Edge%202016.pdf, accessed May 2017.

Turkle, S. (2016) *Reclaiming Conversation: The Power of Talk in a Digital Age.* London: Penguin.

UNICEF (2013) New UNICEF report ranks children's well-being in 29 of world's richest countries, http://www.un.org/apps/news/story.asp?NewsID=44613#.U439JCimVBO, United Nations, accessed May 2017.

Voogt, J. and Roblin, N.P. (2013) *21st Century Skills.* Twente: University of Twente.

WHO (1997) *Life Skills Education in Schools.* Geneva: World Health Organization.

PART 4

Across the curriculum

18

Literacy: more than reading and writing
BETHAN MARSHALL

Introduction

There are two ways in which the topic of literacy is discussed. One, which is in some ways the most conventional, is how we teach children to read and write. The other is linked with our view of society and how we conceive the role of education and what it can do. As we shall see, these two aspects of our understanding of the word literacy are linked, because, to quote the poet T.S. Eliot, '[we] derive our theory of education from our theory of life' (Eliot, quoted in Tate 1998: 3–4). In some ways, then, given that we have oscillated politically in the UK between Labour and Conservative governments, talk of literacy may be confusing and far from clear because the respective theories of 'education' and therefore 'theories of life' may differ considerably between the political parties. In addition, Labour may not always be progressive in their ideas and the Conservatives might not always have traditional views. Governments may set up enquiries into the teaching of reading or language across the curriculum which do not echo the convictions of the majority of MPs in that party and often the solutions can just seem a muddled mishmash of ideas.

Broadly speaking, however, there are two views of education, and therefore of literacy, that can be defined. The first is progressive, the other traditional and, within that polarity, others exist that tend towards one point of view or the other. We will begin by looking at the progressive view of literacy and education, then consider one in the middle and then look at the traditionalist's perspective before considering ways in which this also influences the teaching of reading.

Theories of life and literacy

Literacy and progressivism

The concept of literacy has become so important that it is now being defined by organizations such as UNESCO:

> Literacy is about more than reading or writing – it is about how we communicate in society. It is about social practices and relationships, about knowledge, language and culture.

Those who use literacy take it for granted – but those who cannot use it are excluded from much communication in today's world. Indeed, it is the excluded who can best appreciate the notion of 'literacy as freedom'.

(UNESCO 2003)

By defining it in this way, that is about 'social practices' and sloganizing it as 'freedom', the writers of this document can be described as taking a progressive view of the notion of literacy. This is because our view of the purposes of education, and what it means to be literate, relate to education and our beliefs about the nature of society and our place within it.

This elision between what might be called a progressive philosophy of education and vision of how society should be organized is evident in the titles of books by two of the leading proponents of progressive education: Lev Vygotsky and John Dewey. In fact, the notion of progressive education was introduced by Dewey. Vygotsky wrote the book *Mind in Society* (1978) and Dewey's most famous work is *Democracy and Education* (1916). It is present also in a pamphlet by Robin Alexander, another, more recent, advocate of progressive education, called *Education as Dialogue: Moral and Pedagogical Choices for the Runaway World* (2006b). In it, he notes that: 'In some countries education has been required to mould individuals into compliant subjects; in others it has attempted to develop active and questioning citizens . . . Thus education may empower and liberate, or it may disempower and confuse (2006b: 5). It is evident on which side of the debate Alexander sits, for he wishes actively to promote dialogue in the classroom because

[It] requires willingness and skill to engage with minds, ideas and ways of thinking other than our own; it involves the ability to question, listen, reflect, reason, explain, speculate and explore ideas . . . [it] lays the foundations not just of successful learning but also social cohesion, active citizenship and the good society.

(2006b: 5)

But it is his views in the *Cambridge Primary Review* that are perhaps the most significant. In defining literacy, he writes:

Literacy achieves our listed aim of empowerment by conferring the skill not just of learning to read and write but to make these processes genuinely transformative, exciting children's imaginations (another listed aim), extending their boundaries, and enabling them to contemplate lives and worlds possible as well as actual.

(Alexander 2009: 269)

Alexander's views chime with those who advocate what is known as critical literacy:

Literacy becomes a meaningful construct to the degree that it is viewed as a set of practices and functions to either empower or disempower people. In the larger sense, literacy must be analysed according to whether it promotes democratic and emancipatory changes.

(Freire and Macedo 1987: 41)

For such writers, the type of literacy detailed in government documentation is simply 'schooled literacy' (Street and Street 1991), i.e. an ability to decode the print on the page but little else. By contrast,

> Critical literacy responds to the cultural capital of a specific group or class and looks to ways in which it can be confirmed, and also at the ways in which the dominant society disconfirms students by either ignoring or denigrating the knowledge and experiences that characterize their everyday lives. The unit of analysis is social and the key concern is not individual interests but with the individual and collective empowerment.
>
> (Aronowitz and Giroux, quoted in Ball, Kenny and Gardiner 1990: 61)

Others, such as Shirley Bryce Heath, have problematized the issue still further by examining the literacy of different social groups and noting how children from certain communities are disadvantaged by narrow definitions of 'schooled literacy' (Heath 1983). As Gee notes, such a perception of what it means to be literate means that 'the ability to talk about school-based sorts of tasks is one way in which Western-style schools empower elites: they sound like they know more than they do' (Gee, quoted in Corden 2000: 27).

Even those with a less overtly radical agenda use the term 'critical literacy' to describe a form of literacy that goes well beyond the basics. Richard Hoggart, who wrote the seminal book *The Uses of Literacy* ([1957] 2009), in his essay 'Critical Literacy and Creative Reading', writes:

> The level of literacy we now accept for the bulk of the population, of literacy unrelated to the way language is misused in this kind of society, ensures that literacy becomes simply a way of further subordinating great numbers of people. We make them literate enough to be conned by the mass persuaders . . . The second slogan has to be 'Critical Literacy for All'. Critical Literacy means . . . teaching about the difficulties, challenges and benefits of living in an open society which aims to be a true democracy.
>
> (Hoggart 1998: 60)

For all these writers, to varying degrees, literacy becomes a means of reading the society in which we live. Integral to this task is a demand that we do not take authority at face value but question and challenge it as part of the democratic process. They do not want passive subjects but active citizens.

Ofsted and literacy

Ofsted's view of literacy may be seen to be somewhere in the middle. Ostensibly not told what to think by the various governments that it has served, Ofsted, and the HMI of which it is a part, nevertheless have both political and pragmatic roles. The desire for a literate population is there in Ofsted's pronouncements. In its *Improving Literacy in Secondary Schools* (2013a), it went beyond England and started the section on 'Making a case for literacy' (2013a: 6) with a quotation from the European Union:

> If smart growth is about knowledge and innovation, investment in literacy skills is a prerequisite for achieving such growth . . . Our world is dominated by the written word, both online and in print. This means we can only contribute and participate actively if we can read and write sufficiently well.
>
> (EU 2012, quoted in Ofsted 2013a: 7)

What is interesting about this quotation is that it takes a slightly more pragmatic approach to what literacy may entail. Its views are more economic. The quote goes on to say:

> But, each year, hundreds of thousands of children start their secondary school two years behind in reading; some leave even further behind their peers . . . Literacy is about people's ability to function in society as private individuals, active citizens, employees or parents . . . Literacy is about people's self-esteem, their interaction with others, their health and employability. Ultimately, literacy is about whether a society is fit for the future.
>
> (Ofsted 2013a: 7)

Rather than espousing 'the notion of "literacy as freedom"' (UNESCO 2003), this document asks about 'people's ability to function in society as private individuals' (Ofsted 2013). True, it talks of 'active citizenship' and 'people's self-esteem' but it does so in the context of 'employability', so when it concludes 'Ultimately, literacy is about whether a society is fit for the future' (Ofsted 2013a: 7), the emphasis is on an economic future rather than on, for example, the emancipatory aspects.

It is significant then that Ofsted leads its section on making a case for literacy thinking of the 'function' (Ofsted 2013a: 7) of literacy rather than any other. All subsequent references are made to something that is practically achievable and something that it can judge. So, for instance, it writes: 'Aspects of literacy are now built into each of the key judgements made in a school inspection: overall effectiveness; achievement; the quality of teaching; and leadership and management' (Ofsted 2013a: 8) and 'Teachers in a secondary school need to understand that literacy is a key issue regardless of the subject taught. It is an important element of their effectiveness as a subject teacher' (Ofsted 2013a: 8).

The need for all teachers to be teachers of literacy can be traced back to seminal reports such as the Bullock Report in 1975 which was subtitled 'A language for life'. It recommended 'more support to combat the problem of adult illiteracy' (Gibbons 2017: 44) and in one of the chapters, called 'Language across the curriculum', it stated: 'every school should develop a policy for language across the curriculum' (DES 1975: 529) and promoted talk as a means of learning. In this respect, therefore, Ofsted can be seen to have progressive tendencies.

Again, we see the desire for all teachers to be teachers of literacy in Ofsted's remark about the new national teaching standards, which had just been set in 2012. It writes about how

> [These] set the benchmark for the evaluation of teaching by school leaders and by Ofsted, [in that they] require teachers to 'demonstrate an understanding of and take responsibility for promoting high standards of literacy, articulacy and the correct use of standard English, whatever their specialist subject'.
>
> (DfE 2012, quoted in Ofsted 2013a: 8)

But what is interesting about this last quotation is that it links the need for promoting literacy with the 'correct use of standard English' (DfE 2012, quoted in Ofsted 2013a: 8). In this respect, Ofsted's view of literacy mutates into something else, whereas those writing the DES Report may have had sympathy with those who linked literacy with a progressive view of education evidenced in statements such as: 'Children learn as certainly by talking and writing as by listening and reading' (Departmental Committee of the Board of Education 1921: 520) or, 'What has been shown is that the teaching of traditional analytic grammar does not appear to improve performance in writing' (1975: 172). It also believed that children should learn about language by 'experiencing it and experimenting with its use' (1975: 173) whereas Ofsted talks about 'the correct use of standard English' (DfE 2012, quoted in Ofsted 2013a: 8).

Literacy and the traditionalists

In linking literacy to 'the correct use of standard English' (Ofsted 2013(a): 8), Ofsted is in some ways promoting a conservative or traditional view of education, and, through this, of society. Again if we look more fully at the quotation from T.S. Eliot, whose views were well to the right, in his essay 'On Modern Education and the Classics', he wrote that education was

> A subject which cannot be discussed in a void: our questions raise other questions, social economic, financial, political. And the bearings are on more ultimate problems even than these: to know what we want in education we must know what we want in general, we must derive our theory of education from our theory of life.
>
> (Eliot, quoted in Tate 1998: 3–4)

The progressive educator John Dewy defined 'the main purpose and objective' of traditional education, such as that espoused by Eliot, as the preparation of

> The young for future responsibilities and for success in life, by means of acquisition of the organized bodies of information and prepared forms of skill which comprehend the material instruction. Since the subject matter as well as standards of proper conduct are handed down from the past, the attitude of the pupils must, upon the whole, be one of docility, receptivity, and obedience.
>
> (Dewey 1966: 18)

The societal and moral implications of this position become clearer when we apply Eliot and Dewey's observations, again, to the literacy debate. John Rae, the former headteacher of Westminster School, wrote, for example, in the *Observer* in February 1982:

> The overthrow of grammar coincided with the acceptance of the equivalent of creative writing in social behaviour. As nice points of grammar were mockingly dismissed as pedantic and irrelevant, so was punctiliousness in such matters as honesty, responsibility, property, gratitude, apology and so on.
>
> (Rae, quoted in Graddol *et al.*
> 1991: 52)

In identifying progressive teaching so closely with the permissive society, Rae appears to locate a problem with literacy developing somewhere around the mid-1960s. His observation is misplaced and there is little evidence that standards have altered over time. From the Newbolt Report of 1921 (the first report on the specific teaching of English), through to the present day, there are continual governmental reports of standards in decline. Yet research, comparing standards over thirty years, carried out by the National Foundation for Educational Research (Brooks 1997), has shown that no such decline in standards has occurred.

Such opinions have also found credence, however, in social commentaries. In her book, *All Must Have Prizes*, written as an invective against what she sees as the failings of the liberal educational establishment, the journalist Melanie Phillips comments, 'The revolt against the teaching of grammar becomes a part of a wider repudiation of external forms of authority' (1996: 69). In a chapter ironically subtitled 'Proper literacy', she lays the blame at the door of radical English teachers:

> English, after all is the subject at the heart of our definition of our national cultural identity. Since English teachers are the chief custodians of that identity we should not be surprised to find that revolutionaries intent on using the subject to transform society have gained a powerful foothold, attempting to redefine the very meaning of reading itself.
>
> (1996: 69)

Both Rae's and Phillips' analyses of the problem are almost certainly more to do with their view of society than literacy standards in schools. There is a subtle but significant elision between rules of language and standards of behaviour where anxiety about the latter requires greater emphasis on the former. Grammatical rules become societal laws. Any suggestion that these might be redefined or abandoned becomes a threat to civil order. For Phillips and Rae, literacy is to be taught as a set of rules in order to reinforce an orderly society.

The elision is found again in the rhetoric of the former Secretary for State for Education, Michael Gove. In his speech to the Tory Party Conference in 2010, in a language that sounds, at first, all-inclusive, he is eager to apportion blame. He talks of the desire for children to be literate, adding:

> Wanting to teach children to read properly isn't some sort of antique prejudice – it's an absolute necessity in a civilized society and I won't rest until we have eliminated illiteracy in modern Britain. The failure to teach millions to read is the greatest of betrayals. But I'll be taking on the education establishment because they've done more than just squander talent.
>
> (Gove 2010)

And he points out that, 'We will tackle head on the defeatism, the political correctness and the entrenched culture of dumbing down that is at the heart of our educational establishment' (Gove 2010). In blaming the 'educational establishment' so firmly he is not differing that much from a Labour Education Secretary, David Blunkett. In a *Daily Mail* article in 1999, he wrote:

> Yet there still remain the doubters to whom these [traditional] methods remain anathema. I still encounter those in the education world who would prefer the quiet life of the past, where education was 'progressive' and where the failure of half our pupils was taken for granted. There are even those who suggest that learning to read properly threatens creativity. Can they really be taken seriously? Are they actually claiming that to be illiterate helps you to become a better artist?
>
> I suspect the real reason why these critics say this stifles creativity is that it ends the ill disciplined 'anything goes' philosophy, which did so much damage to a generation.
>
> (Blunkett 19 July 1999)

In both Gove's and Blunkett's comments, the idea of a 'civilized society' is contrasted with 'ill discipline' and an 'anything goes philosophy' and thus we see that the perspectives of a Labour and a Conservative politician unite, albeit that the Tory is attacking Labour. Both are, however, criticizing the so-called progressive educational establishment or world.

Literacy and learning to read

This desire to teach children to read can also be seen in terms of progressive and traditional. Most of the attempts to bring about a literate society have in recent years been of the latter persuasion.

Synthetic phonics

For both political parties, becoming literate is a matter of being able to decode the print on a written page. The method that both advocate using is synthetic phonics. In 2006, the Rose Report, commissioned by a Labour government, declared that:

> Despite uncertainties in research findings, the practice seen by the review shows that the systematic approach, which is generally understood as

'synthetic' phonics, offers the vast majority of young children the best and most direct route to becoming skilled readers and writers.

(DES 2006: 4)

Moreover, this method was to be exclusive:

For beginner readers, learning the core principles of phonic work in discrete daily sessions reduces the risk, attendant with the so-called 'searchlights' model, of paying too little attention to securing word recognition skills. In consequence, the review suggests a reconstruction of the searchlights model for reading.

(2006: 4)

This is because, according to the report,

If beginner readers, for example, are encouraged to infer from pictures the word they have to decode, this may lead to their not realising that they need to focus on the printed word. They may, therefore, not use their developing phonic knowledge. It may also lead to diluting the focused phonics teaching that is necessary for securing accurate word reading.

(2006: 36)

The 'searchlights' model of learning to read was one advocated by the National Literacy Strategy (NLS), which is now defunct. The NLS was introduced in 1997 by, again, the Labour government and sought to improve the literacy rates of primary-age children. Although it took a predominantly phonics approach to the teaching of reading, it did suggest other strategies as well, for example, looking at pictures to decipher a word or using grammatical knowledge to work out what was being said in a sentence. With the Rose Report this strategy ended and synthetic phonics was introduced across the board. Primary school teachers were retrained and beginner teachers are now only taught synthetic phonics as an aid to reading. The teaching of synthetic phonics in primary schools began in 2007.

So what exactly is synthetic phonics? Advocates of this method argue that there are 44 phonemes in the English language, in other words, the sounds that letters can make. If we take the letter A, for example, this has three phonemic sounds:

å as in cat
ah as in bath (if you speak English with a southern or RP accent)
ae as in plate

Children need to learn each phonemic sound first and then they can learn to identify digraphs. These are when two letters are combined together like 'sh', or 'th'. From here they progress to trigraphs where three letters are combined like 'thr'. And so it continues. Children are only introduced to books when they have mastered all 44 phonemes, the rest are introduced as they go along. Special reading scheme books have to be written for the scheme as only words that can be decoded phonemically can at first be introduced.

Synthetic phonics differs from analytic phonics, the other main use of phonics in teaching children to read. Analytic phonics also identifies phonemic sounds but relies also on a pupil's propensity to make analogies. In particular, it depends on onset, the initial phonemic sound, and an analogous sound, usually rhyme. The Dr Seuss books, such as *The Cat in the Hat*, are a good example of analytic phonics. The title itself is an illustration of onset and rhyme in the words 'cat' and 'hat' but other reading schemes rely heavily on analytic phonics, too, *The Oxford Reading Tree* being one such example. The academic Usha Goswami, who sympathizes with analytic phonics, was involved in writing them when she was based at Oxford University.

Phonics testing

The Coalition government took the teaching of synthetic phonics one stage further and in 2011 Michael Gove introduced a phonics tests for 6-year-olds. Children are already assessed on their reading at age 7. The phonics test, or check, is additional and mandatory and will, the Conservatives presume, teach them to 'read properly'. As the DfE put it, 'The purpose of the phonics screening check will be to confirm that all children have learned phonic decoding to an age-appropriate standard' (DfE 2012). Children are asked to read a series of words, some of which are regular words and some of which are called 'alien' or non-words that have a phonic clue in them but are not part of the English language. So, for example, in the government's video on the phonics test, they have words like 'yed', 'emp', 'sheb', 'muzz' or 'roopt' (YouTube, accessed 19 May 2015). In order to achieve a pass rate a child has to score more than 30 correct answers.

The phonics screening check has faced considerable opposition. The United Kingdom Literacy Association (UKLA), for example, published a letter in 2012 in which it claimed that

> The government is proposing to spend millions of pounds of taxpayers' money every year on a test which will increase workload, undermine teaching time, fail in its core purpose of accurately identifying children's needs in reading and is unnecessary in promoting the already present teaching of phonics.

Even the All-Party Parliamentary Group had doubts about the efficacy of a phonics alone approach, 'There was a great concern that phonics . . . and reading . . . were being used interchangeably by policy makers when they were not the same thing at all: reading isolated words is not reading for meaning' (APPG 2011: 14). Nevertheless the phonics test came in and is going strong.

Clackmannanshire

Both the Labour government and the current Conservative administration favour synthetic phonics largely because of a report on the teaching of literacy in the schools in Clackmannanshire (2005). Clackmannanshire is a small authority in Scotland, having 19 primary schools in total. The researchers Johnson and Watson originally began their work in 1997, but they reported on it seven years later as the report was intended as longitudinal research. The programme started off in just three primary schools but after 16 weeks it expanded to include all 19 primaries, as the results appeared so good. Seven years later Johnson and Watson compared the results of the pupils in Clackmannanshire with other comparable students elsewhere. What they found was that although the Clackmannanshire primary pupils, at the age of 11, were three and a half years ahead in their ability to decode print, in comprehension they were only three months ahead. In the main, however, all that was reported was the first set of data, not the second. Synthetic phonics was the apparent silver bullet politicians had been searching for in terms of improving literacy.

There were, however, several problems with the research. First and foremost, it was never intended to be an all-encompassing defence of synthetic phonics. Sue Ellis (2007), who submitted evidence to the Rose Report, claimed,

> The Clackmannan phonics research reported by Watson and Johnston (2005) was an experimental trial to compare different methods of teaching phonics. It wasn't designed (despite media reports) to investigate whether phonics instruction provides a more effective 'gateway' to reading than a mixed-methods approach. The researchers did not collect the range of data nor conduct the sorts of fidelity checks that would be required to address such a question.
>
> (Ellis 2005, quoted in Rosen 2006)

And although the schools did use synthetic phonics, local authority money was put in as well so that 'These staff carried out home visits, ran story clubs and after-school homework clubs, worked with parent groups, set up library visits and borrowing schemes as well as working in classrooms' (Ellis 2005, quoted in Rosen 2006), as well as 'Schools [being] involved in a separate and concurrent initiative, the New Community Schools Initiative, [which] introduced personal learning planning. This included some, but not all, of the early intervention schools' (Ellis 2005, quoted in Rosen 2006).

Nor was it a peer-researched project. Traditionally, when published, research projects are peer-reviewed by fellow academics and they tend to have advisory committees during the research process that both guide and comment on the research as it progresses. The Clackmannanshire research had neither but research undertaken by the American National Reading Panel (National Institute of Child Health and Human Development 2000) did. It looked at hundreds of peer-reviewed articles in its analysis of whether or not analytic or synthetic phonics was a better way of teaching reading and it found that there was no difference between the two.

But this finding should be set beside, perhaps, a more fundamental difficulty with any phonics teaching of reading and that is that English is not a particularly consistent phonetic language. There are numerous exceptions to any phonic rule. Moreover, meaning can and does play an important part in teaching children to read. If we take the word 'read', we have to know the context and meaning of the phrase in which it occurs to know how it is pronounced – is it read as in *reed* or read as in *red*? Then again, in that sentence, it could be both or either. Take another example – *tear* and *tear*. Is it a word that makes us cry or one that rips us apart? Is it a verb or a noun? Only when we know what it means, can we interpret it correctly. Or the start of so many children's tales and stories: 'Once upon a time there was . . .'. How is one supposed to read that ever-familiar phrase using synthetic phonics? The 'O' is pronounced as a 'w' and the verb 'was' is actually pronounced 'woz'. Teaching children to read based on phonemic sounds alone, without any heed to meaning, could be seen as flawed, as the results in Clackmannanshire seem to indicate.

Reading for meaning and progressivism

Margaret Meek advocated a completely different way of becoming literate. She thought that children would learn to read using 'real books' rather than reading schemes. She took what she calls a social constructivist, or Vygotskian, perspective on early reading (see, for example, Meek 1988; 1991). In other words she has sought to build on what young children already know, which includes their knowledge of how books work and how print conveys meaning. In this way reading and writing are always taught within a clearly defined context. They do not exclude phonics but do not wholly rely on it either. The work of the Centre for Language in Primary Education (CLPE) has built on this work. Research publications such as *The Reader in the Writer* (Barrs and Cork 2002) show how children use their readerly knowledge of how stories and texts work in their writing.

This is very different from the phonics approach to reading, either analytic or synthetic, and it sees literacy as far more than simply decoding print. It is an approach that is found in CLPE's more recent publication and assessment arrangements, *The Reading and Writing Scales* (CLPE 2016),which among other things, again link the reader and the writer and, just as importantly, the meaning of the text pupils are reading. Indeed, there is some indication that viewing literacy as simply decoding print can prevent children from taking pleasure in reading. In 2005, an Ofsted report on English teaching was published. It was written before the Rose Report but after the first cohort of children to complete primary school using the NLS and it makes for interesting reading. While it never actually criticizes the literacy hour, it does virtually everything but. Hints that all was not well with the framework were already to be found in the annual reports of the then Chief Inspector David Bell (3 March 2005). Six months before the review on the teaching of English, he bemoaned the lack of reading in schools, particularly in primaries. Children, he complained, were not encountering enough whole texts during lessons, being given instead extracts from novels. He worried, therefore, that they would lose out on the pleasure of reading. The previous year he had noted that the creative curriculum was being constrained by teachers teaching to the Key Stage 2 test.

While, as has been said, the criticism is never overt, in the Ofsted review on English teaching (2005a), what becomes increasingly evident is that if teachers actually use the framework as their guide in the classroom, their performance will be merely satisfactory or worse. Quoting from the HMCI's annual report, the review notes, in its section on the quality of teaching, that trainee teachers tend 'toward safe and unimaginative teaching . . . partly because [they] use the structure and content of the strategy too rigidly' (Ofsted 2005b: 16). And again, 'For too many primary and secondary teachers . . . objectives become a tick list to be checked off because they follow the frameworks for teaching too slavishly'(Ofsted 2005b: 16–17).

The effects of such approaches are made clear throughout the review. If we look, for example, at the comments on reading, the authors cite research evidence in support of its inspection findings. The Progress in International Reading Literacy Study (PIRLS) found that while 10-year-olds in English schools had comparable reading standards to those in other countries, they were less interested in reading for pleasure. There was also a decline in whether or not they found reading enjoyable between 1998 and 2003. The National Foundation for Educational Research (NFER) also found in its 2003 survey that 'children's enjoyment of reading had declined significantly in recent years' (2003: 22) (see Ofsted, 2005a: 21).

While reading for pleasure may seem an inessential but pleasant by-product in the business of raising literacy standards, research evidence of the last 30 years suggests otherwise. As the Ofsted review notes, the Bullock Report of 1975 found that a major source of adult illiteracy was that, 'they did not learn from the process of learning to read that it was something other people did for pleasure' (Bullock 1975, cited in Ofsted 2005a: 24). The Programme for International Student Assessment (PISA) also found that: 'Being more enthusiastic about reading, and a frequent reader, was more of an advantage on its own than having well educated parents in good jobs', concluding, 'finding a way to engage students in reading may be one of the most effective ways to leverage social change' (OECD 2002, quoted in Ofsted 2005a: 2). Yet Ofsted's own report on the situation in England, *Reading for Purpose and Pleasure*, observed that reading was 'negatively associated with school' (Ofsted 2004, quoted in Ofsted 2005a: 23), particularly for boys and their parents.

Concluding thoughts

All of us want literacy for society and the majority of us want to read, not as a chore but as something pleasurable. But the problems with literacy or being literate do not stop at the edge of the printed page. They are about so much more. For now, in schools, synthetic phonics reigns. Yet those who deem that literacy stops at the functional will, perhaps, always disagree with those who see literacy as being about 'making and exploring meaning' (Alexander 2009: 269). This chapter explores the debate, the two opposing sides and something in the middle. Whenever the issue of literacy comes into the public domain, it is worth starting by considering which side, if any, they are on and then deciding what we think.

References

Alexander, R. (2006) *Education as Dialogue: Moral and Pedagogical Choices for a Runaway World*. Cambridge: Dialogos.

Alexander, R. (2009) *Children, Their World, Their Education: Final Report and Recommendations of the Cambridge Primary Review*. London: Routledge.

All-Party Parliamentary Group for Education (2011) *Report of the Enquiry into Overcoming the Barriers to Literacy*. London: HMSO.

Ball, S.J., Kenny, A. and Gardiner, D. (1990) Literacy policy and the teaching of English, in I. Goodson and P. Medway (eds) *Bringing English to Order*. London: Falmer.

Barrs, M. and Cork, V. (2001) *The Reader in the Writer: The Influence of Literature upon Writing at KS2*. London: Centre for Language in Primary Education.

Bell, D. (2005) Speech. A good read, World Book Day, 3 March.

Blunkett, D. (1999) Commentary: moaners who are cheating your children, *Daily Mail*, 19 July.

Brooks, G. (1997) Trends in standards of literacy in the United Kingdom 1948–1996. Conference paper. British Educational Research Association, University of York, 11–14 September.

Centre for Language in Primary Education (2016) Reading and writing scales, https://www.clpe.org.uk/library-and-resources/reading-and-writing-scales, accessed 15 November 2016.

Corden, R. (2000) *Literacy and Learning Through Talk*. Buckingham: Open University Press.

Departmental Committee of the Board of Education (1921) *The Teaching of English in England: Being the Report of the Departmental Committee Appointed by the President of the Board of Education to Inquire into the Position of English in the Educational System of England* (The Newbolt Report). London: HMSO.

DES (Department for Education and Skills) (1975) *A Language for Life* (The Bullock Report). London: HMSO.

DES (Department for Education and Skills) (2006) *Independent Review of the Teaching of Early Reading: The Final Report* (The Rose Report). London: HMSO.

Dewey, J. (1916) *Democracy and Education*. New York: Macmillan.

Dewey, J. (1966) *Experience and Education*. London: Collier Books.

DfE (Department for Education) (2012) *Teachers' Standards*. London. HMSO.

DfE (Department for Education) (2015) *Initial Teacher Training Handbook*. London. HMSO.

Ellis, S. (2005) *The Wider Context for Synthetic Phonics in Clackmannanshire: Evidence to the Rose Committee of Inquiry into Methods of Teaching Reading*. Glasgow: University of Strathclyde.

Ellis, S. (2007) Policy and research: lessons from the Clackmannanshire Synthetic Phonics Initiative, *Journal of Early Childhood Literacy*, 7(3): 281–97.

European Union (2012) *Final Report of the EU High Level Group of Experts on Literacy*, ec.europa.eu/education/literacy/resources/final-report/index_en.htm, accessed 15th March 2017.

Freire, P. and Macedo, D. (1987) *Literacy: Reading the Word and the World*. London: Routledge.

Gibbons, S. (2017) *English and its Teachers: A History of Policy, Pedagogy and Practice*. London: Routledge.

Gove, M. (2010) Speech, http://www.conservatives.com/News/Speeches/2009/10/Michael_Gove_Failing_schools_need_new_leadership.aspx, accessed 4 December 2010.

Graddol, D., Maybin, J., Mercer, N. and Swann, J. (eds) (1991) *Talk and Learning 5–16: An Inservice Pack on Oracy for Teachers*. Milton Keynes: Open University Press.

Heath, S. (1983) *Ways with Words*. Cambridge: Cambridge University Press.

Hoggart, R. ([1957] 2009) *The Uses of Literacy: Aspects of Working Class Life*. London. Penguin.

Hoggart, R. (1998) Critical literacy and creative reading, in B. Cox (ed.) *Literacy is Not Enough: Essays on the Importance of Reading*. Manchester: Manchester University Press.

Meek, M. (1988) *How Texts Teach What Readers Learn*. Stroud: Thimble Press.

Meek, M. (1991) *On Being Literate*. London: Bodley Head.

National Institute of Child Health and Human Development (NIH, DHHS) (2000) *Report of the National Reading Panel: Teaching Children to Read (00-4769)*. Washington, DC: U.S. Government Printing Office.

OECD (2002) *Reading for Change: A Report on the Programme for International Student Assessment*. Paris: OECD.

Ofsted (2005a) *English 2000–5: A Review of the Inspection Evidence*. London: HMSO.

Ofsted (2005b) *The Literacy and Numeracy Strategies and the Primary Curriculum: HMCI*. London: HMSO.

Ofsted (2013) *Improving Literacy in Secondary Schools: A Shared Responsibility*. London: HMSO.

Phillips, M. (1996) *All Must Have Prizes*. London: Little, Brown and Co.

Rosen, M. (2006) http://www.michaelrosen.co.uk/kingstalk.html, accessed 3 December 2010.

Street, B. and Street, J. (1991) The schooling of literacy, in D. Barton and R. Ivanich (eds) *Writing in the Community*. London: Sage.

Tate, N. (1998) What is education for? The fifth annual education lecture, King's College London.

UNESCO (2003) Statement for the United Nations Literacy Decade 2003–12, New York: UNESCO.

Vygotsky, L. (1978) *Mind in Society*. Cambridge, MA: MIT Press.

Watson, E. and Johnston, R. (2005) *Accelerating Reading Attainment: The Effectiveness of Synthetic Phonics*. St Andrews: University of St Andrews.

19

Numeracy, mathematical literacy and mathematics
EVA JABLONKA AND KAREN SKILLING

Introduction

Today, a student in a member country of the Organisation for Economic Co-operation and Development (OECD) spends on average 1200 hours in a mathematics classroom during their primary and lower secondary education. In most European Countries, mathematics accounts for between 15 per cent and 20 per cent of total instruction time in primary education. While in almost all countries the proportion of time allocated to mathematics decreases at secondary level, it is still large in comparison with other subjects (Education, Audiovisual and Culture Executive Agency 2011). The significant position of mathematics in the compulsory school curriculum is related to both individual and social benefits associated with this school subject. These expected benefits, however, vary across countries and often change in the course of major curriculum reforms. Benefits cited in policy debates relate to the alleged need for national or supra-national economic competitiveness based on the use of mathematics in particular occupations in science, technology and engineering, and, related to this, the widening of participation in higher education in particular subjects for which advanced mathematics is needed. It is also claimed that mathematics provides a training ground for logical thinking and critical thinking skills; contributes to informed citizenship; and is useful in everyday practices and employment. In this context, *mathematical* (or *mathematics*) *literacy* are terms that have been used to express a range of goals for compulsory mathematics education that transcend mastery of calculation techniques and knowledge of definitions, properties and relations of mathematical objects. Those goals concern the capacity to make use of mathematical concepts, procedures, methods and theories in extra-mathematical contexts. Hence a focus on numeracy and mathematical literacy might be seen in tension with a focus on the study of abstract concepts in pure mathematics. However, these goals provide a justification for mathematics education for everyone.

This chapter addresses a range of issues relevant to the development of *numeracy* or *mathematical literacy* in school mathematics, including the origins and use of these terms and the underlying goals for mathematics education. It explores the place of numeracy and mathematical literacy in formal curriculum documents from England and makes comparisons with other English-language documents from countries such as Australia, New Zealand, South Africa and the USA. The chapter then discusses some suggestions that have been made for teaching practice in mathematics as well as in other school subjects with the aim of developing numeracy and mathematical literacy as envisaged in various curriculum documents, in policy discourse or by mathematics educators. These suggestions are not matters only for teachers of mathematics, the arguments presented in this chapter are intended for all those who are involved in teaching because all students require numerical competencies so that they can become fluent and active participants in their society.

Numeracy and mathematical literacy as goals for mathematics education

The terms *numeracy*, *mathematical* (or *mathematics*) *literacy* (hereafter referred to as N/ML) are used to refer to a range of goals for compulsory mathematics education that transcend mastery of calculation techniques and understanding of intra-mathematical structures. In policy texts, numeracy often refers to using basic mathematical skills and concepts as a tool in situations that occur in everyday life and in professions that do not rely on specialized training in mathematics. This understanding of numeracy as basic functional mathematics is used in particular in the context of adult education (Coben and O'Donoghue 2014), but may also refer to arithmetic-related competencies that are typically acquired in primary education (Office for Standards in Education, Children's Services and Skills 2011).

The notion of mathematical (or mathematics) literacy became popular in the context of international comparative achievement surveys. The Third International Mathematics and Science Study (TIMSS – in recent cycles of the survey, the abbreviation stands for Trends in International Mathematics and Science Study) conducted by the International Association for the Evaluation of Educational Achievement (IEA) included a mathematics and science literacy test for students in their final year of secondary school in 21 countries with the aim 'to provide information about how prepared the overall population of school leavers in each country is to apply knowledge in mathematics and science to meet the challenges of life beyond school' (Mullis *et al.* 1998: 13). A similarly ambitious definition of mathematical literacy is found in the OECD's framework for the Programme for International Student Assessment (PISA):

> With mathematics as its primary focus, the PISA 2012 assessment measured 15-year-olds' capacity to reason mathematically and use mathematical concepts, procedures, facts and tools to describe, explain and predict phenomena, and to make the well-founded judgements and decisions needed by constructive, engaged and reflective citizens.
>
> (OECD 2014: 28)

N/ML concerns the application of mathematics in a range of practices in which students and adults are assumed to participate. Hence education for N/ML can have different emphases, such as fulfilling new demands for a skilled workforce in STEM-related professions, fitting individuals with the skills for dealing with their personal finances, raising awareness for sustainable development through choice of particular contexts for mathematical investigations, or educating critical citizens and promoting distributive justice particularly in the context of the teaching of statistics. Consequently, N/ML cannot be conceived of exclusively as a neutral set of skills independent of a point of view on the main purpose of (mathematics) education.

Based on this observation, Jablonka (2003), in a review of literature, identified five agendas on which conceptions of N/ML rest. These include developing human capital to match assumed labour market needs, maintaining cultural identity particularly in contexts of post-colonial curriculum development, pursuing social change through critical pedagogy, creating environmental awareness and recognition of the limitations of technological solutions for global problems, and developing the capacity to critically evaluate mathematical applications especially those that are used to maintain social and political positions. These agendas draw attention to the underlying viewpoints or focuses, such as quantitative literacy (Steen 2001), critical mathematical numeracy (Frankenstein 2010), mathemacy (Skovsmose 1994), matheracy (D'Ambrosio 2003), statistical literacy (Gal 2002) and techno-mathematical literacy (Hoyles *et al.* 2010).

While there are different evaluations of the breadth and depth of mathematical knowledge and skills needed for successful participation in everyday practices, all the authors cited above have stressed that a certain level of proficiency in mathematics is necessary for developing those diverse mathematical literacies. Also, even though based on different agendas for education, all conceptions of N/ML except those exclusively driven by labour market demands, are associated with developing a critical stance towards taken-for-granted assumptions of a range of practices, including those that rely heavily on applications of mathematics.

The main arguments, however, for broadening the scope of school mathematics in order to develop N/ML were initially independent of the overall goals of mathematics education. One major driver was based on the observation of students' difficulties in making sensible use of their mathematical school knowledge to solve problems in extra-mathematical contexts. A substantial body of research had shown that school students did not automatically consider extra-mathematical conditions and use their out-of-school experiences when solving such problems (see, for example, Verschaffel, Greer and De Corte 2000), but also found that relying too much on their experiences and non-mathematical knowledge from the respective out-of-school practices was likewise unhelpful. While the 'blame' for this may be put on the quality of school mathematics tasks that are supposed to resemble 'real-life' problems where mathematics might be of use, these issues also point to the principal limitation of fully acknowledging out-of-school experiences and non-mathematical considerations. At the same time, the constitution of school mathematics in terms of 'products' – definitions and naming of concepts and results of mathematical research in the form of theorems and techniques for solving sets of similar tasks – was challenged. Product-oriented curricula were complemented, or partly substituted, by descriptions of mathematical processes or strategies, such as heuristics for mathematical problem-solving, mathematical modelling, mathematical argumentation, constructive and critical mathematical reasoning, and communicating mathematical matters (Niss and Jablonka 2014). What we are arguing is that the expectations and assumptions for developing N/ML in compulsory mathematics education have been and are contested. In National Curriculum documents, the rationales behind the type of mathematics instruction as constituted through a particular framework are not always made fully explicit, but comparative studies reveal different emphases.

Numeracy and mathematical literacy in the curriculum

Now we turn to explore how N/ML are positioned in official curriculum documents of selected countries; in other words, we will consider how some of this contestation is embedded in National Curriculum documents. This exploration reflects on the curriculum objectives and emphasis on N/ML in terms of the suggested content and processes for teaching and learning. We focus on mathematics curriculum documents mainly in early secondary years up until the time mathematics is no longer compulsory. However, we note that for some countries the mathematics curriculum is presented as a continuum from the start of school to Year 8 (New Zealand and the USA) or to Year 10 (Australia), whereas in other countries the curriculum is focused on stages or groupings by school years (e.g. the secondary curriculum for England includes Key Stages 3 and 4). We begin by looking at the English National Mathematics curriculum and then explore comparable mathematics curriculum documents from a range of other English-speaking countries, including Australia, New Zealand, South Africa and the United States, in order to illustrate the ways that N/ML are articulated and emphasized. Some curriculum documents explicitly mention (personal) finances as a topic to deal with in mathematics education. If this is the case, we also examine the idea of financial literacy education.

The English context

The National Curriculum for England (DfE 2014a), commissioned by the Department for Education (DfE), sets out programmes of study and expected outcomes for all 12 subject areas across four Key Stages of schooling. Before outlining the programmes of study for individual subjects, the contents page of the National Curriculum makes several statements. One of these statements is for Numeracy and Mathematics (DfE 2014a: 10). Two points are detailed: the first states, 'Teachers should use every relevant subject to develop pupils' mathematical fluency. Confidence in numeracy and other mathematical skills is a precondition of success across the national curriculum.' The second point emphasizes numeracy and mathematical reasoning in all subjects, highlighting that students need to 'understand and appreciate the importance of mathematics'. Some mention of developing skills in arithmetic, problem-solving, measuring, estimation and sense making is made, alongside the application of geometric and algebraic understanding, probability and notions of risk as well as a number of skills related to the collection, presentation and analysis of data (DfE 2014a). Unfortunately, the guidance is quite general and there are no explicit examples of how numeracy and mathematical skills should apply to the other subject areas or how teachers (of mathematics or any other subject) could or should judge which particular aspects would be most appropriate to emphasize.

The National Curriculum also sets out individual programmes of study, of which mathematics is one. In this chapter, our focus is the mathematics curriculum for Key Stages 3 and 4, which apply to school Year 7 (age 11) to Year 11 (age 16). In the context of widening participation of young adults between 16 and 18 years in education and training, recent initiatives in England require all students to remain studying mathematics until they reach a certain proficiency level. Government initiatives include expectations that all students will continue to study mathematics in some advanced form and this has led to the introduction of a new Core Mathematics qualification. This qualification is described as a practical and everyday mathematics course and is designed for students not intending to take mathematics at A level (Educational Development Trust 2017). One of the arguments for increased post-16 participation in mathematics study is the improved earning capacity when these students become active in the labour market (10 per cent greater than non-post-16 participating peers) and the importance of mathematical skills for employment (Adkins and Noyes 2016). Government influences for the introduction of the Core Mathematics qualification are reflected in this agenda, which assumes an increased importance of mathematical skills across a range of practices, in particular, for applying mathematics to analyse situations as adults, such as financial transactions (e.g. mortgage payments), as well as grasping applications of statistics, financial mathematics and modelling (e.g. to understand investments) (DfE 2014b). However, despite the focus of this course emphasizing everyday mathematics use and functional applications, the emphasis of N/ML is not specifically mandated (DfE 2015).

It is also relevant here to mention an increased focus on financial literacy education (FLE) for school-aged students in England. Prior to 2014, most financial education taught in English secondary schools was delivered by themed units within the Personal Social, Health and Economic (PSHE) curriculum, which was a suggested but non-compulsory subject. However, in 2014, it became a statutory requirement to teach financial education in mathematics as well as Citizenship as part of the National Curriculum. In this context, not only some specific mathematical content was emphasized (such as operations with numbers, percentages and statistics), but also financial concepts (such as unit pricing). FLE was added to the Citizenship Curriculum, including: teaching students the 'functions and uses of money, the importance and practice of budgeting, and managing risk' at Key Stage 3; and 'Income and expenditure, credit and debt, insurance, savings and pensions, financial products and services, and how public money is raised and spent' at Key Stage 4 (DfE 2014a). Although financial education has become a statutory requirement, specific guidance on how teachers are to acquire the knowledge and skills to equip students with FLE is not detailed, however, links to teaching resources and professional development are available.

Returning to the individual programme of study for mathematics in the National Curriculum, mathematics is positioned as a 'creative and highly interconnected discipline' and claims that 'it is essential to everyday life, critical to science, technology and engineering, and necessary for financial literacy and most forms of employment' (DfE 2014a: 108). Additionally, mathematics 'provides a foundation for understanding the world, the ability to reason mathematically, an appreciation of the beauty and power of mathematics, and a sense of enjoyment and curiosity about the subject' (DfE 2014a: 108). Although there is no specific mention of numeracy or mathematical literacy in the programme of study, the idea of the relevance and power of mathematics and mathematical reasoning as a means for understanding 'the world' reflects the goals of mathematics education associated with N/ML.

These overarching purposes are followed by the three key aims of the mathematics National Curriculum (DfE 2014a). The first is to be fluent in the fundamentals of mathematics so that conceptual understanding, recall and application of knowledge can occur rapidly and accurately. The second notes the importance of being able to reason mathematically to conjecture, to generalize and develop arguments, justifications or proof using appropriate mathematical language. The third aim pertains to solving problems by applying mathematical knowledge and understanding to complex problems, which suggests development of numeracy or mathematical literacy but without specifying any particular conception of N/ML. Notions of working mathematically are outlined more specifically in the mathematics curriculum from Stage 3 onwards, again emphasizing building 'connections across mathematical ideas to develop fluency, mathematical reasoning and competence in solving increasingly sophisticated problems'. It is also suggested that pupils 'apply their mathematical knowledge in science, geography, computing and other subjects' (DfE 2014a: 153) although, as we have already indicated, no specific guidance is provided for relevant applications or appropriate methods to use. Despite including *Numeracy and Mathematics* as a separate overarching section in the National Curriculum, there are no clear links to the mathematics curriculum (which mainly lists mathematics topic material). The lack of specificity for ways in which numeracy could be developed within mathematics and interconnected to other subject areas does little to support teachers both in clearly understanding the intentions of the curriculum or enacting them. In many ways, there seems to be a separation between the official curriculum (aims, objectives and content) and how it is envisaged to operate in classrooms, therefore weakening the stated purpose of the mathematics curriculum itself.

Australian context

The current Australian Curriculum (Australian Curriculum and Assessment Reporting Authority 2014) is the first national curriculum implemented at a federal level. Initial development of this curriculum began with a focus on four key subjects (English, history, mathematics and science), and was built through a series of national consultation processes (Way *et al.* 2016). Although a national curriculum has now been established, currently each state and territory is responsible for its implementation and so in effect this allows for variations in curriculum delivery between the states and territories (Way *et al.* 2016).

The Australian Curriculum includes three dimensions: *learning areas* (eight key content areas, one of which is mathematics); *general capabilities* (one of which is numeracy); and *cross-curricular priorities* (acknowledging Aboriginal and Torres Strait Island history and culture, engaging with Asia and sustainability) (ACARA 2014). The key purpose of the general capabilities and priorities is to lift and extend the eight learning areas across each year level, from foundation (equivalent to reception in England) through to Year 10 (equivalent to Year 11). The document includes the rationale, aims and structure of the mathematics curriculum. The structure details three content strands describing what should be taught and what students should learn, with some emphasis on relevance to 'real-life' contexts. Teachers are also expected to consider instructional approaches that support four proficiencies, namely: understanding; fluency; problem-solving; and reasoning. However, there is a lack of specificity as to how these approaches translate into classroom pedagogy and there is reliance on teachers interpreting the curriculum content and making decisions in using appropriate teaching practices (Way *et al.* 2016).

N/ML is more obviously a fundamental component of the Australian Curriculum than the English one, and is positioned as one of the *general capabilities*. The rationale for the *general capabilities* dimension emphasizes readying young people for their future lives and careers so that they can be successful citizens in the twenty-first century (ACARA 2014). As a general capability, numeracy is embedded in all subjects so that it is practised in multiple contexts, and is detailed more carefully than in the English curriculum. However, although some specifications about prescribed content are available in each subject, little detail is included in relation to specific numeracy requirements or the opportunities that teachers might recognize and identify in their teaching that may develop numerical activities that are relevant in the 'real world' (Geiger, Forgasz and Goos 2015). In fact, specific teaching strategies are not clearly articulated. The lack of curriculum guidance in terms of cross-curricular applications means that there are no sets of typical or well-established practices for applying mathematics to other subject areas and teachers need to use their own networks and recourses to develop these. However, without a deep understanding of mathematical methods or theories, it will be difficult for non-expert teachers of mathematics to identify effective opportunities for developing numeracy or, for example, knowing if particular teaching strategies should be utilized over others (Way *et al.* 2016).

Concerns have also been raised about the social and cultural appropriateness of a programme of financial literacy, recently added to the Australian Curriculum (Blue, Grootenboer and Brimble 2014; Blue 2016). Notably, the MoneyStart programme and MoneyStart Teaching Strategy have been developed and implemented by the Australian Securities and Investment Commission (ASIC), which is the corporate market and financial services regulator in Australia. The aim of this strategy is to 'develop consumer and financial literacy capabilities in young Australians' (ASIC 2017a). Examples of units of work include a Year 9 unit of work for mathematics called 'How can we obtain more money?' and a Year 10 English unit called 'Teens talk money' (ASIC 2017b).

As there are currently no FLE courses during pre-service teacher education, questions have been raised about whether the professional development offered by the MoneyStart programme is sufficient to equip teachers to meet the aims of financial literacy and education (Blue *et al.* 2014). Further concerns relate to some of the suggested financial literacy tasks, for example, questioning the relevance for Year 5 students (aged 10–11 years) to develop a financial plan and budget, which appear to be based on assumptions that young students are in possession of and responsible for managing money (Blue 2016). In particular, Blue (2016) notes that many programmes for financial education are generic and so do not necessarily attend to the cultural norms of indigenous communities who may hold different views about community resources and the extent to which making financial decisions influences the whole community. Blue cites the work of Lucey, Agnello and Laney, who describe *thin* and *thick* views of financial literacy: the conventional *thin* view focuses on an individual's ability to make effective financial decisions whereas a *thick* view recognizes that such decisions 'occur within a social system and affect the lives of other participants' and 'result from a degree of care or control that one experiences towards society' (2015: 1).

New Zealand context

The current *New Zealand Curriculum for English-Medium Teaching and Learning in Years 1–13* (Ministry of Education 2007), which was introduced in 2007 and fully implemented in 2010, combines three interconnected streams to structure the curriculum. In contrast to the Australian Curriculum, the New Zealand one takes a holistic approach in the form of a multi-strand curriculum with an overarching vision supported by underlying principles (Way *et al.* 2016). The eight underlying principles embody national and local beliefs about what is important in a school curriculum and should be considered by schools when making decisions for teaching. The principles comprise 'high expectations', 'learning to learn', 'the Treaty of Waitangi', 'community engagement', 'cultural diversity', 'coherence', 'inclusion' and 'future focus'. Hence there is some explicit recognition of New Zealand being linguistically and culturally diverse, emphasizing the expectation that teaching involves helping students to respect diverse viewpoints and customs. With this revised curriculum comes an expectation that five overarching competencies (thinking; relating to others; using language, symbols and texts; managing self; and participating and contributing) should be integral to all learning areas including mathematics.

Mathematics is one of eight subject areas, and in the New Zealand Curriculum it is designated as *Mathematics and Statistics*, which is a distinctly different emphasis from other countries we have considered in this chapter. The document explains that both mathematics and statistics 'equip students with effective means for investigating, interpreting, explaining, and making sense of the world in which they live'. Although the mathematics and statistics learning area is structured according to broad mathematical strands – number and algebra, geometry and measurement, and statistics and problem-solving – each set of related objectives states an expectation for student engagement in thinking mathematically and statistically in relation to practical applications (Ministry of Education 2007). It is worth noting that the weighting of the three strands varies for different academic years in school, for example, a higher proportion of number objectives are aimed for in earlier years and a higher proportion of geometry in later years. The New Zealand Curriculum also allows schools to design and shape their curriculum according to the needs/progression of their students, offering greater flexibility, authority and responsibility for operationalizing the curriculum than in the other two settings discussed (Education Review Office 2013).

The National Standards (NZ) set out broad expectations of achievement and are structured according to the strands of the mathematics and statistics learning area detailed for school years 1–8. Therefore, the New Zealand Curriculum and the National Standards are intended to complement each other. They both play a role in developing N/ML, which have been informed by the Numeracy Development Projects (NDP). The NDP were conceived as an evidence-based initiative and have generated a wave of reform in several phases over nearly 20 years in New Zealand mathematics education (MoE 2015). This reflects the importance placed on teaching for and developing students' N/ML and reflects ongoing concerns of education policy in NZ for meeting numeracy expectations at school level and among the current adult workforce. As in the English and Australian settings, N/ML is viewed as important for young people as they approach adulthood, with weight placed on being able to manage the social, emotional, physical and economic aspects of their lives (Ministry of Education 2007). However, both the Australian and New Zealand Curriculum documents provide details about what is meant by numeracy or mathematics literacy and examples of where and how appropriate activities can be incorporated across other curriculum subjects. Another commonality between these two documents is the acknowledgement of cultural diversity evidenced in the cross-curricular priorities (Australian Curriculum 2014) and underlying principles (New Zealand Curriculum 2010), which recognizes and respects students' cultural identities in the development of N/ML.

A specific focus in the application of numerical skills is developing 'financial capability' (interchangeable with the term 'financial literacy'), which is given as an example of a theme for cross-curricular activities. Here financial literacy is defined as 'the ability to make informed judgements and effective decisions regarding the use and management of money'. The intention is to equip students with skills, knowledge and strategies enabling them to make such decisions and be responsible managers of money so that they can live, learn, work and contribute to their communities (MoE 2007). The strategy for financial literacy is not compulsory and its uptake depends on individual schools. With the assistance of various providers, teaching resources are available via links on the Ministry of Education website.

South African context

In South Africa, several curriculum reviews since 2000 culminated in the implementation of the Curriculum and Policy Statements (CAPS) in 2012. The CAPS is a single comprehensive document for all subjects listed in the National Curriculum Statement Grades R-12. The curriculum grades are organized into four phases and include: Foundation Phase (reception to Grade 3); Intermediate (Grades 4–6);

Senior Phase (Grades 7–9); and the Further Education and Training (FET) Phase (Grades 10–12). For mathematics in the first three phases five key content areas are specified, including: numbers, operations and relationships; patterns, functions and algebra; space and shape; measurement; and data handling. The fourth phase includes several compulsory subjects and a range of additional subject choices. It is compulsory for students to study mathematics, but students can choose to take either 'Mathematics' or 'Mathematical Literacy'.

The subject 'Mathematics' comprises ten mathematical topics that build on the five mathematics content areas of the three previous phases and is intended to provide the link between the Senior Phase and Higher Education. The CAPS for this phase states that the purpose is for learners to 'acquire a functioning knowledge of the Mathematics that empowers them to make sense of society. It aims at ensuring access to an extended study of the mathematical sciences and a variety of career paths' (Department of Basic Education 2011: 10).

'Mathematical Literacy' is a separate subject, which aims at developing competencies that: '[a]llow individuals to make sense of, participate in and contribute to the twenty-first century world – a world characterized by numbers, numerically based arguments and data represented and misrepresented in a number of different ways' (Department of Basic Education 2011: 8). The competencies list the importance of reasoning, decision-making, problem-solving, managing resources, interpreting information and using technology. The core elements of 'Mathematical Literacy' (ML) involve using elementary mathematics, authentic real-life contexts, solving familiar and unfamiliar problems, decision-making and communication, and integrating appropriate content and skills in a variety of contexts. Several reasons are espoused for the introduction of mathematical literacy including: becoming 'a self-managing person, a contributing worker and a participating citizen in a developing democracy', being able to work mathematically to solve problems and 'to engage mathematically . . . to become astute consumers of mathematics' (Department of Basic Education 2011: 8). The topics for ML are assigned as *basic skills topics* and *application topics*, with the expectation that learners will integrate the content and skills of the former to make sense of the context of the latter. The application topics include finance, data handling, measurement, probability and maps, plans and representation of the physical world. Therefore, there is a connection made between specific mathematic content, and contexts where students should be able to apply a set of named skills and competencies.

This level of specification is more detailed than information provided by the curriculum documents of Australia, New Zealand and England. The opportunity to choose 'Mathematical Literacy' as an alternative subject to 'Mathematics' resembles the strategy in England for introducing the Core Mathematics qualification. Both place emphasis on equipping individuals with a level of mathematical competency to gain employment, contribute to society, manage their finances and solve problems.

Financial education for this phase of learning is also a focus within the 'Mathematical Literacy' programme. For the senior phase of learning (Grades 7–9) provision for consumer financial education is situated in Economic and Management Sciences. This area aims to equip learners with skills for personal and community development and sustaining economic growth and includes topics such as saving, budgeting, income and expenditure, accounting concepts and cycles, and financial management and record-keeping (Department of Basic Education 2011).

United States of America context

In the USA, the National Governors Association (NGA) and the Council of Chief State School Officers (CCSSO) in 2010 released the Common Core State Standards (CCSS) for English Language, Arts and Literacy and Mathematics for children from kindergarten (reception stage in the UK) to grade 12. The CCSS set clear goals about the knowledge and skills that students are expected to acquire in mathematics but did not indicate how these should be implemented or the way that teachers should teach these aspects (Common Core State Standards Initiative 2010).

The preamble to the CCSS for Mathematics (Common Core State Standards Initiative 2010) highlighted a number of key aspects that were influential in their development. Similar to the English official rationale for introducing curriculum changes, considerations of the results of high-performing countries such as Singapore and Hong Kong (measured by international tests such as PISA and TIMSS) played a role in the policy discourse. The importance of developing numeracy and geometric skills in the early years of schooling and establishing a more focused and coherent mathematics curriculum was stressed. This was based on the assumption that a less strictly organized curriculum might distort the mathematics presented, and a focus on mathematical procedures could lead to student dissatisfaction and lack of interest. Therefore, the current CCSS emphasizes conceptual understanding of key mathematical ideas and mathematical organizing principles of content areas to structure the ideas as students develop skills and knowledge cumulatively (Common Core State Standards Initiative 2010). Although it is stated that the main aim of the CCSS is to improve the mathematics achievement of all students in the United States, the mathematics curricula that students experience in low-income areas across different states may still remain more similar than those offered in schools in higher-income areas in the same state.

The CCSS Mathematics Standards include two components – the Standards for Mathematical Content and the Standards for Mathematical Practice – and there is an expectation that a connection is made between them. The Standards for Mathematical Content aim at balancing skills and understanding in ways that students can engage with the discipline of mathematics as they develop and gain expertise throughout their years at school (Common Core State Standards Initiative 2010). The Standards for Mathematical Practice describe key processes and proficiencies, drawing on ideas from previous standards: for example, the process standards of problem-solving, reasoning and proof, communication, representation and connections espoused by the National Council of Teachers of Mathematics (NCTM). Strands regarding mathematical proficiency are based on the specifications of an influential National Research Council report entitled *Adding It Up* (2001) and include: adaptive reasoning, strategic competence, conceptual understanding, procedural fluency and a productive disposition (Common Core State Standards Initiative 2010).

High school standards, which come into play after Year 8, specify topics that students are required to study in preparation for college and further careers. These include: number and quantity; algebra; functions; geometry; and statistics and probability. In addition to these topics, developing mathematical models of (real) situations ('modeling') is included as a Standard for Mathematical Practice. With no explicit mention of N/ML, the curriculum focus appears to be on academic mathematics, but under 'modeling' there are some typical examples given of situations amenable to descriptions by mathematical models the results of which should be interpreted in terms of the context.

As in the other settings, finance ('money') is included in the mathematics curriculum as an example of the application of mathematical skills under 'measurement and data', 'functions', but also appears under 'modeling'. In addition, there are National Standards for Financial Literacy (2017a), established by the Council of Economic Education (CEE). The CEE has correlated selected lessons to the English Language Arts and Mathematics Common Core Standards. Currently, however, only 17 states require students to take a course in personal finance and 20 states require students to take a course in economics (CEE 2017b).

N/ML: contested practice

This section has reviewed mathematics curriculum documents from five countries and noted the diversity in the conceptualization and structure of N/ML. Some countries provide particular mathematics-related courses focusing exclusively on N/ML such as the post-16 Core Mathematics qualification in England and the Mathematical Literacy subject offered to Grades 10–12 in South Africa. Such programmes highlight a tension between subordinating examples of the use of mathematics to mathematical structuring principles, or subordinating mathematical structures to a range of practices, in which sensible use of any mathematics could be made.

Other countries focus more obviously on N/ML in cross-curricular activities, such as seen in the Australia and New Zealand Curriculum documents. When N/ML is construed as a cross-curricular aim, it is assumed that a suitable mathematical 'toolkit' is available to both students and teachers in the other school subjects. However, if such toolkits are not available, to which resources and networks can teachers turn to access relevant and appropriate mathematics information? A key question then arises about the extent to which understanding of the mathematical principles upon which the functioning of particular numerical or algebraic calculation techniques, geometrical constructions or other relevant mathematical techniques rest, is necessary for the choice and judgement of their suitability. A related issue concerns the identity of teachers as experts for particular subjects, as guidance for teachers in deciding when, where and how to apply or integrate N/ML is not detailed.

As typical topics for N/ML, some examples of themes for financial literacy education are included in the mathematics curricula we reviewed, such as dealing with personal finances, budgets, insurances, consumer credits and mortgages, or investment and saving. On the other hand, some mathematics is included in programmes that aim at financial literacy. Neither of these, however, include a reflection of differences in socio-economic status and cultural affiliation among groups of students. This absence points to some general difficulties teachers might face in the classroom when engaging in activities that aim at developing N/ML through mathematics task that are relevant for 'real life' as the 'real lives' of their students might be quite different.

N/ML in the classroom

Through some necessarily brief accounts of different national curricula we have illustrated the ways in which N/ML are argued for as part of mathematics education, as cross-curricular topics or as a separate subject. While dealing with money is a traditional area of N/ML included in mathematics education, we have also noticed a trend in stressing financial literacy. These short examples of curriculum aims and guidelines illustrate a number of tensions and dilemmas in terms of outcomes in practice. For example, curriculum frameworks usually do not offer much detail about classroom practice as teachers are expected to select appropriate activities in accordance with their particular students' out-of-school experiences, previously acquired school knowledge, interests and school ethos, etc. While there appears to be agreement that mathematics education should provide the skills and knowledge necessary for further mathematical studies and some specialized professions, it should also teach skills that will be useful in the students' adult lives, that is, to develop the students' N/ML. However, there is yet to be agreement on what this should or could look like in teaching practice, as, for example, Askew (2015) notes. Or indeed, which groups of students should engage in this curriculum, or who should take responsibility for delivery – should this be all teachers of all subjects, specialist mathematics educators or any other people? In addition, the case studies have also highlighted questions about when or at what age/stage this provision should start and which topics should be included.

For instance, the development of *number sense* (McIntosh, Reys and Reys 1992) has been considered to be a crucial topic in the pre-algebraic classroom. It includes aspects of quantitative reasoning that mediate between symbolic representations of quantities and their interpretations in particular practices, such as the knowledge of situation-specific quantities, skills in employing numbers as measures, estimation of quantities and making order-of-magnitude approximations, and strategies for rounding. Similarly, other researchers have pointed to the importance of developing *symbol sense*, which mediates between algebraic representations and their context-specific interpretations, and includes the facility to generate numeric, graphic or computer representations of algebraic expressions (Fey 1990; Arcavi 1994). Managing the transition between specific context-based procedures, on the one hand, and generalized mathematical problem solutions, on the other, is a continuing concern.

Studies of workplace mathematics (e.g. Bessot and Ridgway 2002; Hodgen and Marks 2013) could be usefully consulted as a basis for developing tasks for the mathematics classroom. In this way some shortcomings of those school mathematics tasks that typically ignore specific conditions, possible variations, and suitability of the outcomes for solving a problem or answering a question may be overcome. Taking these variables into account would require some knowledge about particular workplace practices or in other (school) subjects, which is not usually the case with those who are subject-specialists in mathematics.

In line with some of the goals expressed in state-mandated curriculum frameworks, as detailed above, a range of strategic skills are needed for the development of N/ML. These include developing specifications of a problem through asking suitable questions, finding symbolic mathematical descriptions of the processes and relationships as well as interpreting and evaluating these with regard to their usefulness in solving the problem. In mathematics education and in some curriculum documents this process is referred to as mathematical modelling or mathematization. As with other strategic skills, these are best acquired by practising them, initially with the aid of a more experienced other. Other skills associated with N/ML are best developed through discussions, acknowledging different points of view, awareness of divergent aims and of alternative perceptions of a problem, and awareness of possible limitations of a mathematical treatment of a problem. This all suggests general pedagogical strategies that foster dialogue. Altogether, these suggestions imply that any choice of classroom activities ought to acknowledge that numeracy and mathematical literacy is a socially and culturally embedded practice.

Concluding thoughts

In some contexts, numeracy (connoting 'numbers') only means a facility in the use of basic arithmetic in the same way as literacy is often taken to mean the essence of the ability to read and write, for example, in the estimated literacy rates for different countries reported by the UNESCO Institute for Statistics. Literacy then might be understood as a skill that is developed and used independently of the social and cultural contexts and associated values in which any reading or writing occurs; but the requirements, conditions, motives and interests involved in being able to construct meaning in reading and writing vary across contexts, as do the social positions of particular speakers or readers, as we have seen in the discussion above. This argument challenges any conception of basic literacy as an assembly of purely technical and cognitive (strategic) skills. One then rather would speak of 'literacies' as the diverse social practices and their conceptions of reading and writing (see Chapter 18).

• Thinking about your own educational development, in which contexts would particular mathematical skills have been useful to learn about? In terms of numeracy or mathematical literacy, why do you think it is often just seen as an assembly of purely technical-mathematical and cognitive (strategic) skills without reference to the social or cultural context in which these skills are used?

One issue that makes for complexity in educational provision of N/ML relates to differences between students. People's private, professional, social, occupational, political and economic lives not only represent a multitude of different requirements, but also different social conditions and identities. For example, in classroom activities aimed at developing numeracy for dealing with financial transactions by means of 'real-life' mathematics tasks, students might be construed as low or as high budget consumers with particular concomitant tastes. Consequently, any attempt to include 'real-life' N/ML tasks in classroom teaching, needs to be sensitive to differences in subject positions, which evoke different experiences with the same out-of-school practice.

> What sorts of different subject positions might need to be taken into consideration in your experience?

Another important issue to think about is the impression conveyed by many school numeracy tasks that the mathematical skills and knowledge are not only helpful, but sufficient for success in a range of practices. This impression is also reflected in the tasks used in the regular OECD mathematical literacy survey in the context of the Programme for International Student Assessment (PISA) (see Chapter 5 in this volume). Based on an analysis of the 17 published questions from the 2012 survey (OECD-PISA 2014), Jablonka (2015) noted that the questions framed were concerned with out-of-school practices, but that the experiences students might have gained in these practices were in fact not helpful for solving them. When numeracy or mathematical literacy is developed in cross-curricular projects, there is a much better chance of including and developing both mathematical and other relevant skills and knowledge, and co-ordinating a range of perspectives.

> Which cross-curricular projects, in which mathematics plays a role, did you or would you have liked to see in your own educational development?

Finally, we want to highlight one more area of complexity. There is some agreement that N/ML is based on knowledge that is or should be accessible to all. As more and more sophisticated mathematical procedures are in play through calculation technology, for example, in the form of tax, loan or pension calculators, currency converters, user-defined online polls etc., the question of the depth of mathematics knowledge needed for understanding how the input relates to the output of such technologies emerges. While the knowledge of the constructor is not the same as the one of the user, it appears to be comparatively difficult to develop criteria for sensible functioning of mathematical computation technology without access to some principles of its operation (Gellert and Jablonka 2007). In general, the relation of mathematical literacy to technological literacy needs to be further investigated.

How well do you think schools and teachers are able to meet these goals of using mathematical concepts, procedures, methods and theories in extra-mathematical contexts?

What does all this mean for teachers' professional training and education?

References

ACARA (Australian Curriculum, Assessment and Reporting Authority) (2014) *Foundation to Year 10 Curriculum: Language for Interaction*, http://www.australiancurriculum. edu.au/mathematics/curriculum/f-10?layout=1, accessed 7 May 2017.

Adkins, M. and Noyes, A. (2016) Reassessing advanced level mathematics, *British Educational Research Journal*, 42(1): 93–116

Arcavi, A. (1994) Symbol sense: informal sense making in formal mathematics, *For the Learning of Mathematics*, 14(3): 24–35.

Askew, M. (2015) Numeracy for the 21st century: a commentary, *ZDM Mathematics Education*, 47(4): 707–12.

Australian Securities and Investment Commission (2017a) *MoneyStart Teaching Program*, https://www.moneysmart.gov.au/teaching, accessed 29 April 2017.

Australian Securities and Investment Commission (2017b) *MoneyStart Teaching Resources for Secondary Schools*, https://www.moneysmart.gov.au/teaching/teaching-resources/ teaching-resources-for-secondary-schools, accessed 29 April 2017.

Bessot, A. and Ridgway, J. (eds) (2002) *Education for Mathematics in the Workplace*. Dordrecht: Kluwer Academic Publishers.

Blue, L. (2016) Financial literacy education with aboriginal people: the importance of culture and context, *Financial Planning Research Journal*, 1(1): 91–105.

Blue, L., Grootenboer, P. and Brimble, M. (2014) Financial literacy education in the curriculum: making the grade or missing the mark? *International Review of Economics Education*, 16: 51–62.

Coben, D. and O'Donoghue, J. (2014) Adults learning mathematics, in S. Lerman (ed.) *Encyclopedia of Mathematics Education*. Dordrecht: Springer.

Common Core State Standards Initiative (2010) *Common Core Standards for Mathematics*, http://www.corestandards.org/wp-content/uploads/Math_Standards1.pdf, accessed 28 April 2017.

Council for Economic Education (2017a) *National Standards for Financial Literacy*, http://councilforeconed.org/resource/national-standards-for-financial-literacy/, accessed 29 April 2017.

Council for Economic Education (2017b) Survey of the States, http://councilforeconed.org/ policy-and-advocacy/survey-of-the-states/, accessed 29 April 2017.

D'Ambrosio, U. (2003) The role of mathematics in building a democratic society, in B.L. Madison and L.A. Steen (eds) *Quantitative Literacy: Why Numeracy Matters for Schools and Colleges*. Princeton, NJ: National Council on Education and the Disciplines.

Department of Basic Education (2011) *Mathematical Literacy. National Curriculum Statement. Further Education and Training Phase. Grades 10–12*, http://www.education. gov.za/Curriculum/CurriculumAssessmentPolicyStatements/CAPSFETPhase/ tabid/420/Default.aspx, accessed 28 April 2017.

DfE (Department for Education) (2014a) *The National Curriculum in England: Key Stages 3 and 4 Framework Document*, https://www.gov.uk/government/publications/ national-curriculum-in-england-secondary-curriculum, accessed 28 April 2017.

DfE (Department for Education) (2014b) *Launch of New High Quality Post-16 Maths Qualifications*, press release, 5 December, https://www.gov.uk/government/news/launch-of-new-high-quality-post-16-maths-qualifications, accessed 28 April 2017.

DfE (Department for Education) (2015) *Core Mathematics Qualifications: Technical Guidance*, https://www.gov.uk/government/uploads/system/uploads/attachment_data/file/450294/Core-Maths-Technical-Guidance.pdf, accessed 28 April 2017.

Education, Audiovisual and Culture Executive Agency (2011) *Eurydice. Mathematics in Europe: Common Challenges and National Policies*, http://eacea.ec.europa.eu/education/eurydice/documents/thematic_reports/132EN.pdf, accessed 6 May 2017.

Education Review Office (2013) *Mathematics in Years 4 to 8: Developing a Responsive Curriculum*, http://www.ero.govt.nz/publications/mathematics-in-years-4-to-8-developing-a-responsive-curriculum/, accessed 28 April 2017.

Educational Development Trust (2017) *Core Maths Support Programme England*, https://www.educationdevelopmenttrust.com/en-GB/case-studies/core-maths-support-programme, accessed 28 April 2017.

Fey, L.T. (1990) Quantity, in L.A. Steen (ed.) *On the Shoulders of Giants: New Approaches to Numeracy*. Washington, DC: National Academy Press.

Frankenstein, M. (2010) Developing critical mathematical numeracy through real real-life word problems, in U. Gellert, E. Jablonka and C. Morgan (eds) *Proceedings of the Sixth International Mathematics Education and Society Conference*. Berlin: Freie Universität Berlin.

Gal, I. (2002) Adults' statistical literacy: meanings, components, responsibilities, *International Statistical Review*, 70(1): 1–25.

Geiger, V., Forgasz, H. and Goos, M. (2015) A critical orientation to numeracy across the curriculum, *ZDM: The International Journal on Mathematics Education*, 47(4): 611–24.

Gellert, U. and Jablonka, E. (eds) (2007) *Mathematisation and Demathematisation: Social, Philosophical and Educational Ramifications*. Rotterdam: Sense Publishers.

Hodgen, J. and Marks, R. (2013) *The Employment Equation: Why Our Young People Need More Maths for Today's Jobs*. London: The Sutton Trust.

Hoyles, C., Noss, R., Kent, P. and Bakker, A. (2010) *Improving Mathematics at Work: The Need for Techno-Mathematical Literacies*. London: Routledge.

Jablonka, E. (2003) Mathematical literacy, in A. Bishop, M.A. Clements, C. Keitel, J. Kilpatrick and F.S.K. Leung (eds) *Second International Handbook of Mathematics Education*. Dordrecht: Kluwer Academic Publishers.

Jablonka, E. (2015) The evolvement of numeracy and mathematical literacy curricula and the construction of hierarchies of numerate or mathematically literate subjects, *ZDM Mathematics Education*, 47(4): 599–609.

Lucey, T.A., Agnello, M.F. and Laney, J.D. (2015) *A Critically Compassionate Approach to Financial Literacy*. Rotterdam: Sense Publishers.

McIntosh, A., Reys, B.J. and Reys, R.E. (1992) A proposed framework for examining basic number sense, *For the Learning of Mathematics*, 12(3): 2–8.

Ministry of Education (2007) *The New Zealand Curriculum*, http://nzcurriculum.tki.org.nz/The-New-Zealand-Curriculum, accessed 28 April 2017.

Ministry of Education (2015) *Numeracy Development Projects Number Framework*, http://dev.nzmaths.co.nz/numeracy-development-projects-number-framework, accessed 28 April 2017.

Mullis, I.V.S., Martin, M.O., Beaton, A.E., Gonzalez, E.J., Kelly, D.L. and Smith, T.A. (1998) *Mathematics and Science Achievement in the Final Year of Secondary School: IEA's Third International Mathematics and Science Study (TIMSS)*. Washington, DC: Boston College.

Niss, M. and Jablonka, E. (2014) Mathematical literacy, in S. Lerman (ed.) *Encyclopedia of Mathematics Education*. Dordrecht: Springer Reference.

OECD (Organisation for Economic Co-operation and Development) (2014) *PISA 2012 Results: What Students Know and Can Do. Student Performance in Mathematics, Reading and Science (Volume I)*, revised edition, February 2014, https://www.oecd.org/pisa/keyfindings/pisa-2012-results-volume-I.pdf, accessed 25 March 2017.

Office for Standards in Education, Children's Services and Skills (2011) *Tackling the Challenge of Low Numeracy Skills in Young People and Adults*, https://www.gov.uk/government/publications/tackling-low-numeracy-skills-in-young-people-and-adults, accessed 25 March 2017.

Skovsmose, O. (1994) *Towards a Philosophy of Critical Mathematics Education*. Dordrecht: Kluwer Academic Publishers.

Steen, L.A. (ed.) (2001) *Mathematics and Democracy: The Case for Quantitative Literacy*. Princeton, NJ: Woodrow Wilson Foundation.

Verschaffel, L., Greer, B. and De Corte, E. (eds) (2000) *Making Sense of Word Problems*. Lisse, The Netherlands: Swets and Zeitlinger.

Way, J., Bobis, J., Lamb, J. and Higgins, J. (2016) Researching curriculum, policy and leadership in mathematics education, in K. Makar, S. Dole, J. Visnovska, M. Goos, A. Bennison and K. Fry (eds) *Research in Mathematics Education in Australasia 2012–2015*. Singapore: Springer.

20

The use of data in schools: how can a teacher manage?
BOB BURSTOW

Introduction

This chapter considers one of the more worrying aspects of becoming a teacher – the rise and rise of the use of data in every aspect of school life. Beginning with an overview of the data landscape, the chapter examines some of the key stages in the growth of data collection and interpretation over the last 50 years. The chapter then examines the implications of this for the classroom teacher and makes some suggestions for turning negativity and confusion into a positive aid to teaching. So, if you are in a hurry, turn to the conclusion.

> The key validity concerns are that the test results are being used for too many purposes and that the high stakes nature of some of these distorts teaching and learning.
>
> (Whetton 2009: 132)

The title of this chapter is appropriate. Data does indeed need to be managed, for it is a two-edged sword. Data can provide useful information, but it is also open to misuse and misinterpretation. A single dataset can be put to many uses, some of which may be appropriate and some of which are potentially dangerous. In one context (inside a single school, say) the collected data may prove to be a vital aid to learning – in a second context (within a single country perhaps), it may be distorted or destroyed at the whim of political ideology.

To illustrate what I mean, consider first this, possibly apocryphal, story (adapted from Smith 1998):

> A successful Head of Maths was appointed to her first Assistant Headship, in a different school. This meant that her (somewhat reduced) teaching timetable would be in the Maths department. During one of her visits to the new school, during the summer term, she was told that she would be given the second set in next year's Year 11 'Because with your experience you can give them the shove that they need to get better grades.'

Being a new Assistant Head, most of the rest of her preparation for the new post concerned life and strategic thinking in the Senior Team, but she duly turned up to her Year 11 Maths lessons ready with both attitude and materials, to push the class forward.

They fought back, of course, and complained bitterly about the amount of homework she was setting and the high expectation she had of them all. But she persevered.

Mock exams were set at the end of the autumn term, and the final department meeting before the end of term was an opportunity to compare results across teaching groups. It was broadly as expected: Set 1 had done best, Set 2 was next and Set 3 came third. However, to everybody's surprise, Set 4 ranked the same as Set 2. The Head of Department turned to the Assistant Head and congratulated her – while she took a while to realize that she had never been informed of the change in her timetable. For this term she had been teaching Set 4 as if they were Set 2 – and to very good effect.

Sadly, this story does not have a happy ending. Once the Assistant Head knew that she was actually teaching Set 4 and not Set 2 (and Set 4 knew that she knew) their performance slowly slipped. By the end of the year they were settled where they 'should be', between Set 3 and Set 5 in their final results.

Pause for thought

Consider your own experience as a teacher.

- Have you ever prejudged a pupil based on staffroom gossip or poor or possibly irrelevant information?
- What might you do to avoid emulating the teacher in this story?

This may well be a fable, but it has been reportedly quite usual to hear teachers in schools who draw their pupil population from disadvantaged estates talk in terms of: 'But what can you expect from children from this sort of background?' How a teacher selects from all the data they have access to and how they then use that data really do require careful and thoughtful management. To give you another example from recent research, a Head of Modern Foreign Languages, interviewed following some carefully targeted professional development concerning the use of ICT in his subject, noted:

We gave the Year 8 Germans the same test, irrespective of their set. The average mark in the lower group actually reflected their National Curriculum and CATs test scores together. We were proud because we produced a test that actually was meant to fit the bill. Because we thought at one point it might be too difficult for my group and so on and parts of it were. But they could all do something in this Year 8 exam and that was a real eye-opener because it actually matched the grades, very well indeed to the CAT scores. It was an unexpected event. We found in the lower set that *there were a half dozen kids that could easily have been in the higher group and vice versa,* the tail end of the higher group could have been in the lower group.

(cited in Burstow 2017, my emphasis)

Here are a well-meaning set of teachers, in a challenging secondary school, who found themselves faced with errors in their practice following the introduction of a different test – and one that was more reliable, judging by the comparison with the pupils' Cognitive Ability Test (CAT) scores. Before this time, the department had fallen into the lazy habit of equating poor behaviour with poor ability when placing pupils into teaching sets. The account given here describes the moment when, as part of a professional learning intervention, and having developed a computer-based test for their classes, the teachers realized how poor their previous practice had been. An error of at least six pupils in 30 suggests that around one-fifth of each class was incorrectly placed.

In the national context, there is much commentary in the press, using data to fuel their stories. For example:

Ministers urged to tackle league table 'gaming' as study finds schools 'manage out' pupils (Santry 2017, *Times Educational Supplement*, 31 January).

The thinking behind exams is crude and simply out of date (Rose 2016, *Guardian*, 24 January).

Genetics accounts for more than half of variation in exam results (Sample 2013, *Guardian*, 11 December).

League tables misrepresent up to 40 per cent of secondaries (Vaughan 2011, *Times Educational Supplement*, 19 August).

Data is crucial to improvement, academic says (Belgutay 2011, *Times Educational Supplement*, 30 September).

So, on the one hand, doubt is being cast on the reliability of some of the data in the public domain (although there are questions to be asked about the meaning of 'misrepresent' in this article). On the other hand, there is commentary on the implications of the same dataset in the life of a modern school.

In a still wider context, in the world of international data collection, British politicians can apparently change the rules in a way that schools in the country are forbidden to do. The news that, in 2015, the Programme for International Student Assessment (PISA) would introduce a new test of collaborative problem-solving that 'requires a different approach to the education system than a hothouse around the acquisition of knowledge' (Peter Millar, cited in Stewart 2011) led to the Secretary of State announcing that England would not participate in that test. Hardly an option that is open to any head of a state school in this country.

Data, then, is not straightforward. It is slippery. It is asked to perform many different tasks, for which one specific dataset may not necessarily be suited. It also needs to be interpreted – and this insertion of a translation stage raises all the dangers and caveats associated with any departure from an original source. For any departure from the original data means an editing stage, a reduction or 'simplification' of the dataset to improve readability, or understanding, or access – depending on the editor's approach. Just as in photography, video and sound editing, once another individual takes data and samples it, or simplifies it, then it will be changed and some of the original meaning – and the ability to make a reasoned judgement on the new interpretation – will be lost.

One thing is clear, data now occupies a central place in educational planning and in the accountability of schools. How has this situation developed over time? This question will be addressed over the next three sections.

Data collection and use: in the days of paper records

Before 1988, there was no statutory state control of the curriculum, nor was there a national system of statutory testing. Schools and teachers were able to implement a curriculum that they felt met the needs of their students (Wyse and Torrance 2009). This seemingly idyllic existence did have its moments, but also its disadvantages. Hargreaves (2000) discusses the 'autonomous teacher', who may have had the freedom to do as they wanted and to sample and cherry-pick materials from a variety of published courses and well-respected sources (Nuffield Foundation, Schools Council, etc.), but they were also alone, unless they were prepared to give up their own time to go to the local teachers, centre to meet other like-minded teachers of their own subject. The Association for Science Education, and similar groups for other subjects, were and are the much-to-be-applauded survivors of this independent spirit.

This sounds like an ideal time to many. A time of freedom – but also a time of great responsibility, except that few were held to account. For many pupils – and their teachers – the first national measure was the 11+ test. The view was that IQ was fixed although there was research in the 1950s to dispute this (Sampson 1965). The next national assessment would not happen until the public exams at 16 – the O (Ordinary) level and CSE (Certificate of Secondary Education) exams. There were, of course, regular tests and end-of-term exams throughout secondary schools, but these were for internal use only and were occasionally passed on to the parents as part of the written report.

In this self-contained and insulated world, then, it is reasonable to assume that individual teachers might have used data to: formulate classroom student learning goals; analyse data and collaborate in joint action planning; change instruction on the basis of data and develop ownership of data use. How far they actually did this is not recorded. In addition, within an individual classroom, students might also work with teachers in examining and understanding their own data and develop ownership of their own results. They might indeed, but there was little incentive or demand that they should.

Typical data available to teachers at this time is illustrated in Figures 20.1 and 20.2. In both cases the data compares individual pupil performance in one subject against that same student's mean performance in the previous summer's GCSE in

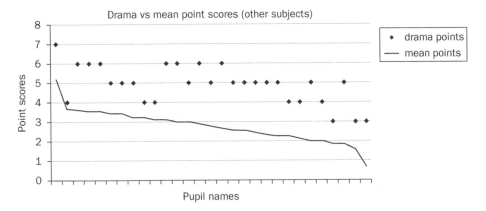

Figure 20.1 Pupil performance (drama)

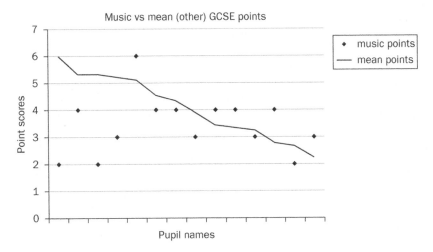

Figure 20.2 Pupil performance (music)

all the other subjects that they had taken. The single line on the graph is a false line, derived by connecting all the student mean scores, whereas the individual plotted points are individual GCSE results. What this was intended to show each head of department was how pupils in their exam group performed compared to their performance in the other subjects they were taking.

So, in Figure 20.1, with all pupil scores in that subject above the line, the Head of Department could be very pleased that their exam group had all performed well against those students' other GCSE subjects. In Figure 20.2, the Head of Music could not be so sanguine, as many of their own exam group had not performed very well as compared with those same pupils' other examination subjects.

Pause for thought

This dataset should raise all sorts of questions of course.

* How reasonable is it to make this comparison at all?
* Should we expect every pupil to perform equally well in all their examinations?
* What about comparing the performance of these cohorts with those in other schools?

These are valid questions. These displays are included to give an example of what sort of things individual schools did to try to evaluate their own performance, to involve the departments in the discussion (apparently by setting one against the other in an implied competitive context – drama here had 'clearly' done better than music, which therefore had questions to answer).

As to comparison with other schools, all that was available were the published GCSE and A level results tables – which were only available months after the exams themselves, and much too late for any school leadership team to factor into their planning for the following year. Anecdotally, in the town where I was a deputy head of a 'school facing challenging circumstances' – as we were later to be described – the significantly better results of our neighbouring schools were, we 'knew', because of their intake. These more popular schools could pick from a very large population of applicants. There was talk – really, just cynical speculation – about whether their results were really that good. Shouldn't highly selective schools be presenting A grades across the board for all their students instead of the 75 per cent A*–C that some published year on year?

All of this was supposition (and some envy). The will, and the means to gain a more informed picture, was not yet apparent at the national level. Two developments were needed.

Data collection and use: some starter factors

The first of these was the introduction of computers into the administrative life of schools. This arguably began with LFM (Local Financial Management) – a subsection of the Local Management in Schools (LMS) initiative in the 1980s (NCSL 2014). To facilitate the increased load on school financial managers, computers were provided, together with training for the relevant staff. It then became apparent that other aspects of school data could be better managed by this technology: attendance records, exam entry and exam results and eventually the whole pupil record dataset.

This development may well have then been a partner to a second starter factor – central government interest. For many years, there had been an annual census of schools, collecting, on paper, basic statistics about each school: its population, by age in lower school, middle school and sixth form and other data concerning the combination of subjects studied, destination of leavers and other items. This was known as 'Form 7' – which added to the tension of every calendar new year of every school in the country. This data was always collected on the third Thursday of every January and was a key factor in deciding how much each school would get in monetary terms. Hence its importance in the minds of every headteacher and of every SLT member who had responsibility for its completion.

What the introduction of computers did was to make this data available to central government, not just for a whole school, but at a much finer-grained individual pupil level. It would now be possible for government statisticians to view the whole of the country's dataset and compare pupils' performance in a forensic manner (Allen 2011; DfE 2016). The paper version was phased out in favour of the PLASC (Pupil Level Annual School Census), which in turn was superseded in 2007 by the School Census, which increased its collection methods to three data sampling points a year.

Some criticisms and commentary on various iterations of data provision by schools

How to interpret all this data was an issue. One of the first people to gain access to the national dataset was David Jesson. He used this as an opportunity to begin to make judgements about the validity of the data he was examining. Consider, for example, the issue of free school meals (for this example and many others, you are recommended to find one of the editions of *The Numbers Game* (Jesson 1999)).

Jesson and his colleague Keith Hedger compared two measures: the percentage of a school's population who were registered for free school meals (FSM), set against the then available GCSE performance measure. Later, Noden (2009) did a similar analysis for the Sutton Trust, using data from the 2005 GCSE cohort. His results are listed in Table 20.1

Pause for thought

Take a moment to look at the pattern you see here – even if (especially if!) you are not a mathematician.

- How would you describe this set of data?
- Is there a clear pattern?

Table 20.1 Percentage of FSM pupils achieving 5+ A*–C grade GCSEs and equivalent

School FSM 'Band' (%)	Pupils on FSM attaining 5+ A*–C (%)
<5	38
5–9	32
9–13	30
13–21	28
21–35	28
35–50	29
>50	37

Source: After Noden (2009: 2).

Table 20.2 Comparing two FSM results ranges

Free School Meal (%)	Lowest GCSE recorded	Highest GCSE recorded
10	24	51
20	25	52
30	21	48
40	19	36
50	20	40
60	21	35
70	22	28

Source: After Jesson (1999: 62).

Table 20.1 shows a 'dish' effect, pupils receiving free school meals are shown to be doing better in schools with both low and high proportions of FSM pupils. Jesson describes his pattern of data as being a 'relatively strong negative association' (Jesson 1999: 62) – but it is the spread or the range of the data that raises many questions as to its validity (that is, is it measuring what it purports to measure?). A clear and consistent negative association would suggest that the higher the percentage of FSM pupils, then the lower the GCSE results would be. The spread (how far the plots vary away from one single neat straight line), however, raises further questions.

Look more closely at Jesson's data (Table 20.2) and take as an example the maximum and minimum marks for the schools with a 50 per cent FSM population. You will see a lowest mark level with 20 on the GCSE scale and a top mark level with 40. Similarly, looking at the 10 per cent set of returns gives a lowest value of 24 on the GCSE scale and a top reading of 51, and so on.

Looking at this sample of data from a slightly different direction shows that most of the range of points of each (between the highest and lowest GCSE scores) are overlapping. That is, between 24 and 40 on the GCSE scores, free school meals are not useful or accurate as a discriminator.

However, this argument has not been understood – or possibly understood but not accepted – by governments and social media. It has been acknowledged for some time that free school meals are only a proxy or shorthand for social class and wealth (Hobbs and Vignoles 2007; Styles 2008; McKinney *et al.* 2012) – so a school reporting a high FSM percentage in its Annual Return will be interpreted as a school with a monetarily and socially poor population. In addition, this false interpretation may be extended to an expectation of performance in examinations – which, as you now know, is not actually the case.

It is worth noting, however, that it is possible to put this same data to a much more positive use. If a school with a 50 per cent FSM population knows this data range, then it should not be satisfied with any GCSE result that is not at the top end of the range. For if other schools can achieve this result with and for their pupils, then surely – the argument goes – so should they. Bear this point in mind for a later section in this chapter.

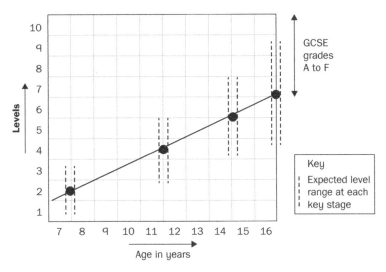

Figure 20.3 Sequence of pupil achievement of levels between ages 7 and 16
Source: Black (1987: 104).

So, if free school meals do not provide a valid measure for comparing school performance, what could? The National Curriculum Task Group for Assessment and Testing (TGAT) (Black 1987) was set up to address exactly this issue. One of the key recommendations of their report was the creation of tests at four points during compulsory schooling, in the years when pupils reached the ages of 7, 11, 14 and 16 (Black 1987: 97). TGAT proposed a relationship between each test to allow for progress to be reported, as in Figure 20.3.

Figure 20.3 shows the mean suggested level for each test (2 at age 7, 4 at age 11, and so on). The dotted lines to either side of each main point show the range of results that might be expected for the whole population. This means that there is considerable overlap between scores at each test level, in the original recommendations. It can also be noted that the range increases with age, from a three-level range at age 7 to a five-level range at age 16. In other words, the original report could see pupils at age 16 who were still performing at the mean level for an 11-year-old. (Some unattributed statistician also suggested that extrapolating these figures back into pre-school years would suggest a zero range – that is all children would be identical – six months before the egg was fertilized. This is a rare example of statistician humour.)

More significantly for all teachers and pupils in England, the TGAT report led to the establishment of the SATs tests, which have become a dominant part of the educational landscape.

Jesson (1999) notes the much improved grouping of data points if GCSE results are compared with a prior attainment test, such as those recommended by TGAT. Table 20.3 shows this (and should be compared to Table 20.2 both for the range of maxima and minima and how much more compact is the grouping, bearing in mind that the same population of schools was used each time – all schools in England and Wales).

Table 20.3 Positive correlation between prior attainment tests and GCSE results (about +0.9)

School prior attainment figure	Lowest GCSE measure recorded	Highest GCSE measure recorded
10	12	30
20	20	34
30	22	35
40	38	46
50	35	50
60	40	56
70	50	58

Source: After Jesson (1999: 62).

This development opened the way for a much more precise examination of pupil and teacher performance over time. Given one key assumption, that the tests remained equally difficult from year to year, it was possible to set expectations for each cohort of pupils, at each level, based on how previous cohorts had performed.

For example, you can plot a scattergram of a set of results (be they class, year group or larger population) and produce a line of best fit (similar to the theoretical one in Figure 20.3). Taking this line (note that this is often a measure of a previous cohort's performance, that is, an indication of potential), a teacher might plot their existing cohort's test scores to see if they were performing better (above the line), worse (below the line) or the same (on the line) as the previous cohort had done. For those who had done better, the term added value was coined – suggesting that the teacher, or the school, had played a part in this improved result. The result for a pupil who had performed worse than expected would have been described as having 'negative value added' which seems a little circuitous. It does, at least, avoid the suggestion that the teacher, or school, had set out with the intention of bringing this pupil's results down – a thought which goes against any reasonable view of teachers and teaching.

It was not long before this value added data was in use, within schools, using not only individual pupil data, but also across whole local authorities, where the dataset of each school had been reduced to a single figure. So, schools as a whole were at one time viewed as having high (or low, or negative) value added. This comparison of schools, within local education authorities, was used, for a while, by school advisors and improvement partners in discussion with senior leaders. It provided evidence for the school's position within the authority – and, unpacked a little, by gender, say, as a crude analytical tool to pinpoint areas of weak performance.

There were issues with this system from a very early stage. Among them was the recognition that to formally test every child in every subject on four separate occasions was an impossible task. It was quickly reduced to a 'core' of maths, English (subdivided into reading and writing) and science. Later on, science was dropped from this core group of subjects.

Then, the fact of publicizing these results in the press almost certainly led to a simplification of the tests themselves – an increased focus on the summative (and hence accountability) aspects of the test, rather than any developmental aspect (Daugherty 1995; Torrance 1995; Wyse and Torrance 2009).

In addition, there were regular comments in the press and by academics concerning:

- Measurement error in marking of work: for example, the questions surrounding KS2 English question setting and marking in 2016 (TES Editorial 2016; Ward 2016).

- Variation in pupil performance: Le Grand (1997) writes of the temptation, or pressure, to 'game' a punitive system – such as the system of national SATs testing in England. Where a school is judged on the success of its pupils over time, the pressure to teach to the test becomes overpowering. Where a school has the operation of tests at both entry and departure, as is the case in the primary sector, then a further manipulation may be possible – to deliberately present poor results for the entry test (Key Stage 1) and then the best possible results on leaving (Key Stage 2) to maximize the public record of progress made by each cohort of pupils. This option is not open to secondary schools, who inherit the entry level test score from their feeder primary schools. Stewart (2015) details evidence for this practice. Knights have indeed become knaves (Le Grand 1997).

- Random cohort variation from year to year: pupil populations are not identical. Their test scores will naturally vary when compared to other cohorts of the same age range in the same school but in different years. To expect year-on-year improvement in test scores is an unrealistic expectation and this is recognized by the inspectorate, who look over at least three-year results before identifying a trend (Ofsted 2012: para. 17).

- Incomplete data collection leading to skewed results: Gorard, Hordosy and Siddiqui (2012) wrote of the possible positive effects for schools of publishing incomplete data. They claimed to have found evidence for this in many of the results for high-ranking state schools. These findings were also echoed in the press by Lipsett (2009) and Mansell (2014), who claimed that around 10,000 pupils were leaving before their GCSE exams and that some schools were showing a 20 per cent drop in their GCSE year cohort, between the January census date and the exam entry. Clearly, if these departing pupils were all likely to have returned poor exam results and all those remaining were to have produced good grades, then this skewed data would show the school in a better light than would have been the case had those pupils remained. Another example of how the system might be 'gamed'. The regret must be, if this is happening, for the waste of time and effort that could have been put into the education of those pupils, rather than aiming to please the inquisitors.

Despite the critics, the use of raw exam results as a comparator held for some time, but doubts were expressed quite early in the process, notably by Goldstein and colleagues (Goldstein and Spiegelhalter 1996; Goldstein and Thoma 1996), concerning the validity of using raw exam data as a comparative measure between schools. Goldstein and Thomas argued that the range of results was a vital component in this comparison. They argued that there would always be an error in the reporting of a school's results, in terms of it being a truly accurate measure of the ability of any given group of pupils. There would, for example, always be a variety of potentially confounding variables (incidence of hay fever in that pupil cohort, say) that would interfere with the validity of the results. They calculated the probable range of results – above and below the reported figure – that each school might have gained, had conditions been different. In effect, from a best possible scenario to a worst. This range they described as a confidence measure. As a consequence, one school could only be distinguished, statistically, from any another if there was no overlap of these ranges of results. The effect of this work was to produce a levelling out of the majority of the schools in the country. There was little, if any, real difference between the majority of the state schools.

Goldsmith (2004) contributed to this argument by suggesting a number of other factors which might well play a part in the difference in performance between schools. These included: the racial and ethnic mix within both the school and the social background (within the sample of 24,000 students from 1000 schools across the USA). One of their findings was that Latino and Blacks' beliefs were more optimistic and pro-school in a segregated environment, especially if those schools also employed minority population teachers. This multilevel modelling, and other examples of a breakdown of the influence of a variety of factors, led to a refinement (or complication, depending on your viewpoint) of the original model which became known, in England, as the Contextual Value Added measure.

This, at its peak, during the first ten years of the twenty-first century, was developed by the government of the day into a seemingly precise set of measures. It was based on a breakdown of national schools data by nine 'characteristics'. They were:

1. Gender – exam results separated by gender across each school's cohort.
2. Special Educational Needs (SEN) – a range of different SEN measures were used here (Figlio and Getzler 2006). A child might be diagnosed as having such a need if they had learning difficulties caused by physical or mental disabilities, emotional or behavioural problems or specific problems with reading, speaking or mathematics (Northern Ireland Department of Education 1997).
3. Ethnicity – based, like all other measures, on the schools' own returns as part of the national school census. This variable was provided by the parents, who had the right not to reply (Gillborn 2010).
4. Free school meals eligibility – remember the earlier discussion, and citations, above.
5. First language – that is, pupils had this as an additional language.
6. Mobility – what proportion of the cohort had arrived at, or left the school at non-standard times? That is, other than arriving in September at age 11 or leaving in July after reaching their 16th birthday (Dobson, Henthorne and Lynas 2000; Cook 2012b).

7. Age – this aimed to cover the recognized difference in exam performance between autumn and summer birth dates in pupil populations (Cook 2012a).

8. In care – the relative attainment of pupils grouped by the nature of their out-of-school principal carer (Carr-Hill 2012).

9. Income Deprivation Affecting Children Index (IDACI) – a postcode-related deprivation measure (Webber and Butler 2007; Stewart and Vaughan 2010). This datum, based on the previous National Census data, was a map, matching postcode to an overall figure for deprivation of the population within that postcode (derived from income, family size and type of housing, for example). The intention was to allow schools to ensure that they were recruiting pupils from across the deprivation spectrum. It did, however, allow schools to make other decisions in practice.

This full dataset was made available to schools through a charity, the Fisher Family Trust (FFT – see www.fft.org.uk for some historical background). Every school – and potentially every teacher of an exam group – could now examine their own cohort and set their performance against a population of 'virtual' neighbours. Choices for comparisons included: schools with broadly similar intakes, schools in the top 20 per cent of exam results and schools within the geographical neighborhood. Thus, schools could set targets based on (apparently) accurate data from previous years, and the targets could in theory be more accurately matched to the ability of the cohort.

For many schools this dataset introduced an element of control over their own destiny and was appreciated by them for this reason. Using FFT data it was possible for senior leaders to mount well-supported arguments to explain their targets for their department and also to explain them, within a context, to parents, governors, inspectors and local government officers.

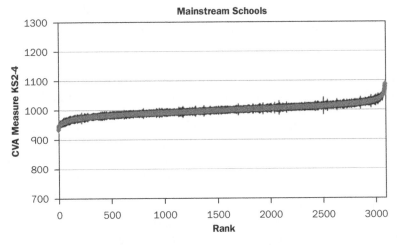

Figure 20.4 Comparison of state school CVA scores: 2005 dataset

Source: After DfE (2010b).

It was not so popular among politicians and the media. Under the CVA system of measures a typical ranking of GCSE performance by school produced the display shown in Figure 20.4.

Now, instead of a clear, steep, single line, which clearly discriminated between schools, there was a fuzzy (thanks in part to Goldstein's confidence measures) and near-horizontal display. It was now possible for a school to drop its score by only a few points and to slide more than 80 places down the ranking. As a result, this removed the clear competitive comparators of raw exam results and, rather than affirming to schools and politicians alike that most schools were actually performing at much the same level, it offered a much less satisfactory presentation of the data from their point of view.

Gorard *et al.* (2012) then demonstrated that poor data collection was a contributor to this fuzziness and flat-lining. Given the way this data is derived, it was only pupils with a complete data record whose data could be plotted. A child who had enrolled at a school at a non-standard time (in Year 10 and age 15, say) would never feature on that school's return, especially if the school had been unable to get a record from that pupil's previous school. Similarly, a pupil who left a school early (before the January of the examination year) would also never feature on that school's record.

Gorard *et al.* (2012) explored CVA scores for all schools (see Figure 20.4) over a number of years and established that:

- All the schools at the top end of the CVA comparative curve were small schools with a highly mobile population.

- Most schools could improve their relative position in CVA enormously by selecting and omitting the least flattering 50 per cent of their pupil scores. This may have happened inadvertently.

- There were no schools at all with consistently and clearly positive CVA that also included at least 99 per cent of their pupils in the calculation.

- There were fewer schools with consistent CVA over five years than would be expected by chance alone.

When CVA was discarded as a national measure, the government of the day gave the reason for doing this as that it had led teachers into a self-fulfilling prophecy mind-set – in other words, that it was 'morally wrong to have an attainment measure which entrenches low aspirations' (DfE 2010a: 6.13). It is interesting to contemplate how this measure became equated with low expectations, rather than a celebration of schools' performance under widely differing circumstances. Readers may care to speculate as to whether it was the apparent over-complication, the lack of immediately obvious discrimination between high-level and low-level performance or other factors that produced this claim.

This view, however, was addressed by Harlen and Deakin-Crick (2002: 40), who noted that 'the introduction of the National Curriculum Tests in England seemed to produce a correlation between low achievement and low self-esteem [which] did not exist prior to the introduction of the tests'. They identified a cause of this as 'a focus on performance outcomes' (Harlen and Deakin Crick 2002: 49) rather than a constructive discussion around the testing process.

Pause for thought

Consider the origins of this outcomes-focused approach.

* Was it schools, the media, the government or other interest groups who were the architects of this interpretation?

In rejecting a multilevel approach, and returning to a reliance on raw exam results, English school education seems to be standing alone. Scottish schools use an online tool called 'Insight' to 'benchmark their performance along several different dimensions' (Scottish Government 2015). There are also similar performance measures in use in Australia, Canada, France, Iceland, Mexico, the Netherlands, Portugal, Sweden and the United States, and in a modified form in Norway, Germany and Spain. In Austria, Denmark, France, Ireland and parts of Belgium, 'official documents stated that national tests should not be used to rank schools' (Wiggins 2016).

Perhaps the Organisation for Economic Cooperation and Development showed some insight when it found that school accountability based on student test results 'can be a powerful tool for changing teacher and school behaviour but it often creates unintended strategic behaviour' (Wiggins 2016)

Data creation: the national testing system in England

So far, we have been considering the interpretation of pupil data. There has been discussion of the factors that might influence the validity of the raw exam results, but so far there has been no consideration of the Standardized Assessment Tests (SATs) themselves. As the mechanism of SATs testing in England developed, so time, and the increasing size of the whole record of results at the different Key Stages, allowed for more measured commentary from the academic research community, rather than the often more excitable press. Although some of the comments from the universities seemed unusually emotive.

Going back to the development of the original SATs tests, following the proposals in the TGAT report (Black 1987), there was a movement away from a teacher-based assessment towards a paper-based externally applied testing system. In addition, there was a cut in the number of levels, down from the TGAT 10-level recommendation to a 7-level range. So, from the start, there was a politically imposed modification to the academically developed proposals. The aim was to produce a centrally administered and nationally moderated set of levels, as opposed to the likely widely varying sets of results that would occur were the testing to be allowed to remain in the hands of the classroom teachers (and which did happen in New Zealand in 2008 (Thrupp 2013)).

> **Pause for thought**
>
> - How important is it to have a standardized set of test results across the country?
> - Has this standardization been successfully achieved?

In a very early commentary, Pollard (1994) found that teachers tended to favour formative, provisional and implicit assessment, but that this ideology was in conflict with the newly arrived national testing which was already changing classroom activities, especially towards the end of each Key Stage as teachers coached and practised for the tests. This was still apparent nearly a decade later, when Harlen and Deakin-Crick (2002) noted at several points in their report, that the high-stakes nature of the testing system resulted in:

- Teachers adopting a teaching style that emphasized transmission teaching of knowledge at the expense of more active and creative learning experiences
- A great deal of time being spent on practice tests, the valuing of test performance and the undervaluing of other student achievements
- Teachers' own assessment becoming summative in function rather than formative.

Even more critical were Webb and Vulliamy (2006) who found that teachers, in their sample, resented the dominance of the national testing system and gave accounts of negative effects on their delivery of the curriculum, as well as stress and pupils' anxiety as consequences of the testing system. They also recorded comments from some senior leaders who identified demotivation of their teaching staff because of the negative effect of performance tables.

So, over time, this combination of government expectation, a continual inspection focused on attainment and a resulting pressure on schools has produced a system which has constrained teaching, frustrated teachers and, according to Richard Vaughan in *The Times Educational Supplement*, misrepresents around 40 per cent of secondary schools (Vaughan 2011).

The government has reacted to this growing body of criticism, in the press as well as from academic writing. As well as the effects on teachers and pupils, there were regular complaints about the reliability of marking (especially of KS2 English). One chosen route was to introduce a range of adjustments, with some of the Key Stage tests being withdrawn or changed. For example, Key Stage 3 tests ceased in 2010, science testing at Key Stage 2 became teacher-assessed for most schools in 2016.

In 2016, a much wider-ranging set of changes were introduced. These measures included the following:

- *Progress 8:* This measure seemed designed to address many of the concerns that have been expressed about raw exam results as a sole measure. Better surely to measure the entry level and exit level of each pupil, in a selection of eight subjects, and from that to derive a measure of their progress through the system. In this simple form, schools could show how well they educate pupils across the whole ability range – using the nationally agreed measures. However, it is not as straightforward as that. The calculation of the figure is not straightforward, being complex and constrained by which subjects are ruled as acceptable contributors to the result. Initial reporting suggests that some schools are finding that because Progress 8 scores are determined by certain subjects only (predominantly English Baccalaureate subjects) that pupils' curriculum choices are being narrowed down to traditional academic GCSEs over creative subjects (Wiggins 2016).

- *Life after levels*: Apparently to avoid the labelling of children as they move between one school and the next – especially from primary to secondary – the SATs levels are no longer being made available to the pupils' new school. Instead, schools will be presented with a score, for each 11-year-old pupil, where a score of 100 will represent the 'national standard'. In the early years of this system, there will be little meaning to be derived from these scores. As a result, secondary schools are returning to other tests (such as the Cognitive Assessment Tests (CATs)) to gain a baseline measure from which to begin their Progress 8 dataset. This measure has also added to the confusion surrounding the calculation of the Progress 8 score.

- *GCSE regrading*: At the same time as both the above measures, the GCSE grading system is being reviewed. In 2016, and for two or three years following, all subjects will transfer from an A*–G grading system to a 9–1 system (the measures are from highest to lowest in both cases). So, the direction of travel along the grading system is reversed, this allows, it is to be supposed, for extra levels to be added at the top end, should further discrimination be needed – it becomes easy to add a level 10 in this new system rather than the confusion of A**, and so on. However, it has been made clear to schools that there is not intended to be any direct mapping of the old system onto the new. Schools, as a result, are currently in a most uncertain place, in terms of their exam preparation. *The Times Education Supplement* suggests that this is 'one policy that even Gove's most ardent supporters still probably wish he had rejected' (Richmond 2016). The skills of the experienced teacher, in predicting their pupils' performance in future public exams, will need to be relearned. This does meet a need, expressed by university admissions bodies, to provide greater discrimination at the top end of the exam grades, but to introduce this at the same time as Progress 8 and the A level changes, considered below, is a unique event. All other major changes in the testing system in England have been phased in over time.

- *Post-16 examination reform*: As mentioned above, at the same time, the existing post-16 system has been refined, so that the one-year AS qualification has now been decoupled from the two-year A level. In other words, pupils can no longer convert their one-year results into a more significant two-year grade with just an extra year's work. What this will mean for curricula, timetables and university entrance requirements remains to be seen, but it may well distract both pupils and teachers from their supposed primary focus on the best possible education for the pupils. It also has the potential for producing an unexpected outcome: while one aim was to reduce the exam overload in post-16 education, it has removed the AS results as a valued indicator of A level performance for the university interview boards. As a result there has been an '*alarming number of university entrance tests* listed on the UCAS website, as university departments decide that they need more concrete evidence than GCSE grades and teacher predictions' (Dunford 2016).

Pause for thought

Consider the issues for a highly selective secondary school working within this performance model.

- What are the issues for it if it wishes to retain a high ranking in a future league table?

At the time of writing (2017) the effects of some of these measures are impossible to determine, as they are only just being implemented. To put this sort of information into a book seems a little strange, but the unique conditions being faced by teachers at this time should be recorded. Readers in future years are urged to extend their understanding of the effects of these measures by a reading of the lay media and the academic journals, as well as inspection of summary documents that will become available.

For the teacher in the classroom, all of this presents a very real problem. This is not for a moment to deny the importance of data to the teacher, for data is crucial. The question is deciding on what other school data is needed (behavior and equity for example) to provide a more nuanced overall measure.

Data collection and use: what should the classroom teacher do?

It may well be concluded from the chapter so far that the understanding and treatment of data are open to question. A simplistic approach, such as reducing the complexity of an individual child's learning to a single data item, cannot give anything more than a simplistic answer. It is important to realize that there are other ways of looking at the same data. For example:

- 80 per cent of all schools show value added significantly higher than might be expected for one or more groups.
- 50 per cent of all schools have at least one subject which would put them in the top 20 per cent nationally (in the subject concerned).
- Struggling and failing schools are not inevitably staffed by struggling and failing teachers.

(Reynolds 2010: 164)

Of overriding importance is the idea that, while all the various data items described above are not necessarily useful at a national level, when they are compressed into one measure for a whole school, it can be a more precise tool when applied within a single school and within a single classroom. Putting this another way, the errors (as described by Gorard *et al.* 2012) cast doubt on the validity of some of the nationally published results, but reflecting a single school's results back on itself can reveal interesting comparisons between teachers of the same pupils and lead to constructive learning conversations – a more precise version of the crude comparative figures that started this chapter (Figures 20.1 and 20.2).

The classroom teacher, then, should never lose sight of the importance of the individual pupil. The more the teacher understands the pupil, the more insight they have into each of their pupil's mind and background, the better their chance of finding the best way of facilitating the learning of every individual. This is not just an ideal. Colleagues who are still classroom teachers and senior staff, and who were consulted for this section of the chapter, were unanimous in this. They all said that teachers should focus on the children as individuals. They should use the available data to inform the future direction of their work. They should use the data not to confirm a negative prejudice about possible performance but to positively show how to enable and facilitate that individual's best possible outcomes (which, note, might not exclusively be examination results).

Concluding thoughts

To summarize, it is possible to use the same data to apparently 'prove' three very different conclusions:

1. The raw results approach: schools with better exam results are better. Therefore, schools do make a difference.
2. The demographic approach: successful schools all have a 'good' socioeconomic mix. Therefore, schools do *not* make a difference.
3. The contextual approach: schools make very little difference, but using the same CVA data there may be up to a four-fold difference between pupil performance in different subjects and classrooms. Teachers are revealed as the critical factor at this level (Wiliam 2008).

We should conclude, therefore, that no teacher should ever forget that the pupils in their class are individuals: human, alive and unique. They are the reason that a teacher is in their classroom. It is the pupils who only get one chance at their education. To select just a few aspects of their whole complexity is to reduce their significance and to deny their individuality. However, to use, with understanding, the rich datasets that are now available, to learn to apply that data to the conundrum that is the effective education of every individual pupil, is potentially to improve both the teacher's insight and their pupils' eventual success.

References

Allen, R. (2011) *National Pupil Database: wiki*. London: Institute of Education, https://nationalpupildatabase.wikispaces.com/, accessed 25 October 2016.

Belgutay, J. (2011) Data is crucial to improvement, academic says. *Times Educational Supplement*, 30 September 2011.

Black, P. (1987) *National Curriculum Task Group on Assessment and Testing: A Report*. London: DfES.

Burstow, B. (2017) *Effective Teacher Development*. London: Bloomsbury.

Carr-Hill, R. (2012) Finding and then counting out-of-school children, *Compare: A Journal of Comparative and International Education*. 42 (2): 187–212.

Cook, C. (2012a) Birthdays and school grades, *Financial Times*, 1 March.

Cook, C. (2012b) The social mobility challenge for school reformers, *Financial Times*, 22 February.

Daugherty, R. (1995) *National Curriculum Assessment: A Review of Policy, 1987–1994*. Hove: Psychology Press.

DfE (Department for Education) (2010a) *The Importance of Teaching: The Schools White Paper 2010*. London: TSO.

DfE (Department for Education) (2010b) *School Performance Tables*, http://www.education.gov.uk/schools/performance/archive/schools_10/s3.shtml, accessed 26 April 2017.

DfE (Department for Education) (2016) School Census, unpublished. London: DfE, https://data.gov.uk/dataset/school-census, accessed 25 October 2016.

Dobson, J., Henthorne, K. and Lynas, Z. (2000) *Pupil Mobility in Schools: Final Report*. London: University College London.

Dunford, J. (2016) Decoupling AS and A level will inevitably prove to be a terrible mistake, *Times Educational Supplement*, 4 May.

Figlio, D.N. and Getzler, L.S. (2006) Accountability, ability and disability: gaming the system? *Advances in Applied Microeconomics*, 14: 35–49.

Gillborn, D. (2010) The colour of numbers: surveys, statistics and deficit-thinking about race and class, *Journal of Education Policy*, 25: 253–76.

Goldsmith, P.A. (2004) Schools' racial mix, students' optimism, and the black-white and Latino-white achievement gaps, *Sociology of Education*, 77: 129–47.

Goldstein, G. and Spiegelhalter, D. (1996) League tables and their limitations: statistical issues in comparisons of institutional performance, *Journal of the Royal Statistical Society. Series A (Statistics in Society)*, 150: 385–443.

Goldstein, G. and Thomas, S. (1996) Using examination results as indicators of school and college performance, *Journal of the Royal Statistical Society. Series A (Statistics in Society)*, 159: 149–63.

Gorard, S., Hordosy, R. and Siddiqui, N. (2012) How unstable are 'school effects' assessed by a value-added technique? *International Education Studies*, 6.

Hargreaves, A. (2000) Four ages of professionalism and professional learning, *Teachers and Teaching: Theory and Practice*, 6: 151–82.

Harlen, W. and Deakin Crick, R. (2002) A systematic review of the impact of summative assessment and tests on students' motivation for learning, *Research Evidence in Education Library*. London: Institute of Education.

Hobbs, G. and Vignoles, A. (2007) *Is Free School Meal Status a Valid Proxy for Socio-Economic Status (in Schools Research)?* London: LSE, Centre for the Economics of Education.

Jesson, D. (1999) *The Numbers Game: The Use of Assessment Data in Primary and Secondary Schools*. London: LSE, Centre for Performance Evaluation and Resource Management.

Le Grand, J. (1997) Knights, knaves or pawns? Human behaviour and social policy, *Journal of Social Policy*, 26: 149–69.

Lipsett, A. (2009) Thousands leaving school before GCSEs, *Guardian*, 23 February.

Mansell, W. (2014) The strange case of the vanishing GCSE pupils, *Guardian*, 21 January.

McKinney, S., Hall, S., Lowden, K., Mcclung, M. and Cameron, L. (2012) The relationship between poverty and deprivation, educational attainment and positive school leaver destinations in Glasgow secondary schools, *Scottish Educational Review*, 44: 33–45.

NCSL (National College) (2014) *CSBM Managing School Finances: Overview and Introduction*, https://www.nationalcollege.org.uk/transfer/open/csbm-managing-school-finances/csbm-5f-s1/csbm-5f-s1-t3.html, accessed 25 October 2016.

Noden, P. (2009) *Attainment Gaps Between Pupils in the Most Deprived and Advantaged Schools*. London: Sutton Trust, http://www.suttontrust.com/wp-content/uploads/2009/05/Attainment_deprived_schools_full.pdf, accessed 25 April 2017.

Northern Ireland Department of Education (1997) *Special Educational Needs: A Guide for Parents*. Belfast: Government of Northern Ireland.

Ofsted (2012) *Inspection 2012: Proposals for Inspection Arrangements for Maintained Schools and Academies from January 2012: For Consultation*. London: Ofsted.

Pollard, A. (1994) *Changing English Primary Schools? The Impact of the National Curriculum and Assessment*. London: Cassell.

Reynolds, D. (2010) *Failure Free Education? The Past, Present and Future of School Effectiveness and School Improvement*. London: Routledge.

Richmond, T. (2016) Will new GCSE grades be popular? The odds are 9-1, *Times Educational Supplement*, 10 July.

Rose, T. (2016) Why do we trust exam results? *Guardian*, 24 January.

Sample, I. (2012) Genetics accounts for more than half of variation in exam results, *Guardian*, 11 December.

Sampson, A. (1965) *Anatomy of Britain Today*. London: Hodder and Stoughton.

Santry, C. (2017) Ministers urged to tackle league table 'gaming' as study finds schools 'manage out' pupils, *Times Educational Supplement*, 31 January.

Scottish Government (2015) *Education and Training, Schools, Insight: Key Features*, http://www.gov.scot/Topics/Education/Schools/curriculum/seniorphasebenchmarking/KeyFeatures, accessed 16 February 2017.

Smith, A. (1998) *Accelerated Learning in Practice: Brain-Based Methods for Accelerating Motivation and Achievement*. Bodmin: MPG Books.

Stewart, W. (2011) Mr Gove fixes PISA's new problems by ignoring them, *Times Educational Supplement*, 7 October.

Stewart, W. (2015) Are schools altering results – to make them look worse? *Times Educational Supplement*, 6 March 2015.

Stewart, W. and Vaughan, R. (2010) Tories would ditch pupil deprivation from tables, *Times Educational Supplement*, 26 March.

Styles, B. (2008) Moving on from free school meals: national census data can describe the socio-economic background of the intake of each school in England, *Educational Research*, 50: 41–53.

TES Editorial (2016) Why the KS2 Sats are flawed. *Times Educational Supplement*, 29 April.

Thrupp, M. (2013) National standards comparisons impossible, *NZ Herald Tribune*, http://www.nzherald.co.nz/opinion/news/article.cfm?c_id=466andobjectid=10884899, accessed 16 February 2017.

Torrance, H. (1995) *Evaluating Authentic Assessment: Problems and Possibilities in New Approaches to Assessment*. Milton Keynes: Open University Press.

Vaughan, R. (2011) League tables 'misrepresent up to 40 per cent of secondaries', *Times Educational Supplement*, 19 August.

Ward, H. (2016) Exclusive: 'Deadening, difficult and unfair' – the experts' verdicts on this year's Sats. *Times Educational Supplement*, 27 May.

Webb, R. and Vulliamy, G. (2006) Coming full circle? The impact of New Labour's education policies on primary school teachers' work, *Journal of Education Policy*, 17(1).

Webber, R. and Butler, T. (2007) Classifying pupils by where they live: how well does this predict variations in their GCSE results? *Urban Studies*, 44: 1229–54.

Whetton, C. (2009) National Curriculum assessment in England: how well has it worked? Perspectives from the UK, Europe and beyond, *Educational Research*, 51: 131–5.

Wiggins, K. (2016) GCSE results day: how Progress 8 works, *Times Educational Supplement*, 26 June.

Wiliam, D. (2008) *Tight but Loose: A Conceptual Framework for Thinking about School Reform at Scale*. London: Kings College.

Wyse, D. and Torrance, H. (2009) The development and consequences of National Curriculum assessment for primary education in England, *Educational Research*, 51: 213–28.

21

Schools and the safeguarding agenda
JENNY DRISCOLL

Introduction

Safeguarding children is a complex and emotionally demanding statutory responsibility for everyone working in schools. Media reports of historical child maltreatment scandals (including that concerning the celebrity DJ Jimmy Savile) and contemporary cases (such as child sexual exploitation groups in Rotherham (Jay 2014)) have tended to encourage a sense of a system in perpetual crisis. The numbers of children who are the subject of a protection plan and received into state care have risen significantly since the death of Baby Peter Connelly in 2007 (DfE/NS 2016a; 2016b). But while child protection services are undoubtedly severely stretched, it is important to acknowledge that, to some extent, the system may be regarded as a victim of its own success. Increases in confirmed cases of child maltreatment are thought to reflect greater awareness and willingness to take action (Bentley *et al.* 2016) among professionals working with children, who are now more likely to identify children at risk of harm and refer their concerns to children's social care services (Gardner and Brandon 2009).

It is extremely difficult to be confident about statistics in this arena because of changes in definitions and thresholds for intervention as well as challenges in interpreting whether changes in reporting represent genuine increases in prevalence or improved recognition of and responses to child maltreatment. However, there are indications that legislation and policy have had some positive effect. In particular, statistics show falls in child homicides in England, Scotland and Northern Ireland in the decade to 2014/15 and in deaths of children aged 14 or under from assault, neglect or where the cause is undetermined but may have been suicide or maltreatment in all four nations (Bentley *et al.* 2016). Some researchers consider that there has been a significant overall drop in child killings since the 1970s (Pritchard and Williams 2010). But the changing social context in which children are growing up appears concurrently to be creating new challenges. There has been a recent increase in suicides among 15–19-year-olds in the UK, as well as apparent rises in a range of online offences against children and emerging recognition of issues such as child trafficking (Bentley *et al.* 2016). In addition, the scope of safeguarding has been broadened in recent years to include protecting children and young people from the risk of radicalization, extending professional responsibilities into a sensitive and contentious area.

It is therefore essential that teachers are well-equipped and confident in undertaking their role in safeguarding children. The harm inflicted by child maltreatment is often devastating in both childhood and adult life but difficult to heal: consequently, there is a strong moral and financial imperative in favour of prevention and early intervention (Munro 2011). Of all professional groups working with children, teachers are particularly well placed to notice changes in the appearance, behaviour or attainment of children which may indicate cause for concern, and to prevent the escalation of problems (DfE 2016). School staff are also in a position to develop relationships of trust and respect with children and young people which may empower those experiencing difficulties to turn to them for help and support (Raymond 2013). The relative importance of schools and education services in the identification of child maltreatment is evident from data on the sources of referrals to children's social care services (Figure 21.1). The significance of safeguarding in the daily work of schools is reflected in a *Times Education Supplement* (*TES*) survey of more than 1,200 head teachers, which found that around two-thirds of teachers had reported safeguarding concerns within the previous 12 months (Morrison 2014).

This chapter first explains the term 'child maltreatment' and considers its prevalence before briefly summarizing the lifetime effects of child abuse and neglect. It then sets out the statutory framework, in which high-risk 'child protection' work is embedded in a wider safeguarding policy intended to promote child welfare and prevent maltreatment. Professional duties at each level of concern are highlighted and particular issues that have come to the fore in recent years are addressed, with particular attention to the anti-radicalization 'Prevent' strategy.

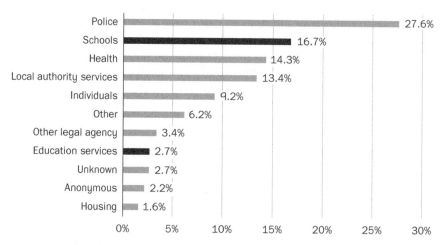

Figure 21.1 Sources of referrals to Children's Social Care Services SFR52-2016, p.6 (total 621,470)

Finally, current challenges facing staff in schools are discussed in the context of an age of austerity, managerialism and performativity. Key points include being alert to the possibility of maltreatment; the importance of a culture of listening to children and of being sensitive to unspoken indicators of need or distress; and the complexity and sensitivity of decision-making in child protection cases.

Although the issues and the principles are broadly the same in all four nations of the UK, child protection is a devolved area of government. In England, the principal piece of legislation is the Children Act 1989, with additional provisions in the Children Act 2004, the Safeguarding Vulnerable Groups Act 2006, the Children and Families Act 2014, and the Children and Social Work Act 2017. Statutory guidance is primarily to be found in *Working Together to Safeguard Children* (HM Government 2015c) and *Keeping Children Safe in Education* (KCSiE) (DfE 2016).[1] Where legislation or statutory guidance is referred to in this chapter, it relates to England and to some extent Wales. In Wales, although the Children Acts 1989 and 2004 and the Safeguarding Vulnerable Groups Act 2006 apply, there is additional legislation in the Social Services and Well-being (Wales) Act 2014 and the guidance is set out in the *All Wales Child Protection Procedures* (All Wales Child Protection Procedures Review Group (AWCPPRG) 2008). In Scotland, the primary legislative provisions are to be found in the Children (Scotland) Act 1995; the Protection of Vulnerable Groups (Scotland) Act 2007; and the Children and Young People (Scotland) Act 2014. These are complemented by the *National Guidance for Child Protection in Scotland* (Scottish Government 2014). In Northern Ireland, the law is set out in the Children (Northern Ireland) Order 1995, and the overarching policy framework in *Co-operating to Safeguard Children and Young People in Northern Ireland* (Department for Health, Social Services and Public Safety 2016).

The nature and prevalence of child maltreatment

Defining child maltreatment

Four categories of child maltreatment are universally identified: physical abuse, emotional (or psychological) abuse, sexual abuse, and neglect. These terms are defined in paragraphs 35–40 of KCSiE (DfE 2016). Under these definitions, both neglect and emotional abuse require maltreatment or a failure to meet a child's needs that is 'persistent' (paras. 38, 40) and '[s]ome level of emotional abuse is involved in all types of maltreatment of a child, though it may occur alone' (para. 38). The current guidance highlights some of the issues that are of particular contemporary concern, including the abuse (particularly the sexual abuse) of children by other children or young people; bullying and cyber-bullying as types of emotional abuse; and non-contact activities or 'grooming' a child in preparation for further sexual abuse, including through the Internet. The guidance stresses that a child who is being sexually abused may not be aware of that fact, which is a significant consideration in relation to disclosure. Paragraph 43 of the guidance sets out a list of issues on which further guidance may be required. These include some more recently identified forms of maltreatment, such as child sexual exploitation (CSE), faith abuse, female genital mutilation (FGM), forced marriage, gang violence, gender-based violence, hate, sexting and child trafficking. A detailed exploration of the nature of these behaviours is beyond the scope of this chapter but further information is included in Annex A of KCSiE (DfE 2016).

It is also important to be aware of the contexts in which child maltreatment may occur. These may be considered under three broad categories: intra-familial, extra-familial and peer-to-peer abuse. While legislation was originally aimed at maltreatment within the family, in the 1990s attention refocused on abuse in institutional and community settings and the notion of the paedophile (Parton 2016). In the twenty-first century, the rise of the Internet, with its attendant opportunities and threats in 'meeting' strangers online and access to and exchange of pornographic material, is rapidly changing the face of child protection. All three contexts may give rise to a criminal investigation and potentially proceedings. Allegations against school staff are taken extremely seriously because abuse constitutes a breach of the duty of care owed by school staff to students. In intra-familial cases, family proceedings under the Children Act 1989 for the removal of a child from their home may be considered and be instituted concurrently with criminal proceedings where appropriate.

The prevalence of child maltreatment

Arguably, child maltreatment is to an extent a socially constructed phenomenon in that the understanding and classification of the concept vary over time and across cultures: for example, attitudes to corporal punishment have changed dramatically in the last few decades. In common with most developed countries, the UK has seen a huge increase in referrals to children's services in the last 30 years (Lonne et al. 2009). Resource issues have led to increased pressure on children's social care services and higher thresholds for referrals and services (Sidebotham et al. 2016), leaving front-line professionals with the burden of managing some cases of significant concern with limited support from social services.

While it is extremely hard to assess the prevalence of child maltreatment given the difficulties outlined above, Gilbert et al. (2009), in a review of literature from the USA and Europe, concluded that official statistics in relation to substantiated allegations of child maltreatment only show around a tenth of cases. They estimated that between 4 and 16 per cent of children are physically abused; around one in ten suffers neglect or psychological abuse; and 5–10 per cent of girls and 1–5 per cent of boys suffer penetrative sexual abuse. In a large-scale UK study, Radford et al. (2013) found that almost 22 per cent of 11–17-year-olds had experienced at least one incident of parental or caregiver maltreatment in their childhood. Twenty per cent of girls aged 15 reported sexual victimization in the previous year, and perpetrators were aged under 18 in nearly two-thirds of childhood contact sexual abuse. The survey of 18–24-year-olds replicated methodology used a decade earlier and comparison suggests that rates of some forms of child maltreatment, particularly severe physical and sexual abuse, have fallen in the intervening years. In the current economic climate, it is also important to be aware of the stress placed on parents by poverty: children who are taken into care tend to be from poorer homes, particularly in cases of emotional abuse and neglect (Neale and Lopez 2017).

The impact of child maltreatment on child and adult functioning

Child maltreatment is associated with significant physical and mental health difficulties across the life-course, such as problematic, aggressive or offending behaviour; substance misuse; obesity and eating disorders (Gilbert *et al.* 2009). In younger children, self-awareness and the ability to attend to their own wishes and feelings may be affected by sustained hypervigilance, while older children may develop severely negative self-perceptions (Harter 2012). Children subjected to lengthy periods of maltreatment may display aggressive behaviour, certain memory problems and symptoms of attention deficit hyperactivity disorder (ADHD) (Glaser 2000). Recurrent episodes of maltreatment and suffering several types of maltreatment aggravate the psychological effects, which are likely to continue into adulthood (Gilbert *et al.* 2009).

Maltreated children are considerably more likely to feel depressed and/or suicidal than others, especially if they have been physically abused (Dunn *et al.* 2013). Physical abuse is also particularly associated with lower educational performance as well as direct physical injury (Gilbert *et al.* 2009). Experience of childhood sexual abuse is associated with poor mental and physical health problems, sexually risky conduct, post-traumatic stress disorder (PTSD) symptoms and unemployment (Fergusson, McLeod and Horwood 2013). Young people's social functioning may be affected by emotional and social detachment (McLean *et al.* 2013), which may negatively impact on their relationships in the future (Harter 2012). Since emotional abuse takes a number of different forms and is often part of a wider pattern of maltreatment, distinguishing its particular impact is challenging, but it is associated with heightened risks of psychological distress, alcohol abuse and suicide attempts in adolescence (Tanaka *et al.* 2011), and poorer life satisfaction and predisposition to illness in adulthood (Gavin 2011).

While the effects of neglect have been less well researched, it seems to be potentially as harmful as other forms of maltreatment (Gilbert *et al.* 2009). Severe neglect in early childhood is associated with slower growth and shorter stature in adulthood (Denholm, Power and Li 2013). Cognitive function may be irrevocably affected by poor stimulation during sensitive periods of brain development, while hypervigilance or aggressive behaviour may emerge later in life where conditions such as depression impact on a parent's ability to provide sufficient sensitivity in interacting with very young children (Glaser 2000).

The likely prevalence of child maltreatment, coupled with the enormous harm it inflicts both during childhood and beyond, prompts statutory guidance to advise school staff to 'maintain an attitude of "it could happen here"' (DfE 2016: para. 19). It also justifies the web of responsibilities imposed on professionals in this arena, considered in the following section.

The statutory framework: child protection within a child welfare framework

The New Labour government (1997–2010) promoted use of the term *safeguarding* in preference to *child protection* to signal a shift in policy intended to embed responses to children suffering or at risk of harm (the preserve of social work) within a broader framework of professional support for families. Although ostensibly a response to the Laming Review (Laming 2003) following the death of Victoria Climbié, which pointed to failures in multi-agency working in the protection of children, it was also motivated by the desire to reduce the rates of school drop-out, teenage pregnancy, anti-social behaviour and youth crime (Parton 2006). Under the Children Act 2004 s10, local children's services authorities must make arrangements to co-operate with 'relevant partners' to improve the well-being of children in their area. All partners – including schools, colleges and academies (added through the Apprenticeships, Skills, Children and Learning Act 2009) – have a duty to co-operate with children's services in these arrangements.

This broad duty is also directly imposed on schools. The Education Act 2002 s175 requires school governing bodies to ensure that their functions are exercised with 'a view to safeguarding and promoting the welfare' of children at the school, and a similar duty is imposed on independent schools and academies (including free schools) by regulations made under s157. 'Children' refers to people under the age of 18 (Children Act 1989 s105; DfE 2016: para. 5). The Teachers' Standards (DfE 2011: 14) reinforce the requirement that teachers have 'regard for the need to safeguard pupils' well-being', but the duty is wider and applies to all staff in schools and colleges. Following the Munro Review (Munro 2011), two key principles apply to safeguarding arrangements in all agencies working with children and families: first, that safeguarding is 'everyone's responsibility', and second, that professionals' approach to safeguarding should be 'child-centred' (DfE 2016: para. 2). This concept is interpreted in KCSiE (DfE 2016) as meaning that professionals 'should consider, at all times, what is in the best interests of the child' (para. 2), while in relation to effective services, it is said to imply that services 'should be based on a clear understanding of the needs and views of children' (HM Government 2015c: para. 14). Ascertaining the best interests of a child in the light of their needs and views may pose a significant challenge in the context of safeguarding work, for example, where the needs of parents distract professionals from the experience of the child.

KCSiE defines:

> safeguarding and promoting the welfare of children as: protecting children from maltreatment; preventing impairment of children's health or development; ensuring that children grow up in circumstances consistent with the provision of safe and effective care; and taking action to enable all children to have the best outcomes.

> (DfE 2016: para. 4)

This continuum of concern is reflected in the Ofsted inspection framework. *The School Inspection Handbook* (Ofsted 2016: 42) descriptor for 'outstanding' in this area includes:

> Leaders and managers have created a culture of vigilance where pupils' welfare is actively promoted. Pupils are listened to and feel safe. Staff are trained to identify when a pupil may be at risk of neglect, abuse or exploitation and they

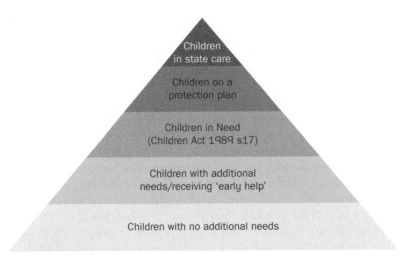

Figure 21.2 Access to services/intervention according to level of need or risk

report their concerns. Leaders and staff work effectively with external partners to support pupils who are at risk or who are the subject of a multi-agency plan.

The continuum of needs or intervention may be depicted by a pyramid model, which maps onto children's legal status in terms of the support which they may be able to access or the extent to which state intervention into family life may be considered justified (see Figure 21.2). The following sections briefly consider the four upper levels of the pyramid, and the implications of children's status for professionals working with children in those groups, but it is important to recognize that children may move up and down the layers of the pyramid over time in response to events and/or the provision of services, sometimes rapidly.

Early help

KCSiE (DfE 2016: para. 9) expects that '[a]ll school and college staff should be prepared to identify children who may benefit from early help', a term which refers to the stage of the problem, not the age of child. *Working Together* (HM Government 2015c) suggests that professionals should be particularly alert to the potential needs of children: with disabilities or Special Educational Needs; exhibiting signs that they may be involved in anti-social or criminal behaviour; in families where there are issues such as substance abuse, adult mental health problems, or domestic violence; showing early signs of abuse and/or neglect; and of young carers. Possible requirements for early help should be discussed initially with the school's Designated Safeguarding Lead (DSL), who is responsible for supporting staff in their safeguarding duties; co-ordinating support for children within the school; and liaising with other agencies, including children's services, health and the police. Local agencies are expected to make arrangements for the assessment of early help needs, which should be carried out by a lead professional identified in consultation with the child and their family (HM Government 2015c). Teachers are often well placed to take on a lead professional role, in which case they are required to access services for the child and/or their family in accordance with the assessment, but it is also critical, should concerns escalate, that they are aware of local thresholds for criteria for referral to children's services under s17 (Children in Need) or s47 (where there is 'reasonable cause to suspect a child is suffering or likely to suffer significant harm') of the Children Act 1989. All staff need to be aware of the process for making a referral to children's services: this should wherever possible be undertaken through the DSL, but any member of staff may make a referral. The non-statutory guidance *What to Do If You're Worried a Child Is Being Abused* (HM Government 2015b) stresses that '[i]f you have concerns about the safety or welfare of a child and feel they are not being acted upon by your manager or named/designated safeguarding lead, it is your responsibility to take action' (para. 32). Additionally, all safeguarding concerns, discussions and decisions should be recorded in writing together with the reasons for reaching any decisions made (DfE 2016: para. 29).

Children in need

Children in need comprise those who are (1) 'unlikely to achieve or maintain, or to have the opportunity of achieving or maintaining, a reasonable standard of health or development without the provision of services by a local authority', or (2) whose 'health or development is likely to be significantly impaired, or further impaired, without the provision of such services'; or (3) who are disabled (Children Act 1989 s17(10)). Children who appear to meet this definition as interpreted in the Local Safeguarding Children Board's local criteria should be referred to children's services in order for them to access social care services following a statutory assessment. If the referral is not accepted, and/or staff consider that the child's situation is not improving, they should press for re-consideration (DfE 2016: 8/para. 24).

Children at risk of harm

There is accessible advice on responding to child protection concerns in *What to Do If You're Worried a Child Is Being Abused* (HM Government 2015b). Professionals are expected to be alert to signs that a child may be being maltreated, to question the conduct of children and parents or carers (where appropriate) and be wary of accepting accounts at face value. *What to Do* provides a list of *potential* warning signs that a child is being maltreated (p. 6/para. 8), which should trigger further consideration, but the age and developmental stage of the child as well as the context and history may also be relevant. Analysis of serious case reviews (SCRs) has identified a 'toxic trio' of parental characteristics very commonly associated with child maltreatment, namely, domestic violence, substance (including alcohol) misuse and mental ill-health (Brandon *et al.* 2008). Poor school attendance should also be regarded as a significant warning sign (Sidebotham *et al.* 2016). SCRs also reveal concern over the fate of children aged 13 or older with long-standing problems such as self-harm, criminal activity, self-neglect, substance abuse, school exclusion or absence, and suicide attempts, who are likely to be regarded by professionals as 'difficult', rather than attempts being made to ascertain the underlying causes of their exhibited distress (Brandon *et al.* 2008; Sidebotham *et al.* 2016).

If at any time there is reasonable cause to suspect that a child is in immediate danger or is at risk of harm, a referral should be made to children's services or the police immediately (DfE 2016: para. 28) in order for emergency protective action or proceedings to be taken, or initiation of a child protection plan. This may be particularly likely to be the case when a child discloses maltreatment.

Disclosure

Dealing with children's disclosures of maltreatment is a sensitive matter for two main reasons. The first is the need to consider that what is said and done may become evidence in criminal proceedings, in which the evidential requirements are stringent. It is particularly important therefore that disclosures by a child are carefully recorded but that children are not asked leading questions (questions which might lead them to consider that a particular answer is expected), nor are any suggestions put to them. The second is a question of respect for the child taking an adult into their confidence. While maintaining children's confidentiality is critical to the development of trusting relationships, which in turn facilitate disclosure, failure to share information across agencies continues to be highlighted in SCRs. Consequently, children must never be promised confidentiality and should be made aware in advance of disclosure that serious concerns about their welfare will have to be shared with others. If the nature or severity of the activity the child reports is unclear, concerns can be discussed initially with the DSL without disclosing the identity of the child. However, although mandatory reporting of maltreatment has not been universally introduced at the time of writing, the issue is currently the subject of a government consultation and there is an exception in relation to Female Genital Mutilation (FGM), discussed later. Failure to report maltreatment may amount to professional misconduct or negligence in an area where professionals are subject to clear statutory duties.

Disclosing maltreatment is a difficult and distressing undertaking for children. Disabled children are a group at particular risk of abuse, in part because they may be less able to understand or to disclose what is happening. Young people have highlighted the importance of being *asked* about their general welfare when they are exhibiting signs of difficulty, in order to provide an opportunity to tell, whether imminently or when they feel ready to do so (Allnock and Miller 2013; McElvaney, Greene and Hogan 2014). Some have reported having to disclose on several occasions before action was taken (Allnock and Miller 2013). There are particular barriers to the disclosure of child sexual abuse, with the literature suggesting that most victims do not disclose until adulthood (McElvaney 2015). Influential factors include shame; self-blame; fear of being disbelieved; and fear of the consequences within the family unit (particularly protecting parents from distress) (McElvaney *et al.* 2014; Reitsema and Grietens 2016). Verbal communication is especially difficult: behavioural and emotional indicators should be regarded as part of the disclosure process (Reitsema and Grietens 2016). As young contributors to an SCR stated: 'we want teachers to notice behaviour changes, to try and talk to us and notice our unhappiness' (Myers and Carmi 2016: 11). Instead, adolescents appear most likely to confide first in a peer, who may provide important encouragement and support to disclose (McElvaney et al. 2014; Reitsema and Grietens 2016). The introduction of statutory Relationships and Sex Education (RSE) (Children and Social Work Act 2017 s34) is therefore extremely welcome as an opportunity to ensure that children themselves are able to recognize harmful sexual conduct and respond appropriately to peer confidences, although it is disappointing that it is expected parents will continue to be able to 'opt out' of these lessons on behalf of their children.

In relation to sexual abuse in particular, the response of the confidant is critical in determining how the disclosure interaction develops as well as having an impact in the longer term (Reitsema and Grietens 2016). Children need to know that they will be believed (McElvaney et al. 2014); consequently, credibility should be assumed by the person to whom disclosure is made.

Children on a protection plan

Once a referral has been made and an assessment initiated by children's services, if there is reason to *suspect* that the child is suffering or likely to suffer significant harm, an inter-agency strategy discussion will be convened by children's services. This will consider the level of risk faced by the child and in particular whether enquiries should be initiated under Section 47 of the Children Act 1989, in which case a social worker will lead the investigation. If the concerns are substantiated by the s47 enquiries and the child is judged to be at continuing risk of significant harm, then the social worker manager will convene a child protection conference. The child's teacher may be invited to attend and participate in decision-making at the conference, at which a core group of professionals and family members most involved with the child (such as a teacher, nurse, youth worker and family support worker) will be appointed to develop a child protection plan and a social worker designated to lead on its implementation. Involved professionals will be required to contribute to child protection reviews. Since children who are the subject of a protection plan have been identified as at risk of harm, all professionals involved in their care should be particularly vigilant in concern for their welfare.

Children in state care

At any stage in the processes above, the local authority may institute emergency proceedings or proceedings for a care or supervision order, under which the child may be removed from the care of his or her parents. A court may only make such an order if it is satisfied

(a) that the child concerned is suffering, or is likely to suffer, significant harm; and (b) that the harm, or likelihood of harm, is attributable to – (i) the care given to the child, or likely to be given to him if the order were not made, not being what it would be reasonable to expect a parent to give to him; or (ii) the child's being beyond parental control.

(Children Act 1989: s31)

Some children, usually older children, may also be in state care through 'voluntary' arrangements between the local authority and the parents under s20 of the Children Act 1989. Such arrangements may include accommodation being provided for children of 16 and 17 years even where their parents object to the child leaving home. Children in care are beyond the scope of this chapter but are likely to have significant additional educational and pastoral needs and their care will be co-ordinated by their school's Designated Teacher for Looked After Children.

Contemporary issues in safeguarding and child protection

There are a number of issues that have come to the fore in recent years that pose new and unique challenges for schools. This section briefly considers three areas of concern which may be particularly sensitive to address: radicalization and the 'Prevent' agenda; gender-based violence regarded as harmful traditional practices; and peer-to-peer abuse, including cyber-bullying.

Radicalization and the 'Prevent' agenda

'Prevent' is the government's policy to tackle the recruitment of terrorists and support for terrorism and is one of four dimensions of the government's counter-terrorism strategy, CONTEST (the others being Pursue, Protect and Prepare). In relation to children, the policy was influenced by concerns about online radicalization, children travelling to Syria and the so-called 'Trojan Horse Operation' that concerned allegations about an Islamic plot in Birmingham to take over failing schools and insert Islamic principles into their practices and management (Long 2016). Despite multiple reports (see Arthur 2015), no evidence of terrorism, extremism or radicalization was found in any of the schools, although some concerns were expressed about aspects such as gender stereotyping, inadequate sex and relationships education, and the lack of education about religious diversity. Partly as a consequence of these concerns, the Prevent strategy includes non-statutory advice to schools to promote 'the fundamental British values of democracy, the rule of law, individual liberty, and mutual respect and tolerance of those with different faiths and beliefs' (DfE 2014b: 5) – although the exclusive 'Britishness' of such qualities may be called into question.

The strategy also includes statutory duties under the Counter-Terrorism and Security Act 2015 s26 known as 'the Prevent Duty'. Schools are included in the list of agencies required to have 'due regard to the need to prevent people from being drawn into terrorism' in carrying out their functions. According to statutory guidance:

> Being drawn into terrorism includes not just violent extremism but also non-violent extremism, which can create an atmosphere conducive to terrorism

and can popularize views which terrorists exploit. Schools should be safe spaces in which children and young people can understand and discuss sensitive topics, including terrorism and the extremist ideas that are part of terrorist ideology, and learn how to challenge these ideas. The Prevent duty is not intended to limit discussion of these issues. Schools should, however, be mindful of their existing duties [under Sections 406 and 407 of the Education Act 1996] to forbid political indoctrination and secure a balanced presentation of political issues.

(HM Government 2015a: para. 64)

But radicalization is a sensitive area of considerable discomfort for many professionals, because it is one in which the boundaries between the protection and the criminalization of children may readily become blurred. Non-statutory advice states that 'protecting children from the risk of radicalisation should be seen as part of schools' . . . wider safeguarding duties' (DfE 2015: 5), yet government policy is motivated by national security concerns rather than the protection of individual children, as is perhaps reflected in reference to a 'culture of vigilance' in the Ofsted inspection descriptors cited above. Concepts such as 'non-violent extremism' may be difficult to define clearly and the National Union of Teachers (NUT n.d.: 1) argues that it is not the province of teachers to 'police' their pupils. Concern has also been expressed that the provisions may result in discrimination against Muslim students, increase their sense of alienation and endanger social cohesion (Coppock and McGovern 2014).

Schools are expected to 'assess the risk of children being drawn into terrorism, including support for extremist ideas that are part of terrorist ideology' (DfE 2015: 56). Assessment should be made on the basis of the risks identified in the local area by the police and/or local authority and take account of online risks. Schools should establish clear procedures to protect children at risk of radicalization (DfE 2015: 57) and staff should be aware of when referral to the Channel programme (a voluntary programme offering early support to people identified as vulnerable to radicalization) may be appropriate. Local area arrangements will be co-ordinated by the Local Safeguarding Children Board, or equivalent body, and core training in this area has been developed by the Home Office in the form of WRAP (Workshop to Raise Awareness of Prevent). DfE (2015) advice suggests that PSHE and citizenship lessons can be used to build children's 'resilience' to radicalization, through critical exploration of political and social issues, knowledge of democratic government, respect for diversity, and understanding of how to resist pressure, manage risk and make safe choices.

Gender-based violence and harmful traditional practices

'Harmful traditional practices' is the collective term used for a range of cultural practices usually imposed on girls and/or women, which may be justified on social or religious grounds in practising communities but are universally regarded as abusive in countries in the Global North. The two practices most likely to be encountered in schools are Female Genital Mutilation (FGM) and early marriage.

In relation to both, teachers should be alert to children being taken abroad, particularly to their families' country of origin, often at the start of the summer holidays in the case of FGM especially, in order to allow time for recovery before the new academic year.

FGM is a crime under the Female Genital Mutilation Act 2003 (as amended by the Serious Crime Act 2015). Multi-agency statutory guidance sets out the expectations on all agencies, including schools (HM Government 2016). Teachers should be aware if their school may include children at risk of the procedure: experimental statistics suggest that more than 90 per cent of 5,702 newly reported cases in 2015–16 with a known country of birth concerned women and girls born in Africa, and Somalia accounted for over a third of cases with a known country of birth (NHS Digital 2016). Teachers are under a mandatory duty to report to the police where, in the course of their professional duties, they are informed by a girl that FGM has been carried out on her (Serious Crime Act 2015 s74).

Since children under 16 are not capable in law of giving valid consent to marriage, any marriage of a child under 16 is regarded as a forced marriage. Marriage of an older child or young person will also be forced if they do not give their full and free consent. Forced marriage is a criminal offence under the Anti-Social Behaviour, Crime and Policing Act 2014 but victims can also be protected through civil proceedings for an injunction under the Forced Marriage (Civil Protection) Act 2007. Although there is an important distinction between the two, forced marriage appears to be more common in cultures in which arranged marriages are usual (Samad and Eade 2003) and it is often difficult to distinguish an arranged marriage from a forced marriage because emotional blackmail is the most commonly used strategy to obtain consent from an unwilling partner to an arranged marriage (Gangoli, Razak and McCarry 2006). In 2016, the most common countries of destination for victims from the UK were Pakistan (43 per cent), Bangladesh, India, Somalia, Afghanistan and Saudi Arabia; 80 per cent of victims were female (Home Office/Foreign and Commonwealth Office 2017).

Peer-to-peer abuse

While bullying has long been problematic in schools, the challenge it presents has been greatly magnified by the rapid increase in young people's social media use. Cyber-bullying appears to be potentially more distressing to young people than traditional forms of bullying, being associated with higher rates of depressive symptomology and suicidal ideation (Bonanno and Hymel 2013). There is non-statutory advice to schools on preventing and tackling bullying (DfE 2014a), which includes guidance on the bullying of Lesbian, Gay, Bi-sexual and Transgender (LGBT) young people. But the Internet and social media have also increased children's access to pornographic material and introduced new forms of potentially abusive conduct, including sexting and 'catfishing' (posing as someone else online for the purposes of sexual exploitation). Despite some alarm over the risks to young people of Internet usage, Livingstone and Smith (2014) conclude that increased access to technology does not appear to have resulted in increased harm, possibly because the new risks are displacing traditional ones, or policy and practice initiatives have been effective, or children have become more adept at self-protection. Others conclude that the Internet has been associated with earlier sexualization and alternative means of sexual harassment, pressure or coercion. Easy access to online pornography is thought to be presenting children with unrealistic body images as well as divorcing sex from intimacy and normalizing sexist and violent sexual behaviours (Temple-Smith, Moore and Rosenthal 2015).

Dealing with underage sexual activity is a difficult and sensitive area. Adolescent sexual experimentation is a normal part of development and has many positive consequences (Temple-Smith *et al.* 2015), but teachers should seek the advice of their DSL if they have any concerns about pupils' sexual activities. While the age at which children can consent *in law* to penetrative sexual activities is 16, children under 13 are deemed unable to consent *in fact*, meaning that sexual intercourse with a child aged under 13 is regarded as rape, even if the child purported to consent (Sexual Offences Act 2003). Although the minimum age of criminal responsibility in England and Wales is 10 (Children and Young Persons Act 1933 s50, as amended), prosecution of mutually consensual activities where both parties are older adolescents is unlikely. The aim of the legislation is the protection of children and the test is whether prosecution is in the public interest, which will depend on considerations such as the age, vulnerability and understanding of each participant and the nature of their relationship (Crown Prosecution Service (CPS) n.d.).

Challenges in the current educational and social policy context

The issue of the sexual abuse of children by their peers highlights the ambiguity evident in social policy around adolescent sexual activity, which appears often to have contributed to an inadequate or inconsistent professional response to child sexual exploitation. SCRs have pointed to schools' failings in recognizing signs of sexual exploitation, particularly where disruptive behaviour, poor attendance, missed schooling and bullying are present (Myers and Carmi 2016).

Moreover, in a 'marketized' education sector, in which schools' performance is measured in terms of concrete educational qualifications, there is a risk that safeguarding may be seen as a distraction from or likely to undermine the principal 'business' of schools (Baginsky, Driscoll and Manthorpe 2015). Reduced emphasis on pastoral support and inadequate access to mental health services hamper schools' ability to engage troubled children and keep them in school (Myers and Carmi 2016). Prevalence statistics suggesting that around one in ten children aged 5–16 have a diagnosable mental health condition (Green *et al.* 2005) are out-of-date,[2] but there appears to be an increased need for mental health services for children and young people, especially in relation to self-harm and emotional difficulties, and only a minority of young people are able to access effective help (Department of Health/NHS England 2015).

Following the Munro Review (Munro 2011), schools have been included in attempts to encourage the exercise of professional judgement in preference to an over-reliance on procedure and process, but this may also be challenging in a performance-driven educational sector (Baginsky *et al.* 2015). SCRs have consistently highlighted failings in information-sharing within and between agencies responsible for child protection (Brandon *et al*. 2008; Sidebotham *et al*. 2016). In relation to schools, these have particularly concerned: uncertainty about responsibilities to share information and thresholds for making referrals; poor communication arrangements within schools; and weak partnership working with children's services (Baginsky 2007; 2014). Government policy to increase the independence of schools through the promotion of academies, including 'free' schools, is likely to exacerbate these challenges (Davies and Ward 2012). This is already evident in the relatively poor representation by academies (as well as independent schools) on Local Safeguarding Children Boards, compared with the maintained sector (Baginsky and Holmes 2015).

Concluding thoughts

Child protection is often regarded as the 'Cinderella' of work with children. Many professionals seem anxious to avoid getting too involved in this aspect of their work, a response which is understandable but troubling. In part, it is likely to be attributable to the distressing nature of the work; the reality of the fact that vulnerable children, particularly adolescents, are often extremely 'difficult'; and to a 'rule of optimism' that militates against professionals thinking the worst about the children and families with whom they work. Yet the role is inescapable, given teachers' unique position in the lives of children and the statutory responsibilities placed upon them as a result. Any teacher who is concerned about their knowledge or skills is this area should raise this as a training need.

Moreover, safeguarding cannot be divorced from the academic work of schools: children's welfare is imperative to their ability to meet their academic potential (Lefevre *et al*. 2013). Best practice in safeguarding from outstanding schools emphasizes the importance of enabling staff to get to know the children in their care well and of promoting student participation in the life of the school and in their own education, to empower them to voice their concerns and provide them with the knowledge and skills to keep themselves and one another safe (Lefevre *et al*. 2013). A student-centred and participatory ethos is not only compliant with children's rights under the United Nations Convention on the Rights of the Child (UNGA 1989), but is also associated with reduced disaffection and improved behaviour, and encourages the development of maturity and decision-making skills. The literature consistently reinforces the importance of school staff who are accessible, non-judgemental, sensitive, alert, curious and prepared to listen to children. Ultimately, teachers who have the confidence and compassion to develop professional relationships of mutual respect, trust and understanding with their students are likely to find their career more rewarding in the round – and, potentially, can make a genuinely life-changing or even life-saving impact on a child's life.

Notes

1 Note that both these documents are regularly updated and it is important to refer to the version in force.
2 The government has promised to improve statistical data on children's mental health in the near future.

References

All Wales Child Protection Procedures Review Group (AWCPPRG) (2008) *All Wales Child Protection Procedures*, http://www.childreninwales.org.uk/our-work/safeguarding/wales-child-protection-procedures-review-group/, accessed 15 March 2017.

Allnock, D. and Miller, P. (2013) *No One Noticed, No One Heard: A Study of Disclosures of Childhood Abuse*, https://www.nspcc.org.uk/globalassets/documents/research-reports/no-one-noticed-no-one-heard-report.pdf, accessed 9 March 2017.

Arthur, J. (2015) Extremism and neo-liberal education policy: a contextual critique of the Trojan Horse affair in Birmingham schools, *British Journal of Educational Studies*, 63(3): 311–28.

Baginsky, M. (2007) *Schools, Social Services and Safeguarding Children: Past Practice and Future Challenges*. London: NSPCC.

Baginsky, M. (2014) Social work in hiding? The views of other professionals on social workers and working with social workers, *Research, Policy and Planning*, 30(3): 143–54.

Baginsky, M. and Holmes, D. (2015) *A Review of Current Arrangements for the Operation of Local Safeguarding Children Boards*. London: Local Government Association.

Baginsky, M., Driscoll, J. and Manthorpe, J. (2015) Thinking aloud: decentralisation and safeguarding in English schools, *Journal of Integrated Care*, 23(6): 352–63.

Bentley, H., O'Hagan, O., Raff, A. and Bhatti, I. (2016) *How Safe Are Our Children?* NSPCC, https://www.nspcc.org.uk/services-and-resources/research-and-resources/2016/how-safe-are-our-children-2016/, accessed 7 March 2017.

Bonanno, R.A. and Hymel, S.J. (2013) Cyber bullying and internalizing difficulties: above and beyond the impact of traditional forms of bullying, *Journal of Youth and Adolescence*, 42(5): 685–97.

Brandon, M., Belderson, P., Warren, C., Howe, D., Gardner, R., Dodsworth, J. and Black, J. (2008) *Analysing Child Deaths and Serious Injury Through Abuse and Neglect: What Can We Learn?* Department for Children, Schools and Families (DCSF), Research Report DCSF-RR023. Nottingham: DCSF.

Coppock, V. and McGovern, M. (2014) 'Dangerous minds'? Deconstructing counter-terrorism discourse, radicalisation and the 'psychological vulnerability' of Muslim children and young people in Britain, *Children and Society*, 28(2): 242–56.

Crown Prosecution Service (CPS) (n.d.) Prosecution Policy and Guidance: Legal Guidance – Rape and Sexual Offences: Chapter 2: Sexual Offences Act 2003 – Principal Offences, and Sexual Offences Act 1956 – Most commonly charged offences, http://www.cps.gov.uk/legal/p_to_r/rape_and_sexual_offences/soa_2003_and_soa_1956/, accessed 14 March 2017.

Davies, C. and Ward, H. (2012) *Safeguarding Children Across Services: Messages from Research*. London: Department for Education.

Denholm, R., Power, C. and Li, L. (2013) Adverse childhood experiences and child-to-adult height trajectories in the 1958 British birth cohort, *International Journal of Epidemiology*, 42: 1399–1409.

Department for Health, Social Services and Public Safety (2016) *Co-operating to Safeguard Children and Young People in Northern Ireland*, https://www.health-ni.gov.uk/

publications/co-operating-safeguard-children-and-young-people-northern-ireland, accessed 15 March 2017.

Department of Health/NHS England (2015) *Future in Mind: Promoting, Protecting and Improving Our Children and Young People's Mental Health and Wellbeing*, https://www.gov.uk/government/publications/improving-mental-health-services-for-young-people, accessed 14 March 2017.

DfE (Department for Education) (2011) *Teachers' Standards: Guidance for School Leaders, School Staff and Governing Bodies*, https://www.gov.uk/government/publications/teachers-standards, accessed 15 March 2017.

DfE (Department for Education) (2014a) *Preventing and Tackling Bullying Advice for Headteachers, Staff and Governing Bodies*, https://www.gov.uk/government/publications/preventing-and-tackling-bullying, accessed 13 March 2017.

DfE (Department for Education) (2014b) *Promoting Fundamental British Values as Part of SMSC in Schools*. Departmental advice for maintained schools, November 2014, https://www.gov.uk/government/publications/promoting-fundamental-british-values-through-smsc, accessed 13 March 2017.

DfE (Department for Education) (2015) *The Prevent Duty: Departmental Advice for Schools and Childcare Providers*, https://www.gov.uk/government/publications/protecting-children-from-radicalisation-the-prevent-duty, accessed 13 March 2017.

DfE (Department for Education) (2016) *Keeping Children Safe in Education, Statutory Guidance for Schools and Colleges*, https://www.gov.uk/government/publications/keeping-children-safe-in-education–2, accessed 24 January 2017.

DfE/NS (Department for Education/National Statistics) (2016a) *Characteristics of Children in Need: 2015 to 2016 SFR52/2016*, available at https://www.gov.uk/government/statistics/characteristics-of-children-in-need-2015-to-2016, accessed 7 March 2017.

DfE/NS (Department for Education/National Statistics) (2016b) *Children Looked After in England (Including Adoption) Year Ending 31 March 2016 SFR41/2016*, available at https://www.gov.uk/government/statistics/children-looked-after-in-england-including-adoption-2015-to-2016, accessed 7 March 2017.

Dunn, E., McLaughlin, K., Slopen, N., Rosand, J. and Smoller, J. (2013) Developmental timing of child maltreatment and symptoms of depression and suicidal ideation in young adulthood: results from the national longitudinal study of adolescent health. *Depression and Anxiety*, 30: 955–64.

Fergusson, D.M., McLeod, G.F. and Horwood, L.J. (2013) Childhood sexual abuse and adult developmental outcomes: findings from a 30-year longitudinal study in New Zealand, *Child Abuse and Neglect*, 37(9): 664–74.

Gangoli, G., Razak, A. and McCarry, M. (2006) *Forced Marriages and Domestic Violence among South Asian Communities in North East England*. Bristol and Newcastle: Bristol University and Northern Rock Foundation.

Gardner, R. and Brandon, M. (2009) Child protection: crisis management or learning curve? *Public Policy Research*, 453: 177–86.

Gavin, H. (2011) Sticks and stones may break my bones: the effects of emotional abuse, *Journal of Aggression, Maltreatment and Trauma*, 20(5): 503–29.

Gilbert, R., Spatz Widom, C., Browne, K., Fergusson, D., Webb, E. and Janson, S. (2009) Child Maltreatment 1: Burden and consequences of child maltreatment in high-income countries, *Lancet*, 373: 68–81.

Glaser, D. (2000) Child abuse and neglect and the brain – a review, *Journal of Child Psychology and Psychiatry*, 41(1): 97–116.

Green, H., McGinnity, A., Meltzer, H. *et al.* (2005) *Mental Health of Children and Young People in Great Britain 2004*. London: Palgrave.

Harter, S. (2012) *The Construction of the Self*. New York: The Guildford Press.

HM Government (2015a) Revised Prevent Duty Guidance: for England and Wales. Guidance for Specified Authorities in England and Wales on the duty in the Counter-Terrorism and Security Act 2015 to have due regard to the need to prevent people from being drawn into terrorism, https://www.gov.uk/government/publications/prevent-duty-guidance, accessed 13 March 2017.

HM Government (2015b) *What to Do If You're Worried that a Child Is Being Abused. Advice for Practitioners*, https://www.gov.uk/government/publications/what-to-do-if-youre-worried-a-child-is-being-abused–2, accessed 13 March 2017.

HM Government (2015c) *Working Together to Safeguard Children: A Guide to Inter-Agency Working to Safeguard and Promote the Welfare of Children*, https://www.gov.uk/government/publications/working-together-to-safeguard-children–2, version last updated 16 February 2017, accessed 7 March 2017.

HM Government (2016) *Multi-Agency Statutory Guidance on Female Genital Mutilation*, https://www.gov.uk/government/publications/multi-agency-statutory-guidance-on-female-genital-mutilation, accessed 13 March 2017.

Home Office/Foreign and Commonwealth Office (2017) Forced Marriage Unit Statistics 2016, https://www.gov.uk/government/statistics/forced-marriage-unit-statistics-2016, accessed 13 March 2017.

Jay, P. (2014) *Independent Inquiry into Child Sexual Exploitation in Rotherham (1997–2013)*. Rotherham: Rotherham Metropolitan Borough Council, http://www.rotherham.gov.uk/downloads/file/1407/independent_inquiry_cse_in_rotherham, accessed 7 March 2017.

Laming (2003) *The Victoria Climbié Inquiry*. Cm 5730. London: The Stationery Office.

Lefevre, P. *et al.* (2013) *Good Practice Guidelines for Safeguarding and Child Protection in Secondary Schools*, Office of the Children's Commissioner (OCC), http://www.childrenscommissioner.gov.uk/publications/good-practice-guidelines-safeguarding-and-child-protection-secondary-schools, accessed 14 March 2017.

Livingstone, S. and Smith, P.K. (2014) Annual Research Review: Harms experienced by child users of online and mobile technologies: the nature, prevalence and management of sexual and aggressive risks in the digital age, *Journal of Child Psychology and Psychiatry*, 55(6): 635–54.

Long, R. (2016) *Counter-Extremism Policy in English Schools*, London: House of Commons Report, No. CBP 07345, 15 January 2016, http://researchbriefings.parliament.uk/ResearchBriefing/Summary/CBP-7345#full report, accessed 15 March 2017.

Lonne, B., Parton, N., Thomson, J. and Harries, M. (2009) *Reforming Child Protection*. London: Routledge.

McElvaney, R. (2015) Disclosure of child sexual abuse: delays, non-disclosure and partial disclosure. What the research tells us and implications for practice, *Child Abuse Review*, 24(3): 159–69.

McElvaney, R., Greene, S. and Hogan, D. (2014) To tell or not to tell? Factors influencing young people's informal disclosures of child sexual abuse, *Journal of Interpersonal Violence*, 29(5): 928–47.

McLean, C., Rosenbach, S., Capaldi, S. and Foa, E. (2013) Social and academic functioning in adolescents with child sexual abuse-related PTSD, *Child Abuse and Neglect*, 37(9): 675–78.

Morrison, N. (2014) Teachers are the front line of children's safety, *Times Educational Supplement*, 26 September (News No. 5114).

Munro, E. (2011) *The Munro Review of Child Protection: Final Report, A Child-Centred System*. London: The Stationery Office, https://www.gov.uk/government/collections/munro-review, accessed 9 March 2017.

Myers, J. and Carmi, E. (2016) *The Brooke Serious Case Review into Child Sexual Exploitation*. Association of Independent LSCB Chairs/NSPCC, available at: https://www.nspcc.org.uk/preventing-abuse/child-protection-system/case-reviews/2016/, accessed 15 March 2017.

National Union of Teachers (n.d.) *Education and Extremism: Advice for Members in England and Wales*, https://www.teachers.org.uk/equality/equality-matters/education-and-extremism, accessed 15 March 2017.

Neale, A. and Lopez, N. (2017) *Suffer the Little Children and their Mothers: A Dossier on the Unjust Separation of Children from their Mothers*. London: Crossroads Books, http://legalactionforwomen.net/2017/02/14/suffer-the-little-children-their-mothers-a-dossier-on-the-unjust-separation-of-children-from-their-mothers/, accessed 15 March 2017.

NHS Digital (2016) *Female Genital Mutilation (FGM) – April 2015 to March 2016, Experimental Statistics*, https://www.gov.uk/government/statistics/female-genital-mutilation-apr-2015-to-mar-2016-enhanced-dataset, accessed 13 March 2017.

Ofsted (2016) *School Inspection Handbook*, https://www.gov.uk/government/publications/school-inspection-handbook-from-september-2015, accessed 15 March 2017.

Parton, N. (2006) *Safeguarding Childhood: Early Intervention and Surveillance in a Late Modern Society*. Basingstoke: Palgrave Macmillan.

Parton, N. (2016) The Contemporary Politics of Child Protection: Part Two (the BASPCAN Founder's Lecture 2015), *Child Abuse Review*, 25(1): 9–16.

Pritchard, C. and Williams, R. (2010) Comparing possible child-abuse-related-deaths in England and Wales with the major developed countries 1974–2006: signs of progress? *British Journal of Social Work*, 40(6): 1700–18.

Radford, L., Corral, S., Bradley, C. and Fisher, H. (2013) The prevalence and impact of child maltreatment and other types of victimization in the UK: findings from a population survey of caregivers, children and young people and young adults, *Child Abuse and Neglect*, 37: 801–13.

Raymond, A. (2013) *The Child Protection and Safeguarding Handbook for Schools: A Comprehensive Guide to Policy and Practice* (2nd edn). London: Optimus Education.

Reitsema, A.M. and Grietens, H. (2016) Is anybody listening? The literature on the dialogical process of child sexual abuse disclosure reviewed, *Trauma, Violence and Abuse*, 17(3): 300–40.

Samad, Y. and Eade, J. (2003) *Community Perceptions of Forced Marriage*. London: Foreign and Commonwealth Office.

Scottish Government (2014) *National Guidance for Child Protection in Scotland*, http://www.gov.scot/Publications/2014/05/3052, accessed 15 March 2017.

Sidebotham, P., Brandon, M., Bailey, S., Belderson, P., Garstang, J., Harrison, E., Retzer, A. and Sorensen, P. (2016) *Pathways to Harm, Pathways to Protection: A Triennial Analysis of Serious Case Reviews 2011–2014*. London: Department for Education, https://www.gov.uk/government/publications/analysis-of-serious-case-reviews-2011-to-2014, accessed 15 March 2017.

Tanaka, M., Wekerle, C., Schmuck, M.L. and Paglia-Boak, A. (2011) The linkages among childhood maltreatment, adolescent mental health, and self-compassion in child welfare adolescents, *Child Abuse and Neglect*, 35: 887–98.

Temple-Smith, M., Moore, S. and Rosenthal, D. (eds) (2015) *Sexuality in Adolescence: The Digital Generation*. New York: Taylor and Francis.

UNGA (United Nations General Assembly) (1989) *United Nations Convention on the Rights of the Child*, http://www2.ohchr.org/english/law/crc.htm, accessed 20 January 2017.

22

Environment, sustainable development and education
MELISSA GLACKIN AND JUSTIN DILLON

Introduction

In September 2015, 193 Member States attending the United Nations (UN) Sustainable Development Summit in New York adopted a new global development framework: 'Transforming our World: the 2030 Agenda for Sustainable Development'. The Agenda consists of 17 Sustainable Development Goals (SDGs) (or 'Global Goals' as they are popularly known) and 169 targets, which commit all signatory countries to tackle issues as diverse and deep-rooted as gender inequality, climate change, access to quality education and the promotion of peaceful and inclusive societies (UN 2015). Education is a key strategy for achieving the Sustainable Development Goals. In this chapter, we examine the tensions and controversies around the term 'Education for Sustainable Development' (ESD), and consider the arguments as to why and how all schools should 'teach', 'do' and ultimately, connect their students' learning to the environment and sustainability.

The environment

Before we go any further, it is worth noting that the word 'environment' is itself contested. Writing in 1996, the Canadian researcher, Lucy Sauvé, summarized different ways of conceptualizing the environment, and indicated how they were related (see Table 22.1). It should be evident from Sauvé's taxonomy how a science teacher, a geography teacher, a warden of an environmental education centre and the head of education at a natural history museum might use quite different conceptualizations of the environment. These different views of the environment might well affect how they teach and what they teach.

So, for example, in *Our Common Future* (WCED 1987) (commonly referred to as the Brundtland Report), a seminal document in the history of education and the environment, the implicit conceptualization of the environment appears to be dualistic and Cartesian, that is, the environment is seen as a *global resource*, to be

Table 22.1 Conceptualizations of the environment

Environment as nature . . .	to be appreciated, respected, preserved: dualistic, Cartesian interpretation, humans are removed from nature.
Environment as a resource . . .	to be managed: this is our collective biophysical heritage and we must sustain it as it is deteriorating and wasting away. As, for example, in the Judaeo-Christian view (Book of Genesis).
Environment as a problem . . .	to be solved: the biophysical environment, the life support system is threatened by pollution and degradation. We must learn to preserve its quality and restore it (problem-solving skills emphasized).
Environment as a place to live . . .	to know and learn about, to plan for, to take care of: day-to-day environment – characterized by its human, socio-cultural, technological and historical components.
Environment as the biosphere . . .	in which we all live together, in the future: 'Spaceship Earth' (Fuller) and Gaia (Lovelock) – self-regulating organism.
Environment as a community project . . .	in which to get involved (that is, a context that affords opportunities for working with others for the benefit of all).
Environment of a human collectivity . . .	a shared living place, political concern, the focus of critical analysis: solidarity, democracy and personal and collective involvement in order to participate in the evolution of the community.

Source: Sauvé (1996).

developed and managed for sustainable profit, and as *nature*, to be revered and respected for the enjoyment and survival of human beings, thus:

> the environment does not exist as a sphere separate from human actions, ambitions and needs and attempts to defend it in isolation from human concerns have given the very word 'environment' a connotation of naivety in some political circles.
>
> (WCED 1987: 6)

There are many who see *Our Common Future* as a simplistic document that tries to be all things to all people. However, one of the positive elements of *Our Common Future* was that it recognized the links between (human) development and the environment, stating that the two were inseparable.

This is an important sentiment because it recognizes that focusing on the physical aspects of the environment without considering social issues such as health, employment, legislation and education is extremely problematic. We would argue that all teachers, across the Key Stages and subject disciplines, need to be aware of the complex interrelationship between the big issues, referred to as 'wicked problems' (Dillon *et al.* 2016), and to reflect that complexity in both what they teach and in what they do. 'Wicked problems' are socio-cultural problems that are often interconnected, involve large numbers of people and opinions, have economic implications and are often defined by contradictory knowledge. As a result, action is focused on improving a situation rather than solving the problem (Dillon *et al.* 2016). Examples of such problems include: inequality, public health, global consumption, capitalism, biodiversity loss and the limits of natural systems. All of which are interconnected. Hence, we would argue that due to the complexity of the problems, it is imperative, either explicitly or implicitly, that teachers of all subject disciplines explore these issues so that students across all Key Stages are prepared to contribute to, stimulate and eventually lead the debate on connected issues such as national and global governance, global citizenship and sustainable resource use (Mace 2014). So rather than the environment *per se*, environmental education connects to sustainability and sustainable development. However, we are getting ahead of ourselves and before we explore further how these issues might be effectively included in a student's education, in the next section we examine the key concepts of sustainability and sustainable development, pointing to some problems with the ways in which the terms are used.

Sustainability and sustainable development

Opinions vary as to what is meant by sustainability or sustainable development. In general, though, the lack of agreement about the terms is glossed over, and policy-makers make bold assertions without much by way of a caveat. So, for example, the UK Government states that it is committed to sustainable development, defining sustainable development as 'making the necessary decisions now to realize our vision of stimulating economic growth and tackling the deficit, maximising wellbeing and protecting our environment, without affecting the ability of future generations to do the same' (Department for Environment, Food and Rural Affairs 2015: para. 1 'Issue').

In essence, then, we can have our cake now as long as we ensure that there will be enough cake for future generations to eat. Although contentious and open to interpretation – just what is meant by 'necessary decisions', for example? – it would be hard to argue that the sentiment was hugely undesirable. However, in this definition there is an implicit priority for economic development over, rather than aligned with, environmental development and well-being. Such a definition does little to address the wicked problems we are facing.

It is therefore unsurprising that in a recent report by the Environment Audit Committee, whose remit includes a responsibility to audit the government's performance against sustainable development and environmental protection targets, a similar observation was made on the role of HM Treasury in sustainable development. The Committee reported that the Department most frequently used the term sustainability in the context of economic growth, commenting, 'it was not clear whether the Treasury's use of the term sustainability aligns with the concept of sustainable development' (House of Commons Environmental Audit Committee 2016: 5). Noteworthy is that the Committee cites *Our Common Future*'s (WCED 1987) definition of sustainable development:

> Humanity has the ability to make development sustainable to ensure that it meets the needs of the present without compromising the ability of future

generations to meet their own needs. The concept of sustainable development does imply limits – not absolute limits but limitations imposed by the present state of technology and social organization on environmental resources and by the ability of the biosphere to absorb the effects of human activities.

(para. 27)

We will discuss the roots of this report later, but the point here is that compared to the government's definition above, here there is an acknowledgement of 'needs', in particular, the essential needs of the world's poor, and the idea of limitations imposed by social organization on the environment's ability to meet present and future needs.

This broader notion, that sustainable development needs to be considered from a global (rather than only national) and longer-term perspective, and that outcomes impact both humans and the Earth, is captured by the United Nations (UN) Secretary-General Ban Ki Moon at the launch of the momentous Sustainable Development Goals Summit in September 2015:

> It is an agenda for people, to end poverty in all its forms. An agenda for the planet, our common home. An agenda for shared prosperity, peace and part-nership . . . To do better, we must do differently. The 2030 Agenda compels us to look beyond national boundaries and short-term interests and act in soli-darity for the long term. We can no longer afford to think and work in silos.
>
> (UN Secretary-General 2015)

In understanding sustainable development from a global position, it becomes clear that it cannot be achieved by technological solutions, political regulation or financial instruments alone. Sustainable development requires individuals, com-munities and nations to change the way they think and act together. For these behaviour changes to occur, quality education and learning for sustainable devel-opment are required at all levels and in all social contexts. It is here that most teachers should be able to see how they might contribute. Later we explore how ESD might effectively be part of a student's education. In the next section we offer some context to the environmental and sustainable development movements.

Some context

Even if it is difficult to appreciate fully the connections between our lives and those of others, it would be difficult not to be aware of the global nature of envi-ronmental problems. The impact of the environment on people's lives whether they be in New Orleans or Fukushima, whether they be affected by storm, volcano or tsunami, is all too apparent. To what extent environmental catastrophes are caused by, or exaggerated by, human impact is not yet known but the scientific evidence points to the need for humans to do more to protect the environment (Mace 2014). Doing more might mean imposing more rules and regulations, it might mean trav-elling by train not by plane, or it might mean teaching other people not to make the mistakes of this and previous generations.

Concern about the environment grew rapidly around the middle of the last century and although the topics of concern have changed, there is still wide public interest in issues such as global warming, climate change, air and water quality, and the impact of development on communities. In recent years, links between food, the environment and health have become much more widely understood. For example, politicians and parents are concerned about immunizations, about what children consume and about the amount of exercise that they get compared to previous generations.

In the 1950s and 1960s, people became increasingly aware that scientific and technological advances sometimes came with undesirable side-effects. Rachel Carson's *Silent Spring* exposed the catastrophic effects of pesticide spraying in the USA and elsewhere (Carson [1962] 1999). The book has rarely been out of print, although Carson was heavily criticized at the time of its publication by politicians, industrialists and the media (Dillon 2005).

In the 1970s and 1980s, a series of international conferences and declarations helped to focus the attention of environmentalists, educators and policy-makers on the key environmental problems and on how education might play a role in their solution. The United Nations Conference on the Human Environment in Stockholm in 1972 was a key event in the development of what became commonly known as environmental education (EE). There are, as you might expect by now, many definitions and conceptualizations of environmental education. There are several reviews of the EE literature which provide a good background to the range and scope of teaching and learning in, for and about the environment (see, for example, Hart and Nolan 1999; Marcinkowski 2009). The differences between environmental education (EE) and Education for Sustainable Development (ESD) are complex and it is beyond the scope of this chapter to do them justice (see, for example, Kopnina 2012). Suffice to say that it is impossible to talk about ESD without understanding that it has its roots in EE as well as in development education, as was mentioned earlier. UNESCO has defined ESD as follows:

> ESD empowers learners to take informed decisions and responsible actions for environmental integrity, economic viability and a just society, for present and future generations, while respecting cultural diversity. It is about lifelong learning, and is an integral part of quality education. ESD is holistic and transformational education which addresses learning content and outcomes, pedagogy and the learning environment. It achieves its purpose by transforming society.
> (UNESCO 2014: 12)

The publication of *Our Common Future* (WCED 1987), by the World Commission on Environment and Development, in 1987, led to the popularization of the definition of sustainable development outlined earlier. As previously illustrated, *Our Common Future*'s conceptualization underpins much current thinking about sustainable development. Five years later, in 1992, the Rio Declaration from the World Conference on Environmental and Development (WCED or 'The Earth Summit') began by stating: 'Human beings are at the centre of concerns for sustainable development. They are entitled to a healthy and productive life in harmony with nature' (WCED 1992).

A decade later, at the World Summit on Sustainable Development, the Johannesburg Declaration announced that world leaders were committed 'to build a humane, equitable and caring global society cognizant of the need for human dignity for all' (UNESCO 2006). The value of education as the foundation of sustainable development was reaffirmed at the Johannesburg Summit, as was the commitment embodied in Chapter 36 of Agenda 21 of the Rio Summit, 1992. In the same year, 2002, the United Nations proposed the Decade of ESD. The Decade was an attempt to get the environment and development into the school curriculum across the world.

The impact of the Decade of ESD on global education is difficult to measure. However, recent international agreements indicate a growing recognition of ESD as an integral element of a quality education and a key enabler for sustainable development. For example, ESD was central in the Muscat Agreement adopted at the Global Education For All Meeting (GEM) in 2014. Further, in 2015, ESD can be identified in the historic 2030 Sustainable Development Goals (SDGs) adopted by 193 countries (United Nations 2015). Later we discuss the impact and the legacy of the Decade of ESD in two countries – England and Scotland. However, now we turn to criticisms of sustainable development and ESD.

Criticisms of sustainable development and ESD

Verbal felicity and practical logic

Sustainable development as a concept has its critics. Speaking at a conference in 2000, the *Guardian*'s architecture correspondent Martin Pawley criticized *Our Common Future*'s definition, and another simpler version which spoke of 'leaving the planet to the next generation in no worse state than that in which the present generation found it', as embodying 'a breathtakingly serious number of contradictions and flaws' (Pawley 2000: para. 5). He added, 'What they gain in verbal felicity they lose in practical logic.' Pawley pointed out that both definitions were 'textbook examples of the political fudge' which combined opposing positions (sustainability and development) by proposing a third (sustainable development). Another critic, Sachs (2015), argued that sustainable development required the conservation of development, not the conservation of nature. This extract from *Our Common Future* hints at another of the tensions in the term sustainable development: 'What is needed is an era of new economic growth – growth that is forceful and at the same time socially and environmentally sustainable' (WCED 1987: 6). That is easy to say but incomparably difficult to achieve. Wals and Jickling (2008) related the contradictions inherent in sustainable development to Orwell's 'double think' – that is, ordinary citizens become brainwashed into accepting contradictory meanings for a term. Sustainability is so hard to pin down that ultimately its utility becomes questionable. Terms such as sustainable development, Stables argues, are 'paradoxical compound policy slogans' (2001: 251). This might not necessarily be a bad thing, argue Scott and Gough (2003), as long as teachers can use the debate about terms to educate students about the use of language in everyday life.

Education 'for' . . .

Critics of Education *for* Sustainable Development have not been reticent in their arguments. When Hopkins wrote that 'education should be able to cope with determining and implanting these broad guiding principles [of sustainability] at the heart of ESD [education for sustainable development]' (1998: 172), Jickling responded by arguing:

> When highlighted in this way, most educators find such statements a staggering misrepresentation of their task. Teachers understand that sustainable development, and even sustainability, are normative concepts representing the views of only segments of our society. And, teachers know that their job is primarily to teach students how to think, not what to think.
>
> (Jickling 2000: 469)

Jickling and Wals (2008) have also expressed their concerns about the lack of educational philosophical analysis in EE and the use of education as a tool for the advancement of sustainable development. That is, they ask that if the purpose of education is for people to think for themselves, then education 'for' anything is inconsistent and should be rejected. Kopnina (2012) calls for ESD to radically change from current discourse which prioritizes environmental protection concerning social issues (for example, poor people) to a moral obligation for caring about species, other than humans, including the entire ecosystem. So, although there are many advocates of ESD, it has its critics. In the next section we will examine what has been suggested that an education about or for sustainability might involve.

What should people learn and how could they be taught?

Despite continued concern about the environment, both local and global, the low levels of public knowledge and understanding continue to worry environmentalists. Relatively recent data indicates that only half of adults in the USA understand the mechanism of climate change. However, perhaps more concerning is that nearly four in ten Americans think there is a great deal of disagreement among scientists as to whether global warming is happening or not (Robelia and Murphy 2012). Such confusion, or scepticism, is on the rise with similar trends tracked in the UK and Australia (Klein 2015). This current course looks likely to continue as Donald Trump, the president of the USA, called global warming a hoax invented by the Chinese (Philips 2017). The challenges facing teachers, in terms of the low-level public understanding about environmental issues, should not be underestimated.

Education for sustainable development is manifest in the curriculum in many countries to differing degrees. As discussed earlier, the Decade of Education for Sustainable Development (DESD: 2005–2014), for which UNESCO (United Nations Education, Scientific and Cultural Organisation) was the lead agency, aimed to change the approach to education so that it integrated the principles, values and practices of sustainable development. ESD was no longer to be an add-on to formal curriculums, rather it was to be integral and integrated. To this end, UNESCO provided ESD guidance through the Global Action Programme with a detailed implementation roadmap, including guiding principles, objectives and priority action areas (UNESCO 2014).

The ESD principles that UNESCO encourages countries to adhere to include: that ESD allows everyone to acquire the knowledge and skills so that they may contribute to, and take informed decisions about, sustainable development; that ESD is grounded in a rights-based approach to education that is relevant today; and that ESD is organized as a transformative education in that it aims to reorient societies towards sustainable development. With UNESCO's enduring and focused steer for ESD in mind, we now turn to review its status in the United Kingdom. We draw on, and compare, evidence of curriculum and practice from two political jurisdictions – England and Scotland – as for countries so geographically close, their ESD offers are distinctly different.

Since the late 1990s the UK Government has devolved responsibility for Scotland's education to a directly elected parliament. Sustainable development is one of the Scottish Government's key national performance outcomes and a 'greener' and 'fairer' nation informs an overarching strategic objective. The country has set ambitious climate change targets alongside an emphasis on the importance of societal change towards a sustainable future.

Within this context, it is unsurprising that Martin and colleagues (2013), following a critique of UK ESD education policy and practice, observed that the Scottish Government was substantially committed to ESD. This commitment was evident in 2011 when the incoming government set a manifesto target to explore the concept of 'One Planet Schools'. That is, the government was receptive to the World Wide Fund for Nature's (WWF) proposal that all schools should take a whole school approach to build pupils' capacity to responsibly contribute to a future where people and nature were able to live in harmony within their fair share of the planet's natural resources (WWF 2012).

Fast forward to 2017, 'Learning for Sustainability' is one of the seven topics that underpin the 'Curriculum for Excellence' (CfE), the recent major revised curriculum in Scotland. 'Learning for Sustainability' integrates ESD, Global Citizenship and Outdoor learning (Education Scotland 2017). The phased introduction of CfE has enabled the integration of ESD across the whole school, as called for by the WWF. Further, with all beginning and in-service teachers now required to address 'Learning for Sustainability' in their teaching, it has now been embedded across the Standards for Registration (General Teaching Council for Scotland 2012).

Turning to England, as previous chapters have highlighted, alongside the country's political change, the school curriculum has undergone substantial revisions over the past six years. Before 2010, teachers were told that ESD was evident within the curriculum as it reflected societal values. Specifically, ESD was included within one of the two overarching curricula aims whereby pupils were to develop an 'awareness and understanding of, and respect for, the environments in which they live, and secure their commitment to sustainable development at a personal, local, national and global level' (QCA 2004). However, rather than being integrated across the whole curriculum, opportunities for understanding sustainable development were prioritized in geography, science, D&T and citizenship programmes of study.

Martin and colleagues (2013) note that since the election in 2010, in England the government's emphasis on sustainable development has declined, with climate change being given less priority. As a potential result, rather than a ramping-up of ESD in English schools as might be expected following the Decade of Education for Sustainable Development, the 2014 revised curriculum saw ESD and EE all but eradicated. That is to say, ESD or EE is no longer a value underpinning the National Curriculum although examples of environmental-related issues and themes feature across subject curricula in science and geography. A similar omission is reflected in the English Teacher Standards leaving ESD passed over (Department for Education 2013).

The lack of legislation for ESD or EE in England, however, should not be taken to indicate that no practice exists. As in Scotland, many schools and teachers in England place ESD at the heart of their teaching both integrated into formal teaching as well as through extra-curricular activities. Much of this work is supported by charities and not-for-profit organizations working to raise public awareness of environmental issues, in particular climate change. Three such groups in the UK that have been particularly active in working with schools and young people are explored in more detail later. However, regardless of how ESD or EE features in a formal or informal curriculum, an important question for beginning teachers is, how should it be taught? As set out earlier, EE and ESD for students are arrived at both from what teachers teach and what teachers do. Although the two are inseparable, below we focus only on what effective teaching is.

What is 'effective' environmental education and ESD?

Effective ESD (which when referred to in this section includes environmental education) is often considered as that which enables pro-environmental decision-making. It has been widely proposed that for ESD to be effective, students need to experience personal relevance and social environment context (Martin and Chen 2016). For example, more than two decades ago, Fettis and Ramsden (1995) argued that one of the best educational experiences for ESD was to have students conduct short research projects on topics directly relevant to or leading to sustainability. One of the 'founding fathers' of ESD, Bill Stapp (2000), who began the Global Rivers Environmental Education Network (GREEN), saw watershed and rivers as linking different interests and cultures together offering environmental problem-solving. Hopkins and McKeown (1999), outlining what they describe as key steps towards sustainability, argued that students in programmes (such as GREEN) that have been offered a new perspective and a reorientation will learn to practise a sustainable lifestyle. The authors go further to say that as the teaching had been locally relevant their new skills were tailored to the conditions of the community. On a similarly positive note, Rauch (2002) saw ESD as providing opportunities for schools to become thematic breeding grounds for innovation. That is, the context of teaching sustainability would act as a vehicle for creative and aspiring interdisciplinary learning.

Later attempts to describe possible pedagogical approaches mixed older ideas of holism and interdisciplinarity with newer ideas such as participatory decision-making. So, for example, according to UNESCO, ESD will aim to be:

- *interdisciplinary and holistic*: learning for sustainable development embedded in the whole curriculum, not as a separate subject;

- *values-driven*: it is critical that the assumed norms – the shared values and principles underpinning sustainable development – are made explicit so that that can be examined, debated, tested and applied;

- *critical thinking and problem-solving*: leading to confidence in addressing the dilemmas and challenges of sustainable development;

- *a multi-method*: word, art, drama, debate, experience . . . different pedagogies which model the processes. Teaching that is geared simply to passing on knowledge should be recast into an approach in which teachers and learners work together to acquire knowledge and play a role in shaping the environment of their educational institutions.

- *a participatory decision-making process*: learners participate in decisions on how they are to learn;

- *applicable*: the learning experiences offered are integrated in day-to-day personal and professional life;

- *locally relevant*: addressing local as well as global issues, and using the language(s) which learners most commonly use. Concepts of sustainable development must be carefully expressed in other languages – languages and cultures say things differently, and each language has creative ways of expressing new concepts.

(UNESCO 2006)

It is noteworthy that the outcomes, such as pro-environmental decision-making, revered when teaching issues relating to sustainability diverge from those, such as knowledge and understanding gains, traditionally assessed by schools (see Rickinson *et al.* (2004) for a comprehensive review of the effects of outdoor learning). However, separating knowledge, or cognitive learning gains, from action, or affective, social and behavioural learning gains, is obtuse. There is a correlation between environmental knowledge and pro-environmental decision-making. In other words, some knowledge is required before people will perform actions to resolve an issue (NEETF 2005). For example, knowing how the burning of fossil fuels impacts climate change might lead to the decreased use of petrol-fuelled cars. Equally, a rudimentary understanding of aquifers and water tables is necessary to understand how ground water can become polluted or how we impact our 'water footprints' through food processing and consumer goods. However, as evident in the recent rise of climate change sceptics, knowledge is not necessarily enough when it comes to environmental awareness or pro-environmental actions. A gap still remains.

Factors influencing environmental decision-making are extremely complex. Alongside knowledge, the determinants include social norms and the social desirability in their personal and professional lifestyles. Kollmus and Agyeman (2002) note three specific reasons as to why people encounter cognitive difficulties in achieving environmental awareness. First, many environmental problems, such as climate change and air pollution are abstract and not easily directly observed. Second, the issues are often slow and change is gradual which over a long period is difficult to appreciate. Third, many environmental issues are concerned with future predictions which due to the intricacy of environmental interactions are complicated and challenging.

These reasons go some way to explain why teaching strategies offering personal relevance and social context are so frequently cited as effective for environmental education. In practice, Kollmus and Agyeman (2002) highlight the importance of images – such as photographs, diagrams and graphs – to help invoke emotional involvement. They cite the visual impact of ozone hole images and 'charismatic mega-fauna' (such as lions and pandas) as creating much broader public support than less visual, more abstract issues such as climate change. This observation led Robelia and Murphy (2012) to conclude that environmental issues with memorable images may seem more pressing than climate change as minute changes on a global scale are impossible to visualize.

In the UK, Gayford (2009), following a three-year longitudinal study of schools' approaches to sustainable development, reported that student attitudes towards sustainability varied depending on the school's approach. Schools in which students showed improvements in knowledge of issues related to sustainability were seen to have several similarities. First, there was an explicit linking of sustainability across the curriculum and into the whole school ethos of school. So, rather than specific subject disciplines, schools might base learning around themes. The Ellen MacArthur Foundation presents an excellent illustration of how school subjects, such as mathematics, geography and English, can be successfully interlinked by a theme such as 'The future of energy' (ellenmacarthurfoundation.org). Second, teachers used innovative approaches which included a significant amount of pupil involvement in planning and presenting. Third, schools engaged families of their students to discuss the importance of learning for sustainability.

It is interesting to note that Gayford (2009) found that schools were more likely to engage students in sustainability when they provided events and activities that interrupted the routine and extended the learners' experience of sustainability, and where international links with developing countries were used to improve students' cultural understanding. Conversely, schools which preached to students about the need for sustainability or continually presented negative images less successfully engaged students. Students in such schools exhibited feelings of lack of interest or hopelessness. Hence, it is the whole school embodiment of ESD that offers most potential.

Several factors determine whether teachers include ESD alongside their everyday pedagogical decision-making. These factors include: the teacher's belief concerning what education is for, how they perceive their subject and how they believe children learn (Glackin 2016). Further, as we have seen in the comparison between England and Scotland above, the inclusion of ESD is influenced by the National Curriculum, the whole-school ethos and by colleagues' beliefs and values. Finally, on a practical note, including ESD in teaching is determined by a subject's allocated curriculum time, professional time for lesson planning and the geographical context of your school (Hill 2012). This list represents a number of potential barriers that teachers might need to overcome if they are to develop ESD in their classrooms.

In the next section we outline three initiatives that are shaping students' experience of EE and ESD in secondary schools in England: (1) the Council for Learning Outside the Classroom; (2) Sustainability and Environmental Education (SEEd); and (3) Eco-Schools. In terms of professional accreditations, while several of these organizations do provide professional development opportunities for teachers, at present there are no formally recognized professional qualifications available to teach EE in schools.

Council for Learning Outside the Classroom

In the light of the success of the Manifesto for Music, the Education and Skills Select Committee recommended that the government should publish an 'Education Outside the Classroom Manifesto'. The manifesto, announced in 2005 by the Department for Education, stated: 'We believe that every young person should experience the world beyond the classroom as an essential part of learning and personal development, whatever their age, ability or circumstances' (DfES 2006: para. 1), The manifesto was an attempt to ensure that all pupils have reasonable access to learning in different contexts. One of the results of the manifesto was the establishment of the Council for Learning Outside the Classroom (LOtC): a body charged with promoting outdoor learning while raising the quality of the experience on offer. Opportunities to address sustainability through learning outdoors are plentiful and the Learning Outside the Classroom website (lotc.org.uk) provides a range of useful links including highlighting research supporting the use and development of the school grounds and links to health and well-being while being in, and learning about, the outdoors.

The Council has developed a Quality Badge scheme that identifies institutions and organizations that provide effective and safe LOtC activities. The argument for the scheme is that it makes it easier for teachers to organize visits by reducing the bureaucracy involved and enables them to celebrate formally the efforts that go into organizing whole-school out-of-classroom teaching and learning.

Sustainability and Environmental Education (SEEd)

The Sustainability and Environmental Education (SEEd) charity is focused on supporting teachers to place sustainability at the core of their work. It claims that it is 'the hub for bringing together, sharing and enhancing best practice in sustainability for environmental education' (SEEd 2017). SEEd's goal is to keep educators thinking and updated as to what is effective practice. The charity also strives to change societal attitudes and norms towards sustainability and environmental issues.

To this end, anyone can become a member of the organization. SEEd's website offers teaching resources which span topics such as: habitats and homes, equality and justice, health and well-being, green economics, design for the future and communication and media. The broad list of topics indicates the reach that sustainable education has across the curriculum subjects. SEEd organizes an annual National Sustainable School Conference and offers Learning for Sustainability leadership courses.

Eco-Schools

Eco-Schools is an international award programme that provides schools with a framework to improve the environment, save money and achieve international recognition (Eco-Schools 2017). In England, the programme is co-ordinated by the environmental charity Keep Britain Tidy. The programme provides a flexible framework for learning and action which schools usually complete outside the formal curriculum. Like SEEd the topics that Eco-Schools span are diverse and include: energy, litter, global citizenship, school grounds and transport.

Students are said to drive the Eco-School programme by leading eco-committees. Schools work towards gaining one of three awards – Bronze, Silver and Green flags – which symbolize excellence in the field of environmental activity. By January 2017, 17,000 schools in England had registered to be Eco-Schools, of which 1,200 had achieved the Green Flag status (Eco-Schools 2017). It is noteworthy that while the number of schools registered has increased over the past seven years by 3000, the number of schools achieving the awards has remained consistent. Perhaps signalling that although schools are keen to participate, in practice implementation is challenging. Fraser (2010) reported that the majority of those registered are primary schools, adding that secondary schools find the initiative more challenging because they tend to be large institutions, have fewer opportunities for cross-curricular work, have a shortage of time, have a lack of awareness of eco-projects available and feel they do not have the skills or expertise.

Concluding thoughts

We have tried to show that we are still struggling to understand whether education for sustainable development is more than a slogan and, if it is, how might it be enacted in schools and beyond. Underlying the debates about the validity of the terms 'sustainability' and 'sustainable development', there are bigger, more philosophical issues to do with what is the purpose of schooling – what or who is education for? The complexity and urgency of ensuring that future generations are offered the opportunities through education to understand and explore their environment and issues concerning sustainable living are captured in the WWF 2016 Living Planet report (2016). Here, the WWF asserts that the UN 2030 Agenda for Sustainable Development combines the economic, social and ecological dimensions necessary to sustain human society through the Anthropocene. But it stresses, 'that these dimensions are all interconnected and must be addressed in an integrated manner' (WWF 2016: 106). Going on to state, 'In the future, a basic fact must therefore inform development strategies, economic models, business models and lifestyle choices: we have only one planet and its natural capital is limited' (WWF 2016: 106).

Education is key to such change and teachers are the change agents. If you believe that you can offer a value-free education, then we believe that you are mistaken. Whether education actually *will* make a difference to the public's view of the environment or will slow our impact on our environment, is another question. But we believe that we need to consider what contribution we are going to make to that goal in our lives as teachers.

References

Carson, R. ([1962] 1999) *Silent Spring*. Harmondsworth: Penguin.

Department for Environment, Food and Rural Affairs (2015) *2010 to 2015 Government Policy: Sustainable Development*, https://www.gov.uk/government/publications/2010-to-2015-government-policy-sustainable-development/2010-to-2015-government-policy-sustainable-development#issue, accessed 24 January 2017.

DfE (Department for Education) (2013) *Teachers' Standards Guidance for School Leaders, School Staff and Governing Bodies* (DFE-00066-2011). London: Department for Education, https://www.gov.uk/government/uploads/system/uploads/attachment_data/file/301107/Teachers__Standards.pdf, accessed 19 January 2017.

DfES (Department for Education and Skills) (2006) *Learning Outside the Classroom Manifesto*. London: DfES.

Dillon, J. (2005) 'Silent Spring': science, the environment and society, *School Science Review*, 86(316): 113–18.

Dillon, J., DeWitt, J., Pegram, E., Irwin, B., Crowley, K., Haydon, R., King, H., Knutson, K., Veall, D. and Xanthoudaki, M. (2016) *A Learning Research Agenda for Natural History Institutions*. London: Natural History Museum.

Eco-Schools (2017) *Eco-Schools*, http://www.eco-schools.org.uk/, accessed 23 January 2017.

Education Scotland (2017) Home page, https://education.gov.scot/, accessed 25 January 2017.

Fettis, G.C. and Ramsden, M.J. (1995) Sustainability – what is it and how should it be taught? *ENTRÉE '95 Proceedings*, 81–90.

Fraser, N. (2010) Eco-schools Scotland: lessons learned from first-hand experiences, *School Science Review*, 92(338): 67–72.

Gayford, C. (2009) *Learning for Sustainability: From the Pupils' Perspective*. Godalming: WWF-UK, assets.wwf.org.uk/downloads/wwf_report_final_web.pdf, accessed 25 January 2017.

General Teaching Council for Scotland (2012) *The Standards for Registration: Mandatory Requirements for Registration with the General Teaching Council for Scotland*. Edinburgh: GTC Scotland, http://www.gtcs.org.uk/web/FILES/the-standards/standards-for-registration-1212.pdf, accessed 18 January 2017.

Glackin, M. (2016) 'Risky fun' or 'authentic science'? How teachers' beliefs influence their practice during a professional development programme on outdoor learning, *International Journal of Science Education*, 38(3): 409–33.

Hart, P. and Nolan, K. (1999) A critical analysis of research in environmental education, *Studies in Science Education*, 34: 1–69.

Hill, A. (2012) Developing approaches to outdoor education that promote sustainability education, *Australian Journal of Outdoor Education*, 16(1): 15.

Hopkins, C. (1998) The content of education for sustainable development, in M.J. Scoullos (ed.) *Environment and Society: Education and Public Awareness for Sustainability; Proceedings of the Thessaloniki International Conference*. Paris: UNESCO.

Hopkins, C. and McKeown, R. (1999) Education for Sustainable Development, *Forum for Applied Research and Public Policy*, 14(4): 25–8.

House of Commons Environmental Audit Committee (2016) *Sustainability and HM Treasury. Fifth Report of Session 2016–17*. Order of the House, http://www.publications. parliament.uk/pa/cm201617/cmselect/cmenvaud/181/18102.htm, accessed 24 January 2017.

Jickling, B. (2000) Education for sustainability: a seductive idea, but is it enough for my grandchildren?, http://www.ec.gc.ca/education/ee_jickling_e.htm, accessed 3 September 2006.

Jickling, B. and Wals, A.E.J. (2008) Globalization and environmental education: looking beyond sustainable development, *Journal of Curriculum Studies*, 40(1): 1–21.

Klein, N. (2015) *This Changes Everything: Capitalism vs. the Climate*: New York: Simon & Schuster.

Kollmuss, A. and Agyeman, J. (2002) Mind the gap: why do people act environmentally and what are the barriers to pro-environmental behavior? *Environmental Education Research*, 8(3): 239–60.

Kopnina, H. (2012) Education for sustainable development (ESD): the turn away from 'environment' in environmental education? *Environmental Education Research*, 18(5): 699–717.

Mace, G.M. (2014) Whose conservation? *Science*, 345(6204): 1558–60.

Marcinkowski, T.J. (2009) Contemporary challenges and opportunities in environmental education: where are we headed and what deserves our attention? *Journal of Environmental Education*, 41(1): 34–54.

Martin, A.R. and Chen, J.C. (2016) Barriers to sustainability in mature-age adult learners: working toward identity change, *Environmental Education Research*, 22(6): 849–67.

Martin, S., Dillon, J., Higgins, P., Peters, C. and Scott, W. (2013) *Education for Sustainable Development (ESD) in the UK: Current Status, Best Practice and Opportunities for the Future*, UK National Commission for UNESCO, http://www.unesco.org.uk/wp-content/uploads/2015/03/Brief-9-ESD-March-2013.pdf, accessed 17 January 2017.

National Environmental Education and Training Foundation (NEETF) (2005) *Environmental Literacy in America: What Ten Years of NEETF/Roper Research Studies Say About Environmental Literacy in the US*. Washington, DC: National Environmental Education and Training Foundation (NEETF), https://www.neefusa.org/resources/publications. htm, accessed 19 January 2017.

Pawley, D. (2000) Sustainability: a big word with little meaning, *Independent*, 11 July, http:// www.audacity.org/Resourcing%t20the%20future.htm, accessed 25 January 2017.

Pawley, D. (2000) "Sustainability: a big word with little meaning." London: Independent Newspaper, July 11, 2000 (Review section, p. 4).

Philips, T. (2017) Trump warming to reality of climate change, says senior Chinese official, *Guardian*, 17 January, https://www.theguardian.com/environment/2017/jan/17/trump-warming-to-reality-of-climate-change-says-senior-chinese-official, accessed 9 March 2017.

QCA (Qualifications and Curriculum Authority) (2004) *The National Curriculum Key Stage 3 and 4*, http://webarchive.nationalarchives.gov.uk/20130401151715/http://www. education.gov.uk/publications/eOrderingDownload/QCA-04-1374.pdf, accessed 18 January 2017.

Rauch, F. (2002) The potential of education for sustainable development for reform in schools, *Environmental Education Research*, 8(1): 43–51.

Rickinson, M., Dillon, J., Teamey, K., Morris, M., Choi, M.Y., Sanders, D. and Benefield, P. (2004) *A Review of Research on Outdoor Learning*. Preston Montford: Field Studies Council.

Robelia, B. and Murphy, T. (2012) What do people know about key environmental issues? A review of environmental knowledge surveys, *Environmental Education Research*, 18(3): 299–321.

Sachs, J.D. (2015) *The Age of Sustainable Development*. New York: Columbia University Press.

Sauvé, L. (1996) Environmental education and sustainable development: a further appraisal, *Canadian Journal of Environmental Education*, 1: 7–33.

Scott, W.A.H. and Gough, S. (2003) Rethinking relationships between education and capacity-building: remodelling the learning process, *Applied Environmental Education and Communication*, 2(4): 213–20.

SEEd (2017) *SEEd About Sustainability and Environmental Education*, se-ed.co.uk, accessed 23 January 2017.

Stables, A.W.G. (2001) Who drew the sky? Conflicting assumptions in environmental education, *Educational Philosophy and Theory*, 33(2): 245–56.

Stapp, W.B. (2000) Watershed education for sustainable development, *Journal of Science Education and Technology*, 9(3): 183–97.

UNESCO (United Nations Educational, Scientific and Cultural Organisation) (2006) *Education for Sustainable Development*, http://unesdoc.unesco.org/images/0015/001524/152453eo.pdf, accessed 9 March 2017.

United Nations (2015) *Transforming Our World: The 2030 Agenda for Sustainable Development* (September 2015), https://sustainabledevelopment.un.org/post2015/transformingourworld/publication, accessed 25 January 2017.

United Nations Educational, Scientific and Cultural Organisation (UNESCO) (2014) *UNESCO Roadmap for Implementing the Global Action Programme on Education for Sustainable Development*, France: United Nations Educational, Scientific and Cultural Organization, http://unesdoc.unesco.org/images/0023/002305/230514e.pdf, accessed 16 January 2017.

United Nations Secretary-General (2015) Secretary-General's remarks at Summit for the Adoption of the Post-2015 Development Agenda, https://www.un.org/sg/en/content/sg/statement/2015-09-25/secretary-generals-remarks-summit-adoption-post-2015-development, accessed 24 January 2017.

Wals, A.E.J. and Jickling, B. (2002) 'Sustainability' in higher education: from doublethink and newspeak to critical thinking and meaningful learning, *International Journal of Sustainability in Higher Education*, 3(3): 221–32.

World Commission on Environment and Development (WCED) (1987) *Our Common Future*. Oxford: Oxford University Press.

World Commission on Environment and Development (WCED) (1992) *Our Common Future Reconvened*. London: WCED.

World Wide Fund for Nature (WWF) (2016) *WWF 2016 Living Planet Report*. WWF, Gland, Switzerland, http://wwf.panda.org/about_our_earth/all_publications/lpr_2016/, accessed 25 January 2017.

World Wide Fund for Nature (WWF) (2012) *One Planet Schools: Connecting School and Community. Research Findings*. Scotland: World Wide Fund for Nature (WWF).

Further reading

Klein, N. (2015) *This Changes Everything: Capitalism vs. the Climate*. New York: Simon & Schuster.

Lucas, A.M. (1991) Environmental education: what is it, for whom, for what purpose and how, in S. Keiny and U. Zoller (eds) *Conceptual Issues in Environmental Education*. New York: Peter Lang Publishing.

Scott, W. and Gough, S. (2003) *Sustainable Development and Learning. Framing the Issues*. London: RoutledgeFalmer.

23

14–19 education: education and training in school and beyond
SIMON GIBBONS

Introduction

The focus of this chapter is that stage of secondary education that has come to be known, relatively recently, as the 14–19 phase. Although education as a whole would appear to be a site for almost continual change of policy and practice, nowhere is this statement more true than in relation to the latter stages of compulsory and non-compulsory education. However, despite the numerous policy developments and initiatives, several pressing concerns remain. What the central aims of this phase of education ought to be, and how these might be reconciled with the perceived needs of individuals, society, employers and higher education establishments, are questions that continue to occupy the minds of educational thinkers and policy-makers. In offering an overview of historical developments in the area, and exploring recent policy initiatives, this chapter should enable you to understand the situation we now find ourselves in, and encourage you to ask yourself such fundamental questions.

Central issues in 14–19 education

Before offering an overview of developments in the 14–19 phase, it is worth pausing to consider some of the reasons why this is a problematic area. Central to this is the issue of what is appropriate education or training for young people in this age range, and within that lie the problems of academic versus vocational education. In *Education and Training 14–19: Curriculum, Qualifications and Organisation* (Hodgson and Spours 2008), the authors offer a comprehensive account of developments in the area over the past 20 years. They hope that an understanding of the differing views over policy in the area might mean mistakes over future direction could be avoided.

Although written some time ago, Hodgson and Spours' critical evaluation of developments helps to shed light on some of the complexities of the issues by showing that in itself the 14–19 phase as an entity has evolved as much in a reactive way to existing problems, rather than as proactive policy-making. Their view about the state of the 14–19 phase might be viewed as somewhat alarming, but there is no little truth in it:

> The 14–19 concept has manifested itself in different ways over the past two decades, has ebbed and flowed in terms of national policy and has found it difficult to establish itself as something that is consistent and easily understood.
>
> (Hodgson and Spours 2008: 20)

In *Education for All: The Future of Education and Training for 14–19 Year Olds* (Pring *et al.* 2009), the authors identify five legacies that have been left by various policy developments affecting the 14–19 phase, legacies which must be addressed in any attempt to create a coherent and successful system. In summary, these five legacies are:

1. The tripartite mentality, dividing young people between 'academic', 'vocational/technical' and 'the rest'
2. The failure to achieve parity of esteem between 'academic' and 'vocational' courses
3. Ambivalence towards the meaning of 'vocational'
4. Lack of recognition of new qualifications among employers and higher education
5. The transient nature of new qualifications.

These legacies do not appear to be mutually exclusive; they offer a helpful summary of the issues in the 14–19 field, and are thus worthy of further exploration. The tripartite mentality undoubtedly has its roots, as we will see, in the 1944 Education Act, while the lack of recognition of new qualifications and the transient nature of these may well be linked; it is hard to see how one could expect employers or universities to develop an understanding of the meaning and value of a qualification when changes in this area have been so frequent. If a new qualification is not allowed to evolve, develop and establish a reputation, it is little wonder that it fails to achieve recognition. At post-16, the problem is perhaps particularly acute; there is little doubt that the A level has the reputation as the 'gold standard' among employers and university admissions tutors and it has been historically difficult for any alternative qualification to gain a meaningful foothold all the time its existence continues.

The ambivalence suggested towards the meaning of 'vocational' is an interesting point. Historically, much 'vocational' education, certainly for young people between 14 and 16 years old, has been very much school-based rather than employer-led. This may contribute to some mixed feelings towards its worth. There is, however, another complication with a paradigm that sets 'vocational' as some kind of opposite of 'academic', a situation that certainly seems to have developed within the education system in England in particular. Such a binary opposition is inclined to collapse under even the merest closer examination; most people would class the study to become a lawyer or a doctor, for example, as highly academic, yet at the same time such study could hardly be thought of as more vocational. How the 'common-sense' division that has evolved between the academic and vocational can be disputed and how fuller understandings of the meanings of these terms might be achieved are complex questions.

The second legacy issue that Pring *et al.* (2009) identify might be seen as the most difficult to reconcile; what has been a seemingly desperate attempt to make academic and other types of qualification in some way hold equal value. *Education for All* suggests that this parity of esteem may well in fact be a 'meaningless aim' (Pring *et al.* 2009: 7) within a system of qualifications that is highly divided. The argument is put forward that a radical approach be taken to overhaul the system of qualifications. This suggestion, as we will see in taking a historical overview, has been put to the policy-makers in various forms at different times.

A brief historical context

One reason that may account for the amount of change affecting the education of the 14–19 age group in England is the fact that the notion of educating or training all children within this range is still a relatively recent phenomenon. Prior to the Second World War only a minority of children would have experienced secondary education as we would typically recognize it today, for in this period, '88 percent of young people had left school by 14' (Tomlinson 1997: 3). It was not until the landmark Education Act of 1944 – commonly known as the Butler Act (after Rab Butler, the then Education Minister) – that secondary education for all up to the age of 15 became compulsory. The Act did in fact suggest schooling should continue to 16 but this aim was not realized for nearly three more decades. The Butler Act suggested a 'tripartite' education system of grammar, technical and secondary modern schools, but gave local authorities the freedom to decide on their own educational structure. In the event, few technical schools were ever opened, probably as a result of financial constraints, and the majority of children found themselves divided between grammar schools, where the so-called academically brightest were schooled towards public examinations, and secondary moderns, where typically children left school aged 15 without formal academic qualifications that were in any case, only offered to students aged 16. There were exceptions; London County Council was one of a small number of councils that took advantage of the Act's flexibility to put in place plans for a comprehensive system of education, where children of all academic abilities would be taught in single establishments, though, as has been noted, this was unusual in the country as a whole (see, for example, McCulloch 2002). Though the London Plan took many years to take effect in full – and indeed some grammar schools remain in the capital to this day – it paved the way for the comprehensivization of schooling in England that gathered pace through the 1960s and 1970s following the government circular in 1965 that asked all local authorities to propose plans for a comprehensive system. By the end of the 1980s, the majority of children in England were being taught in comprehensive schools, with a relatively small number of grammar schools remaining within the state education system.

Secondary education for all, the raising of the school-leaving age to 15 and then to 16 in 1972 (under the legislation known as ROSLA – the Raising of the School Leaving Age) meant that a new group of children remained in the school system. The traditional curriculum was geared towards the 'academic' child, and thus not seen as appropriate for many in the new 'fifth form'. A high proportion of the 'less academic children' would have experienced 'one year outward looking, life-adjustment courses' (Chitty 2009: 173) which would have been extended from those provided in the fourth year of many secondary modern schools. The growth in the staying on rates in the school population goes some way to explain, no doubt, the plethora of new policy initiatives affecting the 14–19 phase since the 1960s in particular; in their review, Wright and Oancea filled 40 pages simply listing the initiatives and policies impacting on the 14–19 phase since 1976 (Wright and Oancea 2005).

Given that the qualification that had generally been on offer in the grammar schools for 16-year-olds – the General Certificate in Education (GCE) O level examination – had been designed for the 20 per cent of children educated within that school system, there was clearly a need to offer an alternative 'academic' qualification for the remaining population, and this arrived through the introduction in the 1960s of the Certificate of Secondary Education (CSE). No doubt in part due to the near total comprehensivization of the school system by the 1980s, the General Certificate in Secondary Education (GCSE) was introduced as a common examination and replacement for the GCE and CSE for students at age 16. This, along with the introduction of the National Curriculum following the 1988 Education Act, meant that in the main all students up to the age of 16 followed what might be called a common curriculum. Post-16, however, GCE A levels – though they have gone through various modifications – have remained a constant, and the dominant academic qualifications, although it might be worth mentioning here that one relatively recent phenomenon in a minority of schools has been the increasing number adopting the International Baccalaureate (IB) as an alternative, or replacement, qualification to the A level. Some view this qualification, first offered in England in private schools, as far richer and wider-ranging than the narrow specialism of A level subject choice, and it is certainly a qualification that has recognition both nationally and internationally. *The Baccalaureate: A Model for Curriculum Reform* (Philips and Pound 2003) offers a comprehensive overview of the qualification and its use internationally, and within Wales in the United Kingdom.

Traditionally, those students not seen to be academically 'bright' enough for A level study would have left school at 16, perhaps moving into work, perhaps into apprenticeships or training schemes, or possibly into further education and sixth form colleges to pursue some form of vocational training. The last 40 years have seen a series of vocational qualifications introduced, initially for students in the post-16 age group, to satisfy the needs of young people not wishing, or thought not able enough, to pursue GCE A level study. These have included Business and Technology and Educational Council (BTEC) and City & Guilds Courses, and more recently General National Vocational Qualifications (GNVQs), so that, by the 1980s:

a three-track system emerged post-16, reflected in a system of awards: the academic route for those capable of pursuing 'A' (Advanced) Levels, mainly on their way to universities; an occupationally specific or 'strongly vocational' route for those who were to acquire the skills relevant to the workplace (reflected, at different levels, in the National Vocational Qualifications or NVQs); and an 'in-between' or 'weakly vocational' route in which young people would pursue a general education, albeit embodied within a vocational area to give a sense of relevance and to contextualize the knowledge (General National Vocational Qualification or GNVQ).

(Pring 2007: 119)

A predominant feature of the vocational qualifications that have been introduced has been the attempt to stress their equivalence with traditional academic qualifications; the intermediate GNVQ was stated to be the equivalent of four GCSEs at grade A*–C, while the advanced GNVQ was equated to two GCE A levels. It is doubtful whether such claims of equivalence have ever fully convinced either employers or universities' admissions tutors. The equivalence claims do point, however, to the bigger issue of the growing divide that has arisen between the academic and vocational routes, a divide that has characterized 14–19 education in England in particular. Successive policy initiatives have attempted to address this divide, with the aim of moving away from what has been viewed by many as effectively a 'two-tier' system, the 'high status' academic pathway and the 'low status' vocational route.

The most concerted attempt to address this status problem came with the publication of the Tomlinson Report (DfES 2004). The working group led by Sir Mike Tomlinson that produced the report was set up by the then Labour government who had genuine concerns over the relatively small proportion of young people remaining in education and training beyond the age of 16. The working group's final report (DfES 2004) contained what for many were welcome, but in some ways radical, solutions to tackle existing problems in the phase. Central to the recommendations was a complete overhaul of the qualifications system: 'The existing system of qualifications taken by 14–19 year olds should be replaced by a framework of diplomas at entry, foundation, intermediate and advanced levels' (DfES 2004: 7).

Essentially, Tomlinson's proposals would mean that between the ages of 14–19, students would take certain core subjects (including literacy, numeracy and ICT) and then select from other options. In an attempt to address the historical problems of the academic/vocational divide, full implementation of the proposals would have enabled students to combine academic and vocational work, with all students obtaining a diploma at one of four levels as a result of their work across the phase. The system would involve an increase in the proportion of internally assessed student work, rather than externally marked examinations, meaning that the clear end point marked by assessment at 16 could be avoided 'At entry, foundation and intermediate levels, in place of existing GCSE-style examinations, teacher-led assessment should be the predominant mode of assessment' (DfES 2004: 9). It was the kind of system for which many within education had been calling. If the 14–19 phase were to be viewed as a whole, with the expectation that all young people remain in some form of education or training throughout the phase, then the existence of terminal examinations for all at 16 was creating an artificial and unhelpful break in the continuum – it was in fact serving accountability purposes, rather than any educational ends. The recommendations, the report suggested, would bring a cohesion to the 14–19 phase, rather than it being made up of 14–16 and post-16 bolted together:

> The interlocking nature of the diploma means that as soon as a diploma is claimed, the learner automatically has some of the components to achieve the next level diploma, thus helping to bridge the pre-16/post-16 divide and providing a motivation to continue in learning and achieve qualifications which are credible with employers and others.
>
> (DfES 2004: 11)

However, from the very day of its publication it was clear that these central recommendations regarding the qualifications framework would not be accepted by the then New Labour administration. My own memory of the evening following the report's publications is exactly that recalled here: 'the very same night the Prime Minister, Tony Blair, in a speech to the CBI stated "GCSEs and A Levels will stay. So will externally marked exams"' (Hodgson and Spours 2008: 34). I listened to that very speech with a dual sense of disappointment but inevitability. Education commentators at the time (see, for example, Baker 2004) clearly saw the government reaction as politically rather than educationally motivated. There was an election looming, and any attempt to water down the perceived 'gold standard' of external A level examinations might have led 'middle England' to feel the government were 'dumbing down' or being 'soft' on standards. It is of course a reality, though none the less disappointing for that, that decisions affecting the education of the nation's children are rarely taken without the potential political cost borne in mind. Tomlinson had suggested that the scale of reform needed would require a ten-year implementation programme – few in UK history are the governments that have had the courage to initiate anything that would fail to bear full fruit within a parliamentary term.

The government's response to the Tomlinson Report came in the form of the Education and Skills 14–19 Paper (DfES 2005). Although in her Foreword the Secretary of State for Education Ruth Kelly acknowledged the 'excellent work of Sir Mike Tomlinson and his Working Group on 14–19 Reform' (DfES 2005: 3), there is no doubt that the core and most far-reaching proposals of Tomlinson were flatly rejected. A central aim of Tomlinson had been to tackle the academic/vocational divide with the introduction of new all-encompassing qualifications, but the 2005 White Paper in fact: 'rejected Tomlinson and proposed academic and vocational routes with their respective qualifications' (Pring 2007: 121).

The White Paper ensured the continued existence of GCSEs and A levels, but in a move that – on the surface at least – seemed to draw on the working group's proposals, and introduced the Diploma as a new vocational qualification. It has been suggested (Hodgson and Spours 2010), this embodiment of the qualification represented a 'cherry picking' by the government of Tomlinson's original proposals. It is difficult to avoid such a conclusion, and to think that an opportunity for real reform was missed. There were plans to develop diplomas that would cover academic as well as vocational areas of study and thus perhaps address the division, but these were never realized as a new administration and new thinking brought further overhaul of the 14–19 phase.

Education for All: The Future of Education and Training for 14–19 Year Olds (2009) was in fact the final summary report of the Nuffield Review, the largest-scale research into 14–19 education and training ever undertaken in England and Wales. The review, ongoing between October 2003 and September 2009, was extremely wide-ranging, covering all aspects of education and training for the 14–19 age group. In addressing the question of why such a large-scale review was needed, the final executive summary made a powerful claim, suggesting that:

> A range of problems need to be addressed: many young people abandon education as soon as they can; teachers feel constrained by constant and (what they see as) inappropriate interventions from government and by the assessment regime; universities worry about the readiness of young people for higher education; and employers complain about lack of preparation for employment in terms of skills, knowledge and attitudes. Despite many initiatives from the respective governments – many of them being both commendable and effective – much more needs to be done. And in many cases, different policies need to be adopted.
>
> (Nuffield Review, Executive Summary 2009: 5)

The Review resulted in a large number of associated publications, ranging from annual reports to briefing and issues papers. The 12 issues papers, dealing with subjects from curriculum to careers education, are a particularly rich source of information to support further study of the 14–19 phase, and all are freely downloadable from the Nuffield Review website (http://www.nuffieldfoundation. org/14-19review). The review covered areas such as funding, curriculum, qualifications and institutional collaboration, and one would hope that, given the support of research, the findings would be taken seriously by policy-makers. The extent to which this may be true might be seen in the later section of this chapter that explores the most recent central policy initiatives in the 14–19 phase.

Raising the age of participation and the question of NEETs

In the latter years of the New Labour government, attention turned more explicitly to the efforts to ensure that more young people stayed in education and training beyond the age of 16. In the 2007 Green Paper, *Raising Expectations: Staying in Education and Training Post-16* (DfES 2007), the case was first explicitly made by government to raise the age of participation first to 17 and then 18 years of age. Although previous 14–19 policy had included aspirations and targets for greater participation, this Green Paper paved the way for the first statutory increase in leaving ages since the 1972 Raising of the School Leaving Age (ROSLA) legislation.

The arguments for this shift presented in the Green Paper included those indicating the potential economic benefit to the individual of staying in education to 18:

> By participating for longer, young people are much more likely to achieve a level 2 qualification and consequently earn more in the future. People with five or more good GCSEs earn on average around £100,000 more over their lifetime than those who leave learning with qualifications below level 2.

> (DfES 2007: 12)

There were also suggestions that society as a whole suffers as a result of relatively low involvement in education and training at post-16: 'Society also benefits from increased participation. Those who participate are less likely to experience teenage pregnancy, be involved in crime or behave anti-socially' (DfES 2007: 12).

There is no doubt that the emphasis placed on post-16 participation had been informed by research carried out on the group of young people who have come to be known collectively as 'NEETs' (Not in Employment, Education or Training). It is difficult to be precise about the number of young people falling into this category. The Labour government commissioned a number of research reviews into this 'difficult to pin down' group of young people (for example, Coles *et al.* 2002; Rennison *et al.* 2005). Some of the difficulty is that although given a blanket name, it is not the case that NEETs are a homogeneous group, since those classified as such might include young people acting as carers, individuals on a gap year, those with illness, or those involved in crime, to name but a few. The EYE Briefing Paper 3, published as part of the Nuffield Review, put the NEET figure at around 10 per cent of the 16-18-year-old population, and explored some of the complexities involved in the attempts to accurately calculate this figure (Nuffield Review 2008).

Given that the NEET group is a complex and heterogeneous one also means it is difficult to envisage a single policy initiative or strategy that could 'solve' the problem of this group. There is, however, enough in the research to suggest that the fact that a significant number of young people fall into this category at one point or another leads to problems both for those individuals and for wider society. The statutory raising of the leaving age might then be seen as the only single policy that could in one sweep address the problem. That the needs of NEETs focused the mind of the government on raising the age of participation is supported by the DfES-commissioned research published soon after the 2007 Green Paper, which concluded: 'Young people most likely to be affected by the proposed legislation are those who, in the absence of the proposed policy, would have probably been NEET or in JWT (jobs without training)' (Spielhofer *et al.* 2007: 1).

The decision to raise the age of participation was made law by the 2008 Education and Skills Act (House of Lords and House of Commons 2008). The legislation was not – as with ROSLA – a raising of the school-leaving age, rather it was a raising of the age of participation. Under the Act, all young people would remain in some form of education until 17 from 2013 and then 18 from 2015 (i.e. those beginning in Year 7 in 2009 would now continue to 18). What is meant by participation covers: full-time education in school or college; work-based learning such as apprenticeships and part-time education or training if employed, self-employed or volunteering for more than 20 hours per week.

Apprenticeships

An alternative to school or college-based education for those of 16 years and over is to take an apprenticeship. Traditionally apprenticeships have been 'on the job' training for those entering industries such as construction. Modern Apprenticeships were introduced by the Conservative government in 1994, with employers given subsidies to take on young people. Modern Apprenticeships were succeeded in 2004 by Apprenticeships, with three levels being available: Apprenticeship (equivalent to five GCSE passes at A*–C); Advanced Apprenticeships (equivalent to two A level passes) and Higher Apprenticeships, leading to qualifications at NVQ level 4 or possibly Foundation Degrees. Most recently, the Apprenticeship, Skills, Children and Learning Act has consolidated the Apprenticeships and sought to substantially increase the number of places available, so that all qualified 16-year-olds have the right to an apprenticeship (DCFS 2009). As has been observed, the Apprenticeship in England differs greatly from those of higher status offered in European countries such as Germany and Holland. Indeed, it has been suggested that two distinct types of vocational education and training (VET) exist: 'a "skill" or "task-based" model dominating in England, and an "occupational" model prevalent in the Netherlands, France and Germany' (Brockman, Clarke and Winch 2010: 113):

> In the occupational model, VET, including apprenticeship, is based upon the principle of enhancing individual capacity or potential within a broadly defined occupational field. Qualifications, developed by the social partners (employers and trade unions), are awarded on completion of a regulated and recognized programme, comprising occupational knowledge and competences as well as general and civic education, thus providing for the development of the person within the occupation and as a citizen in the wider society . . . By contrast, in England, competence refers to the performance of prescribed tasks to an acceptable standard without the reflective use of knowledge.
>
> (Brockman *et al.* 2010: 113)

For these authors, the results are stark – for example, an apprenticeship in the construction industry in Germany would allow a young person to develop a range of skills that might be needed within the broad field of that industry, whereas one in England would simply give a participant knowledge of basic tasks, such as bricklaying. It is difficult to disagree with the views of these researchers that fundamental changes need to be made to the Apprenticeship, including broader educational content, for the option to obtain greater status and be more appealing to both students and employers.

A further dimension to the Apprenticeship is the Young Apprenticeship, which was also introduced in 2004. Under this initiative (see DfES 2006a; 2006b), a small number of students at age 14 are given the opportunity to spend two days, or equivalent, out of school in a work environment. While in school they study core National Curriculum subjects (such as English, maths and ICT) to GCSE level, and when in the work environment they pursue vocational qualifications at level 2 (equivalent to GCSE grades A*–C).

Recent policy initiatives around 14–19 and their emerging effects

Recent political change has, somewhat inevitably, meant further developments focused on the 14–19 phase. Within weeks of assuming power in 2010, the Conservative/Liberal Democrat Coalition administration announced that the planned diplomas in academic subjects – which had been scheduled for first teaching from 2011 – would no longer be introduced. The cost saving of this intervention was highlighted by the Schools Minister, Nick Gibb, along with the suggestion that government should not be dictating to schools about the nature of qualifications offered to students. The Coalition's first education White Paper *The Importance of Schools* (DfE 2010) also had recommendations that had the potential to affect the 14–19 phase, though the messages may have been viewed, at best, as somewhat ambiguous. The rhetoric of the paper did acknowledge the problems within the phase, particularly the issue of NEETs, and insisted that there should be high expectations of all children, 'ensuring they continue their education until age 18 and beyond' (DfE 2010: 41). There was, however, the revelation that legislation would be brought forward to allow the enforcement of compulsory education and training to age 18 to be introduced at a slower rate, 'to avoid criminalising young people' (DfE 2010: 50) – so there seemed to be an acknowledgement here that in the short term at least, there would still be significant numbers of young people leaving school at 16. There was support for apprenticeships, and for vocational qualifications, with an acknowledgement that: 'This country suffers from a long-standing failure to provide young people with a proper technical and practical education of a kind that we see in other nations' (DfE 2010: 49).

However, this assertion was followed by the accusation that vocational education had become pseudo-academic, with students following courses that were easy for schools to deliver, or those that 'confer advantages in the accountability system' (DfE 2010: 49). The implication was that qualifications like the Diploma were taken due to their equivalency to a number of GCSEs, thus enabling schools to climb performance league tables without students having to take subjects that might be viewed as more academically challenging. Also within the paper was the suggestion that there should be the introduction of an English Baccalaureate, a certificate awarded to any student obtaining five good GCSE passes, including English, mathematics, a science, a modern or classical language, and a humanities subject. The plan was for this qualification to be featured in school performance tables. The message from the new administration was clear; they wanted more students to follow traditional academic subjects – the drive was towards a more, so-called, rigorous education up to the age of 16 at least.

In a bid to address the various problems he perceived with the 14–19 phase, particularly around the alternatives to academic curriculum and assessment, the then Secretary of State for Education, Michael Gove, announced in autumn of 2010 that a review of vocational qualifications would be undertaken, led by Professor Alison Wolf of King's College London. In announcing the review, Mr Gove suggested that there should be the creation of 'university technical colleges', academies which students could attend from age 14 to follow predominantly vocational courses, with some core academic study (Sharp 2010). For many, this sounded very reminiscent of the technical schools proposed as part of the tripartite system recommended by the 1944 Butler Act.

The Wolf Review (Wolf 2011) was hailed by Gove on its publication as 'brilliant, and ground breaking' (Wolf 2011: 4). In offering the case for fundamental reform of the phase, the report established three core principles: first, that vocational qualifications needed to be directly relevant for the labour market; second, referring to previous well-meaning attempts to claim parity between vocational and academic qualifications, that there needed to be honesty about the value of qualifications; and third, there needed to be simplification of the phase that had been overly complicated by what was described as 'twenty years of micro-management' (Wolf 2011: 9). Wolf made a total of 27 far-reaching recommendations. These recommendations ranged from those relating to the nature of vocational qualifications that ought to be available, to how such qualifications might contribute to school performance indicators, to the teaching of maths and English at post-16, and to the status of FE-trained teachers. Significantly, too, there were recommendations about the funding of post-16 education.

There has been a relatively rapid implementation of the vast majority of the reforms recommended by the Wolf Report, so that within four years the government was able to publish a progress report which stated that 20 of the 27 recommendations had been met in full while six were in the process of being met, with one being met in part (DfE 2015). The actions taken have certainly had effects on schools, colleges and students in the 14–19 phase in a number of key areas.

Whether or not it was the case that schools had been playing the system by entering students for allegedly easy vocational-type qualifications that were judged to be equivalent to GCSE is debatable, but the changes made have addressed this. The government has moved to a system of approving Technical Awards that awarding bodies wish to offer to schools with the proviso that these cannot include subjects that are included in the EBacc. Any given Technical Award can only be equivalent to one GCSE and the changes made in parallel to the school performance indicators have had an effect. Essentially secondary schools are now judged by the proportion of students attaining in four key areas: the EBacc; English and maths GCSE; attainment across eight subjects (called Attainment 8); and progress across eight subjects (called Progress 8). It is the last of these that is perhaps the most important as it will be Progress 8 that is the measure of the floor standard for schools. This measure is a calculation of how much progress students have made in up to eight subjects; five of these are the EBacc subjects while three may come from a so-called open group of approved academic, arts and vocational subjects. Since a maximum of three vocational subjects can contribute to the performance scores, the thrust now is on all students to be following a relatively academic programme in Key Stage 4. In 2016, the government's White Paper,

Educational Excellence Everywhere, made clear its aim to 'continue to embed reforms to assessment and qualifications including more robust and rigorous GCSEs and A Levels' with the expectation that 'the vast majority of pupils will study the English Baccalaureate (EBacc)' (DfE 2016a: 88). The stated aim is to ensure all students receive education in a common core of subjects that allow for progression. Whether one views this as a desirable move or not, it clearly removes any incentive schools might have had to enter students for those vocational qualifications which, in the past, may have been equivalent to four or five GCSE 'C' grades.

Following Wolf, it is now a requirement for all students failing to gain a pass grade in maths and English to continue to study these subjects post-16, with this being a condition of funding for providers. While this clearly affects the experience of students in this group, the wider change to post-16 funding following Wolf, with funding now calculated by student rather than by qualification, may have profound effects on schools and colleges. This method of funding may well affect the viability of smaller sixth forms, and within sixth forms will also affect the viability of less popular subjects. The results can already be seen with schools reducing the available options for sixth form subjects and with more and more students having to move between schools that have co-ordinated in consortiums to offer a fuller range of post-16 subjects taught across different institutions.

So, while Wolf and its implementation explicitly referred to vocational education, there have been resulting, or at least concurrent, changes to the academic diet for students in the 14–19 phase. Up to the age of 16, these have no doubt been driven in part by changes to assessment, to equivalence of qualifications and to the performance indicators used in school league tables; changes that have been implemented in the wake of Wolf. Post-16, other notable changes have been implemented; the decoupling of AS and A2 has meant schools having to significantly rethink aspects of curriculum organization in the sixth form. Interestingly, too, the Extended Project Qualification (EPQ), which is in some ways a legacy of the Diplomas, is becoming increasingly popular for A level students and beginning to gain recognition with university admissions tutors. For those students taking A level examinations, in their new linear design with greater weighting now given to terminal examinations, the Extended Project is perhaps the only opportunity now to genuinely develop independent study and learning skills and to afford students opportunities to pursue topics and subjects for which they have personal passions. This may be particularly the case as the reforms to the curriculum at post-16 have seen a large number of what might be seen to be less academic subjects being discontinued; there are now no longer A levels available in such subjects as creative writing, performance studies and applied art and design.

Most recently, in July 2016, following a review led by Lord Sainsbury (Sainsbury 2016), the government launched its Post-16 Skills Plan (DfE 2016b), the latest bid to bring reform to the area of vocational, or more correctly technical, education. Under the proposals in this plan, the ambition is that 'every young person, after an excellent grounding in the core academic standards and a broad and balanced curriculum to age 16, is presented with two options: the academic or the technical option' (DfE 2016b: 7). The central proposals are to streamline the system so that 15 technical routes are developed, with standards guided by the industries and occupations themselves leading to qualifications up to level 5, combining work in college and the workplace through apprenticeships. If the timetable for implementation is met, then these new qualifications will be available for delivery in September 2019 and they will, according to the announcements in the spring 2017 budget, be named 'T levels' (for a fuller explanation of these proposed new qualifications, see http://feweek.co.uk/2017/03/06/making-sense-of-the-plans-for-t-levels/).

Apprenticeships themselves have, too, been the target of very recent reform with new apprenticeships standards introduced that ensure, for example, that all apprenticeships have a minimum of 20 per cent off the job training, an assessment that covers theoretical and practical aspects and a focus on English and maths. The changes, with employers leading the development of the standards, began as a result of the independent review of apprenticeships led by Doug Richard which was published in 2012 (Richard 2012). The review's recommendations continue to be implemented.

With the scale and rapidity of recent change it can be difficult to keep pace with current arrangements for study and assessment in the 14–19 range. The 'Handy Guide' to qualification reform produced by Pearson is a useful resource in this respect (Pearson 2016).

Concluding thoughts

I have tried to show in this chapter the ways in which fundamental issues relating to the 14–19 phase continue to exercise policy-makers, and offer some reasons to explain this. Striking a balance between the academic and the vocational is a recurring problem and arguably it is not one that has been lessened by the most recent initiatives that again seem to confer more status on the academic route. What can only honestly be described as the stranglehold of the accountability framework does mean that schools have little option but to restrict choice for students in Key Stage 4; the effects of this on students' motivation and attitudes to education will no doubt become clear over the next few years. It is almost inevitable that data will point to more 16-year-olds attaining the EBacc; whether this is in their, or society's, best interests is another question. The nature and status of the EBacc also have the potential to further limit the scope for pupils in schools to follow arts or cultural subjects, like dance, art, drama and media studies. Indeed, a review commissioned by the National Union of Teachers (Neumann et al. 2016) has already shown how students' choices have been restricted and that this has had negative consequences for things like behaviour. So while official policy rhetoric claims to be devolving more power over curriculum to schools, and while the effective deregulation of the school landscape through such initiatives as academization and the free schools programme offers scope for innovation at the level of individual institution, the ways in which schools are judged undoubtedly means that for students between 14–16 at least, it is likely that there will be more conformity of experience.

For those that support a perhaps more innovative approach to curriculum, with more diverse academic and vocational options open to students in this phase of their education, recent policy moves may seem less than support-ive. For supporters of the reforms, however, the aims are to ensure all young people get what be might called a strong grounding or foundation in a full range of key academic subjects. As you begin your teaching career it will be interesting for you to see how these changes are affecting not only your own subject's status and position, but the overall levels of motivation and engagement among the students you encounter. There is evidence that so-called middle-attaining students might be most affected by new reforms (Hodgson and Spours 2015); is this a phenomenon that you notice in schools?

Ensuring that hundreds of thousands of young people do not drop out of the system completely remains a central issue, too. Moves to address the perceived problem of the NEET population do not seem, so far at least, to have had the desired effects. Government figures from November 2016 revealed that 11.9 per cent of the 16–24 age group were classified as NEETs, an increase on the previous year, despite the raising of the age of participation (House of Commons Library 2016). Clearly there is still an issue here and it is perfectly fair to argue that the effects of the pressures on the 14–16 phase may do little to help in the resolution of the problem.

Given the ongoing concerns, it is highly unlikely that – even in the short term – we have seen the last of central policy reform affecting the 14–19 phase. As you move through your training year and into your first post, it would be best to keep a watchful eye on developments affecting this phase and to be sensitive to the potential impact on the students you teach.

References

Baker, M. (2004) Why Tomlinson was turned down, http://news.bbc.co.uk/1/hi/education/4299151.stm, accessed 1 May 2017.

Brockman, M., Clarke, L. and Winch, C. (2010) The Apprenticeship Framework in England: a new beginning or a continuing sham? *Journal of Education and Work*, 23(2): 111–27.

Chitty, C. (2009) *Education Policy in Britain*. London: Palgrave Macmillan.

Coles, B., Hutton, S., Bradshaw, J., Craig, G., Godfrey, C. and Johnson, J. (2002) *Literature Review of the Costs of Being 'Not in Education, Employment or Training' at Age 16–18*. London: DES.

DCSF (Department for Children, Schools and Families) (2009) *Functional Skills: Nuts and Bolts Series*. London: DCFS.

DfE (Department for Education) (2010) *The Importance of Teaching: The Schools White Paper 2010*, https://www.gov.uk/government/uploads/system/uploads/attachment_data/file/175429/CM-7980.pdf, accessed 1 March 2017.

DfE (Department for Education) (2015) The Wolf Report: recommendations final progress report, https://www.gov.uk/government/uploads/system/uploads/attachment_data/file/405986/Wolf_Recommendations_Progress_Report_February_2015_v01.pdf, accessed 1 May 2017.

DfE (Department for Education) (2016a) *Educational Excellence Everywhere*, https://www.gov.uk/government/uploads/system/uploads/attachment_data/file/508447/Educational_Excellence_Everywhere.pdf, accessed 1 March 2017.

DfE (Department for Education) (2016b) *Post 16 Skills Plan*, https://www.gov.uk/government/uploads/system/uploads/attachment_data/file/536043/Post-16_Skills_Plan.pdf, accessed 1 March 2017.

DfES (Department for Education and Skills) (2004) *14–19 Curriculum and Qualifications Reform: Final Report of the Working Group on 14–19 Reform (the Tomlinson Report)*. London: DfES.

DfES (Department for Education and Skills) (2005) *14–19 Education and Skills*. London: DfES.

DfES (Department for Education and Skills) (2006a) *Young Apprenticeships for 14–16 Year Olds: A Guide for Education, Skills and Training Professionals*. London: DfES.

DfES (Department for Education and Skills) (2006b) *Young Apprenticeships for 14–16 Year Olds: Information for Pupils*. London: DfES.

DfES (Department for Education and Skills) (2007) *Raising Expectations: Staying in Education and Training Post-16*. London: DfES.

Hodgson, A. and Spours, K. (2008) *Education and Training 14–19: Curriculum, Qualifications and Organization*. London: Sage.

Hodgson, A. and Spours, K. (2010) Vocational qualifications and progression to higher education: the case of the 14–19 Diplomas in the English system, *Journal of Education and Work*, 23(2): 95–110.

Hodgson, A. and Spours, K. (2015) *The Missing Middle: How Middle Attaining Students in 14–19 Education Are Being Overlooked and Squeezed by Policy*, http://kenspours.org/uploads/3/6/0/5/3605791/missing_middle_hol_2015.pdf, accessed 10 February 2017.

House of Commons Library (2016) *Briefing Paper: NEET: Young People Not in Education, Employment of Training*, http://researchbriefings.parliament.uk/ResearchBriefing/Summary/SN06705, accessed 21 December 2016.

House of Lords and House of Commons (2008) *Education and Skills Act*. London: HMSO.

McCulloch, G. (2002) Local authorities and the organisation of secondary schooling 1943–1950, *Oxford Review of Education*, 28(2/3): 235–46.

Neumann, E., Towers, E., Gewirtz, S. and Maguire, M. (2016) *A Curriculum for All? The Effects of Recent Curriculum, Assessment and Accountability Reforms on Secondary Education*, https://www.teachers.org.uk/sites/default/files2014/curriculum-for-all-64pp-10845.pdf, accessed 10 February 2017.

Nuffield Review (2008) *EYE Briefing Paper 3: Rates of Post-16 Non-participation in England*. London: Nuffield Review of 14–19 Education and Training, England and Wales. http://www.nuffield14–19review.org.uk, accessed 1 September 2010.

Nuffield Review (2009) *Executive Summary*, http://www.nuffield14-19review.org.uk, accessed 1 September 2010.

Pearson (2016) *14–19 Qualification Reform 2010–19: A Handy Guide*, https://uk.pearson.com/content/dam/region-core/uk/pearson-uk/documents/about/news-and-policy/handy-guides/handy-guide-to-14-19-qualification-reform-2010-2019.pdf, accessed 12 January 2017.

Philips, G. and Pound, T. (eds) (2003) *The Baccalaureate: A Model for Curriculum Reform*. London: Kogan Page.

Pring, R. (2007) 14–19 and lifelong learning, in L. Clarke and C. Winch (eds) *Vocational Education: International Approaches, Developments and Systems*. London: Routledge.

Pring, R., Hayward, G., Hodgson, A., Johnson, J., Keep, E., Oancea, A., Rees, G., Spours, K. and Wilde, S. (2009) *Education for All: The Future of Education and Training for 14–19 Year Olds*. London: Routledge.

Rennison, J., Maguire, S., Middleton, S. and Ashworth, K. (2005) *Young People Not in Education, Employment or Training: Evidence from the Education Maintenance Allowance Pilots Database*. London: DfES.

Richard, D. (2012) *The Richard Review of Apprenticeships*, https://www.gov.uk/government/uploads/system/uploads/attachment_data/file/34708/richard-review-full.pdf, accessed 12 February 2017.

Sainsbury, D. (2016) Report of the Independent Panel on Technical Education, https://www.gov.uk/government/uploads/system/uploads/attachment_data/file/536046/Report_of_the_Independent_Panel_on_Technical_Education.pdf, accessed 1 June 2017.

Sharp, H. (2010) Vocational education has 'lost its way', says Gove, http://www.bbc.co.uk/news/education–11229469, accessed 2 December 2016.

Spielhofer, T., Walker, M., Gagg, K., Schagen, S. and O'Donnell, S. (2007) *Raising the Participation Age in Education and Training to 18: Review of Existing Evidence of the Benefits and Challenges*. London: DfES.

Tomlinson, S. (1997) Education 14–19 divided and divisive, in S. Tomlinson (ed.) *Education 14–19 Critical Perspectives*. London: DfES.

Wolf, A. (2011) *Review of Vocational Education: The Wolf Report*. London: Department for Education.

Wright, S. and Oancea, A. (2005) *Policies for 14–19 Education and Training in England 1976 to the Present Day: A Chronology*. Briefing Paper for the Nuffield Foundation Review of 14–19 Education and Training, www.nuffield14–19review.org.uk, accessed 12th December 2016.

24

Learning with digital technologies
MARY WEBB

Introduction

The twenty-first century is characterized by rapid change. This change is led by people, not by technologies, but new technologies have provided scope for new ways of communicating, interacting, creating, working, socializing, playing and learning. In order to live and work in this changing society, people need the understanding and skills to take advantage of these new developments. Our education system, therefore, is having to respond to the challenges provided by new technologies and educators are trying to decide what these changes mean for learning as well as how to prepare young people to take their place in a society that is changing rapidly. While new technologies can make many aspects of life easier and work more productive, for teachers they can add to the complexity of pedagogical decision-making. Having some understanding of the debates around the use of new technologies in learning and the issues and practical concerns that have been identified will help you to navigate the policies and practices in your school. It will help develop your own and your students' skills to make appropriate use of technologies to enable and enhance or perhaps transform your students' learning.

The current situation of policy and practice in relation to the use of digital technologies in schools varies greatly between schools. For you, as a beginning teacher, this means that an important first step is to find out about policy and practice in relation to digital technologies in your placement school. However, you cannot assume that such practice is the norm and you may well find that students in other placements experience very different facilities and expectations. In some schools, for example, there is an expectation that students will bring their own mobile devices to school and use them to access information, take photos to document their work, run apps (applications) to explore new concepts and use social media to communicate with teachers and peers. However, in other schools, mobile phones are banned and students use the school computers only when instructed to by their teacher. This divergence of mobile phone policy illustrates the wide-ranging views that exist across the education system of how best to respond to new technologies.

You may be experienced in deploying a range of technologies in your life and in your own learning and may be keen to explore how you can support your own teaching and your students' learning with digital technologies. On the other hand, you may feel overwhelmed by the range of different technologies and varying possibilities for supporting your students' learning. Certainly, there are many experienced teachers who find the complexity of selecting from the wide range of new opportunities provided by technologies challenging or even confusing. Thus, in this chapter, I review what we know about how developments in digital technologies influence learners, teachers and education more generally. Furthermore, I examine opportunities and challenges for using new technologies in education, both at the time of writing this chapter and looking ahead a few years. I hope this will encourage you to look carefully at what technologies are available in your own school and others and to reflect on how you might try using a range of different resources in your own practice. I will not be providing you with specific examples of how to use technologies in your own teaching because that varies from subject to subject and topic to topic. Indeed, pedagogical practices are often subject-specific but at the same time some general pedagogical principles in relation to the use of digital technologies can be discerned.

In this chapter I review evidence of learners' characteristics, capabilities and expectations in relation to the use of new technologies in their daily lives and particularly for learning. Then I consider the implications for teachers' pedagogical knowledge and practices and the development of students' digital skills. Subsequent sections discuss particular aspects of learning, teaching and assessment that are being affected by new technological developments.

It is important to be clear about the language being used in this field because a range of different terms have been used in the UK over the last few years. The term Information and Communication Technologies (ICT) has been used in the UK and elsewhere to refer to the use of new technologies to support learning. ICT across the curriculum (ICTAC) has also been used to refer to the cross-curricular use of technologies. Rather confusingly, until recently ICT was also a curriculum subject but a report by the Royal Society (2012) recommended major reforms including changing the name of the curriculum subject to computing. The new curriculum for computing in schools incorporates three elements: (1) computer science as the underlying academic discipline; (2) information technology as the use of computers in business and industry; and (3) digital skills. The use of ICT to support learning across the curriculum is additional to the computing curriculum and is sometimes referred to as Technology Enhanced Learning (TEL) especially in further and higher education.

Learners in the Internet Age

The changes in society and access to technologies mean that learners are now very different from generations prior to the 'digital age'. The extent and nature of these changes and their implications for teaching are much debated in the research literature and popular media, and are often misunderstood, ignored or oversimplified by educators. For example, the term 'digital natives' has become quite widespread in education to refer to a set of perceived characteristics of young people, who have been immersed in technology throughout their lives, that sets them apart from previous generations in terms of their skills, expertise and expectations with new technologies. The perception appears to be supported by the ways in which young people, often at a very early age, become adept at using mobile phones, etc. and seem to be constantly interacting and socializing through social media, gaming environments, and so on. However, this perception is critiqued by many researchers, including Kirschner and van Merriënboer, who go as far as to say in relation to young people's Internet searching behaviour:

> What we may actually be seeing is a generation where learners at the computer behave as butterflies fluttering across the information on the screen, touching or not touching pieces of information (i.e., hyperlinks), quickly fluttering to a next piece of information, unconscious to its value and without a plan.
>
> (2013: 171)

Green and Hannon (2007) conducted interviews and focus groups with 60 children and young people between the ages of 7 and 18 in the UK to explore their use of technologies and uncovered a more interesting and complex picture. While the majority of children and young people had integrated the use of technologies into their daily lives, the ways in which they used technologies varied. They categorized young people into four groups and they found relatively few in the groups with significant expertise, i.e. groups 1 and 2:

1. *Digital pioneers* were blogging before the phrase had been coined.
2. *Creative producers* are building websites, posting movies, photos and music to share with friends, family and beyond.
3. *Everyday communicators* are making their lives easier through texting and MSN.
4. *Information gatherers* are Google and Wikipedia addicts, 'cutting and pasting' as a way of life (2013: 11).

Green and Hannon's study is now some years old and we might expect there to have been further changes over the last 10 years. A Canadian study that involved only a relatively small number of teenagers (age range 12–14) looked in depth at their perspectives on their use of new technologies (Li, Snow and White 2015). This research suggests that young people's use of technology has continued to increase and they regard this as important for their social activities but its use for learning remains much more limited. However, Li, Snow and White's study did show that the older students in their study (aged 14) were able to discuss the potential for using technology in their learning. In particular, they claimed that being able to bring in their own computers to school would enable them to feel more comfortable in using technology to support their learning. The issue of how computer facilities should be provided in school, i.e. whether students should be allowed to bring in their own devices (BYOD), which presents some technical challenges for schools as well as potentially class management issues, or whether access to computers is best provided through school-owned computers, is an ongoing debate.

In summary, studies suggest that young people vary in their uses of technologies and there are age differences in their perceptions of the potential for technology to support learning. The implication for teachers is that it is important to find out about students' skills, preferences and experiences in relation to using new technologies in their learning. Furthermore, it is important to ensure that appropriate opportunities are provided to develop students' skills and understanding, i.e. to develop digital skills/digital literacy as discussed later in this chapter.

Government initiatives for digital technologies in education

Since the 1980s, when computer technologies started to become available in schools, successive UK governments have invested in initiatives to promote their use in learning. These funded initiatives have frequently been associated with claims and expectations that using new technologies would support learning and improve standards (Department for Education and Employment 1997; DfES 2003; 2004; 2005). More recently, the UK government has devolved most decision-making, including that relating to the use of technologies, to schools. Nevertheless a UK government view of the relevance of technologies for learning is presented regularly at the annual BETT Show in London, which is the major UK show focused on education and technology. For example, in 2017, the Skills Minister emphasized the importance of digital skills for equipping everyone for work (Department for Education and Halfon 2017). In 2016, the UK Education Minister emphasized: (1) the importance of access to broadband in schools for all children; (2) the new computing curriculum designed to enable the next generation to compete in the global jobs market; and (3) the key role of technology as an aid to running schools and adaptive assessments (Department for Education and Morgan 2016). In addition to these specific initiatives the Minister stated that 'we see education technology as an aid to excellent schools and excellent teachers, not a replacement for them' (Department for Education and Morgan 2016). This emphasis on technology being used to support teachers and not replacing them is important. This is because over time many claims have been made for technologies, including, for example, artificial intelligence having the potential to save money in education by taking over aspects of teaching. There is no doubt that aspects of artificial intelligence will be extremely useful in education in the future, for example, voice input such as that provided by Siri, is heavily dependent on AI techniques. However, it is beyond the scope of this chapter to review the potential for AI in education but it is encouraging to note that the AI community sees its potential to support teachers and enhance learning rather than to replace teachers (see, for example, Timms 2016).

Adopting new pedagogical approaches with digital technologies

There have been many claims that digital technologies can transform learning and teaching across the curriculum by providing: (1) greater flexibility in the place and time for learning; (2) access to almost unlimited information and knowledge;

(3) personalized learning; and (4) new ways of interacting. These new opportunities can support existing teaching and learning practices and/or generate new pedagogical approaches. For example, in a 'flipped classroom' approach, the teacher might provide a digital resource for students to study in advance of a lesson so that the lesson itself can focus on identifying and discussing particular aspects of the topic that students find difficult. Other pedagogical approaches that have been identified as new or at least significantly transformed by digital technologies include game-based learning, peer learning, and adaptive learning in which delivery of online content is adapted to the needs of each individual learner. Decisions about which pedagogical practices to use need to be based on sound pedagogical principles including understanding of learners' needs and capabilities.

Ideally teachers would like to ensure that any new pedagogical practices that they adopt are based on evidence that such practices support, enable or preferably enhance students' learning beyond what could be achieved through previous practices. However, identifying which technologies to use in which situations, based on evidence, can be difficult. There have been many studies of the effects of interventions with new technologies. Hattie examined more than 800 meta-analyses of studies that investigated the effects of various different types of interventions on achievement including 76 meta-analyses that were based on approximately 4500 studies using digital technologies (Hattie 2009). Hattie made his comparisons using 'effect size' which is a quantitative measure of the difference between two groups and can be used to compare effects from different studies. While Hattie did find clear evidence for some teaching approaches having positive effects on achievement, he found much variation and no clear patterns with regard to the value of using different types of technologies to support learning. His analyses of effect sizes of interventions with new technologies (Hattie 2009) did suggest that key attributes leading to the highest effects were:

- a diversity of teaching strategies;
- multiple opportunities for learning;
- the pupils are in control of the learning rather than the teacher;
- peer learning is optimized;
- the tasks are challenging;
- there is well-explained and focused feedback.

(Hattie 2009: 221)

This list provides some useful pointers towards positive outcomes of using technology to support and promote learning but it needs to be interpreted with caution. Hattie's findings are based on a synthesis of meta-analyses from many studies. Each separate meta-analysis would have been derived from studies that met certain criteria so many studies would have been excluded. (See Hattie 2009: Chapter 2, for an explanation of effect sizes and the limitations of meta-analysis.) In particular, many qualitative studies that examined practice in depth as well as most practitioner-based research will not have been incorporated. In addition, new opportunities, provided by, for example, new online resources or mobile applications (apps) become available all the time, making it impossible for research to provide detailed up-to-date evidence of their value for learning. Therefore, it is important to continually examine the pedagogical potential of new technological innovations to enhance or transform your students' learning, to think about where they might support your teaching and to try out new approaches as well as to learn from the findings of previous research.

Teachers' knowledge, skills, understanding and decision-making for deploying digital technologies

In a review of research into ICT and pedagogy together with the study of 'best practices', Cox and Webb (2004) identified the following skills and understanding that are needed by teachers in order to make effective use of digital technologies.

- Teachers need to understand the relationship between a range of ICT resources and the concepts, processes and skills in their subject.

- Teachers need to use their subject expertise to obtain and select appropriate ICT resources which will help them meet the learning objectives of a particular lesson. Resources include subject-specific software as well as more generic resources.

- Teachers need knowledge of the potential of ICT resources, not only in terms of their contribution to pupils' presentation skills but in terms of their facilities for challenging pupils' thinking and extending pupils' learning in a subject.

- Teachers need confidence in using a range of ICT resources, which can only be achieved through frequent practice with more than one or two uses of ICT.

- Teachers need to understand that some uses of ICT will change the nature and representations of knowledge and the way the subject is presented to and engages the pupils (Cox and Webb 2004: 7).

The list may be daunting to some teachers but the way to start is to try one approach focusing on your learning intentions for your pupils using one piece of software or web-based resource and try to reflect on and evaluate the outcomes. You can gradually expand your expertise through observing other teachers, finding out about good practice, e.g. through online discussion boards, and experimenting in your own lessons. In this way you gradually improve your decision-making regarding the use of technologies as well as your overall pedagogical repertoire.

In order to take account of teachers' decision-making in interactions that enable learning, Lee Shulman developed a model of 'pedagogical reasoning' based on his many years of experience of teaching and teacher education (Shulman 1987). Shulman also coined the term 'pedagogical content knowledge' (PCK) which is now in common use to describe the practical, subject-related, knowledge that teachers develop through their experience to design their teaching. Shulman's work, which was seminal in understanding teachers' decision-making, proposed that teachers need both generic and subject-specific knowledge of various types. His model of pedagogical reasoning focused

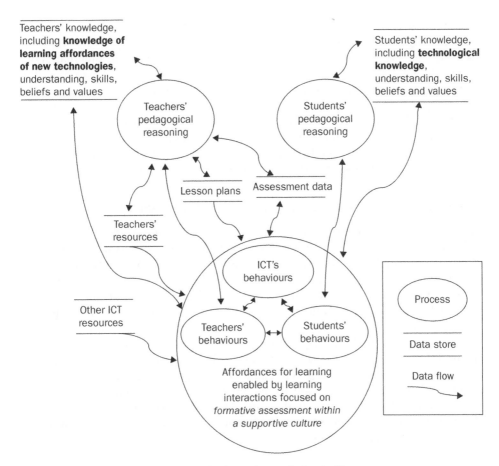

Figure 24.1 Framework for pedagogical practices relating to IT use

Source: Adapted from Webb and Cox (2004).

predominantly on teachers and underplayed the opportunities for pupil involvement in planning and managing their learning as well as the importance of interactions in learning. Therefore, Webb and Cox (Cox and Webb 2004; Webb and Cox 2004b; Webb 2005) refined Shulman's framework of knowledge and reasoning to incorporate the use of new technologies and recognize the potential involvement of pupils in pedagogical decision-making, as shown in Figure 24.1. We know that some students make extensive use of new technologies for learning, often without their teachers' knowledge. For example, a study by Jared (2013) of interactions on a website for mathematics learning (NRICH) showed that students aged 14–16 were regularly using the discussion board to explore problems that they had been set for homework. Generally their teachers were unaware of the activities of their students.

The framework in Figure 24.1 looks complex because pedagogical decision-making requires teachers to use a wide range of knowledge and skills, not only in planning their lessons but also in the minute-by-minute decisions that they make as they interact with their students. The availability of an expanding range of resources and learning opportunities provided by new technologies increases the knowledge that teachers need in order to deploy them effectively. Therefore, it is particularly important to harness and build on students' own knowledge and experience of new technologies. An important aim is to build students' capabilities for autonomous learning through using new technologies. The framework incorporates affordances for learning, a term that has been adopted by many researchers, to refer to possible uses enabled by technologies within any particular learning context, as will be discussed in the next section.

Providing affordances for learning with digital technologies

Affordances for learning are dependent on a combination of the whole environment for learning together with the characteristics of the learner (Cox and Webb 2004; Webb 2005; Gibson 2014). Table 24.1, which is adapted and updated from previous findings of how specific affordances were enabled by teachers (Cox and Webb 2004; Webb and Cox 2004) categorizes affordances in order to identify the main types of digital technologies involved and a range of different learning that can be supported.

There is evidence of positive effects on learning of most of the affordances in Table 24.1 but the effects are dependent not on the technology itself but, crucially, on how it is deployed in the learning situation (Webb and Cox 2004). Table 24.1 also shows whether the types of digital technologies are generic, implying that similar knowledge and skills are needed to deploy these types of digital technologies across a range of subjects, or whether subject-specific pedagogical knowledge is essential in order to choose and use the resource. This categorization shows that generic types of digital technologies, e.g. web browsers, discussion boards or mind-mapping software, can provide many affordances for learning. Using some of these generic tools could support learning in a range of different topics and contexts. Therefore, you may be able to provide additional affordances for your students' learning by developing your use of just a few types of generic software. In addition, all subject areas have subject-specific software that is useful for learning particular topics and aspects of the subject matter. For example, simulation and animation software is available for learning topics in science, history and geography. For learning modern foreign languages, software has been developed for practising grammar and vocabulary. Some subject-specific software can be acquired through a one-off purchase whereas other software is available on subscription. There is also a massive and rapidly increasing amount of free software available on the web. Some apps are genuinely free because they have been developed by educators who would just like to see them used; other apps are paid for by advertising or as free versions of a more sophisticated product.

For you as a beginning teacher looking for apps to support your students' learning, a first step might be to identify software that the school has purchased and/or identified as being useful for its curriculum. You might also identify other potentially useful software resources through discussion with your peers, tutors and from online recommendations, e.g. from websites of subject associations.

Table 24.1 Categories of affordances for learning supported by digital technologies

1. Categories of affordances	2. Learning supported	3. Types of digital technologies used	4. Generic or subject-specific digital technologies
Researching information	Acquiring knowledge, consolidating understanding, developing researching and critical evaluation skills	Internet, web browsers, web cams, content-specific databases, geographical information systems	Generic/subject specific
Communicating, collaborating	Collaborative learning, peer interaction, peer feedback, teacher feedback, distance learning, developing social skills	Discussion boards, chat rooms, microblogging (e.g. Twitter), social networking sites, videoconferencing	Generic
Creating digital working models	Learning through creating: models, programs, games, animations. Includes analysing, designing, evaluating and formulating and solving problems.	Programming languages including beginners' block-based languages, programming a robot, modelling tools, game design software	Generic/subject specific
Visualizing processes/ideas	Ability to mentally visualize processes, understanding dynamic processes, reflecting, reviewing, comparing, evaluating, consolidating understanding	Simulations, animations, virtual worlds, 3-D models, haptic-enabled virtual reality	Subject specific
Investigating relationships, testing hypotheses	Thinking about relationships between variables, reflecting, reviewing, comparing, evaluating, consolidating understanding	Simulations, spreadsheets, data-logging packages, specific modelling packages, virtual worlds with haptics	Generic/subject specific
Feedback	Knowing what aspects need more learning, thinking, predicting, self-assessment	Simulations, mind-mapping software, interactive whiteboard, shared blogs, microblogging (e.g. Twitter), discussion boards, content-specific tutorial systems	Generic/subject specific

(Continued)

Table 24.1 continued

1. Categories of affordances	2. Learning supported	3. Types of digital technologies used	4. Generic or subject-specific digital technologies
Preparing presentations and producing digital content	Organizing ideas, reflecting, reviewing, evaluating, consolidating understanding	PowerPoint, wikis, blogs, word processors, video editing software, web design software	Generic
Presenting	Presentation skills, organizing ideas, reflecting, reviewing, evaluating	PowerPoint, interactive whiteboard	Generic
Making a drawing	Thinking about what they already know about composition	Drawing package	Subject specific
Taking turns	Social skills, sharing	Robot, shared computer	Generic
Broadening experience	Generalizing from examples, extending their ideas, clarifying, generating new ideas	Internet, web browsers, web cams, videoconferencing, shared blogs, microblogging, discussion boards	Generic
Drawing graphs	Thinking about relationships between variables	Spreadsheets, data-logging packages	Generic

Source: Adapted from Cox and Webb (2004); Webb (2005).

Much has been written about evaluating educational software and a web search will provide you with various checklists of questions to consider. Generally these approaches to evaluating software are aimed at heads of department and others who are deciding whether or not to purchase or recommend the software for the school. For you as a beginning teacher identifying software that might be useful for lessons that you are expecting to teach in the near future is your main challenge. A study by Baran, Uygun and Altan (2017) examined in detail the thinking, pedagogical decision-making and other considerations that pre-service teachers discussed when evaluating mobile apps for use in their lessons. The key findings that emerged from this study, and from other studies of approaches to software evaluation, were questions related to a fit with pedagogy, technical usability, content, connectivity and contextuality. Baran *et al*. also concluded that the activity of evaluating mobile applications was useful for the development of pre-service teachers' understanding of the uses of ICT for learning and their own pedagogical decision-making.

Digital skills/digital literacy/computational thinking

In addition to you developing your knowledge, experience and confidence in using digital technologies to support your students' learning, you need to check that your students have adequate skills for the activities you are planning. Furthermore, there is an expectation that all teachers will play a part in the development of the digital skills all students need to take their place in society. The nature of these skills and understanding is debated in the literature and the various terms used to describe them include: basic digital skills, digital literacy, information literacy. The UK government, during 2016, undertook an inquiry into digital skills in the UK, resulting in a report entitled 'Digital Skills Crisis' (House of Commons Science and Technology Committee 2016). This report identified a skills gap throughout education and training as well as in industry and business. In this report 'digital skills' referred to the broad range of skills needed to make use of digital technologies and the report also referred to the importance of the computing curriculum as well as to the need to develop digital skills across the whole curriculum.

The National Curriculum for Computing defines being digitally literate as students being 'able to use, and express themselves and develop their ideas through information and communication technology at a level suitable for the future workplace and as active participants in a digital world' (DfE 2013: 1). Analysis of global curricula and frameworks for the skills needed for participation in a digital world show a consensus regarding digital literacy but also includes skills in the related aspects of communication, collaboration, problem-solving, critical thinking, creativity and productivity (Voogt *et al*. 2013).

There is also a specific set of thinking skills and processes described as 'computational thinking', which refers to the thinking involved in identifying, analysing and formulating problems in such a way that a computer can be deployed to solve the problem. Developing and being able to deploy such computational thinking not only gives people insights into the capabilities and limitations of computers but also encourages a logical approach to solving everyday problems. For these and other reasons computational thinking has been described as a third literacy which is crucial for everybody (Wing 2006). However, beyond this general idea of solving problems using concepts and techniques from computer science and computing, there is no generally agreed definition of computational thinking. Nevertheless, in England, computational thinking was incorporated in 2014 as a key component of the new 'computing' curriculum. Key concepts mentioned in the computing curriculum in relation to computational thinking include abstraction, logic, algorithms and data representation, and there is a strong emphasis on writing programs. However, while there is value in developing computational thinking through specialist computing lessons where students can evaluate their thinking by implementing computer programs, computational thinking does not depend on programming and is important for most other subjects. Thus, for example, abstraction, i.e. identifying and defining the key elements of something at an appropriate level of detail and removing unnecessary information, is regarded as one of the key processes in computational thinking. Abstraction is also a key process in modelling of ideas and systems which is also crucial for learning science, history and geography. Increasingly in learning science, in particular, students are expected to develop and work with computational models. Currently, globally, there is very strong interest in the value of computational thinking over the specialized computing curriculum and across a range of other subjects (see, for example, Weintrop *et al.* 2015; Angeli *et al.* 2016; Webb *et al.* 2017).

Online reading and researching

A major change for learners in the twenty-first century associated with what is sometimes called the digital age or knowledge society is access to almost unlimited information through the Internet. While simple access to information obviously does not ensure learning, it does mean that learners are no longer dependent on teachers and books, etc., to provide access to the ideas that they need in order to learn. In nearly all curriculum subjects, online research is likely to be a useful learning approach on frequent occasions. At the same time the skills needed for online reading and research differ from those required for print-based reading (OECD 2015; Dwyer 2016). Therefore, you might think about how to enable your students to approach Internet-based research. For example, Dwyer (2016: 384 has suggested some specific strategies for supporting students in Internet-based research because she claims that 'reading online introduces new challenges for the reader and requires deeper levels of higher order processing skills, strategies, practices, and dispositions'. Dwyer's strategies can be summarized as: (1) create authentic online inquiry opportunities; (2) dig deeper with students' self-generated inquiry questions; (3) observe and analyse: assess students' strengths and needs; (4) scaffold key stages of the Internet inquiry cycle; and (5) encourage peer-to-peer collaboration. Do you think the strategies are appropriate? Why/why not? Can you come up with a good example of such an approach that you might use in a lesson?

Links between home and school – any time, anywhere learning

One of the potential benefits of digital technologies is provided by mobile technologies together with Internet access which enables 'any time anywhere learning'. There is a fairly large literature on mobile learning and how it has transformed learning for many groups of people. A useful definition, by Pachler, Bachmair and Cook, which characterizes mobile learning as providing opportunities for significant change to learning practices, is as follows: 'Mobile learning – as we understand it – is not about technology or delivering content to mobile devices but, instead, about the processes of "coming to know" and "being able to operate successfully in and across" new and ever changing context and learning spaces' (2009: 6).

For teachers and schools in developed countries, responses to mobile learning vary widely from a total ban on mobile phones in schools to embedding of mobile use into the curriculum. More generally, mobile learning provides important learning opportunities for people in a wide range of contexts but optimizing its use presents challenges. For example, a report to UNESCO states: 'Just because mobile technology will be more accessible, affordable and powerful does not necessarily mean it will be used productively or to its full potential' (Shuler, Winters and West 2013: 35). The report goes on to list key questions for us in relation to using mobile technologies effectively:

- Has the education community recognized the vast potential that lies within informal learning spaces, and is it leveraging the ubiquity of mobile technologies to afford new breakthroughs in bridging school, after-school and home environments?
- How do we effectively train educators to use mobile technologies to advance and ensure high-quality learning?
- How do we build capacities for learners to exercise greater control and choice over their own learning?

For schools, an important benefit of mobile learning is the increased opportunity for bridging between home and school learning and other types of informal learning. Such bridging is also supported by Learning Platforms.

Learning Platforms

Learning Platforms are Internet-based environments that support learning by providing a set of software tools for presentation and sharing of materials as well as communication between learners, teachers and parents. They are also called Virtual Learning Environments (VLEs), Learning Management Systems (LMSs) and Personal Learning Environments (PLEs), depending on how they are viewed within the educational establishment, e.g. whether they are primarily there to support personalized learning or to support management. Generally over the last few years Learning Platforms have continued to expand their functionality and try to offer a 'complete solution' for schools to manage their students' learning and assessment. A range of different Learning Platforms is available but they tend to provide similar learning opportunities. Anecdotal reports from teachers suggest that the use of the various tools available is patchy and Learning Platforms generally are not fulfilling their full potential of supporting and enhancing learning in the classroom and beyond. In a self-report study of 50 teachers in UK secondary schools, Underwood and Stiller identified three key barriers to the use of learning platforms: the functionality of the software, workloads and personal interest (Underwood and Stiller 2014). One of your first steps in familiarizing yourself with policy and practice in relation to digital technologies in your school is to identify the school's Learning Platform, ensure that you have appropriate access and examine how this is used by students, teachers and parents.

Learning through game playing

Teachers have long recognized the benefits of using games, simulations and game elements in their lessons for the purposes of increasing students' engagement and motivation. Digital games can now incorporate a range of features which may engage and motivate users as well as enabling them to explore scenarios that were previously not easily accessible. These new features include virtual reality, augmented reality where digital information is superimposed on the user's environment, haptic (virtual touch) interfaces and gesture control. Since the advent of digital games, many have advocated their use in learning while others have focused on their potential dangers. Systematic reviews of the many studies of game-based learning reveal a complex picture in which well-designed games can support learning better than more traditional methods (Connolly *et al.* 2012; Girard, Ecalle and Magnan 2013; Hamari *et al.* 2016). Over many years a range of educational games and simulations have been designed for use in schools and more recently a variety of free or low-cost apps based on games or incorporating game elements have become available. A web search will reveal a plethora of games and game-based approaches to learning and suggestions about how they might be used in various curriculum subjects. Key interrelated aspects of the game playing experience that may support learning are engagement, challenge, immersion and matching the game to the skills of the learner (Hamari *et al.* 2016). However, currently the majority of studies show the benefits of using games to support manipulative skills and lower cognitive skills rather than understanding of complex concepts. As with other elements of TEL the main benefits are dependent on how teachers deploy the various resources, including games, to support their planned learning outcomes.

Computer-based assessment

IT offers enormous scope for transforming assessment practices but we are currently in only the early stages of this process. According to Bennett's review of the evolution of educational assessment, from a paper-based technology to an electronic one (Bennett 2015), the current state of educational assessment is between a first generation focused largely on infrastructure building and the second generation driven by efficiency. It will be the third generation of assessments, not driven by technology, but focused on cognitive principles and theory-based domain models, that will enable assessments to serve both the needs of learners and those of institutions and this evolution is likely to take many years. Scenarios for IT-enabled assessments may take many different forms, some of which hold much promise for supporting learning (Gibson, Webb and Forkosh-Baruch 2012). Thus, while much effort in institutional and national testing systems is focused on harnessing the power of automated systems in order to reduce costs and increase efficiency, a range of different assessment scenarios have been the focus of research and development for some years. IT-enabled assessments may involve, for example, a pedagogical agent acting as a virtual coach patiently tutoring someone and providing feedback in anything they would like to learn (Johnson and Lester 2016); an analysis of a learner's decisions during a digital game or simulation (Clarke and Dede 2010; Bellotti *et al.* 2013); students reviewing and commenting on one another's digital creations through an online discussion (Ertmer *et al.* 2007; Webb 2010); a multimedia-constructed response item created with an online animation and modelling application (Mislevy, Steinberg and Almond 2003; Lenhard *et al.* 2007); students receiving remote asynchronous expert feedback about how they worked with one another via IT to solve a problem and communicate their understandings (Rissanen *et al.* 2008) or an emotionally engaging virtual world experience that unobtrusively documents progression of a person's leadership and ethical development over time (Turkay and Tirthali 2010). This set of vignettes, while not all focused on secondary education, begins to outline a broad range of possibilities that place IT in a variety of roles, including becoming a medium for communication, learning assistant, judge, test item and performance prompt, practice arena, and performance workspace (Webb, Gibson and Forkosh-Baruch 2013).

While much effort from examination boards and other authorities is focused on developing IT-based summative assessment, as a teacher you have many opportunities to use IT to support formative assessments. For example, this can be done by using digital communication tools to feed back to groups of students through your school's Learning Platform.

Internet safe practices and cyber-bullying

This chapter would be incomplete without some mention of safety in relation to Internet use because there are strong and valid concerns among parents and teachers. A review by Tanya Byron (Byron 2008) identified important issues and actions needed for Internet safety while acknowledging the value of using the Internet and other new technologies for learning. It is beyond the scope of this chapter to explain the issues and consequences for policies and practice but most schools have implemented comprehensive Internet safety policies and a useful online resource for teachers is provided by the National Crime Agency (CEOP) at: https://www.thinkuknow.co.uk/Teachers/.

Looking ahead

Predicting the future is always difficult and there are many examples regarding digital technologies in education that have proved to be wildly inaccurate.

Nevertheless attempting to foresee future trends is important for planning and influencing developments. A report, the Horizon Report, that attempts this foresight using a Delphi research approach, which captures the key ideas and their priorities, from a group of experts, is produced each year. The Horizon Report looks at current trends as well as likely longer-term trends (five years plus). The 2016 Horizon Report (Adams *et al.* 2016) identified short- and medium-term trends as a focus on programming and computational thinking as well as developing understanding through creating artefacts and solving problems. Furthermore, they identified an increase in collaborative learning using digital technologies to support interactivity and a corresponding focus on deeper learning supported by these approaches. Longer-term trends identified were redesigning learning spaces to accommodate more learner-centred interactive learning and collaboration. Alongside these new learning approaches the report identified a trend towards more flexible school experiences including curricular ones that incorporate more real-world problem-solving. While these trends are visible in various innovative schools and the experts in the study verified their value, they also identified a number of challenges for the widespread adoption of these innovations. A key challenge was confirmed as rethinking the role of teachers away from that of providing expert knowledge towards designing learning environments that develop twenty-first-century skills such as creativity, collaborative problem-solving and digital literacy.

Concluding thoughts

- Which ICT facilities – hardware and software – have you identified in your current placement school that you think you might use soon in one of your lessons?
- What affordances for your students' learning do you think they might provide?
- What range of uses of ICT for learning have you observed in your placement school?
- In what ways do they enable better learning than previous pedagogical approaches?
- What is the functionality of the Learning Platform in your school?
- How do students, teachers and parents use the Learning Platform?
- What do you think a school day in the life of a 14-year-old will be like in five years' time?
- In 10 years' time?

References

Adams, T., Becker, S., Freeman, A., Giesinger Hall, C. *et al.* (2016) *NMC Horizon Report: 2016 K-12 Edition*. Austin, TX: The New Media Consortium.

Angeli, C., Voogt, J., Fluck, A., Webb, M. *et al.* (2016) A K-6 computational thinking curriculum framework: implications for teacher knowledge. *Journal of Educational Technology and Society* 19(3): 45–57.

Baran, E., Uygun, E. and Altan, T. (2017) Examining preservice teachers' criteria for evaluating educational mobile apps, *Journal of Educational Computing Research*, 54(8): 1117–41.

Bellotti, F., Kapralos, B., Lee, K. *et al.* (2013) Assessment in and of serious games: an overview, *Advances in Human-Computer Interaction*, 20: 131–41.

Bennett, R.E. (2015) The changing nature of educational assessment, *Review of Research in Education*, 39(1): 370–407.

Byron, T. (2008) *Safer Children in a Digital World: The Report of the Byron Review*. Nottingham: Department for Children, Schools and Families.

Clarke, J. and Dede, C. (2010) Assessment, technology, and change, *Journal of Research in Teacher Education*, 42(3): 309–28.

Connolly, T.M., Boyle, E.A., MacArthur, E. *et al.* (2012) A systematic literature review of empirical evidence on computer games and serious games, *Computers and Education*, 59(2): 661–86.

Cox, M.J. and Webb, M.E. (2004) *ICT and Pedagogy: A Review of the Research Literature*, Coventry and London: British Educational Communications and Technology Agency/Department for Education and Skills.

Department for Education and Department for Employment (1997) *Connecting the Learning Society*. London: HMSO.

Department for Education and Halfon, R. (2017) Speech: Robert Halfon: BETT Show 2017, BETT Show, ExCel Centre, London.

Department for Education and Morgan, N. (2016) Speech: Nicky Morgan: BETT Show 2016, BETT Show, ExCel Centre, London.

DfE (Department for Education) (2013) *National Curriculum in England: Computing Programmes of Study*. London: DfE.

DfES (Department for Education and Skills) (2003) *Fulfilling the Potential. Transforming Teaching and Learning through ICT in Schools*. London: Department for Education and Skills.

DfES (Department for Education and Skills) (2004) *A National Conversation about Personalised Learning*. London: Department for Education and Skills.

DfES (Department for Education and Skills) (2005) *Harnessing Technology: Transforming Learning and Children's Services*. London. Department for Education and Skills.

Dwyer, B. (2016) Engaging all students in internet research and inquiry, *The Reading Teacher*, 69(4): 383–9.

Ertmer, P.A., Richardson, J.C., Belland, B. *et al.* (2007) Using peer feedback to enhance the quality of student online postings, *Journal of Computer-Mediated Communication*, 12(2): 1–15.

Gibson, D., Webb, M.E. and Forkosh-Baruch, A. (2012) Global perspectives on information and communications technology and educational assessment. Paper presented to the IFIP Working Conference: Addressing educational challenges – the role of ICT, Manchester Metropolitan University, Manchester, UK.

Gibson, J.J. (2014) *The Ecological Approach to Visual Perception: Classic Edition*. Hove: Psychology Press.

Girard, C., Ecalle, J. and Magnan, A. (2013) Serious games as new educational tools: how effective are they? A meta-analysis of recent studies, *Journal of Computer Assisted Learning*, 29(3): 207–19.

Green, H. and Hannon, C. (2007) *Their Space: Education for a Digital Generation*. London: Demos.

Hamari, J., Shernoff, D.J., Rowe, E. *et al.* (2016) Challenging games help students learn: an empirical study on engagement, flow and immersion in game-based learning, *Computers in Human Behavior*, 54: 170–9.

Hattie, J.A.C. (2009) *Visible Learning: A Synthesis of Over 800 Meta-Analyses Relating to Achievement*. London: Routledge.

House of Commons Science and Technology Committee (2016) *Digital Skills Crisis*, http://www.publications.parliament.uk/pa/cm201617/cmselect/cmsctech/270/27002.htm, accessed 9 June 2017.

Jared, E. (2013) PhD thesis, Department of Education and Professional Studies, King's College London.

Johnson, W.L. and Lester, J.C. (2016) Face-to-face interaction with pedagogical agents, twenty years later, *International Journal of Artificial Intelligence in Education*, 26(1): 25–36.

Kirschner, P.A. and van Merriënboer, J.J.G. (2013) Do learners really know best? Urban legends in education, *Educational Psychologist*, 48(3): 169–83.

Lenhard, W., Baier, H., Hoffmann, J. and Schneider, W. (2007) Automatic scoring of constructed-response items with latent semantic analysis, *Diagnostica*, 53(3): 155–65.

Li, J., Snow, C. and White, C. (2015) Teen culture, technology and literacy instruction: urban adolescent students' perspectives, *Canadian Journal of Learning and Technology*, 41(3): online. Available at https://www.cjlt.ca/index.php/cjlt/article/view/26967, accessed 6 May 2017.

Mislevy, R.J., Steinberg, L.S. and Almond, R.G. (2003) On the structure of educational assessment, *Measurement: Interdisciplinary Research and Perspective*, 1(1): 3–62.

OECD (2015) *Students, Computers and Learning: Making the Connection. PISA.* Paris: OECD Publishing.

Pachler, N., Bachmair, B. and Cook, J. (2009) *Mobile Learning: Structures, Agency, Practices*. London: Springer Science and Business Media.

Rissanen, M. J., Kume, N., Kuroda, Y. *et al.* (2008) Asynchronous teaching of psychomotor skills through VR annotations: evaluation in digital rectal examination, *Studies in Health Technology and Informatics*, 13(2): 411–16.

Royal Society (2012) *Shut Down Or Restart? The Way Forward for Computing in UK Schools*. London: Royal Society.

Shuler, C., Winters, N. and West, M. (2013) *The Future of Mobile Learning: Implications for Policy Makers and Planners*. Paris: United Nations Educational, Scientific and Cultural Organization.

Shulman, L. (1987) Knowledge and teaching: foundations of the new reform, *Harvard Educational Review*, 57(1): 1–22.

Timms, M.J. (2016) Letting artificial intelligence in education out of the box: educational cobots and smart classrooms, *International Journal of Artificial Intelligence in Education*, 26(2): 701–12.

Turkay, S. and Tirthali, D. (2010) Youth leadership development in virtual worlds: a case study, *Procedia Social and Behavioral Sciences*, 2(2): 3175–9.

Underwood, J.D.M. and Stiller, J. (2014) Does knowing lead to doing in the case of learning platforms? *Teachers and Teaching*, 20(2): 229–46.

Voogt, J., Erstad, O., Dede, C. and Mishra, P. (2013) Challenges to learning and schooling in the digital networked world of the 21st century, *Journal of Computer Assisted Learning*, 29(5): 403–13.

Webb, M.E. (2005) Affordances of ICT in science learning: implications for an integrated pedagogy, *International Journal of Science Education*, 27(6): 705–35.

Webb, M.E. (2010) Beginning teacher education and collaborative formative e-assessment, *Assessment and Evaluation in Higher Education*, 35(5): 597–618.

Webb, M.E. and Cox, M.J. (2004) A review of pedagogy related to ICT, *Technology, Pedagogy and Education*, 13(3): 235–86.

Webb, M.E., Davis, N., Bell, T., *et al.* (2017) Computer science in K-12 school curricula of the 21st century: why, what and when?, *Education and Information Technologies*, 22(2): 445–68.

Webb, M.E., Gibson, D. and Forkosh-Baruch, A. (2013) Challenges for information technology supporting educational assessment, *Journal of Computer Assisted Learning*, 29(5): 451–62.

Weintrop, D., Beheshti, E., Horn, M., *et al.* (2015) Defining computational thinking for mathematics and science classrooms, *Journal of Science Education and Technology*, 1–21.

Wing, J. (2006) Computational thinking, *Communications of the ACM*, 49(3): 33–6.

25

Beyond the subject curriculum: the form tutor's role
JANE JONES

Introduction

Your mental image of yourself teaching probably involves you explaining key elements of your subject. However, you will spend a significant amount of time in school doing something for which you may have had little preparation and which opens up innumerable opportunities to frustrate and fulfil. Government policy means that schools are pressed to deliver national policies on such diverse matters as teenage pregnancy, safeguarding, bullying, correct use of ICT and responsible use of social media, the respect agenda, healthy eating, gender-neutral language and behaviour, etc., and it is frequently the form tutor who has to manage this response. Almost certainly, you will be involved as a form tutor within weeks of starting to teach. With the pressures on young people seemingly increasing with each generation, you will play a major part in the lives of large numbers of pupils in ways in which it is hard to imagine now. This chapter is an attempt to help you to prepare for the challenges that lie ahead beyond your role as subject teacher in your school. The work of the form tutor cuts across subject specialisms and emphasizes study and coping strategies as well as personal, vocational and life skills, creating a multidimensional role (Startup 2003; Cefai 2008). Thus, the form tutor needs to provide support and act as first port of call and a guide – in short, be available on a daily basis to provide stability for the pupils. Increasingly the form tutor is also a first port of call for parents as well as students, through the planners and high contact relationship expected and demanded by parents. Consequently, the role of the form tutor, which has recently changed significantly as will be explored later in the chapter, is challenging, unique and rewarding.

The character and ethos of a school are, according to Tattum, determined by 'decisions about the curriculum, the allocation of resources, the grouping of pupils and the arrangements made for guidance and welfare' (1988: 158). While government policy and funding largely determine factors such as school resources and the content of the curriculum, pupil grouping, student welfare and personal guidance, under the guise and auspices of the pastoral system, still remain within the decision-making processes of individual schools and teachers. Partly in response to teachers' legitimate complaints, over many years, about administrative overload (but mainly as a response to a DfES-commissioned report (Smithers and Robinson 2003) on continuing high rates of wastage from the teaching profession), the government published, in 2003, *Raising Standards and Tackling Workload: A National Agreement* (DfES 2003), which brought in a process referred to as 'workforce remodelling'. This initiative was designed to ensure some non-contact time for all teachers and to shift many of their administrative functions, as well as some aspects of the former tutor role, to support staff and to non-teaching staff (Cooper 2005). These members of staff may be referred to as pastoral assistants, behaviour managers or student development leaders, among other things and often have a non-teaching background.

The agreement was followed by the introduction, in January 2006, of teaching and learning allowances (TLRs). The agreement required all management allowances to be replaced by TLRs by September 2008 with new job descriptions to be agreed with the relevant staff. Since allowances can only be given for teaching and learning responsibilities, with which the existing concept of pastoral support sits uneasily, traditional pastoral posts of responsibility can no longer be remunerated and even the term 'pastoral' is falling out of use. Bottery and Wright (2000) found that, in a large number of secondary schools, the pressure of targets, performance management and the focus on delivering the National Curriculum meant that wider aspects of being an extended professional, for example, in the tutor role, were being displaced. Such a shift, potentially threatening jobs, and also challenging a core belief of many teachers in the pastoral role, has met with some opposition.

Schools were directed to introduce changes in pastoral structures, programmes and roles of responsibility, and have implemented them in diverse ways. Many are structuring their organizational and pastoral support in ways that reflect the school's strategic awareness, priorities and its culture. Some have, in fact, added a new layer of support teachers working closely with form tutors while other schools have invested in more senior office staff to take on some of the admin functions that were previously part of the form tutor's brief. The social and emotional aspects of learning (SEAL) programme promoted by the government was designed to promote the skills that underpin effective learning and positive behaviour and the emotional health and well-being of the whole school community. An evaluation by the DCSF (2010) found some lack of coherence in provision but maintained the importance of such a focus. As part of a research project undertaken in 2010 to monitor recently introduced arrangements, a deputy head contributed this thought-provoking view:

> My experience of learning mentors is a bit vicarious. I have talked with colleagues in other schools and there have been mixed results. Generally, at secondary level, the success depends to a large extent on the student's motivation and the parental support. So it tends to work better for those students who are maybe academically weaker or have organisational problems but who genuinely want to do well. It has been less successful with disaffected pupils (generally boys) who although sometimes more able, are less motivated.

This is why in certain schools, the preference has been to recruit learning mentors with a direct link to industry, to see if they could make pupils see the link between learning and future employment. I know from colleagues in some schools that recruiting high quality learning mentors continues to be a challenge. I personally feel that resolving the problem of pupil attitudes will take a lot more than just learning mentors, although this is a valuable contribution in some cases.

(Jones 2010)

The form tutor's role has certainly changed to some degree from the traditional pastoral role to something a little different, involving liaising with a team of support staff and agencies outside of school, and using more electronic means to deal with administration and monitoring, thus providing the tutor with the best overview regarding the progress and general development of pupils. One teacher and form tutor in an Essex school commented on the wider framework of the monitoring of pupil progress and welfare:

As they consider individual progress and targets, tutors also need to be mindful of whole school target grades, mentoring, for example, each half term students who have 'negative' progress or low effort grades in any subject and set targets with the pupils to raise their attainment.

However, even with a diffusion of the role and ongoing substantial changes that you, as a new tutor, have to be aware of, the role is one that remains vital to the well-being of pupils and central to that of being a teacher (Rees 2010). As another deputy head said:

Even with new admin staff, peer counsellors, learning mentors and so on, the pupils still always gravitate to their form tutor. Some schools have changed the name from form tutor to learning manager or other things, but we are old-fashioned and are sticking to the name that everyone understands.

(Jones 2010)

This pull towards the tutor is something that was also commented on by an experienced teacher, in her form tutor (called 'mentor' in her school) role, with reference to the aforementioned 'gravitation' when she emphasized that: 'You are often the only adult the student sees every day. Some students don't see their parents (not always through choice!) and knowing you will be the same is key.'

The tutor within the school system

There are more than 4500 secondary schools in England and, within each one, the headteacher faces the demanding task of organizing the pupils, staff and other resources to produce an effective learning environment. During the setting up of the comprehensive system in the 1950s and 1960s, considerable thought was given to developing an organizational system in which individual pupils would feel valued, noticed and encouraged in their learning. Some schools – but not many state schools – set up vertical systems, in which three or four pupils from each year group were placed in the same tutor group, resulting in a mixed-age group somewhat akin to a (very large) family, where younger pupils could rely on the help and support of older pupils, as well as on their tutor. In return, older pupils took care of the younger ones in the tutor group, which assisted the development of their social and life skills. However, while the vertical system provided a strong integrating system to support individual pupils, it also created problems, particularly administrative ones.

During research in a Kent school, in 2006, which was about to change from a year (horizontal) group system to a vertical system (Jones 2006), pupils in a Year 7 class stated that they would prefer to be in a form of their own age because that was how they made friends. Their tutor's view was that the group dynamics were crucial in a vertical system, and that the mix of pupils needed to be arranged very carefully. She also stressed that continuity of tutoring was important, as pupils needed time to develop their confidence and to share their feelings, a factor also emphasized by Hornby, Hall and Hall (2003) and Brougham (2007).

By far the most common arrangement found in schools is the horizontal system, in which tutor groups contain pupils from only one year group, which is the system normally found in primary schools (with the form tutor replacing the class teacher). Such a system, with Heads of Year, often supported by non-teaching pastoral leaders, working with a group of form tutors, creates a pastoral management structure which may, or may not, integrate well with the academic system of heads of department and subject teachers. While this structure brings stability, some Year 10 pupils in the school mentioned above reflected that it was 'unfair if you are stuck with a tutor you don't get on with'.

There are, of course, exceptions to the rule, and some schools have combined horizontal and vertical systems with pupils belonging both to a house *and* a year group. In these schools, the year group is the main organizational division, with the house system bolted-on for activities such as competitive sports. In recent times, the house system and inter-form competitions of all kinds are finding some favour again and are key elements being brought from independent schools' practice into some new academy schools to emphasize achievement in more than just sports. It is, however, a focus on making provision for personal growth and achievement rather than the particular type of system that is the key to success (Standish, Smeyers and Smith 2006).

Learning to be an effective form tutor

A form tutor is the one person, probably in conjunction with a pastoral assistant, who has daily contact with a group of pupils, monitoring their general well-being and possessing an exclusive overview of their progress across all subjects. It is, as Purdey (2013: 2) writes, 'a priceless relationship' that gives the form tutor a unique insight into the individual pupils' interests, needs, struggles and achievement, perhaps more than any other adult in their lives. Just 'being there' is an important factor, providing pupils with what might be the only point of security in the case of those with chaotic lives. When a pupil mistakenly calls a tutor 'Mum' or 'Dad', it can be a powerful reminder of how few adults actually talk *with* rather than *at* their children.

Your own education, in terms of school studies and degree work, may not have prepared you for the variety of routine and not-so-routine tasks that a form tutor may face. Discussing the death of a friend or relative of a pupil, monitoring a target or explaining notices, might well constitute the daily 'pastoral agenda' of a form tutor – all within a very brief time slot. The range of issues raised in those few minutes may be greater than in the rest of your day in school. Admitting to not knowing the right answer may work in lessons, but pupils expect their tutor to follow up the issues they discuss with her or him.

Pupils in a form may come from very different backgrounds to you, may hold very different attitudes and may have faced a range of emotional experiences that you may never encounter, except through them. The lives of some pupils may be so fraught with problems that you may wonder how they manage to cope. Trying to empathize without direct experience is challenging, and cannot be learnt quickly. In these litigious times, some issues need to be referred to more senior staff higher up the chain and it is essential to know this chain of support to deal with serious issues arising from contemporary lifestyles (Purdey 2013). Learning to be a good form tutor may be more demanding than learning to be a teacher of your subject. The role is a highly skilled one, requiring a range of personal qualities, skills and attitudes. One headteacher interviewed by Jones (2006) described a 'good tutor' as 'one who knows the pupils well, is highly structured and organized, and that includes the fun bits like the end of term parties, sets boundaries so the pupils are clear and well informed, and is fair'.

Observing experienced tutors, taking part in target setting and reviewing sessions, attending parents' evenings, talking to colleagues about your concerns, listening to pupils and hearing their views and keeping up to date with official documentation with regard to pastoral concerns – and developing your own expertise – will help you to become an effective tutor. To learn effectively needs commitment on your part, as well as access to information such as https://www.gov.uk/government/collections/departmental-advice-schools, the website for the National Association for Pastoral Care in Education (www.napce.org.uk/) and helpful advice from teacher and professional unions. Form tutoring is essentially about listening, 'noticing' and maintaining a dialogue with youngsters.

Tutor knowledge and skills

In addition to invaluable experience in the classroom, there are many publications and other resources available on PHSE, for example, Best's review (2001) of research in the pastoral domain and Carroll's analysis (2010) can be used to develop your knowledge and skills in this role. Relevant publications, for example, the *Journal of Beliefs and Values*, contain articles on issues such as sexuality and bereavement, and *Pastoral Care in Education* is a particularly rich resource for tutors. In this journal, you find discussions about topics such as work planners, careers education, citizenship, bereavement courses, the development of study skills, personal development, behaviour management, and bullying. The latter has become, in recent years, a considerable social problem in various areas of life and in schools in particular, and there is no shortage of literature on the topic (for example, Rigby 2010).

Evidence, collected over many years, and in many countries, shows that bullying is usually a much bigger problem than most teachers realize. Bullying is increasingly taking the shape of cyber-bullying with the ever-increasing use of social networking sites, mobile phones and other technology (Shariff 2009). Form tutors need to be up to date with such technologies and the uses and abuses of these, and develop what Mason (2002) calls the 'discipline of noticing' if things seem to be remiss in this respect, such as mobile phone pictures causing distress. A pupil who claims to have been bullied, whether in school or off-site, must always be taken seriously and a pupil asking for help needs time and reassurance, even if it is not immediately available. This gives a potent message, first to those pupils who are bullied and, even more importantly, to would-be bullies who may be deterred by visible, decisive and speedy action by form tutors. Schools are required to have an anti-bullying policy and the form tutor needs to be familiar with this and with the associated procedures. Furthermore, as a form tutor, you are not alone, for you will invariably have recourse to the support of experienced colleagues. As long as bullying is endemic to school life, many pupils will experience unhappiness as a result of incidents generated by the school culture. They need to be made aware that the form tutor is the one named person to whom they can turn and who will be fully informed. With sensitive issues, counselling skills are needed and the form tutor, who is categorically not a counsellor, may well have to act as counsellor at times in situations where individual pupils need personal responses. As King writes:

> The emphasis now is on equipping teachers with basic counselling skills: not training them as counsellors or to work as counsellors, but helping teachers perform their 'pastoral' work more effectively, and enabling them to recognize problems which need referring on to a specialist or a specialist agency.
>
> (1999: 4)

Pellitteri et al. (2006) call this 'emotionally intelligent school counseling'. Such basic skills, King (1999: 4) suggests, would involve 'listening skills, the skills of empathetic understanding, responding skills and a clear awareness of boundary limits'. Child Protection is paramount in schools (all schools have a designated Child Protection Officer) and it is necessary that pupils understand that confidentiality cannot be guaranteed, although we can guarantee to listen and to ensure support. Tutors must take care not to put themselves at risk and, for example, never speak to pupils on sensitive issues or in potentially dangerous circumstances without a witness. It is not so much trust that is at stake here but common sense and concern for each individual's rights, both the pupil's and the tutor's as is further discussed in Chapter 21.

Some schools have experimented successfully with peer counselling whereby older pupils are trained to listen to and to provide support for younger pupils.

The practice has now become widespread and peer mentoring is considered a way to engage pupils in developing a sense of responsibility and pupil leadership (Cartwright 2007). In one school, for example, each form has two older peer mentors attached to it: interestingly, these pupils also have a modest supervisory role in marshalling the dinner queues, which they carry out with great seriousness. Investigating such initiatives in other schools and keeping an eye on the education press can alert you to strategies that others have used successfully to deal with what, for you, might seem an intractable problem.

During the 1960s and 1970s, some schools were able to appoint counsellors, but their numbers declined as budgets were tightened in the decades that followed. In recent years, some schools have recognized the value of providing counselling services and have reconsidered the budgetary implications in terms of the value for money in respect of pupil well-being and the impact on learning. Nonetheless, counselling pupils will normally be part of the form tutor role, but lack of time and expertise will mean that many issues will, by necessity and perhaps to the benefit of a greater number of pupils, be explored within the tutor group context. The task here is to create a supportive environment and learning community (Watkins 2005) and to nurture support through activities such as role play, debate and discussion. One-to-one counselling, with all the time implications involved, should still be the right of pupils, particularly those for whom the form tutor is the only caring adult whom they encounter on a daily basis.

Responsibilities and problems take up a fair share of the tutoring time available, but there are humorous moments to be shared within the form group and many occasions when you will be uplifted by their spontaneity, their acts of generosity and by the care that they show for one another. Tutors should also celebrate the full range of achievements of their pupils, sometimes with due pomp and circumstance if certificates are to be awarded, for example, or a quiet word of praise to an individual pupil in another situation. Many pupils tend to dislike being praised in front of their peers – possibly because they are embarrassed or because there is more status in receiving a reprimand. However, good behaviour and good work benefit from reinforcement through appropriate praise and feedback.

The negative self-image that results from inadequate feedback about a pupil's ability can manifest itself when it is time to write self-assessments, for example, for a record or statement of achievement, or student portfolio. Pupils are notoriously lacking in confidence when it comes to identifying their strengths and achievements, which are often considerable. It is the form tutor who, as the teacher with an overview of a pupil's progress across all subjects, can coax these strengths out, thereby helping pupils to increase their self-esteem and construct a more positive, more accurate self-image and self-assessment. Following the 'remodelling of the workforce' initiative and in the light of teacher accountability and responsibility for the delivery of school targets, monitoring and assessment to focus on individual pupil requirements and learning needs are becoming, increasingly, the key function of the role of the form tutor, as more of the traditional pastoral aspects are devolved to support staff, including as one tutor said 'some of the nice bits'.

Monitoring and assessing

The integration of electronic communication into the everyday life of schools facilitates collecting the tracking of data relating to registration, and the recording and monitoring of progress. Once a crucial function of the form tutor, with schools now obliged to report their attendance rates, filling in the register and 'chasing up' absences have become key tasks of the school central administration using appropriate technological support systems. Essentially, the form tutor's role in relation to attendance consists of a single act of entering pupils' presence and absence electronically. One system found in schools is Bromcom, which uses codes for reasons for absence when these have been evidenced by parents or carers (for example, M = medical). Given the greater efficiency of electronic registration, paper registers are rapidly being replaced, at least in secondary schools, and some schools have initiated self-registration, using swipe cards, for their post-16 students. The information is instantaneously available to the school administration, where the designated attendance manager pursues unaccounted absences by phone or email. The attendance manager also enters reasons for absence which have been notified to the school by phone or email.

Schools have facilitated communication with parents by setting up telephone numbers offering a menu that allows parents to report lateness or absence by voicemail rather than handwritten note, and text-messaging is also widely used for home–school communication. A pupil's presence/absence and the reason are therefore available centrally to the form tutor and other staff who teach the pupil. A *bona fide* appointment is an 'authorized absence', although many schools are restricting such absences in the school day and expressly forbid their pupils to go on holiday in term time. From a school's point of view, the absence of even one or two pupils can affect the national test results or, indeed, GCSE percentages. In addition to the 'record book' or 'homework diary' used to monitor and to communicate with parents and guardians, schools have started to use email as a mode of communication with parents. Teachers can now use their laptops to communicate using email between year teams as well as between members of a department and receive whole-staff communication rather than putting up notices in the staff room (which has the added benefit of increasing pupils' privacy: only those who need to know are given personal information about pupils). Technological advances can, thus, assist tutors in identifying irregular attendance patterns and acting quickly in response to this and other behaviours of concern that contribute to pupil unhappiness and underachievement. As with any continuous monitoring, these methods help to identify problems sooner rather than later, allowing for solutions to be negotiated, targets set and achievements recognized and rewarded.

In addition to information on attendance, you will, in your role as form tutor, receive assessments made by colleagues of other subjects on your tutees' learning. Based on this information, and taking the 'whole' pupil into consideration, you may need to work out with the pupil, parents and colleagues an individualized learning plan. The importance of the personalized learning agenda in developing teachers' leadership and mentoring capability, with a view to creating and supporting student autonomy, self-assessment and a sense of pupils' responsibility for their own learning, has been highlighted in the National College for School Leadership's (2005) paper *Leading Personalised Learning in Schools: Helping Individuals Grow.*

Many schools have moved away from the end-of-year summative report and now build in progress reviews, on a one-to-one basis, in tutorial time, in accordance with the widespread adoption of formative practices in classrooms (part of an assessment for learning framework discussed in Chapter 14). This system has generally been targeted at older pupils, who may have GCSE support tutorials (Year 10 is a major transition time for pupils who may be launched into a different pace and style of learning and may quickly come to grief without support), but in an increasing number of schools, academic tracking and support start in Year 7. In fact, target setting and progress reviews are now well established in most schools with proper timetabled slots that enable pupils to have, what one tutor called, 'private quality time for all, not just those seen to be in trouble and singled out' (Jones 2006). While the focus of the system is on academic progress, this tutor also commented that 'it is the form tutor who, alone, sees how personal issues impact on learning' (Jones 2006).

Typically targets will relate to academic matters (for example, spelling in English or developing revision strategies), social concerns (for example, lateness or a lack of organization) and extra-curricular activities (after school contributions or interests and responsibilities outside of school). Each pupil will then specify, 'How I am going to achieve this target'. The review provides an opportunity for the pupil to consider 'How am I doing?', and to set new targets. Increasingly, schools organize tutorial days, an arrangement by which the timetable is suspended on particular days so that pupils and their parents can attend interviews with the form tutor to discuss any concerns, as well as progress across their subjects and target setting. This can build on recent developments in primary schools where pupils in need have one-to-one support for literacy and maths and, although not quite a learning mentor model, it is close and probably quite effective in that it gives pupils the tools to fully engage with education throughout their schooling drawing on, for example, Hattie's (2008) concept of 'visible learning' through a holistic teaching approach.

Personal, health, social and citizenship education[1]

The concept of spiritual, moral, social and cultural (SMSC) education, which underpins the National Curriculum, emphasizes the need for a whole-school approach to the drawing up and delivery of a pastoral curriculum (Best 2000; Prever 2006). All dimensions of a school, and the curriculum as a whole, contribute to the personal and social development of the pupils in some way, as is elaborated in a briefing paper 'The link between pupil health and wellbeing and attainment' for head teachers, governors and staff in education settings, produced by the NAHT and the Department of Health (PHE 2014). This report contains evidence that pupils with better health and well-being are likely to achieve better academically and emphasizes the importance of the impact of the whole school culture, ethos and environment to this end. Nonetheless, pastoral programmes will be

clearly identifiable in most schools, and many topics, issues, activities and outcomes will be considered best handled by form tutors, as part of a tutorial programme. The tutor's role, which up to now may appear sometimes reactive and
random, becomes coherent within the whole-school personal, health, social and
citizenship education (PHSCE) structure. In the best systems observed by Ofsted,
teams of tutors worked alongside a pastoral leader/student development manager
on a range of issues related to personal development relevant to each age group.
This strategy often results in a pastoral curriculum built on the identification of
issues deemed relevant to a particular age range. Thus, a Year 7 group may undertake an induction programme and focus on transition; Year 9 may focus on 'options';
and Year 11 may look at study skills or careers. A spiralling model, whereby themes
are constantly revisited (but to different degrees and in different ways) optimizes
learning opportunities and deepens understanding of the issues. Crucially, the success of the PHSCE programmes depends, to a large extent, on a school's commitment to them. Effective PHSCE delivery requires:

- An adequate time allocation
- Ownership of materials (participation by staff in their creation)
- A variety of inputs (outside speakers, videos, debates, etc.)
- Managerial support.

Unfortunately, you will find that all these factors are not always available, and for
historical and financial reasons, the programmes are typically delivered by form
tutors as an 'add-on' to their subject. Schools with a more strategic awareness of
the purpose of TLRs,[2] are devising more effective and imaginative ways of delivering PHSCE; for example, timetabling whole days or even weeks, for teaching the
programmes and developing the expertise of a team of selected form tutors to
teach them, enabling them to show the initiative and creativity that they invariably demonstrate in their subject teaching. One school, for example, has taken a
theme such as 'liberty' or 'discovery' and the whole school has worked in tutor
groups to explore meanings and have then presented their ideas to their peers in
other groups. In such cases, tutors can seek to develop skills that can enhance the
learning environment for all the pupils, and enable them to take advantage, on a
daily basis, of all that the school offers. In the longer term, tutors help pupils to
feel that they are an integrated and important part of classroom and school life
and to develop the skills and understanding needed to live confident, healthy and
independent lives.

Whole-school worship and moral education

The majority of schools have experienced some difficulty in responding to the
legal requirement for a collective act of worship, although as Gill (2000: 110) asserts:
'Most schools claim to make a regular provision for their pupils which, taken over
a year, incorporates a broadly religious dimension.' The provision might include
whole-school assemblies, tutor and year group assemblies, and opportunities for

individual silent reflection. In county primary, denominational and independent schools, Gill found that assemblies were considered an opportunity for the pupils 'to encounter the possibility of religious commitment' (2000: 109). In some schools, notably denominational ones, teachers were able to demonstrate, and share, their faith, while in others teachers experienced a personal dilemma, as Gill explains: in the conflict they experience between their desire to be seen by pupils to uphold the law in respect of a religious activity in which they feel unable to participate, while retaining their standing with pupils as individuals of personal and professional integrity (2000: 110).

It will be important for you to assert your beliefs and to recognize your own personal dilemmas, but also to resolve and accommodate these within the culture and ethos of the school in which you have chosen to work. At the very least, you will be expected to accompany pupils to assemblies, support them in form assemblies, and undertake whatever tasks are required of you in that aspect of tutor time that comprises the collective act of worship.

Gill discovered a more fulsome acceptance by teachers of a responsibility to contribute, generally, to the moral development of the pupils. This aspect of the teacher's role, for example, took place in PHSCE or form time, and focused on social interactions and the application of moral principles, such as justice and respect, and the discouragement of prejudice, bullying and racism. According to Gill, the teachers sometimes organized structured debates, while on other occasions, spontaneous discussion arose as a result of 'critical incidents' in school.

Marland and Rogers suggest that the tutor's role is to identify issues and prompt group discussion, enabling pupils not just to arrive at decisions, but to focus on how to arrive at decisions. They argue that: 'The process of tutoring is empowering the tutee, but with the giving of self-power must go the development of the ability to be sensitive and appropriately generous. Morality and ethics are at the heart of tutoring' (1997: 26).

In my research with adolescent girls (Jones 2006), many said that they liked the opportunity to gather in a larger group, especially if pupils were presenting an assembly, or if they had a special visitor, or if the focus of an assembly was an issue of concern and interest to them. Likewise, they enjoyed debates on similar themes in PHSCE, especially where they had an opportunity to air their views (and for these not to be scorned by tutors), and to be listened to with seriousness and respect. Gill, in her research, found that 'what young people value most is sincerity and relevance' (2000: 114). Pupils had strong feelings about apparent injustices and the problems of modern society, and were greatly moved by natural catastrophes and other disasters, possessing an instinctive desire to want to help. As Gill suggests: 'Contemporary issues, current affairs and a wider discussion about the problems which confront the young in an imperfect world should receive a much greater emphasis' (2000: 115). She echoes Marland and Rogers' suggestion for the need to create opportunities for pupil participation and involvement in the exploration of such issues. You, as form tutor, have a role in helping to create such opportunities within the whole-school spiritual, moral, social and cultural (SMSC) development framework and in helping the pupils to relate these concerns to their own lives.

Pupils' perceptions

The pastoral system, as part of your new school's ethos and culture, provides a framework for initiating and sustaining shared perspectives of individual pupils. In secondary school, pupils are frequently taught by ten, or more, teachers and may be perceived differently by each one. This atomistic approach does little to help them to create a sense of identity as learners and as participants in the school system. The form tutor's role within the system is to mediate between the teachers, parents and learners. By presenting a more complete picture of the pupils in a class to its teachers, you may ensure that future interactions take place in an informed and stable environment – neither marred nor exaggerated by uncharacteristic episodes or behaviours. Such behaviours will often be picked up in the reporting system where teachers write their comments. The form tutor's role here is to collate the comments and meet with parents to set targets going forward for the student's support and improvement.

It is useful to know how the organization, in this case the school, is perceived by the individual, that is the pupils, since this perception is, as Handy and Aitken (1988) point out, one of the most important factors in organizational theory. To investigate this issue, for this revised chapter, I collected new data from 12 schools, with a total of 413 pupils, 290 at KS3, 79 at KS4, 44 at KS5 (post-16) (Jones 2016). I asked the same two questions as I had asked smaller numbers of pupils in surveys in 1995, 2006 and 2010 for previous editions of this book:

1. What do you think is the role of a form tutor?
2. What are the qualities of a good form tutor?

To question 1, almost half of all the pupils questioned felt the most crucial role of a form tutor was to be supportive, helpful and understanding to pupils – in particular for the pupils at KS3 and KS4. At KS5, the pupils felt the most important role of a form tutor was ensuring pupil safety, a more nuanced emphasis, a reflection of the times perhaps. Sample KS4 comments were that tutors should 'act as a person of support to members of the form and as a friend. They help to make sure that everyone is alright and they're coping'; 'to assist students not necessarily in particular subjects but rather in a more general sense which may include school life or even home life' and 'to support their form throughout the years, and help to guide them through their academic studies'. An interesting comment came from a KS3 pupil who felt that the form tutor's role was 'to be a sort of "parent" to the pupils in the form . . . as pupils spend most of their time in school the form tutor has to be a secondary guardian. Most pupils tend to get stressed so a secondary guardian is helpful.'

Other key ideas on the form tutor's role identified by most KS3 and KS4 pupils were enforcing rules and taking the register. Most pupils said their role also included passing on messages/information and taking the register, helping the pupils to prepare for the day and be 'up to scratch'. Pupils in KS5 suggested that form tutors had a role in helping them prepare for further study and future careers, being supportive and providing reassurance at all times with regard to personal concerns.

In response to question 2, approximately a third of all the pupils questioned thought the most important quality a form tutor should have is to be caring and supportive – this was the case across the three Key Stages. The second and third most important qualities for KS3 were, respectively, to be funny/happy and an effective disciplinarian (but not 'shouty' or 'moany'). However, KS4 and KS5 pupils suggested that the second most important quality was for a form tutor to be approachable and easy to talk to, followed, third, by being an amusing and happy tutor. It is noticeable that 13 per cent of all the pupils mention discipline in some way although these comments were tempered by reference to teachers as follows: 'not strict (since it's not a lesson and we should relax)' and 'not too much shouting'. Pupils across the board did, however, want teachers to be 'strict when people misbehave', 'nice but strict' and capable of 'controlling the class'. This would indicate that the pupils understand the need for rules and regulations but that it all depends on how the form tutor puts this across to the group.

Over a period of 21 years since the first edition of this book, the results from the current survey were broadly in line with the previous samples that always highlighted administrative functions, the caring role and the perceived central disciplinary function of the tutor role. In all the surveys, pupils were quite clear that their first point of contact when in need was the form tutor. The overarching image of the effective form tutor is, as in the description of her form tutor by one KS4 pupil: 'He's funny and he helps his tutor group and he's good at keeping order' and 'He's funny, but strict but he makes you laugh when he's strict.' The pupils put great store by fairness – 'no faves' – dependability and kindness in their form tutors. Several KS3 pupils expected to be entertained by their form tutors!

You can carry out a similar exercise to find out and verify the expectations your pupils have of you as their tutor. The results from the research I undertook reflect two very basic pupil needs: first, individual care and support, and, second, the need for the teacher to maintain orderliness within the peer group. This conclusion concurs with Delamont's enduring assertion that the 'main strength of a teacher's position is that, in general, pupils want her to teach and keep them in order' (1983: 90). While the demands the pupils put on teachers may seem simple, the means of providing for their needs remains a challenging and diversified task in the case of the form tutor. Sizing up pupils is a continuous and evolving task for you, as form tutor, as you will be in a unique position – perceiving pupils in a holistic manner, mapping their strengths and weaknesses, and recognizing their successes and needs. With this perspective in mind, the form tutor fosters and supports the classroom interactions to assist pupil learning and development.

Concluding thoughts

The form tutor's role then, in conjunction with year/house/pastoral team colleagues, is to cohere all aspects of the pastoral and academic curricula. The tutor is, accordingly, 'the integrative centre for the school's whole curriculum' (Marland and Rogers 1997: 6). Research such as that by Weare (2005) shows that schools that focus on this aspect of their work with young people actually enhance pupil attainment. These schools are also aware of changes and developments and, after critical analysis, integrate these into their work. Currently, there is an upsurge of interest in emotional intelligence and literacy, and helping youngsters to be happy, resilient and confident through enhancing their self-understanding, their capacity to understand others, their ability to manage and reduce conflict and stress and thus to be successful learners (Claxton 2008). Thinking back to the data provided in this chapter on pupil views on form tutors, where do you see the stress points and how do they seem to change as the pupils get older and move through the school? The role of the tutor continuously reconfigures according to school and societal change and need, and an important task for experienced and new form tutors, like yourself, is to consider how you can elaborate the developmental and creative potential of this role and the special contribution you can make in each of your tutees' personal development. Drawing on your early experiences of form-tutoring during your training, what do you think your special contribution could be and how could you develop this?

The dependence of many students on the form tutor for a successful school career is tangible in this comment from a KS3 pupil: 'If the tutor is a good one, they can act as quite a positive foundation for each school day.' It is a role that, though challenging and changing, in essence remains actually very stable and is immensely rewarding, and a good form tutor, who adheres to being firm, friendly and fair, and funny if possible, is rarely forgotten. The final reflection for the reader is to ask you to think back to your form/personal tutors throughout your education, identify those you feel really had an impact on you and reflect on why this was so.

Notes

1 Many schools now deliver citizenship as part of the pastoral, health and social education programme (PHSE). Accordingly, more schools now refer to what they call the PHSCE curriculum.
2 The Workforce Remodelling Agreement's teaching and learning allowances (TLRs) can only be awarded for teaching and learning responsibilities. Many schools have appointed behaviour managers/counsellors to manage behaviour issues and attendance problems. The cost of employing these non-teaching personnel is cheaper than paying a teacher for non-contact time to undertake this work. Thus, the traditional binary role of the pastoral team, academic mentoring and behaviour management, has been divided up and reallocated. These sorts of ongoing changes will continue to influence and shape pastoral work in the future.

References

Best, R. (ed.) (2000) *Education for Spiritual, Moral, Social and Cultural Development.* London: Continuum.

Best, R. (2001) *Pastoral Care and Personal-Social Education: A Review of UK Research.* Southwell (Notts): British Educational Research Association.

Bottery, M. and Wright, N. (2000) *Teachers and the State.* London: Routledge.

Brougham, R. (2007) *Be a Better Form Tutor.* London: Teach Books.

Carroll, M. (2010) The practice of pastoral care of teachers: a summary of published outlines, *Pastoral Care in Education*, 28(2): 145–54.

Cartwright, N. (2007) *Peer Support Works: A Step by Step Guide to Long Term Success.* London: Continuum.

Cefai, C. (2008) *Promoting Resilience in the Classroom.* London: Jessica Kingsley Publishers.

Clarke, P. (2000) *Target Setting.* London: RoutledgeFalmer.

Claxton, G. (2008) *What's the Point of School? Rediscovering the Heart of Education.* Oxford: Oneworld.

Cooper, V. (2005) *Support Staff in Schools: Promoting the Emotional and Social Development of Children and Young People.* London: National Children's Bureau.

DCSF (Department for Children, Schools and Families) (2010) Social and emotional aspects of learning: national evaluation. Research Report DFE- RR049. London: DCSF.

Delamont, S. (1983) *Interaction in the Classroom.* London: Methuen.

DfES (Department for Education and Skills) (2003) *Raising Standards and Tackling Workload: A National Agreement,* http://www.remodelling.org/remodelling/nationalagreement. aspx, accessed 5 September, 2006.

Gill, J. (2000) The act of collective worship, in R. Best (ed.) *Education for Spiritual, Moral, Social and Cultural Development.* London: Continuum.

Handy, C.B. and Aitken, R. (1988) *Understanding Schools as Organizations.* London: Penguin.

Hattie, J. (2008) *Visible Learning: A Synthesis of Meta-Analyses to Achievement.* London: Routledge.

HMSO (2002) *A Time for Standards.* London: The Stationery Office.

HMSO (2004) *The Children Act.* London: The Stationery Office.

Hornby, G., Hall, C. and Hall, E. (eds) (2003) *Counselling Pupils in School: Skills and Strategies for Teachers.* London: RoutledgeFalmer.

Jones, J. (1995) What makes a good form tutor? King's College London: unpublished paper.

Jones, J. (2006) Student perceptions of in-school tutoring and mentoring. King's College London: unpublished paper.

Jones, J. (2010) Exploring the changing role of the form tutor. King's College London: unpublished paper.

Jones, J. (2016) Exploring changing teacher roles and pupil attitudes to the form tutor role. King's College London: unpublished paper.

King, G. (1999) *Counselling Skills for Teachers. Talking Matters.* Buckingham: Open University Press.

Marland, M. and Rogers, R. (1997) *The Art of the Tutor. Developing Your Role in the Secondary School.* London: David Fulton.

Mason, J. (2002) *Researching Your Own Practice: The Discipline of Noticing.* London: Sage.

NAHT and the Department of Health (2014) *The Link between Pupil Health and Wellbeing and Attainment.* London: Public Health England.

NCSL (National College for School Leadership) (2005) *Leading Personalised Learning: Helping Individuals Grow.* Nottingham: NCSL.

Pellitteri, J., Stern, R., Shelton, C. and Muller-Ackerman, B. (eds) (2006) *Emotionally Intelligent School Counseling.* Mahwah, NJ: Lawrence Erlbaum.

Prever, M. (2006) *Mental Health in Schools: A Guide to Pastoral and Curriculum Provision.* London: Paul Chapman.

Public Health England (PHE) (2014) *The Links Between Pupil Health and Well-Being and Attainment: A Briefing for Head Teachers, Governors and Staff in Educational Settings.* London: NAHT and PHE Publications.

Purdey, N. (ed.) (2013) *Pastoral Care 11–16. A Critical Introduction.* London: Bloomsbury Academic Press.

Rees, G. (2010) *Understanding Children's Well-being: A National Survey of Young People's Well-being*. London: Children's Society.

Rigby, K. (2010) *Bullying Interventions in Schools: Six Basic Approaches*. Camberwell, Victoria: ACER Press.

Shariff, S. (2009) *Confronting Cyber-bullying: What Schools Need to Know to Control Misconduct and Legal Consequences*. Cambridge: Cambridge University Press.

Smithers, A. and Robinson, P. (2003) *Factors Affecting Teachers' Decisions to Leave the Profession*. Nottingham: DfES.

Standish, P., Smeyers, P. and Smith, R. (eds) (2006) *The Therapy of Education: Philosophy, Happiness and Personal Growth*. Basingstoke: Palgrave Macmillan.

Startup, I. (2003) *Running Your Tutor Group*. London: Continuum.

Tattum, D. (1988) Control and welfare: towards a theory of constructive discipline in schools, in R. Dale, R. Fergusson and A. Robinson (eds) *Frameworks for Teaching*. London: Hodder and Stoughton.

Watkins, C. (2005) *Classrooms as Learning Communities: What's in it for Schools?* London: Routledge.

Weare, K. (2005) *Improving Learning Through Emotional Literacy*. London: Paul Chapman.

Further reading

Baginsky, M. (2008) *Safeguarding Children and Schools*. London: Jessica Kingsley Publishers.

Bullock, K. and Wilkeley, F. (2004) *Whose Learning? The Role of the Personal Tutor*. Maidenhead: Open University Press.

Hamblin, D. (1993) *Tutor as Counsellor*. Oxford: Basil Blackwell.

O'Brien, J. and Macleod, G. (2010) *The Social Agenda of the School*. Edinburgh: Dunedin Academic Press.

Pring, R. (1984) *Personal and Social Education in the Curriculum*. London: Hodder and Stoughton.

Qualifications and Curriculum Authority (QCA) (1997) *The Promotion of Pupils' Spiritual, Moral and Cultural Development: Draft Guidance for Pilot Work*. London: QCA.

Tindall, J.A. (1994) *Peer Programs: An In-Depth Look at Peer Helping, Planning, Implementation and Administration*. Bristol, PA: Accelerated Learning. Available at: http://www.bera.ac.uk/pdfs/BEST-PastoralCareandPSE.pdf, accessed 16 September 2010.

26

Continuing as a teacher

MELISSA GLACKIN, SIMON GIBBONS, MEG MAGUIRE, DAVID PEPPER AND KAREN SKILLING

Continuing to learn

> As the most important profession for our nation's future, teachers need considerable knowledge and skill, *which need to be developed as their careers progress.*
> (DfE 2016: 3, our italics)

In 2016, the Department for Education (DfE) published *The Standards for Teachers' Professional Development* setting out guidance for school leaders and organizations to support effective professional development for teachers. Taken from this guidance, the extract above highlights the societal importance for teachers' continual professional development (CPD) – that is, the outcomes of CPD need to reach further than just for the individual teacher or the school. What is less clear is what is meant by 'considerable knowledge and skill' . At the end of Chapter 1, we asked you to consider what a 'good' teacher might look like. Perhaps, after further reading, you have now come to a conclusion. Or perhaps, through your school placement experiences, you agree with Kennedy (2010), who suggests that the effective qualities of teachers are, to some extent, context-specific and are not easily defined. In many countries, governments have set out Teachers' Standards, or competences, that beginning and in-service teachers are expected to demonstrate before they are certified for practice. Teachers' Standards, in their broadest sense, reflect what a government/society values in its teachers while offering a tool to judge effectiveness. For example, in England, Teachers' Standards (DfE 2011: 7) state:

> Teachers make the education of their pupils their first concern, and are accountable for achieving the highest possible standards in work and conduct. Teachers act with honesty and integrity; have strong subject knowledge, keep their knowledge and skills as teachers up-to-date and are self-critical; forge positive professional relationships; and work with parents in the best interests of their pupils.

This extract draws into sharp focus the idea that alongside personal attributes such as concern, honesty and integrity, effective teaching requires keeping up to date with subject knowledge, general teaching knowledge and skills. In a complex context of continuous education reforms, what constitutes effective teaching is ever-changing, hence the requirement for on-going professional development (Guskey 2002). Further, even if schools were in a vacuum insulated from change, teaching is not simply a skill which can be mastered in a finite period of time; it is a complex professional art which you will continue to develop throughout your teaching career. Continuing professional development (CPD) should be just that, a process of professional development which continues throughout your career. Here are some of the types of CPD in which you might engage:

- Learning specific skills, such as the use of some new technology or a new examination foci
- Updating your subject knowledge either to make it part of your teaching repertoire or to bolster your own background knowledge
- Developing your general teaching methods or introducing new ones, such as questioning skills, behaviour management, or teaching for high-level thinking
- Preparing you for increased responsibilities, for example, a course for new heads of department.

Of these, only the first could be regarded as a relatively straightforward matter of acquiring new skills which you will acquire with adequate practice. All of the others require some conceptual development and possibly even changes of belief on your part. They will inevitably take time and, if effective, will lead to changes in your practice and to changes in your students, such as better learn-ing, better thinking, or better behaviour (Guskey and Yoon 2009). Such changes are not earned lightly and in this chapter we will explore some of the key indica-tors of *effective* professional development and try to offer some sort of 'buyer's guide' to help you judge when professional development is worth pursuing and when it is not.

Drivers of professional development

Your development as a professional has parallels with the ways in which your students develop their understanding of your subject area, but it also has unique features. Professional development involves *conceptual change*, and this is of the same type as the conceptual change you are trying to engender in your students (as explored in Chapter 10 by Heather King and Jill Hohenstein's chapter). It also requires *reflection on practice* and this may have a parallel in your students' learning, if you are in the habit of encouraging them to be meta-cognitive (for example, asking them to think back to how they learned some-thing, or what mistakes they made and how they corrected them). Finally, professional development requires you to practise new skills so that they become 'second nature' to you and this feature is more specific to the develop-ment of professional skills. This section will consider each of these three strands to CPD in turn.

Conceptual change

Borko and colleagues (2010) approach professional development from a cognitive-psychological perspective in which change in practice is associated with changes in the inner mental workings of teachers and their constructions of new understandings of the processes of learning. An example of thinking about professional development in the context of conceptual change is provided by Mevarech (1995). She describes the U-shaped learning curve which teachers go through when trying to replace one skill, and the epistemology on which it is based. Glackin (2016), building on Adey *et al.* (2004), also approaches the professional development of teachers from a constructivist perspective, showing how teachers need to interrogate their beliefs about the nature of teaching and learning before they are ready to construct new positions. This conceptualization of teacher change draws on what we already know about conceptual change and attitude change in students. It focuses on teachers' prior conceptions and recognizes that you are unlikely to make significant changes in practice unless you recognize and, if necessary, challenge some of your 'core' deep-rooted beliefs about the nature of learning. Such change is likely to be a slow and difficult process, and thus, real change in practice will not generally arise from short programmes of instruction, especially when those programmes take place in a centre removed from your own classroom (Pedder and Opfer 2011).

In focusing on the need to tackle some of our taken-for-granted assumptions about teaching and learning, we are not suggesting that this is the first thing that must happen before changes in teaching practice can occur. As Bandura (1997) explained through his theory of self-efficacy, if an action did not necessarily reflect a teacher's belief but resulted in a positive outcome, and if the actions were maintained and the positive feedback continued, a long-term consequence might be some change in beliefs. Guskey (1986) found that professional development programmes were usually unsuccessful in bringing about any change in beliefs unless teachers could be convinced to trial procedures which resulted in improvements in student achievement. He proposed that changes in beliefs followed, rather than preceded, changes in teaching practice. That said, we suggest that the relationship is bi-directional, that is, beliefs shape pedagogical decisions and pedagogical decision outcomes shape beliefs. Nevertheless, whether they are a precursor or a consequence, changes in beliefs may only be temporary. A change in context or an end to positive student feedback might halt the process of pedagogical change and return teachers' perspectives to their original state (Mischel and Shoda 1995). Furthermore, the process might be affected by the type and depth of the belief – whether it is 'core' or 'peripheral' to the teachers' wider belief system (Rokeach 1968).

Reflection on practice

The idea of the teacher as a reflective practitioner has a long and respectable history in the literature. Stenhouse (1975), for example, argues that effective teacher professionals have the capacity and commitment to engage in autonomous self-development, through systematic self-study, reflection and research. Further, Baird and colleagues (1991) have shown the central role that reflection – both on classroom practice and on the phenomena of teaching and learning – has in the pedagogical development process of both beginning and experienced teachers engaged in programmes of professional development.

At face value, reflection might seem simple. However, reflective practice is a complex, multifaceted phenomenon. Zwozdiak-Myers (2012) considers reflective practice as professional development when it consists of an enquiry that incorporates a broad set of processes. These include the ways that teachers' structure and restructure their actions, beliefs, knowledge and theories that blend together to inform their teaching. Zwozdiak-Myers (2012: 4–5) identifies nine key dimensions of reflective practice where teachers do the following:

1.   Study their own teaching and personal improvement
2.   Systematically evaluate their own teaching through classroom research procedures
3.   Link theory with their own practice
4.   Question their personal theories and beliefs
5.   Consider alternative perspectives and possibilities
6.   Try out new strategies and ideas
7.   Maximize the learning potential of all their students
8.   Enhance the quality of their own teaching
9.   Continue to improve their own teaching.

Reflection may be accomplished through the use of diaries or other forms of logs, or orally at 'feedback' sessions with colleagues and course leaders as well as from supportive dialogue about teaching observations (McIntosh 2010). You can benefit from such feedback sessions through putting your experiences and associated feelings, both positive and negative, into words and discussing them with peers. If you remain less aware of your own assumptions about teaching, there is no way that they can be inspected and, if necessary, challenged. However, this process does require confidence, trust and self-efficacy, that is a belief that by going through the process, your practice and your students' learning, will benefit. This is by no means an easy task.

Intuitive knowledge in teaching practice

Expert practitioners build up a complex personal knowledge base that can become 'second nature' to them and which they draw upon, sometimes in an intuitive way. This knowledge base is acquired through training and experience but individuals may not always be able to articulate why they do what they do (Atkinson and Claxton 2000; McMahon 2000). Such implicit knowledge may be an influence for good or for ill in the direction it proposes for action. For example, implicit knowledge can be built up from working in a traditional context rooted in an authoritarian view of teacher–student relationships and based on a simple transmission epistemology. On the other hand, it may be derived from a combination of a personal philosophy of guided democracy with some experience of the process of constructivism, and the observation of colleagues who have shown how all students can be encouraged to contribute to the construction of their own understandings (Wilson 2009).

In discussing the intuitive nature of much of the procedural knowledge of teaching, it is important not to confuse the ideas of 'intuitive' and 'instinctive'. The latter implies a 'taken-for-granted' and perhaps unconscious reaction. 'Intuitive', on the other hand, implies a behaviour which occurs without there always being explicit cognition at the moment at which it arises but which, over time, honed by experience, reading and discussion, has become part of the professional repertoire of the teacher. The basis of the behaviour remains in the subconscious. The term 'implicit knowledge' is sometimes used for this type of understanding which gives rise to intuitive behaviour (Tomlinson 1998). Intuition is how, as teachers, we deal with situations as they arise in the complex social environment of the classroom. It would be impossible to proceed through every classroom moment entirely on the basis of rational and conscious decision-making or problem-solving. The 'professional' response in such situations depends much on intuition, a process described by Brown and Coles (2000: 173) as 'concentrated, condensed, interpretations' of different experiences of problem-solving. The important point here is that intuitive behaviour is based on our implicit knowledge, informed by previous situations and on the constructs we have built over time from such experiences but which have not necessarily been externalized or made conscious.

These three strands of thought on the nature of professional development (concept change, reflection and intuition) that we are discussing here intertwine and feed into one another. What is an effective way of inducing a process of conceptual change? Why, to encourage reflection. And what is the basis of the intuitive knowledge which guides action? It is the underlying conceptions and beliefs of the individual. Guided reflection assists the process of conceptual change, and conceptual change re-structures the intuitive knowledge upon which teaching practice rests. In his seminal work on professional development, Schön (1987) shows how reflection is an essential part of the process by which teachers incorporate the perceived needs of a situation within their own system of beliefs, and this is all part of the development of their 'professional artistry'. This is a good description of practice arising from intuitive understandings. Perhaps the real challenge is to tease out how this intuitive understanding can be prised open to further analysis and exploration.

The practicalities of effective professional development

All teachers should have access to powerful professional development that helps them to thrive, and their students to succeed. To ensure this, we need a clear idea of what powerful teacher development looks like.

(Sir John Holman, Teacher Development Trust (TDT) 2015: 5)

Within the myriad of experiences that contribute towards teacher learning, identifying features that provide 'powerful professional development' can be challenging. Notwithstanding this ambiguity, several recent literature reviews concur as to the essential elements for teacher professional development (Desimone 2009; van Driel *et al.* 2012; TDT 2015). In this section we want to explore some of the key components of effective CPD. To do this, we first consider the type of professional development programme (such as what is being introduced and how it is introduced) and then review what is an effective CPD environment. Finally, we discuss the range of professional development opportunities that you might consider – offering these only as examples as the sector is continually in flux.

Type of CPD programme

What is being introduced?

First, the material or method being introduced by the professional development must itself have proven value. That is, 'professional development should be underpinned by robust evidence and expertise' (DfE 2016: 8). Or, as van Driel and colleagues (2012) explain, well-researched programmes are evidence-based or evidence-informed. The Teacher Development Trust (2015) emphasizes the pointlessness of organizing professional development for an innovation which is not itself worthwhile or of established quality. An example of innovation failure often cited is the post-Sputnik reforms (1957–80) in science education in the USA and the fact that the programmes of change were driven by politicians and had not been established as educationally sound. In selecting a professional development experience from those on offer, ask yourself: Does the innovation being introduced have any sound theoretical foundation? Is any good evidence offered for the effectiveness of the innovation? As an example, a professional development programme introducing the idea of 'learning styles' (visual, auditory, kinaesthetic) may be fun, may be well presented and may appear plausible but you will not find many psychologists who give any credence to the validity of learning styles, nor will you find any evidence (in peer-reviewed academic journals) for the efficacy of labelling children with a supposed learning style (Coffield 2012). As Adey and Dillon (2012) suggest in their book *Bad Education*, there are multiple myths in education that require debunking.

How is it being introduced?

Second, the quality and quantity of the professional development programme matter. The one-shot, in-service education and training (INSET) day is universally recognized as not necessarily bringing about any sustained changes in teaching practice or student learning, but how many 'shots' are needed to be effective? Guskey and Yoon (2009) think that two years is a minimum time needed for real change to occur. That is, before a new pedagogic skill becomes 'second nature'. The Teacher Development Trust's (2015) review of international research points to at least a minimum of two terms being needed to promote sustainable development. This estimate of a minimum requirement is consistent with the notion that real change in practice requires conceptual change in the teacher, and conceptual change is well known to be slow. Time is needed to assimilate the new practices.

As for the quality of presentations on professional development courses, nothing is less convincing or more ironic than a formal lecture on the benefits of constructivist teaching. It seems obvious that a teacher is unlikely to be encouraged to use active methods in the classroom because of a monologue delivered from the front of the room. If you want to promote teachers' use of questioning, then present your teacher audience with some 'effective' questions at their own level. If you want to encourage teachers to promote collaborative learning in their classrooms, the professional development course should have activities for teachers which can only be solved by collaboration with colleagues. Coherence between the underpinning programme theories with the programme practice is essential.

Finally, a professional development programme which fails to reach into the classroom will fail. There must be some mechanism by which, as you try new methods in your own classroom, you can enlist a critical friend to observe your efforts and provide coaching – returning us to the need for reflection. From a meta-analysis of nearly 200 studies of the effect of professional development, Joyce and Showers (2002) concluded that of all the features which are usually incorporated into professional development programmes, it was coaching which proved to be an essential ingredient when the outcome measurement was student change. Coaching in innovative teaching methods can be provided by peers, by senior colleagues, by the professional development tutors, and it may be managed using video recordings. But it must, emphatically, be distinguished from appraisal or inspection (Cox 2010). Coaching is a friendly, supportive, and non-judgemental process. Coaching can work as a source of self-efficacy, influencing teachers' confidence, offering verbal persuasion to take risks and try new practices (Palmer 2011). But all this needs to take place in an environment that is conducive to enquiry, learning and change.

An effective environment

Collaborative learning

Notwithstanding the focus of this book is on the teacher, it is clear from the literature and from experience that teachers are rarely if ever able to make real changes in their pedagogy unless the school environment in which they find themselves is, at the very least, tolerant of innovation. Hence for active learning to take place, collective participation (Desimone 2009) or collaborative teacher learning (van Driel *et al.* 2012) is required. Desimone (2009: 184) suggests that 'such arrangements set up potential interaction and discourse, which can be a powerful form of teacher learning'. Teachers who are trying to change their practice find it extremely difficult to be 'different' from their colleagues in the same school. Schools which are more successful in taking on an innovation are ones in which there is much communication between teachers in the department about the new methods (Little 2012). No one individual, however well motivated and energized, can maintain a new method of teaching if they feel isolated. McLaughlin (1994: 33), quoted by Fullan (1995), reported that:

> as we looked across our sites at teachers who report a high sense of efficacy, who feel successful with today's students, we noticed that while these teachers differ along a number of dimensions ... all shared this one characteristic: membership in some kind of strong professional community.

Just what collegiality looks like on the ground can be described on a scale from teachers having virtually no professional conversations with one another, through informal chats about the innovation in the corridor or over coffee, to the situation where one or two members of a department have responsibility for overseeing the implementation, and can act as sounding-boards for others as they try out novel approaches. Better again is the addition of regularly scheduled meetings devoted to assessing progress in implementing the innovation, and best of all is some form of peer-coaching. Units of collegiality within schools form subcultures which may be productive (as in the case of a department that happily shares both professional and social experiences) or may be 'Balkan' (Stoll and Fink 1996), a carping and disruptive influence that limits professional experimentation and growth.

School organization conditions

The senior leadership team is critical to establishing a school ethos supportive of change and development. The Teacher Development Trust (2015) highlights the core role of schools leaders in effective professional development as: developing a vision, managing and organizing, promoting a challenging learning culture and encouraging teachers as leaders. For example, there are two particular aspects where the headteacher's role is essential, without which professional development is unlikely to be effective. The first is in recognizing the time required for in-school professional development, and the second is in building the innovation into the structure of school, or at least the relevant department. These points correspond to two of the key features which Fullan and Stiegelbauer (1991) report as being essential if an innovation is to become institutionalized: the commitment of the headteacher and the incorporation of structural changes into school and classroom policy. Let us consider each of these in turn.

All of the strategies described in the last section for maximizing productive collegiality depend critically on recognition by school leaders – typically the headteacher and the head of department – that investment in time for sharing among teachers is at least as important as is time for professional development provided by external organizations. We have, from time to time, been quite surprised to find that a headteacher who is prepared to find a significant sum of money for a professional development programme then baulks at creating the time for teachers to meet together to share experiences and to develop their practice collaboratively within the department. This type of headteacher seems to act as if paying the money was all that was required for magic to follow. The best professional development programme in the world will have no deep-seated effect on practice if there is no active support mechanism for teachers introducing new methods, to ensure that the hard work involved in high-quality teaching is recognized, and to establish methods of sharing practice.

The second aspect that can limit the impact of CPD is the absence of any structural sustainability built into the culture of the school. It is the responsibility of senior leadership in the school to provide systems which ensure that a method or approach that has been introduced and which is still considered positively is maintained. Practical signals that an innovation has been adopted into the structure include requests from the headteacher for updates on the implementation, attention by the leadership to timetabling requirements, and the inclusion of the innovation in departmental policy documents and development plans. Without the establishment of such sustaining structures, efforts put into teachers' professional development are in danger of being lost when key teachers who may be most committed to the changes leave the school.

Where to now?

Currently there is a wide range of different types of CPD on offer to schools. Many of the subject associations offer short courses to support developments and policy reforms in their disciplines. Multi-Academy Trusts (MATs) and Teaching Schools regularly deliver their own sessions to enhance the professional development of their staff. Most new teachers come into the profession with Master-level credits and many more practitioners now anticipate studying for a higher degree either in their discipline or an interdisciplinary area such as Effective Management or Assessment. There is also a growing number of freelance consultants and companies that provide different forms of often tailored CPD. Taken from a teacher's blog, we want to include a visionary and perhaps utopian approach to CPD that highlights the need for professional development really to be *continual* – a point to which we all subscribe.

> I dream of a day where CPD is so inherently established that it becomes part of every teachers' bloodstream; that accumulating a feathered-cap of personal development becomes the norm, not a desire for the determined and those with funds liberally allocated for Inset courses, master's degrees and those with time on their hands. That this approach to development becomes so ingrained that we cannot work without it. So vital is our development and routinely established as part of our working week, that we cannot secure jobs, promotions, pay-rises or any credibility without an accurate log of our own reflective journey.
>
> (McGill 2013: n.p.)

Concluding thoughts

As you progress through your career, accruing new responsibilities in the pastoral and subject areas, then increasingly demanding leadership posts, possibly back into academia, or into education consultancy roles, or out to curriculum projects, or through union activity, or straight through the school system to becoming a headteacher, at every step you will be meeting new challenges. You will need to acquire new skills and new understandings, learn to see things from new perspectives, occasionally even to change camps perhaps from poacher to gamekeeper. At every step, grab opportunities for professional development. As a rough guide to finding your way through the maze of professional development on offer, ask these questions (all based on principles summarized in this chapter):

- Will there be an opportunity to share the professional development experience with others, or is it likely to remain an individual personal experience?
- Looking at what a professional development programme offers, ask about theoretical bases, whether the programme shows any evidence of positive effects on students, and whether the teachers who are to use it find the materials accessible and relevant.
- Find out whatever you can about the quality of delivery. Does it use active workshop approaches?
- Does the programme claim to lead to changes in students' achievement, motivation, or other characteristics on the basis of a short one-off intensive course? If so, be sceptical. Effective programmes should provide for follow-up which explores implementation and supports you in trying new methods in your own classroom.
- Look to your school: are senior leaders prepared to make any structural changes to the timetable and/or to school and department development plans to maximize the chance of an innovation becoming a deep-rooted feature of the school?

And as you progress through your career, and find yourself in a position where you are allocating professional development funds within a school, bear in mind the difficulties of managing effective (as opposed to stylish) professional development for yourself and colleagues. It may be better to distribute the funds 'unfairly' across some departments in order to concentrate funds where they have a chance to root and grow than to be 'fair' in the distribution of one-day INSETs, which may have limited effects on classroom practice.

You will not have got it all sorted out in a couple of years' time. If you are fortunate you will continue to learn and develop more complex subject knowledge, pastoral understanding and leadership capabilities throughout your career. That's a pretty exciting prospect.

References

Adey, P. and Dillon, J. (eds) (2012) *Bad Education: Debunking Myths in Education.* Maidenhead: Open University Press.

Adey, P., Hewitt, G., Hewitt, J. and Landau, N. (2004) *The Professional Development of Teachers: Practice and Theory*. Dordrecht: Kluwer Academic.

Atkinson, T. and Claxton, G. (eds) (2000) *The Intuitive Practitioner. On the Value of Not Always Knowing What One is Doing*. Buckingham: Open University Press.

Baird, J.R., Fensham, P.J., Gunstone, R.F. and White, R.T. (1991) The importance of reflection in improving science teaching and learning, *Journal of Research in Science Teaching*, 28(2): 163–82.

Bandura, A. (1997) *Self-efficacy: The Exercise of Control*. New York: W.H. Freeman and Company.

Borko, H., Jacobs, J. and Koellner, K. (2010) Contemporary approaches to teacher professional development, in E. Baker and B. McGaw (eds) *International Encyclopedia of Education* (3rd edn). Oxford: Elsevier, pp. 548–56.

Brown, L. and Coles, A. (2000) Complex decision making in the classroom: the teacher as an intuitive practitioner, in T. Atkinson and G. Glaxton (eds) *The Intuitive Practitioner: On the Value of Not Always Knowing What One is Doing*. Buckingham: Open University Press.

Coffield, F. (2012) Learning styles: unreliable, invalid and impractical and yet still widely used, in P. Adey and J. Dillon (eds) *Bad Education: Debunking Myths in Education*. Maidenhead: Open University Press.

Cox, E. (2010) *The Complete Handbook of Coaching*. London: Sage.

Desimone, L.M. (2009) Improving impact studies of teachers' professional development: Toward better conceptualizations and measures, *Educational Researcher*, 38(3): 181–99.

DfE (Department for Education) (2011) *Teachers' Standards* (DFE-00066-2011), https://www.gov.uk/government/publications/teachers-standards, accessed 23 May 2017.

DfE (Department for Education) (2016) *Standards for Teachers Professional Development*. London: Department for Education, https://www.gov.uk/government/publications/standard-for-teachers-professional-development, accessed 23 May 2017.

Fullan, M. (1995) The limits and potential of professional development, in T.R. Guskey and M. Habermann (eds) *Professional Development in Education: New Paradigms and Practises*. New York: Teachers College Press.

Fullan, M.G. and Stiegelbauer, S. (1991) *The New Meaning of Educational Change*. London: Cassell.

Glackin, M. (2016) 'Risky fun' or 'authentic science'? How teachers' beliefs influence their practice during a professional development programme on outdoor learning, *International Journal of Science Education*, 38(3): 409–33.

Guskey, T.R. (1986) Staff development and the process of teacher change, *Educational Researcher*, 15(5): 5–12.

Guskey, T.R. (2002) Professional development and teacher change, *Teachers and Teaching*, 8(3): 381–91.

Guskey, T.R. and Yoon, K.S. (2009) What works in professional development, *Phi Delta Kappa*, 90(7): 495–500.

Joyce, B. and Showers, B. (2002) *Student Achievement: Through Staff Development* (3rd edn). New York: Longman.

Kennedy, M.M. (2010) Attribution error and the quest for teacher quality, *Educational Researcher*, 39(8): 591–8.

Little, J.W. (2012) Professional community and professional development in the learning centered school, in M. Kooy and K. van Veen (eds) *Teacher Learning That Matters: International Perspectives*. New York: Routledge, pp. 22–46.

McGill, R.M. (2013) Professional development for teachers: how can we take it to the next level? *Professional Development. Teachers' Blog*, https://www.theguardian.com/teacher-network/teacher-blog/2013/jan/29/professional-development-teacher-training-needs, accessed 31 May 2017.

McIntosh, P. (2010) *Action Research and Reflective Practice: Creative and Visual Methods to Facilitate Reflection and Learning*. London: Routledge.

McLaughlin, M. (1994) Strategic sites for teachers professional development, in P. Grimmett and J. Neufeld (eds) *Teacher Development and the Struggle for Authenticity: Professional Growth and Restructuring in a Context of Change*. New York: Teachers College Press.

McMahon, A. (2000) The development of professional intuition, in T. Atkinson and G. Glaxton (eds) *The Intuitive Practitioner: On the Value of Not Always Knowing What One is Doing*. Buckingham: Open University Press.

Mevarech, Z.E. (1995) Teachers' paths on the way to and from the professional development forum, in M. Hubermann (ed.) *Professional Development in Education: New Paradigms and Practises*. New York: Teachers' College Press.

Mischel, W. and Shoda, Y. (1995) A cognitive-affective systems theory of personality: reconceptualizing the invariances in personality and the role of situations, *Psychological Review*, 10(2): 246–68.

Palmer, D.H. (2011) Sources of efficacy information in an inservice program for elementary teachers, *Science Education*, 95(4), 577–600.

Pedder, D. and Opfer, V.D. (2011) Are we realising the full potential of teachers' professional learning in schools in England? Policy issues and recommendations from a national study, *Professional Development in Education*, 37(5): 741–58.

Rokeach, M. (1968) *Beliefs, Attitudes, and Values: A Theory of Organization and Change*. San Francisco: Jossey-Bass.

Schön, D.A. (1987) *Educating the Reflective Practitioner*. San Francisco: Jossey-Bass.

Stenhouse, L. (1975) *An Introduction to Curriculum Research and Development*. London: Heinemann Education.

Stoll, L. and Fink, D. (1996) *Changing Our Schools: Linking School Effectiveness and School Improvement*. Buckingham: Open University Press.

Teacher Development Trust (2015) *Developing Great Teachers*, http://tdtrust.org/about/dgt, accessed 23 May 2017.

Tomlinson, P. (1998) *Implicit Learning and Teacher Preparation: Potential Implications of Recent Theory and Research*. Brighton: British Psychological Society Annual Conference.

van Driel, J.H., Meirink, J., Van Veen, K. and Zwart, R. (2012) Current trends and missing links in studies on teacher professional development in science education: a review of design features and quality of research. *Studies in Science Education*, 48(2): 129–60.

Wilson, J. (2009) *Learning for Themselves: Pathways to Independence in the Classroom*. London: Routledge.

Zwozdiak-Myers, P. (2012). *The Teacher's Reflective Practice Handbook: Becoming an Extended Professional Through Capturing Evidence-Informed Practice*. London: Routledge.

Index